PUBLICATIONS OF
THE WELLCOME INSTITUTE OF THE HISTORY OF MEDICINE

(*General Editor:* F. N. L. Poynter, Ph.D., D.Litt., Hon.M.D.(Kiel))

New Series, Volume XXI

THE CULT OF THE SEER
IN THE ANCIENT MIDDLE EAST

THE
CULT OF THE SEER
IN THE
ANCIENT MIDDLE EAST

A Contribution to
Current Research on Hallucinations
drawn from Coptic and other Texts

by

Violet MacDermot

LONDON
WELLCOME INSTITUTE OF THE HISTORY
OF MEDICINE
1971

First published 1971

© The Wellcome Institute of the History of Medicine, 1971

Made and printed in Great Britain by
William Clowes and Sons, Limited, London, Beccles and Colchester

CONTENTS

FOREWORD AND ACKNOWLEDGMENTS   ix

PREFACE   xi

INTRODUCTION   1

  I   THE FACULTY OF VISION   1
  II   THE DECLINE OF ORACLES   13

Chapter I   *WITHDRAWAL FROM THE*
    ENVIRONMENT OF THE SENSES   22

    Preliminary Considerations   22

  I   THE ASCETIC WAY OF LIFE   26   (272)

    1   Ascetic Practices   26   (272)
    2   Discipleship   29   (283)

  II   SELF-ISOLATION   31   (290)

    1   Prolonged Solitude   31   (290)
    2   Self-enclosure   34   (296)

  III   SELF-MORTIFICATION   36   (301)

    1   Fatigue and Weakening of the Body   36   (301)
    2   Pain   37   (305)
      (i)   Self-infliction of Pain   37   (305)
      (ii)   Disregard of Pain   37   (312)
      (iii)   Devices for Preventing Rest   38   (316)

  IV   FOOD DEPRIVATION   39   (322)

    1   Restriction of Diet   39   (322)
    2   Days of Fasting   40   (327)
    3   Heavenly Food   42   (333)

  V   SLEEP DEPRIVATION   43   (338)

    1   Complete Deprivation   43   (338)
    2   Nights of Vigil   47   (340)
    CONCLUSION   48

Chapter II *THE ESTABLISHMENT OF A*
NON-MATERIAL ENVIRONMENT   49 (344)

I MENTAL POWERS   49 (344)
   1 Prayer and Meditation   49 (344)
   2 Attainment   53 (350)
   3 Vision   54 (355)
   4 Gifts   57 (363)
     (i) Prophecy   57 (363)
     (ii) Memory   58 (376)
     (iii) The Gift of Tongues   59 (378)
     (iv) The Gift of Knowledge and Wisdom   62 (381)

II DEMONIC VISITS   64 (383)
   Preliminary Considerations   64
   1 Forms   74 (383)
   2 The Devil as Deity   76 (394)
   3 Mode of Activity   78 (398)

III DISCERNING SPIRITS: DISPELLING EVIL   80 (411)
   1 Recognition   80 (411)
   2 Distinguishing Good and Evil in Fellow-Men   82 (415)
   3 Possession and the Casting out of Devils   83 (424)
   4 Dispelling Evil   86 (428)
   CONCLUSION   89

Chapter III *THE REPRESENTATION OF A*
NON-MATERIAL WORLD   90 (438)

   Preliminary Considerations   90
I HEAVENLY VISITATIONS   93 (438)
   1 Personal Appearance to Ascetics   93 (438)
   2 Appearance at the Eucharist   95 (449)
   3 Interpretation of Doctrine   96 (453)
   4 Healing   98 (457)
   5 The Foretelling of the Birth of Holy Men   100 (461)

II HEAVENLY COMMUNICATIONS   102 (465)
   Preliminary Considerations   102
   1 The Recognition of a Holy Man   103 (465)
   2 The Call to the Ascetic Life   104 (472)
   3 The Call to Found a Monastery or Church   105 (476)
   4 The Call to the Ministry   106 (486)
   5 Admonition   107 (490)

III   THE DEATH OF A HOLY MAN   108   (498)

Preliminary Considerations   108
1   Death Foretold   110   (498)
2   The Last Words   113   (507)
3   The Fetching of the Soul   114   (511)

IV   THE JOURNEY TO PARADISE   117   (538)

Preliminary Considerations   117
1   The Separation of the Soul from the Body   124   (538)
2   The Experiences of Souls in the Life after Death 127   (549)
3   The City and Thrones of Heaven   132   (555)
4   The Foundations of Heaven; The Paradise of
      the Third Heaven; the Earthly Paradise   137   (562)
CONCLUSION   142

Chapter IV   *THE REPRESENTATION OF*
NEGATIVE EXPERIENCES   144   (576)

I   DEATH AND JUDGMENT   144   (576)

Preliminary Considerations   144
1   The Death of the Wicked   148   (576)
2   Abbaton, the Angel of Death   155   (583)
3   The Meeting with Those of Heaven   159   (589)

II   AMENTE   161   (594)

Preliminary Considerations   161
1   The Torments   167   (594)
2   The Remission of Punishments   171   (605)
3   Purification after Death   174   (618)
CONCLUSION   177

Chapter V   *THE ESTABLISHMENT OF*
COMMEMORATIVE RITUAL   179   (626)

I   THE MARTYR CULT   179   (626)
Preliminary Considerations   179

1   Martyrdom Foretold   183   (626)
2   Rewards in Heaven   184   (642)
3   The Boat Journey   188   (656)
4   The Execution   190   (663)
5   Instructions on Burial; on Building a Shrine   192   (671)
6   The Cult of the Shrine   193   (677)
      (i) Writing and Preaching   193   (677)
      (ii) Services to the Martyr   195   (682)
7   Favours Granted at the Shrine   198   (702)

CONTENTS

II SALVATION FROM DEATH   201   (708)

    Preliminary Considerations   201
    1 Identity Announcement   203   (708)
    2 Greeting   205   (713)
    3 Releasing   207   (717)
    4 Restoring   210   (727)
    5 Raising from the Dead   212   (741)

III HEAVENLY SIGNS   219   (747)

    1 Heavenly Light   219   (747)
    2 Heavenly Fire   223   (765)
    3 Heavenly Beauty   225   (771)
    4 Miraculous Events   228   (774)
    CONCLUSION   232

Postscript *ARCHAISM IN THE TWENTIETH
CENTURY*   234

NOTES ON CHAPTERS I–V   238

ABBREVIATIONS   261

*ABBREVIATIONS USED IN REFEFENCES TO THE
    TEXTS IN SECTIONS I–V*   262

INTRODUCTION TO THE TRANSLATED TEXTS   269

THE TEXTS: SECTIONS I–V. See Chapter Headings
    above for page numbers (in Brackets)

NOTES ON SECTIONS I–V   786

BIBLIOGRAPHY (GENERAL)   790

BIBLIOGRAPHY (MEDICAL)   798

INDEX OF QUOTATIONS IN CHAPTERS I–V   801

    I   AUTHORS   801
    II TITLES   804

INDEX OF QUOTATIONS IN SECTIONS I–V   807

GENERAL INDEX TO CHAPTERS I–V   811

FOREWORD AND ACKNOWLEDGMENTS

The 'seeing' of 'visions' is generally thought to involve only the realm of subjective experience. The problems of seership lie in a dimension where the fields of psychology, language and religion overlap. In this sphere, the methods of science and scholarship are not usually considered appropriate. In the ancient world, however, subjective experiences appear to have had an objective validity. I have attempted, in this book, to investigate the possibility that the significance of these 'visions' is not only ascertainable, but is relevant to some problems of today. I have based my studies almost entirely upon the internal evidence of the appropriate texts. It has been necessary to bring to bear upon these records the disciplines of a number of branches of learning, in particular those mentioned above. Today, it is difficult to have more than a superficial knowledge of any field, including one's own. I hope, therefore, that specialists will be forbearing where I have offended against some of the canons of scholarship.

I wish to express here my gratitude to a number of people who have helped with this book, while absolving them at the same time from any responsibility for the views which it contains. To Dr. James Drescher, for his painstaking care in reading all the sections containing the translated texts and the Coptic word groups, I am deeply indebted. I would like to record my gratitude to the late Professor J. Černý for much help with problems in the Coptic texts, to Professor J. B. Segal for advice on the Syriac texts, Mr. Cyril Spaull and Professor H. S. Smith for suggestions on Egyptian sources. To Mr. Harry Rutherford, who read the final manuscript, I am especially grateful. My thanks are due to the Trustees of the Wellcome Foundation, without whose generous financial assistance this work could not have been done. I most particularly thank Dr. Poynter, not only for his unfailing kindness and help, but for his readiness to support such an unorthodox undertaking. Finally, I have to thank Mrs. P. Barnden for her invaluable advice and assistance in preparing the book for publication and Mr. J. Dent for the indexing of the book and for help with proof-reading.

I am grateful for permission granted, by the late Professor J. Černý and Messrs. Hutchinson, to quote from *Ancient Egyptian Religion*; by Dr. J. Drescher, to quote from *Apa Mena*; by Dr. G. Vermes and Pelican Books, to quote from *The Dead Sea Scrolls in English*; by G. A.

ix

Williamson and Penguin Books, to quote from *Eusebius: The History of the Church*; by Miss G. H. Turnbull and the Oxford University Press, New York, to quote from *The Essence of Plotinus*; by Professor F. C. Grant and Bobbs Merill and Co., to quote from *Hellenistic Religions*; by Father A.-J. Festugière, to quote from *Les Moines d' Orient*; by the Woodbrooke Council, to quote from the *Mingana Woodbrooke Studies*; by Professor R. McL. Wilson and the Lutterworth Press, to quote from *New Testament Apocrypha*; by Dr. H. Chadwick and the Cambridge University Press, to quote from *Origen: Contra Celsum*; by the SPCK, to quote from G. W. Butterworth *Origen: On First Principles*; G. H. Box *Testament of Abraham*; by the Committee of the Egypt Exploration Society, to quote from *Oxyrhinchus Papyri XI*; by W. Heinemann and Sons, to quote from F. H. Colson *Philo*; F. C. Conybeare *Philostratus: Life of Apollonius of Tyana*; H. N. Fowler *Plato: Apology, Phaedo, Phaedrus*; W. R. M. Lamb *Plato: Minos, Epinomis*; A. H. Armstrong *Plotinus*; H. Rushton Fairclough *Virgil*; by Methuen and Co., to quote from A. E. Taylor *Plato: Timaeus and Critias*; by J. M. Dent and Sons, to quote from A. D. Lindsay *The Republic of Plato*; R. V. Tasker *Saint Augustine: The City of God*; by Professor O. Chadwick and the SCM Press, to quote from *Western Asceticism*.

For permission to reproduce Coptic text, I am grateful to the editors of the 'Corpus Scriptorum Christianorum Orientalium de Louvain-Washington', the 'Publications de l'Institut Français d'Archéologie Orientale', Cairo and the Patrologia Orientalis, Paris.

PREFACE

A disturbing feature of modern literature on hallucinations and hallucinogenic techniques is the increasing tendency to assume that experiences
achieved by such methods as drug-taking are comparable or even identical with those of the seers of ancient religious history. It is also argued
that because drug-induced hallucinations play an important role in
primitive cultures in initiation and other rituals, drug-taking in modern
culture would be beneficial in promoting social relations. Similarly,
because subjective feelings of 'oneness' or 'timelessness' occur under
the influence of hallucinogenic drugs, it is thought that these feelings
entitle the drug taker to consider that he has undergone the same experiences as the ascetic seers of ancient times. It is argued, furthermore
that, by means of drugs, all personal effort is rendered unnecessary.
Learned and responsible writers, from William James and Aldous
Huxley to those of the present day, have encouraged this attitude, and
few psychologists or theologians have come forward to oppose it.

It seems, therefore, timely to present a detailed study of the lives,
the ascetic practices and the 'visions' of a group of seers of the early
Christian period on whom a considerable body of literature exists.
The subject of the recording of visions is also considered together with
the social value of such records. The aims and attitudes of the seers can
be seen from these writings and the question of the relevance of these
aims and attitudes to modern life is raised. At the same time, the features
which distinguish the visions of the seers from the modern 'psychedelic'
experiences may become clearer.

Workers in the field of 'sensory deprivation' have included the early
seers among those whose visionary experiences could be ascribed to
sensory deprivation. It is well known that hallucinations can occur in
normal subjects when the surroundings are monotonous, when sensory
stimulation is reduced to a minimum and the individual is isolated from
all social contact. The conditions can be produced in the laboratory
and the phenomena have been extensively studied in connection with
'space-medicine'. It has been suggested that these induced hallucinations have some similarity to those of the ancient seers. The only common
feature is the fact that the early ascetic lived in conditions super-
ficially resembling those described in modern work on sensory deprivation. The difference in the attitude of the ancient seer to his physical

environment, from that of the modern individual, has not been taken into account.

The chief sources of our present knowledge of the seers of the early Christian period are the writings of the Church Fathers and monks of that time. These writings contain many descriptions of ascetic practices and visionary experiences and a number of extracts from these writings is here presented. The collection of extracts from edited and translated texts is, it is hoped, a representative sample of a vast literature. The extracts are mainly derived from Coptic and Syriac texts, the background of the majority of the narratives being Egypt, Syria and Palestine. Quotations from the extracts are grouped together under headings which cover the most frequently described types of ascetic practices and visionary experiences.

Although this book is intended in the first instance as a contribution to medical-historical studies, the bringing together and classification of these texts may perhaps be of use to Coptic and other scholars. The explanatory notes and comments on the texts are chiefly related to the medical-historical problems under consideration. Thus many aspects of the subject, which are beyond the scope of this book, have been ignored. It does, however, appear relevant to study the peculiarities of language which appear in these texts. The outstanding feature is the repetition, in the corresponding situations of different texts, of certain groups of words. These are reproduced for special study in the original Coptic in a supplementary volume. The word-groups and a list of the most frequently used words together form a 'vocabulary' of the subject of seership.

It is hoped that this study will help to clarify the subject of the possible contribution to modern social life, to art or to individual enlightenment, of self-induced hallucinations. The question for serious consideration is whether drug-taking and similar techniques may not represent both an atavistic return to the cults of primitive societies and an irresponsible reawakening of primitive faculties—and whether they may not be liable in modern life to be destructive both to society and to the individual.

INTRODUCTION

I THE FACULTY OF VISION

Today the word 'vision' can be used in three ways. It can denote the ordinary act of seeing or the faculty of eyesight. It can be used metaphorically for an imaginative conception in the mind of an artist or thinker. Finally, a vision can mean an appearance, often of a religious or prophetic character, which is seen otherwise than by ordinary sight and which presents during an abnormal state of mind. A hallucination, on the other hand, is defined as the apparent perception of an external object when no such object is present.

In the ancient world, these distinctions which, for us, depend upon our insight into our own faculties, were less clear or non-existent. The recognition of a faculty, whether physical or mental, depends on a degree of self-consciousness. Self-consciousness, in turn, depends on some intellectual development. It is during the period preceding the emergence of intellectual knowledge that vision is regarded as a revelation both of the natural and of the supernatural worlds. In ancient cultures, 'vision' was a complete experience, involving sight, hearing and knowledge while the natural and supernatural elements were inseparable. Different peoples and civilisations developed in different ways and faculties, which were highly regarded in one culture, were often ignored in another. Ancient cultures were essentially religious and their survival depended to a great extent on their internal religious unity. For self-preservation, therefore, religious groups in the ancient world maintained themselves distinct and in sharp contrast to their neighbours for long periods of time. Three such religious cultures, which developed in their early stages in relative independence of one another, were the Egyptian, the Greek and the Jewish. As a result of their conflicting views on the different spheres of human activity, it happened that when they confronted one another during the Hellenistic period, there was an unprecedented inquiry into human faculties. It became a matter of importance to know whether knowledge, obtained in the form of visions or revelations, had a greater validity than that acquired by study of the world of natural phenomena. The early Church was particularly anxious to exert authority in this field, in view of the claim of Christianity to be a new revelation. A feature of this period was the widespread rise of cults, concerned with the promotion of seership.

1

For a better understanding of the background and significance of these cults, it is necessary to review certain features of the religions of Egypt, Greece and Israel, especially those which contributed to the thought and practices of the early Christian era.

(i) *Egypt*

The oldest of these ancient religions was the Egyptian. It had survived, with some modifications, for nearly three thousand years and had, by the time of the Greek and Roman occupation, entered a period of decadence. A characteristic of Egyptian religion was an ability to assimilate and absorb new influences from without and from within. This was not an intellectual synthesis of conflicting elements, but an amalgamation, over a long period of time, of old ideas, beliefs and practices with innovations and importations. The Egyptian religious attitude was one of worship, extending to the whole of life. It was an attitude of inclusiveness, on the one hand, and of inability to discard old beliefs and observances on the other. With increasing political unity, local deities were transformed into, or fused with, those of the dominant regime; deities lost, or assumed, importance from one period of time to another.

In the earlier period of Egyptian religion, life was seen as a unity, as a co-operation of the divine and the human. There was no sharp distinction between the dimensions in which the divine and the human acted. The Egyptian possessed an innate sense of analogy, which enabled him to 'see' the world in both divine and human terms. The sky, the earth, the air and the River Nile were deities; all natural phenomena were gods or parts of gods; human and animal faculties were personified. Deities were represented pictorially, in human or animal form, or as humans with animal heads. Only the king appeared as an animal with a human head (the so-called Sphinx). This anthropomorphic world was unified by the king, who was the earthly embodiment of divinity. By re-entering the world of the gods after death, the king was a link, uniting human and divine life. Whereas, in the world of men, the king alone was the unifying factor, in the world of the gods, triads of deities were usually supreme. These triads varied, and were composed of different gods, at different periods of Egyptian history. The most famous of these triads was that of Osiris, Isis and Horus, whose worship became, in Hellenistic times, widespread throughout the Graeco-Roman world.

In the solar religion, the king, as representative of his people, was identified with the sun and after death joined the sun in the daily journey across the sky. The means by which this life process of men and gods was maintained was ritual. Like the sun, man continued to live after death and like the sun, he could be caused to 'come forth by day',[1] by

2

means of the right invocations. The ritual of the identification of the dead with the sun was originally the prerogative of the king, but was in early times extended to the nobles. The ritual for promoting the annual renewal of vegetation, and thus of life for man, was the basis of the cult of Osiris. The deity whose birth, death, dismemberment and final resurrection were celebrated, was the representative of both plant and human life. The cult of Osiris was universal, in that it included the general population as well as the king, and it was practised at all periods of Egyptian history. Judgment of the individual's life took place after death and identification with Osiris depended on his being 'true of voice'.[1]

The exercise of divine power, whether by man or deity, was believed to be achieved by speech. In one account, the creation of the world was said to be the work of the heart and tongue of the god Ptah. The knowledge of the name of a person or situation was felt to be a source of power. By pronouncing the name, a person could be recalled to life or obliterated, a difficulty could be overcome. The name of a man was, in a sense, synonymous with his personality and the recollection of the name of a man after death ensured the continuation of his 'life'.[2] One of the greatest fears of a man was that his name should be forgotten. The Egyptian funerary rituals and memorial inscriptions both commemorated the dead and maintained the sense of community of the living with the dead. On the one hand, the deceased were enabled to know the correct names and formulae, by means of which they could pass through the world of *Amente* (the underworld whose entrance was in the West); on the other hand, both in speech and in writing, the names of the deceased would be remembered on earth. Ritual also ensured the expulsion and aversion of malevolent influences during life and after death. Evil beings were depicted in monstrous, mainly animal forms and much of funerary ritual consisted in spells to overcome them.

Writing was also a means of achieving destructive effects, through the divine power inherent, not only in the words but also in their component hieroglyphs. The funerary inscriptions of the burial chambers and coffins were intended as a form of communication between the living and the dead. They were effective, not only when spoken aloud, but in themselves as a form of speech. In addition to formulae to ensure for the dead continuity of life, renewal of life and overcoming of obstructions, a number of inscriptions were concerned with the re-establishment of the person of the deceased.[3] His name, epithets, attributes, and achievements were enumerated. His limbs and organs were invoked and said to be joined together. To some extent, the funerary ritual was a recapitulation of the process of creation; in this case the members of the human world recreated the divine person of the deceased.

In ancient Egyptian religion, the experience of 'life, health and prosperity'[4] in the fields of the Nile valley was the highest form of happiness; life after death was a continuation of the same pleasures and occupations. Such an attitude was dependent on a form of consciousness in which individual self-consciousness, as we know it, did not exist. Their experience can perhaps be interpreted by us as one of identity, maintained by ritual, of the human world, the world of nature and a 'post-mortem' world, all of which were divine. When such a civilisation was no longer able to expel outside invaders, its disintegration was inevitable. The final decay of Egypt was occurring during the Hellenistic period.

(ii) *Greece*

In ancient Greece, as in Egypt, religion was first manifested as ritual, and in classical times, there existed two independent forms: the Olympian and the chthonic.

> Those of the gods who are source to us of good things have the title of Olympians, those whose department is that of calamities and punishment have harsher titles; to the first class both private persons and states erect altars and temples, the second is not worshipped either with prayers or burnt-sacrifices, but in their case we perform ceremonies of riddance (*apompai*).
>
> Isocrates, *Oration*, V.117

The Olympian deities were anthropomorphic and in their forms and activities were represented the range and interplay of human passions and aspirations. Men were able to participate in, and to experience, this emotional drama by hearing the recitations of the poets, by performing the ritual acts of worship and by seeing or creating their forms in works of art. The Olympian gods were distinct from man in being immortal and in having supernatural powers, with which they intervened in human affairs. The human and divine worlds, however, remained separate and man did not desire either to become a god or to be like a god. The ability of men to pass moral judgments on their gods did not detract from their belief that the myths of the poets contained 'eternal truths'. Greek education at all periods involved the learning by heart and study of the poems of Homer. The detachment and objectivity with which the Greeks were able to view their own emotions was the result of reliving, through art and ritual, the experiences of the gods. Human emotions and aspirations were embodied in visible forms; both harmony and conflict were represented through the medium of art. In the architecture, sculpture, poetry and drama of classical Greece, harmony was achieved and realised by the exercise of the imagination.

Plato gave philosophical expression to an imaginative vision of the universe, in which divine harmony is akin to human thought:

> And the motions akin to the divine within us are the thoughts and revolutions of the universe. So it is they to which each of us must conform.
>
> Plato, *Timaeus*, 90D

The divine harmony is also embodied in the visible world, as in a living creature:

> For this our world has received its full complement of living creatures, mortal and immortal, and come to be in all its grandeur, goodness, beauty and perfection,—this visible living creature made in the likeness of the intelligible and embracing all the visible, this god displayed to sense, this our heaven, one and only begotten.
>
> Plato, *Timaeus*, 92C

The anthropomorphic and harmonious conception of the world was, however, the vision of a privileged few; it was the background of a culture which is still regarded as one of the peaks of human achievement. Nevertheless, long after the disappearance of this culture, the Platonic vision of a divine world, underlying the world of the senses, continued to exert influence.

While the Olympian deities were recognised as 'the source of good things', it was known that there existed other powers of a more dangerous nature, from whose presence man needed protection.[5] These chthonic deities, the object of popular rituals of 'riddance', were primarily the ghosts of the dead. In Greece, there was no sense of unity of the living and the dead, and the dead were seen as hostile and vengeful. To get rid of these spirits was to undergo purification, and to be pure was to have performed the ceremonies to placate and avert them. During the festival of the Anthesteria the spirits were feasted and then were bidden to depart.

When the religions connected with the names of Dionysus and Orpheus entered Greece they had no influence on the Olympian cult, but they gave new meanings to the popular rites for aversion of evil and for purification. The essence of the Dionysiac religion was the belief that man could become a god[6]; the new ritual was the communal eating of the body of the god. In the worship of Dionysus, the conviction that man could become a god was realised by the ritual incarnation of the god in one of his worshippers. Drunkenness was a necessary accompaniment of the ritual, in order to obliterate self-consciousness and restraint.

1

Orphic religion was based on the Dionysiac belief that man could become a god, but the means of achieving divinity differed. The means still involved the obliteration of self-consciousness, but the method was not physical intoxication but emotional ecstasy, induced by music and rhythm. The experience of identity with the physical organism was replaced by a vision, realised by the soul. The 'vision', experienced and portrayed in the Orphic cosmogony, was an ordered system based upon a series of triads. The system had some affinities to that of Pythagoras, who had proposed that the universe had a mathematical ground-plan, that qualitative differences were due to different underlying mathematical forms. As in the Pythagorean cult, preparation for Orphic initiation included ascetic abstinence and purification rites. The candidate was enthroned and the revelation was the human shape of the god Orpheus, as musician. In a state of ecstasy induced through music, man saw himself in control of the animal world, which lay at his feet.[7] The Orphic religion conceived the spirits of the old religion as inhabiting the underworld in monstrous forms, part human and part animal, implacable and vengeful in the life after death.

Another figure in Greek tradition, who gave to man a special significance, was the hero. The hero was portrayed in poetry and drama as a man who, by the exercise of human powers and virtues, was able to be victorious over both natural and supernatural obstacles.[8] The essential quality of the hero was his readiness to die, either for his own glory or for that of his cause. Through heroic poetry, other men who possessed some measure of the same qualities, shared in a vision of the meaning of the individual man in the universe. The hero was not a god, but a man who overcame his own limitations and those imposed on him by Destiny. (The relation of the hero to the Hellenistic solar cults is discussed in Chapter III.IV.4.)

After their death, the shrines of the heroes became the centres of local ritual cults. The heroes reigned over the inhabitants of the underworld and could be invoked to intervene in the life of the community, to act as oracles, or to heal the sick. The healing ritual was one of the most important of these shrine cults. The essential act was the sleep within the sanctuary. The hero appeared to the patient in a dream and either healed him or revealed to him the means of healing. The dream oracle was proper to the earth-born heroes and was distinct from the rites of the Olympian gods.

Plato recognised that the poets did not speak out of their own wisdom, but because they were inspired and, like the prophets and givers of oracles, they were not conscious of what they were saying:

That divination is a gift to the witless in man we have abundant

6

proof. No man, in fact attains to inspired and true divination in his full senses, but only when understanding is fettered by sleep or distraught by disease, or it may be, by possession. 'Tis for one in his wits to recall and understand the deliverances of divination and possession, waking or sleeping and to discern the significations of all their visions, what evil or good, past, present or to come, they figure and to whom; but 'tis no work for him who has been distraught and is yet in that case to judge of that which he sees or utters; rather . . . to know himself belongs only to the sober. Whence also our usage sets prophets over the deliverances of inspired divination. Some call these men themselves 'diviners', all-unknowing that they are interpreters of the riddling speech and vision and should most rightly be called not 'diviners' but spokesmen (*prophetai*) of divination.

Plato, *Timaeus*, 71E–72B

He praised the kind of possession or madness, which came from the gods, as superior to sanity. He allowed that, by its means, public affairs were influenced and future generations educated:

In reality the greatest of blessings come to us through madness, when it is sent as a gift of the gods. For the prophetesses at Delphi and the priestesses at Dodona, when they have been mad, have conferred many splendid benefits upon Greece both in private and in public affairs, but few or none when they have been in right minds; and if we should speak of the Sibyl and all the others who by prophetic inspiration have foretold many things to many persons and thereby made them fortunate afterwards, anyone can see that we should speak a long time. And it is worth while to adduce also the fact that those men of old who invented names thought that madness was neither shameful nor disgraceful; otherwise they would not have connected the very word mania with the noblest of arts, that which foretells the future, by calling it the manic art. . . . The ancients then testify that, in proportion as prophecy (*mantike*) is superior to augury, both in name and in fact, in the same proportion, madness, which comes from god, is superior to sanity, which is of human origin.

Plato, *Phaedrus*, 244A–D

He claimed that his own life work, as philosopher, had been the result of commands given to him through dreams and oracles:

I have been commanded to do this by the God through oracles and dreams and in every way in which any man was ever commanded by divine power to do anything whatsoever.

Plato, *Apology*, 33C

To Plato, the pursuit of wisdom and the perfection of the soul were the most important duties of a man. The attainment of knowledge was comparable to physical death and therefore, for a philosopher, death was less to be feared than for other men. Pure knowledge was an experience of the soul and, for this reason, the body was a barrier to attaining truth:

> When the soul makes use of the body for any inquiry, either through seeing or hearing or any of the other senses,—for inquiry through the body means inquiry through the senses,—then it is dragged by the body to things which never remain the same, and it wanders about and is confused . . .
>
> But when the soul inquires alone by itself, it departs into the realm of the pure, the everlasting, the immortal and the changeless, and being akin to these it dwells always with them whenever it is by itself and is not hindered, and it has rest from its wanderings and remains always the same and unchanging with the changeless, since it is in communion therewith. And this state of the soul is called wisdom.
>
> Plato, *Phaedo*, 79C,D

The vision of the philosopher involved the separation, in some sense, of the soul from the body. The body was a tomb in which the soul was imprisoned:

> . . . being permitted as initiates to the sight of perfect and simple and calm and happy apparitions, which we saw in the pure light, being ourselves pure and not entombed in this which we carry about with us and call the body, in which we are imprisoned like an oyster in its shell.
>
> Plato, *Phaedrus*, 250C

The organ of knowledge and vision for Plato was the soul. The soul, not the universe, was immortal and self-moving:

> Every soul is immortal. For that which is ever moving is immortal; but that which moves something else or is moved by something else, when it ceases to move, ceases to live. Only that which moves itself, since it does not leave itself, never ceases to move, and this is also the source and beginning of motion for all other things which have motion.
>
> Plato, *Phaedrus*, 245C

The language, in which Plato expressed the relationship of the soul to the divine world and to the world of the senses or body, continued to be used in the Alexandrian schools by Greek, Jewish and finally by

8

Christian writers in the Hellenistic period. More than those of any other Greek philosopher, the thought forms of Plato, through the Neo-Platonic schools, influenced the early Church Fathers.

In the third century A.D., Neoplatonism represented the culmination of the philosophic approach, deriving from Pythagorus, Plato, Aristotle and Philo, in which, through philosophy itself, an experience of reality was attained. To Plotinus, the chief exponent of Neoplatonism, the whole cosmos was united by the common participation in one soul. Through the soul, the wills of all members were united in a common will:

> This All is one universally comprehensive living being, encircling all the living beings within it, and having a soul, one Soul which extends to all its members; every separate thing is an integral part of this All by belonging to the total material fabric, while in so far as it has participation in the All-Soul, it possesses spiritual membership as well. Each several thing is affected none the less by all else in virtue of the common participation in the All.
>
> This One-All, therefore, is a sympathetic total and stands as one living being. As in an animal the separate parts are not continuous and yet are effectively near, so here with corresponding things not side by side but separated by others, the sharing of experience by dint of like condition—this is enough to ensure that the action of any distant member be transmitted to its distant fellow. Where all is a living being summing to a unity there is nothing so remote in point of place as not to be near by virtue of a nature which makes of the one living being a sympathetic organism. The concern must be for the whole of which each item is a member.
>
> The entire cosmos puts its entire life into act, moving its major members with its own action and unceasingly setting them in new positions; by the relations thus established of these members to each other and to the whole, the minor members in turn are brought under the system as in the movement of some one living being, so that they vary according to the relations, positions, configurations.
>
> For ourselves, while yielding to the action of the All whatever in us belongs to it, we realize too that the whole man is not thus bound that our submission must be only within limits. . . . The will of any organic thing is one; but the distinct powers that go to constitute it far from being one; yet all the several wills look to the object aimed at by the one will of the whole; for the desire which the one member entertains for another is a desire within the All.
>
> Plotinus, Enneads, IV.4.32, Problems of the Soul, II

In man, the soul was the means of knowledge and the aim of the philosopher was to separate the soul from the body, so that the vision of the soul was directed away from sense-perception:

> As long as we have agent and instrument, there are two distinct entities; if Soul uses the body, it is separate from it,—part of the Soul, at least—while another part is in contact, the disjoined part ranking with the instrument or thing used. It will be the double task of philosophy to direct this lower soul towards the higher, and except in so far as the conjunction is absolutely necessary, to sever the agent from the instrument, the body, so that it need not forever have its act through this inferior.
>
> Plotinus, *Enneads*, I.1.3, *The Animate and the Man*

Whereas for Plato, communion with the divine could be attained by the use of the memory of concepts reached through reason, Plotinus demanded that all memories be forgotten. For Plotinus, the goal of philosophy was not contemplation of the divine, but an experience of identity. The *Phaedrus* expressed the attitude of Plato:

> For a human being must understand a general conception formed by collecting into a unity by means of reason the many perceptions of the senses; and this is a recollection of those things which our soul once beheld, when it journeyed with God and, lifting its vision above the things which we now say exist, rose up into the real being. And therefore it is just that the mind of the philosopher only has wings, for he is always, so far as he is able, in communion through memory with those things the communion with which causes God to be divine. Now a man who employs such memories rightly is always being initiated into perfect mysteries and he alone becomes truly perfect.
>
> Plato, *Phaedrus*, 249B,C

Plotinus required the extinction of individual consciousness:

> Of things of earth it (the soul) will know nothing. There can be no memory in the Intellectual World; all is presence there; there is no passage, no transition from one thing to another.
>
> There will not even be memory of the personality, no thought that the contemplator is the self. In contemplative vision, especially when it is vivid, we are not at the same time aware of our own personality; the activity is towards the object of vision with which the thinker becomes identified.
>
> Plotinus, *Enneads*, IV.4.1. *Problems of the Soul*, II

Plotinus described how the seer was able to create a mental picture of a unified universe, and then to imagine that there existed another universe, without any attributes derived from sense perception. Of this second universe, God was the creator but man was able to identify himself with the divine creative power. In union with the divine, man lost the consciousness of himself as a separate individual, and the identity of the seer and the seen was experienced in the soul. That this was the goal for the few and was only rarely attained, is clear from the writings of his pupil, Porphyry:

> And this goal he attained four times, I believe, while I was living with him—not potentially, but actually, though by an actuality which is beyond the power of language to describe. . . . His writings are the record of these researches and revelations given him by the gods.
>
> Porphyry, *Life of Plotinus*, 23.15

For the many, the dilemma of the Hellenistic world remained unresolved. With intellectual development, there was increasing individual self-consciousness. Only by loss of this consciousness of self, was it possible to attain an experience of the divine as inspiration or incorporation, and this within the circle of a cult. Among those who attempted to solve the problem confronting men of that period were the gnostic groups. Within the scope of this book it is only possible to mention briefly the gnostic movements (see Chapter IV.II); their existence caused the early Church Fathers to intensify their efforts to formulate their own intellectual standpoint and system of ethics.

(iii) *Hebrew*

To the ancient Egyptian, the divine world was manifested in the daily round of human activities. Through his religious ritual, he felt in unison both with the organic world of nature and with the human world, alive and dead. His only aim was the prolonging of his state of happiness for as long as possible. The Hebrew religion, in contrast, was the means by which a people separated themselves from their neighbours, became animated with a sense of purpose and, in order to achieve their goal, developed a close religious and racial unity.

From the time of Abram, who separated himself from the polytheistic practices of Haran on hearing the command of his God, Hebrew religion was essentially obedience to authority. Within this authority was a legal element, the covenant. The earliest acts of obedience were the creation of a racial group, united by ties of blood, and the rejection of polytheistic practices in favour of a strict monotheism. Continuity of life was seen in the physical terms of race, and intermarriage with neighbouring tribes was forbidden. Whereas the ancient Egyptian

11

himself addressed and invoked his many deities, believing in the power of the words which he spoke, in the Hebrew religion, man felt that it was the deity who spoke, that power resided in the deity and that disobedience was followed by retribution.

The second 'separation' of the Hebrew people was from Egypt. Under the leadership of Moses, the Children of Israel, the twelve tribes descended from Jacob, received the laws by which henceforth they were bound. Moses was the first of a long line of leaders, through whose inspired speech came the divine commands and revelations. The Law, a moral code, was revealed to Moses under conditions suggesting alteration of consciousness,—upon a mountain top in fire and earthquake (see Chapter V.III.4). The Law was received by the people as externally imposed rules of conduct, which included prohibition of the making of visible images of the deity. Thus only through the intellect could the Deity be understood by those who were not prophets, and knowledge of God was limited to knowledge of his Laws. Under Moses, the advance from oral tradition to written law was made; the Law covered both the revelations received in the desert of Sinai and the accounts of the origins and rise of a 'holy nation' as embodied in the Pentateuch, traditionally all the writings of Moses.

The means by which a national historical self-consciousness was developed was the continual revelation of the will of their God to the people of Israel. The prophets were the channel by which the nature and purposes of the deity were made known; prophetic utterances, which began with Moses, continued to be made until the post-exilic era. The terms 'prophet' and 'seer' were used synonymously[9]; throughout the period, prophets were known as seers and their revelations were spoken of as 'visions'. A definite cult of seership existed; the prophets formed guilds and received a training. The prophet felt he was called to his role, that prophecy was a gift, and in this role he was known as 'a man of God'. Self-preparation in the form of prayer, fasting, even self-mutilation were practised and a special garment of skin or hair was worn. The prophets received their revelations under abnormal conditions of consciousness in states of ecstasy, trance or dream and they spoke under the influence of the 'spirit of Jahweh' or the 'hand of Jahweh' (see Chapter V.III.4).[10] The experiences, recorded in the books of the prophets, included both the hearing of 'the voice of Jahweh' and the seeing of visionary worlds. The visions showed the divine world in which Jahweh operated and also the future events of this world. The communications of the prophets continually recalled the people of Israel to their national-historical role. From Moses, they learnt that they would 'inherit' a 'promised land', an earthly paradise, and through

Elijah, it was announced that God was not only God of Israel but of all nations. Isaiah foretold the rise of a New Jerusalem, a Kingdom, embracing all the earth, over which the Messiah would rule, the nucleus of which new kingdom would be in Zion.

Experience of the divine, in the Egyptian, Greek and Hebrew religions, was recognised as essential for human life on earth. The technique or ritual by which such experience was achieved invariably precluded individual self-consciousness. Whereas both Egyptian and Greek religions saw the gods and the universe in anthropomorphic forms, Judaism prohibited such a view. In Judaism, the Deity was an expression of nationhood rather than the image of man or the universe.

II   THE DECLINE OF ORACLES

Plutarch's *On the cessation of Oracles* drew attention to a phenomenon, which was apparent in different forms throughout the Hellenistic world, for which men were unable to account:

> The assertion that the Oracles are lying idle and dumb, because the daemons have migrated or deceased starts another yet more important inquiry into the cause and power, whereby they render prophets and prophetesses possessed with inspiration, and capable of seeing visions. For it is not possible to lay the blame on their desertion as the cause why the Oracles are dumb, without first explaining in what way the daemons, when they do preside at them, and are present, render these same Oracles active and able to speak.
>
> Plutarch, *On the cessation of Oracles*, XXXVIII

He also commented on the decline of poetic inspiration and on the use of prose, rather than poetry, for expression:

> . . . For the use of language is like the exchange of a coin that acquires a different value at different times . . . There was a time when people used for the currency of speech verses and tunes and songs, converting into music and poetry, all history, all philosophy, every passion, and to speak generally, every circumstance that required more dignified utterance. For things that nowadays few people listen to, everybody then used to hear, and took pleasure in their being sung . . . Nay, through this aptitude for poetry, most persons admonished others by means of the lyre and song: they spoke their minds, they comforted others, they did their business with fables and with songs; furthermore

they caused to be made in verse and songs the hymns of the gods, prayers, and thanksgivings; partly from natural aptitude and partly from old custom.

Plutarch, *On the Pythian Responses*, XXIV

Only when it appeared to be declining, did men become explicitly conscious that they possessed a faculty for apprehending the divine. In Jewish religious circles, this consciousness was expressed in the writings which declared that the message of prophecy was no longer available.[11] The failure of vision, dreams and prophecy was mentioned as a fact in *i Samuel*[12] and foretold in *Ezekiel*.[13] *Psalm* 74(73).9 was a lament that a source of knowledge and direction no longer existed. In the Rabbinic writings, it was said that prophetic inspiration had ceased since the days of Haggai, Zechariah, Malachi and Ezra.[14] The Jewish historian Josephus (*c.* A.D. 100) wrote that prophetic inspiration had ceased in the reign of Artaxerxes (fifth century B.C.).[15] With the decline of prophecy, the interpretation of the earlier prophecies became an increasingly important activity.

The prophetic utterances were probably originally memorised by disciples and transmitted, first as oral tradition, and later put in writing; thus the composition of the 'book' of a prophet would be the work of a guild. The organised study of the Torah or Law began during the time of Ezekiel. After the end of the Captivity (538 B.C.), began a period of intense preoccupation with the collection together and study of both written and unwritten traditions: the books of the laws, the chronicles and the prophetic writings. These eventually together formed the written Torah.[16]

Intellectual activity in the Hellenistic world was increasingly dominated by tradition and habitual practices. Both in the Greek and Jewish centres of learning, study was based on the learning of texts by heart. In the Jewish schools, the written Torah, when studied, had to be learnt from a book[17]; thus reading was necessary. The aim of study was firstly the perfect memorisation of the text; secondly, it was necessary to learn to read it aloud with accurate cantillation. The oral Torah (or tradition) was also memorised. The text was repeated by a teacher until the hearers were able to recite it alone. Thus the traditional material was imprinted on the memory and was kept alive by constant repetition. Only after the complete text was memorised, was either oral or written Torah subjected to examination or interpretation by a student.

The method of exegesis was two-fold[18]: on the one hand, every word and phrase were examined separately, independently of their context, on the other, allegorical interpretation was used. The canon of the Pentateuch and the prophetic writings began to be defined about 200

B.C. and from this time, the acceptance of fresh prophecy became increasingly difficult. The oracle, as a source of knowledge, fell into disrepute as a result of the spread of mystery cults, of Persian and Babylonian origin, which were regarded by the Jewish authorities as idolatrous. There was a hope, expressed in *i Maccabees*,[19] that the gift of prophecy would be renewed and that a prophet would appear, who would be the precursor of the Messiah. The hope was connected, through the earlier prophetic writings, with the names of Moses and Elijah.

In the Greek schools, learning was based on the memorisation and interpretation of Homer and the classical poets. The 'divine madness' described by Plato[20] was no longer felt. A bard of the ancient Greek tradition, when telling a story, would recreate the familiar images and situations, so that the resultant was a fresh work of art. In the recitation of a written text, there was merely a passive re-experiencing of familiar emotions. Contained within these religious and poetic narratives, however, were those symbols and images which constitute 'myth'. The mythology of the ancient world had arisen in the form of visions, oracles and revelations. The desire to give intellectual and moral interpretations to these traditions occupied both Greek and Jewish thinkers.

The centre of philosophy and culture of the Hellenistic world, from about 250 B.C., was Alexandria. One of the leading Jewish thinkers was Philo, whose lifetime covered the beginning of the Christian era. His purpose was to set forth an allegory of the human soul and its relations to God, based on interpretation of the scriptures. He used the language of Greek philosophy, drawing from the different schools to illustrate his thesis. Like Plato, he considered the body to be the prisonhouse of the soul and that the soul or mind alone were capable of relationship with God. Relation with the divine for Philo, however, involved ecstasy or possession and the obliteration of the light of the human mind:

> Admirably then does he (Moses) describe the inspired when he says 'about sunset there fell on him an ecstasy'.
>
> Philo, *Who is the Heir?* LII.263

> 'Sun' is his name under a figure for our mind. For what the reasoning faculty is in us, the sun is in the world, since both of them are light-bringers, one sending forth to the whole world the light which our senses perceive, the other shedding mental rays upon ourselves through the medium of apprehension. So while the radiance of the mind is still all around us, when it pours as it were a noonday beam into the whole soul, we are self-contained, not possessed. But when it comes to its setting, naturally ecstasy and divine possession and

15

madness fall upon us. For when the light of God shines, the human light sets; when the divine light sets, the human dawns and rises. This is what regularly befalls the fellowship of the prophets. The mind is evicted at the arrival of the divine spirit, but when that departs the mind returns to its tenancy. Mortal and immortal may not share the same home. And therefore the setting of reason and the darkness which surrounds it produce ecstasy and inspired frenzy. . . . For indeed, the prophet even when he seems to be speaking, really holds his peace, and his organs of speech, mouth and tongue are wholly in the employ of Another, to shew forth what He wills.

Philo, *Who is the Heir?*, LIII.263–266

In the post-exilic period, coincident with the decline of prophecy, appeared another Jewish tradition, that of the apocalyptic writings. The books of *Daniel* and *I Enoch* were the fullest expression of this type of literature.[21] The language and symbolism showed the re-use of pre-existing forms; the imagery was drawn, not only from Old Testament sources, but from Babylon, Persia and Greece. Although the figures and images were stereotyped, they varied between one apocalyptic tradition and another in their manner of presentation. Among the classical prophets, *Ezekiel* was an important source of imagery, but themes were also drawn from *Jeremiah*, *Zechariah 1–8*, and *Isaiah 24–27*. Themes included the regions of the cosmos, cataclysm and judgment, the Day of the Lord, the coming of the Golden Age and the Resurrection of the Dead, the life after death and the divisions of Hell and Paradise. There was particular concern with the 'beginning' and 'end' of human and cosmic history. The apocalyptic writers were concerned with events in time; the coming of the Messiah and its relation to the origin and future, both of the Jewish people and of mankind. Throughout the apocalyptic literature, the thought and imagery of the prophets was fitted into a new pattern of ideas. The traditional phraseology was regarded as being of divine origin; the words and images were the medium of divine revelation. Thus arose a method of writing, in which the language pre-supposed a knowledge of an earlier literary background, and in which 'seership' was claimed on the basis of the writer's relationship to a patriarchal figure.

A characteristic of apocalyptic writers was the practice of ascribing a given line of tradition to a great figure of the past.[22] This use of names depended on the idea of corporate personality, which existed among the Jewish people. The group included members past, present and future and could be represented by an individual at any time. The sense of kinship entitled a writer to attribute experiences to one who could have been his ancestor. Like the Egyptians, the Jews thought of historical time as a recurrent series of cycles, so that events from the past could be related to similar events in the present. Thus the three main lines of apocalyptic tradition were associated with critical turning points, connected with the names of Enoch (with Noah), Moses (with Ezra) and Daniel.[23] In the same way, laws were attributed to Moses, even in the post-exilic period, psalms were credited to David, and the books of *Proverbs*, *Ecclesiastes* and *Wisdom* to Solomon. Thus, as in Egypt, the name of a man was the possession, not only of the individual but of the family or group. A father gave his name to his son and continued to live in the son; the qualities attached to a famous name were received by whoever inherited the name. In this way, to adopt the name of a seer of the past, was to be identified with him, to re-experience his vision and to continue, in new circumstances, to proclaim his message.

The apocalyptic writers claimed to have received their inspiration, as did the classical prophets, in the form of dreams, visions or trances. A phenomenon, commonly described in Greek literature but unknown in the Old Testament prophets, was that of the soul or spirit of a man leaving the body and travelling through the places of Heaven and Hades. Such an experience was not described by the prophets who did not think of the soul apart from the body,[24] as a separate conscious entity. Man was regarded as a unity by the prophets; psychic powers resided within the organs[25] and members of the body, the heart, the bowels and the reins or kidneys. The apocalyptic writers, however, thought of the soul apart from the body, as leading a conscious life of its own and communing with the Deity. The words 'soul' and 'spirit' were used interchangeably:

> And it came to pass after this that my spirit was translated and it ascended into the heavens, and I saw the holy ones of God.
>
> *I Enoch*, 71.1 (Charles)

In other writings, bodily transportation of the seer was described. Christian writers adopted the form of Jewish apocalyptic writings and, on occasions, 'Christianised' Jewish texts (see Chapter III, 'Conclusion').

The Alexandrian 'Catechumen School', in the second and third centuries, was a centre of Christian scholarship and of religious and philosophic discussion. It had been a centre of Greek learning since the Ptolemaic period, and Greek rational methods were the basis of much early Christian writings. The works of Clement of Alexandria were attempts to prove, by reasoned argument, that Christianity fulfilled the demands of Greek philosophy and of 'gnosticism'. For Clement, salvation depended on knowledge and knowledge ultimately was 'vision'; the true 'gnostic' was one who, through his will to know, enlightened himself.

The use of the terms 'vision' and 'sight' in the writings of Clement appears to have been figurative, a deliberate use of the vocabulary of his non-Christian opponents. The 'gnostic' perfected himself in accordance with the 'vision' of God:

> . . . The gnostic therefore, being naturally disposed to love God who is truly One, is himself a truly perfect man and a friend of God, being ranked and reckoned as a son. These are names, expressive of nobility and knowledge and perfection, in accordance with that vision of God which is the crowning height attainable by the gnostic soul, when it has been perfectly purified, being now deemed worthy to behold for ever the Almighty, face to face. For there having been made entirely spiritual, it departs to its kindred sphere and there, in the spiritual Church, abides in the rest of God.

> Clement, *Stromateis*, Book VII.xi.68

The 'apprehensive vision' of the 'gnostic' arose from his service to God:

> . . . Only I say that those gnostic souls are so carried away by the magnificence of the vision, that they cannot confine themselves within the lines of the constitution, by which each holy degree is assigned and in accordance with which the blessed abodes of the gods have been marked out and allotted; but being counted as holy among the holy, and translated absolutely and entirely to another sphere, they keep on always moving to higher and yet higher regions, until they no longer greet the divine vision in or by means of mirrors, but with loving hearts feast for ever on the uncloying, never-ending sight, radiant in its transparent clearness, while throughout the endless ages they taste a never-wearying delight, and thus continue, all alike honoured with an identity of preeminence. This is the apprehensive vision of the pure in heart. This then is the life-work of the perfected gnostic, viz. to hold communion with God through the great High Priest, being made like the Lord, as far as may be, by means of all his service towards God,

> Clement, *Stromateis*, Book VII.iii.13

Nevertheless, faith was said to be the precondition of knowledge; as human attainment was limited, faith was the substitute for knowledge for those to whom knowledge was not available.

From the time of Clement, the Alexandrian tendency, derived from Plato, to lay emphasis on knowledge as the chief factor in spiritual development, was checked and more importance was attached to the will to believe. The doctrine of 'gnosis' was increasingly strongly opposed by the Church Fathers, as it was thought likely to encourage the idea that salvation could be acquired by the efforts of the individual, apart from the Church. In the Patristic writings, from the time of Clement onwards, appeared the Stoic doctrine of self-repression, the use of the rational powers to overcome the irrational elements of man's nature:

> Now the sacrifice which is acceptable to God is unswerving abstraction from the body and its passions. This is the really true piety.
>
> Clement, *Stromateis*, Book V.xi.1

Thus, by assuming divine authority over the intellect and will of the individual, the Church placed herself as mediator between man and the divine.

To Origen, the way to knowledge was through the Bible. He developed a method of allegorical exegesis, which later became the model for biblical exegesis for the Eastern Church. The narratives of the Old Testament were shown as allegories of the soul in its ascent towards knowledge. The interpretation of the scriptures was said to be possible by three methods, according to the level of the soul's understanding:

> The right way, then, to read the Scriptures and extract their meaning, so far as we have been able to discover from examining the oracles themselves, appears to be as follows: ... A man ought then, in three ways, to record in his own soul the purposes of the Holy Scriptures; that the simple may be edified by, as it were, the flesh of Scripture (for thus we designate the primary sense), the more advanced by its soul, and the perfect by the spiritual law, which has a shadow of the good things to come.
>
> Origen, *Philocalia*, II

To Origen, the understanding of Scripture was 'the art of arts' and 'the science of sciences'.[26] The mysteries, contained within the Scripture, were only revealed to those who sought the right interpretation with insistent prayer. Such a personal approach to revelation was discredited by the later Church Fathers.

In concluding this brief summary, it can be seen that the early Christian world of Alexandria was the scene of conflicting views on human faculties and abilities. It is only possible to pursue here those aspects of the subject which concern the availability of vision, knowledge or revelation to the individual. From Greek philosophy, through Neoplatonism, came a tradition that by individual effort, through intellectual means, a vision or experience of immaterial reality was possible. The method, which was available only to a few, was described as a 'separation of the soul from the body'. Earlier examples of such an approach were the Pythagorean and Orphic mysteries, in which, through the activities of a group, the individual experienced the universe and himself as divine, or immaterial. These methods all involved the obliteration, to some degree, of individual self-consciousness.

A similar type of approach to knowledge was that of the dream vision of the Jewish apocalyptic seer. As in the Greek tradition, the sense perceptions were not employed in obtaining the vision. During the experience, however, the seer maintained his identity; there was no union of the seer with the divinity. Understanding of the revelation was limited to those few who were familiar with the symbolic language. Nevertheless, the vision was a confirmation of the existence of an immaterial world, at a time when prophetic sources had ceased.

The emotional or moral approach of man to the divine was made possible through the histories and dramas of the gods and men of Greek mythology. Participation, through art and ritual, in their conflicts and assessment of their virtues was an experience, not of individuals, but of groups who shared a common background and history. A similar approach was that of the Jewish people, to whom their own history and destiny was made known by the visions of the prophets. The experience, whether of divine approval or condemnation, was shared by all; the group experienced the consequences of its actions. Whereas, to the Greeks, the world of the senses expressed the immaterial world of emotions and moral laws, for the Jewish people, strict rules governed the use of material objects. Images were associated with polytheism, which was a constant threat to the idea of one nation united in the worship of one God. This idea of 'unity' was the concept which enabled the Jewish people to separate themselves from their neighbours. Polytheistic religious expression was based on sense-perception. The ability to conceive of one God, transcending a plurality of gods, was the earliest manifestation of conceptual thought. The struggles of the Jewish people to maintain this idea, against the temptation to return to more primitive forms of religion, is embodied in the Old Testament narratives. The Dionysiac and other similar cults were the means, in Hellenistic times, by which more developed peoples sought to preserve archaic means of attaining knowledge.

The ancient Egyptian civilisation was unique in that it perpetuated, to a relatively late date, an archaic pattern of life. Egyptian religion was not primitive; it was highly developed and formalised. Nevertheless, it was concerned with maintaining those faculties, possessed by primitive man, before the development of conceptual thought. These faculties operated through the senses and depended on the integration of the individual within the group. There was thus a group-consciousness of man as a divine entity, of co-existent human and divine worlds and of the embodiment of divinity in the world of nature.

The early Church adopted an approach to knowledge of the divine similar to that of Judaism; that revelation had taken place in the past and that this revelation was contained in the Scriptures. The interpretation of the Old and New Testaments became increasingly the prerogative of the Church, rather than of the individual. By emotional and moral arguments, men were urged to adopt the new revelation through faith. Both individual man and the physical world were regarded as alienated from their divine origin; only through the Church could man's communication with the divine be restored. Whereas to Clement of Alexandria and Origen, the will of the individual enabled him to strive for perfection, the later Fathers stressed the necessity for obedience to the divine authority of the Church. In Judaism, when prophecy as a source of national guidance declined, the interpretation of the Law gained increasing power. To the Christian Fathers, the authority of the Church rested on its interpretation of the revelation contained in the Scriptures.

CHAPTER I

Withdrawal from the Environment of the Senses

Preliminary Considerations

The narratives of the lives of the early Christian saints and martyrs form a large volume of literature preserved during the centuries by the Church. Their original purpose was to record the lives and the manner of death of the heroic figures of early Christian times. They were intended to be read aloud so that the hearers participated emotionally in the events depicted. Thus the Christian biography served a similar function to the ancient hero-legends: the representation to the hearers of a non-material world. For this reason they appealed to and inspired listeners for many centuries. Modern critical research has revealed that much fictitious literature has accumulated around the historic facts. Certain literary patterns occur in the narratives and these were used again and again by hagiographers.[1] Only a certain prescribed form of life befitted a saint and thus these stylised biographies grew up round the names of their subjects. Great emphasis was laid upon the events connected with the death of the saint and the life stories were often, in the martyrdoms, reduced to a minimum. It was a pictorial and dramatic means of presenting the death of the individual; death was not a tragedy, as in Greek hero stories, but the means of entry into an eternal and divine life. The early Christian Church needed a new mythology as inspiring as that of the ancient world and the martyr and saint replaced the hero and sage. Whereas the early mythologies arose spontaneously in ancient times, the stories of saints were composed deliberately and for a purpose by men of culture.[2] The fact that their form was preserved by later imitators, however ignorant, suggests that the form itself was important.[3] The same literal or religious truths could have been expressed in other ways; it may therefore be worth examining those very elements which make the stories valueless as historical records.

The forms of biography can be distinguished: the martyrdom and the life of the ascetic. Of the former, the martyrdom of Polycarp (d. 156), written within a few years of his death, is the earliest, and was the model for many later writings. The subject of martyrdoms will be considered in Chapter V; the earliest martyrologies, both in the east and west, date from before the fifth century. The biography of Anthony by Athanasius, written *c*. 357, began the tradition of the lives of ascetic saints of the early Christian period. Historical biographies were well known in the Graeco-Roman world and it was the purpose of such writers as Suetonius, Sallust and Salpicius Severus to depict, against a recognisable background of events, the moral characters of their subjects. Plutarch (d. 102) was a philosopher as well as a moralist; his concern was with the meaning and significance of actions:

> We do not give the actions in full detail and with scrupulous exactness, but rather a short summary since we are not writing histories but lives. Nor is it always in the most distinguished achievements that men's virtues or vices may be best discerned, but very often an action of small note, a short saying or a jest, shall distinguish a person's real character more than the greatest sieges or the most important battles.
>
> Plutarch, *Alexander*, I

Athanasius, in his biography of Anthony (*c*. 357), drew upon earlier models[4]; one was the *encomium*, in which a figure in public life was praised for his achievements and services to the state (see Chapter V). Another literary model was possibly the life of Apollonius of Tyana by Philostratus (*c*. 217), a sophist, whose subject was a neo-Pythagorean sage who had lived a hundred years earlier. Apollonius was said to have practised and preached strict asceticism, to have had authority over demons and to have visited and reformed the centres of ancient religions. Athanasius used his biography as a vehicle for his attacks on heresies within the Church, on Neoplatonism and in particular on the cults and mystery religions in Egypt. Certain elements, peculiar to the life of Anthony, reflected the special circumstances of the writer and above all his background of Greek culture.[5] The Church of Alexandria was Greek-speaking and the biography was intended for other Churches of the Greek-speaking world. The notion of the practice of philosophy as a form of death, or withdrawal from the life of the senses, was found in the writings of Plato; some biographies represented the ascetic life in similar terms:

> If it (the soul) departs pure, dragging with it nothing of the body, because it never willingly associated with the body in life, but avoided it and gathered itself into itself alone, since this has always been its constant study—but this means nothing else than that it pursued philosophy rightly and really practised being in a state of death; or is not this the practice of death?
>
> Plato, *Phaedo*, 80E

23

Although Greek-speaking Christians were present in Egypt from an early date, conversion of the Egyptian people probably began in the middle of the third century. In the latter half of this century began the withdrawal of individuals to the desert for a life of isolation. The original meaning of *monachos* was 'man alone, in isolation from his fellows'. The first solitary ascetics were the chief subjects of the stories which later circulated in the settlements of monks in the western desert. The earliest communities were those of Cellia and Nitria[6] and many of their members lived an almost completely solitary life. A similar colony was founded in 330 by Macarius; meanwhile the coenobitic community of Pachomius had been in existence since 323, situated at Tabennesi in Upper Egypt. Thus within about a century, a movement which had been originally towards complete isolation of the individual, developed a communal form. The sayings and lives of the solitary ascetics were collected by their disciples and circulated as an oral tradition. Many were in the form of aphorisms and characteristic actions. They were thus memorised and recited as short episodes each concerning a named individual. In the fourth century the collecting together of these scattered narratives began. In the case of some communities, visitors were the means whereby these narratives were conveyed to the outside world.

In 388 Palladius came to Egypt from Galatia and his *Lausiac History*, which appeared *c.* 420, contained the stories collected by the monks of Cellia and Nitria. The *Historia Monachorum in Aegypto*, concerning the same communities, was a similar collection by an unknown visitor and was translated into Latin by Rufinus (*c.* 400). The *Apophthegmata Patrum* was a collection of narratives made about the middle of the fifth century. Scetis was devastated by barbarians (407–8) and the stories concerned Scetis during the period prior to the devastation. These narratives, when presented to the world, were in Greek and translations were made throughout the Christian world. The Coptic versions which made no attempt at literary elegance, are probably closest to the originals. In the case of the monastic foundations in Upper Egypt, the scattered narratives concerning their founders, Pachomius at Tabennesi and Shenute at Atribe, were collected and arranged by their successors. Thus the original language of these *Lives* was Coptic (Sahidic). They appeared as a collection of episodes in juxtaposition rather than as consecutive narratives. Biographies of non-Egyptian ascetics included the *Life of Hypatius* by Callinicus (mid-fifth century) and the anonymous *Life of Daniel the Stylite*, both from the region of Constantinople. In the sixth century, Cyril of Scythopolis was the author of a number of *Lives* of Palestinian monks. In the same period, John of Ephesus wrote a Syriac *History of the Eastern Saints* on monastic life in Mesopotamia.

Translation of the Bible into Coptic (the last form of the ancient Egyptian language) began from the second half of the third century. Until the Council of Chalcedon in 451, Greek was the liturgical language of the Church in Egypt. After this date, Coptic (Sahidic and later Bohairic) was used in the services and has remained the liturgical language until today. Although Greek was the language used for administration in Egypt until the Arab conquest, the people of Egypt were largely unable to speak Greek and were unconcerned with Greek culture. Thus for the majority of the Egyptians, the Bible in Coptic translation became the literary model and source of inspiration. Copies of the Scriptures were not numerous and thus adoption of Christianity necessitated learning portions of the Bible by heart. The earliest ascetics were probably illiterate (Anthony was described as being ignorant of Greek and unable to write). The texts were therefore memorised aloud, phrase by phrase, in the traditional manner of the early schools. Thus a system of Biblical recitation evolved in which phrases, or sequences of phrases, were the units. The language and vocabulary of the Bible thus became a common idiom between Christians. Such language was not used for daily affairs but was considered suitable for the commemoration of holy men. Just as the Bible was understood to contain an 'inner' as well as an 'outer' meaning, so the language of the Bible could be used to describe the actual events of the life of a saint as well as his subjective experiences.

It was accepted as Christian teaching that the events in the Gospels were a recapitulation and fulfilment of certain events in the Old Testament.[7] The biography of a Christian saint was intended as evidence that he also, during his lifetime, had 'relived' these events. Whereas the Alexandrian schools had shown that the Old Testament narratives could be given an allegorical interpretation as experiences of the soul, the Egyptian ascetics made the scriptures the basis for a way of life. The divergence of approach between the Alexandrian Fathers and the people of Egypt was due to their different cultural backgrounds. The Alexandrian culture was intellectual, based on Greek philosophy and Jewish theology. The Egyptian people were the inheritors of an ancient polytheistic tradition, in which the human and the divine were interpenetrating worlds. For the Egyptian, asceticism was a renunciation of his ancient religion and culture and a reversal of his attitude toward the natural world. Whereas to the Greek philosopher, the life of the senses was a distraction or impediment to higher thought, to the pagan Egyptian, the senses were his means of communication with the divine. The Egyptian ascetic, like the Jewish people of old, had literally to withdraw from the land of Egypt, to spend forty years of privation in the desert,[8] in order to overcome his psychic enslavement by his former way of life. The outcome of the struggle was not the gaining for himself and others of the power of conceptual thought, or of the ability to recognise the divine as a non-material unity. The ascetic went beyond the experiences of the Old Testament without, however, leaving his desert cell; he found the meaning of the Kingdom of Heaven by the control of his own faculties.

Under the headings 'Withdrawal from the Environment of the Senses' and 'The Establishment of a Non-material Environment', an attempt has been made to reinterpret the biographies of the ascetics. A distinction is made, from time to time, between what was represented by the biographers and what, with hindsight, it is perhaps possible to decide as to the nature and significance of the actual experiences of the individuals. This distinction is made, on the one hand, by reference to pre-Christian mythology, whose 'image' the Christian writers tried to efface, and to pre-Christian tradition whose influence nevertheless persisted. On the other hand, from modern knowledge on the production of hallucinations, an attempt has been made to deduce the possible results to the individual of the environmental and other factors described.

The ascetic movement took place at a time when the possibility of attaining direct knowledge of the divine was being denied by the Church Fathers. It is suggested that the ascetics sought to show that man alone, by his own efforts, could attain 'perfection' and that individual man was the new revelation of the divine.

I THE ASCETIC WAY OF LIFE

1 Ascetic Practices

The biography of the saint was originally composed as the proof of a new relationship between man and the divine; asceticism was the preparation necessary for living 'the life of the angels'.[9] The form of the biography was frequently a 'confession', or recapitulation of his life, said to have been made by the saint at his death-bed or in expectation of death (see Chapter III.III.2). Such a confession was rather of acts which he had performed or avoided than of his dogmatic beliefs. This rendering of an account of his life by one about to die had certain resemblances to the Egyptian *Book of the Dead*, wherein the deceased enumerated the acts from which he has refrained during his life.[10] The confession by the saint was made to a disciple, a fellow-ascetic or a visitor, on whom fell the responsibility that the words were preserved. These life-histories, which are here quoted as 'episodes', varied in form. Some were eye-witness accounts of meetings with ascetics and included stories of journeys into the desert; others repeated stories which were already traditional. The same forms were used to describe the way of life within the coenobitic and monastic establishments.

The 'themes' of the accounts of the ascetic way of life illustrated the experiences of the saint during his withdrawal from the world of the senses. Each aspect of his life—habitation, posture, diet, clothing, sleep and prayer—represented a sphere of conflict, a field in which he performed certain practices in a new way. For each of these changes, the Bible was cited as the model and the source of inspiration.[11] In the daily life of the Egyptian community of the first centuries A.D., ritual was still the means whereby the social and religious vitality was preserved. Thought and imagination were directed towards maintaining and renewing physical life. For the Egyptian of that period who adopted Christianity, the ascetic life was a necessary consequence of his special physical and social circumstances. The practice of a life based on non-material values was impossible in a community to whom the material world was the vehicle for divine manifestation, to whom conformity to the communal patterns was essential for all its members. The Egyptian withdrew from this milieu from necessity. Christianity made demands on the individual which, in his case, could only be fulfilled in total isolation. Whereas the group required the conformity of all its members, the ascetic was attempting to live in opposition to all group traditions. The extremes of self-imposed discipline were evidence of the efforts required to maintain this 'separation from the world'.

In addition to creating for himself a new way of life, the ascetic had to impress on his memory a completely new world of thought and imagination. In adopting the Bible, he inherited a religious background on which he modelled his own life. The history of the Jewish people in their progress from polytheism to monotheism was represented as the source from which he found guidance for his own efforts. The ancient Egyptian religion, unlike the Hebrew, held the view that death was the means of entry into a divine life, that the soul after death was able to participate in this world. The ascetic saw in Christianity the means of entry into the divine world in this life. The ascetic life was essentially a witness to the experience that there existed a non-material dimension, the entry to which was a form of death. The themes of 'The Ascetic Way of Life' illustrate the extent to which the saint approached the condition of death. In relation to the physical world, the ascetic was a dead man; he left the society of men, abandoning all his possessions. His habitation was the desert, the traditional Egyptian burial place. In so far as he was able, he aimed to live as if he were deprived of a physical body. The separation of the soul from the body was seen, not as the end of earthly life, but as a condition to be maintained by daily exertion.

The use of certain numbers to denote the duration of time or the repetition of ritual acts was widespread in ancient religions. From the time of Daniel onwards, the use of numbers in apocalyptic literature occurred.[12] The numbers three and a half, seven, seventy and four hundred and ninety were most frequently mentioned in connection with divisions of time. It was believed that the number and duration of the periods of time were divinely appointed, the pattern of the past would be the pattern of the future and the End would resemble the Beginning; thus these numbers revealed the divine purposes. (See Chapter III, 'Preliminary Considerations', for the relation of ritual, based on the Zodiac, to the physical life of the community). Since the ascetic life was deliberately based on Biblical patterns, the symbolism of the numbers used in these biographies referred to manifestations of the divine to the ascetics. These numbers were a replacement of those used in pagan mythology, and in the lives of the ascetics, the numbers acquired a new meaning. The biographies were written by and were intended for those to whom the Biblical symbolism was apparent. Thus forty years, the period spent in the wilderness by the Children of Israel, was the time when the Deity manifested to his people and the time when the Children of Israel were led by a column of fire. Forty days, the duration of the fasts of Moses, of Elijah and of Christ, was, in the early Christian period, regarded as the time spent by the soul after death in its return to the divine world (see Chapter III.iv.2). In the Torah, and especially in the apocryphal literature, the relationship between the calendar and prophecy or vision was demonstrated. The fiftieth day of the Feast of Weeks[13] was, according to the *Ezra Apocalypse*[14] and the *Book of Jubilees*,[15] the time of the revelation given to Moses on Sinai, and in the third-century Church it became the Feast of Pentecost.[16]

In certain Jewish sects, devoted to the minute study and observance of the Law, there is evidence that fifty-day periods were counted throughout the year.[17] The Therapeutae, described by Philo and located in Egypt, showed a combination of Pythagorean influences with Jewish thought:

> ... following the truly sacred instructions of the prophet Moses. First of all these people assemble after seven sets of seven days have passed, for they revere not only the simple seven but its square also, since they know its chastity and perpetual virginity. This is the eve of the chief feast which Fifty takes for its own, Fifty the most sacred of numbers and the most deeply rooted in nature, being

28

formed from the square of the right-angled triangle which is the source from which the universe springs.

Philo, The Contemplative Life, VIII.64, 65

In the writings of the Slavonic Josephus,[18] it was said that the Essenes (a community possibly identical with that of Qumran) celebrated the seventh day, the seventh week, the seventh month and the seventh year. These sects lived in expectation of the return of prophecy.

The most frequently mentioned units of time in the lives of the ascetics were the hour, the day, the week and the year. The biographies gave a new significance to calendar periods of time; they represented the achievements of the ascetics and were a measure of human powers of endurance and self-control. They also symbolised periods during which the ascetics were in communication with divine world, and were thus a measure of subjective time.

2 Discipleship

The master-disciple relationship was an important feature of early asceticism. During the third century A.D. in Egypt and elsewhere in the Christian world, groups of ascetics were separating themselves from the community life of their native villages. Men such as Anthony, who later became hermits, first placed themselves under the guidance of recognised holy men. Not only among the early communities, but also in the writings of Clement and Origen,[19] the superiority of the solitary life to that within the community, as a means of personal attainment, was maintained. The first Christian ascetics had, as their goal, the perfection of the individual and the attainment of the power to contemplate the divine world. The early monastic communities were regarded as a training ground and a necessary preparation for the life of the hermit. Community life was a period of probation[20] in which obedience to the commands of an elder and to a common discipline were a prelude to life alone without the support of external rules. The solitary life was a precondition to communication with the divine world. The existence of hermits who could describe their experiences was a guarantee that such revelations were possible. The disciple of the holy man was in the position of hearer of his master's revelations.

Just as the Church Fathers, after the fourth century, made the Church into the intermediary between man and the divine, so later monasticism rejected the idea of the superiority of the hermit's life over that of the community.[21] The monastic community, as an end in itself, was exemplified in Egypt by the coenobitic movement, initiated by Pachomius. From the fourth century onward, the monastery was no longer a place of preparation for a life of complete isolation. Monastic life thenceforth involved life-long obedience to the rule[22] of a community invested in a superior. Monasticism spread rapidly throughout Egypt, Palestine, Asia Minor and the Christian world of the West. The ideal of the monk was, however, not that of the solitary seeker after perfection; his aim was not to rule himself, but to obey the rule of his order.

Two factors encouraged the creation of enclosed monastic communities. Firstly, the early groups and hermits were defenceless against attacks by desert tribes or non-Christian enemies. The high walls of the monastery offered a certain measure of protection from a hostile world. The second factor was the liability of those in isolation to delusions and even to insanity:

> The solitude of which Saint Evagrius spoke when he said that 'solitude is good and acceptable, etc., but let him who is unable to meet the abysses of evil thoughts take care not to be injured in his mind' refers to neither the solitude that takes place in the communal life of the Brothers, nor to that of the week-days, nor to that of the Seven Weeks, nor even to the solitude imposed by some monks upon themselves in the monasteries, but it refers to the solitude which is kept in the desert and remote wastes. This solitude does not benefit everybody, but only those perfect people who have been seasoned with the salt of knowledge, who have abundantly acquired the love of solitude and endowed themselves with great endurance.
>
> Dadisho', *On Solitude* (Woodbrooke Studies, VII, p. 81)

> There are three great and mighty fights which specially beset a lonely life in the desert: a great fear at night, a severe and cruel weariness in daytime, and the mental deception caused by the demons. If these three fights occur to a man in the desert, and if he be ignorant, devoid of love for our Lord, not endowed with much endurance, and lacking a leader, his mind will easily be injured.
>
> Dadisho', *On Solitude* (Woodbrooke Studies, VII, p. 82)

The above quotations and those of Sub-section 1.2 concerned the period preceding the development of enclosed monasticism. The relationship between holy man and disciple was that of father-son and also of master-servant. The existence of faithful disciples, who brought them food, enabled some ascetics to spend long periods of time in complete isolation. The disciple would bring his master bread at the necessary intervals.

The reception of a disciple often involved the bestowal on him of a robe of office (Quotations 1, 3, 6). The garment of the monk symbolised, as did the mantle of Elijah, his ability to communicate with the divine world and that this power could be passed from holy man to disciple. The angels as bodiless beings typified the monk and his garment was known as the angelic robe (see Chapter III.ii.2).

The instructions of the master to the disciple concerned, not doctrinal matters, but the personal qualities required for a life of solitude and the austerities to be practised in daily life. Learning consisted in obedience to commands to carry out certain ascetic procedures. The life of the holy man himself was the example and incentive to progress for the disciple. The imagery of the stadium was used by the monks who, like athletes, were said to strive to outdo one another in their achievements (see Chapter V.i.3). Oral teaching included certain books of the Bible and prayers, all of which had to be memorised by the pupil. Finally, at the end of his period of instruction, the disciple, if he wished to become a hermit, had to find his own place of dwelling apart from his master. In some cases, disciples formed groups in the neighbourhood of holy men in order to profit by their sayings. A large number of the *Apophthegmata Patrum* took the form of answers to questions on the ascetic life put by disciples to the elders. At the death of the holy man, his last words and instructions were received by his disciple and it was the disciple who wrapped and buried his body (Quotation 7).

An important function of the older monks towards their disciples was the recognition of certain ill-effects on the mind arising in consequence of the solitary life (Quotations 19–22). A number of accounts show that the ascetics were subject to hallucinations which, with proper training, they were able to recognise and reject. (See Section II, Subsections II, III). Those monks who accepted the illusory appearances as divine revelations were treated by the elders as suffering from delusions of grandeur. The treatment consisted in a humiliating return to community life together with physical restraint and manual labour. It is clear from the accounts that not all the cures were successful and that the end was sometimes death or insanity.

II SELF-ISOLATION

1 Prolonged Solitude

In Hellenistic times a dualistic view of the world was widespread; man and nature possessed material and non-material dimensions: the body or physical and the soul. The psychic life of the community manifested itself in the will of the group to survive through future generations and to retain control of all its members. In addition, group memory stretched back to ancestors whose influence continued invisibly among

31

the living. In cutting himself off from the community life of his village, the Egyptian ascetic aimed to make himself independent of the powerful psychic forces by which he was united with his fellows. In renouncing the possibility of heirs, he deprived himself of that form of immortality in which a man felt that he continued to live in those of his descendants who bore his name. He renounced the support of all rituals by which the forces of the visible world were controlled in this life and by which his survival was ensured in the life after death.

To the ascetic, the dimension which the soul experienced corresponded to that of the life after death or of life in eternity; it differed from it, in that it was entered consciously during life. Just as the soul was believed to separate from the body after death in order, after passing through the stages of the after-life, to enter the heavenly worlds, so the soul of the ascetic had to be released from its dependence on sensory impressions. The sense-world of the Egyptian was not that of modern man; the psychic experiences or images revealed by the objects of the physical world corresponded to the divinities of the ancient world. Asceticism demanded that they be disregarded; Christianity required that they be rejected as demons. (See Chapter II.ii, 'Preliminary Considerations'). The mystery cults of the Hellenistic world sought to continue and to intensify the archaic faculties of man, to keep human imagination directed to the worlds of hallucinations and of dreams. The ascetic aimed to develop within himself the power to be independent of the physical world on the one hand and of all outer authority and guidance on the other. He believed that the 'Kingdom of Heaven' lay within himself and that in isolation a new means of experiencing the divine could be found.

Only by the most strenuous efforts could the ascetic liberate his soul from its involvement with his kinsmen, his property and his religious rituals. Thus the ascetic life, for him, could only effectively be practised in complete physical isolation. This method of self-perfection required that a man should experience his own identity apart from any group. The group characteristically found its fulfilment not in the attainment of the individual but in the growth of its numbers or increase of its power. Thus the ascetic regarded his own salvation as his first duty and, in leaving his family and possessions, he felt that he followed the example of the apostles.

A measure of progress in the ascetic life was the ability to endure solitude. The coenobitic life enabled each monk to spend periods of time alone in his cell and gradually to increase the time spent alone:

At the beginning, a man should accustom himself to the solitude of a single week only, and never go out of his cell in the middle of the week, nor allow anybody to go to him; and, if possible, no one should speak to him even from the aperture of his cell, until he has inured himself against the trials which come upon him from the demons and the passions that beset the solitude of the week-days. ... He will later go up gradually to the solitude which is higher than this, and which is that of the Obligatory Seven Weeks. At the end, if he is capable and willing, he will be perfected by the complete and perpetual solitude of all his life.

Dadisho', *On Solitude* (Woodbrooke Studies, VII, pp. 80, 81)

The spending of a life-time in complete solitude was evidence of the monk's ability to endure isolation from the community to which he belonged; his death in isolation showed his independence, even in death, of group rituals.

Some hermits carried their desire for independence of the material world to the extent of casting off their clothing and, like animals, eating the wild vegetation (Quotations 11–16). Hairy anchorites appeared in various pre-Christian myths.[23] In certain Biblical characters, growth of hair was associated with exceptional powers (Elijah and John the Baptist) or with dedication (the Nazirites). Nebuchadnezzar lived with the beasts of the field and ate grass until 'seven times' had passed over him, as a prelude to the return of his 'understanding'. In the case of the ascetics, the growth of hair was a sign that they no longer felt the effects of outer conditions; it was regarded as a divine gift and as a result of their exertions.

The permanent withdrawal of monks from the sight and sound of other men denoted the change from the coenobitic to the solitary life. Coenobitic communities of the pre-Christian period, as described by Philo, arose as an escape from the decadence and corruption of the Alexandrian world. Such groups were free from economic and political domination and could evolve their own way of life:

They pass their days outside the walls pursuing solitude in gardens or lonely bits of country, not from any acquired habit of misanthropic bitterness but because they know how unprofitable and mischievous are associations with persons of dissimilar characters. This kind exists in many places in the inhabited world, ... but it abounds in Egypt in each of the nomes as they are called and especially round Alexandria.

Philo, *The Contemplative Life*, II.20; III.21

Christian communities withdrew to secluded places from similar motives but they were less concerned with developing a community life than with changing man's relationship to himself. For this reason silence as well as withdrawal was practised as an ascetic discipline. In the ancient world, silence had been practised by the followers of Pythagoras and also by the Neo-pythagoreans. It was said of Apollonius of Tyana that he kept silence for five years, after which time he assumed the role of oracle and teacher:

> When he conversed he would assume an oracular manner . . . And his sentences were short and crisp, and his words were telling and closely fitted to the things he spoke of, and his words had a ring about them as of the dooms delivered by a sceptred king.
>
> Philostratus, *Life of Apollonius of Tyana*, I.XVII

The concentrated brevity of speech, which appeared in the *Apophthegmata*, was their characteristic quality. That the practice of consulting the gods as oracles was widespread in Egypt was noted by Herodotus (*c*. 450 B.C.).[24] Literary and archaeological evidence confirm that the practice continued into the Christian period. The narratives represented the desert fathers as an authoritative source of advice to the populace, a role in society similar to that of the oracles. In contrast to the pagan oracles, the 'revelations' of the holy men appear to have been spoken as ordinary human communications. The discipline of silence ensured that a high value was placed upon speech. Although they saw themselves in line with the prophetic tradition, the ascetics spoke only for themselves and not as the mouthpieces of God.

2 Self-Enclosure

In Egypt, the desert was at all periods the burial place of the dead; the tomb was the place where the relatives made contact with the deceased members of the family. In general, the tomb represented a house or dwelling with a superstructure of stone or brick and a subterranean chamber in which the coffin was placed. At certain periods of Egyptian culture, rock-hewn tunnels or natural caves were used as burial places. In order to enclose himself, the monk either built himself a cell from stones or entered a tomb. In either case, he aimed to isolate himself completely from the world of the living. He anticipated his natural death by separating himself physically from life as he had hitherto known it. The wandering ascetic maintained his relationship with the world of nature but was independent of the community for his food. The enclosed ascetic depended for his supply of bread and water on the visits of a disciple. To bring gifts of food was the duty of a disciple towards his master, as in the past it was the obligation of the relatives towards the deceased.

By excluding the light, the ascetic cut himself off, not only from physical involvement with the outside world, but also from the rhythms of day and night. His sense of time was thus necessarily a subjective one. His environment, whether or not he was in the dark, was one of un-relieved monotony; sensory experiences were reduced to a minimum. In this situation, the adoption of the standing posture and the use of devices to promote discomfort ensured that the ascetic remained awake. Thus conscious withdrawal from the world of the senses was only possible on the basis of the self-infliction of physical pain (see Chapter I.III).

The likening, by Tertullian, of the prison to the place of retirement of a monk ignored the motive which impelled the Egyptian to enclose and to inflict pain upon himself:

The prison does the same service for the Christian as the desert did for the prophet. Our Lord Himself spent much of His time in seclusion, that He might have greater liberty to pray, that He might be quit of the world. It was in a mountain solitude, too, that He showed His glory to the disciples. Let us drop the name of prison; let us call it a place of retirement. Though the body is shut in, though the flesh is confined, all things are open to the spirit. In spirit, then roam abroad; in spirit walk about, not [setting before you shady paths or long colonnades, but the way which leads to God. As often as in spirit your footsteps are there, so often you will not be in bonds. The leg does not feel the chain when the mind is in the heavens.

Tertullian, *ad Martyras*, 2

The tomb was the focus of the ancient Egyptian cult of the dead, a cult in which the life of the living was intimately connected with that of the dead. It was in order to free himself from the domination of these ancestral influences that the ascetic adopted this way of life. The ancient Egyptian reverenced and preserved the human body as the means by which, in life, he experienced a divine world. The Christian ascetic endeavoured to transform his physical organism in such a way that sensory experience lost its value to him as a source of revelation. His self-training was directed towards ignoring, first, the demands upon him of the living pagan community and, secondly, those of the dead. It was his effort to succeed in the latter which was represented by his bio-graphers as his fight against the demons (see Section II.II).

III SELF-MORTIFICATION

1 Fatigue and Weakening of the Body

By isolating himself, the ascetic established himself as an individual, capable of living apart from the community and to a certain extent, independent of the natural world. Self-mortification was the means by which he withdrew his attention from the world of the senses. His aim was to cause his own soul to become as detached from, or unconscious of, his body, as if he were literally dead. In order to experience the existence of a world of imagination which was independent of his physical sense perceptions, it was first necessary for the ascetic to withdraw his entire attention from the physical world. The divine, for him, was related to and expressed in terms of the world around him. He had hitherto regarded his life in the world of sense perception as a participation in a divine life; like the recurring seasons, this life had an inevitability in which, by his rituals, he had participated. Only with an effort of will, could he, by not performing the ancient rituals, reject those powers and beings which he formerly was accustomed to regard as divinities. Whereas the pagan Egyptian was dominated by his natural environment and by his community, asceticism represented his effort to emancipate himself from this state of subjection.

In this process of detachment of his psychic and intellectual powers from their intimate relation with his physical environment, the ascetic lived through, in imagination, the experiences of the soul leaving the body after death. Whereas in the post-mortem world of ancient Egypt, external powers judged and tormented the soul, the ascetic was his own judge and task-master. Self-mortification thus induced, in life, experiences felt at the releasing of the soul from the body after death.

If consciousness was to be directed to a world which had no immediate physical counterpart, it was necessary to reduce, as far as possible, the demands of the physical organism. This was accomplished by fatiguing the body with physical labour and by preventing the recuperation of bodily powers, thus producing a state of physical weakness. The labours performed were often of a useless nature, in order that there might be no incentive for doing them other than the desire to weaken the body. The weakness of the body, occurring naturally before death from sickness or old age, was thus self-induced, and was held to be a pre-condition of 'releasing the soul'.

2 Pain

(i) Self-infliction of Pain

The pains experienced by the ascetic were derived from both outer and inner sources. Those from within were the effects of deprivation of food, sleep and rest. Pains from without included self-inflicted injuries and irritations, and the pains resulting from exposure to heat and cold, prolonged standing or confinement in cramped surroundings. The essential characteristic was that the pains were self-inflicted and self-maintained. Although self-mortification was practised by many ascetics for periods of years, it was not regarded as an end in itself by the monks of Egypt. For these ascetics in the early period of their history, self-mortification was merely a means of achieving a degree of conscious control of the imagination.

The *Apophthegmata* contain accounts of ascetics of both Syria and Egypt. The forms which self-mortification took in Syria differed in some respects from those in Egypt. Among the Syrian ascetics were the 'stylites' and 'dendrites'[25] who spent their ascetic lives upon columns and in trees respectively. Others enclosed themselves in small cages or weighed themselves down with chains. The result of such practices often were severe physical deformities or mutilations, sometimes only discovered at the death of the holy man. Such accounts suggest that these ascetics existed in a trance-like condition to which their self-mutilations contributed. Syrian asceticism contained tendencies towards fanaticism and mysticism and thus differed from that of Egypt. The stylites became, in their lifetimes, centres of cults which derived more from paganism than from Christianity.

The tears of the ascetic were not an emotional release; they were a compulsory part of his regime of self-mortification. He expressed emotions which were not related to his own personal experience. Tears were regarded as a sign of 'perfection'. They were evidence that the soul of the ascetic was identified with that of mankind (Quotations 35–38).

(ii) Disregard of Pain

Detachment of the soul and intellect from the physical organism involved, not only the disregarding of the demands of the body for food and sleep, but also the ignoring of pain. The natural man from the ancient world of the Middle East was shielded from conscious experience of extreme pain by the onset of a dream-like hallucinatory state. Techniques involving painful applications to the body were widely used in ancient cults in order to induce such states.[26] In contrast, the early ascetic trained himself to endure pain in full wakefulness. The ability to disregard pain without diminution or loss of consciousness was the test of his freedom from involvement with the world of physical sensation.

The dualistic views of Neoplatonism and of later Christian mysticism were of the soul held within the body; the aim of the philosopher or mystic was to release the soul from its imprisonment in order to achieve a union of the soul with the divine. In doing so, he became oblivious, both of the material world and of himself as a separate individual. The Egyptian ascetic, on the other hand, sought to avoid any diminution or loss of consciousness. He remained aware of and disregarded the damage he inflicted upon his own body. In assuming, as far as possible, the condition of one already dead, he anticipated his own death and promoted the dissolution of his body. The pains of his self-mortification continued to be felt by the ascetic so long as his attention was directed to his body; thus burning heat in this life corresponded to the fires of the life after death.

Just as the desert was regarded by the Egyptian as the earthly counterpart of the world of death, so the noon-day sun was an image of death and the middle of the day was a time when the malevolent powers of the dead were at their strongest. The ascetic, therefore, placed himself in the sun and in hot places in order to experience to the full and, by ignoring them, to overcome these powers. Thus the essential character of self-mortification, as practised by the Egyptian ascetics, was the deliberate performance of those actions which, in the ancient religion, brought him into relation with his divinities; instead of propitiating the powers of this world, he trained himself to ignore them.

(iii) Devices for Preventing Rest

The standing posture,[27] later adopted by the Eastern Church as the attitude of prayer, was, for the ascetic, the means of ensuring wakefulness. The physical effort of maintaining the standing position for long periods of time was, in itself, a means of self-mortification. Physical pain was one means of preventing sleep; another was the practice of weaving strips of palm-leaf while standing in prayer. The monotonous, semi-automatic nature of the work ensured that it was no mental distraction.

By constantly exercising his mind in the repetition of prescribed numbers of prayers, the ascetic excluded dreams and hallucinations. The enumeration of the number of days spent in self-mortification, or of the numbers of prayers repeated, represented to the biographer a measure of the progress or achievement of the ascetic. That the sufferings of the ascetic were expressed in physical terms, was the result of his peculiar circumstances of mind and body. The struggle of the ascetic was for control of his psychic life and the conflict was with his own physical organism. Because of their Biblical associations with revelations three days or forty days represented periods of time during which it was necessary that the ascetic should remain consciously awake; the fact that he was able to do so was evidence of his ability to reject unwanted psychic experiences. (See Chapter II.III.4.)

IV FOOD DEPRIVATION

1 Restriction of Diet

Ancient Egypt was an agricultural country and its life centred round the producing of food, both animal and vegetable. The wealth of the community lay in the food it produced; it was the product of the fertility of the land, the crops and the animals. The cults of Osiris, the god of vegetation, and of the Apis Bull and other animals were essentially fertility cults. Thus food not only played a major part in the social life and religious practices of the Egyptians, but it was also an essential means, for the living, of communicating with the dead. The cult of the dead involved funerary banquets at which a variety of ritually prescribed foods were consumed. The liturgy of funerary offerings[28] included bread, cakes, beer, wine, meat, fowls and fruit. Through the ceremony of the funerary meal, the relationship between the living members of the community and their ancestors was periodically renewed. Whereas vegetable foods were generally partaken freely by all, animal foods were subject to religious restrictions, often based on the fact that, according to districts, different animals were sacred for different communities. The sacred animals were not eaten and were often mummified after their death. The mummification of animals dated back to the predynastic period of Egyptian history as did the association of particular animals with localities and their inhabitants. The eating of animals ritually killed was described by Herodotus[29]; the burning of the carcase was preceded by the pouring of oil over the offering. Thus the eating of animal food was intimately connected with the most ancient elements of Egyptian religion.

Because fasting was widespread among both pagans and Christians in the Hellenistic world, the Christian biographers took care to establish the motive for which their subjects abstained from meat; the eating of a small quantity of meat 'for the sake of others' was held to be a proof of orthodoxy.[30] In abstaining from meat, the Egyptian was said not to be acting from the motive of the Manichaean ascetics,[31] to whom the taking of animal life was forbidden, nor, as his Greek-speaking biographers sometimes portrayed him, because he wished to be a philosopher. By rejecting meat and oil[32] from his diet, the Egyptian dissociated himself from his community, from his own district and from his ancestors. The cooking of meat on the fire was a ritual part of the preparation of food-offerings for the dead, and cooked meat was therefore unacceptable to the ascetic. He regarded it as the eating of food offered to idols,[33] a practice forbidden to the Jews in the Old Testament. The avoidance of fruit, as food subject to fermentation, and particularly of wine represented his rejection of intoxication[34]; for him, intoxication was a physical means of experiencing his identification with the community and its divinities. That drunkenness was prevalent in Egypt can be seen from the writings of Pachomius[35] and other early Fathers. Any food or drink which contributed to loss of waking consciousness or to orgiastic self-immersion in the community rituals was thus rejected by the ascetic. In abstaining from meat and wine he had a Biblical precedent in the Jewish sect of the Nazirites who 'separated themselves unto the Lord'.[36]

Bread was, on the one hand, a food universally eaten and on the other was, like dates and pulses, the normal diet of the poor. The eating of these foods emphasised the ascetic's lack of concern with worldly wealth and his independence from any local community or cult. Restriction of diet to a minimum quantity of vegetable food with periods of complete abstention was thus part of the process of self-mortification. Great emphasis was laid, in the biographies of the ascetics, on their feats of endurance in the sphere of fasting. If a miraculous element was introduced, the intention of the biographers was possibly to stress the victory involved. Because eating was not merely a physiological but also a psychological experience, fasting caused, not only physical deprivation but also the enhancement of the sense of isolation. Thus, in restricting his diet, the ascetic not only weakened his body but he cut himself off from the way of life of his community. In so doing he closed for himself a channel of communication with the divine world of his ancestors.

2   Days of Fasting

In the early Church, apart from the fast of forty days before Easter, it was usual to fast twice a week, on Wednesdays and Fridays.[37] The latter practice distinguished the Christians from the Jews, who fasted on Mondays and Thursdays, and also associated these days with the Easter week events. A day of fasting began at midnight and lasted until the ninth hour (3 p.m.). Among the ascetics arose the practice of extending the fast beyond the usual time, either to sunset or for two, three or more days. As Saturday and Sunday were not normally days of fasting, the ascetics sometimes fasted for the remaining five days of the week.

It has already been seen how, in ancient Egypt, the feast was regarded as the means of participating in the divine world; the same was true in the earlier periods of Greek history. By the time of the early Christian era, educated Greeks and Jews regarded the polytheistic cults of paganism as superstitious and as something remote from their own experience. They rejected a sense-based revelation of the divine and both Greeks and Jews regarded fasting rather than feasting as a means of approaching the deity. To the Neoplatonists, the soul was the organ through which the divine could be contemplated and fasting was a means of increasing the soul's receptivity. From the writings of both Greek philosophers and Jewish prophets, it can be seen that the experiences or revelations occurred when the subjects were, to some extent, in a condition of trance, ecstasy or dream. (See Introduction I.)

During the Hellenistic period, dreams were highly regarded as a source of divine revelation; fasting was held to be an essential preparation. Philostratus, in his *Life of Apollonius,* expounded the view that since the soul was influenced by the diet, only by abstemiousness and avoidance of meat and wine, could the soul receive unconfused dreams.[38] Fasting was part of the ritual preparation for the incubation sleep of the mystery cults in which dreams were deliberately sought in answer to prayer. Iamblichos[39] and Plutarch[40] described the preparatory fasts which were carried out by those who were consulted as oracles. From these accounts, it appears that, in relation to revelatory experiences or oracular utterances, fasting was an essential preliminary. Fasting appears to have affected, not only the physical organism, but also the psyche, in such a way that dream-experiences assumed, to the subject, the significance of revelations.

That the number of days of abstention from food was regarded as important in relation to prophecy, is seen from the numerous references to them in both Greek and Jewish literature. They were particularly emphasised in the Old Testament; Moses fasted for forty days on Sinai, Elijah fasted for the same period on his journey to Horeb, Daniel fasted for three weeks.[41] In the Apocalyptic Literature, the writer of *II Esdras* fasted for three periods of seven days[42]; in *II Baruch* the prophet underwent three fasts of seven days.[43] In the *Life of Adam*

41

and Eve, Adam spent forty days fasting.[44] Philo described three- and six-day fasts as a preparation for the study of philosophy in his life of the sect of the Therapeutae:

> None of them would put food or drink to his lips before sunset since they hold that philosophy finds its right place in the light, the needs of the body in the darkness. . . . Some in whom the desire for studying wisdom is more deeply implanted even only after three days remember to take food. Others . . . hold out for twice that time and only after six days do they bring themselves to taste such sustenance as is absolutely necessary.
>
> Philo, *The Contemplative Life*, IV.34.35

The forty-day period was officially adopted by the Church at the beginning of the fourth century as a time of preparation for Easter. It was spoken of by Leo the Great as *quadraginta dierum exercitatio*. Based on Christ's fast in the wilderness, it represented a period of conflict with demonic powers. This is confirmed by the fact that the forty days before Easter was, in the early Church, the final period of preparation of catechumens for Baptism; this was a ritual in which the exorcism of demonic powers played a large part. Prior to its adoption by the Church, the period of forty days as a time of fasting had already been in use among the ascetics: it was the time of their most intense conflict against the powers of their ancient religion.

3   Heavenly Food

The Egyptian ascetic did not consider fasting as a preliminary measure, either for a revelation or for a union of his soul with God. He was not preparing himself for a future relationship with the Deity; he himself was the realisation of divinity, within the limits of his situation. The divine life necessitated his independence, not only of earthly food, but of all relationship with the outside world. To the extent that he withdrew himself from outer life he found his nourishment from a non-material source within himself. The taking of no earthly food during the three days of self-withdrawal before death (narrative III.III.3:11; see also III.III.1:12) was also described in the case of the seer of the *Enoch* apocalypse; this period represented the final separation of the soul from the body:

> . . . from the time when the Lord anointed me with the ointment of his glory, there has been no food in me, and my soul remembers not earthly enjoyment, neither do I want anything earthly.
>
> *II Enoch*, 56.2 (Charles)

A similar fast lasting forty days was described in the *Apocalypse of Abraham*:

> And we went, the two of us together, forty days and nights, and I ate no bread and drank no water, because my food was to see the angel who was with me, and his speech—that was my drink.
>
> *Apocalypse of Abraham*, XII, (Box, p. 50)

In the mythology of ancient Greece, there existed certain legendary figures whose god-likeness lay in their independence of all earthly needs, including food; among these philosophers and seers were Abaris, Epimenides and Pythagoras.[45] This ideal of god-likeness was revived in Hellenistic times among the Neoplatonist writers and was still held by the Greek hagiographers of the Christian period. Unable to understand the achievements of the Egyptian ascetics but wishing to depict them as manifesting the divine, their biographers ascribed to them a god-like ability to live without earthly food.

In the representations of the heavenly banquets, as of those of ancient Egypt, the good things of the earth were transformed and became heavenly foods: the bread, the basket of fruits, the fruits of the Tree of Life or the meal served on a table. These descriptions of miraculous manifestations were similar to those in 'The Journey to Paradise' (Section III.iv.4).

V SLEEP DEPRIVATION

1 Complete Deprivation

The ascetic life was essentially an attempt by the individual to overcome in himself his attachment to the ancient Egyptian religion and social system. Because it was a non-intellectual religion, based on shared experience and inherited traditions, the efforts required to effect this were, in the first place, of a physical nature. Sleep deprivation, together with fasting and self-mortification, played an essential part in weakening the body and in contributing towards bodily 'death'. The aim of the ascetics, however, was the final demonstration of the overcoming of death, of resurrection from death. The overcoming of death was, for them, the conscious experience in this life of a dimension in which death did not exist. That sleep and waking were to be regarded as models of death and resurrection, was also expressed by Tertullian: .

> Sleep ... is formed into the model of death which is general and common to the race of man. ... Accordingly, when the body shakes

43

off its slumber, it asserts before your eye the resurrection of the dead by its own resumption of its natural functions.

Tertullian, *de Anima*, LII

In claiming that the ascetics slept little or not at all, their biographers indicated that they maintained themselves in a state of conscious wakefulness. Sleep, in this connection, was the image of death because during sleep and unconscious states, in the old religion, the world of the gods was experienced. Such experiences were recognised by the ascetics to be illusory and to constitute a threat to their conscious life.

Throughout the ancient world, dreams were held to be the vehicle for divine revelations. In the Old Testament, the commands of the Deity were made known through dreams. In the mystery rites and the incubation cults of the Hellenistic period, the messages of the gods were received by the participants while they were in a state of sleep or trance. Similarly, the oracular interpretations of dreams were the result of such states. In a relatively non-intellectual age, dreams played a prominent part in men's lives; from dreams they hoped to derive knowledge of a super-human world or to obtain solutions to their daily problems.

The view that in sleep, as during philosophical thought, the soul was free and detached from the body, was stated by Iamblichos:

> The soul, having a two-fold life—the one along with the corporeal body, and the other separate from everything corporeal—we, in the case of the other mode of living, when we are awake, make use of many things pertaining to the life belonging with the body, except we, after a manner, detach ourselves from it in every respect by pure principles of thought and understanding. In sleep, however, we are completely set free as from fetters lying by us, and bring into activity the life which is separate from the sphere of generated existence. Hence, therefore, this form or ideal of life, whether it is spiritual or divine, which is the same, or only one existing individually by itself, is awakened in us and puts forth its energy according to its own natures.

Iamblichos, *The Egyptian Mysteries*, III.vii (Wilder, p. 111)

In its state of detachment from the body, the soul, according to Iamblichos, was in a condition in which it could receive knowledge applicable to all spheres of earthly life:

> When (the soul) is united to the gods through such liberated energy, it receives on the instant abundances of perceptions ... and henceforth establishes the absolutely genuine principles of knowledge. ... It not only takes a view of every period of time, and examines events

that are to take place in the period, but it likewise participates in the arranging, management and correcting of them. It not only heals diseased bodies, but also restores to order many things among men which were discordant and disorderly. It also gives forth discoveries of arts, proper regulations for the administering of law, and institutions of customs. Thus, in the temples of Asklepios, not only are diseases brought to an end by dreams of divine origin, but through manifestations by night the medical art is combined with the sacred visions.

> Iamblichos, *The Egyptian Mysteries*, III.vII (Wilder, p. 112)

That knowledge received from dreams was dependent on the condition of the body was held by Plutarch and other writers:

> ... But especially does the imaginative part of the soul show itself to be mastered by the body, and to sympathize with its changes; as is apparent in the case of dreams. For sometimes we are involved in numerous and infinitely varied visions, whilst at other times, on the contrary we have complete freedom and peace from anything of the sort.
>
> Plutarch, *On the cessation of Oracles*, L

According to Plato, whose views were expressed by Cicero, only to those who lived abstemiously were dependable visions given in their dreams:

> Pythagoras and Plato, authors most worthy of belief, command that, in order to have dreams to be depended upon, we should retire to rest after having prepared ourselves by a certain mode of life and diet;
>
> Cicero, *de Divinatione*, 2.58.119

The dependence of the soul, and hence of dreams, on bodily states was also recognised by the Neopythagoreans; this dependence on the body was thought to be the cause of the unreliability of dreams as divine revelations:

> And more than this, as a faculty of divination by means of dreams, which is the divinest and most godlike of human faculties, the soul detects the truth all the more easily when it is not muddied by wine, but accepts the message unstained and scans it carefully. Anyhow the explainers of dreams and visions, those whom the poets call interpreters of dreams, will never undertake to explain any vision to anyone without having first asked the time when it was seen. For if it was at dawn and in the sleep of morning-tide, they calculate its meaning on the assumption that the soul is then in a condition to

divine soundly and healthily, because by then it has cleansed itself of the stains of wine.

Philostratus, Life of Apollonius of Tyana, II.xxxvii

The soul was recognised by Plato to have both rational and irrational components. According to Cierco, the rational soul participated in dreams when the other parts were restrained:

> When (a man) takes his rest, that part of the soul which is the seat of judgment and reason is active, alive, and gratified by the meal of good thoughts, while the second part of the soul, which indulges in sensual pleasure, is not worn out either by want or excess of food, and also the third part, in which burns the fire of passion, is at ease and restrained. In such a man, because the two irrational parts of the soul are kept in their places, the third, which is the rational and judicious part, can shine forth and participate lively and vigorously in the act of dreaming. Only then visions will occur which are undisturbed and truthful.

Cicero, de Divinatione, 1.29.60f

The effect on dreams of food and wine as stimulants of the irrational soul was shown by Plato:

> When the rest of the soul, the reasoning, gentle, and ruling part of it, is asleep, then the bestial and savage part, when it has had its fill of food or wine, begins to leap about, pushes sleep aside, and tries to go and gratify its instincts. You know how in such a state it will dare everything, as though it were freed and released from all shame or discernment. It does not shrink from attempting incestual intercourse, in its dream, with a mother, or with any man or god or beast. It is ready for any deed of blood, and there is no unhallowed food it will not eat. In a word, it falls short of no extreme of folly or shamelessness.

Plato, Republic, IX.571

The world of the gods was, in Egypt, also the world of the dead. Through dreams, the dead communicated with the living and the practice of sleeping in the tombs for the purpose of receiving such communications was current in Egypt. At an earlier period such practices had been condemned by the prophets of the Old Testament in their efforts to overthrow the polytheistic cults of Canaan. To the Egyptian ascetic therefore, sleep represented a time when his soul was subject to his body and to those influences which derived from his old religion. He endeavoured to regulate his sleep in such a way as to lessen its dangers for himself; his ideal was to sleep for as short a time as possible. He rejected the dreams of the 'irrational soul', as described by Plato, not only on moral grounds, but because such practices were implicit in his religious rituals. In dreams, he felt himself subject to the ancestral forces and nature powers with which, through such practices, he had in the past been identified.

2 Nights of Vigil

By spending the night in vigil, the ascetic remained awake at those times when he was most susceptible to influences from his old religion. Only by keeping himself awake could he overcome the temptation to submit to these influences; like the Psalmist, he regarded the gift of wakefulness as a weapon:

> They used to say about Abba Pachomius that he spent much time in striving with devils like a true athlete, and after the manner of Saint Anthony. And because many devils came against him in the night season, he asked God to keep away sleep from him both by day and by night, so that he might not sleep at all, and might be able to bring low the might of the Enemy. . . . Now this gift was given unto him, even as he had asked.
>
> Palladius (Budge I, *Sayings of the Fathers*, 106)

The forty days of fasting were essentially a period of wakefulness helped by self-mortification. Thus the ascetic used all means available to him in his efforts to maintain his waking consciousness for as long a period as possible.

In the practice of ceaseless activity and wakefulness, the ascetic likened his life to that of the angels. He also took for his model the four bodiless, living creatures, surrounding the heavenly throne. In basing his life on patterns taken from the Scriptures, the ascetic made himself, as far as possible, independent of the natural rhythms of his body and at the same time of the rhythms of the earth and sun. As the times of sunset and sunrise were of particular importance in a solar religion, the ascetic arranged that these should be times of prayer and he ascribed to them a Christian meaning:

> They also said about him that on the night of the Sabbath which would end in the dawn of Sunday, he would leave the sun behind him, and would stretch out his hands towards heaven, and would pray (in this position) until the sun rose in his face, when he would satisfy his eyes with a little slumber.
>
> Palladius (Budge I, *Sayings of the Fathers*, 105)

The vigil of the night of the Sabbath was the commemoration of the Easter vigil.

CONCLUSION

In this chapter on the ascetic way of life, the regime of the solitary monk has been considered. From the standpoint of modern medicine, the techniques of asceticism resemble those used in experimental 'sensory deprivation'. (See Postscript.) The isolation of the individual, the removal of external sensory stimuli and the stereotyping of the environment are conditions which, in modern man, are hallucinogenic. When, to these, are added the factors of sleep and food deprivation, it becomes clear that what are here described are also the conditions conducive to the production of the dream visions of the pre-Christian religions. There is Scriptural evidence that the prophets of the Old Testament, to whom the ascetics were compared, followed such a regime. It is probable that the actual 'way of life' described in the quotations of the present section was based on that practised in relation to the Hellenistic incubation cults.

Here is seen the anomaly which is apparent in the biographies of both saints and martyrs. The holy men were given credit for actions and experiences which were appropriate, not to Christianity, but to the paganism which they were rejecting. This discrepancy between the aim of the holy men and the manner in which they were represented arose from two factors. Firstly, as has been seen, the biographies of early times were written on pre-existent models. The holy man of the ancient world was recognised because he manifested the divine according to certain patterns. These took the form of miracles, feats of endurance and communications with the gods. The language of these models largely belonged to mythology and described the experiences of ritual trances and dreams. The biographers of the ascetics did not distinguish clearly the characteristics which made the feats of the saints and martyrs of Christianity different from those of the holy men of earlier times. The Christian saints, unlike their pagan predecessors, rejected the patterns of the ancient world and freed themselves from their domination. The second factor, which is more fully discussed in Chapter III, was the desire of the biographers to obliterate the memory of pagan practices. The method used was that of superimposing 'Christianised' versions, with new names, upon the already existing narrative forms. In so doing, it was apparently not recognised that it was not merely the names which gave Christian significance, but the manner in which experience of the divine was represented.

CHAPTER II

The Establishment of a Non-material Environment

I MENTAL POWERS

1 Prayer and Meditation

This chapter attempts to restate the possible nature of the experiences of the ascetics. The assumption is made that, amongst the doctrines put into the mouth of Anthony by Athanasius,[1] the following correctly represented the attitudes of the ascetics:

> The Lord has told us in advance; The Kingdom is within you. Virtue therefore has need only of our will, since it is within us and springs from us.
>
> Athanasius, *Life of Anthony*, 20

The Kingdom of Heaven was an immaterial dimension of life whose existence had been foretold in the Old Testament and whose realisation was described in the Gospels. The ascetic believed that since it was revealed in the Scriptures that man's nature was divine, it was his duty to become to some degree conscious of himself as an individual. For him, the New Testament was the guarantee that human perfection was a possibility. The ascetic saw the Scriptures as the revelation of his own nature and meditation on them as necessary for any degree of self-consciousness. The attainment of 'a measure of divinity' was an experience which he could only achieve by the exercise of his own will, in most cases gradually, by daily effort (see Quotation 8). In reciting the Scriptures, he recreated for himself part of the panorama of the Old Testament and saw parallels to his own struggles in those of the Jewish people.

Just as the Jews in the Old Testament had to give up the making of images and to apprehend the Deity as non-material and imperceptible to the senses, so the Egyptian ascetic had to develop the ability to abstract his thoughts of the divine from material objects:

> In the sphere of its spirituality, mind has no material image and likeness. If the hope of the watchful monks reaches no farther than

the state in which the vision of their mind, in the sphere of spirituality, does not rise above material likenesses and images, they are the most unhappy of men. This, however, is not so, but the contrary is the case; that is to say, we monks expect and hope that in the sphere of spirituality we shall see a thing that in its greatness is high above the senses of the body and the faculties of the soul.

'Abdisho' Hazzaya, *Treatises* (Woodbrooke Studies, VII, p. 159)

In this he was impeded by his own language. The Greek language had long been the instrument of philosophic thought, and in Greek it was possible to speak of ideas and concepts which had no material counterpart. The Coptic language, on the other hand, was the last phase of one which had existed for three thousand or more years.[2] Many of the word-roots had persisted since the earliest stages of the language. Words were, by long tradition, associated with images of the material world; the powers latent in natural objects could be evoked by pronouncing their names. For the Egyptian, it was difficult to separate words from images. Nevertheless, since the divine world was immaterial, he had to exclude from his mind, not only thoughts derived from without, but also those images which words themselves aroused. Thus, for the ascetic, the overcoming of his attachment to his old religion and his assertion of his will towards perfection began in his mind (Quotations 1–7). Freedom was not freedom to think arbitrarily, but freedom to decide what should and should not be the content of his thoughts. Until he was able to exercise this control, he was not able to experience the divine world.

> When a thought has come against the soul, and the soul has, with great difficulty, been able to drive it out, another makes ready to come, and in this manner the soul is occupied the whole day long in a war against the thoughts and is unable to occupy itself with the sight of God.
>
> Palladius (Budge II, *Questions and Answers*, 559)

> And the old man said unto me: '. . . I have cleansed my thoughts according to my power, and I resist the thoughts which rush upon me. And in this manner, afterwards, there dawned upon me the spirit of visions.'
>
> Palladius (Budge II, *Questions and Answers*, 562)

Thus the atavistic faculty whereby the Egyptian people were able, to a later date than their neighbours in the Middle East, to see a divine presence in the material world, was dispelled by the ascetic life. This process of liberation took place in the sphere of the senses and that of the imagination—in the former, by physical methods, and in the latter by control of thought.

Early Christianity was greatly influenced by the Judaism of the Old Testament, in particular by the belief in a transcendent God who imposed moral law upon man and demanded obedience. Through Neoplatonism, which derived not only from Greek philosophy but also from Judaism, there entered into the teachings of the early Church Fathers the view that the divine could only be experienced in the mind (see Quotations 11–13).

> What else is 'to see God in the heart' but to understand and know him with the mind, . . . ? For the names of the organs of sense are often applied to the soul, so that we speak of seeing with the eyes of the heart, that is, of drawing some intellectual conclusion by means of the faculty of intelligence. So too we speak of hearing with the ears when we discern the deeper meaning of some statement. So too we speak of the soul as being able to use teeth, when it eats and consumes the bread of life who comes down from heaven. In a similar way we speak of it as using all the other bodily organs, which are transferred from their corporeal significance and applied to the faculties of the soul.
>
> Origen, *de Principiis*, I.I.9 (Butterworth)

Persistence of this belief, especially among the Alexandrian Fathers, is seen in their mystical writings, in which experience of the identity of the human mind with an external divine counterpart was described. What the mystic experienced was ascribed to the intervention of an external deity with whom he felt himself united. The Church, however, laid increasing emphasis on the necessity for man to believe in the received revelation of the Scriptures, rather than in mystical experiences; it was held that the mind or intellect should not only receive the doctrine, but should be man's dominant faculty. Asceticism, to the Church Fathers, thus became a means of self-conditioning in order to prepare the mind for indoctrination. The 'mental' powers of the ascetic were therefore extolled. If the authority of the doctrine were to be upheld, it was necessary to discourage disobedience; thus arose the emphasis by the Church on judgment in the life after death, with rewards for the righteous and eternal punishment for sinners. Such doctrines were circulated as exhortations by the Church Fathers, and appeared among the *Apophthegmata* of the desert monks:

> And make thy cell a hall of judgment of thyself, and a place for striving against devils and evil passions, and let there be depicted therein the kingdom (of Heaven), and Gehenna, and death and life,

and sinners and the righteous, and the fire which never is quenched, and the glory of the righteous, and the outer darkness, and the gnashing of the teeth, and the light of the righteous, and their joy in the Holy Spirit, and the Passion of our Lord, and the memorial of his Resurrection.

Palladius (Budge II, *Questions and Answers*, 579)

Among the exponents of this 'Judaistic' Christianity was Evagrius Ponticus, a deacon from Constantinople who spent, from A.D. 382, seventeen years in the Egyptian desert of Scete (see Chapter II.1.4.iv). He sought to introduce to the monks the mystical teachings of Origen, of whom he was a follower. The writings of Evagrius were originally in Greek and influenced, among others, Palladius and John Cassian, both writers on Egyptian monasticism.[3] Stories bearing the name of Evagrius occurred among the *Apophthegmata* and are evidence of his attitude (see Quotations 9, 10). That Evagrius disregarded the religious background of the Egyptians appears from his writings on the demons. He was one of the chief exponents of the view that the demons corresponded to the seven (or eight) chief vices of man.[4] From this arose the widely held belief that the Egyptian ascetics spent their days struggling to suppress thoughts arising from lust. Such an interpretation of the ascetic life could only be applicable to the repressive forms of monasticism which arose later.

The quotation above, from Palladius, shows the monk depicting to himself in imagination the torments of hell compared with the joys of heaven. This emphasis on hell and the use of the imagination for self-intimidation was not a characteristic of Egyptian asceticism. In the latter, self-mortification was only directed at the physical body. The pagan Egyptian believed in human happiness and that happiness was implicit in experience of the divine. The underworld of the next life in ancient Egyptian religion had been a purgatorial stage which the soul had to pass in order to reach the divine world. The Christian Hell was seen as a necessary purification on the way to heaven rather than an alternative to it. His way of life enabled the ascetic, as an individual, for the first time, to control his own imagination. Under his old religion, his imagination had been tied to rigid traditional formulae. As a result of his ascetic practices, his thought was no longer fettered by its association with the images of the past. He was thus able to create for himself, in his imagination, a non-material world, based on the events in the Scriptures. This was the 'vision' of the ascetic; it was not 'seen' in a dream or trance, it could be shared with others, and it concerned this life as well as the next. It was a world, not only of thought, but of emotion.

For the Egyptian, the Scriptures performed, in a very different context, something of the function which the Homeric myths had done for
the Greeks. They provided for him an education of the emotions and
an insight into the morality of both the Old and New Testaments.
Participation in imagination in the Biblical events was an emotional
experience and also a means of self-knowledge. Possibly the athletics
of the Greeks had originally played for them a role similar to that of
the ascetic practices of the banishment from daily life of the ancestral
spirits. The Erinyes were the inhabitants of the Orphic underworld,[5]
as has been seen on p. 6, and they were transformed in Christianity
into the tormenting angels of Hell. When the Egyptian ascetic imagined
Hell, he peopled it with the ancestral and nature powers of his own previous religion. His motive for asceticism was, however, not the avoidance of Hell, but the desire to experience the world of Heaven. The
Scriptures were the source from which he drew the imagery with which
he created, in his imagination, a new dimension: that of the Kingdom
of Heaven or Paradise. The desert of Scete was known as the 'Paradise
of the Fathers',[6] and it is evident that they believed that man could live
in happiness on earth, inspired by the best which he could imagine. The
ascetic movement in Egypt can be understood as a sudden intuition among
men that a non-material Paradise was an attainable reality on earth.

The ascetics were capable of finding an apparently limitless source of
inspiration within themselves. Whatever they wished to know, it was said
that they were able to obtain the answer (Quotations 15–30). By means
of their asceticism, they were able to achieve, by their own efforts,
both a vision of a divine life and an insight into human problems.
The powers of the ascetics were, however, misunderstood—not only by
their visitors from the sophisticated circles of Alexandria and Constantinople, but also by their own pagan and Christian communities.
The populace, as can be seen from the *Life of Anthony*,[7] were always
ready to ascribe miracles to the holy men. In a non-intellectual milieu,
during a period of profound social and psychological changes, divine
intervention was sought as the solution to problems and holy men were
regarded as being in an especially privileged position in regard to the
divine powers. In ancient Egypt, such natural phenomena as the flood-
ing of the Nile were held to be promoted by human agency. Therefore,
by virtue of their prayers (Quotations 16, 17) the existence of holy men
was often felt, even by pagan communities, to be beneficial.[8]

2 Attainment

Attainment of 'perfection' in this life was the aim of the ascetics;
it was regarded as their highest achievement as individuals. It was for

this end that they entered the solitary life and that they trained their disciples. Perfection appears, from the accounts, to have included the possession and exercise of divine powers and gifts, but to have depended rather on humility than on the manifestation of miraculous faculties. To some extent, perfection included the ability to recognise the attainment of others. If it was possible for an ascetic to create a divine world in his imagination, it was necessary for him, not only to distinguish those brethren who possessed a similar ability: he had also to be able to include his fellow ascetic in his own vision. Certain stories illustrated the occasions on which such recognition occurred. The recognition of an elder by his disciples sometimes took place at his death-bed (Quotation 2); at other times the occasion was a visit by a disciple to his master alone (Quotations 3, 4). Conversely, the attainment of a disciple would lead to his recognition by an elder who saw him in a vision (Quotations 7–9).

Unfortunately, in their passage through many hands, much of the subtlety and irony of these accounts has been lost. Originally their outstanding qualities were probably, not only their wisdom, but also their wit. If they have survived chiefly as illustrations of morality and of miracles, they still also demonstrate an appreciation of human perfection as a razor's edge, rather than as a permanent state.

3 Vision

The distinction between the seeing of visions in a state of dream ecstasy, or trance, and the exercise of the conscious imagination, was not clear to the writers of the Hellenistic or early Christian period. That asceticism was a preliminary to both forms of vision, probably made it appear to the biographers of the Egpytian ascetics that, in visions, they were describing phenomena familiar to them from the writings of antiquity. Such were the dream visions and ecstasies remembered and related afterwards by those who had experienced them. The recall of such visions was believed to be dependent on the faculty of memory[9]; the divine was experienced in dreams and recalled as a memory:

> They keep the memory of God alive and never forget it, so that even in their dreams the picture is nothing else but the loveliness of divine excellences and powers. Indeed many when asleep and dreaming give utterance to the glorious verities of their holy philosophy.
>
> Philo, *The Contemplative Life*, III.26

Memory was also thought by Plutarch to contain knowledge of the future as well as of the past. In dreams, or at the moment of death, the obscuration of the contents of the memory by the body was said to be overcome:

> For just as the Sun doth not become bright, when he bursts through the clouds, but is so perpetually, yet he appears to us, when in a mist, dull and obscure, in like manner the soul doth not acquire the prophetic power, when it passes out of the body, as out of a cloud, but possesses it even now, though it is dimmed by its mixture and confusion with the body. We ought not to wonder or disbelieve this, when we observe if nothing else, the faculty of the soul which is the converse of Foreknowledge, that is what we call the Memory: how great an operation doth it perform in preserving and storing up things gone by, or rather, things that are. For of things past, none is or subsists, but all things are born and die together ... but this faculty of the Soul, laying hold upon them, I know not how, invests things not present with visible form and existence. ...
> No wonder then, as I have said, if that which holds tight the things that be no more, should anticipate many of those that do not yet exist. ...
> Souls therefore possessing this faculty inherent in their nature, though obscured, and hardly showing itself, do nevertheless put forth blossom, and recover this power—in dreams often, on the point of death, some few—either that the body becomes purified, or assumes a new temperament on these occasions, or else that the reasoning and thinking parts of the soul are unbound and released ... from the Present and turn towards the Future.
>
> Plutarch, *On the cessation of Oracles*, XXXIX

The trance proper was a state in which memory, in the sense of power to recall the experience afterwards, was partially or completely obliterated. In such states the subject either became the mouthpiece of the divinity with which he was possessed, or he assumed the physical identity of the deity whom he impersonated. It is likely that 'speaking with tongues',[10] as described in the New Testament and as practised later by such groups as the Montanists, was a self-induced trance state (see p. 59). Such speech was related to that of the oracles and prophets of antiquity, and in it the speaker assumed the role of the divinity of his community.

A further type of visionary experience, to be differentiated from that of the Egyptian ascetics, was the mystical. The distinction here lay in the degree of self-consciousness which was maintained. In the dream vision, the dreamer experienced himself as a spectator, or actor, in a situation; his level of consciousness was that of a sleeper. The true mystic aimed to obliterate his own self-consciousness in an identification of himself with a universal or divine entity. His experience of divinity coincided with the loss of his consciousness of himself as a separate individual. Such mystical experiences were the aim of the Neoplatonic philosophers and were achieved by intellectual effort. The influence of such an approach to the divine continued among the early Alexandrian Fathers, among whom was Evagrius Ponticus[11] (see p. 52). It is known that Evagrius was a friend of Macarius of Alexandria; his influence can be seen in the account of the attempt by Macarius to concentrate his thought upon God for five days (Quotations 1–3). The Coptic version reveals that his aim was to unite himself with God as the Trinity; in this he was more like the mystics of the Alexandrian school than his fellow ascetics of Egypt.

In the typical visions, the Egyptian ascetic described himself as seeing various personalities, places or events. He pictured himself as an actor in a situation based upon Biblical precedent. It was, however, frequently recorded that, during the vision, he was in a dream or trance. It is also probable that the difficulty of remaining awake and the temptation to relapse into a less conscious state was too great in many cases, and that dream and trance visions also occurred. Nevertheless, the emphasis on wakefulness, in the accounts of the ascetic lives, strongly suggests that the aim was a waking experience, and as such, the vision was a conscious creation of the imagination. In attributing dreams and trances to the ascetics, the biographers described the visions of these men from the point of view of Greeks of the early Church of Alexandria or Constantinople, rather than from that of Egyptians. The use of the imagination by the individual, as a means of self-discipline, was a new phenomenon among the Egyptians. That the imagination could be used consciously, in order to make manifest the divine, appears to have been overlooked by the early Church Fathers so completely that the existence of such a practice can only be inferred indirectly. The early Church endeavoured to suppress ecstatic speech and regarded such practices as pertaining to paganism rather than to Christianity. Visions were, however, accepted by the Church Fathers, since they appeared to be the result of an intervention of the Deity towards man. The activity of the divine was held by the Church to come from a source outside of man; it was not admitted that man, from within himself, could become the conscious creator of his own visions of the divine.

The imparting of their 'visions' by the ascetics to their fellow hermits or disciples was different from the transmission of the prophecies or oracles of antiquity. In the latter case, the prophet or seer, as the channel of the divine communication, felt no personal responsibility for the message; he spoke freely to his audience as the mouthpiece of the deity. The ascetics, as creators of their 'visions', often showed reluctance to speak, lest they should do so from motives of pride or vanity. Nevertheless, it appears to have been the custom to insist that every monk should share his vision with his fellows[12]; the created vision was regarded as having not only a subjective but an objective value.

4 Gifts

(i) Prophecy

The powers of the ascetics were portrayed by their biographers as gifts bestowed upon them by the Deity. Among these gifts were the ability to foretell the future, the gifts of exceptional memory, of inspired speech, and the possession of wisdom. New qualities or abilities were not shown as the outcome of personal effort, but as rewards for faithful service or even as consolations for hardship endured. In these lives, the biographers implied that asceticism, practised with the hope of a reward in heaven, was doubly rewarded with special gifts in this life. The accounts of the ascetics were derived, not only from the monks, but also from the communities among whom circulated 'miracle stories' derived from various sources. That, by the use of their own powers of intellect and imagination, the ascetics were able to make predictions about events in everyday life, and to foretell disasters, would appear miraculous to a non-intellectual populace. It is probable that the miraculous powers attributed to holy men were based on already existent miracle stories. For those to whom the experiences of the ascetic were an unknown dimension of life, it was nevertheless necessary to portray the relationship of the holy man to the divine. The possession of certain gifts implied that he had attained to this relationship, and miracle stories became an essential ingredient of a biography. Such stories appear to have either been included uncritically by the biographers, or to have been added at a later period. However, their presence in so many biographies suggests that they produced for the populace an acceptable picture of a holy man based upon traditional models. The accounts showed the holy man, like an Old Testament prophet, as an agent of the Deity, not as one who was conscious that within himself was the source of the divine.

Few, if any, of the prophecies of the monks contained expectations of a future expansion of Christianity. On the contrary, from the time of Anthony onwards, they foretold the decay of monastic life, together with the destruction of the Church (Quotations 13–29). Whereas, in the *Life of Anthony*, the menaces to the Church were ascribed to 'heretics', in the visions of Pachomius, the monasteries were destroyed by 'barbarians'. The ascetics were said to have foreseen that later generations of monks would not have the 'wings of fire' which had enabled them, as pioneers of monasticism, to rise to a new dimension of life. It was thus with no hope that their vision of Paradise would be continued by their successors, that the ascetics continued to recreate it. In his vision of times to come, Pachomius saw that in those days, the monks would be in a hell from which they could not escape; monasticism did not solve the conflict between Christianity and its opponents.

(ii) *Memory*

The learning by heart and recitation of texts was the traditional method of education in the Hellenistic period; in this way, as has been seen, Jewish and Greek students absorbed their own respective cultural heritages. When the Egyptian ascetics learned the Scriptures, they were transforming their whole mental background; they deliberately replaced everything which was derived from their traditional religion and culture by the contents of the Old and New Testaments. Thoughts and images which were not connected with the Scriptures were gradually eliminated from their minds. Thus the recitation of the Scriptures was, for the Egyptians, an ascetic exercise, necessary as a means of introducing a new element into their inner life. By daily repetition, the impact of these texts on the inner life of the ascetics was reinforced. The ascetic life was a slow conditioning of the whole personality towards functioning as an individual. The Scriptures were first memorised and gradually formed the basis for thought and imagination.

Pre-Christian groups which practised asceticism, and whose main activity had been the study of the Scriptures, were the Essenes and the Therapeutae.[13] They differed from the Egyptian ascetics in having an intellectual approach; according to Philo the Therapeutae found the Scriptures a source of allegorical meanings:

> They read the Holy Scriptures and seek wisdom from their ancestral philosophy by taking it as an allegory, since they think that the words of the literal text are revealed by studying the underlying meaning.
>
> They have also writings of men of old, the founders of their way of thinking, who left many memorials of the form used in allegorical interpretations and these they take as a kind of archetype and imitate the method in which this principle is carried out.
>
> Philo, *The Contemplative Life*, III.28,29

THE ESTABLISHMENT OF A NON-MATERIAL ENVIRONMENT

Among the early Christian Fathers, Origen was perhaps the most outstanding for his devotion to the study of the Scriptures. As a preparation for his studies, Origen practised strict asceticism:

> For many years he (Origen) persisted in this philosophic (ascetic) way of life, putting away from him all inducements to youthful lusts, and at all times of the day disciplining himself by performing strenuous tasks, while he devoted himself most of the night to the study of Holy Scripture. He went to the limit in practising a life given up to philosophy; sometimes he trained himself by periods of fasting, sometimes by restricting the hours of sleep, which he insisted on never taking in bed, always on the floor. Above all he felt that he must keep the Gospel sayings of the Saviour urging us not to carry coats or wear shoes and never to be worried about the future. He displayed an enthusiasm beyond his years, and patiently enduring cold and nakedness, went to the furthest limit of poverty, ... Not once did his determination weaken; it is said that for several years he went about on foot without any shoes at all, and for a much longer period abstained from wine and all else beyond the minimum of food, so that he ran the risk of upsetting and even ruining his constitution.
>
> Eusebius, *History of the Church*, VI.3.9

This description by Eusebius was a model for later biographies of ascetics. However, unlike Origen and the pre-Christian cults, the Egyptian ascetics were not concerned with allegorical interpretations of the Scriptures; their chief endeavour was to recite them daily. Whereas for the pre-Christian Jewish sects and for Origen and his followers, the Scriptures themselves were a source of revelation which could be attained by intellectual exertion, for the Egyptian ascetics the Scriptures were the form through which they exercised their imagination. Like pre-Christian sages, they acquired the reputation of having remarkable memories. It has, however, been seen that the ability to remember and repeat what was learned was a characteristic of Hellenistic schools. What was significant was that the ascetics memorised, not what belonged to their own cultural background, but something completely new.

(iii) *The Gift of Tongues*

Among the powers ascribed to the ascetic were those 'gifts of the Spirit', described in the New Testament, which followed the event of Pentecost. Among the earliest Christians, 'prophecy' and 'speaking tongues' were regarded as manifestations of the working of the Spirit.

The former appears to have been a form of ecstatic speech in which the speaker felt himself inspired by the Spirit in whose name he spoke. The speaker was thus the mouthpiece of the Spirit and his words were accepted as revelations by his audience, 'Speaking with tongues' was not, at least in the majority of cases, the speaking of foreign languages, but the making of incomprehensible sounds in a state of trance. The possession of the Spirit was regarded by the earliest Christians as a characteristic which distinguished them from non-Christians. Nevertheless, the more irrational manifestations of such 'inspired' speech were condemned by the Church during its first centuries of existence.[14]

In the middle of the second century, a revival of 'prophecy', as practised among the first Christians, occurred in Asia Minor among a group of Christians led by Montanus:

> (A recent convert named Montanus) was filled with spiritual excitement and suddenly fell into a kind of trance and unnatural ecstasy. He raved, and began to chatter and talk nonsense, prophesying in a way that conflicted with the practise of the Church handed down generation by generation from the beginning. Of those who listened at that time to his sham utterances some were annoyed, regarding him as possessed, a demoniac in the grip of a spirit of error, a disturber of the masses. They rebuked him and tried to stop his chatter, remembering the distinction drawn by the Lord, and His warning to guard vigilantly against the coming of false prophets. Others were elated as if by the Holy Spirit or a prophetic gift, were filled with conceit, and forgot the Lord's distinction. They welcomed a spirit that injured and deluded the mind and led the people astray: they were beguiled and deceived by it, so that it could not now be reduced to silence. . . . Then he secretly stirred up and inflamed minds closed to the true Faith, raising up in this way two others—women whom he filled with the sham spirit, so that they chattered crazily, inopportunely, and wildly, like Montanus himself.
>
> Eusebius, *History of the Church*, V.16.6–10

This was a cult practising strict asceticism and claiming that their speech, during their self-induced trances, was inspired by the Spirit. They spoke in the first person as God the Father, the Son or the Paraclete. They also were said to practise sleeping in temples in order to obtain revelations. Montanism reached North Africa by A.D. 200 and Tertullian became one of its followers.[15] Thereafter, the movement declined and only in Asia Minor did it persist till the fifth century.

Although there is no direct evidence that the Egyptian ascetics were influenced by Montanism, the fact that they were credited with 'prophecy' and 'speaking with tongues' shows that their biographers were familiar with these terms. As has already been seen, the solitary ascetics either avoided speech with other men or spoke in carefully chosen words. A few among them, in particular Pachomius and Shenute,[16] the founders of monastic institutions, undoubtedly possessed outstanding powers of speech. These powers acquired by them, their biographers described as gifts of 'prophecy' and 'speaking with tongues'.

In the case of Ephraim the Syrian, 'speaking with tongues' perhaps referred to the large number of hymns which he had composed and for which he was famous.[17] The hymns of Ephraim survive in Syriac; those of his Egyptian contemporaries probably all perished in their original form. Nevertheless, the large collection of hymns of the Coptic Church,[18] many dating from the early monastic period, were probably originally derived from those composed by the ascetics. The ascetic not only created a non-material heavenly world, but he himself lived within this Paradise of his imagination. He used the words of the Scriptures, and in particular the Psalms, to express not only his thoughts but his emotions. Thus he himself created the emotional atmosphere of his heavenly world:

> (The fathers) applied all the Psalms to their own lives and works, and to their passions, and to their spiritual life and to the wars which the devils waged against them. Each man did thus according to his capacity, whether he was engaged in a rule of life for the training of the body, or of the soul, or of the spirit, . . . he acquires daily the faculty of singing a song mingled with the meditation of God and with the gaze (which is fixed) upon Him, . . . and which is like that of angels.
>
> Palladius (Budge, II, Appendix 35)

> He will make the thoughts of the psalms his own. He will sing them no longer as verses composed by a prophet, but as born of his own prayers . . . fulfilled in his daily life.
>
> Cassian. *Conferences*, X.11 (Chadwick)

In their method of singing, the ascetics differed from other non-Christian sects. That choral singing was used as a means of inducing ecstasy is suggested in the account by Philo of the Therapeutae:

> (They become) a copy of the choir set up of old beside the Red Sea in honour of the wonders there wrought. . . . This wonderful sight and experience, . . . so filled with ecstasy both men and women that forming a single choir they sang hymns of thanksgiving to God their

Saviour, the men led by Moses and the women by the prophetess Miriam.

> Philo, *The Contemplative Life*, XI.85,87

But it is well that the Therapeutae, a people always taught from the first to use their sight, should desire the vision of the Existent and soar above the sun of our senses and never leave their place in this company which carries them on to perfect happiness. And those who set themselves to this service ... carried away by a heaven-sent passion of love, remain rapt and possessed like bacchanals or corybants until they see the object of their yearning.

> Philo, *The Contemplative Life*, II.11, 12

Choral song was an expression of shared emotions, whereas the hymns of the ascetics were their personal expression of feeling. A further difference in the two methods of singing lay in the fact that the Therapeutae met to commemorate particular occasions with their singing; the ascetics aimed to maintain a continuous attitude of praise:

> Abba Isidore, who was the priest in Scete, said: 'When I was a young man and stayed in my cell, I made no limit to the number of psalms which I used in the service of God. Night and day alike were spent in psalmody.'
>
> Palladius (Chadwick, *Sayings of the Fathers*, XI.17)

> Abba Hyperichius said: 'Keep praising God with hymnody, and meditate continually.'
>
> Palladius (Chadwick, *Sayings of the Fathers*, VII.20)

To the ascetic, the fitting response, on his part, to the knowledge of himself as a divine being was not, like the Montanists, arrogant self-assertion. Those who spoke as mouthpieces of the Persons of the Trinity[19] were, as has been seen, thought to be of unsound mind (p. 60). It was therefore with the angels who were, according to the Scriptures, constantly singing praises to the Trinity that the ascetics, in their imagination, aligned themselves.

(iv) *The Gift of Knowledge and Wisdom*

The knowledge which the ascetics actually possessed was not great intellectual knowledge; it was wisdom derived from their personal experiences. The knowledge which was ascribed to them was, on the one hand, that of the Alexandrian schools, and on the other, that of pre-Christian oracles and healing cults. Through his practices of self-mortification, as has been seen, the ascetic released himself from and 'overcame' the various powers within himself which bound him to his community and made him dependent on natural phenomena. As a result, he was no longer dominated psychically by what he perceived through his senses. In so far as he was able to make himself independent of the world which his senses had previously presented to him, he was able to exercise control over his thoughts and emotions. Self-knowledge enabled the ascetic to control, not only his own inner life, but that of others. This was the source of his power as a healer. Individual self-knowledge and self-control had been an ideal of Greek philosophy; it had depended on exceptional intellectual attainment among a few individuals and on the creation of an exceptional environment. The self-knowledge of the Egyptian was the outcome, not of exceptional development of any one faculty, but on the achievement of a measure of control over those which he had. His great achievement in this respect was the liberation of his faculties from their domination by influences derived from his community and previous environment.

In achieving their own freedom, the ascetics were the 'saviours' of their fellows; it was not necessary for all to pass through the experiences of self-mortification. An individual who was manifestly free himself could influence others indirectly. This was possibly the real basis of the accounts of the ability of the ascetics to heal the sick. To the populace, however, the ascetic played the role of the miracle-performing saviour who intervened in human affairs; those who were healed by him were not able to explain how it happened.

Throughout this book, evidence is brought forward to show that, because of the forms of expression used by their biographers, it was, and is, possible to misinterpret the achievements of the ascetics. Some barriers to communication arising from the great differences in background have already been discussed. Among these was the language difference (p. 50). Perhaps the most important cause of misunderstanding was the inability of the ascetics to express themselves in conceptual terms. The early Egyptian ascetics not only had no background of intellectual training, but they rejected for themselves the book learning of the Alexandrian schools. The ascetics were therefore limited in their ability to communicate with the outside world. Whereas personal experiences could be shared and understood among those who had undergone similar experiences, the vehicle of conceptual language was necessary to express these unfamiliar subjective events to others. Failure to appreciate the importance of conceptual thought precluded the possibility of objective criticism and judgment between the desert and the outside world. It also contributed to the situation which arose later in the monasteries of the Eastern Church. The high value set upon stereotyped devotional observances tended to debar the monks from further intellectual development.

II DEMONIC VISITS

Preliminary Considerations

A belief in demons and in their penetration into all aspects of life was widespread in the late Hellenistic period:

The whole world and the circumambient atmosphere were filled with devils; not merely idolatry, but every phase and form of life was ruled by them. They sat on thrones, they hovered around cradles. The earth was literally a hell, though it was and continued to be a creation of God.

Harnack, *Mission and Expansion of Christianity*, Ch. III, p. 131

Conflict with demons played a prominent part in the lives of the ascetics and it is possible to see in this the struggle of the individual against the powers of his old religion. A belief in demons was not peculiar to Christianity and it is necessary to seek its origins from Egyptian, Jewish and Greek sources. A characteristic of the Hellenistic period was a desire to preserve or revive archaic forms of religion, in particular, cults in which there was obliteration of consciousness. The eruption of irrational manifestations into social life and the fear of the demonic world was a consequence of this desire to turn back the clock.

In Egypt, a return to earlier forms of worship occurred in the Saite period. About 750 B.C. an Ethiopian (or Nubian) dynasty of rulers from the South conquered Egypt.[20] The Ethiopians, in forming their kingdom, considered themselves heirs to the old Egyptian religion and civilisation. The Nubians had been conquered and reconquered from the period of the Old Kingdom onwards, and the Egyptian religion had been more than once introduced among them. How far 'Egyptianisation' affected their own primitive culture is not known. Nevertheless, in the Saite period, they impressed the outside world with the archaic quality of their practices. Thus arose the idea among the Greeks and others, as seen in the account of Apollonius of Tyana, that the Ethiopians were the wisest and most pious of men and that Ethiopia was the cradle of Egyptian civilisation.

The Ethiopian dynasty of kings instituted a religious revival in Egypt, taking as their model the period of the Old Kingdom.[21] Old beliefs and practices were revived and it was this that gave the last period of Egyptian religion the archaic character which was admired by the Greeks. The outstanding characteristic of the late Egyptian religion was the revival and spread of the worship of animals. Animal cults belonged to prehistoric periods of Egyptian history and the deities

were essentially regional. Their re-introduction during the Saite period
had the effect of strengthening local community ties and reviving the
hostilities and differences between local groups. The adoption of
aspects of more universal gods as local deities was begun in the New
Kingdom and was continued during the Graeco-Roman period. Thus,
in its last phases, Egyptian religion, as practised by the great majority
of Egyptian people, had reverted to an earlier phase and was a cult
intended to reinforce community ties. Foreign gods made little impression on the Egyptians and the Greek (and later the Roman) invaders
were, as regards religion, brought under the influence of Egypt.[22]
From the time of Alexander the Great, the foreign rulers of Egypt
assumed the role of divine kings and had, by this means, achieved
political unity. The Egyptians opposed the military strength and cultural
superiority of their rulers with the power of their religion.

The 'Egyptianisation' of the Greek settlers began in the third century
B.C. Like Herodotus,[23] they thought they saw analogies between
Egyptian and Greek gods, and they ascribed to Egyptian deities
meanings based on Greek mythology:

> The ceremonies the priests perform in public when they are conveying
> the body on a raft, at the burial of the Apis, differ in nothing from
> the Bacchanalea.
>
> Plutarch, *On Isis and Osiris*, XXXV

Osiris became the subject of intellectual speculations and dream-
visions:

> (The vulgar) have the idea that the sacred and truly holy Osiris
> dwells in the earth, and under the earth, where are hidden the
> corpses of such as seem to have come to an end. But he Himself
> dwells at the greatest distance from the earth, being unmixed,
> undefiled, and pure from all nature admitting of corruption and
> of death; but the souls of men here below, enveloped in bodies and
> passions, have no participation in the Deity, except as far as lies in
> grasping Him by conception, like an indistinct dream, by means of
> philosophy; but where they are set free to migrate to the Formless,
> Invisible, Impassive, and Good, then this God becomes leader and
> king over them, whilst they hang, as it were, upon him, and contem-
> plate without ever being satiated.
>
> Plutarch, *On Isis and Orisis*, LXXIX

The cult of Egyptian deities with new names and forms began in several
centres in Egypt. The name of the cult of Osiris (*Usar*) and the Apis
Bull (*Hapi*) was changed to the Greek form, Serapis, and the deity took
the aspect of the Greek Pluto, a god with curling hair and a long beard.[24]

65

Osiris, as worshipped by the Greeks, was not only the god of the dead, but also a solar deity. Since the end of the New Kingdom, an important change had been taking place in Egypt in the worship of Osiris. He was still the deity with whom man was identified after death, but by the Saite period he had also assumed the role of the sun god Rē. The Apis Bull had, in the New Kingdom, been so closely associated with Osiris that he eventually merged with him as one deity, *User-Hapi* (Serapis). In the Ptolemaic period, Osiris, together with the goddess Isis and Horus the Child, was worshipped as a solar deity. The cult spread, not only among the Greeks in Egypt, but throughout the Greek-speaking Mediterranean world. The worship of Isis and Serapis continued in the Roman empire until the fourth century A.D.[25]

The transformation of Osiris and Isis into solar deities is linked in the writings of Plutarch with the idea of the promotion of Greek heroes to the rank of gods. He associates this change of status with the interchangeability of the divine and the demonic natures:

> And she (Isis), together with Osiris, having been translated from the rank of good daemons up to that of gods, by means of their virtue (as later was done with Hercules and Bacchus) receive, not inappropriately, the united honours of gods and of daemons everywhere, both in the regions above earth, and in those under ground, possessing the supreme power.
>
> Plutarch, *On Isis and Osiris*, XXVII

In classical Greek culture, the view that the nature of demons was that of intermediaries between the divine and human worlds was expressed in the writings of Plato. In the Hellenistic period, there was a desire to relate the cults of Egypt to Greek ideas. Plutarch, in alluding to the ambivalent nature of demons, noted that Xenocrates had described them as potentially either malevolent or benevolent. He also quoted from Empedocles the idea that through punishment the demonic nature could be purified and returned to a higher place in the moral hierarchy of such beings:

> Xenocrates thinks that the unlucky days of the month, and whatever festivals are accompanied with stripes and blows, abusive or obscene language, have nothing to do with honouring the gods or good daemons; but that there are certain Powers of Nature existing in the circumambient air, great and strong indeed, but malignant and ill-tempered, who take delight in such things, and if they obtain them, betake themselves to nothing worse. But the good ones, on the contrary, Hesiod styles 'pure daemons' and 'guardians of men'. . . .

And Plato terms this species 'Hermeneutic' and 'Daemonaean', a middle class between gods and men, conveying up thither vows and prayers from mankind, and bringing down from thence to earth prophesies and gifts of things good. Empedocles even asserts that daemons suffer punishment for their sins both of commission and omission, ... until having been thus chastened and purified, they obtain once more their natural place and position.

Plutarch, On Isis and Osiris, XXVI

Within the cult of Osiris, the Greeks were able to accept the presence of animal deities by assigning to them the role of demons or inter-mediaries. Plutarch thus described the function of Anubis, the jackal god of the Egyptians:

And he that reveals the things of heaven, the word of those that move above, is named 'Anubis', sometimes 'Hermanubis', the former as belonging to those above, the latter as belonging to those below; for which reason people sacrificed to the one a white cock, to the other a saffron coloured one;

Plutarch, On Isis and Osiris, LXI

Plutarch further suggested that the link between the divine and the demonic lay in the fact that the bestial part of the soul of the god was divided among the animals sacred to him:

For the Apis, along with a few others, is reputed sacred to Osiris, and if this explanation be true, I am of opinion it indicates what we are in search of in the case of the animals that are acknowledged and have joint honours with him, for instances, the ibis, the hawk, the baboon, and the Apis himself; for so do they call the goat, that is, at Mendes.

Plutarch, On Isis and Osiris, LXXIII

The Greeks and others who participated in these cults no longer lived, like the Egyptians, in closed communities. The rituals were performed by the non-Egyptians, not to enhance their feeling of community life, but in order to attempt to return to more archaic experiences. For the individuals of the Graeco-Roman world, attempts to reinstate the gods in the natural phenomena of the world led, on the one hand, to gross superstition, and the propitiation of gods and demons replaced more rational conduct.[26] On the other hand, the spread of cults using techniques for diminishing self-consciousness rendered their partici-pants susceptible to irrational influences capable of dominating the personality. Thus arose states of consciousness in which men felt themselves 'possessed' by demons, and demonic possession became a widespread phenomenon in the Hellenistic world. Consciousness of a demonic world replacing the divine world had become so strong by the second century A.D., that Tertullian was able to write:

> Acknowledge that there is but one species of such beings, namely, demons, and that the gods are nothing else. Look out then, for gods. For now you find that those whom you formerly took for such, are demons.
>
> Tertullian, *Apologeticum*, XXIII

To the Egyptians themselves, the archaic practices of the late phases of their religion were merely a reinforcement of a way of life which they had never abandoned. On the one hand, the animal world was seen as anthropomorphic and was invested with human attributes and roles. On the other hand, the animal and the human being were seen as particularly related through the faculties of sense perception which they had in common. The senses were regarded as organs of knowledge through which the will of the gods was made known. Animals were recognised and deified as possessors of senses more perfectly developed than those of man. The Egyptian divinities were ultimately those which controlled the rhythms of the universe, the sun, moon and stars. The sensitivity of certain animals to seasonal events was the basis of the use of these animals and their organs for divination.[27] Animals were thus regarded as the interpreters to man of the divine world.

In the Egyptian rituals for the dead, the fact that the individual passed through the actual experience of death alone is reflected in his encounter with monstrous demonic beings during his journey through the underworld of *Amente*. In passing from one state to another, he was temporarily separated from the community; he no longer shared the experience of the living and had not yet reached the community of the heavenly worlds. Thus only by the individual, isolated by death from his community, were the demonic beings experienced. The same demonic world was revealed to the living who participated in the rituals for ensuring the passage of the dead through the regions of *Amente*.

When the world was not experienced as a shared totality, when an individual or group confronted it in isolation, man became conscious of a demonic world. Thus the attempt by man to separate himself from the community coincided for him with the loss of his vision of the world as divine and with the entry into his consciousness of the demonic world. Natural objects, no longer seen in a divine context, appeared to be the habitations of menacing beings. The characteristic of the demonic world was its unpredictability; the demons might be either benevolent or malevolent. and had either to be propitiated by gifts and sacrifices or else exorcised. Cults for the propitiation of demonic beings were the basis of the practices of the Canaanite tribes from whom the Children of Israel tried to keep themselves separate.[28] Among the tribes, all land, whether desert or fertile, was seen as inhabited by demons. Fertile districts were the sphere of the Baalim or 'Lords of the land', who were potentially beneficent to those who cultivated the soil; for the nomads, the harshness of life in the desert was paralleled by the malevolence of its demonic inhabitants. In this patriarchal society, men were united by blood ties; among the nomads, blood was seen as uniting men not only with one another but with their animals, who were regarded as ancestral figures. Among the nomads, the ritual killing of an animal and the consumption of its flesh and blood were the means of experiencing this relationship.[29] After the change to agricultural life, a different meaning was given to animal sacrifice; animals were killed and their blood was shed upon the ground in order to propitiate the demonic powers and procure the fertility of the earth. Animal sacrifice was thus a means of bargaining with the demonic powers, of obtaining material benefits for the tribe and for ensuring the continuance of these favours. The worship of the God of Israel included ritual animal sacrifice; the propitiation of one deity replaced that of the demonic powers. The function of the sacrifice, as a bargain or covenant to ensure certain favours, remained the same.

The central feature of the Jewish religious practices was the endeavour to transform man's experience of the world so that it was no longer regarded as being under demonic influences. In order to achieve this certain objects and actions were designated as being clean and acceptable to the Deity; they were distinguished from others which were unclean and therefore to be avoided. As has been seen, ritual purity concerned the removal of demonic influences. By ritual actions the temporarily unclean could be transformed into the clean. The prohibitions relating to the unclean were the basis of the Jewish moral code. Some of the strictest laws concerned the types of food which might be eaten. The eating of blood, which was regarded as the soul[30] and thus the expression of man's link with the animal world, was prohibited. The animals rejected by Mosaic law were a subject of speculative writing by the Church Fathers; to Origen, they were those which had been used for divination by the Egyptians.[31] Clement, following a Jewish tradition,[32] saw a moral distinction between the animals which chew the cud and those which do not. It is, however, also likely that the chosen animals were made clean and their previous association with demonic cults obliterated, by the fact of their inclusion within the cult of the God of Israel. A deity with supreme power could exorcise the

6

demons from his cult objects. The demons were cast out of all those things in the human and natural worlds which were said to be clean. The remainder continued to have demonic associations.

The effect of Judaism was the abolition, for the Jewish people, of any consciousness of the divine within the visible world; the Creator was seen as being outside His creation. Judaism thus sought to prohibit the search for the divine in the human world, either living or dead, or in the world of nature. Whatever powers lay within man or in the external world, they were not to be regarded as divine, and their worship was forbidden. The demons of the Graeco-Roman world, discussed above, had been seen as beneficent or malevolent according to their effects; no moral stigma was attached to man for engaging in cults designed either to invoke, propitiate or avert them. In Judaism, on the other hand, those who returned to the practices of their ancestors, or were tempted to join in the cults of their more primitive neighbours, were not only the objects of censure, but were also regarded as the cause of divine retribution upon the whole people. The ills which befell the Jewish nation were attributed to divine vengeance for its disobedience.

That the gods of one religion became the devils of another is seen in the well-known example of the Persian word *daevas*.[33] In the ancient religion of Persia this word signified 'demon', with the connotation of evil. Etymologically, the word is identical with the Sanskrit *deva*, meaning 'deity'. Among the Children of Israel, the gods of the Canaanite tribes were condemned by the prophets as demons. The ambivalence of these god/demons lay, not so much in their own nature, as in the case of the demons of Empedocles, but in the attitude of their worshippers. To the prophets, they were the source of evil, but to the Jewish people, they clearly gave satisfactions not found in the cult of the one God. The transition from one form of religion to another was not, in this case, the abandonment of practices which involved diminution of consciousness; as has been seen, the prophets cultivated techniques of this nature. However, the prophets were not regarded as divinities; they were merely the mouthpieces of the divine. The Law of Judaism involved the renunciation by man of divinity for himself and the world; henceforth divine intervention in human affairs was seen to come from a source completely external to man.

The prohibitions of Judaism are relevant to the present theme, because many of them continued unchanged in the Christianity of the early Church. Among the dimensions of life in which it was forbidden to see any manifestation of the divine, was the sexual act. In ancient Greece, every aspect of sex had divine significance; it was a worship of life itself, and was seen as an experience shared by man with the whole world of nature. It was the essential core of both the popular festivals and such cults as Orphism. In the religion of ancient Egypt, sex was seen as if from the point of view of a child. A man's closest relationships were those within the family, and in particular to his mother and sister. A Pharaonic dynasty was matrilineal,[34] and a king might ensure his right to rule by marrying his mother or sister, or even both. The titles of Father, Mother, Son and Daughter were all seen as relationships with the divine; the king was the Son of Rē, and similar titles were those of Father, Mother, or Daughter of the God.[35] The Egyptians were more preoccupied with birth than with the sex act itself, and 'birth' rituals were the enactment of the king's entry into the divine world.

In Judaism, in order to ensure racial purity, exogamous marriage was forbidden and any breach of this law was condemned as 'fornication'. This law was probably a continuation of earlier tribal custom whereby marriage outside the tribe was forbidden.[36] If this was the case, 'fornication' was then doubly illegal; it was a breaking of both Mosaic law and tribal custom. The signification of 'fornication' and the reason for its condemnation by Judaism lay in the rituals for propitiating demons and for ensuring fertility, with which it was associated. When immortality for the individual depended on having male heirs, fertility was all-important. That propitiation of demons for the sake of fertility precluded the possibility of moral law is seen by the fact that these rituals of 'fertility' included the sacrifice of infants as burnt offerings.[37]

Terms which denote sexual promiscuity appear to have been used in the Old Testament to condemn cults associated with divinities other than the God of Israel. Infidelity to the God of Israel was thus defined and condemned in sexual terms. The Jewish 'nation' was an artificial creation based, on the one hand, on the worship of a single Deity and, on the other, on the tradition of the descent of the whole nation from a single ancestor. That the nation, in fact, arose from the confluence of a number of tribes, is suggested by the tendency of the Jewish people, throughout the period covered in the Old Testament, to turn to the cults of neighbouring tribes. Among primitive patriarchal peoples, demonic influences included the dead who, unless given their due, were a source of misfortune, including infertility, to the living.

That tribal ancestor worship was the greatest threat to the integrity of the Jewish nation is reflected in the vehemence of the language with which such practices were prohibited. It is therefore likely that the practices designated as 'whoring', 'fornication' and 'adultery' were tribal rites for ensuring fertility by communication with the dead, and that the gods condemned were the tribal ancestors. Because the only

71

means, by which the will of the God of Israel was declared, was through the prophets, all prophecy, dreams and visions which came through tribal ancestor cults were condemned as false. For this reason, the consulting of those who had 'familiar spirits' was forbidden, and the penalty for wizards and necromancers, who themselves had 'familiar spirits', was death.[38] The making of material images, through which the god or ancestral spirit could manifest, was condemned in strong terms.[39] The endeavour of Judaism to remove from the material world any divine connotation is seen in the description of idols as mere wood and stone, without human faculties.[40] Their worship was seen as a 'snare',[41] or deception, and this term (frequently repeated in the Psalms) passed into Christian writings, where it was applied to the activities of the Devil.

Terms of abuse, denoting sexual promiscuity, were the means of expression of a society in which communal integrity depended on maintaining racial purity. Thus such language was the strongest condemnation of any practice which threatened that society. The essential aim of Judaism was the creation of one nation, related by blood ties; it was therefore necessary to destroy, among its members, any consciousness of mere tribal identity and replace it with one of nationhood. When the Old Testament was adopted as a Scripture by the early Christian Church, 'fornication' lost its original meaning of (sexual) infidelity to the God of Israel, and the Church Fathers condemned the sexual act itself. Paganism was identified with sexual licentiousness and the pleasure obtained through the senses, and Christianity with sexual chastity in obedience to a divine law. The *Lives* of the Egyptian ascetics represented, as can be seen in the *Life of Anthony* by Athanasius,[42] the desire in the minds of the Fathers to relate this image to the practices of the ascetics. Like the descriptions by Plutarch of the cult of Isis and Osiris, those of the Greek visitors to the Egyptian deserts were often only interpretations of what they found in terms of their own background.

In the Old Testament, the God of Israel, as the representative of the divine for the Jewish people, contained within himself the aspects of both judge and executioner. In the latter role of destroyer of the disobedient, or manifestor of wrath and vengeance, he was partly replaced, in the post-exilic apocalyptic literature, by demonic powers. In the places of punishment, it was the demonic powers which both experienced and administered torment (see Chapter IV). That Jewish apocalyptic writings were influenced by Greek ideas is seen, not only in the accounts of the life after death, but also in those which made the air the place of operation of the demons (see Chapter III):

Here Satanail with his angels was thrown down from the height. And one from out the order of angels, having turned away with the order that was under him, conceived an impossible thought, to place his throne higher than the clouds above the earth, that he might become equal in rank to my power.

And I threw him out from the height with his angels, and he was flying in the air continuously above the bottomless.

II Enoch, 29.4,5 (Charles)

Satanail was one of several names for the chief of the powers, who in apocalyptic literature, were cast by the Deity into places of punishment. In the Old Testament, Satan was mentioned in three documents, all of the post-exilic period.[43] In his role as 'son of God' or 'adversary', Satan was closely associated with the Deity; like the demonic powers in Greek literature, his function appeared to be that of intermediary between the divine and man. The Satan of the New Testament was seen, not only as chief of the demonic powers, but as a power of evil of a different order from any which appeared in the Old Testament. In the New Testament the demonic powers which invaded and possessed men appear to have been the cause of physical rather than of moral ills. It is perhaps significant that, in the *Book of Job*, the appearance of Satan coincided with the emergence of a man who, like Satan in the apocalyptic literature, set himself in opposition to the Deity. The ultimate evil in the Old Testament was represented as the aspiration of man to divine status; in the New Testament it was the non-recognition of divinity in man. The necessity was shown that this recognition should be enacted consciously and not while 'possessed' by demonic powers.[44]

To summarise this preliminary discussion, there appears to have been an eruption of a disturbing religious experience in the pre-Christian Hellenistic world: the 'demonic'. In the ancient religions of the Egyptians and, at an early period, of the Greeks, a man felt that to injure his fellow-men or an animal was to injure himself. The harmony was based on a shared 'life of the senses'. By an act of separation, man broke this relationship with his surroundings, and thus, as a result of his own guilt feelings, experienced the outer world as inhabited by hostile demons. Experience of the demonic coincided with the growth of individual self-consciousness and of the intellect. For the use of the latter, it was thought necessary for men to achieve a certain independence from sense-based relationships. The relationships, whose rupture caused most guilt feeling, were those with deities experienced in dream and trance states. The Semitic nations possessed an outstanding capacity for 'separating themselves' from their surroundings and neighbours.

73

Among the Jews, guilt feelings for their own actions led to the exaggerated performance of propitiatory rites. By the sacrifice of first-born children, or substitute victims, the vengeance of tribal deities was thought to be averted. The utterances of the prophets, condemning tribal cults, created guilt feelings for the Jews in relation to the God of their nation. The experiences of the individual, overwhelmed by conflicting guilt feelings, were expressed most clearly in the Psalms. The religion of Judaism involved the individual in a conflict between the demands of a national and a tribal religion. The Jews placed both God and those who were 'no gods'[45] outside of man. The ascetics carried 'separation from the world' further than the Jews; they also renounced nationhood. Like the Jews, they knew the experiences of guilt caused by separation from their old religion. The demonic world, which had only appeared to them in their ancient religions during the passage through *Amente* after death, now became their daily experience. Just as Satan began as an intermediary between God and man and became hostile to both, so the senses became the source of demonic illusions when man separated himself from the community. Only as temptation to return to the old religion was the 'life of the senses' seen as evil by the early ascetics. The guilt feelings for breaking the old religious unity were not removed by repressing them with the intellect and by self-sacrificial actions, as Judaism attempted to do, but by restoring the broken relationships in a dimension which was non-material.

1 Forms

The demonic forms which appeared to the ascetics were derived either from Biblical sources, from the rituals of the ancient Egyptian religion, or, occasionally, from Greek paganism. The ascetics were trying to obliterate from their experience all hallucinatory appearances, even of Biblical personages. They rejected all mental images which they did not themselves consciously create, and the seeing of demonic forms was regarded as an illusion of the senses.

The association in the Old Testament of 'fornication' with paganism led the Church Fathers to interpret the demons, against which the ascetics fought, as sexual temptations (Quotations 9–12). In Egypt, laws of inheritance required a man's marriage with his nearest female relatives; such a marriage was forbidden in Jewish and Greek cultures. To the Egyptians therefore, sexual relations with strange women would be as much an offence against their old religion as against their ascetic rules. Ancient Egyptian religion contained at least as many female as male deities. It is therefore unlikely that the female figures seen by the

74

ascetics were anything other than demonic appearances of the deities of their old religion. The large number of accounts of the sexual temptations of the ascetics appears to be due to the fact that the lives of the ascetics became, for the early Church, a form of propaganda in favour of chastity. The idea of the Neoplatonist philosophers, that intellectual communion with the divine could be attained by withdrawal from the life of the senses and by practising sexual continence, was adopted by the early Church Fathers. Sexual continence became the precondition of a holy life, whether intellectual or not, and the conflicts of the ascetics with the demons were held up as the 'way of perfection'.

A demonic form associated with the ancient religion of Egypt was that of the Nubian, who appeared to the ascetic as a black figure (Quotations 15–22, 27). The Nubian was seen, in some accounts, as having blood-shot or fiery eyes, a spinous body and the smell of a he-goat; he was often associated with the temptation to unchastity. The black figure is perhaps some form of the Egyptian deity, Osiris. The Egyptians themselves were in part of African origin, and, as pointed out by Plutarch, Osiris was sometimes depicted as black-coloured because of his relation to the soil of Egypt:

> They (the priests of Egypt) fable that Osiris was black-coloured because all water blackens earth, clouds and garments, when mingled therewith. . . . And the Ox that is kept at Heliopolis, which they call Mnevis (sacred to Osiris, and which some believe to be the sire of the Apis) is black, and receives secondary honours to those paid to Apis.
> Plutarch, *On Isis and Osiris*, XXXIII

The 'Ethiopian', however, appeared in various writings and, in the present context, was probably a fusion of the Greek satyr with a Nubian, as an 'image' of sexual licence.[46]

The dragon as a demonic form (Quotations 23–26) had Biblical associations.[47] Serpents, however, had played a large part in Egyptian rituals since early times, especially in connection with the passage of the dead through the underworld of *Amente*. Monstrous serpent forms, some with multiple heads, were depicted in the texts of these rituals.[48] It was probably because of its significance in relation to the king that the serpent was associated with the life after death. In life, the cobra was an emblem of royalty and divinity, not only for the king, but for the queen, who was identified with the cobra goddess. The cult of the cobra, as a female deity, persisted in Egypt from pre-dynastic times until the Graeco-Roman period.[49] Another of the most ancient deities, who appeared in the underworld of *Amente*, was the crocodile. In life, in the Pyramid texts, the king was identified with the crocodile as the deity concerned with the Nile floods [50]; in various centres the cult of this deity continued until late times. The overcoming of the dragon within the waters, which was later adopted as a theme in the Christian iconography of Baptism, probably represented the victory of Christianity over paganism. (For discussion on the dragon in relation to the Zodiac, see Chapter IV.II.1.)

The 'changing forms' of certain of the demonic hallucinations were described in the *Life of Anthony* and in some other ascetic *Lives* (Quotations 28–30); demonic beings which 'change their form' were found also in some descriptions of death-bed experiences (see Chapter III.IV; IV.I). The similarity between these accounts suggests that in the experience of 'death in this life', which the Egyptian ascetics consciously underwent, it was from the rituals connected with the passage of the soul through *Amente* that the demonic forms were derived. The ancient Egyptian communities had, by their rituals, protected themselves as far as possible from these demonic experiences. They occurred as an inevitable consequence of separation of the individual from the community, and it was by their own efforts in isolation that the ascetics succeeded in 'exorcising' these demonic forms. The changing forms of the apparitions were, by later writers, sometimes given a moral significance. The change of a beggar into a Nubian (Quotation 27) illustrated the dangers of such apparently virtuous actions as almsgiving to strangers of the opposite sex.

In the mystery cults, gods were said to be unchangeable, whereas demons appeared in different shapes:

> Moreover, the figures of the gods in regard to size, aspect, external appearance and everything around them, are absolutely unchangeable. Those of the archangels are very near to those of the gods in these respects, but some short of being actually the same. Those of the angels are inferior to these, but are unchangeable. Those of the demons are seen in different shapes and appear great and small at different times; but the manifestations are the same. Those of the archons who are rulers are unchangeable, but the apparitions of those that belong to the realm of Matter are apt to change into innumerable forms. Those of the half-gods are like to those of the demons and those of the souls conform in no small degree to changeableness, peculiar to the demons.
>
> Iamblichos, *The Egyptian Mysteries*, II.v (Wilder, p. 83)

2 *The Devil as Deity*

The accounts of the appearances of the Devil to Diocletian (Quotations 1–7), and to King Erodianus (Quotation I:26) belong, as does the story of the saving of the woman by Saint Theodore (Quotation 1:27) to the martyrdom narratives. They are included here for completeness, as illustrating both forms in which the Devil was thought to appear, and the moral attitudes of the writers. The 'fall' of Diocletian was seen to lie in his pact with the Devil: in return for worshipping the Devil, Diocletian would himself be given worship. The Roman Emperor was seen by the Christian Church as Anti-Christ, the personification of man's mis-appropriation of divinity. In usurping the worship due to Christ, the Emperor was re-enacting the fall of Satan. In the Jewish Apocalyptic literature, one of the causes of the fall of Satan was said to be his aspiration to be the Deity. Diocletian was said to have also made himself subject to the pagan gods whose worship he promoted. In one account (Quotation 4), the Devil appeared to Diocletian 'clothed like an Egyptian', thus associating with the devil those Egyptians who acquiesced in Emperor worship or pagan cults.

The accounts of the infestation of pagan temples by demons (Quotations 10–12), and the more legendary stories of the slaying, by Christian saints, of monsters which terrorised the countryside, may possibly have had a similar basis. When pagan communities, in early Christian times, changed their attitudes towards their ancient gods and adopted other values, their deities, in becoming the objects of guilt-feelings and fears, were seen as hostile. Without outside intervention, the communities were unable to rid themselves of these attitudes. The Egyptian deity Bes,[51] who is mentioned by name in one account (Quotations 10), was a household god, a bandy-legged dwarf of hideous appearance; as a demon, he was inflicting upon men those very ills which his presence, as a talisman, would be expected to avert.

The prohibitions of Judaism against the worship of false gods were, in the main, directed against those who tried to deify their personal ancestors. In Christianity the prohibition included, not only ancestors but living rulers. In Egypt, every phase of life was, in some way, connected with a divinity. Thus the coming of Christianity precipitated among the Egyptian people widespread fear; manifestations of the devil were seen in all aspects of their environment.

In the early Church, it was the idea that man himself was, in any sense, divine that was surrounded with the strictest prohibitions. For the ascetic, self-consciousness did not at all imply self-divinisation. He became conscious that withdrawal from his old religion based on the experience of the senses resulted in demonic illusions. In realising himself as the source of these images, he differed from the Jews of the Old Testament, to whom all divine and demonic manifestations came from without. Unlike the righteous man of Judaism, he did not try to justify himself, but saw in his 'separation from the life of the senses' a means of perceiving that which was demonic in him:

> It is written concerning the idols, 'They have a mouth and speak not, and they have eyes and see not, and they have ears and hear not'; even thus is it right for a monk to be. And because idols are an abomination, a man must hold himself abominable in his own sight.
>
> Palladius (Budge I, Sayings of the Fathers, 480)

At the end of the fourth century, the desert ascetics were condemned by the Alexandrian Church for the heresy of Anthropomorphism[52]: the giving of a human form to the Deity:

> A few days after, ... arrived the customary festal letter from Bishop Theophilus of Alexandria (A.D. 399). ... He concluded in the letter a long refutation of the absurd heresy of the Anthropomorphites. Nearly all the monks in Egypt, being uneducated and therefore holding wrong ideas, received this with bitterness and hostility; ... because (by denying that Almighty God was formed in the fashion of a man, when Scripture bears clear witness that Adam was created in his image) he seemed to be attacking the text of Holy Scripture.
>
> Cassian, Conferences, X.2 (Chadwick)

By this time the Church Fathers, in their conflict with paganism, had adopted a standpoint with regard to man's divinity, similar to that of Judaism: that the divine was separate from and transcendent to the human. The ancient Egyptian religion was based on anthropomorphism; what was new for the ascetics was that man could, alone and outside his community, have the experiences of Heaven and Hell.

3 Mode of Activity

The form of demons varied from one culture to another; they made their appearance, as has been seen, to the individual at the time when he no longer participated in the rituals of his community. For the Jewish people, this feeling of 'expulsion from Paradise' related to an event which had taken place at a remote period in their history. The Book of Jubilees, an apocryphal post-exilic writing, expressed their feeling of isolation from the animal world:

> And on that day was closed the mouth of all beasts, and of cattle, and of birds, and of whatever walks, and of whatever moves, so that they could no longer speak; for they had all spoken one with another with one lip and with one tongue.[53]
>
> Book of Jubilees, 3.28 (Charles)

THE ESTABLISHMENT OF A NON-MATERIAL ENVIRONMENT

In ritual, not only the benevolent, but also the aggressive and destructive aspects of divinity could be experienced and expressed. An ancient religion, such as that of Egypt, provided a framework for the imagination of the community. Men's thoughts and feelings were bound up with the physical experiences of their rituals. In ritual, the distinction between subjective and objective experiences was unclear, and in performing identical actions, men felt a physical identity. Thus man was prevented by ritual from seeing himself distinct from his fellows and from nature; in other words, he was shielded from knowing himself as an individual. The individual, on separation from his group, remained at first confused between the subjective and objective worlds, but his imagination was no longer controlled by the community. The demons were the manifestations of the uncontrolled imagination of the individual. As has been seen, they were associated with feelings of guilt and fear. The demonic images, or hallucinations, precluded conscious thought and action. In communal ritual, the individual was not in full conscious control of himself; he was 'possessed' by the communal deity. Anger and aggression were expressed in ritual, but the individual was protected from the impact of these negative emotions. In Judaism, aggression and destruction were regarded as the prerogative of a transcendent Deity, and these emotions were expressed through the prophets alone. Thus the community 'received', it did not share in 'expressing' the divine anger and vengeance. The ascetics not only had to expose themselves to the demonic attacks, they had to direct their own aggression in such a way that they did not destroy themselves.

The mode of activity of the demonic forms was not, as was thought by the Church Fathers, that they were a temptation to immoral thoughts and actions. Their danger lay in the possibility that the ascetic might become possessed by the demonic aspect of one of his old deities. The conflict with the demons was essentially the attempt, by the ascetic, to maintain conscious control of his personality. As has already been seen, conscious wakefulness was the aim of ascetic self-mortification. The practices themselves were a deliberate means, for the ascetic, of testing his own powers of maintaining consciousness. In the ancient Egyptian ritual, it appears to have been mainly in relation to the death of the individual that the destructive aspect of the deities was manifested. The life of the ascetic, from a physical point of view, was an act of self-destruction; it was, however, performed consciously with a purpose unrelated to that of physical survival. If, however, the ascetic was not able to develop and maintain self-consciousness he became liable, literally, to destroy himself. The result of demonic possession

79

could be, not only physical injury, but risk of death (Quotations 31–39). The descriptions of demonic assaults accompanied by human voices shouting, the sound of tumults and the shaking of walls (Quotations 22–25) suggest that the ascetic, in a trance state without the controlling presence of the community, was directing his own aggression against himself. Among the demonic experiences of the ascetic was that of feeling himself the centre of a circle of wild animals about to attack him (Quotations 29–31). That such experiences were known to the Jews is suggested by the Psalmist's description of his feelings of being among ravening lions, or compassed about by bulls, dogs or bees.[54] It is possible that the language of the descriptions in the *Life of Anthony* and in other *Lives* was derived from that of the *Psalms*. The parallel, seen by the ascetics themselves, between their own experiences and those of the writers of the *Psalms*, accounted for the popularity of this Scripture among them.[55]

III DISCERNING SPIRITS: DISPELLING EVIL

1 Recognition

The aims of Egyptian asceticism included, as has been seen, the detachment of thoughts and feelings from dependence on sense perceptions. It involved, therefore, their recognition as human faculties whose functioning depended on man as their author, and not on the surrounding world. In the Egyptian pagan community, a man's thoughts and feelings were shared with other members of the group and were related to objects perceived through the senses; the objects were given divine and human characteristics. Thus the 'objects' and the related thoughts and feelings were experienced by the group as a whole. The breaking of this unity by one member resulted in his perceiving, in place of the original experience, its menacing hallucinatory counterpart. Thus he encountered, without the 'controlling' effect of the group, the embodiment of his own thoughts and emotions; these embodiments which he felt unable to control, appeared to approach him from without.

The experience of the Jews, in relation to the laws and revelations of their Deity in early Judaism, was that these came from without. Thus ultimate control over the thoughts and actions of the people of Israel was vested in the Deity. In Judaism, the possibility of disobedience to divine law was seen to lie within man; the chief occasion for such action was the desire to return to more archaic tribal cults. The notion of a transcendent authoritarian Deity was, for the community as a whole, never successful in producing a unified and obedient people. Only in such groups as the Essenes,[56] who separated themselves from the general community, was the principle of obedience to external divine authority realised in practice.

The preliminary training of the ascetic, before he entered the solitary life, was essentially one of control of his thoughts and feelings by submission to authority. The disciple thus accepted his master as authority in place of his former community; this outer authority was not only over the actions of the disciple, but over his thoughts and feelings:

> The fathers used to admonish the brethren to ask the old men questions continually, and to learn from them, and to reveal to them their thoughts and to live according to their directions.
>
> Palladius (Budge II, Appendix, 68)

The only means by which the ascetic could finally rid himself of hallucinatory experiences was by seeing himself, not only as ruler over his thoughts and feelings, but as their author and source. Thus the solitary life was the final and necessary stage in this form of self-training.

The writings of the early Church Fathers continued to maintain the attitude of Judaism: that divine authority was external to man, and that the Deity and the Devil intervened from without in man's subjective life. Thus man's thoughts and feelings were never completely under his own control; in acting, man was obeying either the Deity or the Devil. In the *Life of Anthony*, Athanasius described the production of, on the one hand, feelings of joy and on the other, those of fear, confusion and disturbance of thought, depending on the source of the visions received (Quotations 1, 10). By noting the state of his feelings, the ascetic was said to be able to distinguish the different types of visions. This doctrine of the relation of visions of gods and demons to the emotions was derived from Greek sources, and was seen in Neoplatonic descriptions of mystery cults. Iamblichos described the feelings of order and tranquillity which were said to proceed from visions of gods, and those of tumult and disorder which accompanied those of demons:

> Further still, to the gods there pertain order and tranquillity; and with the figures of the archangels there exists a dramatic representation of order and quietude. With the angels there is present the disposition for order and peacefulness, but they are not free from motion. The figures of the demons are accompanied by tumult and disorder. With those of the archons there are objects to be seen analogous to each class which we have already mentioned: those

of the realm of Matter being borne along tumultuously. Those of the half-gods are constantly in motion and are never exempt from change, and these of the Souls resemble the figures of half-gods, but at the same time are inferior to them.

Iamblichos, *The Egyptian Mysteries*, II.v (Wilder, p. 83)

Such descriptions concerned dream experiences, and the Church Fathers did not distinguish the difference between such experiences and those of waking consciousness. In the *Life of Anthony*, the visions were said to be the source, not only of emotional effects, but also of virtues and vices. Thus, according to Athanasius, man's imaginations came to him from without; the good were those which made him happy, but moral responsibility for their production was removed from him. This method of 'distinguishing spirits' according to their effects upon the soul was also found in the second-century Judeo-Christian apocalypse, the *Shepherd of Hermas*.[57] In this case, two angels, one of righteousness and the other of wickedness, were said to enter the heart. The doctrine of two angels or spirits, one of light and the other of darkness, who ruled mankind, was found in the *Rule of the Community*[58] of the Qumran sect, and in a number of Jewish apocryphal writings. Thus the doctrines on the 'distinguishing of spirits', claimed by their biographers to be those of the Egyptian ascetics, were essentially a continuation of those of late Judaism and of the Mystery cults.

2 Distinguishing Good and Evil in Fellow-Men

The recognition of offenders within the early monastic communities and the attitudes of the elders towards the misbehaviour of their disciples were the subject of Narratives 1–5. Narratives 6–13 and 15–22 probably illustrated controversies within the early Church, concerning the re-admission of lapsed Christians and penitents to the congregation.

The early Church, as distinct from the monastic communities, tended towards severity in excluding those who had offended from participating in the Eucharist.[59] This practice of expelling offenders and exacting periods of penance, before re-admission to the congregation, had a precedent in Judaism in the rules of the Qumran community. In the latter, any member who broke his oath of obedience could be given periods of penance for varying periods up to two years, during which time he was excluded from the 'Pure Meal of the Congregation'.[60] Anyone who 'murmured' against the authority of the community could be expelled completely. Those who were admitted as members were first examined on their deeds and understanding. *The Rule of the Community* was thus a discipline of mind and action.

THE ESTABLISHMENT OF A NON-MATERIAL ENVIRONMENT

Within the monastic communities, these narratives suggest that, in addition to authoritarian measures, other means were known for transforming men's behaviour. These measures depended on the presence of elders who, as a result of their ascetic training, were able to place their own human situation imaginatively in a divine context. Until the monks were able themselves to exert their own imagination, the representations of their heavenly environment were created for them by the elders, together with the effects of misbehaviour.

The Narrative (6, 7), said to concern Paul, the predecessor of Anthony, may have been the model for the other stories, (8, 9, 15) on a similar theme. They all illustrated the idea that, to one who could recognise the divine, a man's physical appearance was expressive of the state of his soul. The depiction of a change in appearance, as a result of participation in the services of the Church, was perhaps a literary device to show that the performance of the liturgy was a recreation of the Heavenly world which alone could effect such a transformation. The depiction of angels recording names (Narratives 10–13) introduced an element which was associated with representations of the Judgment of the Soul (Chapters IV.1; V.1.7). Thus their presence at the Eucharist was linked with the idea that, in this human and divine assembly, the state of each soul was revealed. The administration, or withholding, of the Sacrament (Narratives 14–22) and the threatening of the inattentive (Narratives 15, 16) by angels, were further illustrations of the idea that, at the Eucharist, a man's true worth was made known. Such stories, as a means of persuasion, were an alternative to the rules of obedience of later monasticism.

3 Possession and the Casting out of Devils

In the non-Christian religions and cults of Hellenism, whether man conceived his authority to lie in the phenomena of surrounding nature, or in a transcendent Deity, this authority was felt as external. Experience of the divine, as has been seen, was mediated and controlled by the community for the community. The individual, deprived of this support, was liable to the invasion of his personality by complex emotional influences, with which he felt identified and which controlled him. The aim of the early Church leaders was to substitute, in men's minds, the authority of the Christian community for that of the pagan one. It was therefore necessary to demonstrate to the populace that the power of the Church was greater than that of any other religion; this power was, in fact, the control of men's imagination.

From the second and third centuries onwards, parallel to the intellectual activity of the Alexandrian Church Fathers, there arose a large body of popular literature. The Christian communities of Syria and Asia Minor were probably the source of those narratives, now known as the *Apocryphal Acts of the Apostles*.[61] They were biographical narratives, somewhat similar in form to the *Life of Apollonius of Tyana*, and composed of material drawn from many sources. It is not necessary here to discuss their relationship to Manichaean and Gnostic writings, except to note that, in these *Acts* as elsewhere, the Christian compilers used and altered unorthodox material for the purposes of their own propaganda. The biographies which have survived were particularly associated with the names of five apostles: Peter, Paul, Andrew, John and Thomas. It is not known how early these writings were introduced into Egypt; written texts date from the sixth century, but the presence of their essential themes in the *Apophthegmata* suggests that they were known to the biographers of the ascetics. Whereas the *Apophthegmata* were read in monastic circles the *Acts* were the literature of the lay communities.

The purpose of the accounts of the Apostles was the demonstration of the ineffectiveness of the demonic powers against those of Christianity. The expulsion, by the Apostles, of the demons which inhabited the temples and images of paganism, was described together with the overthrowing of these temples and their replacement by churches. Accounts of exorcism, especially of women, suggest that, to the authors of these narratives, sexual continence was the essential message of Christianity. Whereas in the New Testament, demonic possession was not seen as having sexual implication, in these *Acts* it was nearly always the demons of unchastity which were expelled. As refusal to fulfil its marriage laws involved expulsion from a pagan community, converts to Christianity had, in order to be protected from demonic assault, to submit to the authority of the Church. The *Apocryphal Acts of the Apostles* were related, through the themes of martyrdom and exorcism, to that other and even larger body of literature, the *Acts of the Martyrs* (see Chapter V). The theme of martyrdom occurs in the *Acts of the Apostles*, both as the story of the death by this means of the apostle himself, and also as the immolation of those converts to whom death was preferable to unchastity. Thus sexual continence was included with martyrdom as a means of achieving the final reward for separation from the pagan community, the resurrection in the life after death.

Stories of cures, similar to that attributed to Saint George (Narrative 1), are typical of the literature of the martyrdoms. The exorcism of the demoniac, while lying unconscious in the shrine where the Christian martyr was buried, was a method of healing essentially the same as that of the pagan incubation cults. By continuing the practices of paganism, the Church ensured that its authority over men's imagination was substituted for that of the pagan communities. The theme of the use of violence in the overcoming and expulsion of demons was a common one in this type of literature; in this case it was possibly a dream-representation of the power required to resist demonic possession. As has been seen, the Egyptian ascetics appear to have resisted consciously the experiences of demonic possession. Dream experiences of the conflict of a deity with a demon may have been, in the incubation cults, a foreshadowing of this conscious power. The ascetics also, by means of pain, rendered themselves more liable to demonic experiences in order that they might consciously resist them. Their biographers, however, interpreted these ascetic exercises as a form of punitive attack on the demons:

> For immediately the devils see the monk afflicting his body with labours, they become afraid, and stagger about, because they are more tormented by the labours than is the man who is engaged in them.
>
> Palladius (Budge II, Appendix, 23)

The expulsion of demons by casting them down from a height was described in a number of narratives in the *Apocryphal Acts of the Apostles*.[62] It was a demonstration that the power of the demons as divinities was overcome, since divine beings were said to be sustained in the air and did not incur damage by falling. Such demons were also associated with the possibility that, unless exorcised, the individual under their influence would destroy himself (Narrative 2). In the *Apocryphal Acts*, exorcism by the use of speech was the method said to have been practised by the apostles, thereby following the precedent of the canonical Scriptures. In the Old Testament, the exorcism of an evil spirit from Saul was said to have been effected by David through music,[63] suggesting that the healing of Saul occurred during a state of reduced consciousness. Josephus provides evidence that such methods were also in use in post-exilic times:

> God enabled Solomon to learn the arts valid against demons, in order to aid and heal mankind. He composed incantations for the alleviation of disease, and left behind him methods of exorcism by which demons can be finally expelled from people, a method of healing which is extremely effective even in our own day.
>
> Josephus, *Antiquities of the Jews*, VIII.2.5

Exorcism by speech implied the conscious recognition, by the exorcist,

7

of the demonic influence. In accounts of exorcism in the New Testament and elsewhere, the demon, and not the possessed individual, was addressed as a personality. In the *Apocryphal Acts*, the demons were said to hold conversation with the apostles and, as in the New Testament, to recognise the superior power of Christianity, even asking not to be destroyed before their time.[64] The demons were thus made to speak with the voice of the pagan communities, whose form of group consciousness was about to be overthrown.

Before disappearing, the expelled demons were often seen, by the newly exorcised persons, as having human or animal forms. Thus the experience of possession was, before full consciousness was reached, succeeded by a hallucinatory state. In the story of Saint George (Narrative 1), the demoniac stated that he did not see the demon until after it was expelled. In the Old Testament, fire and smoke were the manifestation of divine wrath; similarly, in the Christian stories, the devil and demons who showed these attributes were embodiments of fury and envy. As fire, the demons represented the offended and envious deities of the old religion of paganism; in other words, they embodied men's experiences of anger and deprivation. When the conflict between the new and the old, and the loss of the old religion, were no longer felt by the individual, the exorcism was complete.

4 Dispelling Evil

In ancient Egypt there was no distinction between religion and magic. Although they developed practical skills and techniques, the ancient Egyptians retained a sensitivity to both the subjective and objective qualities of their surroundings. As has seen been, physical sensations were to them a source of divine knowledge. This divine knowledge consisted both in the experience of subjective unity and in the exertion of power within that unity. Inside this 'system', a multiplicity of deities and rituals existed, in order to ensure that for all events, the most propitious circumstances prevailed. The aversion and dispelling of malevolent influences was, as has been seen, achieved by ceremonies and invocations, and also by the avoidance of unfavourable circumstances. The latter involved knowledge of the movements of the heavenly bodies and the interpretation of terrestial signs.

Both astrology and divination were widely practised throughout the Hellenistic Middle East (see Chapter III, 'Preliminary Considerations'). In the Graeco-Roman world, the revival of archaic cults was a conscious attempt to use Egyptian 'magic' in order to avert malevolent influences from the individual. The cult of Serapis, which was essentially one of

THE ESTABLISHMENT OF A NON-MATERIAL ENVIRONMENT

'incubation' and of dream-visions, involved the subjection of the individual to the power of the priestly sect. In the hope of benefit, individuals placed themselves in circumstances over which they had no control. It is significant that it was recognised that the power of the group operated, not only at rational but at irrational levels of consciousness. There was, however, in such cults, only a partial and limited awareness of the irrational divine world in which the ancient Egyptians were able to operate.

It was not only to the decadent cults of Hellenism that Christianity was opposed, but to the faculties which these cults sought to revive and imitate. The essential character of Christian exorcism was that it was consciously performed. It implied the exercise of divine power by the individual, in the first place on himself, and it did not depend for its effectiveness on the presence of a group. The ascetic, in overcoming the demonic influences, knew himself as divine, not as the recipient of divine authority, but as its source. In establishing itself as the mediator of divine authority, the early Church adopted and Christianised the 'magic' formulae for averting evil of the pagan cults which it supplanted. By using the techniques of pagan ritual, it was possible to demonstrate that the powers of paganism were subject to the Church.

In exemplifying the unfailing victory of Christianity over the demonic powers, the *Apophthegmata* resemble the *Apocryphal Acts of the Apostles*. Among the techniques borrowed by the Church from the religion of ancient Egypt were those for the aversion of malevolent influences. The methods attributed to the ascetics included the use of amulets (the Egyptian *ankh* became the Coptic Cross), of curses and spoken formulae (Narratives 25, 26), and of names (Narratives 22–28). Narratives 6–11 differ from the others in showing the influence of the teaching of Evagrius; victory over a demon implied the overcoming of the corresponding vice. In the remainder of the quotations, it is implicit that, in order to dispel the images of his old religion, the ascetic created for himself a divine environment, either entirely in his imagination (Narratives 4, 13, 15), or with the aid of external devices (Narrative 5). The demonic powers were either 'bound' (Narratives 18–21), or caused to disappear by the exertions of the ascetic. For this purpose the recitation of certain books of the Old Testament, especially the *Psalms*, was held to be particularly effective (Narratives 16–17). Perhaps the most conclusive demonstration of the control of the ascetic over his own imagination was his ability to ignore or mock the hallucinatory forms (Narratives 12, 14, 17, 23).

Whereas their physical surroundings appeared menacing to the populations of the Graeco-Roman world, to the early Church Fathers they appeared polluted and corrupt. The practice of exorcising the objects of daily life arose as a safeguard against demonic influences:

'Why were the Fathers in the habit of making the sign of the blessed Cross over such of (the creatures which God hath made) as they ate as food?' The old man said: '. . . Because sin obtained dominion, every one of them became polluted; then came the advent of our Lord . . . and everything became sanctified. . . . But because the blessed Fathers knew the harmful disposition of Satan, who even by means of such things as are used as food carrieth on a war to our injury, they sealed their foods with the holy sign of the Great Cross.'

Palladius (Budge II, Appendix, 104)

The corruption of paganism lay in the conscious revival of archaic techniques for purposes other than that of the revelation of the divine to man. The Church Fathers saw the Church as the recipient of the true revelation in regard to man's divinity. In supplanting the cults of paganism, the early Fathers had to present to men's imagination an image of the divine, more compelling than that of their rivals. The image which was upheld was, however, often that of the authoritarian God of Judaism, in whom alone resided divine power; man was the channel, not the source of divine power:

Every demon, exorcised in the name of the Son of God, . . . is mastered and subdued. Whereas if you exorcise in the name of any king or righteous man, or prophet, or patriarch, who has been one of your-selves, no demon will be subject to you.

Justin Martyr, *Dialogue with Trypho*, II.lxxxv

Associated with the idea of divine authority was that of punishment for disobedience. Exorcism was seen, by the early Latin Fathers, as the infliction of pain on the demons themselves:

This goes on today as well, in the scourging and burning and torturing of the devil at the hands of exorcists, by means of the human voice and the divine power,

Cyprian, *Letters*, LXIX.15

As has been seen, the use of pain was, in early religions, a means of inducing trance states. For the Egyptian ascetics, the endurance of pain was an ascetic exercise, during which consciousness had to be maintained. In later periods of the Church, assaults on the demons, in the name of Christianity, were the pretext for the causing of suffering to those believed to be under demonic influence.[65] The 'overcoming' of the Devil by exorcistic self-mortification became one of the practices of later monasticism.

CONCLUSION

The Church, in its conflict with paganism, based its claim to supremacy on its superior 'spiritual' powers. The early Fathers strove to demonstrate, either that the powers possessed by paganism were false, or else that the Church possessed similar powers in greater measure. The biographers of the ascetics set out to prove that in a situation where oracular and prophetic cults were unreliable, a renewal of these gifts had taken place among Christian ascetics. They showed that the ascetic life was as conducive to visions as the dream cults and mystery religions of paganism. That the manner in which the visions were experienced was the vital issue has been almost completely obscured by the method of presentation.

In an age when men were dominated by fears of a demonic world, the Church claimed to possess powers to command and exorcise demons stronger than those of paganism. In these biographies, it was shown that the ascetic life was a means by which 'demons' could be exorcised. The demons, however, were here represented, as in the religions of the ancient world, as powers external to man. In so far as demons were admitted to be subjective, they were identified with vices, of which lust was the chief. It was not clearly recognised that the demonic world was that which, irrespective of its content, was experienced when the imagination of the individual was not under his own conscious control.

In this chapter, an attempt has been made to reassess the achievements of the ascetics. It has been suggested that the 'real' aim of the ascetic movement in Egypt was an attempt, spread over at least one generation, to reverse the psychological effects of the ancient religion. In ancient Egypt, the imagination of the population was impressed through ritual, so that the physical universe was seen as having human faculties. In this situation, the individual had not only no control of his own psychic workings, but he was incapable of thought or imagination which was not 'sense-bound'. In this chapter, the 'real' purpose of the life of the ascetic and the nature of his experiences has been suggested. In the next two chapters, the content of the 'visions' attributed to him, and the manner of their representation, is discussed.

CHAPTER III

The Representation of a Non-Material World

Preliminary Considerations

The liturgical writings of Egypt, the books of the Old Testament and the records of the cults and shrines of Greece had in common that they depicted a confrontation of the 'human' and the 'divine'. The deities of Egypt were shown addressing or being addressed by the deceased person; the God of Israel appeared to the patriarchs and prophets; the gods and heroes intervened in the lives of their worshippers. Liturgies, in general, were the re-enactment of the circumstances of a divine manifestation, the theurgic reproduction of the original experience in the imagination of the participants. The totality of such an experience formed an 'image' in their consciousness; recall of the 'image' reproduced the experience among those who had shared in it. An example of a late development in the creation of an 'image' was the ikon of the Eastern Church. The ikon, as a record of a divine manifestation, was for him who confronted it a means of communion with the heavenly world.

In ancient Egypt, the psychic life of the community was related at an early period to the motions of the stars. The annual passage of the sun through the constellations of the ecliptic was celebrated in ritual dramas, thus identifying the whole community with each 'image' in turn. The psychic well-being of the group was achieved by the subjection of all to the periodically recurring 'images'; all were bound by the law of the universe to behave in certain ways at certain times of year. The relating of the communal psychic life to the annual cycle of the sun was the means of ensuring that internal conflicts were expressed and resolved ritually. Not only man, but the whole natural world, was seen as participating in this cycle. Animals and birds, being more sensitive to the will of the 'gods', were sources of oracular knowledge (see p. 68). Included in the natural world was the earth itself, and the sacred places of the Nile valley played their part in the annual celebrations. Much of the ritual of ancient Egypt consisted of processions concerned with obtaining oracular manifestations.[1] The figures of deities, or of deified statues of the kings, were transported from one shrine to another; their

90

passage was sometimes ritually barred by obstructions.[2] In the course of these processions, oracular responses and pronouncements by the deities were made through the medium of the officiating priests (see p. 107). The manner of receiving the divine communications precluded the possibility of conscious thought by the participants, and the authority of the oracles was regarded as indisputable. Thus the community experience was bound and controlled by a series of 'images', which, although they related man to the universe, allowed no freedom to the individual (see p. 79).

In cultures such as the Egyptian, in which events were not explained by logical and conceptual thinking, all subjective processes were experienced as a sequence of 'images'. The 'rules' by which one 'image' succeeded, or could be substituted for another, were originally based on ritual experiences, and became fixed by tradition (see p. 104). Ritual was the means by which man related his subjective life to the movements of the stars and the behaviour of natural phenomena. Ritual thus determined the sequence of 'images' and the psychic value of each. The physical world thus played the role of regulator of man's psychic processes, and the sequence of physical events was translated into the imagery of ritual. These 'images', based on a fixed sequence of experiences, persisted in this sequence until man was able, by his own intellectual processes, to manipulate the 'images' and to re-order them for a conscious purpose. The Old Testament contains much evidence of the use, by a collective, of traditional images for national purpose. Ancient Egyptian inscriptions, in contrast, show how apparently easily the names of deities could be substituted for one another, while preserving unchanged the traditional sequence of 'images'. The Coptic writings were expressions of this non-conceptual method of thought, which persisted into the Christian period. The 'Lives' of the ascetics and martyrs consisted, as has been seen (p. 22ff.), of a series of 'images'. These narratives show evidence of the traditional ancient Egyptian sequence patterns, as found on biographical stelae. The 'images' themselves, while being recognisably Christian, show sufficient of the Egyptian substratum for it to be apparent when the Christian 'images' have 'overcome' the pagan ones. Whereas the people of an ancient culture were able to incorporate the 'images' of another culture into their traditional pattern, only the individual could impose upon 'images' a pattern of his own.

In the Hellenistic period, the power of the 'image' in controlling men's behaviour was recognised by Greek and Jewish thinkers. The laws of psychic life, as causally connected processes, had been expressed as the Zodiac. The source of the images was not fully appreciated, but in the incubation cults, it was found that dream images followed predictable patterns and could be related to the cycle of the Zodiac. Jewish apocalyptic literature shows that, in late Judaism, dream revelations were an important means of interpreting the relation between psychic processes and external events. The theme of the journey of the seer through the places of heaven and hell showed a conscious attempt to use the imagery of the Zodiac for eschatological purposes.[3] The Jews, in forming themselves into a nation, had abandoned the cult of the stars as rulers of their psychic life, and they had based their communal rituals on a lunar calendar. In the post-exilic period, the image of Jahweh as ruler of the world was expressed by depicting angels, replacing the stellar gods, as rulers of the defeated nations.

The emergence of the hierarchy of the angels, as the messengers of Jahweh and thus as the 'image' of his victory,[4] can be traced in the later books of the Old Testament. In *Job*,[5] the angels were identified with the stars. The phrase 'host of the height'[5] appeared instead of the pre-exilic term for the stars: 'the host of heaven'.[5] The struggle for supremacy of the Jewish nation was depicted as a cosmic conflict in which the sun, moon and stars were overthrown by the Lord.[5] In this struggle, nationhood was identified with the monotheistic belief in a supreme deity, to whom other gods (whose existence was not denied) were subordinated. In *Zechariah*,[5] there appeared for the first time the differentiation of angels into a hierarchy, and this notion recurred in *Daniel*. In addition, in *Daniel*,[5] the angels in charge of nations were designated as 'princes'. The archangels Michael and Gabriel were, in this book, given proper names and thus appeared, as the re-named gods of other nations, now acting as the agents of Jahweh. Jahweh, enthroned with the angelic hierarchy, was the 'image' of a victory, both external and subjective.

The ancient device of relating man's psychic life to the movement of the stars served, both as a means of regulating and stabilising community behaviour, and as a method of deterring individual eccentricity. Thus the individual who withdrew from his community life went counter, not only to his own people and ancestors, but to the cosmic powers. The problem of representing such an individual act, in terms of the overthrow of a previous way of life, lay in the fact that the new experiences had to be expressed with a vocabulary inherited from the past. The words created 'images', and it was essential to demonstrate that the new 'images' were evidence of greater divine power than the old. Nevertheless, the new 'images' of Christianity, like those of paganism, held a potential danger to the individual. On the one hand, the 'images' were still a deterrent to the individual against leaving the group. Thus the more compelling image of a heavenly kingdom, to which access could be had through the Church, replaced nationalistic images of world conquest. On the other hand, even in isolation, the individual was always liable to be controlled by, rather than to control, the images.

I HEAVENLY VISITATIONS

1 Personal Appearances to Ascetics

From the texts, three main problems emerge, which have continually to be discussed and presented in relation to one another. First, with regard to the seers themselves, the question arises, not only of what they 'saw', but of how they 'saw' it. The second question is the extent to which the written descriptions of the biographers are actually concerned with the experiences of the seers. The third problem is the relation of the writings on 'visions' to the prevailing attitudes of Christian and pagan authorities. Throughout this chapter and those which follow, an attempt has been made to correlate these three aspects of the subject.

The ascetics were represented, by their biographers, as individuals who conquered the demonic powers of the desert. To these writers, the 'visions' were a means of demonstrating the overcoming and replacing of the 'images' of paganism by those of Christianity. Demonic and angelic 'visions' were, however, 'images' of the divine, experienced in states of dream or trance (see p. 54ff.). To experience the divine through the imagination, it was necessary for an individual to avoid losing consciousness. The ascetics, in their daily 'meditations', recited aloud the Scriptures which they had memorised. If they relived the events in their imagination as they did so, they exposed themselves to the danger that they might identify themselves with the 'images' and that they might become 'possessed' by them.[6] As has been described, the ascetics, at times, appeared to undergo states of demonic possession; in some cases, they suffered from delusions that they were favoured persons (Section I.1.2: 19–22). Cases were described which suggest that complete disintegration of the personality and insanity also occurred (p. 79ff.). The biographers, and the ascetics themselves, appear to have been unable to express conceptually the relationship of the individual to his inner source of inspiration. In Biblical language, the ascetics were said to have spoken face-to-face with Christ, and the apostles and prophets. Such descriptions were appropriate for the experiences of collective ritual. Nevertheless, because of their Scriptural associations, this language and imagery were used as if they were equally applicable to the individual. Thus when the ascetics appreciated the implications of the Scriptures as a personal revelation, this was described in their biographies as a 'visitation' by a Biblical figure.

If the early ascetics achieved for themselves the power to appreciate the divine, through the imagination rather than through the senses, it was at great personal cost and in complete isolation. This combination of imagination and insight was, in each case, an individual achievement. The accounts of the first founders of the monasteries suggest that they made strenuous efforts to share their imaginative conceptions with their communities. Examples of their efforts to transmit their knowledge to their disciples can be seen in Quotations 1, 2, 4–7, 9–11, 14. The episodes in Quotations 1, 2, 4 (5), 14 appear to be variations of the same narrative, as do those in Quotations 6, 7 and 9–11, which respectively have the same apparent common bases. These groups of stories may perhaps be interpreted as showing that, in the enclosed type of monastic life, the conditions for the domination of the individual by the community were inevitably created.

The Kingdom of Heaven was represented as containing, not only the figures of the Old and New Testaments, but also the martyrs and Patriarchs of the early Church, as well as fellow-ascetics. Meditation, like martyrdom, appears to have been regarded as a means of 'joining' this community; the martyr did so in the literal sense of physical death. The idea that insight, derived from these meditations, could solve human affairs, is suggested in Narrative 15. Quotations 6, 7 and 8 perhaps illustrate the conception of the liturgy as a celebration in which, not only the living, but also the dead participated.

Solitary asceticism was necessarily a temporary phenomenon in Egypt. The emergence of individuals among the early ascetics appears to have been unique, and the outcome of the first impact of Christianity on Egyptian paganism. The men of subsequent generations were in a different psychological and political situation. Walled enclosures were built, in Egypt, to ensure the physical survival of the monks in a hostile environment. The monastic literature shows that, from about the fifth century, there grew a cult surrounding the names of holy men acknowledged to be seers. Although their miraculous powers were important attributes, in these stories, the essential characteristic of the saints and martyrs was the fact that they had seen 'visions' and had communicated with the divine world. Their lives were perhaps a reassurance to those who, unable to create such a world for themselves, might doubt its existence. The seeing of visions was represented as being the reward for victory over the 'devil', or the powers of paganism. Thus arose the anomaly that, whereas the ascetics had in fact striven to maintain wakefulness, their 'lives' depicted them as seeing dream-visions and hallucinatory apparitions, in a manner similar to that of the devotees of pagan cults. Only the content of the visions was 'Christianised'; the manner of receiving them, as represented, was the same as that of paganism. As in pre-Christian times, 'visions' were the vehicles of both intellectual and moral ideas; they conveyed the answers to doctrinal disputes, they carried reprimands and advice and they forecast the future. Instead of the visitation being that of a pagan deity, there appeared either a Biblical figure or the holy man himself.

2 Appearance at the Eucharist

The earliest writings on the forms of Eucharist used in Egypt were explicit in identifying the elements with the body and blood of Christ.[7] The transformation was seen as the manifestation of the Spirit, whose intervention was invoked. The accounts of 'visions' of light, fire or of the heavenly companies over the altar, during the Eucharist, were perhaps composed in support of the fifth century Monophysite Church[8] leaders against their opponents. Certain of the latter maintained that the elements retained their own nature and that the 'change' was a question of 'grace', whereas the orthodox Coptic Church resisted any doctrinal attempt to deny to the physical elements a divine transformation.[9]

The narratives appear as an attempt to convey to the congregation the notion that, during the performance of the liturgy, a visible manifestation of the divine took place. Such an event was the expected consequence of performing a ceremony in pre-Christian times. The light on the altar and the celestial hierarchies were represented as externally 'visible'. Only the holy man performing the ceremony was, in some narratives, shown as capable of 'seeing' his heavenly surroundings. Such an association of 'visions' with the performance of ritual was appropriate to paganism rather than to Christianity.

By the seventh century, the probable date of the dialogue recorded in the *Questions of Theodore* (6),[10] the priest, asking the question on visions seen at the altar, was speaking from hearsay. He was given the answer by the Archbishop that only at the final dispensation would such a descent of the powers of heaven occur. The priests and congregations were, by this time, dependent on faith and traditional 'images'; perhaps ritual failed to evoke any more 'visions' (see Introduction II. The Decline of Oracles).

3 Interpretation of Doctrine

It is posited that the creation, by the exercise of the imagination, of a divine dimension gave the ascetics a new insight into human nature. Implicit in the notion of a heavenly world was the idea that, within it, all human conflicts would be resolved and difficulties overcome. In the pre-Christian cults of Hellenism, as in Judaism proper, the solution of certain human problems was regarded as outside the sphere of man's capacity. Such important matters concerned, not only the individual, but also the group to which he belonged. Thus, for guidance on the future of their nation, the Jews, following the example of the prophets, prayed to the God of Israel. The participants in the Graeco-Roman cults applied for answers to their problems to the various oracles. These methods of obtaining answers or revelations were often, as has been seen, promoted by physical disciplines, including fasting. Because of their dependence on ideas held in common, the revelations to each of several individuals of one group, with similar problems, might be expected to be the same. The answers to prayer arose in the contexts of communities who each indoctrinated their members from their own sources. Such ideas were in the nature of mythology, rather than intellectual dogmas. Resource to oracles prevailed in societies which turned to past revelations, rather than to intellectual inquiry, for guidance in their affairs.

For the Egyptian ascetics, the Bible formed a common basis of ideas and, within the framework of these ideas, they may have been able, by their own efforts, to reach solutions to problems. Their thoughts were the outcome of their meditations, but were often represented as having been spoken to them by Biblical personages. Their thoughts were the result of a lifetime of effort and were transmitted to their disciples; like oracles, these sayings were represented by biographers as having come from a divine world. This attitude can be seen in narratives 4–6. Intellectual debate on doctrine, such as took place in the schools of Alexandria,[11] was thus unknown among the desert ascetics.

Evidence that revelation, if given to more than one person in response to prayer, was held by the early Church writers to be authoritative, can be seen in the so-called *Muratori Canon* (c. A.D. 200). The document was a form of catalogue of the New Testament writings and dealt with the exclusion of those considered heretical:

> When his fellow-disciples and bishops urged him (the disciple John), he said: 'Fast with me from today for three days, and what will be revealed to each one, let us relate to one another.'
>
> *Muratori Canon* (Wilson, I, p. 43)

Revelations achieved in a similar way were described by later writers in connection with the controversies which surrounded the Council of Chalcedon[12]:

> Acacius, the Archbishop of Constantinople, writing to Peter, the Archbishop of Alexandria. . . .
> I was standing and I lifted up the Holy Offering at the third hour of the 15th day of Paopi. Then, when we had sung the Trisagion of God, there appeared above me a great light, indescribable and never before seen by me, and it covered me over together with the whole altar, and I saw in truth our Lord Jesus Christ, like a child, wearing a white linen garment. I saw the mark of the nails upon Him and He lay upon the plate and the chalice which were upon the altar, as if on a couch. And He removed again my fear and trembling from me. And He filled me with joy. For I thought that I was not placed upon the earth at all. I heard Him saying thus, as God knows: 'Have courage my priests and have courage all my people, I have removed from you the shame of the writing of the renunciation, which you wrote in the impious Tome of Leon,[13] which is accursed, together with the Council of Chalcedon.' And after this I did not see Him, nor did I hear His voice, nor did I see the blessed light.
> *Lettres de Pierre Monge et d'Acace* (Amelineau, Miss. IV, p. 223)

In this text, purporting to be the correspondence between the heads of the Churches of Alexandria and Constantinople, the revelation received by both men was similar to that described in the narrative on which are based Quotations 1, 2. The same miraculous occurrence was also said to have been seen at the shrine of Saint Theodore (Section V.1.7), in this case resulting in the conversion of a Jew.[14] The revelation, in these narratives, concerned a 'mystery' and was expressed in mythological language. Authority to the revelation was given, in the first example, by the elevated position of the Church leaders, in the second, by the fact that the subjects were renowned holy men, and in the third, that it occurred at the shrine of a martyr. In all three instances, the same revelation was received by more than one person.

For the meaning of the narrative in Quotation 3, see II.3. The end of the story concerns the prophecy that a people would be the spiritual fruits of the labours of the holy man. The giving of a man's name to a place[15] ensured that he would be remembered by future generations, whenever the name was spoken. Quotations 7 and 8 are included in this section as illustrations of communications, said to have been received by the ascetics without visualisation of a heavenly personage. The interpretations, given to ascetics on the passage of souls through the places of heaven and *Amente*, are discussed in connection with Subsection III.

4 *Healing*

Egyptian asceticism differed essentially, in its attitude to the physical body and to the natural world, from that of the Alexandrian Church Fathers and of the Syrian monks. The latter were influenced by Manichaean asceticism, in which the 'image' of spirit imprisoned in matter led to an extreme antagonism to everything physical.[16] Spirit, or light, and darkness were seen as cosmic forces, external to man. Ahriman, the opponent of light, was said, in the *Pahlavi* texts, to be the producer and maintainer of bodily forms and material existence[17]; the inducing of birth and the propagation of the race was regarded as co-operation with Ahriman. The task of man was, by withdrawal from the material world, to promote the liberation of the light. Manichaeism spread from Persia and Mesopotamia and influenced both the Christian communities of Palestine and the Christian and other schools of Alexandria. Its exaltation of the intellect, on the one hand, and denigration of physical existence, on the other, were attitudes held in common by many late Hellenistic movements. Many were seeking either solutions from human problems, or justification of their beliefs, by the elaboration of systems of knowledge. Among a number of these groups, sexual continence was obligatory. The so-called *Pseudo-Clementine* letters, of Syrian origin, in Coptic translation, not only identified the Christian life with one of continence, but gave to eunuchs together with virgins the highest place in heaven:

> For He gives in His House a place more excellent than that of sons and daughters to eunuchs and virgins; for they are more excellent than those who dwell in honourable marriage and in a pure bed; God will give an incorruptible kingdom of angels to those who have made themselves eunuchs, and to virgins, because of this great witness.
>
> *Pseudo-Clementines: ad Virgines*

It is recorded that certain of the Manichaean 'elect' were castrated[18]; among the Church Fathers, only Origen took this extreme step.[19] The intellectual achievements of this age appear to have been accomplished at a great price and with much difficulty. The individual, in order to live an intellectual life, had to apply to himself measures the reasons for which, today, are not easy to appreciate. Narratives 1 and 2 perhaps represented a 'Christian' version of the operation.

The form of Narratives 4–6, which concerned the healing of internal organs,[20] was similar to that discussed above (II.III.3:1) and was based on descriptions of the incubation cults, and also possibly of techniques of preparing the body for mummification. The narrative contained in the story of Onnophrius,[21] said to have been told by the fourth-century ascetic Paphnutius, re-appeared again in the life of the sixth-century Bishop Pisentius.[22] In the same manuscript, of Upper Egyptian origin, was contained the following quotation, which concerned the subject of healing. It expressed mythologically a viewpoint which may be relevant to the attitude of the Coptic ascetics, to whom the ancient Egyptian medical knowledge was no longer available:

> It happened in the time of Solomon, the King, that he compelled all the demons to tell him the manner of all the remedies and the manner of the plants which were given for sicknesses, that they were healed. Solomon wrote them all on the wall of the House of God. Any man who was sick with any sickness was wont to go into the Temple and look at the wall. He would find the remedy which was written upon the wall, according to his sickness. It happened that when Solomon, the King, died, Hezekiah plastered the walls of the Temple with lime and they were not found again. Hezekiah, the King, when he was sick, he rubbed, he could not find the remedies for healing his sickness. Since it was he who had plastered with lime the walls of the Temple, on which he could not again find the remedies written, he went into the House of the Lord, he lay down, he looked at the wall, he wept, saying: 'Lord, let not what I have done be a sin. I have plastered with lime the walls on which were written the remedies. I was saying: "If they beseech God with faith, they will be healed." Surely I will find remedies that I may be healed.' The Lord heard, He had compassion on him, He sent to him Isaiah, the Prophet, he spoke to him saying: 'Take a cake of figs and smear thyself with it and thou shalt have relief.' Now therefore, O John, he who will do (the will) of God, He will not forsake him.
>
> *Mysteries of Saint John and the Holy Virgin* (Budge, Coptic Apocrypha, p. 69(252))

Ancient Egyptian medicine was a large corpus of knowledge, some contained in temple libraries,[23] the main bulk in manuscript form. It gave detailed instructions on the recognition of diseases and on the preparation and administration of remedies. Knowledge of human anatomy was linked to the rituals of mummification and related different parts of the body to various stellar deities. From an intellectual point of view, Egyptian medicine was not systematic; it was based on traditions concerning their own experiences, psychic and physical, of natural substances in relation to bodily processes. It differed from Greek medicine, which was linked to philosophy and which employed incubation cults as a method of therapy. The thought behind late Greek medicine was deterministic and expressed the influence on the human body of an environment which extended to include the heavenly bodies.[24]

The Alexandrian Fathers despised the human body, with its astrological connections, as a source of evil, and for the same reason, condemned the mystery cults and pagan science. Healing, in the Christian world, was therefore dependent, on the one hand, on divine intervention, and on the other, on the efficacy of exorcism. The *Apocryphon* quoted above expressed the situation of the later Coptic monks, among whom the knowledge of their traditional remedies had been deliberately forgotten. For the early ascetics, the consequence of their self-discipline was represented as control over the workings of natural processes:

> And he said unto them: 'Forgive me, O my fathers, if ye possess purity of heart, every living thing will be subject unto you, as it was unto Adam before he transgressed the commandment of God.'
>
> Palladius (Budge I, *Sayings of the Fathers*, 603)

Narratives 10–12 illustrated the belief that suffering, resulting from the ascetic life, was healed without the need of human remedies. During the later centuries of the Coptic Church, faith in miracles, expected at the shrines of saints, replaced healing due to ascetic effort (see Chapter V.I.7). Quotations 7 and 8 exemplify a healing cult, in which the intervention of an archangel was the Christian equivalent of the visit of a pagan deity. In Narrative 9, the divine visitor, as in incubation dreams, gave instructions on the use of a remedy.

5   The Foretelling of the Birth of Holy Men

In the stories of the Christian seers, inconsistent and contradictory notions, inherited from Greek and Egyptian paganism and from Judaism, continued side by side with one another. In the Old Testament, man's role as begetter of a great race was represented as given to him by a divine command.[25] Nevertheless, the birth of the Patriarchs was depicted as the overcoming, by divine intervention, of female barrenness. Sarah, Rebecca and Rachel[26] were all, in the first instance, unable to bear children—the result, perhaps, of a new racial grouping. The conception of the Patriarchs was represented as the manifestation of divine activity, and the Jewish Patriarch was thus, with the help of the

Deity, the founder of his race. Hebrew Law consisted mainly of injunctions favourable to racial development, and self-destructive practices for the propitiation of pagan deities were prohibited. The Law forbade the shedding of human blood within the group, and thus prevented such rites as the sacrifice of new-born children. Racial purity was ensured by forbidding the mixing of blood by external marriage. Thus, in Judaism, the destiny of the race was dependent on the fruitfulness of its members, and this fruitfulness was promoted by obedience to the Law.

In Pharaonic Egypt, the birth of the king was an event in which the fatherhood of the Pharaoh was ascribed to a deity.[27] In the ceremony, described in the inscriptions of Amonhotep III and Hatshepsut in the temple of Deir el-Bahari,[28] the queen was said to have been chosen by a council of twelve gods (the number of the divisions of the heavens). The birth of the king was thus the result of the impregnation, of a chosen human mother by a god. At Abu Simbel, the mother of Ramses II was said to have been visited by the god Ptah, in his form as the Ram, Lord of Mendes.[29] References to great men who were the result of the union of women with gods (or animals) occurred, not only in Egyptian, but also in Greek and Hebrew mythology. The account, in *Genesis*, of the sons of gods who took the daughters of men[30] and became fathers of the heroes of ancient days, was connected with pre-Judaic ideas of the divine ancestry of man. In ancient Egypt, the person of the Pharaoh was the link between the human order and that of the gods; earthly events were sometimes coincident with certain appearances in the heavens and omens upon earth.[31] In Narrative 1, the light accompanying the birth signified that a manifestation of the divine had occurred, as it did in the New Testament nativity account.

In the New Testament and apocryphal nativity stories, in those concerning Mary and Anna,[32] the emphasis was placed on the woman as the mother of the divine individual, a role for which she had been chosen. The accounts of Elizabeth, on the other hand, emphasised the part played by her husband, in invoking divine aid to overcome her barrenness. The birth of John the Baptist, a prophetic figure, was thus depicted as occurring in a manner similar to that of the Patriarchs. The second of these two methods of representing the birth of holy men was mainly used in the birth stories of, and associated with, the martyrs and saints. These accounts of barren women, who invoked divine aid, had a precedent in the numerous records of incubation cults in Greece, Egypt and elsewhere.[33] In Christian times, the anomaly was seen of the saint who was venerated as an example of asceticism, but was nevertheless invoked to cure infertility. The fast of the pregnant woman (1) perhaps represented an attempt to reconcile the two attitudes by juxtaposing the two 'images'. In Quotations 5 and 6, the influence of the Old Testament can be seen; the infant was promised as an offering to the Deity (5) and sterility was regarded as a cause for reproach (6).[34]

II HEAVENLY COMMUNICATIONS

Preliminary Considerations

Communications from the divine to man were well known in the literature of the pre-Christian religions of Hellenism. The loss of prestige of the pagan oracles as sources of revelation, reported in Jewish and Greek writings, has already been discussed. In contrast, numerous narratives of Christian origin gave the impression that, to the early ascetics and martyrs, communications from heaven were not only frequent but also authoritative and 'genuine'. Such stories represented an attempt to create around the Church a body of 'evidence' that a new relationship with the divine was possible. The means described, of receiving communications by visions or dreams, were similar to those of the cults of pre-Christian religions and, as in early Judaism, the Deity who had no visible form, was heard as a voice. Nevertheless, the visions differed from those of paganism in their imagery; the messengers were invariably of Biblical origin and their communications, in some way, placed the recipient in a Biblical context.

The narratives of early Christianity introduced a mythology which differed from that of Judaism; it contained the idea that the individual, apart from nation or race, could have a relationship with the divine. In late Judaism had appeared the idea of a universal theocracy; the whole world would be a kingdom ruled by the God of the Jews. Such a picture, which gave pre-eminence to a chosen race as recipients of divine guidance, was replaced in the imagery of Christian asceticism by emphasis on the ultimate importance of the subjective experience of the individual. From the fifth century onwards, when Christianity was no longer subject to persecution, there arose a widespread cult of individuals. Narratives multiplied, extolling the founders of the monastic establishments, and depicting them as the patriarchs of a new race. There also appeared the use of the 'image' of angels as mediators in the dialogue between man and the divine.

Philo recognised a relationship between the angels of Jewish tradition and the demons of Greek philosophy.[35] The demons of Greek philosophy represented man's psychic relationship to the divine, often through the imagery of the Zodiac.[36] Menander[37] had stated that by every man, at birth, a good demon took his stand to initiate him in the mysteries of life. According to Plato, every man had a distinct demon which attended him during his life and after death[38]; each demon had his own allotted sphere of operation and watched over his appointed charge, like a shepherd over a flock.[39] The adoption of the Zodiac, in late Judaism, was an 'image', demonstrating the 'victory' of the intellectually conceived transcendent God over a divinity, experienced subjectively, under a multiplicity of aspects. The 'image' of the demon, as indicator of a predetermined destiny, was replaced in Judaism by that of an angel as revealer of a divine purpose. Both 'images' concerned the control of the collective psyche rather than the free-will of the individual. The early Alexandrian Fathers described angels in the terms of Jewish Apocalyptic literature (see III.IV. 'Preliminary Considerations') and adopted the doctrine of good and evil angels appointed to watch over individuals and institutions.[40] The use of angelic messengers, to describe the subjective experiences of the ascetics, thus perpetuated the 'image' of man's relation to the divine, as expressed in Judaism. The angels were the messengers of the transcendent authoritarian deity; the depiction of such angels could only imply a relation to the divine, based on dreams or other abnormal states of consciousness.

A feature of the writings of the Alexandrian Church Fathers was the historical interpretation of figures of the Old Testament as 'types' foreshadowing the New Testament.[41] The New Testament was seen as a historical recapitulation of the Old, and the acts of the Christian community as a realisation of Exodus. Neoplatonic writers had interpreted the Old Testament as an allegory of subjective events in the life of the soul, and their methods had been followed by Clement and Origen.[42] Later writers, in attempting to present history as a unified process leading up to and developing from the New Testament events, neglected the psychological changes involved.

1   The Recognition of a Holy Man

According to the traditional ancient Egyptian autobiographical stelae, to do right was to do 'what men loved and what the gods praised!'[43] Man's actions were performed in the context of his community with the host of heavenly and earthly deities as spectators. Appointment to any office was made, in the first instance, by the gods, and what the gods decided, men approved. The gods also gave directions for the location and building of their own shrines and those of the beatified dead. These manifestations of the divine approbation were, as has been seen, made through the various types of oracle.

The recognition of a hero or holy man, by the divine manifestations

103

which occurred at various stages of his life, was a well-known feature of pagan mythology. In the Old Testament, the divine communications to the Patriarchs took place at intervals and coincided with stages in the historic progress of the Jewish people. Implicit in the 'images' which depicted these events, was the fact that they occurred in some form of dream or trance state. The essential difference between the manner of recognition of the ascetics and that of the Old Testament character lay in the dependence of the holy man on his acceptance, not by the Deity, but by his fellow ascetics. Mutual recognition occurred on the basis that each saw the divine in his fellow:

Thou hast seen thy brother, thou hast seen the Lord thy God.
Historia Monachorum in Aegypto, VIII.55

The placing of two 'images' side by side in a narrative was a pre-logical means of identifying them, or of explaining one by the other. It was possible for the narrator to bring the 'images' into juxtaposition by virtue of their psychic content. Thus to depict, in a story, someone beside a Biblical personage was a means of expressing, by analogy, his status in relation to the divine world. This use of Biblical imagery is seen in the present texts.

In a narrative, the 'image' of angels as intermediaries with the divine, as has been seen, left in doubt the question whether the individual concerned was subject to external law or to his inner voice. A similar ambiguity applied to the imagery of angels as protectors. The pagan community, by ritual, created the experience of a universe of divine beings who, provided they were obeyed, protected their worshippers. Pagan man's 'protection' was his power, collectively, to imagine a beneficent universe. For the individual ascetic, security lay in his ability to create his environment in the imagery of his choice. The community, in harmony with the will of the 'gods', and the individual, in harmony with his own inner law, were thus 'safe', not by virtue of the 'images' which they created, but because they had the power to create these 'images'. His consciousness of his own power to create and order his own psychic imagery was the faculty which enabled the individual to maintain himself apart from the group and its ritual. To the community, the source of this power was unknown, and its members remained in permanent subjection to the 'images' of their own creation.

2 The Call to the Ascetic Life

It has been seen that, in the biography of the ascetic, Christianised 'images' replaced those of paganism. The underlying imagery of the episodes concerned with the calls to the ascetic life and those to found a monastery or church, was that relating the life of the holy man to the life after death (see p. 32ff.). A dwelling-place was allocated to the holy man, in a manner corresponding to ancient practices for determining a burial site.[44] The locality was determined: upon a mountain, by trying first one side and then the other (2), by going on a river journey (5), or a land journey (6), in each case with an angelic messenger as a guide. The subject of funerary journeys made to the South is discussed in Chapter V.I.3. In this Sub-Section, Part 1:7, 8 and Part 2:1, the winged cherubims were possibly substitutions for the winged deities of Egypt who protected the deceased.[45]

In Narratives 7–9, the call to the ascetic life was depicted as given to a disciple, through the person of an elder, as the result of divine instruction. In Narrative 4, of Syrian origin, the master-disciple relation was represented as a vision, in which the disciple was called to succeed his master. Narratives 7–9 were concerned with the monk's robe, which after death became his shroud and thus was an 'image' which replaced that of the elaborate wrappings of the ancient burial. This garment was therefore 'sanctified' by the Christian imagery. However, as in pagan ritual, an externally visible divine manifestation was said to have occurred during the ceremony, in which it was placed upon the candidate. The 'image' of the robe of Elijah (9) carried with it the notion of prophetic power given to the holy man, called to be both a seer and a spokesman for the Deity. The characteristic of these calls to the holy men, as depicted, was their compelling quality, suggestive of the dream-visions of the Old Testament. They conveyed the notions, both of divine vocation and seership, as conditions of entry into the ascetic life. The inadequacy of this imagery to represent the experiences of the individual is again apparent.

3 The Call to Found a Monastery or Church

Narratives concerning the call to build monasteries or churches contained imagery based on the Egyptian funerary cult. The West (1, 10) was the bank of the river on which, in ancient times, was situated the necropolis.[46] The paying of funeral expenses, and the drawing up of legal covenants to provide for the future maintenance of shrines, played a large part in the funerary practices of the late period.[47] In Narrative 2, the gold *solidi* were probably payments 'Christianised' by introducing the number three. Money, miraculously found in a jar (15), was made available for use in building a monastery. The promise that miracles would occur at the church of the holy man (10) was a feature of stories of the shrines of martyrs, and one which had antecedents in the accounts of the sanctuaries of pagan gods of healing. In Narratives 11, 16, the holy man was addressed as if he were preparing for a martyr's death, as an athlete, for whom was prepared the heavenly crown. (See Chapter V.i.3.)

The funerary stelae of ancient Egypt were testimonies for the preservation of the memory of the deceased to an indefinite future. This 'image' was replaced by that of the holy man, as founder of a new community, among whom his name would be remembered for generations to come (1, 2, 5, 10, 13, 16). In Narratives 2, 5, 16, the building itself was called by the name of the holy man and, in 12, his grave was the site of the proposed monastery. The imagery of the Old Testament Patriarchs, as founders of a new race, was much used in connection with the founding of monasteries. By a covenant, the holy man would have multitudes of sons (2), he would beget a holy people (8), his seed would increase (17), and they would become a great race (18). By identifying the idea of immortality with that of a new community, the founding of the monasteries was seen as the initiation of a new sequence of events which would lead into a historic future, according to the pattern of the Old Testament narrative (see p. 25). Like Moses, the holy man was commanded to legislate to his people and was given a tablet on which was inscribed the rules of the monastery (14). The leading of a people through the desert, and the desert as 'the Land of the Inheritance' (1), were 'images' drawn from the Exodus story. The Old Testament 'images' thus replaced the ancient Egyptian 'images' of the shrine cult. They represented the new race as a guarantee of immortality and the deceased holy man as a divine ancestral figure to his descendants.

The life of the monastery was thus, through the imagery of stories, established, for the populace, in the place of the ancient funerary cult. The latter was, especially in the late period, the centre of the religious life of the community and its images were derived from the ritual of antiquity. This funerary cult depended on manifestations of divine power and guidance, through dreams, visions and oracles. The later monastic literature is evidence that reliance on these methods as mediators of the divine persisted, and that the cult of the Christian shrines was a replacement of one ritual by another (see Chapter V.i.6).

4 The Call to the Ministry

Monasticism in Egypt was essentially a movement of laymen. There had been a division, in ancient Egypt, between professional priests and those laymen who performed certain functions in the ceremonies. The latter, known as 'pure ones', carried the figure of the deity in procession and were the mediums through whom the oracular pronouncements were made known to the people (see p. 91). There is evidence that the 'pure ones' spent some of their time in the desert and underwent purification ceremonies.[48] This traditional distinction between the roles of professional, priest and layman may have been the basis, in Christian times, of the great reluctance on the part of monks to undertake priestly duties (4, 5, 6). Their attitude may perhaps be ascribed to a fear lest, in substituting the sacraments for direct experience of the divine, they lose their independence of external ritual. Palladius[49] gave an account of a monk who cut off his ear and threatened to slit his tongue rather than be made a priest. Pachomius himself remained a layman and did not wish his monks to take orders. The first monastic establishment of Pachomius did not at first possess a church, and a neighbouring priest came weekly to the monastery to celebrate the liturgy.

The orders mentioned in the present texts are Deacon, Priest, Hegumen, and Bishop. Narratives 4 and 5 concerned the appointment to the order of Deacon, 3 of Priest, 6 of Hegumen, and 2 and 7 of Bishop. The role of the Deacon was to handle the liturgical vessels, to unlock the doors of the church, and to light the altar lamp[50]; possibly the imagery of such a role was seen to have pagan associations. The call to the ministry, in the form of a vision, may have been a literary device to give the service of the Church the same status as the life of the monastery.

5 Admonition

The 'inner' dialogue of the holy man with the divine was chiefly represented, in the narratives, in the imagery of the Scriptures. Numerous instances occur, in the Old Testament, of admonitions and instructions given in the forms of visions and dreams. The apparently conscious superimposition of Christian over pagan imagery, in these narratives, appears to be mainly concerned with the obliteration of 'images' of the Egyptian funerary cult. From the period of the Old Kingdom onwards, funerary inscriptions admonished and threatened the living, with regard to their duties towards the deceased.[51] Among the consequences of failure, on the part of the living, to fulfil their duties to the dead, were punishment in this life by the deceased himself. Therefore, while the welfare of the dead in the after-life depended on the recitations and other ceremonies performed by the living, life and prosperity in this world could be promoted or overthrown by the intervention of the dead.

In these narratives, a reprimand conveyed by an angel, or apostle, or a voice, was the result of neglect of duty (6, 7), mistaken action (2), or rebellion (1–5). In the ancient inscriptions, threats to the living included their exclusion from participation in rites and ceremonies, and thus their ultimate non-survival. In Narratives 2 and 3, a similar fate was ordered for the wrong-doers within the monastery. Funerary inscriptions also promised vengeance to those who spoke against the deceased, such retribution being carried out by the deceased. Thus 'to receive a spirit' (4, 5) appears to be a Christian formula, replacing a traditional funerary curse. In addition to disasters, the funerary inscriptions also promised that the dead would return for the prayers of the living, bestow benefits. In Narrative 7, the deceased holy man appeared to and admonished his living successor for having neglected his prayers; a return to duty was rewarded by rain. Narratives 8, 9, 10, 16 contained formulae appropriate to stories of the martyrs and the cult of their shrines: the foretelling of death within three days (16), the encouragement of the holy man (8, 9, 10), the rewards for charitable actions (8), the promises of help (8, 10) and renown (10). (See Section V.I.) Narratives 11 and 12 were possibly based on a story from an incubation cult in which the sufferer was told of a cure and a recipe for long life.

The reception of a disciple (13–21) and the appointment of a successor (13, 17) were events which were often depicted as taking place shortly before the death of a holy man. In Narratives 18 and 21 were mentioned the journeys of the disciple to the death-bed of the holy man, in response to instructions in a vision. The role of the disciple, as recipient of the last words of the holy man, has already been discussed (see p. 31). In the stories concerning the appointment of the successor to the head of a monastery, the 'legacy' was not the testimony of the holy man, but the duties of his office. The choice of the successor was represented as having been made by divine guidance. Under the ancient religion, the control, exercised by the wishes of the dead upon the living and the desire of the living for immortality, led to a system of morality in which the dead were felt to judge the living. Right living depended on the fulfilment of obligations towards the dead. Thus each generation felt judged by, and dependent on, its predecessors and ancestors. A mere substitution of 'images' between the old and new religions failed to represent the change of attitude towards death and immortality, which occurred among the ascetics.

III THE DEATH OF THE HOLY MAN

Preliminary Considerations

The remainder of this chapter and Chapter IV are a commentary on narratives concerning 'journeys', said to have been made by the ascetic or his soul to the places of heaven and hell. An attempt is here made to determine the background and sources of these accounts.

The complexity of the ancient Egyptian funerary ritual makes it impossible to describe it in any detail, and its remoteness from modern ways of thought make interpretations extremely hazardous. Nevertheless, its importance, in relation to Christian texts concerning death, make it necessary to attempt a brief analysis. The funerary ritual of the Graeco-Roman period[52] was an amalgam of texts of previous ages, some dating from the Old Kingdom, which had been partially systematised from the time of the New Kingdom onwards. Life after death, which had been seen in the Old Kingdom as lived in relation to the stars, was, from the Middle Kingdom onwards, associated with the night journey of the sun in the underworld of *Amente*. Divinity was a transformation which each man underwent, after death, by uniting with the underworld deity Osiris. Divinity achieved by this means precluded self-consciousness, for which a body and sense-perception was necessary. In so far as the funerary ritual was spoken or performed, the union with Osiris was enacted by the living only by proxy, or by the 'deceased' only in anticipation. The funerary texts were inscribed on the coffin and walls of the tomb as a perpetuation of the ritual.[53] This ritual was the means by which hostile and destructive powers were overcome and relationships achieved, by the deceased, with the various entities of the underworld.

The process of mummification included the removal of the internal organs, which were ritually related both to human faculties and to various deities.[54] These material counterparts of human and divine powers were placed in jars like miniature mummies. In the Christian period, certain ceremonies and invocations from the ritual of the underworld became of particular importance as 'images' of paganism to be 'overthrown'. Of these, Chapter XXX of the *Book of the Dead* called upon the heart to speak on the man's behalf at the judgment; Chapter CXXV contained the 'negative confession', a list of actions with ritual rather than moral implications, which was addressed to each of forty-two assessors[55]; the representation accompanying the latter was of the weighing of the heart of the deceased, in the presence of Osiris and the forty-two assessors; at the end of the seventy-day period of mummification, the ceremony of 'opening the mouth', with a metal instrument, ritually enabled the deceased to partake of the funerary meals provided at his tomb.[56]

The tomb cult of ancient Egypt was concerned with the attainment of immortality through the preservation of the physical body, which acquired divine status after death. Man's continued survival after death

THE CULT OF THE SEER IN THE ANCIENT MIDDLE EAST

was achieved, not only by the mummification of his body, but by the ritual offering of food and the recitation of formulae at prescribed intervals. Immortality, conceived as resulting from the continued performance of rituals, thus depended, for any individual, on the funerary endowments which he made at his own shrine before death. Responsibility for commemoration rituals belonged to professional priests and the wealth of the individual determined the quality of these services. From the Ptolemaic period, there were also local cults of the bodies of certain persons without wealth.[57] Their tombs were regarded as beneficial to their neighbourhood and especially to their guardians and to those who contributed to their upkeep. Among these persons were the drowned, mentioned by Herodotus,[58] who were possibly regarded as having suffered, in drowning, the fate of Osiris. Of the others, whose status perhaps approximated to local 'saints', little is known, apart from the fact that their tombs were a source of income to their guardians and thus the subject of litigation.

1 Death Foretold

The death of the holy man, in the *Life of Anthony*, was given no more importance than any other event in his life. This attitude, found in other early 'lives', was an alternative to that of Egyptian paganism, in which preparation for death was one of life's major activities. The final act in the lives of the desert ascetics included the dispensing with any funerary ritual and the request that the whereabouts of their bodies be unknown:

'Do not allow anyone to take my body into Egypt lest they should keep it in their houses.[59] . . . Therefore (carry out my obsequies yourselves) and bury my body in the earth . . . that no-one will know the place but you alone.'

Athanasius, *Life of Anthony*, 91 (Garitte)

It was essential, if the traditional practices were to be forgotten, that the body of the holy man should 'disappear'. Later literature, however, contained many accounts of the 'invention' of the bodies of saints (see Chapter V). The desire, moreover, of Christian writers to superimpose new 'images' on those of the ancient cult led to the proliferation of 'lives' in which the climax was the departure of the saint or martyr from this world. 'Images' which were literary conventions, and not individual experiences, had little effect in effacing the ancient attitudes which continued under new names.

The life of the desert ascetic has been shown to have been a conscious enactment of the experiences of the 'life after death'. In the sayings reported as those of the ascetics, two differing attitudes to death were expressed. The first, seen in the *Life of Anthony*, contained the notion of detachment, not merely physical but also psychic, as a way of life:

He exhorted them . . . to live as though dying daily.

Athanasius, *Life of Anthony*, 89

'And thus let it be with thyself. If thou wishest to live, become dead, so that thou mayest care neither for the reviling of men nor for (their) praise, for the dead care for nothing; in this wise thou wilt be able to live.'

Palladius (Budge I, *Sayings of the Fathers*, 438)

'And thou must keep hold upon thy grave as if thou wert already dead, and as if death were thy neighbour every day, in the mountains, and in the caves, and in the holds of the earth.'

Palladius (Budge II, *Questions and Answers*, 119)

The old man Macarius used to say; 'Strive for every kind of death—for the death of the body; that is to say, if thou hast not the death which is in the spirit, strive for the death of the body and then shall be added unto thee the death which is in the spirit. And death of this kind will make thee die to every man, and henceforward thou wilt acquire the faculty of being constantly with God in silence.'

Palladius (Budge II, *Questions and Answers*, 162)

In the second, achieved by meditation on the negative 'images' of death, fear of the Last Judgment precluded detachment:

An old man used to say: 'I await death evening, and morning and every day.'

Palladius (Budge I, *Sayings of the Fathers*, 330)

He also said: 'If you always remember your death and do not forget the eternal judgment, there will be no sin in your soul.'

Palladius (Chadwick, *Sayings of the Fathers*, XI.10)

'Keep in thy remembrance always three moments, and forget them not; the first is the moment of death, with its sorrow and grief and trouble, which is immeasurable, that overtaketh every man, when (a man shall stand) before the awful throne of Christ; the second moment is the moment of fear and quaking when men and angels shall rise up, when a man doth not know what command shall come forth concerning him, whether it shall be for life everlasting or for torment everlasting; and the third moment is that when the penalty shall come forth upon us.'

Palladius (Budge II, *Questions and Answers*, 580)

111

The notion of rewards and punishments implied the subjection of the individual to external authority. It finally denied, to men, the exercise of their own moral judgment to assess their achievements.

In the ancient world, man's life was regarded as subject either to Fate or to the rule of divine power. No death took place, therefore, which was not predetermined.[60] The holy man, as being in touch with the divine, was represented as having been foretold his own death. The manner was expressed in the language of the Old Testament in which, to the Patriarch, death was 'sleeping with his fathers', 'being gathered to his people'.[61] This language was reproduced in the Apocalyptic literature as a literary formula, with which to precede instructions:

> The copy of the Testament of Reuben, even the commands which he gave his sons before he died in the hundred and twenty-fifth year of his life. Two years after the death of Joseph his brother, when Reuben fell ill, his sons and his sons' sons were gathered together to visit him. And he said to them: 'My children, behold I am dying, and go the way of my fathers.' And seeing there Judah and Gad and Asher, his brethren, he said to them: 'Raise me up, that I may tell to my brethren and to my children what things I have hidden in my heart, for behold now at length I am passing away.' And he arose and kissed them, and said unto them: 'Hear my brethren, and do ye, my children, give ear to Reuben, your father, in the commands which I give unto you.'
>
> *Testament of Reuben*, 1.1–6 (Charles)

In the *Life of Anthony*, the foretelling of his death was expressed in this language, thus giving recognition to the Old Testament Patriarchs as his fore-runners:

> After a few months he fell sick. He called those who were with him— there were two there who had been ascetics for fifteen years and looked after him because of his great age—and said to them: 'I am going the way of my fathers, . . . for I see myself called by the Lord.'
>
> Athanasius, *Life of Anthony*, 91.

The messengers by whom death was foretold to the ascetics were depicted either as angels, or, in later texts, as Fathers of the Church. The foretelling of his death to the seer by angels appeared in the first-century *Apocalypse of Enoch* in terms very similar to those used later in the biographies of holy men:

> My children, behold, the day of my term and the time have approached. For the angels who shall go with me are standing before me and urge me to my departure from you; they are standing here on

earth, awaiting what has been told them. For tomorrow I shall go up
on to heaven, to the uppermost Jerusalem to my eternal inheritance.

II. Enoch, 55.1–2 (Charles)

The form of the visitation was often similar to that of the premonitory
visits to the martyrs (see Section V.I.1). The identification of the
visitors was followed by the announcement that the time was approaching or that a certain number of days remained.[62] Narratives 12, 15, 16
suggested that the intervening time before death was spent, not in
material preparations, but in meditation. The descriptions (15, 16) of
the two rows of monks on thrones and the notary with a pen in his hand
were perhaps attempts to put a Christian 'image' in place of that of the
Egyptian judgment scene in which the ibis god, Thoth, was the scribe.[63]

The visit of one solitary ascetic to another, in time to hear his last
words and to bury him in his own garment, was depicted as the occasion
of a miraculous event (17–23). To the thought of that time, such a
manner of death would involve not only physical but spiritual annihila-
tion. The testimony of the surviving brother was to the fact that the
deceased lived, to the end, in the dimension of the heavenly world,
which was manifested to others at his death. The stories of the deaths
of the ascetics, in isolation, are perhaps the strongest evidence of the
desire, of some individuals, to maintain themselves without the support
of ritual.

2 The Last Words

The gathering of the brethren of the dying holy man to his bedside
was an occasion to which, in Christian writings, new significance had
to be given. In Judaism, the procedure had been established of the
handing on, at death, of his position as leader, his prophetic gifts and
his mission, by one patriarch or prophet to another. The death of such
a figure was also the occasion for receiving his benediction, his admonitions, and his prophecies concerning the future. In apocryphal
writings,[64] his death-bed was, in retrospect, made the background to an
autobiographical account, by the patriarch, of his past life and moral
failures, and the effect of his actions on the life of his people.

The death-bed accounts of the ascetics, as founders of a new
patriarchal tradition, contained many of the above features (see
Chapter I.I.1). In addition, the imagery of death, as a subjective experience for the individual, was introduced. The death of the martyr
implied his immediate entry to heaven, and his subjective experiences
were represented in terms of the imagery of heaven. A number of

accounts of the deaths of ascetics were in similar terms. In others (1–4), death was represented as a terrifying experience, feared by the holy man:

> When he was soon to commit his soul to God, they saw him weeping, and said, 'Truly, Father are you afraid, even you, of death?' And he said: 'Truly. The fear which possesses me now has been with me since I became a monk; and I am very afraid.' So he slept in peace.
> Palladius (Chadwick, *Sayings of the Fathers*, XV.9)

The significance of the imagery is discussed in Section IV, but, as in the accounts of the conflicts with the demons, (Chapter II.ii) the holy man was represented as, even at death, victorious over the figures of the ancient religion.

The Egyptians probably preserved, in their funerary texts, the super-seded public rituals of their prehistoric past. The texts contained references to barbaric practices and much of their imagery was im-pressive and terrifying. The public rituals perpetuated the relationships of the community to its total environment, and modes of expressing that relationship had replaced one another with the passage of time. According to the rubrics to certain texts of the funerary ritual, the 'knowing' of the words and pictures ensured the safety of the deceased. These instructions suggest that, at death, when failure of sense-perception isolated the individual from communal rituals, he encoun-tered subjectively the chaotic imagery of his past. Knowledge of certain formulae perhaps enabled him to endure the experience. The holy man was represented as being aware of the figures of *Amente* (see Chapters IV.i.1, 2 and V.i.7), but nevertheless as entering heaven in a manner similar to that of the martyrs.

3 The Fetching of the Soul

The Apocalypses of Enoch, Isaiah, Abraham and other Old Testa-ment figures, depicting the translation to heaven of the seer, appear to have been well known in Egypt and to have existed in Coptic transla-tion. Much of the imagery surrounding the death of the ascetics was derived from these sources. In the schools from which they originated, the dream vision or trance of the seer was a vehicle for prophetic writings. In the present writings, the 'vision' was represented as an experience shared among those present at the time of death. The 'fifty men of the sons of prophets[65]' in *ii Kings* awaited the death of Elijah and witnessed afterwards that his body had disappeared. The disciples of the seer[66] Isaiah, the forty prophets and sons of prophets, were told later of 'the things that Isaiah saw'. Elisha was represented as inheriting the prophetic powers of Elijah, because he saw the departure to heaven of the seer. In the present narratives, the spectators, who were witnesses of the death of the holy man, were, like Elisha, represented as having shared his final vision, by virtue of their own powers. However, the type of attainment expressed by the ability to see souls conveyed to heaven and to hear the voices of angels (55–65) was that of an Old Testament prophet.

A feature peculiar to these accounts of the death of ascetics was the appearance, to the holy men, of their predecessors in the ascetic life. The latter announced to the ascetic the time left to him upon earth and returned again to fetch his soul. It was thus represented that, at death, the ascetic broke his final ties with his racial origins. His forefathers, by adoption, were the saints who came to fetch him and his descendants were the disciples who, like him, experienced the reality of eternal life before their physical death. This gathering of saints, past and present, was represented as accepting and giving recognition to the holy man. The latter, in effect, thus received a judgment by his peers before death. In some narratives, the personages brought into context with the holy man included the martyrs (8), the prophets and apostles (2, 7, 8, 12, 13), the cherubim, angels and Christ. However, the imagery of these narratives was invariably that of the visitations by external deities, as found in pre-Christian writings.

In Narratives 27 and 43, the soul in heaven resumed the personality of the deceased, and it was necessary to follow the Coptic in using the masculine pronoun 'he'; similarly, in Narrative 47, concerning the Virgin, the feminine pronoun was used. Elsewhere the neuter pronoun 'it' was used for the separated soul, although in Coptic, as in Greek and Hebrew, the soul is feminine grammatically. In Narrative 25, in which the soul was addressed as the 'daughter' of God, the original translation from the Hebrew, using the feminine pronoun, was followed.

Not only gender but also person presented difficulty to the biographer of the seer. In the present accounts, the 'vision' of the entry of the soul into heaven was described from the standpoint of those on earth. The experiences in heaven, of the seers of the apocalyptic writings, were mainly in the first person. In many apocalypses, changes of person occurred[67]; this may in part be due to the fact that they were composite writings by different authors. The narrative of the *Ascension of Isaiah* began and ended in the third person, with a change to the first person for the actual vision. For those parts of the narrative in which the experiences of the seer were not shared with the spectators, literary devices were used in the present texts. In Narratives 1, 11, 12, an interval of self-withdrawal was represented between the announcement of death and the fetching of the soul. In Narratives 9 and 10, the names of those who fetched the soul were indicated by angels. The use of the first person to describe dream or trance experiences, as in the apocalyptic writings, was continued by the biographers of the ascetics. Testimonies in the first person were inserted for greater effect. Thus in Narratives 7 and 8, a child and a demoniac respectively were represented as witnesses of the heavenly visitations. (In pre-Christian cults, both were regarded as able to receive revelations).

The words 'soul' and 'spirit' were, in these texts, used almost interchangeably; however, only the soul was wrapped, carried to heaven, crowned and given as a gift to God. The spirit was given forth through the mouth (3, 4, 11). The soul either leapt forth with joy (1, 22) or came forth with reluctance (25) or difficulty (20, 21). The music which had dispelled the evil spirit from Saul was represented as liberating the soul of the holy man (20, 21). In some narratives the holy man was described as 'labouring' (12), 'as one about to bear a child',[68] thus relating the notion of death to that of birth. The giving of Baptism by angels to a monk before death (23, 24) suggests that, to the ascetics, the monastic life had a sanctity equal to that of the Sacrament.

The anointing of the body (15–17), the coming forth of the soul into the hands which received it, and the wrapping of the soul (15–19) were all imagery which could have been a replacement of that of Egyptian paganism, as could also the spread of perfume at the time of death. On the evidence of Herodotus,[69] it is known that after removal of the internal organs, the abdominal cavity was filled with myrrh, cassia and other aromatic substances. According to Diodorus,[70] the body was also anointed with oil and rubbed with fragrant materials. The seventy-day period of dehydration with natron was followed by elaborate wrapping and bandaging of the body. The mummy cloths, on which were inscribed texts from the *Book of the Dead*,[71] related the various parts of the body to deities and to regions of the physical universe. The use of silk (18, 19) as a wrapping for the dead began in the fourth century, and its mention serves to place the text at, or after, this date. Linen (22, 53–55) was the traditional material used from ancient times for wrapping the body. The procession was an essential feature of the ancient Egyptian funerary cult[72]; the mummy or statue of the deceased was carried to the tomb, and records of this ceremony on the walls of tomb chapels bear witness to its complexity. Ceremonial processions also occurred at festivals and were the occasion, according to Herodotus, both of singing and of ritual battles.[73] References were made in a number of Christian texts, not only to the singing of angels on the journey to heaven, but to the dangers to be overcome on the way through the air (18, 19; see also Chapter IV.I). The imagery of the chariot as the vehicle of the soul is discussed on p. 121. Accounts of processions of angels and saints conveying the soul of the holy man to heaven were mainly confined to texts of the fifth century and later. In general, the further removed these narratives were from their original meaning as subjective experiences, the more elaborate was their imagery and the more it resembled the paganism it replaced.

IV JOURNEY TO PARADISE

Preliminary Considerations

Within the cults of the Hellenistic world, there had occurred a transition, from a naive acceptance of the revelations of the prophets and poets, to a realisation that the content of these revelations had some relation to the soul of man. Plato, from the background of the Pythagorean and Orphic schools, had expressed philosophically that the powers which worked in man's soul were identical with those which created and moved the universe. The ultimate forms through which the divine worked were said to be those of number:

> If we should deprive human nature of number we should never attain to any understanding. For then the soul of that creature which could not *tell* things would never any more be able one may say, to attain virtue in general; and the creature that did not know two and three, or odd or even, and was completely ignorant of number, could never clearly *tell* of things about which it had only acquired sensations and memories. From the attainment of ordinary virtue—courage and temperance—it is certainly not debarred: but if a man is deprived of true *telling* he can never become wise, and he who has not the acquirement of wisdom—the greatest part of virtue as a whole—can no more achieve the perfect goodness which may make him happy.
>
> Plato, *Epinomis*, 977C,D

In the Hellenistic period, Plutarch, drawing on neo-Pythagorean sources, depicted the universal truths as revolving geometrical figures (see also Plato, *Timaeus*, 53–57):

> He told me in fact, that there were neither an infinite number of worlds, nor a single one, nor yet five, but one hundred and eighty-three, arranged in the form of a triangle, each side of which contains sixty worlds. Of the remaining three, one is placed at each angle; and those in line touch each other, revolving gently as if in a dance. The

area within this triangle is the common hearth of them all, and is named 'Plain of Truth', in which the reason, the forms, and the pattern of all things that have been, and that shall be, are stored up not to be disturbed.

Plutarch, *On the Cessation of Oracles*, XXII

Philo also saw the soul of the sage as the counterpart of heaven:

For he wished to picture the soul of the Sage as the counterpart of heaven, or rather, if we may say so, transcending it, a heaven of earth having within it, as the ether has, pure forms of being, movements ordered, rhythmic, harmonious, revolving as God directs, rays of virtues, supremely starlike and dazzling. And if it be beyond our powers to count the stars which are visible to the senses, how much more truly can that be said of those which are visible to the mind.

Philo, *Who is the Heir?*, XVII.88

Inherent in the neo-Platonic attitude was the notion that the wisdom of the universe was the pattern for the harmony which the philosopher created within his own soul.

The relation of the imagery of the 'visions' of the universe to that of the ancient stellar cults necessitates a review of the origins of the latter. Worship of the heavenly bodies in Babylon antedated the keeping of exact records.[74] In their movements, the stars were seen as manifestations of a universal divine will. By synchronising their activities with those of the stars, men could participate in fulfilling that will. In the eighth century B.C., at a relatively late period in their history, the Babylonians developed an exact chronology. The era of Nabonassar, 747 B.C., marked the beginning of records on which calculations and predictions could be made. The records of the movements of the moon, the synodal revolutions of the planets, and the heliacal risings of stars were not mere observations. The Babylonians regarded both time and number as being of divine significance. Thus the division of the ecliptic into 360 degrees, and of the solar year into twelve months, and the recognition of seven planets, which included the sun and moon, gave a theological meaning to these numbers. The seven planets were known as the 'interpreters' of the divine will; the 36 decans, or ten-degree divisions of the ecliptic (see Chapter IV.1.2) were named 'counsellors', and the 24 stars, twelve in the Northern and twelve in the Southern hemispheres, were called 'judges'. A divine significance continued to be seen in these names and numbers by other nations, among whom the cult was later developed. Babylonian religion remained polytheistic, the triad of the sun, moon and Venus being regarded as the most powerful deities. In Babylon arose the notion of Necessity, that man's life was determined for him in advance. However, in Babylonian religion, as in that of the neighbouring Canaanite peoples, divine powers could be propitiated by sacrifices and gifts.

In the sixth century B.C., 'Chaldean' ideas reached Greece[75] and influenced, at first, only the philosophic schools. The view of the universe held in the classical period was of three spheres: the fixed stars, the planets and the earth. The highest sphere consisted of the stars, or of the ether beyond the stars, and regulated the movements of all the spheres below it. According to Plato, man could observe in the universe a divine counterpart of his own soul; the mind of the beholder was related to the highest sphere:

(The region above the heaven): For the colourless, formless and intangible truly existing essence, with which all true knowledge is concerned, holds this region and is visible only to the mind, the pilot of the soul. Now the divine intelligence, since it is nurtured on mind and pure knowledge, and the intelligence of every soul which is capable of receiving that which befits it, rejoices in seeing reality for a space of time and by gazing upon truth is nourished and made happy until the revolution (of the heaven) brings it again to the same place. In the revolution it beholds absolute justice, temperance, and knowledge.

Plato, *Phaedrus*, 247C,D

Man achieved a relationship with this highest sphere by intellectual effort and ascetic withdrawal from sense experience (see Chapter II.ı). Eternal life was seen as participation, in thought, in the workings of the divine mind:

There are housed in us three several components of soul, each with its own motions. . . . And of the sovereign component of soul . . . we are wont to say, (it) is in the high place of the body and it lifts us on high to our kindred above. . . . But if (a man) gives his heart to love of learning and true wisdom and exercises that part in himself in thinking thoughts immortal and divine, by equal necessity, if he but attain truth, so far as 'tis given to humanity to achieve immortality, he can fall nothing short of that goal; seeing that he is giving tendence to the divine and keeps the guardian spirit that dwells with him in good trim, he must be blest beyond all others. Now there is but one way of tending anything whatever it be—to give it the victual and the

119

motions proper to it. And the motions akin to the divine within us are the thoughts and revolutions of the universe. So it is they to which each of us must conform.

Plato, *Timaeus*, 89E—90D

The conquests of Alexander resulted in the widespread adoption, by the Greek populace, of the stellar cults of the Semitic peoples. The planets were renamed and their qualities identified with those of the Olympian deities of Greek mythology, probably themselves originally stellar deities. At the same time as the popular diffusion of astrology, intellectual interchange continued between the Greek and Chaldean schools. The essential difference between the Greek and Oriental viewpoints lay in their attitude towards eternal life. In Babylon, divinity and eternity were synonymous with endless repetition in time. Hellenistic Greek philosophers, among whom was Posidonius of Apamea,[76] endeavoured to reconcile their ethical belief in a future life, dependent on merit, with their views on the nature of the universe. Moral qualities were thus ascribed to the heavenly bodies. Seven planetary spheres were distinguished, to which corresponded a seven-fold division of the soul. The qualities of the planets were deduced both from their apparent motions and from those of the mythological deities associated with them. The planets thus held potentialities for good and evil. In each sign of the Zodiac were also the deities of the three decans, each associated with qualities and giving three 'faces' to the planet as it passed through the sign.[77] Heaven itself, as Ouranos or the eighth sphere, was the highest sphere. Taking the properties of the fixed stars, Heaven was the sphere of continuous revolution, which was not subject to error or deviation. Below the planetary spheres were the zones, in which operated the four elements, fire, air, water and earth, together with the four cardinal points and the four seasons. The Greeks recognised the sidereal divinities of other nations as being similar to their own, and thus arose the notion that these divinities were of universal significance and applicable to the whole world.

The Persian, Greek and finally the Roman conquests of the Middle East resulted in the spread of ideas, not only of universal religion, but of universal monarchy. The transition from a deterministic polytheism to monotheism was a preliminary stage. It required an abstraction of the notion of divinity from its physical manifestations. In the Roman period, a further development was made, from monotheism to the deification of the Emperor, in the context of the stellar cult.[78] In the late Hellenistic period, the sun was seen as supreme among the heavenly bodies. In becoming the image of the sun upon earth, the Emperor partook of its powers and himself became the central figure of the cult of the 'invincible and eternal sun'.

The basis of the cult of the sun was its apparent influence on the movements of the moon and other heavenly bodies. As 'the chief star of heaven', the sun was seen as the regulator of the movements of the stars. Surrounded by the other planets, the sun was the 'leader of the chorus'. As the 'heart' of the universe, the sun was thought to be the cause of the movements of progression and retrogression of the planets, impelling them forwards and arresting them.[79] These powers of the sun were seen as manifest by virtue of the fact that the sun was the origin of reason and intelligence. The sun was also regarded as the abode of souls and the place to which they ascended after death.

In the popular cults, the imagery inherited from earlier mythology depicted the soul as ascending to heaven in a number of ways: on foot, on horseback, by carriage, by flying, by ladder, or by chariot. The Emperor was driven to heaven in the chariot of the sun. The eagle, as the bird of the sun, also bore the Emperor to the skies. The purification of the soul took place first in the elemental zones, under the influence of air, water and fire:

> Therefore are they schooled with penalties, and for olden sins pay punishment: some are hung stretched out to the empty winds; for some the stain of guilt is washed away under swirling floods or burned out in fire.
>
> Virgil, *Aeneid*, VI.739

The elemental zone of the air was of particular danger to the ascending soul and to this region were assigned demons. Safe passage could be ensured by the knowledge of passwords or by the presence of a divine escort. The latter role was often taken by the planetary deity Hermes. Thus places of purification or torment, in earlier mythology placed beneath the earth, were included in the elemental zones. The Stoics placed Acheron in the sphere of the air, and Tartarus in the region of fire and hail.[80] In the planetary spheres, the soul was divested of bad qualities, each sphere being concerned with a particular soul-quality:

> ... D'abord, dans la dissolution du corps matériel, tu livres ce corps lui-même à l'altération, et la forme que tu avais cesse d'être perçue, et tu abandonnes au démon ton moi habituel désormais inactif, et les senses corporels remontent à leurs sources respectives, dont ils deviennent des parties, et sont de nouveau confondus avec les Energies, cependant que l'irascible et le concupiscible s'en vont à la nature sans raison. Et de cette façon l'homme s'élance désormais vers le haut à travers l'armature des sphères, et à la première zone il abandonne

la puissance de croître et de décroître, à la seconde les industries de la malice, fourbe désormais sans effet, à la troisième l'illusion du désir désormais sans effet, à la quatrième l'ostentation du commandement démunie de ses visées ambitieuses, à la cinquième l'audace impie et la témerité présomptieuse, à la sixième les appétits illicites que donne la richesse, désormais sans effet, à la septième zone le mensonge qui tend des pièges. Et alors, dénudé de ce qu'avait produit l'armature des sphères, il entre dans la nature ogdoadique, ne possédant que sa puissance propre; et il chante avec les Etres des hymnes. . . . Et alors, en bon ordre, ils montent vers le Père, s'abandonnent eux-mêmes aux Puissances, et, devenus Puissances à leur tour, entrent en Dieu. Car telle est la fin bienheureuse pour ceux qui possèdent la connaissance: devenir Dieu. Eh bien, à cette heure, que tardes-tu? Ne vas-tu pas, maintenant que tu as hérité de moi toute la doctrine, te faire le guide de ceux qui en sont dignes, afin que le genre humain, grâce à ton entremise, soit sauvé par Dieu?

Hermes, I. *Poemandrès*, I.24–26 (Festugière)

In this extract from the Hermetic literature, the ascent of the soul was an account of the change from an earthly to a divine nature achieved through the possession of 'knowledge'; the attainment of divinity, as a consequence of 'inheriting' a doctrine, thus placed the divine in the sphere of the intellect.

The movements of the heavenly bodies were seen by the Egyptian and Babylonian peoples as manifestations of divine will, with which the community, through ritual, must identify itself. The popular cults of the Hellenistic period were attempts to participate in the workings of this divine power. (See 'Introduction.') The seer was one who, by heredity or training, was able to identify himself with the national will and thus to be an 'interpreter' of the 'planetary' power. As a result of dream or trance experience, he was able to speak as if he were the deity controlling this 'sphere' and to use the appropriate imagery. In contrast, the philosophic schools of Greece gave highest place to the divine intellect, with which the human soul or mind could establish a relationship and, from a universal standpoint, survey the spheres below. This identification of the faculty of reason, or intellect, with the highest sphere of the universe, continued to be made in Neoplatonic and in Hermetic writings.

In spite of the condemnation of star worship by the Jewish leaders, the books of the Old Testament contained much of the imagery and numerology of the stellar cults of their neighbours. The prophets not only employed the vocabulary of their own people's past, but also used that of religions supplanted by Judaism. The close association, created by ritual, between a people and the movements of the heavenly bodies, was both prescribed and limited by Jewish Law. Although worship of the sun and moon was forbidden, the lunar cycle was the basis of the Jewish feasts, and the number seven, with its multiples, remained of particular religious significance. The year of twelve lunar months gave to the number twelve and its multiples a similar sacred meaning. These numbers were incorporated into Jewish social and religious organisation, the records of which acquired historical significance in the books of the Old Testament.

In the Old Testament, the heavens and their hosts (the stars) were regarded as the domain of the Lord.[81] He sat on His throne and the host of heaven stood on His right and left.[82] The displacement of the nations in the land which the Children of Israel 'inherited' was intended to include the destruction of the local stellar cults.[83] The worship of the Baalim, together with that of the sun, moon, planets and stars, nevertheless continued.[84] The period of national disasters and exile coincided with the contact of the Jewish people with the Babylonian and Hellenistic astrology. Reaction to these latter was influential in the production of the apocalyptic writings.

In the Hellenistic cults, the system of the Zodiac was a means whereby both the individual and a group could participate in the workings of the divine. In Judaism, it was a means of demonstrating the supremacy of the Jewish over other religions. The stars of the Hellenistic system were not only indicators of future events, but were seen to dominate all aspects of life. In contrast, the Jewish apocalypses mainly embodied predictions concerning the national future and also that of the whole world. Systems of angels and archangels, obedient to the divine will, replaced the stars and planets. As intermediaries between God and man, the angels represented the dominion of the Jewish religion over both the heavenly and earthly spheres (see p. 92).

The Hellenistic ethical system, which gave to the heavenly bodies potentialities for good and evil, was replaced, in apocalyptic literature, by a division between those angels and heavenly bodies who had sinned, and those who were obedient. Two angels, one good and one evil, were assigned to both individuals and nations. For the disobedient, who had been led astray by their guardian angels, destruction was predicted. The Hellenistic accounts of the heavenly spheres described the purification of the soul in the elemental and planetary zones. In the apocalyptic literature, the elemental zone of fire was transformed into a place of punishment, with scenes of fiery torment and destruction. Not only the disobedient of the human race, but the whole universe was depicted as involved in a final scene of conflagration. It was necessary that the 'Age to Come', the 'New Heaven' and the 'New Earth', should replace the 'Present Age'.[85] Blessedness in the future age, in which the Lord ruled supreme, was the destiny only of the righteous elect. The apocalyptic literature was an expression of the political and moral crisis of Judaism; it also contained and perpetuated the imagery of the Zodiac. This method of writing, in which the ascent of the soul of the seer was depicted in the language of the Scriptures, was rejected by Judaism after the first century A.D. Its influence continued in Christian circles and further apocalypses were written, even after the adoption of the canonical books of the Bible.

1   The Separation of the Soul from the Body

The traditional methods, by which visionary experiences were attained, has already been discussed ('Introduction', pp. 6–13). The situations of dream, trance, torture, death and ritual were the occasions in pre-Christian writings for such revelations. As literary forms, because of their Biblical associations, either directly or through the Apocalyptic literature, they were re-used by Christian writers and are exemplified in the present texts.

Vision, as an experience of the soul, was held to be obscured by the body. According to this tradition, quoted by Tertullian, the experiences of the heavenly world at death, by the soul, occurred during a gradual separation of the soul from the body. While this separation was incomplete, the soul was able to see the heavenly world more clearly, and because it could still use its bodily organs, was able to communicate what it saw:

> Where however the death is a lingering one, the soul abandons its position in the way in which it is itself abandoned. And yet it is not by this process severed in fractions; it is slowly drawn out; and whilst thus extracted, it causes the last remnant to seem to be but a part of itself. . . . And the last of the whole is the whole; because while it is less, and the latest, it yet belongs to the whole and completes it. Hence indeed, many times it happens that the soul in its actual separation is more powerfully agitated with a more anxious gaze and a quickened loquacity; whilst from the loftier and freer position in which it is now placed, it enunciates by means of its last remnant still lingering in the flesh, what it sees, what it hears, and what it is beginning to know. In Platonic phrase, indeed the body is a prison, but in the apostles it is 'the temple of God' . . . But by reason of its enclosure it obstructs and obscures the soul, . . . when the soul, by the

124

power of death, is released from its concretion with the flesh, it is by the very release cleansed and purified; . . . it recovers its divinity. . . . Then it tells out what it sees; then it exults or it fears, according as it finds what lodging is prepared for it, as soon as it sees the very angel's face, that arraigner of souls, the Mercury of the poets.

Tertullian, de Anima, LIII

Death was thus the moment, according to Tertullian and other Christian writers, when the saint or martyr bore witness to the heavenly places and knew himself as divine (see Quotations 5–9). This imagery was, however, derived from pre-Christian sources.

Not only was the separation of the soul from the body represented as connected with death, but its return was depicted as a process of 're-incarnation'. Both these events were said to be related to the faculty of memory. According to Plato, man's capacity for beholding the divine was due to the fact that he had seen this vision before his birth. Earthly life was either a forgetting, or a recollection, of that which had already been seen; (the relation of memory to the experience of dream visions was discussed on p. 54ff.).

For, as has been said, every soul of man has by the law of nature beheld the realities, otherwise it would not have entered into a human being, but it is not easy for all souls to gain from earthly things a recollection of those realities, either for those which had but a brief view of them at that earlier time, or for those which, after falling to earth, were so unfortunate as to be turned toward unrighteousness through some evil communications and to have forgotten the holy sights they once saw. Few then are left which retain an adequate recollection of them; but these when they see here any likeness of the things of that other world, are stricken with amazement and can no longer control themselves; but they do not understand their condition because they do not clearly perceive.

Plato, Phaedrus, 249E–250A

Recollection of the divine was a condition of 'amazement', the 'madness' or inspiration of the seer. Initiation was described by Plutarch as a means of reminding man of the heavenly places:

The best of our initiatory rites here below are the dreamy shadow of that spectacle, and of that rite; and the words used therein are ingeniously devised for the purpose of reminding us of the beauties of that place.

Plutarch, On the cessation of Oracles, XXII

According to Plato[86] man's life was not only dependent on Necessity, ruled by the stars, but on his own choice, made on the basis of his experience in the heavenly world. The return of the soul from the heavenly to the earthly world was thus bound up with this choice. The theme of the seer, confronted with a choice to be made, appeared both in non-Christian and Christian writings. In the latter, this event often took the form of a vision of the places of heaven, contrasted with those of hell. In Quotation 1, the dreamer was required to choose between the ways of life of her father and her mother, after seeing the respective fates of both.

The return of the soul to the body after a journey to heaven, in order to communicate its experiences to others, was described by Plato.[87] The seer, after twelve days of apparent death upon a funeral pyre, came to life and told the onlookers what he had seen. In the Jewish apocalyptic writings, the visions of the 'seers' were intended, by their authors, as instructions for their readers. The command to Isaiah to return to earth was represented as having come from the heavenly spheres (11); in the Christian narratives (9, 10) the command to return to the body was associated with the prophecy of martyrdom. In Narrative 12, in which the vision was represented as occurring in the context of the liturgy, the seer was commanded to return to build an earthly shrine for the martyr.

The traditional guide of the soul, Hermes, mentioned above by Tertullian, was replaced, in Christian literature, by figures of angels, archangels or Christ. As discussed above (p. 102), these figures were Christian forms of the planetary or solar deities. A similar interpretation was probably applicable to the tall and terrifying figure, seen by the dreamer in Narrative 1. In Narrative 2, two figures of great size and glory appeared to the seer (compare Sub-Section iv.2:1). In the Ethiopic version of the *Ascension of Isaiah*, the glorious angel sent 'to make him see' was said to be 'not of this firmament, nor was he of the angels of glory of this world, but he had come from the seventh heaven'. Gigantic figures were traditional representations of stellar deities; the 'Watchers' or fallen angels of Jewish mythology were said to be of great size.[88] Their relation to the 'disobedient' stars was made clear in *I Enoch*.[89] In general, in the ancient world, tall stature was evidence of superior or divine power:

I, Ezra, saw upon mount Zion a great company, which I could not number, and they all praised the Lord with songs.
In the midst of them was a young man, tall of stature, towering above all the rest, and he set a crown upon the head of each one of them, and he waxed ever taller.
So I asked the angel, saying, 'Who are these, Lord?'
He answered and said to me, 'These are they who have laid aside

their mortal clothing and put on the immortal and have confessed the name of God. Now are they crowned and receive palms.

And I said to the angel, 'Who is that young man who setteth crowns upon them and giveth them palms in their hands?'

He answered me and said, 'This is the Son of God whom they have confessed in the world.' And I began to praise them who had appeared so valiant for the name of the Lord.

V Ezra, 42–47 (Wilson, II, p. 695)

2 *The Experiences of Souls in the Life after Death*

Apocalyptic writing, which began in the latter half of the second century B.C. with the books of *Daniel* and *I Enoch*, was followed by a further period of literary activity in the first century A.D. To this time are ascribed the apocalypses known under the names of *Adam and Eve*, *Abraham*, *II Enoch*, *Moses*, *IV Ezra* and *II Baruch*. During the second century A.D., the last of the apocalypses in the names of Old Testament figures were probably written. To this period belonged the Christian Sibylline books, the *Ascension of Isaiah* and the *Apocalypse of Peter*. The fourth-century apocalyptic writings here quoted, ascribed to Paul and Bartholomew, like the *Apocalypse of Peter*, show evidence of Egyptian origin. Their contents suggest that they were compilations of material from various sources; repetitions in the *Apocalypse of Paul* even indicate the possible juxtapositions of two versions of the same text. The fourth-century Christian apocalypses probably represented the thought forms of the preceding centuries of Christianity in Egypt, including the era of the martyrs and that of the solitary ascetics.

Derived as they were from both Judeo-Christian and Greek sources, the fourth-century apocalypses contained diverse stellar imagery. The Zodiac as a system of expressing the experiences of the soul was widely understood in the Hellenistic world. The stellar imagery of the Graeco-Roman and other cults depicted the ascent of the soul through the spheres of the four elements, the seven planets and the fixed stars. In abstract terms, these three regions represented the physical, emotional and intellectual regions of man's psychic life. The system, derived from Egyptian ritual, expressed the experiences of the soul, between death and rebirth, in terms of the twelve divisions of the night traversed by the sun. The Zodiac, although its numerology was based on divisions of time and space, was a form in which subjective events could be understood. These events were, for the philosophers of the Hellenistic period, the distinguishing or separation of the activities of 'mind', 'soul' and 'will'. The imagery of these three spheres was that of the stars, the

THE CULT OF THE SEER IN THE ANCIENT MIDDLE EAST

planets and the elements respectively, and the stars were regarded as the highest sphere.

The first 'death' of Man was represented, by Plutarch, as a separation of the mind and soul from the body; the second was a separation of the mind, with which consciousness was associated, from the soul. The first separation was said to be violent and the second gentle. Purification of the soul, in the region of the air, preceded attainment of the lowest planetary sphere, the moon. The sun was represented as the highest sphere, only attainable by the mind, unmixed with the natures of soul or body:

> ... Man, most people rightly think a composite being, but wrongly think a composite of two parts only.... Of these three combined things (body, soul and mind), the earth furnished for the birth the body, the moon the soul, the sun the mind....
> The (first) death which we die makes the man two instead of three, the second (death) makes him one out of two. The first takes place in the region of Demeter, (because the earth) and also the dead are subject to her.... The second (death) takes place in the moon, the dominion of Persephone; and of the former the consort is the earthly Hermes, of the latter, the heavenly. The former separates the soul from the body hastily and with violence; but Persephone gently and slowly loosens the mind from the soul, and for this reason she has been named the 'Only-Begotten', because the best part of the man becomes single when separated from the rest by her means.
> Each of these changes happens, according to nature, as follows: every soul, whether without mind, or conjoined to mind, on departing from the body, is ordained to wander in the region lying between the moon and earth for a term, not equal in all cases; but the wicked and incontinent pay a penalty for their sins; whereas the virtuous, in order, as it were, to purify themselves and to recover breath, after the body, as being the source of sinful pollution, must pass a certain fixed time in the mildest region of air, which they call the 'Meadow of Hades', Then, as though returning to their native land after enforced banishinent, they taste of joy, such as the initiated into the mysteries feel, mingled with trouble and apprehension; ... and they also see the ghosts of people there turned upside down, and, as it were, descending into the abyss. Such as are arrived above, and have got firm foot-hold there (on the moon), like victors in the games, crowned with wreaths, encircle their heads with crowns called 'crowns of constancy' ... because the irrational and passionate part of the soul they have ... kept in restraint. ...

They contemplate, in the first place, the magnitude and beauty of the moon; and also her nature, which is not simple and unmixed, but as it were a combination of star and earth. . . . Like as our earth has deep and great gulfs, . . . in a like manner, there are deep places and gulf-like in the moon, . . . in which the souls either suffer or inflict punishment, for the things they have either done or endured; . . . as for the two smaller depths, because the souls pass through them on the way towards heaven and towards earth back again, the one is denominated the 'Elysian Plain' and the other the 'Passage of Persephone, the Terrestrial'. . . .

The mind separates itself out of a desire of reaching the Image in the sun, through which shines forth the Desirable, and Beautiful, and Divine, and Blissful, to which every unmixed nature aspires in different ways.

Plutarch, *On the apparent Face in the Moon's orb*, XXVIII–XXX.

Origen described a 'paradise' for souls on earth as a place in which they would receive instructions concerning the future life. He described the ascent of the soul in terms similar to those of Neoplatonism:

I think that the saints as they depart from this life will remain in some place situated on the earth, which the divine scripture calls 'paradise'. This will be a place of instruction and, so to speak, a lecture room or school for souls, in which they may be taught about all that they had seen on earth and may also receive some indications of what is to follow in the future; just as when placed in this life they had obtained certain indications of the future, seen indeed 'through a glass darkly', and yet truly seen 'in part', which are revealed more clearly and brightly to the saints in their proper times and places. If anyone is 'pure in heart' and of unpolluted understanding he will make swifter progress and quickly ascend to the region of the air, until he reaches the kingdom of the heavens, passing through the series of those 'abiding places', if I may so call them, which the Greeks have termed spheres, that is globes, but which divine scripture calls heavens. In each of these he will first observe all that happens there, and then learn the reason why it happens; and thus he will proceed in order through each stage.

Origen, *de Principiis*, I.xi.6 (Butterworth)

Origen re-expressed the Neoplatonic notion, that experience of heaven consisted in understanding the nature of the stars:

When the saints have reached the heavenly places, then they will see clearly the nature of the stars, one by one, and will understand whether they are living creatures or whatever may be the truth about

129

them. . . . And when they have gone through everything connected with the reason of the stars and with those ways of life that exist in heaven they will come to 'the things which are not seen', or to those whose names alone we have as yet heard, and to the things 'invisible'.

Origen, *de Principiis*, I.xi.7 (Butterworth)

In the Hermetic literature, the experience was an expansion of the scope of the intellect, so that the ordering of the visible universe was comprehended from the point of view of the divine:

Plût au ciel qu'il te fût donné d'avoir des ailes et de t'envoler vers l'air, et là, placé au milieu de la terre et du ciel, de voir la masse solide de la terre, les flots répandus de la mer, les cours fluents des fleuves, les mouvements libres de l'air, la pénétration du feu, la course des astres, la rapidité du ciel, son circuit autour des mêmes points. Oh, que cette vue est la plus bienheureuse, enfant, quand on contemple en un seul moment toutes ces merveilles, l'immobile mis en mouvement, l'inapparent se rendant apparent au travers des œuvres qu'il crée. Telle est l'ordonnance du monde et tel, le bel ordre de cette ordonnance.

Hermes, I. *Poemandrès*, V.5 (Festugière)

In the thought which lay behind Jewish apocalyptic, the divine will was given the supreme place. The deity was surrounded with the imagery of the elemental spheres: fire, wind, cloud, earthquake, etc. The divine intellect which exercised judgment was not clearly differentiated from the divine will and shared the imagery of the latter (see p. 122ff.). In the *Apocalypse of Abraham*, the seer was said to have been raised above the firmament, which appeared beneath his feet:

And He said to me: 'Look now, beneath thy feet at the firmaments and understand the creation foreshadowed in this expanse, the creatures existing on it, and the age prepared according to it.'

Apocalypse of Abraham, XXI (Box, p. 66)

This view was the occasion for foretelling the expansion on earth of the Jewish race:

And the Eternal Mighty One said to me: 'Abraham, Abraham.' And I said 'Here am I.' (And He said:) 'Consider from above the stars which are beneath thee, and number them (for me), their number.' And I said. 'When can I? For I am but a man (of dust and ashes).' And He said to me: 'As the number of the stars and their power, (so will) I make thy seed a nation and a people, set apart for me.'

Apocalypse of Abraham, XX (Box, p. 65)

THE REPRESENTATION OF A NON-MATERIAL WORLD

In the apocalyptic writings, both Jewish and Christian, the prayer of the seer was shown as effective in obtaining a view of the heavenly world, while still in the body. Enoch, Elijah (and Paul) were the proto-types of seers, who had been taken to heaven 'in the flesh'. In the *Testament of Abraham*, the patriarch was represented as asking to see all creation while in the body (see p. 133ff. for discussion on the chariot of the seer):

> Thus saith Abraham, thy servant, O Lord God: O Lord God, in every deed and word which I have asked of thee thou hast heard me, and hast fulfilled every desire of mine. . . . Now Lord God, hear my request; while I am yet in this body, I would fain see all the world and all created things which thou didst stablish together, through one word, O Lord, and when I have seen these, then cheerfully will I depart from life. . . . When the Most High heard this request, he again commanded the archangel Michael, and said unto him: Take a cloud of light and those angels that bear command over the chariots, and go down, and take the just man Abraham on a chariot of the cherubim and exalt him into the air of heaven so that he may see all the world.
>
> *Testament of Abraham*, IX (Box, p. 14)

In the *Apocalypse of Paul*, the Virgin and Saints in heaven were depicted as having asked that Paul might appear to them in the flesh:

> For all the saints have implored my son Jesus, who is my Lord, that you might come here in the body so that they might see you before you depart out of the world; and the Lord said to them: Wait and be patient. Just for a short time and you will see him and he will be with you for ever. And again all together they said to him: Do not sadden us for we wish to see him while he is in the flesh;
>
> *Apocalypse of Paul*, 46 (Wilson, II, p. 790)

The revelations in Narratives 1 and 2 were said to have been given to the holy men in answer to prayer, as were also those given to Pachomius (Narratives 3–5; see text).

Correlation was made, in Narratives 1 and 2, between the experiences of the soul after death and the days of mourning. Such a correlation had existed earlier, in the funerary cults of both Egypt and the Graeco-Roman world.[90] In Narrative 1, the soul spent three days in the region of the air, seeing the whole of creation. On the third day, when the soul was taken to the heavenly throne, an offering was made on earth. A second offering was made on the ninth day, when, after seeing the places

131

of torment, the soul was taken to judgment. In Narrative 2, the soul remained in the neighbourhood of the body for three days and spent the time between the third and ninth day in seeing the places of heaven. The remaining thirty days were passed in the places of torment. The final offering was made on the fortieth day.

The fortieth day after death was the period when, in ancient Egypt, the process of mummification was completed.[91] (See p. 116.) It was celebrated, in Christian times, as the completion of the soul's journey. Another link with Egyptian custom was the mention, in Narrative 2, of the benefit to the soul, of the prayers and offerings made for it on earth. In Narrative 2, the desire of the soul to return to the body and to revisit its former dwelling places were notions of Egyptian origin. The ascension of the soul on the third day was represented as a Christian obligation, and the separation from the body, as an affliction which the soul forgot in heaven. The significance of three, six and forty days, in relation to the experiences of the soul after death, was the basis of the fasting periods of the ascetics (see Section I.IV). The forty-day period, between the Crucifixion and the Ascension was, in gnostic texts, the occasion for the instruction of the Apostles. The Mount of Olives, on which the teaching was said to have been given, was the situation for receiving revelations in the Apocalypses ascribed to Paul and to Bartholomew. The 'school for souls' of Origen was also a sphere for the instruction of the soul on its own nature.

3   The City and Thrones of Heaven

The imagery of the city and thrones of heaven, in late Christian apocalyptic writings, was mainly derived from the Book of Revelation. The representation of the highest heavens showed differences from that in essentially Jewish apocalypses. In addition, in the present texts, the choice of imagery suggests an Egyptian background.

In ancient Egypt, permanent buildings were mainly of a funerary character and the various cemeteries were 'cities of the dead'. The notion of a 'holy city' developed within Judaism and was associated with entering the 'promised land', and with building a tabernacle or temple as a shrine for the deity. The predictions of a 'New Jerusalem', which would be the city of the Messiah in the 'Age to Come', were features of Jewish prophetic and apocalyptic writings. In the building of the ark, the tabernacle and the temple, divinely dictated measurements were incorporated into their structure. The dimensions of the building were thus an earthly manifestation of those numbers of universal significance, here previously discussed in connection with the Zodiac (p. 118ff.).

The throne, as a vehicle for the deity, was known in the religions of Egypt, Babylonia and Canaan. In Egypt, the hieroglyphic names of Osiris and Isis had the 'determinative' of a throne.[92] The ritual enthronement of Osiris took place after his death and resurrection. The names of the Pharaoh and his titles as a divinity were inscribed on his throne. The throne, in Egypt, was also a means of transport, either on the shoulders of men, or on a boat. During these journeys, the oracular pronouncements and judgments of the enthroned deity were made.[93] In the tomb paintings of the New Kingdom, enthroned deities received the homage of the deceased. The human-headed goddess Maat was represented, with eagles' wings, behind seated deities (Tomb of Nefertari, Thebes). The deity who led the deceased before the enthroned god was Horus (Tomb of Rameses I), or Isis (Tomb of Nefertari). The deceased in Paradise was shown seated, in the neighbourhood of a tree (Tomb of Sennefer), which might be fruit-laden (Tomb of Userhat). The deceased also appeared surrounded by his family, similarly seated (Tomb of Ramose). In the imagery of the funerary cult, enthronement generally implied divine status (compare Narratives 1, 2, 4 and 6).

The part played by the throne in Canaanite religion is known from the Ras Shamra texts from the ancient city of Ugarit, contemporary with the New Kingdom of Egypt[94]. The autumnal New Year festival included the ritual triumph of the god Baal over his enemies, his enthronement after his death and resurrection, and the building of his temple. The New Year festival of Israel was known as the Feast of Tabernacles. A number of Psalms contain imagery which suggests that the 'day of Jahweh' was the day on which His enthronement was celebrated, and that this festival supplanted the New Year enthronement of Baal.[95] Enthronement, in this context, thus contained the notion of immortality or renewal of life.

In the Old Testament, the tabernacle and the throne were the situations from whence the will or Judgment of Jahweh were made known. The elements, in particular fire, featured in the descriptions of the revelations. The association of fire with prophecy and with trance states, seen in the Old Testament, was further developed in Jewish apocalyptic writings. The Deity was represented, either as seated on a throne, or as an empty throne, a vision whose fiery nature was impossible to endure:

When we were at prayer, there came to me Michael the archangel, a messenger of God. And I saw a chariot like the wind and its wheels were fiery and I was caught up into the Paradise of Righteousness, and I saw the Lord sitting and His face was flaming fire that could not be endured. And many thousands of angels were on the right and the left of that chariot.

Vita Adae et Evae, XXV.1–3 (Charles)

The imagery of the fiery chariot, on which the seer was conveyed to heaven, was derived from Ezekiel:

And as the fire raised itself up, ascending into the height, I saw under the fire a throne of fire, and round about it all-seeing ones, reciting the song, and under the throne four fiery living creatures singing, and their appearance was one, each one of them with four faces. And such was the appearance of their countenances, of a lion, of a man, of an ox, of an eagle; four heads (were upon their bodies) (so that the four creatures had sixteen faces); and each had six wings; from their shoulders, (and their sides) and their loins. . . . And as I stood alone and looked, I saw behind the living creatures a chariot with fiery wheels, each wheel full of eyes round about; and over the wheels was a throne; which I saw, and this was covered with fire, and fire encircled it round about, and lo, an indescribable fire environed a fiery host. And I heard its holy voice like the voice of a man.

Apocalypse of Abraham, XVIII (Box, p. 62)

The description of a fiery throne, in the form of a series of steps of increasing height, in Narrative 6, suggests an affinity with Jewish mysticism (see below). The imagery is similar to that of *I Enoch*, in which the heavenly house, containing the throne, was depicted in terms of the sun and stars:

And as I quaked and trembled, I fell upon my face. And I beheld a vision.
And lo, there was a second house, greater than the former, and the entire portal stood open before me, and it was built of flames of fire. And in every respect it so excelled in splendour and magnificence and extent that I cannot describe to you its splendour and its extent.
And its floor was of fire, and above it were lightnings and the path of the stars, and its ceiling also was flaming fire.
And I looked and saw therein a lofty throne: its appearance was as crystal, and the wheels thereof as the shining sun, and there was the vision of cherubim.
And from underneath the throne came streams of flaming fire so that I could not look thereon.

And the Great Glory sat thereon, and His raiment shone more brightly than the sun, and was whiter than any snow.

None of the angels could enter and could behold His face by reason of the magnificence and glory, and no flesh could behold Him.

I Enoch, 14.14–21 (Charles)

Texts from Midrashim of the fifth and sixth centuries A.D., which refer to this fiery throne chariot, suggest that the cult of trance states continued in Jewish mystical circles.[96]

The thrones, as subordinate powers and part of a heavenly hierarchy, was a notion which was adopted by Christianity from Jewish apocalyptic sources:

And in the highest of all dwelleth the Great Glory, far above all holiness.

In (the heavens next to) it are the archangels, who minister and make propitiation to the Lord for all the sins of ignorance of the righteous;

Offering to the Lord a sweet-smelling savour, a reasonable and a bloodless offering.

And (in the heaven below this) are the angels who bear answers to the angels of the presence of the Lord.

And in the heaven next to this are thrones and dominions, in which always they offer praise to God.

Testament of Levi, 3.4–8 (Charles)

The seven archangels were also seen as part of this hierarchy. They were said, in apocalyptic writings, to be associated, not only with mankind, but also with the spheres of the universe:

And these are the names of the holy angels who watch.

Uriel, one of the holy angels, who is over the world and over Tartarus.

Raphael, one of the holy angels, who is over the spirits of men.

Raguel, one of the holy angels who takes vengeance on the world of the luminaries.

Michael, one of the holy angels, to wit, he that is set over the best part of mankind and over chaos.

Saraqael, one of the holy angels, who is set over the spirits, who sin in the spirit.

Gabriel, one of the holy angels, who is over Paradise and the serpents and the Cherubim.

Remiel, one of the holy angels, whom God set over those who rise.

I Enoch, 20.1–8 (Charles)

Emphasis was laid on the function of the heavenly hosts, in ceaselessly guarding and encircling the throne of the Deity:

> And round about were Seraphim, Cherubim, and Ophanim; and these are they who sleep not and guard the throne of His glory. And I saw angels who could not be counted, a thousand thousands, and ten thousand times ten thousand, encircling that house.
>
> *I Enoch*, 71.7–8 (Charles)

Their second function was the constant singing of praise:

> Of the singings of the angels, which it is impossible to describe.
> In the midst of the heavens I saw armed soldiers serving the Lord, with tympans and organs, with incessant voice, with sweet voice, with sweet and incessant voice, which it is impossible to describe, so wonderful and marvellous is the singing of these angels, and I was delighted listening to it.
>
> *II Enoch*, 17.I.A (Charles)

The singing of praise, in company with the heavenly host, was a practice perpetuated by the desert ascetics (p. 62).

The whole human community, as the embodiment of the mythology and numerology of the hosts of heaven, was a notion peculiar to Christianity and was made explicit in the apocalyptic writings. A way of life, in accord with the annual cycle of days, weeks and seasons, had been practised in pre-Christian times by the Qumran[97] and similar Jewish communities. Their purposes were, however, limited to national salvation and their underlying principle was that of obedience to the Mosaic Law. Observance of the solar, rather than the lunar year, was a feature of the Qumran cult; community groups had a numerical relationship to the calendar:

> And Israel shall form groups of at least ten men, by Thousands, Hundreds, Fifties and Tens.[98] And where the ten are, there shall never be lacking a Priest learned in the Book of Meditation; they shall be ruled by him.
>
> *The Damascus Rule*, XIII (Vermes, p. 115)

The introduction of the solar year, in Judaism, coincided with the period of apocalyptic writings: the similarity of terminology in *I Enoch* to that of the *Damascus Rule* above can be seen:

> And the leaders of the heads of the thousands, who are placed over the whole creation and over all the stars, have also to do with the four intercalary days, being inseparable from their office, according to the reckoning of the year, and these render service on the four days which are not reckoned in the reckoning of the year.
>
> *I Enoch*, 75.1–2 (Charles)

THE REPRESENTATION OF A NON-MATERIAL WORLD

The Qumran community also saw themselves as an immaterial building, related to the heavenly hosts:

> He has joined their assembly to the Sons of Heaven to be a Council of the Community, a foundation of the Building of Holiness, an eternal Plantation throughout all ages to come.
>
> *The Community Rule*, XI (Vermes, p. 93)

The essential difference between the 'vision' of heaven, in the Jewish and Christian apocalypses, lay in the relating of the universal 'system' to the whole of humanity in the latter. The city of gold with twelve walls, in Narratives 7 and 8, may have referred to the city of the *Book of Revelations*,[99] whose wall was 144 (12 × 12) cubits, the 'measure of a man'. The number twelve contained the notion of wholeness, whether applied to the universe, the year, mankind or the individual. Its use gave a context to the confrontation of the individual with other men, similar to that which, in pre-Christian texts, applied to the meeting with the divine in the universe.

4 The Foundations of Heaven: The Paradise of the Third Heaven: The Earthly Paradise

The mythology of Paradise is so extensive that it is only possible briefly to mention those aspects relevant to seership. In the various accounts from the ancient Near East, Paradise was characterised by its resemblance to, or presence in this world. Its separation from this life was due, either to distance in time, in the past or in the future, to spacial inaccessibility, or to the barrier of death. The separation, in general, divided the sphere of time from that of eternity, the human from the divine.

In ancient Egypt, the difference between this life and the life after death was ritually minimised. 'Life', for the dead, was a replica of life on earth. Work in the gardens, fields and canals was performed by and for the dead; food and family life was enjoyed as on earth. The 'Fields of Reeds' or 'Fields of Peace'[100] were said to be situated in the West, or in the path through *Amente* followed by the sun.

The mythology of ancient Greece also contained references to the West, as the place to which the souls of heroes departed; this was the site of the Isles of the Blest. The region of the sunset was the place of the Garden of Hesperides, whence Herakles fetched the golden apples after killing the dragon.[101] This solar myth represented the passage of the sun through one of the four signs of the Zodiac which corresponded to the equinox or solstice. It was derived from early ritual observance of

137

a festival enacted at one of these four seasons. The fourfold division of the year was represented by the four Zodiacal animals[102]: the lion, the bull, the scorpion and the water-snake. Their ritual 'death' ensured the fruitfulness of the earth and brought human effort into relationship with the divine. In this myth, access to Paradise was shown as achieved through heroic action.

Another group of Greek myths gave man the right of entry to Elysium by virtue either of his kinship with the gods, or of their special favour. The Elysian plain, to which man was translated, was the abode of the immortals, but, like Olympus, was on earth and not in heaven.

> The immortal gods will send thee (Menelaus) to the Elysian plain and the verge of the world where fair-haired Rhadamanthys dwells, where life is easiest for man. No snow falls there, nor any violent storm, nor rain at any time; but Ocean sends forth the clear, shrill blast of the West wind to refresh mankind; because . . . they count thee to be son-in-law to Zeus.
>
> Homer, *Odyssey*, IV.561

The island of Atlantis, described by Plato, was said to be populated by the sons born to Poseidon and a mortal woman.[103] The island prospered as a result of divinely bestowed fruitfulness and human effort, to which combination its beauty was ascribed:

> Poseidon, then, thus receiving as his lot the isle of Atlantis, settled his sons by a mortal woman in a district of it. . . . By the sea, in the centre of the island, there was a plain, said to have been the most beauteous of all such plains and very fertile, and again, near the centre of this plain, at a distance of some fifty furlongs, a mountain which was nowhere of any great altitude.
>
> Plato, *Critias*, 113C

The fruitfulness of the earth, referred to in Narratives 10, 11, 12, 15, 17 and 20, is described in imagery which bears considerable likeness to that in the writings of Plato, depicting Atlantis:

> Besides all this, the soil bore all aromatic substances still to be found on earth, roots, stalks, canes, gums exuded by flowers and fruits, and they throve on it. Then, as for cultivated fruits, the dry sort . . . we call the various kinds pulse . . . the fruit of trees that ministers to our pleasure . . . all these were produced by that sacred island, which then lay open to the sun, in marvellous beauty and inexhaustible profusion.
>
> Plato, *Critias*, 115A,B

According to Plato, man's soul, by virtue of its affinity with the eternal, was able to 'rise above' the heavens, thus transcending time. Man could thus view the earth from the standpoint of eternity:

> But there the whole earth is of such colours, and they are much brighter and purer than ours; for one is golden and one is white, whiter than chalk or snow, and the earth is made up of the other colours likewise, and they are more in number and more beautiful than those which we see here. For those very hollows of the earth which are full of water and air, present an appearance of colour as they glisten amid the variety of the other colours, so that the whole produces one continuous effect of variety. And in this fair earth the things that grow, the trees, and flowers and fruits, are correspondingly beautiful; and so too the mountains and the stones are smoother, and more transparent and more lovely in colour than ours. . . . And the earth there is adorned with all these jewels and also with gold and silver and everything of the sort.
>
> Plato, *Phaedo*, 110C–E

In this experience of Paradise, the imagery was of beauty rather than of fruitfulness. From this viewpoint, the earth and man were seen in their true nature:

> And in sight and hearing and wisdom and all such things (people there) are as much superior to us as air is purer than water or the ether than air. And they have sacred groves and temples of the gods, in which the gods really dwell, and they have intercourse with the gods by speech and prophecies and visions, and they see the sun and moon and stars as they really are, and in all other ways their blessedness is in accord with this.
>
> Plato, *Phaedo*, 111B,C

In Judaism, the Garden of Eden, as the place where God, man and animals had once walked together, was the image of Paradise, which in post-exilic times was transferred to the future age. In the period of the occupation of Canaan, the 'Promised Land' and the 'Land of the Inheritance',[104] flowing with milk and honey, had been images of an earthly kingdom. In apocalyptic writings, the Garden of Eden represented the 'Age to Come'. The Tree of Knowledge was shown as the means by which the seer acquired his wisdom and power of prophecy (Narrative 11):

> And I came to the Garden of Righteousness, and saw beyond those trees many large trees growing there and of goodly fragrance, large, very beautiful and glorious, and the tree of wisdom whereof they eat and know great wisdom.
>
> *I Enoch*, 32.3E

... when I had eaten of the tree of the knowledge, and knew and perceived what will come to pass in this age; what God intends to do to his creation of the race of men.

Vita Adae et Evae, XXIX.2–4 (Charles)

The imagery of the Old Testament, of the Jewish race as a tree with 'roots' and 'branches', was adopted in the Hymns of Qumran; in this case the tree was the community;

They shall send out a bud (for ever) like a flower (of the fields) and shall cause a shoot to grow into the boughs of an everlasting planting. It shall cover the whole (earth) with its shadow (and its crown) shall reach to the (clouds).
Its roots shall go down to the Abyss (and all the rivers of Eden shall water its branches).

Hymns, VI.10 (Vermes, p. 170)

The extraordinary fruitfulness of the trees of Paradise was depicted in an unknown apocalyptic text from Papias, quoted by Ireneus:

Wherefore the aforesaid blessing (of Jacob by Isaac) relates un-questionably to the times of the Kingdom, when the Just shall reign, rising again from the dead; when also the creature, being renewed and delivered, shall bring forth plenty of all kind of nourishment, of the dew of Heaven, and of the fatness of the earth: as the Presbyters who had seen John the Lord's disciple remembered that they had heard of him, how the Lord used to teach concerning those times, and to say, 'Days shall come, wherein vineyards shall grow, having each 10,000 main shoots: and in one main shoot 10,000 branches and in one main shoot again 10,000 sprigs, and upon every sprig 10,000 clusters, and in every cluster 10,000 grapes, and every grape when pressed shall yield twenty five measures of wine. And when any one of those saints shall lay hold of a cluster, another cluster shall exclaim, I am a better cluster, take me, by me bless the Lord.' In like manner also that a grain of wheat would bear 10,000 ears, and that every ear would have 10,000 grains, and every grain ten pounds of clear clean flour; and the fruits too, and seeds, and the grass, in the proportion following on this: and that all animals using as food the things which are received from the earth, should come to be at peace and agreement one with another, submitting themselves to men with entire submission.

Irenaeus, *Adversus Haereses*, Book V, 33.3

Similar imagery found in Narratives 6, 7 and 9, expressed the expansion of the message of Christianity. That Paradise and its trees were the saints themselves was expressed in the *Psalms of Solomon*:

The Paradise of the Lord, the trees of life are his Saints and the planting of them is sure for ever; nor shall they be rooted up all the days of heaven.

Psalms of Solomon, 14.2

The description of the beauty of Moses and Elias (Narrative 15), in its emphasis on their physical appearance, suggests that it was derived from a Greek source.

The vision of the universe by the philosopher, described in the *Phaedo*, was a transformation of the earth which depended on an understanding of its nature. Part of the vision of the seer, in apocalyptic writings, was in the form of a journey, during which the elemental constituents of the world were viewed. The idea of an Ocean or River, encircling the world, was derived from Greek sources; it represented the watery element of the universe (see Narratives 1–3). In the Apocalypse of *I Enoch* (Narrative 4), the regions of all four elements were visited by the seer and mention was made, in this account, of the seasons and the cardinal points, all of which 'belonged' to the sphere of the elements. Four places of Sheol, designated for the souls of the dead, were also described in *I Enoch* (Narrative 5). In Quotation 14, the four rivers of Paradise, corresponding to those of the earth, were seen. The four rivers were thought to flow through the four regions of the world, according to the contemporary geography. Thus the vision was extended to include the whole earth. In the *Apocalypse of Abraham*, Adam, as the ancestor of the whole human race, was seen as a gigantic figure:

And I looked into the picture, and mine eyes ran to the side of the Garden of Eden. And I saw there a man very great in height and fearful in breadth, incomparable in aspect.

Apocalypse of Abraham, XXIII (Box, p. 69)

The whiteness of the land of Paradise and the light by which it was illuminated (Narratives 8, 9 and 21) were said to be due to light other than that of the sun. The notion was thus expressed of Paradise as the state of eternal life; time in the form of the heavenly bodies, had passed away. (See Plato, *Timaeus* 38)

The notion of an earthly Paradise has been extensively developed among the Greek poets. In Hellenistic times, the writing of biographical accounts, such as that of Apollonius of Tyana,[105] included journeys to visit holy men in distant and inaccessible places. The Christian story of the voyage of Zosimus to visit the sons of Jonabdad was based on this type of biography (16–19). The island in the ocean, as the dwelling place of a holy community of people, had certain affinities with Plato's Atlantis. In Narrative 20, a similar story, in connection with Macarius, described his visit to an earthly Paradise of ascetics in the Egyptian desert. In these accounts, the experiences of the soul were expressed in terms of an earthly rather than of a heavenly journey. The literary form was that of an allegory, not an apocalypse.

Access to Paradise, in the ancient world, was achieved in this life through ritual, through philosophy or through dream experience. The Paradise imagined by the ascetics was represented in similar imagery. The vision was not, as in pre-Christian experiences, of the divine nature of the universe, but of this same divinity in man himself and in the human community, past and present.

CONCLUSION

The 'Paradise vision' of the ancient religions concerned the nature of the whole universe, in respect, not of its objective but of its subjective qualities. The latter were ritually attributed to the universe, on the basis of a subjective correspondence between the mode of action of heavenly bodies and that of the human psyche. Whereas in Egypt and Babylon, the qualities attributed to the universe were psychophysiological, the Greeks ascribed to it moral qualities. The 'deities', corresponding to the various parts of the universe, were thus derived from these two levels of experience. The totality of the experience was that of the whole nature of man from a subjective, but non-personal point of view.

The control of this 'universal man' was felt, by the Greeks and the Jews, to be at the periphery of the universe, and by the Egyptians to be in its visible parts. The vision was expressed in images whose content and sequence was determined by ritual. The reactivation of the 'image' reproduced the experience of the 'deity'. Meeting or identification with the 'one' supreme deity, or with one of the 'gods' was achieved in dream or trance states, in which the appropriate series of images was seen. The 'control' of the 'universe' was, in fact, that exercised by the community on the imagination of its members. Such control was only possible in a society in which individual self-consciousness either did not exist or could be temporarily abolished.

Christian writers continued to use the methods of representing religious experiences of the ancient world. The Christian experiences were expressed as traditional image sequences and the deity was depicted as approaching man from without. The 'image' of an external deity was not, however, appropriate to the Christian experience. A deity in the 'peripheral universe' could only be a 'real' experience to someone who, in a trance state and unconscious of his actual surroundings, 'saw' the images previously impressed on his imagination. The pagan community was unconscious of its role as creator of its own vision of the divine. The ascetics spent their lives in recreating and maintaining a different vision from that of paganism. From the narratives, it appears that the content of these visions was a new human community. It can only be deduced indirectly that the 'visions' were experienced in a new manner. It is here suggested that the 'visions' of the ascetics, in which they 'saw' their forerunners and fellows, were conscious experiences of the imagination. The visions, which were often ascribed to the ascetics by their biographers, appear to have been 'Christianised' versions of traditions derived from Egyptian, Greek and Judaic sources.

CHAPTER IV

The Representation of Negative Experiences

I DEATH AND JUDGMENT

Preliminary Considerations

Judgment, in ancient Egypt, was regarded as the prerogative of the gods rather than of men. The function of divine judgment lay, on earth, in settling disputes between men and, after death, in pronouncing a man's right to divine status. During life, judgment was exercised by the gods or the dead, acting through oracles. Judgment, by oracle or dream, was successful in situations where the guilt of an individual member was apparent to the rest of the community; as a method it nevertheless was open to abuse.[1] At his final judgment in the underworld of *Amente*, the individual hoped that his accusers would be overcome by the witnesses and advocates who would speak on his behalf.

In Judaism also, judgment was regarded finally as the role of the Deity. The notion was rejected that judgment on human affairs could be obtained either from the stars (see Chapter III.iv, p. 118), or from communications from the dead. On the Deity was placed the responsibility for the decisions made by the community. Disobedience to the Law resulted in judgment, pronounced against the community rather than the individual. Within the community, lesser matters were settled by men appointed as judges[2] and this practice was followed by the Qumran community. The community groups were thus judged by their chiefs:

> At the age of thirty years he may approach to participate in lawsuits and judgments, and may take his place among the chiefs of the Thousands of Israel, the chiefs of the Hundreds, Fifties, and Tens, the Judges and the officers of their tribes, in all their families, (under the authority of) the sons of Aar(on) the Priests.
>
> *The Messianic Rule*, I (Vermes, p. 119)

Judgment of man's final worth, according to Plato, took account of the appearance of his soul. Impartiality depended on both judges and

144

judged being stripped of all advantages derived from inheritance and wealth.[3] Plato held that only men who had been most just during their lives were able to judge the dead:

> For if a man when he reaches the other world, after leaving behind these who claim to be judges, shall find those who are really judges who are said to sit in judgment there, Minos and Rhadamanthus, and Aenaeus and Triptolemus, and all the other demigods who were just men in their lives, would the change of habitation be undesirable?
>
> Plato, *Apology*, 40E–41A

He stressed the importance of correct assessment of men and the impiety of wrong judgment:

> There cannot conceivably be anything more impious or more to be guarded against than being mistaken in word and deed with regard to the gods, and after them, with regard to divine men; you must take very great precaution, whenever you are about to blame or praise a man, so as not to speak incorrectly; . . . nay the good man is the most sacred of all these things (stocks and stones and birds and snakes).
>
> Plato, *Minos*, 318E–319A

Porphyry, in his *Life of Plotinus*, suggested that a 'company of heaven' existed to which went the noblest of mankind; these were the judges of the souls of men:

> Thus much the oracle has told about Plotinus' activity and fortunes while he was still in the body. After his deliverance from the body the god says that he came to 'the company of heaven' and that there affection rules and desire and joy and love kindled by God, and the sons of God hold their stations, who are judges of the souls, as we are told, Minos and Rhadamanthus and Aenaeus; to them, the god says, he went not to be judged but to be their companion, as are the other noblest of mankind. These are their companions, Plato, Pythagoras, and all who 'set the dance of immortal love'.
>
> Porphyry, *The Life of Plotinus*, 23.25

Christian apocalyptic writings followed those of Judaism, in presenting divine judgment as determining the different fates of the righteous and the wicked in the life after death. In the *Apocalypse of Paul*, the souls of the righteous and wicked were seen brought before God for judgment. The angel, present with each soul during life, was its advocate and the deeds of the past life of the deceased were his witnesses.[4] The nature of the soul was made manifest by the angels and its fate was pronounced by the Deity:

And then I heard the voice of myriad upon myriad of holy angels . . . And they were greatly amazed at that soul . . . And they led it until it worshipped in the presence of God. And when it had ceased, at once Michael and all the host of angels fell down and worshipped the footstool of his feet and displayed the soul, . . . However an angel ran on ahead of it and declared, . . . And in the same way the spirit said: . . . It behaved according to thy judgment. And the voice of God came and said: . . . Let it therefore be handed over to Michael, the angel of the covenant, and let him lead it into the paradise of jubilation, that it may be there until the day of resurrection and become also a fellow-heir with all the saints. And after that I heard the voices of a thousand times a thousand angels and archangels and the cherubim and the twenty-four elders who sang hymns and glorified God. . . . And the angel answered and said to me: Have you believed and understood that whatever each of you has done, he sees it in the hour of his need?

Apocalypse of Paul, 14 (Wilson, II, p. 766)

The *Apocalypse of Paul* contained the notions of two judgments, the second determining the final fate of the soul[5]; the torments were experienced during the intervening period:

And after that I heard voices in the height of heaven which said: Present the unfortunate soul to God that it may know there is a God whom it has despised. Therefore when it had entered heaven, all the angels, thousands of thousands of them, saw it (and) they all cried with one voice: . . . Let such a soul be sent away from our midst; for since it came in, its foul stench has gone through to all the angels. And then it was taken away to worship in the presence of God, . . . But its angel ran on ahead . . . And in the same way the spirit said: . . . Judge it, Lord, according to thy judgment. And the voice of God came forth to it and said: . . . Let him therefore be handed over to the angel Tartaruchus, who is appointed over punishments, and let him send him into outer darkness where there is wailing and gnashing of teeth, and let him remain there until the great day of judgment.

Apocalypse of Paul, 16 (Wilson, II, p. 768)

The difference of attitude, between one which regarded men's fate as determined by the stars, and one in which the role of human free-will was seen, was reflected in the literature on heavenly writing. Tablets, or (later) books, written in heaven,[6] were said to contain either the pre-destined fate of mankind, or the record of the earthly actions of men. In Babylonian mythology, man's destiny, ruled by the stars, was written on heavenly tablets. In Jewish apocalyptic writings, God's plans for mankind were said to be written in heaven.[7] These revelations were also a secret teaching, either made known to the seer,[8] or written by him in heaven.[9] They contained, in astrological terms, the nature and impending destruction of the universe and the fate of its human inhabitants.

Tablets on which were recorded men's actions by which they were judged were described by Plato.[10] The Jewish apocalyptic *Book of Jubilees* mentioned two books; in the Book of Life were written those who would survive, and in a book of adversaries those who would be destroyed. (For further discussion on the Book of Life, see Section V.I.2):

> And we remember the righteousness which the man fulfilled during his life, at all periods of the year; until a thousand generations they will record it, and it will come to him and to his descendants after him, and he has been recorded on the heavenly tablets as a friend and a righteous man. All this account I have written for thee, and have commanded thee to say to the children of Israel, ... but if they transgress ... they will be recorded on the heavenly tablets as adversaries, and they will be destroyed out of the Book of Life, and they will be recorded in the book of those who will be destroyed and with those who will be rooted out of the earth.
>
> *Book of Jubilees*, 30.20–23 (Charles)

The *Ascension of Isaiah* contained the notion that in the seventh heaven everything done on earth was known:

> ... showed me a book, (but not as a book of this world) and he opened it, and the book was written, but not as a book of this world. And he gave (it) to me and I read it, and lo! the deeds of the Children of Israel were written therein, and the deeds of those whom I know (not), my son Josab.
> And I said: 'In truth, there is nothing hidden in the seventh heaven, which is done in this world.'
>
> *Ascension of Isaiah*, IX.22, 23 (Charles)

The Christian *Apocalypse of Elias*, which contained much Egyptian imagery, represented an accusing angel who had to be overcome, a scroll whose writing had to be erased[11] and a judgment scene in which good and evil were weighed in scales.[12]

The ascetic life, as the 'life after death', was the means of removing the act of judgment from the sphere of oracles or dream visions, and transferring it to that of consciousness. By regarding the Old Testament Patriarchs, not only as the ancestors of the Jews, but as forerunners of Christianity, the individual could give them a new significance. In the present texts, however, their role appeared to be that of the just men of the writings of Plato, who judged souls after death. As the leaders of mankind, the Patriarchs were represented as being among those who received the souls of men in heaven (Sub-section I.3). The living were thus shown as dependent on the judgment of the dead.

1 The Death of the Wicked

The ritual of the ancient world protected man from experiencing the self-destructive aspects of those powers which he attributed to the universe around him. The mythology of early periods depicted divine retribution on man as wrath, vengeance or punishment in the life after death. The effects on man of this confrontation with the divine, or demonic, counterparts of himself were depicted, by the seers of antiquity, as the experiences through which the soul passed in the life after death. The redress, in the after life, of wrongs or misfortunes in this world, was the subject of one group of such accounts. The fate of the wealthy, on the one hand, and the poor and virtuous, on the other, exemplified in the Christian Narratives 2–6, had parallels in the stories of Pharaonic Egypt:

> Setme marvelled at those things which he saw in Amente. And Si-Osiri walked out in front of (?) him. And he said to him, 'My father Setme, dost thou not see this great man who is clothed in raiment of royal linen, standing near to the place in which Osiris is? He is that poor man whom thou sawest being carried out from Memphis, with no man following him, and wrapped in a mat. He was brought to the Tê[13] and his evil deeds were weighed against his good deeds that he did upon earth; and it was found that his good deeds were more numerous than his evil deeds, ( ) And it was commanded before Osiris that the burial outfit of that rich man, whom thou sawest carried forth from Memphis with great laudation, should be given to this same poor man, and that he should be taken among the noble spirits as a man of God . . . (But) that great man whom thou didst see, he was taken to the Tê, his evil deeds were weighed against his good deeds, and his evil deeds were found more numerous than his good deeds that he did upon earth. It was commanded that he should be required in Amente, and he (is that man) whom (thou didst see), in whose right eye the pivot (?) of the gate of Amente was fixed, shutting and opening upon it, and whose mouth was open in great lamentation.[14]

Second Tale of Khamuas (Griffith, Stories of the High Priests, p. 48)

THE REPRESENTATION OF NEGATIVE EXPERIENCES

The contrast between the fates of the righteous and the wicked was also the subject of much of the literature of Judaism. In *IV Ezra*, the imagery of the journey of the soul through the planetary spheres (see p. 123) was used to describe seven 'orders', in which only the righteous dead rested; for the wicked, wandering was a state of punishment for their sins: (compare the wandering of unguided souls in Plato's *Phaedo* in the quotation following).

> The state of the soul after death and before the Judgment.
> And I answered and said: If I have found favour in thy sight, O Lord, show this also to thy servant: whether after death, even now when every one of us must give back his soul, we shall be kept in rest until those times come, in which thou shalt renew the creation, or shall we suffer torture forthwith?
> And he answered me and said: . . .
> And concerning death the teaching is: When the decisive decree has gone forth from the Most High that man should die, as the soul from the body departs that it may return to him who gave it, to adore the glory of the Most High, first of all: if it be one of those that have scorned and have not kept the ways of the Most High, . . . Such souls shall not enter into habitations, but shall wander about henceforth in torture, ever grieving and sad, in seven ways . . . Of those, however that have kept the ways of the Most High this is the order, when they shall be separated from this vessel of mortality. . . . First of all they shall see with great joy the glory of him who receives them; and they shall rest in seven orders. . . .
> And I answered and said: Shall time, therefore be given unto the souls, after they are separated from the bodies, that they may see what thou hast described to me?
> And he said to me: Seven days they have freedom, that during these seven days they may see the things aforesaid, afterwards they shall be gathered together in their habitations.
>
> IV *Ezra*, 7.75–101 (Charles)

The interval between judgment and 'reincarnation' was described, by Plato, as a complex path in which the soul had need of divine guidance. The purpose of the journey was that the soul should 'understand its circumstances'. The 'wandering' of the souls, without guidance, resulted in their departure by necessity to their final habitations:

> And so it is said that after death, the tutelary genius of each person, to whom he had been allotted in life, leads him to a place where the dead are gathered together; then they are judged and depart to the other world with the guide whose task it is to conduct thither those

who come from this world; and when they have there received their
due and remained through the time appointed, another guide brings
them back after many long periods of time. And the journey is not as
Telephus says in the play of Aeschylus; for he says a simple path
leads to the lower world, but I think the path is neither simple nor
single, for if it were, there would be no need of guides, since no one
could miss the way to any place if there were only one road. But
really there seem to be many forks of the road and many windings;
this I infer from the rites and ceremonies practised here on earth.
Now the orderly and wise soul follows its guide and understands its
circumstances; but the soul that is desirous of the body, as I said
before, flits about it, and is in the visible world for a long time, and
after much resistance and many sufferings is led away with violence
and with difficulty by its appointed genius. And when it arrives at the
place where the other souls are, the soul which is impure and has done
wrong, by committing wicked murders or other deeds akin to those
. . ., wanders about alone in utter bewilderment, during certain fixed
times, after which it is carried by necessity to its fitting habitation.
But the soul that has passed through life in purity and righteousness,
finds gods for companions and guides, and goes to dwell in its proper
dwelling.

Plato, *Phaedo*, 107D–108B

In Christian apocalyptic writings, torments began for the wicked at,
or even before the moment of death. In the *Apocalypse of Paul*, as in
Narratives 1–6, and 13, emphasis was laid on the pitiless nature of
the angels which appeared to the soul in its 'hour of need'; only for the
righteous were the accompanying angels a defence against the attack of
demonic powers:

And the angel answered and said to me: Follow me and I shall show
you the place of the righteous where they are brought when they are
dead. And I went behind the angel and he led me to heaven and I saw
the firmament and I saw there the Power(s). . . . And the princes of
wickedness were there. These I saw under the firmament of heaven.
And again I looked and I saw angels who were pitiless, who had no
compassion; their faces were full of wrath and their teeth projected
from their mouths; their eyes flashed like the morning star in the
east, and from the hairs of their head and out of their mouth went
forth sparks of fire. And I asked the angel, saying: Who are these,
sir? And the angel answered and said to me: These are those who are
appointed for the souls of the wicked in the hour of need. . . . And I
looked into the height and I saw other angels with faces shining like

the sun; their loins were girt with golden girdles and they had palms in their hands, and the sign of God; . . . And I asked the angel and said: Who are these, sir, who have so much beauty and pity? And the angel answered and said to me: These are the angels of righteousness; they are sent to lead in the hour of their need the souls of the righteous who believed God was their helper. And I said to him: Must the righteous and the sinners meet the witnesses when they are dead? And the angel answered and said to me: There is one way by which all pass over to God, but the righteous, because they have a holy helper with them, are not troubled when they go to appear before God.

Apocalypse of Paul, 11, 12 (Wilson, II, pp. 763–4)

The amelioration, through ritual, of the experiences of the soul in the life after death, was a feature of the ancient Egyptian funerary cult. Prayers, by the dying, for their own safety and visualisation of their passage through *Amente* appeared in some late Christian apocalypses. The following extracts concern the deaths of the Virgin and of Joseph the Carpenter:

Remember her who brought thee forth, O my Lord, for indeed the forms of death have drawn near to me. I pray thee, O my beloved Son, let the powers of death and the forces of darkness flee from me. Let the angels of light draw near to me. Let the worm which does not sleep be still. Let the outer darkness become light. Let the accusers of *Amente* shut their mouths before me. Let the Dragon of the Abyss close his mouth as he sees me coming to thee. O my beloved Son, command that the Ministers of the Abyss flee away from me, and that they do not terrify my soul. The stones of stumbling which are in those paths, let them be dispersed before me. The tormentors with changing faces, let them not see me with their eyes. The River of Fire, which raises waves in thy presence like the waves of the sea, in which are distinguished the two sides, the righteous and the sinners, when I pass over it, let it not turn my soul. Let me be worthy to worship thee with a face in which is no shame. For thine is the power and the glory until the age of all ages. Amen.

de dormitione Mariae (Lagarde, 11)

Now therefore, O my Lord, let thine angel stand with my soul and my body, until they are separated from one another without trouble. Cause not the angel, appointed to me from the day that thou didst form me until now, to burn in his face with anger towards me in the path, as I come to thee, but let him be at peace with me. Let not those with changing faces trouble me in the path as I come to thee. Let not those who are upon the gates restrain my soul, neither let them put me to shame at thy fearful judgment seat. Let not the waves of the River of Fire, in which are souls purified before they see the glory of thy godhead, be wild towards me. O God, who givest judgment to each one in truth and righteousness, now therefore, my Lord, let thy mercy be a consolation to thee, for thou art the Fountain of all Good. Thine is the glory for ever and ever. Amen.

de morte Iosephi (Lagarde, 13)

These prayers implied a belief that *Amente*, the underworld of the ancient funerary cult, was still an experience necessary for all in the life after death (see Section IV.i.2).

The accounts of the experiences of the soul after death, as represented by the gnostic text, *Pistis Sophia*,[15] showed certain similarities to those in the *Apocalypse of Paul*. Both texts contained the imagery of the Zodiac and in both, the chastisement of souls was shown as taking place in relation to the powers represented by these images. In both texts, the experiences of different souls were contrasted. In the *Pistis Sophia*, the life of the soul after death began with its release from the powers represented by the Zodiac:

When the time of the coming forth from the body of that soul is completed, the Spirit Counterpart[16] follows after that soul, he and the Fate follow after it in the Road on which it will go to the Height. And before it approaches the Height, it says the Mystery of the releasing of the Seals with all the bonds of the Spirit Counterpart, these with which the Rulers bound him to the soul, and when they are said, the bonds of the Spirit Counterpart are released and he ceases coming in to that soul. And he releases the soul according to the commands which the Rulers of the Great Destiny ordered him, saying to him, Do not release this soul unless it says to thee the Mystery of the releasing of every Seal, these with which we bound thee to the soul. When therefore it happens that the soul says the Mystery of the releasing of the Seals with all the bonds of the Spirit Counterpart, he ceases coming in to the soul and he ceases being bound to it. And in that hour (it) says a Mystery and dismisses the Fate to its place at the feet of the Rulers which are upon the Road of the Midst.[17] And it says the Mystery and dismisses the Spirit Counterpart to the feet of the Rulers of the Destiny, to the place to which they bound it. . . . And in that hour, the soul becomes a great effluence of light and it takes wings of light completely and it passes through every place of the Rulers with all

THE REPRESENTATION OF NEGATIVE EXPERIENCES

the ranks of the Light, until, it goes to the place of its Kingdom from which it received (its) Mystery.

Pistis Sophia, 262a–263a

In contrast to the *Pistis Sophia*, the *Apocalypse of Paul* showed man's salvation after death as lying in his righteous deeds and in angelic helpers; the latter were said to overcome the powers of the air:

... and I said to the angel: I wish to wait for the souls of the righteous and of sinners and observe in what way they go out of the body. And the angel answered and said to me: Look down at the earth. ... and I looked and saw a man at the point of death. And the angel said to me: This man whom you see is righteous. And again I looked and I saw all his deeds which he had done for the sake of the name of God; and all his desires which he remembered and which he did not remember, all of them stood before him in the hour of need. ... and before he left the world holy and wicked angels stood together by him; and I saw them all; however, the wicked found no dwelling in him, but the holy had power over his soul, directing it until it left the body. ... They received therefore the soul from the body and at once kissed it just as if they had known it every day. ... And the angel that watched over it day by day came to meet it. ... In the same way also the spirit advanced to meet it ... and its angel took it up and led it into heaven. ... And there went to meet it the evil powers who are under heaven. ... And there was a fight between the good angels and the evil angels. ... And all the powers and evil spirits came to meet it, even up to it. But they did not find anything of their own in it.

Apocalypse of Paul, 14 (Wilson, II, p. 764–5)

The *Pistis Sophia* distinguished Destiny or Fate as a power or dimension, from which it was necessary that men should set themselves free. In the accounts of souls subject to Destiny, punishment or destruction were shown as the inevitable results of men's inability to liberate themselves.

Now therefore, when the time comes of the completion of the time of that man, first indeed the Fate comes forth to harness the man within death, through the Rulers and their bonds, these with which they bind through Destiny. And afterwards the avenging Receivers come and they bring that soul forth from the body. And afterwards the avenging Receivers spend three days[18] going round with that soul in all the places, sending it to all the Aeons of the World, while the Spirit Counterpart and the Fate follow after that soul. ... And after three days, the avenging Receivers bring that soul down to *Amente* of the Chaos and when they bring it down to the Chaos, they give it into the hands of those who punish. And the Receivers withdraw to their places, according to the arrangement of the works of the Rulers regarding the coming forth of the souls. And the Spirit Counterpart becomes the Receiver of the soul, striking it and reproving it in punishments, according to the sins which it caused it to commit. And it becomes in a great rage against the soul. And when the soul has completed the punishments in the Chaoses, according to the sins which it committed, the Spirit Counterpart brings it up in the Chaoses, striking it and reproving it in each place, according to the sins which it committed. And it brings it forth upon the Road of the Rulers of the Midst. And when (it) reaches them, they ask it the Mysteries of the Fate. And when it does not find them, they visit their Fates (on it). And those Rulers punish that soul according to the sins for which it is worthy (to be punished). These I will say to you, the type of their punishments in the distribution of the Universe.

Pistis Sophia, 259b–261a

Christian apocalyptic writings depicted demonic experiences as divine retribution for human disobedience. In the *Apocalypse of Paul*, unrighteous deeds were emphasised as the cause of the domination of the demonic powers over the soul:

And he said to me: Look down again at the earth and wait for that other soul of an ungodly man as it comes forth from the body. . . . And I looked and saw all the scorn of the sinner and all that he had done and that stood before him in the hour of his need. And I saw that that hour was more bitter to him than the future judgment. . . . And then holy and wicked angels came together and the soul of the sinner saw both, and the holy angels found no place in it. The wicked angels had power over it; and when they led it out from the body, the angels admonished it three times, . . .

And when they led it out, its familiar angel went before it . . . And the spirit afflicted it and the angel troubled it. However when it reached the powers, as already it went to enter heaven, there was laid on it one evil burden after another.

Apocalypse of Paul, 15, 16 (Wilson, II, pp. 767–8)

The imagery with which the passage of the soul through the powers of the air and of *Amente*, in the *Life of Anthony* and elsewhere (Narratives 7–10; 11–13), was represented, was derived from descriptions of the elemental spheres of the Zodiac.

THE REPRESENTATION OF NEGATIVE EXPERIENCES

The significance of the *Pistis Sophia* document lay in its emphasis on the inevitability of negative experiences. It described the 'post mortem' life of men who had subjected themselves to 'images' of their own creation. It depicted experiences of demonic retribution, following in a sequence pattern as inevitable as that of the movements of the stellar universe. The authors of the *Pistis Sophia*, the Christian apocalyptic writings and the lives of the ascetics, in depicting hell, were each describing an experience known at that time to both the pagan and Christian worlds. A surrounding universe of hostile demons was an impression from which community life and physical health protected men to some extent. Isolation and the decline of bodily powers produced and intensified the experience. The full impact of the 'demonic world' was felt, by the individual, in the 'absence' of the physical body, in the 'life after death'.

2 Abbaton, the Angel of Death

The word *abbaton* or *abaddon*, derived from the Hebrew verb 'to destroy',[19] was used, with the meaning of 'destruction' or *Sheol*, in the Old Testament.[20] In the New Testament,[21] it is found with the meaning of 'destroyer' or 'Angel of the Abyss', equivalent to the Greek Apollyon.

A late Coptic apocryphal text (1,2) described the setting up of Abbaton as a punishment to mankind. It was said that none would escape seeing the terrifying form of death. The powers which appeared, preceding death, also caused terror by their change of form. This 'change of form', or more often, of 'face' was a description frequently applied to the demonic apparitions, seen at the time of death (2, 3, 4). The 'changing faces' were also said to be present to the soul, in its passage through *Amente*:

> Woe is me, my sons, who can encourage me that God is at peace with me, that I may be delivered from this hour. I have also been told that there is a gloomy darkness in the path and there are pitiless tormentors in it, whose faces change very much, whom God has sent to teach the lawless on the way, as it is written. Shall I be saved from such as these? There is also in that place the worm that does not sleep, which eats the lawless more than any cancer.
>
> *Of the falling asleep of Mary*, II (Robinson, p. 96)

In Quotations 4 and 5, the 'changing faces' were said to be those of decans.

155

The word 'decan' was used in the Hellenistic period to denote the stellar deities, which ruled over each ten degree division of the Zodiac. There were thus three decans in each sign. These thirty-six decans[22] of the ecliptic corresponded to the thirty-six (and a half) weeks of ten days into which the Egyptians divided the solar year. The effect, on man, of the movement of the planets within each sign of the Zodiac, was thought to be influenced by the decans which the planets 'faced'.[23] The 'changes of face' were associated with changes of effect, favourable and unfavourable. 'counsellors' (4) was a term used for the thirty-six decans (see Chapter III.ɪv, 'Preliminary Considerations', p. 118). Ancient Egyptian religion related the various parts of the body to the thirty-six decans. According to Origen, the decans were invoked in times of sickness (and presumably in the event of death):

> They (the Egyptians) say that the body of man has been put under the charge of thirty-six daemons, or ethereal gods of some sort, who divide it between them, that being the number of parts into which it is divided (though some say far more). Each daemon is in charge of a different part. And they know the names of the daemons in the local dialect, . . . and by invoking these they heal the sufferings of the various parts.
>
> Origen, *contra Celsum*, VIII.58 (Chadwick)

In the *Testament of Abraham*, Death was given a divine command to assume a beautiful form and to appear to the righteous man Abraham, in order to persuade his soul to leave his body:

> So the unseen God said to Death: . . . Go down to Abraham my friend, and take him and lead him to me. . . . take possession of him with coaxing, for he is my very friend. When Death heard this, he went out from the presence of the Most High and girded about him a most glorious robe, and made his countenance like unto the sun, and became comely and blooming, passing the sons of men, having assumed the form of an archangel, with his cheeks flashing like fire, and he went away unto Abraham.
>
> *Testament of Abraham*, XVI (Box, p. 27)

Abraham, himself, requested Death to appear in his other aspect, a sight hard for men to behold:

> Abraham said: I pray thee, since thou art Death, tell me, comest thou thus unto all in such comeliness, glory and fairness? Death said: Nay, my Lord Abraham; for thy righteousness and the measureless sea of thy hospitality and the greatness of thy love towards God have

THE REPRESENTATION OF NEGATIVE EXPERIENCES

become a crown upon my head, and in beauty, and in great peace and winsomeness come I to the righteous, but to sinners I come in great corruption and fierceness and very great bitterness, and with a fierce and pitiless glance. Abraham said: . . . show me thy fierceness, and all thy corruption and bitterness. Death said: Thou wilt not be able to behold my fierceness, most righteous Abraham. Abraham said: Yea, I shall be able to behold all thy fierceness, because of the name of the living God, for the power of my God which is in heaven is with me.

Testament of Abraham, XVII (Box, p. 29)

Death was described as appearing to Abraham a second time, this time in his fearsome aspect:

Then Death put off all his beauty and fairness, and all his glory, and the form that was like unto the sun, wherewith he was clad, and girded about him his robe of tyranny, and made his countenance gloomy, and fiercer than all manner of wild beasts, and more foul than every kind of foulness; and he showed Abraham seven fiery serpents' heads, and fourteen faces, of the most burning fire, and of great fierceness, and a countenance like unto darkness, and a most gloomy countenance of a viper, and a countenance of a most horrible precipice, and a countenance fiercer than an asp, and a countenance of a dread lion, and a countenance of a horned serpent (cerastes) and of a basilisk. He showed him too a countenance of a fiery sword, and a scimitar-bearing countenance, and a countenance of lightning that flashed forth lightning fearfully, and an echo of fearful thunder. He showed him too another countenance of a fierce, billowy sea, and a fierce river plashing, and a monstrous three-headed serpent, and a wine-cup mingled with poisons; and in a word, he showed him great fierceness and bitterness unendurable, and every deadly disease as of the odour of death. And from the great fierceness and bitterness there died servants and maidservants in number about seven thousand.

Testament of Abraham, XVII (Box, p. 30)

In the description of the second aspect of Death, some of the features were similar to those of Narrative 2. The seven heads and fourteen faces of Death were, like the seven heads of Abbaton, references to the seven planets, as were the seven thunders. The seven headed dragon[24] of the *Ode of Solomon* 22, quoted in the *Pistis Sophia* 147, which was 'overthrown' and 'destroyed', may have had a similar significance. The animal and other faces of Death,[25] would, if this interpretation is correct, have referred to the constellations within the signs of the Zodiac (see also Quotation 3). The universality of the experience of death was represented, in Narrative 2, by allusions to the four sides of the earth and the four dimensions of space. In this context, Abbaton and the figure of Death appear to have represented the demonic aspect of the entire Zodiac, which confronted the individual at the moment of death. In his beautiful aspect, Death was said to have made his face 'like the sun'.

The appearance to the soul, at death, of two angels, one of light and one of darkness, was described in a number of texts (see Chapter III.ii, Preliminary Considerations, p. 103); the following quotation from the apocryphal *Death of the Virgin* is from a speech by the Virgin:

> What shall I say concerning the separation of the soul from the body? O that hour full of fear and trembling; they say that two powers come after the soul, one of light, another of darkness, ugly and full of shuddering and trembling. If it be a righteous soul they bring it forth by persuasion, being compassionate and gentle towards it, because they see its Maker peaceful towards it. If indeed it be a sinner, the (powers of) the light withdraw themselves and those of the darkness approach it in anger, slaying them and carrying (them) off in haste and beating (them). They are grinding their teeth and sending forth flames of fire from their mouths into its face, knowing that its works are ugly.
>
> *Of the falling asleep of Mary*, II (Robinson, pp. 94–96)

The significance of the two angels appears to have been similar to that of the two figures of Death. To those who were dominated by the images of the stellar powers, these images appeared in demonic form at death.

In the *Testament of Abraham*, an apocryphon of Jewish origin, Abraham claimed to be able to withstand the sight of Death, through the power of God within him. The ability to behold Death, through the presence of Christ, was described in Narratives 4–7. These apocryphal accounts were perhaps written to suggest that some, on account of their merit, would be spared the sight of the demonic form of Death (see Chapter V.ii). Quotations 4 and 5, two versions of the death of Joseph the Carpenter, were written in the first person, with Christ as narrator. In these accounts, Christ and Death were the two figures which appeared to Joseph, demonstrating that the power to command or transform Death was the prerogative of the divine. The victory over Death, however, was represented as occurring, not in man, but as an event enacted by two 'deities', external to him.

3   The Meeting with Those in Heaven

The meeting of the seer with the dead, as depicted in the *Odyssey*[26] and in the *Aeneid*,[27] was the occasion of prophetic utterances. Similarly, oracular pronouncements from the dead were a feature of ancient Egyptian ritual. The dead of the pre-Christian world, generally, were regarded as having fulfilled their destiny; in Egypt, one term for death was 'fulfilling the will of Rē'.[28] Nevertheless, destiny, ruled by the stars, was not always consistent with human notions of justice, and the dead were feared by the living as liable to seek either vengeance or redress of their wrongs. In contrast, in the *Apocalypse of Paul*, the message of those of heaven was that those on whom pain or injustice were inflicted on earth would not be afflicted in the next world (8; see also Chapter V). A feature of late Christian apocalypses was the embracing of the 'living' by the 'dead' (Narratives 3, 4, 6, 9, 10, 11). In Egyptian funerary paintings, the dead were shown being embraced by the gods of the underworld. In the Odyssey[26] and the Aeneid,[27] embraces between the living and the dead were represented as impossible. The reunion in heaven thus implied a change of attitude of the living towards the dead and the overcoming of the separation between the two worlds. The status of the living was still, however, shown as dependent on the judgment of the dead. In the earlier apocalypses, no such reunions between the living and the dead were depicted; in *I Enoch*,[29] the righteous were assured only of becoming companions of the hosts of heaven. In the Jewish writings, the 'Age to Come' was represented in terms of a new Paradise; only with Saint Paul[30] did Adam take his place in this new Garden of Eden.

The passage of the soul through the regions of heaven was, in the Mithraic cult,[31] regarded as being barred by seven gates, each of a metal corresponding to a planet. The seventh gate, that of the sphere of the sun, was of gold. The image of heaven, as having gates of gold, was also used by Christian writers (Narrative 11). The alternate rejoicing and weeping of those at the gates of heaven (4, 11) was imagery similar to that of the *Apocalypse of Abraham*. In the latter, Adam, the First Man, seeing the righteous and wicked entering the two gates of heaven, alternately rejoiced and wept:

So Michael turned the chariot, and brought Abraham to the east, to the first gate of heaven. And Abraham saw two ways, the one way narrow and compressed, and the other broad and spacious; and there also he saw two gates, one gate broad on the broad way, and one gate narrow on the narrow way. And outside the two gates there I saw a man seated upon a golden throne, and the appearance of that man was terrible, like unto that of the Lord. And I saw many souls being driven by angels and led in through the broad gate; and other souls I saw, few in number, that were being borne by angels through the narrow gate. And when the marvellous being who sat upon the Golden throne saw few entering in through the narrow gate, but many entering in through the broad gate, straightway that marvellous man did pluck the hairs of his head . . . and hurled himself on the ground from his throne, weeping and wailing. And when he saw many souls entering through the narrow gate, then he arose from the ground and sat upon his throne, rejoicing and exulting with great jubilation. Then Abraham asked the chief-captain: My Lord, who is this all-marvellous man, who is in such majesty, and sometimes weeps and wails, and sometimes rejoices and exults? The (bodiless one) said: This is Adam, the first created man, who is in such majesty, and he beholds the world, for all are sprung from him.

Testament of Abraham, XI (Box, p. 17)

The notion that those of heaven were concerned with the welfare of the living became widespread in later Christian times.

Gates separating the regions of the underworld were an important feature of Egyptian funerary texts. Passage through these gates depended on the pronouncement of the correct names or spells. In the *Ascension of Isaiah*, the descent of the Lord past the gates of the three lowest heavens was said to have been achieved by giving the password.[32] In the *Apocalypse of Paul*, as in the *Ascension of Isaiah*, the gates were guarded by angels whose role was the recognition of those who passed. At the gates of heaven, in Narrative 11, were tablets on which were inscribed the names of the righteous, who thus were enabled to enter. In the *Apocalypse of Elias*, the judgment of the dead was depicted as taking place at the gate of heaven, on the basis of their deeds written on scrolls by the angel of the Accuser:

I said to the Angel: 'Who are these?' He said: 'These are the angels of the Lord Almighty who are writing all the good works of the Righteous upon (their) scroll, (sitting) before the Gate of Heaven. Then I (am wont) to take them by the hand to bring them (with me) before the Lord Almighty that He should write their names in the Book of the Living.

Apocalypse of Elias, 3.3

In some accounts of the journey through the places of heaven, it was not the view of the universe which was changed, but the seer himself. Spells for the transformation of the deceased into the forms which he wished to assume were found in the Egyptian *Book of the Dead*.[33] Transformations into every form they desired was the reward foretold for the righteous in *II Baruch*:

> For they shall behold the world which is now invisible to them, and they shall behold the time which is now hidden from them; and time shall no longer age them.
> For in the heights of that world shall they dwell, and they shall be made like unto the angels, and be made equal to the stars, and they shall be changed into every form they desire, from beauty into loveliness, and from light into the splendour of glory.
>
> *II Baruch*, 51.8–10 (Charles)

In *II Enoch*, the effect of the anointing and robing of the seer, which was performed in heaven, was a transformation of his appearance:

> And the Lord said to Michael: 'Go and take Enoch from out his earthly garments, and anoint him with my sweet ointment, and put him into the garments of My glory.'
> And Michael did thus, as the Lord told him. He anointed me, and dressed me, and the appearance of that ointment is more than the great light, and his ointment is like sweet dew, and its smell mild, shining like the sun's ray, and I looked at myself, and was like one of his glorious ones.
>
> *II Enoch*, 22A.8–10 (Charles)

In Narrative 14, the effect of the heavenly garments in transforming the Patriarchs was described. In the *Ascension of Isaiah*, a transformation was said to have taken place at each heaven in turn:

> ... for the glory of my appearance was undergoing transformation as I ascended to each heaven in turn.
>
> *Ascension of Isaiah*, VII.25 (Charles)

The gates and regions of heaven were thus the context for describing the effects of divine transformations, both on those entering and on those within (see also the *Apocalypse of Elias*).[34]

II AMENTE

Preliminary Considerations

In the ancient Egyptian religion, the human body was the centre of reference for all experience. In life, man felt himself to be 'inside' the body of the universe whose various parts surrounded him. The Afterlife was the experience of the organs of his own body. The twelfth division of the *Book of Gates*,[35] the text describing the divisions of the *Dēt*, or Afterlife, showed a picture of Osiris with his body bent backwards so that his toes touched his head. Within the circle, so formed, was written: 'Osiris, whose circuit is the *Dēt*.' The deified individual, or Osiris, thus contained his experience of the Afterlife, or *Dēt*, within his own body. At death, the individual participated in the disintegration of his own body as, in life, he had entered into the processes of the outer world. His experience of the divine was thus 'bound' to physiological processes and rhythms. For the Egyptian, the animal perhaps typified perfection, because, having no individual consciousness, it was completely absorbed in its own psycho-physiological processes.

In the *Pistis Sophia*, the notion of man bound or enclosed within the circle of his body was described in terms of a Zodiac of hostile powers. The 'outer darkness' was depicted as a dragon, with its tail in its mouth, whose body contained twelve 'Treasuries' of punishments. The Rulers of the Treasuries, like those of the corresponding signs of the Zodiac, had animal faces which 'changed' according to the hour:

Maria continued, she said to Jesus, My Lord, of what type is the Outer Darkness, or else rather, how many places of punishment are there in it? Then Jesus answered, He said to Maria, The Outer Darkness is a great dragon with his tail in his mouth, outside the whole world and it surrounds the whole world, with a multitude of places of judgment within it, having twelve Treasuries of cruel punishments, with a Ruler in every treasury, the faces of the Rulers being different from one another. And the first Ruler who is in the First Treasury (has) a face of a crocodile with his tail within his mouth, with all ice coming forth from the mouth of the dragon, with all cold, with all fever, with every sickness which changes. The authentic name of this one is called Enkhthonin. And the Ruler who is in the second Treasury, a face of a cat is his authentic face. He is called in their place Kharakhar. And the Ruler who is in the third Treasury, a face of a dog is his authentic face. He is called in their place, Arkharokh. And the Ruler who is in the fourth Treasury, a face of a snake is his authentic face. He is called in their place, Akhrokhar. And the Ruler who is in the fifth Treasury, a face of a black calf is his authentic face. He is called in their place, Markhour. And the Ruler who is in the sixth Treasury, a face of a mountain pig is his authentic face. He is called in their place Lamkhamor. And the Ruler who is in the seventh Treasury, a face of a bear is his authentic face. He is called by his authentic name in their place, Lukhar. And the Ruler in the eighth Treasury, a face of a vulture is his authentic face. He is called by his name in their place, Laraokh. And the Ruler

162

in the ninth Treasury, a face of a basilisk is his authentic face. He is called by his name in their place, Arkeokh. And in the tenth Treasury, there are a multitude of Rulers with seven heads of dragons to each one of them (as) their authentic faces. And he who is over them all is called in their place Zarmarokh. And of the eleventh Treasury, there are a multitude of Rulers of that place with seven heads with a face of a cat to each one of them as their authentic faces. And the great one who is over them is called in their place Rokhar. And in the twelfth Treasury, there are a multitude of Rulers who are exceedingly many, with seven heads with a face of a dog to each one of them as their authentic faces. And the great one who is over them is called in their place Khremor. These rulers therefore of these twelve Treasuries are within the dragon of the outer darkness. And to each one of them there is a name according to (the) hour. Each one of them changes his face according to (the) hour. And also these twelve Treasuries have, each one of them, a door which is open to the Height, so that the dragon of the Outer Darkness has twelve Treasuries of darkness, there being a door to every Treasury which is open to the Height. And there is an angel of the Height who watches each one of the doors of the Treasuries.

Pistis Sophia, 287a–289a.

In ancient Egypt, the dissolution of the human body at death was the basis of the demonic hallucinatory experiences, preserved in the texts concerning the Afterlife. Thus the passage of the Sun, past the favourable and hostile powers occupying this 'invisible' ecliptic, was the expression of the soul's 'view' of the body as both its dwelling place and its destroyer. The ascetic released himself from the domination of his own inner processes and rhythms. He exposed himself to all the situations liable to produce the disturbances and changes which normally occurred at death. Self-mortification was the means by which the tendency to hallucination, with dissociation of consciousness from sensory experience, was overcome. By constantly repeated efforts, conscious disregard of pain was achieved, together with detachment of the imagination from physiological processes (see Chapter I.III.2). In the ancient religion, the twelve divisions of *Amente*, or the *Dēt*, were, nevertheless, the path to experience of the divine for the deceased. The twelve Treasuries of the dragon of outer darkness of the *Pistis Sophia* were said each to have a door to the Height. The ascetic regarded the conflict with the demons as an essential preliminary to attainment.

Apocalyptic Judaism recognised the dominance on man exercised by the stellar cults. The dependence was attributed to external powers in the stars and in the elements of the universe. The remedy for man's psychic situation was seen in terms of a dissolution of the Zodiac and the elements. This event was given an eschatological meaning in terms of the future of the Jewish people. Fire, as the element, man's physical experience of which was pain, was depicted as the instrument of divine justice. In *I Enoch*, the luminaries of heaven were seen in the context of a river of fire:

> And they took and brought me to a place in which those who were there were like flaming fire, and, when they wished, they appeared as men. And they brought me to the place of darkness, and to a mountain, the point of whose summit reached to heaven. And I saw the places of the luminaries and the treasuries of the stars and of the thunder, and in the uttermost depths, where were a fiery bow and arrows and their quiver, and a fiery sword, and all the lightnings. And they took me to the living waters, and to the fire of the west, which receives every setting of the sun. And I came to a river of fire in which the fire flows like water and discharges itself into the great sea towards the west.
>
> *I Enoch*, 17.1–6 (Charles)

Both the stars, who were said to have transgressed, and their ruling angels were condemned to punishment by fire:

> And I proceeded to where things were chaotic. And I saw something horrible: I saw neither a heaven above nor a firmly founded earth, but a place chaotic and horrible. And there I saw seven stars of the heaven bound together in it, like great mountains and burning with fire. . . . Then said Uriel, one of the holy angels, who was with me, and was chief over them, and said: '. . . These are the number of the stars of heaven, which have transgressed the commandment of the Lord, and are bound here till ten thousand years, the time entailed by their sins, are consummated.' And from thence I went to another place, which was still more horrible than the former, and I saw a horrible thing; A great fire there which burnt and blazed, and the place was cleft as far as the abyss, being full of great descending columns of fire: neither its extent or magnitude could I see, nor could I conjecture. . . . And he (Uriel) said unto me: 'This is the prison of the angels, and here they will be imprisoned for ever.'
>
> *I Enoch*, 21.1–10 (Charles)

The righteous archangels were said to be the agents by which the chief of the unrighteous angels and his 'hosts' were cast into the fiery abyss:

> And I looked and turned to another part of the earth, and saw there a deep valley with burning fire. . . . And I asked the angel of peace

who went with me, saying: 'For whom are these chains being prepared?' And he said unto me: 'These are being prepared for the hosts of Azazel, so that they may take them and cast them into the abyss of complete condemnation, and they shall cover their jaws with rough stones as the Lord of Spirits commanded.

And Michael, and Gabriel, and Raphael, and Phanuel shall take hold of them on that great day, and cast them on that day into the burning furnace, that the Lord of Spirits may take vengeance on them for their unrighteousness in becoming subject to Satan and leading astray those who dwell on the earth.

I Enoch, 54.1–6 (Charles)

The punishment of the angels who had led mankind astray was associated with destruction of the elements of the earth:

And I saw that valley in which there was a great convulsion and a convulsion of the waters. And when all this took place, from that fiery molten metal and from the convulsion . . . that valley of the angels who had led astray (mankind) burned beneath that land. And through its valleys proceed streams of fire, where these angels are punished who had led astray those who dwell upon the earth.

I Enoch, 67.5–7 (Charles)

The Qumran community saw themselves as the agents through which the overthrow of the disobedient angelic and stellar powers would be effected. The powers of evil in the world were identified as the seven nations who were subject to the 'fallen' planetary angels:

By the hand of Thine anointed, who discerned Thy testimonies, Thou hast revealed to us the (times) of the battles of Thy hands that Thou mayest glorify Thyself in our enemies by levelling the hordes of Satan, the seven nations of vanity, by the hand of Thy poor whom Thou hast redeemed.

The War Rule, XI (Vermes, p. 138)

A battle was depicted, lasting forty years, between the powers of Light and of Darkness, in which the community, organised as the hosts of heaven, participated:

. . . for that shall be the day appointed from ancient times for the battle of destruction of the sons of darkness. At that time, the assembly of gods and the hosts of men shall battle with the company of darkness amid the shouts of a mighty multitude and the clamour of gods and men to (make manifest) the might of God. . . . In three lots shall the sons of light brace themselves in battle to strike down

12

iniquity, and in three lots shall Satan's host gird itself to thrust back the company (of God. And when the hearts of the detach) ments of foot-soldiers faint, then shall the might of God fortify (the heart of the sons of light). And with the seventh lot, the mighty hand of God shall bring down (the army of Satan, and all) the angels of his kingdom, and all the members (of his company in everlasting destruction).

The War Rule, I (Vermes, p. 124)

The imagery of warfare was apparently used for the ritual of the community.[36]

Christian apocalyptic writings, like those of Judaism, contained the imagery of a Last Judgment, followed by the destruction of the universe, prior to a final state of blessedness; (see Chapter III.IV: 'Preliminary Considerations', pp. 123–124). In the early texts, the stars were included with the elements involved in this event:

From east and west and north and south. And then a great river of burning fire shall flow down from heaven and consume every place, earth and great ocean and the grey-blue sea, lakes and rivers, springs and relentless Hades and the heavenly sphere. And the lights of heaven shall be dashed together into a form all-desolate; for the stars shall all fall from heaven into the sea. And all souls of men shall gnash with their teeth, burning in the river of pitch and the raging fire.

Christian Sibyllines, II.195, 200 (Wilson, II, p. 714)

The Treasuries (of the sun, moon and stars) were said to appear at the Last Judgment:

Immediately, when Mary sat upon the judgment seat, the earth was moved, the thunders sounded, the lightnings flashed. The dead arose, they came forth from the tombs, they came to the judgment seat, they stood and they did not speak. The Abyss appeared. The Treasuries and the (regions of) Tartarus appeared. The avenging angels stood like flames of fire. The Treasuries full of pitch and the places of brimstone appeared. And Michael came with his angels, some having crowns in their hands and others robes.

Of the Life of the Virgin, III (Robinson, pp. 22–24)

The four directions of space were described as sources of destruction (see the description of Abbaton in I.2):

Behold—clouds from the east and from the north right to the south. And their appearance was exceeding terrible, full of wrath and storm. . . .

166

THE REPRESENTATION OF NEGATIVE EXPERIENCES

... And after that many clouds
from the south and from the north and another part from the west
shall rise up. ...
And there shall rise up great and strong clouds, full of wrath and
storm, to destroy the whole earth and its inhabitants.

VI Ezra, 34–40 (Wilson, II, pp. 697–698)

The last days, in the *Apocalypse of Peter*, were described as a condition of
total chaos, in which cataracts of fire dissolved the heavens and the earth:

Behold now what they shall experience in the last days, when the day
of God comes.
... cataracts of fire shall be let loose; and obscurity and darkness
shall come up and cover and veil the entire world, and the waters
shall be changed and transformed into coals of fire, and all that is
in it shall burn and the sea shall become fire; under the heaven there
shall be a fierce fire that shall not be put out and it flows for the
judgment of wrath. And the stars shall be melted by the flames of
fire, as if they had not been created, and the fastnesses of heaven shall
pass away for want of water and become as though they had not been
created. And the lightnings of heaven shall be no more and by their
enchantment, they shall alarm the world. And the spirits of the dead
bodies shall be like to them and at the command of God will become
fire. And as soon as the whole creation is dissolved, the men who are
in the east shall flee to the west (and those in the west) to the east;
those that are in the south shall flee to the north and those in the
(north to the) south, and everywhere will the wrath of the fearful fire
overtake them; and an unquenchable flame shall drive them and
bring them to the judgment of wrath in the stream of unquenchable
fire which flows, flaming with fire.

Apocalypse of Peter (Ethiopic), 4, 5 (Wilson, II, pp. 670–1)

In the Last Judgment, the imagery of the demonic assaults in the life
after death was transferred from the individual to the universe. Man's
own destructive powers were attributed to the universe, together with
the responsibility for his attachment to his physical organism. Future
blessedness was therefore seen to be preceded by an obliteration of the
physical world. The final image, therefore, was that of attainment of the
divine at the cost of abolishing consciousness.

1   The Torments

Tartarus, as an abyss of the earth, was said by Plato to have been
known to Homer:

And there are everlasting rivers of huge size under the earth, flowing with hot and cold water; and there is much fire, and great rivers of fire, and many streams of mud. . . . Now a kind of oscillation within the earth moves all these up and down. And the nature of the oscillation is as follows: One of the chasms of the earth is greater than the rest, and is bored right through the whole earth; this is the one which Homer means when he says: 'Far off, the lowest abyss beneath the earth'; and which elsewhere he and many other poets have called Tartarus.

Plato, Phaedo, 111D–112A

Phlegethon, the river of fire of the underworld, was an entity whose description, in the literature of classical Greece, was perhaps based on actual rivers of volcanic origin[37]:

Suddenly Aeneas looks back, and under a cliff on the left sees a broad castle, girt with triple wall and encircled with a rushing flood of torrent flames—Tartarean Phlegethon that rolls along thundering rocks. In front stands the huge gate, and pillars of solid adamant, that no might of man, nay not even the sons of heaven, may uproot in war; there stands the iron tower, soaring high, and Tisiphone, sitting girt with bloody pall, keeps sleepless watch o'er the portal night and day. Therefrom are heard groans and the sounds of the savage lash; withal, the clank of iron and dragging of chains. Aeneas stopped, rooted to the spot in terror of the din.

Virgil, Aeneid, VI.548

The underworld of mythology and initiation cults, with its avenging deities and animal forms, was described by Virgil:

Gnosian Rhadamanthus holds here his iron sway; he chastises, and hears the tale of guilt, exacting confession of crimes, whenever in the world above any man, . . . has put off atonement for sin until death's late hour. Straightway avenging Tisiphone, girt with the lash, leaps on the guilty to scourge them, and with left hand brandishing her grim snakes, calls on her savage sister band. Then at last, grating on harsh, jarring hinge, the infernal gates open. Seest thou what sentry sits in the doorway? What shape guards the threshold? The monstrous Hydra, still fiercer, with her fifty black gaping throats, dwells within. Then Tartarus itself yawns sheer down, stretching into the gloom twice as far as is yon sky's upward view to heavenly Olympus.

Virgil, Aeneid, VI.566

The Afterlife was depicted, in the Christian Sibylline writings, in the terms of classical Greek literature. Gehenna was, however, named in place of Phlegethon:

The angels of the immortal, everlasting God shall punish fearfully with flaming whips, binding them tightly about with fiery chains and unbreakable fetters; then in the dead of night shall they be flung into Gehenna among the beasts of Tartarus, many and fearful, where darkness has no measure. But when they have laid many torments upon all whose heart was evil, later again the fiery wheel from the great river shall close in upon them.

Christian Sibyllines, II.285–295 (Wilson, II, p. 717)

The designation of Gehenna and Tartarus as places of punishment was also made by Hippolytus.[38]

The indirect influence of Greek sources on the imagery of Christian writings can be seen in descriptions of the punishments. The association of punishment with the wheel of Necessity was made by Plato:

Now of this kind, he said, were the punishments and penalties, and the rewards corresponding to them. Each company passed seven days in the meadow, and on the eighth they had to rise up and go on their way, and after four days they came to a place whence they could look down on a straight beam of light, extended like a pillar through heaven and earth, more like the rainbow than anything else, but brighter and purer. To this they came after a day's journey, and there from the middle of the light they saw extended from heaven the ends of the chains which compose it. For this light chains heaven, holding together the whole circumference as under-girders bind a trireme. And from those ends is hung the spindle of Necessity, by means of which all the circles revolve.

Plato, *Republic*, X.616

The imagery of the column round which men circulated appeared in the description of the Afterlife in the biography of Pachomius (1). The wheel to which men were bound re-appeared in later writings as an instrument of punishment:

Some roll a huge stone, or hang outstretched on spokes of wheels;

Virgil, *Aeneid*, VI.616

In Christian apocalypses, the wheel was depicted as fiery (16, 18):

And there are wheels of fire, and men and women hung thereon by the power of their whirling.

Apocalypse of Peter (Ethiopic) 12 (Wilson, II, p. 678)

Darkness, as a condition of the life after death, was a feature of Jewish writings. *Sheol* was depicted in the Old Testament as a place of darkness. In *II Enoch* (2, 3), the place of torment of those imprisoned was said to be in darkness. Darkness was described in the Christian narratives 1, 5, 6. The notion of the dead as shades appears in the Old Testament. In Homer, their insubstantial quality was in itself a torment to the dead. (See p. 159.) The unreality and dreamlike quality of the images seen in Tartarus was described in the *Aeneid*:

> In the midst an elm, shadowy and vast, spreads her boughs and aged arms, the home which, men say, false Dreams hold here and there, clinging under every leaf. And many monstrous forms besides of various beasts are stalled at the doors, Centaurs and double-shaped Scyllas, and the hundredfold Briareus, and the beast of Lerna, hissing horribly, and the Chimaera armed with flame, Gorgons and Harpies, and the shape of the three-bodied shade. Here on a sudden, in trembling terror, Aeneas grasps his sword, and turns the naked edge against their coming; and did not his wise companion warn him that these were but faint, bodiless lives, flitting under a hollow semblance of form, he had rushed upon them and vainly cleft shadows with steel.
>
> Virgil, *Aeneid*, VI.282

The depiction of pits as places of punishment appeared in ancient Egyptian descriptions of the Afterlife.[39] Their occurrence in the *Apocalypse of Paul* is suggestive evidence of the Egyptian origin of this document. Rivers and pits of fire and other tortures were a feature of Christian Egyptian writings on places of punishment (4–9, 15).

The infliction of punishment in Tartarus by executioners of justice of fiery appearance was described by Plato:

> And whenever any one of those who had sunk into incurable wickedness, or any one who had not paid his punishment in full, tried to ascend, the mouth bellowed. And then, he said, fierce men, like coals of fire to look upon, who were standing by and had heard the sound came forward, and some they took in their arms and dragged away, but Ardiaeus and others they bound hand and foot and head, threw them down, and flayed them. They dragged them out of the way to a place apart, and there carded them on thorns, saying to all that passed that they were being taken away to be plunged into Tartarus, and explaining why this was done to them.
>
> Plato, *Republic*, X.615

In the Jewish *Testament of Abraham*, pitiless angels were depicted with fiery faces:

> And while I was thus speaking, Lo, two angels fiery in visage and pitiless in intent, and harsh in looks, were even (now) driving on a thousand souls, pitilessly beating them with fiery lashes.
>
> *Testament of Abraham*, XII (Box, p. 19)

THE REPRESENTATION OF NEGATIVE EXPERIENCES

In the Christian *Apocalypse of Elias*, the description of the avenging angels resembled that of the Greek Erinyes (see p. 53):

> I now walked with the Angel of the Lord, I looked before me, I saw a place there (filled) with a thousand and ten thousand times ten thousand angels who are going within by means of it; their faces being like leopards, their teeth outside their mouths (like wild swine), their eyes clouded with blood, their hair spread out like the hair of women, having whips of fire in their hands.
>
> *Apocalypse of Elias*, 4.13

Tormenting angels were said to rejoice in inflicting punishment and to be pitiless (4, 5, 8, 11).

The Angel of the Abyss, like Abbadon, the Angel of Death, appeared with a glorious aspect to the righteous:

> Then I rose, I stood up, I saw a great angel who was standing before me, whose face gave light like the rays of the sun in his glory, whose face was like Him who is complete in its glory, and he was girded with a girdle of gold upon his breast, his feet were like copper which is melted in the fire.
>
> When I saw him, I rejoiced, because I thought that the Lord Almighty was He who had come to visit me. I cast myself down upon my face, I worshipped him. He said to me: 'Take heed, do not worship me. I am not the Lord the Almighty, but I am the great Angel Eremiel, who dwells below over the abyss and *Amente* in which all the souls are enclosed from the end of the Deluge which happened upon the earth until today.' [40]
>
> *Apocalypse of Elias*, 9.11

He also appeared as a fiery tormenting angel (15). In the *Apocalypse of Paul*, the abyss which was sealed with seven seals was opened by its guardian in order that the apostle might see it by virtue of his merit. The imagery of the Angel of the Abyss suggests that, like the figure of Death, this angel represented the experience of the Zodiac. In the *Apocalypse of Paul*, the opening of the Abyss by an angel was imagery suggesting the control and confinement of demonic by divine powers. Both, however, were represented as situated external to man. In the *Apocalypse of Elias*, the abyss which held the souls of men was said to be controlled by an angel.

2 *The Remission of Punishments*

It has been suggested that an essential achievement of the ascetic life was the ability to withstand demonic and hallucinatory experiences, arising in consequence of isolation or self-mortification. Attainment, for the individual, was the ability to 'immerse' himself in any of the 'elements' of the sense world without losing conscious control of his imagination. Self-control enabled him to guard himself against unwanted experiences and to apprehend the world in the dimension of his own choosing.

On this basis, those who were unable, of themselves, to achieve the separation of the imagination from physical experience, were protected against disturbing experiences through the rituals of the Church. In proportion as the Church gained control over men's minds and imaginations, abolition of demonic experiences in relation to the physical world could be achieved through ritual. When Baptism was established as essential for salvation, subjection of the imagination to the Church became the pre-condition of freedom from demonic attacks. Only those 'sealed' by Baptism were thought to partake of Eternal Life.[41] According to Clement, the gnostics also had a ritual of Baptism. It had the acknowledged purpose of liberating men from domination by the physical Zodiac. It also required the knowledge of man's divine origin:

> Until baptism, they say, Fate is real, but after it the astrologists are no longer right. But it is not only the washing that is liberating, but the knowledge of who we were, and what we have become, where we were or where we were placed, whither we hasten, from what we are redeemed, what birth is and what rebirth.
>
> Clement, *Excerpta ex Theodoto*, 78.1–2

In the dialogue between priest and monk, in the *Questions of Theodore*,[42] the attitude of the Church, in the seventh century, to Baptism is shown:

> The priest said: 'If he is a man who was never baptised (but) was doing works pleasing to God, praying, fasting, alms-giving, will he also be taken down to *Amente*?'
> The bishop said: 'Has he prayed like Jeremiah, the prophet, who spent all the time when he was within the tomb, praying to God until he brought back the captives of the Children of Israel to Jerusalem? Or has he given alms like Job who said: "I have never turned away a man who begged from me"? Or has he received strangers like Abraham? Or has he fasted like Moses who spent forty days fasting until God gave the Law to him? And all these descended into *Amente* because they did not receive baptism, until the Son of God came forth from His Place without limits and incarnated in the Holy Virgin, was crucified, went down to *Amente*, and brought them all up. . . . Behold, here are Abraham and Isaac and Jacob and Moses and the prophets.

They all descended into *Amente*, they who spoke with God face to face. And their good works were not able to save them because they had not received baptism.'

Questions of Theodore, 3 (Van Lantschoot, p. 19)

Evidence that, as a result of the *Descensus*, Adam and the Patriarchs of the Old Testament were regarded as having been raised to heaven, is found in many apocryphal texts.[43]

The recalling to life of pagans, in order to give them Baptism, was described in Quotations 13, 14 and 16. These accounts suggest that, for salvation, Baptism was regarded as effective even after death (see Section III.III.3; 23, 24). In Quotations 1–5 and 13–16, remission of punishments, for those in the Afterlife, was effected or witnessed by an ascetic or martyr. These accounts involved the recalling to life of a dead person, who described his experiences in *Amente*. Similar stories were current in pre-Christian Egypt, of which the first *Tale of Khamuas*[44] is an example. The deceased returned to inform the living of the wrongs to which they had been subjected in life. The influence of the prayers of the living on the fate of the deceased, in their passage through *Amente*, has been discussed in connection with the ancient funerary ritual (p. 151). In Quotations 3–5, the prayers of the holy man were shown to have been effective in relation to the Christian After-life. The respite on the Sabbath and Lord's Day, granted to those in the torments (2, 13, 14, 17), may perhaps have been an image representing that the infliction of punishments was ultimately controlled from heaven and not from Amente.

The righteous dead themselves were regarded as being able to procure remission of punishment for those in *Amente*. In some Jewish and Christian apocalypses, the Patriarchs in heaven were depicted as intercessors:

Abraham said to the chief-captain: What is lacking to the soul for it to be saved? The chief-captain said: If it win one righteousness over and above its sins it enters into salvation. Abraham said to the chief-captain: Come hither, chief-captain Michael, let us make a prayer on behalf of this soul, and see if God will hearken unto us.

Testament of Abraham, XIV (Box, p. 23)

The cult of angels as intercessors is discussed in Chapter III.II. p. 103. The archangel Michael was regarded as the chief intercessor on behalf, both of mankind and of the world of nature (6). In the *Apocalypse of Elias*,[45] Michael was associated with the Patriarchs in interceding for those in the punishments.

173

3 Purification after Death

The River of Fire and the Acherusian Lake, according to the context in which they appeared, held various meanings in Christian times. If the use of these terms is traced to classical literature, Acheron and Pyriphlegethon can be seen to have been two of the three rivers to which went the souls of the dead:

Now these streams are many and great and of all sorts, but among the many are four streams, the greatest and outermost of which is called Oceanus, which flows round in a circle, and opposite this, flowing in the opposite direction, is Acheron, which flows through various desert places and, passing under the earth, comes to the Acherusian lake. To this lake the souls of most of the dead go and, after remaining there the appointed time, which is for some longer and for others shorter, are sent back to be born again into living beings. The third river flows out between these two. . . . This is the river which is called Pyriphlegethon, and the streams of lava which spout up at various places on each are offshoots from it. Opposite this the fourth river issues, . . . called the Stygian river, and the lake which it forms by flowing in is the Styx. And . . . circling round in the direction opposed to that of Pyriphlegethon, it meets it coming from the other way in the Acherusian lake.

Plato, *Phaedo*, 112E–113C

The crossing of the Acheron, as depicted by Virgil, was effected by the ferry of the boatman Charon:

Hence a road leads to the waters of Tartarean Acheron. Here, thick with mire and of fathomless flood, a whirlpool seethes and belches into Cocytus all its sand. A grim warden guards these waters and streams, terrible in his squalor—Charon, on whose chin lies a mass of unkept, hoary hair; his eyes are staring orbs of flame; his squalid garb hangs by a knot from his shoulders. Unaided, he poles the boat, tends the sails, and in his murky craft convoys the dead—now aged, but a god's old age is hardy and green. Hither rushed all the throng, streaming to the banks; mothers and men and bodies of high-souled heroes, their life now done, boys and unwedded girls, and sons placed on the pyre before their father's eyes; thick as the leaves of the forest that at autumn's first frost dropping fall, and thick as the birds. . . . They stood, pleading to be the first ferried across and stretched out hands in yearning for the farther shore. But the surly boat-man takes now these, now those, while others he thrusts apart, back from the brink.

Virgil, *Aeneid*, VI.295

The Acherusian Lake was said by Plato to be a place of punishment in which the wronged decided the term of punishment of the wrong-doers:

Now when the dead have come to the place where each is led by his genius, first they are judged and sentenced, as they have lived well and piously, or not. And those who are found to have lived neither well nor ill, go to the Acheron, and embarking upon vessels provided for them, arrive in them at the lake; there they dwell and are purified, and if they have done any wrong they are absolved by paying the penalty for their wrong doings, and for their good deeds they receive rewards, each according to his merits. But those who appear to be incurable . . . are cast by their fitting destiny into Tartarus, whence they never emerge. Those, however, who are curable, . . . these must needs be thrown into Tartarus, and when they have been there a year the wave casts them out, . . . and when they have been brought by the current to the Acherusian lake, they shout and cry out, calling to those whom they have slain or outraged, begging and beseeching them to be gracious and let them come out into the lake; and if they prevail they come out and cease from their ills, but if not, they are borne away again to Tartarus and thence back into the rivers, and this goes on until they prevail upon those whom they have wronged; for this is the penalty imposed upon them by the judges.

Plato, *Phaedo*, 113D–114B

To the desert ascetics, the River of Fire was, perhaps, a general term which covered the demonic experiences, to which those who abandoned their ancient religion were subject. The crossing of, or immersion in, the River of Fire was regarded as the experience which all must undergo in the 'life after death' (see p. 38). In the present quotations, the Acherusian Lake appeared to have a similar connotation to the River of Fire. Crossing of the River of Fire (1, 4, 6) and of the Acherusian Lake (4) was made by boat. Baptism in the River of Fire (1) and washing in the Acherusian Lake (4) were performed after the crossing. Triple immersion in the Lake of Fire (7) and in the Acherusian Lake (6) were also mentioned in the Jewish *Apocalypse of Moses*:

But when the angels had said these words, lo, there came one of the seraphim with six wings, and snatched up Adam and carried him off to the Acherusian lake, and washed him thrice, in the presence of God.

Apocalypsis Mosis, 37.3 (Charles)

In the above mentioned quotations, the ability to cross the River or Lake of Fire was shown as evidence of divine protection, achieved in

175

various ways. The crossing by boat (1, 2) was said to be the reward for services to the shrine of John the Baptist. In the *Apocalypse of Elias*, the boat journey, as in ancient Egyptian texts, followed a judgment in which an Accuser was overcome:

> They gave me their hand, they mounted me in that boat and they began to sing before me, namely a thousand times a thousand and ten thousand times ten thousand angels. I also clothed myself in an angelic garment. I saw all the angels there as they were praying. I also began to pray with them together. I understood their language in which they were speaking with me: 'Now therefore, my son this is the conflict (that) the good and the evil are weighed in a scales.'
>
> Then a great angel came forth with a trumpet of gold in his hand. He began to blow it three times above my head, while he spoke thus: 'Be strong thou who hast been strong. Be powerful thou who hast been powerful. For thou hast overcome the Accuser, thou hast come forth from the Abyss and *Amente*. Thou shalt cross now at the Crossing-place. For thy name is written in the Book of the Living.'
>
> *Apocalypse of Elias*, 13.1–14.6

In Quotation 3, the martyr protected himself, by a prayer of exorcism, from the River of Fire. A similar form of prayer was spoken by the Virgin on her death-bed:

> Now therefore, my Lord and my God, the hour has come that thou shouldst come to me and have mercy on me and remove from me the stones of stumbling and all the changing faces. Let those that are on thy left hand fall before me, and those on the right stand up with joy. Let all the powers of darkness be ashamed today, because they have found nothing of theirs on me. Open to me the gates of righteousness, and I will enter into them and be manifested to the face of my God. Let the Dragon hide himself before me, as he sees me coming boldly to thee, the only true God. Let the River of Fire, in which are tested the two portions, the righteous and the sinners, be still until I pass by it.
>
> *Of the Life of the Virgin*, IV (Robinson, p. 38)

As a result of these measures, the River of Fire was either not felt at all, or the nature of the experience was altered (1, 6).

Triple immersion, washing or Baptism, in these quotations, were depicted as experiences of the life after death. With the exception of that in Quotation 7, they were said to have taken place before entering the places of heaven. In Quotation 7, the purification took place in heaven, in a vision prior to the martyrdom on earth. The purificatory immersion of earthly Baptism was a ritual exorcism of the physical body and of the water in which the body was immersed. In the rite of the Coptic Church, the body of the candidate was anointed in thirty-six places (the number of the decans of the Zodiac).[46] The prayer for the sanctification of the water recalled the 'breaking of the head of the dragon upon the water'.[47] The control of the human soul and imagination, in relation to experiences of the demonic world, was thus assumed by the Church. The individual was ritually isolated from his old 'physical' rapport with the universe and with his fellow men. In the new situation, he was 'protected' from negative repercussions of his actions in this life and from direct experience of either the demonic or the divine.

This confrontation was 'postponed' until the life after death. In Christian writings, as in those of Judaism, demonic attacks were presented as the punishments awaiting those who disobeyed authority. As seen in the present narratives, evasion of these punishments was the constant preoccupation of some individuals. In the exorcism of Baptism, the Church performed an act by which the individual transferred his allegiance from one authority to another. The obliteration of the demonic world by proxy still left the individual subject to powers inside and outside himself.

CONCLUSION

Egyptian ritual was based on the subjective correspondence between the rhythms of the sun, moon and stars and the physiological rhythms of the body. Psychic attachment to the processes of the body was the basis of the ancient Egyptian religious experience. Breakdown in bodily functioning, either self-induced or due to natural causes, produced a state of psychic disintegration. Prevention of this state with its attendant hallucinatory manifestations was the purpose of the funerary cults. The practice of mummification was probably based on the view that if the body was kept intact, the soul would be preserved from demonic experiences in the Afterlife.

Demonic experience was essentially one of destructive powers whose source appeared, to the ancient world, to be external to man. These negative experiences were regarded as inevitable, but to arise in consequence of inability or failure to perform the right ritual. In Judaism, negative experiences were attributed to the Deity and were regarded as evidence of his wrath. The association of negative experiences with ritual itself appears to have been recognised by some gnostic sects.

Demonic assaults were depicted as the inevitable experiences of those who were unable to liberate themselves from the rule of Destiny, the 'divine' authority of the stars.

Christianity, like Judaism, was concerned to obliterate the stellar cults. Negative experiences were linked with morality, so that they were represented as divine retribution for adherance to these cults. It was not the performance of ritual itself which was regarded as the ultimate cause of the negative experiences, but the performance of the wrong ritual, with divine vengeance as the consequence. Christian ritual was therefore established on the basis that it was a more effective preventative of demonic assaults than the ritual of paganism.

To the individual, the revelation of the demonic experiences was of the destructiveness of his own uncontrolled psychic powers. The revelation to their respective communities, by the Judeo-Christian apocalyptic seers, was of these same destructive powers, exercised by the Deity against the disobedient. The association of demonic experiences with divine retribution placed the ultimate responsibility for the control of these powers outside the human sphere. 'Divine' judgment was represented as acting from the post-mortem world and human destructiveness was attributed to a Deity external to man.

In the case of the 'journey' of the ascetic to heaven, the immediate source of the imagery of hell in the biographies was the Judeo-Christian apocalyptic literature. In these narratives, the ascetic was represented, like the seers of late Judaism, as a witness to the alternative states which awaited men in the life after death.

CHAPTER V

The Establishment of Commemorative Ritual

I THE MARTYR CULT

Preliminary Considerations

The stories of the martyrs often have little apparent relation to history and, as in the case of the ascetics, the events of their lives were recorded in the language of the pre-Christian worlds. Nevertheless, as the scene of action was the historic world situation, a short review of this background is necessary.

Persecutions of Christians, as in the case of those in Rome under Nero, were at first local. The widespread events, on which the martyr cult in the Middle East was founded, took place during a period of a century and a quarter, beginning with the imperial edict in A.D. 202 of Septimus Severus. In the hope of limiting the number of adherents to these religions, conversion to Christianity or to Judaism was forbidden. Persecutions in North Africa, resulting from the edict, were recorded by Tertullian[1] and, in Egypt, by Eusebius.[2] In 250, Decius issued an edict requiring all inhabitants of the Empire to take part in sacrifices to the gods and to invoke protection for the Empire. Those who participated received certificates, or 'libelli', which exempted them from retribution. The Decian persecutions were followed by a period of relative toleration which lasted until the reign of Diocletian. In the calendar of the Coptic Church, the year 284, in which began the reign of Diocletian, was designated as the 'Year of the Martyrs'.[3] In fact, the persecutions began in 303, perhaps under the influence of his general, Maximian. An edict ordered the destruction of all Christian places of worship and the burning of all books. In 304, a further edict imposed sacrifices to the gods.[4] Persecutions began on a large scale in Nicomedia, Syria, Palestine, Phrygia, Egypt and North Africa:

But words cannot describe the outrageous agonies endured by the martyrs in the Thebais. . . . In this way they (the executioners) carried on, not for a few days or weeks, but year after year. Sometimes ten or more, sometimes over twenty were put to death, at other times at least thirty, and at yet others not far short of sixty; and there were occasions when on a single day a hundred men as well as women and children were killed, condemned to a succession of ever-changing punishments.

I was in these places, and saw many of the executions for myself. Some of the victims suffered death by beheading, others punishment by fire. So many were killed on a single day that the axe, blunted and worn out by the slaughter, was broken in pieces, while the exhausted executioners had to be periodically relieved. All the time I observed a most wonderful eagerness and truly divine power and enthusiasm in those who had put their trust in the Christ of God. No sooner had the first batch been sentenced, than others from every side would jump on to the platform in front of the judge and proclaim themselves Christians.

Eusebius, History of the Church, VIII.9.4

In 311, an edict of Galerius ordered the cessation of persecution. Religious toleration was only partial until the accession of Constantine to the position of sole Emperor in 324.[5]

The Era of the Martyrs, thus briefly outlined, was a period when individuals took part in historic conflict against pagan society. The individuals, to whom the way of life of the Roman world was intolerable, who rejected property, family life and state worship, were a threat to that society. The violence of the persecutions was a reflection of the insoluble conflict of two opposing and mutually exclusive viewpoints. The ascetics demonstrated their ability to survive in complete separation from the community. The martyrs adopted the attitude that death was preferable to life.

The desire of the state to destroy those who, for one reason or another, threatened its security met, on the one hand, a will to self-immolation among some sections of the people. The choice of death as a valid expression of contempt for a way of life demanded a maturity of which the majority of the populations were not capable. A widespread wish for death[6] arose, and it was found necessary to restrain groups of people from provoking the authorities to sentence them:

> We ourselves blame those who have leapt on death; for there are some who are not really ours but share only the name, who are eager to deliver themselves over in hatred against the Creator, poor wretches, passionate for death. We say that these men commit suicide and are not martyrs, even if they are officially executed.

Clement, Stromateis, Book IV, IV.17

On the other hand, according to the writings of Dionysius of Alexandria[7] and Cyprian of Carthage, the number of those who met the demand of the edict of Decius, especially in Egypt and North Africa, far exceeded those who refused it:

> (Many of our brethren), vanquished before the fight, did not even make a show of sacrificing under compulsion. They ran of their own account to the Forum, as if they were indulging in a long-cherished desire. There you could see them entreating the magistrates to receive their recantations.
>
> Cyprian, *de Lapsis*, 8

During the period of reconciliation of Church and State within the Byzantine Empire, there arose the cult discussed in the present Section. The substitution of ritual for the inner conflict of the individual was discussed in Chapter IV.II.3, in connection with Baptism. In the case of the martyr, the conflict of the individual against a theocratic society was, by means of a cult, ritually commemorated and resolved by the succeeding theocracy. With the martyrs as objects of veneration, the community resumed practices very similar to those which the martyrs themselves had rejected.

The writings commemorating the lives of the martyrs were originally based on panegyrics delivered at the anniversaries of their deaths. The speeches of the fourth-century Church Fathers were the models for their descendants. The form of these speeches was that of the *encomium*,[8] the early Fathers having been trained as rhetoricians in the classical tradition. In depicting the life of a famous man, the *encomium* followed a certain pattern as regards subject matter. Two aspects of the *encomium* form, used by the early Fathers, are here relevant. In the *syncresis*, or comparison, the martyrs were compared to 'athletes' who ran their course and were finally crowned. They were also likened to noble warriors, to whom was applied the imagery of war and armour. The *ecphrasis*, or description, was a means by which the rhetoricians gave colour to their panegyrics. In the oratory of the Church Fathers, the subject described in most vivid detail was that of the torments suffered by the martyrs. The panegyric was also made the vehicle for discourses and exhortations on moral and theological subjects. These orations suggest that the form of the martyr cult which arose, although influenced by local funerary rituals, was promoted by the early Church Fathers themselves.

Authority to their hearers to appeal to the martyrs for blessings in this life appeared in the orations of the Fathers from the fourth century onwards. Exhortations to invoke the martyrs as intercessors on behalf of the dead and as benefactors to the living were contained in the discourses of Basil the Great,[9] Cyril of Jerusalem,[10] Gregory of Nazianzus,[11] Gregory of Nyssa,[12] John Chrysostom,[13] and Theodoret of Cyrus,[14] together with details of the benefits conferred. Affirmation that the bodies of the martyrs possessed divine powers was also given by the early Fathers. According to Basil the Great,[15] the touching of a martyr's body involved participation in his powers. The most universally recognised power which the martyr, in life, was said to have demonstrated, was against demons. The martyr's relics were proclaimed, in the writings of John Chrysostom,[16] Jerome[17] and others, as exercising this same power on behalf of the living. In addition to exorcising those possessed with demons, the martyr's relics were also said to have the power of curing disease and of promoting fertility. In recounting the miracles associated with the name of a particular martyr, the rhetorician described the cures said to have been performed at his tomb. Miraculous cures, said to have occurred at the shrines of martyrs, were cited from the fourth century onwards, as seen in the writings of Augustine.[18]

The martyr cult thus assumed some of the features of the cult of the dead hero or healer of pre-Christian times. The martyr, even if he had more than one shrine, was associated with the region to which the presence of his tomb or shrine was beneficial.[19] To the shrine was attributed the power of protecting the neighbourhood and its inhabitants from demonic assault. Protection extended, not only to the living, but to the dead. Tombs were therefore placed in close proximity to that of the martyr. Since the power of the martyr was thought to reside in physical remains of his body, it was possible for a district to 'acquire' a martyr by finding and reburying his remains. Dream revelations by martyrs of the whereabouts of their own bodies and instructions concerning their reburial were included in the panegyrics of the early Fathers.

From the fifth century onwards, local bishops and priests either read copies of speeches of the Fathers of the Church, or composed their own on this model. A vast literature arose which was mainly either anonymous in authorship, or written under the pseudonym of an early Father. In these orations of later origin, the tendency, already discernible in the early oratory, to depict the martyr as a type, rather than an individual, became more apparent. The martyr, with the aid of supernatural powers, felt none of his torments, was delivered from all dangers, and was repeatedly restored to life or health. In proportion as his dependence on external aid was stressed, the moral value of the martyr's stand against pagan authority was diminished. Through the martyr cult, the Church thus appropriated the power to designate the sources of divine power. The martyr himself was shown, in life, as dependent on super-natural aid. Only after death did his corpse assume a power of its own. The environment, in the imagination of the populace, was purged of its pagan associations with either gods or demons. Finally, the assignment of the anniversaries of saints to the days of the year obliterated the memory of earlier pagan festivals.

In the martyr stories of the Eastern Church, and especially in those originating in Egypt, emphasis was laid on the subjective experiences, both of the martyrs themselves and of those to whom, in later times, the martyrs appeared. The vision of the heavenly worlds seen by the martyr before death,[20] was, in these writings, preceded by a series of visions during the course of the martyr's life. Experiences were also described of those to whom the martyrs appeared in dreams. The present series of quotations is concerned only with the subjective experiences of the martyrs and the worshippers at their shrines. From this very large field, narratives which were common to a number of texts were selected. Their stereotyped pattern is confirmation that the form of these accounts was rigidly traditional and that subjective experiences were described according to patterns as fixed as those determining the life histories.

1 Martyrdom Foretold

Three literary traditions possibly account for those characteristics which distinguish some of the present quotations from the martyrdom stories of the Western Church. These are firstly traditional Egyptian stories of the deeds of gods and men, secondly Egyptian funerary inscriptions and ritual, and thirdly Christian apocalyptic writings of Egyptian origin. Egyptian texts of the Ptolemaic period contained religious stories[21] in which, as in the present narratives, persons entered and returned from the life after death. Those who had suffered in this life returned in various forms to set right their wrongs. Human lives followed the course determined by Fate and indicated by divine pre-dictions. Egyptian funerary inscriptions were, as has been seen (p. 110), invocations to be said by the living on behalf of the dead. Like the present quotations, they contain detailed lists of the possible benefits and rewards in this life and next, or alternatively, the misfortunes and punishments.

Christian apocalyptic writings essentially presented, through the medium of a 'seer', the 'vision' of the different states of man's soul (see Section III). The Coptic martyr stories appear to have been a form of 'popular' apocalyptic literature, in which the martyr took the place of the 'seer'. He was told of and shown the places of heaven and the rewards awaiting him there. The descriptions of hell of the apocalypses were replaced by accounts of the torments undergone by the martyr and of his miraculous delivery. The vision of heaven was thus juxtaposed to the images of torment and death in these narratives. As a result of their stereotyped character, the effect of these stories probably depended on the fact that they presented the divine world in a manner familiar to the population. The martyr cult was, for the populace, a ritual, during the course of which divine manifestations were possible. The Church, however, assumed the guardianship of the form of the ritual and of the power to invoke the martyr himself.

Themes and episodes derived from Biblical narratives were common to the martyr stories of both East and West. Classical Greek mythology, in particular the stories of heroes and healers, was another source of material found in these narratives. As has been seen, the hero, after death, might be the object of an incubation cult (p. 6). The relation of the stellar cults to Biblical and other pre-Christian literature has already been discussed (p. 118ff.). The visit of a deity to encourage a warrior to fight and the prediction of the outcome of the conflict were themes common to all the above-mentioned sources.[22]

In the present texts concerning George of Diospolis (Lydda) of Cappadocia, the relation of the predictions of martyrdom to the numerology of the Zodiac can be seen (10, 11, 13, 14, 15). The period of 'trials' was seven years, and the number of victories seventy. An incomparable victory was foretold, the result of death and resurrection four times undergone. A prediction of resurrection repeated three times was made for Macarius of Antioch (12). The place and type of trials to be suffered, the place of death and the manner of burial were all set forth, together with the assurances concerning the fate of the martyr's soul. The soul was said to be a 'pledge' or property to be returned to its owner after death in Narratives 13–15. The foretelling of the martyrdom was thus, in some stories, a summary in anticipation of the events which followed. This 'divine' predictability of the martyr's life suggests its relation to the cosmic events of the Zodiac. The resurrection of the martyr was depicted as occurring with the same certainty as the rising of the heavenly bodies.

2 Rewards in Heaven

It was stated by Plato that discipline of the mind was a 'motion' which conformed with the motions of the universe; the corresponding bodily movements were best controlled from the same source:

He that applies himself to science or other severe discipline of the mind must likewise give the body its proper motion, . . . Further the best of motions is that produced in self by self, which has most affinity with the movement of the movement of thought and of the universe as a whole. Motion produced by another is worse, but worst of all that in which the body lies passive and its several parts are set in movement by other agents.

Plato, Timaeus, 88C–89A

The situation of those who, within their cults, submitted themselves to the external domination of the movements of the heavenly bodies, has been discussed (Chapter IV.ii.1). The rites of the martyr cult were the formalised expression of man's effort to free himself from this domination. The struggle was expressed in terms of a conflict between two worlds. On one hand was a heavenly world, formed of a community of those who had experienced death; on the other was a demonic world, from which operated the powers to which the pagan rulers were subject. The Church gave ritual form to this conflict within man; but by so doing protected him from direct experience of it. Performance of the ritual freed man from the immediate necessity to do more than submit to authority; in the ambience of the Church his world was freed from demons. New relationships with the divine were created for him, not with his fellows on earth, but with the beatified martyrs in heaven.

Immortality in the ancient world was expressed in terms of endless and predictable repetition in time. The dead in ancient Egypt were made 'like Rē for ever'.[23] In Jewish apocalyptic writings, the righteous were 'made like the stars'.[24] The imagery of the stars had enabled men of earlier times to portray a divine and immortal world with which the human world had an affinity. The avoidance of the imagery of the stars for depicting the heavenly world in Christian writings resulted in the use of other means of conveying immortality. Using the more 'earthly' imagery of the Old and New Testaments, the heavenly community was represented in a setting of either a city or a garden.

The use of the crown and robe as means of indicating a role to be performed was seen in Jewish apocalyptic writings:

And there again I saw a vision as the former, after we had spent there seventy days. And I saw seven men in white raiment saying unto me: Arise, put on the robe of the priesthood, and the crown of righteousness, and the breastplate of understanding, and the garment of truth, and the plate of faith, and the turban of the head and the ephod of prophecy.

Testament of Levi, 8.1–3 (Charles)

185

The vision of thrones, crowns and garments as rewards for righteousness, for the seer himself and for others, appeared in the Judeo-Christian *Ascension of Isaiah*:

> For above all the heavens and their angels has thy throne been placed, and thy garments and thy crown which thou shalt see.
>
> *Ascension of Isaiah*, VII.22 (Charles)

> And I saw there many garments laid up, and many thrones and many crowns.
> And I said to the angel: 'Whose are these garments and thrones and crowns?'
>
> *Ascension of Isaiah*, IX.24, 25 (Charles)

The promise of a crown as a reward for righteousness occurred in the *Testament of Benjamin*:

> See ye, therefore, my children, the end of the good man. Be followers of his compassion, therefore, with a good mind, that ye also may wear crowns of glory.
>
> *Testament of Benjamin*, 4.1 (Charles)

A parallel to the foretelling of rewards in heaven to the martyr occurred in the Judeo-Christian *Apocalypse of Isaac* (Quotation 1). The death and future status of the Patriarch was depicted in the terms used in the martyr's lives. In the heavenly world of the martyr, the notion of reward for the victorious athlete, at first applied to the crown, was extended to the throne, diadem, and robe, originally signs of rank or office.

In ancient Egypt, the heavenly world was depicted as a place of banquets and feasts. The orgy as an archaic means of experiencing the divine has been discussed ('Introduction I'). In the *Republic*, Plato derided the notion of heaven as an eternity of drunkenness, at the same time condemning those who believed in this means of attaining to heaven:

> And still more delightful than these are the blessings which Musaeus and his son bestow on the just men from the gods; for they take them in their story to Hades, where they seat them on couches and prepare a banquet for the saints, making them spend all their time garlanded and drunken, as though they thought an eternity of drunkenness the fairest reward of virtue.
>
> Plato, *Republic*, II.363

Nevertheless, the banquet in heaven as an image of the state of the soul of the dead persisted in Christian times; Ireneus combined the idea of eternal rest with that of a feast in heaven:

186

All this is in the times of the Kingdom, that is, in the seventh day . . .
wherein they shall do no earthly work, but shall have set by them a
table prepared of God, feeding them with a perfect feast.

Irenaeus, Adversus Haereses, Book V, 33.2

Angels in heaven were said, in the *Testament of Levi*, to offer bloodless
sacrifices in heaven, in propitiation for the sins of men.[25] In the present
texts was expressed the notion of an eternal Eucharistic Offering made
in the Church of the martyred infants in the heavenly Jerusalem.

The imagery of the tablets in heaven, on which were written the names
of men, has already been discussed (Chapter IV.I. 'Preliminary Considerations'). In the present texts, the writing in the *Book of Life* of the
names of those worthy to enter the heavenly world was said also to
involve the erasing of the 'hand-written list' of their sins.[26] The notions
of the martyr as an heir to the Kingdom, or ruler of the Land of the
Inheritance, were derived from the Old Testament. The deprivation of
the Egyptian population of their lands, by the Greek and Roman
conquerors,[27] may possibly account for the frequency with which this
reward was mentioned. During the Ptolemaic period, a man's 'lot' was
the land apportioned to him.[28] As a result of taxation under Roman
rule, ownership of land became increasingly less profitable, and many
Egyptians abandoned their lands. In the Old Testament, Books of the
Living were registers of Israelites with rights to the temporal blessings
of the chosen people. The list of the Elect of the Qumran community
referred to those destined to participate in the Messianic Kingdom:

> . . . The sons of Zadok are the elect of Israel, the men called by name
> who shall stand at the end of days. Behold the exact list of their
> names according to their generations, and the time when they lived,
> and the number of their trials, and the years of their sojourn, and the
> exact list of their deeds.

The Damascus Rule, IV (Vermes, p. 100)

Rejoicing at the appearance of a deity was a traditional mode of
expression, found in many ancient Egyptian laudatory texts. The
following, in praise of Rē, is typical:

> Adoration of Rē when he rises in the eastern horizon of heaven with
> his followers. . . . How beautiful it is when thou arisest on the
> horizon and lightenest the Two Lands (Egypt) with thy rays. All gods
> rejoice when they see thee as the King of all heaven. . . . Those who
> are in the Nether-world come forth at thy approach to see this
> beautiful apparition.

Černý, Ancient Egyptian Religion, p. 56

The representation of the heavenly world as a scene of joyful reception of the martyr by those of heaven, was characteristic of the present narratives. The place of judgment was depicted as being, not in heaven, but in the context of the torments. In the heavenly world, the writing of the name of the martyr in the Book of Life and the erasing of his sins replaced a heavenly judgment and was shown as giving the martyr the right of entry to the Land of Inheritance.[29]

3   The Boat Journey

In his 'trials', the martyr was represented as successfully 'overcoming' his persecutors and thus discrediting the ancient pagan cults. The imagery of the stadium,[30] in which he was the victorious athlete, was that of a circuit, whose predetermined course he followed. In Ptolemaic Egypt, the nomes were associated with the constellations of the Zodiac,[31] the river forming the link between these districts. The boat journey, like the race, were thus images which originally represented the course of the sun.

The boat journey not only had a relationship, by tradition, with the stellar cult, but also with that of Osiris. In making boat journeys to the North or to the South, the martyr used the route followed by the funerary processions of ancient Egypt.[32] At the death of the king, two funerary journeys were made, one to Busiris in Lower Egypt, and the other to Abydos in Upper Egypt, the centre of the cult of Osiris. In late periods, when the rites of the king's burial were adopted by non-royal persons, the scenes of two boat journeys were represented in their tomb paintings. Boat journeys, most frequently to the South (Quotations 1–5, 7, 12), but also to the North (8), were described in the Egyptian martyr stories. An episode in the biography of St. Menas may also have had a link with the rites of Osiris and Isis. When the day of the Saint's martyrdom was foretold, he was commanded to tell his sister what to do after his head had been cut off and his body dismembered. She should collect his remains, put them together, sew them up in a basket and then embark with them on a ship.[33]

In ancient Egypt, the boat journey[34] through the twelve divisions of *Amente* was the means by which the soul, like the sun, passed to a new life. Assaults on the soul after death, in its passage through the air, have already been discussed (pp. 116; 121). In the *Encomium* on St. Menas, whose body was brought from Phrygia to Alexandria by boat, the assault on the martyr by monstrous animal forms was described:

It happened that when they were in mid-ocean, there came out of the sea fearsome beasts with necks raised aloft and faces like those of

188

camels. And they stretched their long necks into the ship, wishing to take the remains of the saint and also the lives of the men on board. Whenever these beasts, as was their wont, raised their necks, fire came from the holy Apa Mena's remains and darted in their faces and they sank beneath the waves.

Apa Mena (Drescher, p. 141)

The destruction of serpents, dragons and other animal forms, during their life-times, featured in a number of martyr biographies. In the case of St. Menas, the victory occurred during a boat journey undertaken after death. The pagan deity superseded by St. Menas is unknown;[35] possibly he was a form of sun god. The trials of the Egyptian martyrs were thus, in some cases, represented as a fusion of motifs from the cult of the life after death of the ancient religion.

The ancient Egyptian use of the oracle, in which natural phenomena were regarded as indicating the will of the gods, appeared in the martyr stories. The state of the wind (Quotations 1 and 2) was represented as a sign indicating the place at which the boat carrying the martyr should land. The sign, in Narratives 1–3, determining the site of the martyr's execution, was the stoppage of oxen. In the case of the body of St. Menas, the inability of camels carrying his coffin to rise and proceed further indicated the burial site.[36] In Quotations 4 and 6, the places were, in one case, designated by an angel and, in the other, by a voice from heaven. The importance of 'divine' rather than 'human' agency in indicating the place lay in the fact that the martyr was a 'stranger' in a strange land (5, 7, 10). He therefore exerted his beneficent influence at the place of his martyrdom. It was necessary for a village claiming a martyr as its local saint that his death had occurred there by divine authority.

The burial of the Jewish Patriarchs with their fathers and the transport of their bodies from Egypt to Canaan was represented in the apocryphal *Testament of the Twelve Patriarchs*:

And Reuben died, having given these commands to his sons. And they placed him in a coffin until they carried him up from Egypt, and buried him in Hebron in the cave where his father was.

Testament of Reuben, 7.1–2 (Charles)

A similar wish to be buried with his fathers (11, 12) or in his own village (6, 7) was represented as having been granted from heaven to the martyr, in certain narratives. Such a removal of a martyr's body after death required an intermediary. A literary device for this purpose appeared in the personage known as Julius of Aqfahs (Kbehes).[37] In a cycle of martyrdoms, including Narratives 10, 11 and 12, he was said to have carried out the wishes of the various martyrs with regard to the disposal of their bodies. He was also said to have written their memorials and thus to have ensured that their requests were made known.

4 The Execution

In ancient Egypt, the head played an important part in the ritual by which the body was 'recreated' after death. Chapter XLIII of the *Book of the Dead* was entitled 'The Chapter of not letting the head of a man be cut off from him in *Amente*'. The text was a spell for preventing the head of Osiris from being taken away from him. In the third ceremony of the ritual 'Opening of the Mouth'[38] of the deceased, it was said to the mummy or statue that he had received his head. These texts carried the implication that the physical union of body and head were essential for the survival, as Osiris, of the deceased.

The reappearance of the saint after death was represented, in the *Acts of Paul*, as occurring subsequent to his decapitation. In this second-century apocryphal text, it was said that Nero singled out Paul for beheading, according to Roman law, rather than for death by fire with the other Christians. The apostle claimed that if he were beheaded, he would rise and appear after death to Nero, in proof that he was not dead. The execution of Paul was described in terms similar to those used in the present texts:

> Then Paul stood with his face to the east, and lifting up his hands to heaven prayed at length; and after communing in prayer in Hebrew with the fathers he stretched out his neck without speaking further. But when the executioner struck off his head, milk spurted upon the soldier's clothing. And when they saw it, the soldier and all who stood by were amazed, and glorified God who had given Paul such glory.
>
> *Acts of Paul*, Martyrdom, 5 (Wilson, II, p. 385)

After the execution, it was said that Paul appeared first to Nero, to whom he prophesied a future of further evil. His second appearance was to two Romans who had said that, if they saw him after death, they would believe in the Resurrection.

The apocryphal *Acts of the Apostles* were widely known throughout the Christian world, including Egypt where texts survive in Coptic. Although the present stories do not all concern Egyptian martyrs, the combination of a boat journey with a martyrdom by beheading is suggestive of Egyptian writing, based on the model of the martyrdom of Paul. The traditional conclusion of a martyrdom story, like that of Paul, was the enumeration of the subsequent appearances of the saint.

A similar account of an execution, performed by soldiers, in the *Acts of Thomas*, also described the appearance of the saint after death. The king, who had disbelieved in the saint during life, was reprimanded by him after death for trying to obtain healing from his relic. The martyr was said to have been given a royal burial (see Quotation 18):

> And when he had prayed, he said to the soldiers: 'Come and fulfil (the command) of him who sent you.' And at once the four smote him and slew him. But all the brethren wept. And wrapping him in fine robes and many fine linen cloths they laid him in the tomb in which the kings of old (were buried).
>
> *Acts of Thomas*, 168 (Wilson, II, p. 530)

Certain features in the present accounts of the beheading of martyrs were common to a number of narratives. The executioners were told, by the martyr, to hasten to pronounce the sentence (2, 4, 11, 13), the appointed place and time for the martyrdom having arrived. The martyr pronounced a prayer of exorcism (6), or crossed himself (12, 14, 21). The executioners were then told by the martyr to fulfil the command (of their impious king) (7–12, 19). After removal of the martyr's head, blood and milk came forth (6–10, 16); the miraculous nature of the latter was mentioned in the *Acts of Paul*.

The importance of the site of the execution has already been discussed (p. 182). On arrival at the appointed place in Narrative 6, as elsewhere, the martyr asked for time to make a prayer. The execution was thus the occasion for the appearance of the Saviour to grant the requests of the martyr (1, 6). The requests concerned the disposal of his body, or, as in Quotation 1, the day of his death. The Saviour gave the martyr an invitation to enter heaven (10, 11), or encouraged him in his trial (13, 14), by describing the joys of heaven.

Two personages who, like Julius of Aqfahs, cared for the body of the martyr and were introduced to account for the arrival of the martyr at the appointed place, were Arianus, the hegemon (2) and Orion, the cursor[39] (3, 16). Both were represented, in the present texts, as Roman officials who had been converted to Christianity and were therefore ready to carry out the wishes of the martyr. Another literary device, whereby the body of a martyr might be transferred from one place to another, was that of the island, to which the body was taken after death (5, 14). As the result of a dream or vision (14), the wishes of the martyr were made known; it thus became possible for the transfer of the body to its rightful place to be effected.

Further instances of the fetching of the soul by angels, the wrapping of the soul and the journey to heaven, already discussed in Chapter III.III.3, are found described in the present narratives. The wrapping of the body prior to burial was discussed in the same Chapter in connection with the ascetics (III.1). The notion of royal honours given to the saint at his burial, seen in Quotations 18 and V.I.5:3, also appeared in the *Acts of Thomas* (see above). In pagan times, the type of funerary ritual was the means of determining the future of the soul. In ancient Egypt, the formulae of the royal funeral were, in the course of time, adopted by non-royal persons for their own use.

5 Instructions on Burial: on Building a Shrine

Service at the martyr's shrine was the expression of the Church's effort to supplant the incubation cult. This cult, in Hellenistic society, as has been seen (p. 88ff.), contributed to that society's decadence and regression towards archaism. The dream vision, interpreted by the priest as a manifestation of the divine will, was a mode of experience appropriate to the ancient theocratic cultures. The dreamer was 'separated' from immediate conscious appraisal of his own experiences. The interpretation of dreams depended on external authority and the premises established by its traditions. Dreams were the manifestation of images, to the pattern of which the dreamer had previously been conditioned by ritual. Dream experiences and their interpretation were thus a self-perpetuating cycle, within which men of antiquity were confined. The mere substitution of new contexts for the archaic rituals and modes of experience only served to continue the trend of ancient society: the promotion of the community without regard to the individual.

The dream revelation was accepted on the authority of the Fathers of the Church, not only as a manifestation of the divine will, but as a means of communication with the dead. The canonisation of the Bishops, who were the authors of the panegyrics commending these practices, gave further authority to their words. Following their lead, the expansion of the martyr cult was accomplished by the 'invention', or finding of martyrs through dream revelations and by the acclamation of these discoveries throughout the Christian world.

The finding of the bodies of two martyrs whose whereabouts had long been unknown was reported by Augustine to be the result of a revelation to a bishop.[40] The disclosure, by this means, of the body of the saint hidden with a pious woman, was described by Gregory of Nyanza.[41] In the biography of Ambrose[42] was described the revelation which led, first to the finding of two martyrs' bodies in the cemetery of the Jews at Bologna, and then to their removal to Florence. Revelations concerning the relics of personages of the New Testament began, in the fifth century, to be of frequent occurrence. Through dreams and visions, the bodies of Stephen, Gamaliel, Nicodemus and John the Baptist[43] were found, and the news of these discoveries was widely circulated. Less well known were the 'inventions' of the bodies of the Old Testament prophets Habakkuk, Micah and Zechariah, and even of Job.[44] Further instances of the contribution of dream visions to the growth of the martyr cult could be multiplied.[45]

In the present texts, the holy man was represented as appearing and giving instructions regarding the disposal of his body and the building of his shrine. In ancient Egypt, it was the practice, during life, to make provision for the future mummification of the body and for the maintenance of the shrine and its cult after death.[46] The construction of the tomb and its equipment was carried out, on their own behalf, by the living. The site and grandeur of the tomb depended on the status of the person concerned. The dream appearance thus enabled the martyr, after death, to give those instructions which he was unable to give during life and to arrange for a shrine in accord with his status. Quotation 7 was taken from a Coptic version of the *Dormition of the Virgin*, describing the death, burial and assumption of the Virgin. Her burial was here depicted in the context of the personages of the Old and New Testaments. This was a form of polemical writing which thus demonstrated, to disbelievers, her status as *Theotokos* or 'Mother of God'.[47]

6 The Cult of the Shrine

(i) Writing and Preaching

The relationship of the martyrdom stories to apocalypses can be seen in those sections of their respective narratives which concerned their commitment to writing. The notion that writing itself was taught by angels (or stars) and that, through writing, men learnt knowledge and fell from their divine status, was expressed in Jewish apocalyptic literature:

And the fourth (angel) was named Penemue: he taught the children of men the bitter and the sweet, and he taught them all the secrets of their wisdom. And he instructed mankind in writing with ink and paper, and thereby many sinned from eternity to eternity and until this day. For men were not created for such a purpose, to give confirmation to their good faith with pen and ink. For men were created exactly like angels, to the intent that they should continue pure and righteous, and death, which destroys everything, could not have taken hold of them, but through this their knowledge they are perishing.

I Enoch, 69.8–11 (Charles)

In *II Enoch*, the writing in heaven of a book for every day of the year was said to reveal to men the fate of all souls before and after their incarnation on earth:

And Pravuil told me: 'All the things that I have told thee, we have written. Sit and write all the souls of mankind, however many of them are born, and the places prepared for them to eternity, before the formation of the world.' And all double thirty days and thirty nights, and I wrote out all things exactly, and wrote three hundred and sixty-six books.

II Enoch, 23.3–6 (Charles)

That written records of the movements of the heavenly bodies were the means by which men knew their destinies, was expressed in the *Book of Jubilees*:

And he (Enoch) was the first among men that are born on earth who learnt writing and knowledge and wisdom and who wrote down the signs of heaven according to the order of their months in a book, that men might know the seasons of the years according to the order of their separate months. And he was the first to write a testimony, and he testified to the sons of men among the generations of the earth, ... And what was and what will be he saw in a vision of his sleep, as it will happen to the children of men throughout their generations until the day of judgment; he saw and understood everything, and wrote his testimony, and placed the testimony on earth for all the children of men and for their generations.

Book of Jubilees, 4.17–20 (Charles)

The attitude to writing, in apocalyptic Jewish texts, differed considerably from that of the Hellenistic Egyptian priesthood. Recitation of what was written was held, in Egypt, to have the power of invoking the gods and of transforming both the soul and the body of man:

(If it be that) thou seekest to pronounce a spell, come to me that I may cause thee to be taken to the place wherein is the book which Thoth wrote with his own hand when he went down following the gods. (There are) two formulae in writing that are upon it, and when thou (readest the first formula thou wilt) enchant the heaven, the earth, the underworld, the mountains, the seas; thou wilt discover all that the birds of heaven and the creeping things shall say; thou wilt see the fish of the deep, there being (power of God resting in water) over them. If thou readest the second formula, though thou be in *Amente*, thou shalt take again thy form upon earth; thou wilt see Ra shining forth in heaven with all the gods of his company, and the moon rising (in) its wise.

First Tale of Khamuas (Griffith, *Stories of the High Priests*, p. 20)

To the ancient Egyptians, speech and writing were essential means by which they participated in the processes of the divine.

In the Christian apocalypses from which Quotations 1–6 are extracts, the rewards were enumerated for writing down the things seen (1, 4, 5, 6), for reciting the apocalypse (1–4) and for preaching it (3, 4). In similar terms, the benefits derived from writing the story of a martyrdom[48] were described (7–10). At this period, writing a book suitable for presentation to a Church was the work of professional scribes. Financial provision for the writing of books to be read in Church was therefore made by the congregation in the hope of future rewards. Books in Church were invariably recited aloud. To an Egyptian, recitation from a reading book appears to have been comparable to pronouncing an invocation. Inducements to read aloud from writings dealing with the heavenly worlds were therefore similar to those given to the martyrs themselves. The sphere of knowledge and writing was thus 'freed' from its pagan associations. The writing and recitation of sacred books were set forth as activities through which the heavenly worlds could be entered, not in this life, but after death.

Power was, however, held to reside in the books themselves. As in ancient Egypt, written words and names were held to be beneficent or malevolent, whether or not they were pronounced. Among the Jews, the wearing of phylacteries,[49] consisting of rolls of inscribed paper, was practised. In Quotation 5, a protective power, similar to that of the phylactery, was attributed to the names contained in the book concerning the Archangel Michael.

(ii) *Services to the Martyr*

In ancient Egypt, the survival of the soul after death was held to be associated with the preservation of the body, the funerary equipment and the tomb itself. Inscriptions were therefore set up at the tomb, from the period of the Old Kingdom onward, cursing those who disturbed or profaned it.[50] (See Chapter III.ii.5.) These imprecatory formulae enumerated the punishments which would follow desecration, both in this world and the next. From the Middle Kingdom onward, formulae of imprecation were juxtaposed to others promising rewards to those who performed acts beneficial to the deceased. In the latter category, came the recitation of the formulae stating that, to the deceased, was granted the favour of 'thousands' of bread and beer, oxen and fowl, alabaster and linen, etc.[51] The recitation of this formula would ensure for him who recited it both benefits in his passage through *Amente* and honourable status and prosperity in this world. He would be the beloved of the king, the favourite of his local god, the chief in his city and nome. The rewards included stability, health, victory over his enemies and perpetuation of his memory on earth. The benefits affected, not only the individual who spoke the formula, but his family and dependents; his successors, moreover, would receive the bequest of his wealth. Thus the beneficial funerary formulae to be recited, the number of punishments in *Amente* averted, the various rewards on this earth and in the future were in the nature of formal lists. The contents of these lists followed a pattern which was dictated by tradition. Similar lists were introduced into the martyr stories.

The relation of the martyr cult to the authority of dreams and visions has been seen in connection with the finding of relics (p. 193). In the present narratives (1–4, 23–24), the form of the cult was represented as having been revealed to the martyr, either during his trials or before his execution. The form of the cult, in Quotations 1, 3–8, 11 and 12, was shown as having been requested by the martyr and confirmed by divine revelation. By means of the vision as a literary device, it was thus represented that it had been divinely authorised that certain practices should constitute the proper cult of the martyr. These practices were derived from the funerary ritual of the pre-Christian religions. Throughout the Christian world, the invocation of martyrs replaced the more general invocation of the dead; the usages depended on the local cults superseded. In Narratives 16–22, the ritual of the shrine cults of the Biblical personages Isaac, Joseph the Carpenter, and John the Baptist, was represented as having been revealed to them; the manner of revelation was described in the same terms as in the martyr stories.

The cult of his shrine was concerned with the preservation and perpetuation of the martyr's name.[52] In this aim and in associating the aim with the preservation of the martyr's body, the cult was related to the ancient Egyptian funerary ritual. The list of services to the martyr set out the acts by which the congregation could commemorate the name of the martyr and benefit by so doing. Children were named after the martyr, not only to perpetuate his name, but also in the hope that his powers to avert evil would protect the child thus named. The chief earthly benefit, to those who served at the shrine, was freedom from the assaults of demonic influences. The invoking of his name and the proclaiming of the effectiveness of his intervention helped to establish the fame of the martyr as an aid to those in trouble. The renown of the shrine was further enhanced by the affirmation that angels and arch-angels participated in its service. It was of great benefit to a district that its shrine should become sufficiently famous that pilgrimages from elsewhere were made to it.[53]

The offering of first-fruits and other gifts and the holding of com-memoration festivals at certain seasons were acts performed, in pre-Christian times, in Jewish and other cults. The guardianship of a tomb was a recognised source of wealth to the priesthood of ancient Egypt.[54] Similarly, gifts to the martyrs' shrines served to enrich the Church. The offering of incense and the lighting of lamps were widely practised funerary rites, relating to the passage of the soul to the next world. The giving of food and alms and the performing of charitable actions was done, in the ancient funerary celebrations, with the intention that those benefited thereby would pray for the soul of the deceased. This practice continued in Christian times; in the context of the martyr cult, the purpose was that the recipients should remember the name of the martyr.

The rewards in heaven, for those who gave services to the shrine and took part in commemorating the martyr, were certainly comparable to those promised to the martyr himself. Of these, the majority have been discussed elsewhere (Chapters III.iv.3, 4 and V.i.2). An interim period of a thousand years before the Last Judgment was a tradition which may have had antecedents in the writings of Plato. In the *Republic*, it was said to be the time spent between one incarnation of the soul on earth and the next: (see also *Phaedrus*, 248E)

> ... Believe that the soul is immortal and able to endure all evil and all good, (and) we shall always hold to the upper road, and in every way follow justice and wisdom. So we shall be friends to ourselves and to the gods, both while we remain here and when, like victorious athletes who go about adding to their prizes, we receive the rewards of our justice; and in the journey of a thousand years which I have described to you, we shall fare well.
>
> Plato, *Republic*, X.621

In the apocryphal *Death of Joseph*, participation in the Banquet of the Thousand Years was related to preservation of the body:

> And I placed my hands upon his body saying: 'Let no evil smell of death have dominion over thee, neither let thine ears stink, nor let corruption ever flow from thy body; neither let thy shroud or thy flesh, in which I have clothed thee, rot in the earth. But let it remain on thy body until the day of the Banquet of the Thousand Years. Let

not the hair of thy head perish, of which I took hold with my hands many times, O my beloved father Joseph, and good will happen to thee.'

de morte Iosephi (Lagarde, p. 26)

Jewish and Christian apocalyptic writings, based on Biblical prophecies, stated that there would be a paradisal time of a thousand years, during which the lamb and the wolf would feed together.[55] In the present texts, an interpretation in keeping with ancient Egyptian views was presented, the deceased reclining as at an earthly banquet.

The exhortations to the laity to write, copy or recite the story of a martyrdom were discussed above (V.I.6.i). Thus at each hearing, the features here presented were reiterated. The repeated performance of the commemorative ritual thus established more firmly the relationship of the cult to the practices and attitudes of pre-Christian times.

7 *Favours Granted at the Shrine*

From Hellenistic times, numerous records survive of the healing cults prevalent at that period. Pausanius, in his *Guide to Greece*,[56] described various sanctuaries, including that at Epidaurus, the centre of the cult of Asclepius. The recollections of the Roman orator, Aelius Aristides, written in the second century A.D., described the visits which he and others made to the shrine of Asclepius at Perganum. He reported the incubation experience of one of the temple ministers:

> The revelation was unquestionable, just as in a thousand other instances the epiphany of the god was felt with absolute certainty. You have a sense of contact with him, and are aware of his arrival in a state of mind intermediate between sleep and waking; you try to look up and are afraid to, lest before you see him he shall have vanished; you sharpen your ears and listen, half in dream and half awake; your hair stands up, tears of joy roll down, a proud kind of modesty fills your breast. How can anyone really describe this experience in words? If one belongs to the initiated, he will know about it and recognize it.
>
> Aelius Aristides, *Sacred Orations*, II.31, 32 (Grant, p. 54)

In Egypt, at this period, similar incubation cults centred round the Hellenised forms of certain Egyptian deities, notably Serapis and Isis. The cult of Imhotep,[57] the healer and architect of the third Dynasty, later deified, was an example of the revival of the names and practices of earlier periods (see Chapter II.II.1). In a second-century Greek papyrus, the account was recorded of the appearance of the god; the narrator was lying sick with his mother beside him:

(My mother) was sitting without enjoying even a short period of slumber, when suddenly she perceived—it was no dream or sleep, for her eyes were open immovably, though not seeing clearly—a divine and terrifying vision, easily preventing her from observing the god himself or his servants, whichever it was. In any case there was someone whose height was more than human, clothed in shining raiment and carrying in his left hand a book, who, after merely regarding me two or three times from head to foot, disappeared. When she had recovered herself she tried, still trembling, to wake me, and finding that the fever had left me and that much sweat was pouring off me, she did reverence to the manifestation of the god, and then wiped me and made me more calm. When I spoke with her she wished to declare the virtue of the god, but I, anticipating her, told her all myself; for everything that she saw in the vision had appeared to me in dreams.

Oxyrhynchus Papyri, XI.1381 (Grant, p. 124)

The document, unfortunately incomplete, from which the above extract was taken, was written in praise of Imhotep. It was designed to set forth the history and miraculous manifestations of the god, together with the benefits which he had conferred upon his worshippers. Records of the personal experiences of visitors who attended the sanctuary of Asclepius at Epidaurus have survived in the form of inscribed votive tablets.[58] These state the condition from which the worshipper suffered and the manner in which the cure was effected. The god was said to have appeared in the course of dreams and to have given reprimands, instructions and advice. Physical sensations were also recorded. In return for these ministrations, payment and gifts were demanded.

Accounts of the cures and miracles performed through the agency of the martyrs appeared in the writings of Augustine. The revelation of the unknown grave of two martyrs was depicted as the occasion of cures and exorcisms:

At that time Thou didst reveal in a vision to Thy famous Bishop the unknown grave of Thy martyrs, Gervasius and Protasius, whose bodies Thou hadst preserved incorrupt for so many years in Thy secret treasury, . . . They were discovered and disinterred, and translated with fitting state to the basilica of Ambrose. And as they were borne along the road, many who were tormented by unclean spirits were healed, the very devils constrained to make confession. . . . (One blind for many years) was allowed to touch with his handker-

199

chief the bier of the saints . . . He laid the kerchief on his eyes, and immediately they were opened.

Augustine, *Confessions*, IX.vii.2

The sources from which Augustine and the later Church Fathers, who described such cures, drew, were the local traditions which arose and were recorded at the shrines themselves:

For if I should but relate all the miracles done on men's bodies by the memorials of St. Stephen, only at Calama and Hippo, it would be the work of many volumes, and yet not be perfect either. I could not relate all, but only such as are recorded for the knowledge of the people, for we desire, when we see our times produce wonders like to those of yore, that they should not be utterly in vain by being lost in forgetfulness and oblivion.

It is not yet two years since the shrine was built at Hippo, and although we ourselves do know many miracles done there since, that are recorded, yet are there almost seventy accounts written of those that have been done from that time to this. But at Calama the shrine is more ancient, the miracles more frequent, and the records far more in number. At Uzalis also, near Utica, have many miracles been wrought by the power of the said martyr, where Bishop Euodius erected his memorial, long before this one of ours. But there they did not use to record them, though it may be they have begun such a custom of late.

Augustine, *City of God*, XXII, viii

The gods of healing, in pagan Egypt, as elsewhere, were visited at their shrines. Certain localities appeared to have been associated by reputation and tradition with the occurrence of cures. When the names of the pagan deities were obliterated, in Christian times, the localities were often occupied by the shrines of martyrs. The latter, in turn, assumed the role of centres of healing and pilgrimage. Such was probably the background of the cult of St. Menas, the oil from whose shrine acquired a reputation throughout the Christian world.[59] Similarly, the shrine of the Saints John and Cyrus at Aboukir was founded on the site of the pagan temple of Isis Medica.[60] The reputations of these shrines of martyrs, like those of the pagan healing centres, increased with the reports of cures effected at them. The *encomium*, recited at the martyr's commemoration festival, invariably, therefore, described the favours, including cures, which had been granted to those who had invoked his name.

The present narratives are a small selection from a vast literature. Healing as a result of a heavenly visitation was discussed in Chapter

III.I.4. In those of the present texts, in which the circumstances of the cures were stated, the night (3, 9), or midnight (1, 5) were specified. The martyr, saint or archangel appeared to the afflicted person during sleep (3, 4, 7, 10), during unconsciousness (1, 11), or during ecstasy (8). Exorcism was performed by making the sign of the Cross (2, 5, 6), or by chastisement (9, 11). In Narrative 9, the offending person was beaten; in 11 (previously discussed in Chapter II.III.3), the demon was chastised by the saint. Narrative 8, depicting the removal of an inscribed copper plate from within the abdomen,[61] may have been related to similar texts concerning the liver (see Section III.I.4). Inscribed models of the liver were used for divination. In Quotation 10, the gift of divine inspiration was represented as bestowed on the author by the saint who was the subject of the biography. The notion that excellence of writing should be ascribed to divine inspiration appeared in the biography of Plotinus by Porphyry:

> . . . Also it is said that the gods often set him straight when he was going on a crooked course 'sending down a solid shaft of light' which means that he wrote what he wrote under their inspection and supervision.

Porphyry, Life of Plotinus, 23.15

In perpetuating modes of healing appropriate to more ancient times, the martyr cult gave recognition to material rather than non-material manifestations of the divine. It also authorised states of sleep or trance as valid levels of consciousness for its apprehension.

II SALVATION FROM DEATH

Preliminary Considerations

The conflict of the Christian convert against the pagan authorities was represented, in the martyr stories, as a series of episodes. Typically, the martyr refused, on demand, to perform pagan rites; he was tried before a tribunal and was then subjected to a number of torments. His survival of these various ordeals 'put to shame' his persecutors and their pagan gods and was proof of the superior power by which he was protected.

The subjective assaults of the hallucinatory and menacing forms of deities, previously experienced within a cult, have been discussed in connection with the ascetics (see Chapter II.II). The torments, which the martyrs were represented as having undergone, corresponded in their imagery to those which the ascetics were said to have experienced. Characteristically, the torments of the martyr were immersion in fire or pits, dismemberment and attacks by wild animals. Similar imagery was used in apocalyptic writings to describe the 'punishments' of the life after death (see Chapter IV.II.1). Experiences of being immersed, dismembered or attacked were also described in the Old Testament, especially by the writers of the *Psalms*. Because these descriptions were relevant to their own experiences, in the accounts of the ascetics the *Psalms* were the most frequently quoted of all the books of the Bible. The imagery of the pit, of the fiery furnace, of overwhelming waters and of the attacks of dogs, lions and bulls was, in the *Psalms*, associated with death and *Sheol*.[62] The *Hymns* of the Qumran community contained similar imagery, including that of dismemberment:

> My arm is torn from its socket (and I can) lift my hand (no more);
> My (foot) is held by fetters and my knees slide like water; I can no longer walk. I cannot step forward lightly, (for my legs and arms) are bound by shackles which cause me to stumble.
> Thy tongue has gone back which Thou didst make marvellously within my mouth; it can no longer give voice.
> (I have no word) for my disciples to revive the spirit of those who stumble and to speak words of support to the weary.
> My circumcised lips are dumb.
>
> *Hymns*, VIII.14 (Vermes, p. 179)

In the communities of Israel, and later of Qumran, these negative experiences, comparable to those of death, were represented as the fate of those in disfavour with the Deity and therefore with the community.

In the context of Judaism, the power which saved and 'raised' the individual from this condition was that of the Deity who was, nevertheless, inseparable from His people. In the Qumran *Hymns*, the community to which the fallen individual was restored was identified with that of the Sons of Heaven, the restored Zodiac (see p. 137):

> I thank thee, O Lord, for thou hast redeemed my soul from the Pit, and from the Hell of Abaddon Thou hast raised me up to everlasting height.
> I walk on limitless ground, and I know there is hope for him whom Thou hast shaped from dust for the everlasting Council.
> Thou hast cleansed a perverse spirit of great sin that it may stand with the host of the Holy ones,
> and that it may enter into community with the congregation of the Sons of Heaven.
>
> *Hymns*, III.5 (Vermes, p. 158)

In the *Psalms* and also in the Qumran *Hymns*, the raising of the individual from this state of torment was represented as 'putting to shame the enemy'. These adversaries were said to require proof that the God of Israel had the power to raise his worshippers and, likewise, were said to reproach a God unable to save and help his people.[63]

The 'salvation' of the individual was not achieved by the intervention of an outside power, but by the recognition of himself as the source of both the demonic and the divine. Thus the same imagery was not applicable to two different subjective events. To the ascetic, 'salvation' was relevant to his continued separation from the community, and to his ability to order his own subjective imagery. To the Jewish psalmist and hymn writer, it implied his restoration to his people and their rituals. In the present section are considered the ways in which the martyr stories depicted the experiences of the individual in relation to the divine and the demonic, not in Christian, but in pre-Christian terms.

1 Identity Announcement

The imagery of the heavenly visitation was derived, as has been seen, from mythology and from descriptions of pre-Christian incubation cults. The visit was, in Narratives 1, 5, 6 and 7, said to have occurred during sleep, at night in 4, 7 and 8, in the middle of the night in 1, 2. The significance of the lighting of the surroundings (1, 2) and of the description of the visitor as a man of light (6), a youth of light (5), and a beautiful youth (8) is discussed in connection with Sub-Section III.1. The non-recognition, by the martyr, of the visitor had its antecedents in classical literature. The purpose of the visit was shown to be, initially the announcement, by the Saviour, of his name.

In ancient Egypt, the pronouncement of names was one of the most essential acts in ritual,[64] and reciprocal naming was the means by which relationships were ritually established with the divine world. The invocation of a deity was effected by recitation of his names and attributes. Hostile powers could be overcome by knowledge of their names. Thus, in ancient Egypt, attention was ritually focused on the act of naming itself, as having potentially a creative or destructive power. Knowledge of names and their ritual use was the prerogative of the Egyptian priesthood. Through the process of naming, man identified his own powers and qualities, while attributing them to the external universe. By means of ritual, man was effectively prevented from seeing himself as the possessor of these powers and qualities. To him, therefore, the utterance of their names was the means by which he caused them to act in his favour.

In Judaism, 'sanctification' of the name of God[65] was seen as the evidence of the power of this name to command reverence. The name of God was said to be 'sanctified' in the eyes of other nations through the achievements of Israel.[66] It was the duty of Israel, therefore, to make the name of God honoured and to prevent its disgrace in the estimate of the world. The individual was thus restrained from behaviour detrimental to the reputation of his national God. Sanctification of the name of God, in later Judaism, implied readiness for martyrdom.[67] God, as it were, ceased to be God, unless Israel, as God's witness, manifested the power of His name to command obedience.

The attitudes of both ancient Egypt and Judaism to the name of the Deity were illustrated in the martyr stories. The martyr, in refusing to sacrifice to pagan gods, was demonstrating the superior compelling power of his own God, in face of other deities. In Egyptian thought, as has been seen, the power of a deity resided in his name. The account of the announcement to the martyr, of the name of his Saviour, used the imagery of a heavenly visitation as a literary device. The narrator thereby established that the martyrdom was enacted to uphold the name of the divine Saviour. The salvation of the martyr, by invoking this name, was a demonstration of its power. A hierarchy of powers was thus established from heaven to the martyr, which were manifestly superior to those of paganism. Fear of immaterial powers of evil, immanent in the surrounding world, was widespread among the early Christian populations. Ancient rituals had surrounded the use of names with the potentiality of making contact with these powers. The martyr stories helped to establish a more powerful name which 'overcame' and obliterated from memory those of its enemies. The displacement of pagan deities by Christianity was thus dramatised. The martyr cult, however, continued the ritual by which 'deities' were created. The martyr himself was established by the same means as had been his pagan predecessors.

The formula of the 'identity announcement' appears to be derived from the Hellenistic mystery cults. The historian Diodorus, in the first century B.C., recorded the inscription on the tomb of Isis, which takes the form of an aretology, or list of divine claims, prerogatives and titles. Similar aretologies, said to be copied from inscriptions at cult centres, are found in the writings of other authors of this period:

> I am Isis, the Queen of every land, she who was taught by Hermes; and whatever laws I have ordained no one is able to annul. I am the eldest daughter of Kronos, the youngest of the gods; I am the wife and sister of King Osiris; I am the one who first found fruit for men; I am the mother of King Horus; I am she who rises in the constellation of the Dog; for me the city of Bubastis was founded. Rejoice, rejoice, O land of Egypt that nourished me.
>
> Diodorus, *Bibliotheca Historica*, I.27.3–6 (Grant, p. 130)

2 Greeting

Plutarch described the greeting given by the god during initiation into the mysteries at Delphi:

> ... It is an address to the god, or an invocation, complete in itself, that together with the utterance thereof puts the speaker in mind of the power of the deity. For the god addresses each one of us here, when approaching him, as if with a salutation, in the words, 'Know thyself', which is neither more nor less than 'Hail', whilst we, in requital to the god, say, 'Thou art', as though paying to him the true, undying, and sole property of himself, the predicate of existence.
> For we ourselves have in reality no part in existence; for all mortal nature being in a state between birth and dissolution, presents no more than an illusion, and a semblance, shapeless and unstable of itself.
>
> Plutarch, *On the E at Delphi*, XVII–XVIII

According to Plutarch, the greeting of the god made the worshipper aware of the illusory nature of his own existence. The experience conveyed that the god alone was immortal; it was nevertheless necessary to recognise the divine:

> But the god is, we must declare; and is with reference to no time, but with reference to the eternal, the immovable, timeless, and indeclinable; that which there is nothing before nor after, nor more, nor past, nor older nor younger, but He being One with the one 'Now' hath filled up the 'Ever'; and that which really is, alone is with reference to Him; neither born, nor about to be, nor growing, nor to have an end. In this way therefore ought we, when worshipping, to salute Him, and to address Him, or even truly, as some of the ancients did, 'Thou art One'.
>
> Plutarch, *On the E at Delphi*, XX

The experience of the divine as eternal unity, discussed already in connection with the writings of the Neoplatonic philosophers (p. 9ff.), was essentially that of the pre-Christian world. The incubation cults provided means of achieving this experience, together with liberation from fears of the after-life.

Amongst means of overcoming fear of the demonic world was, in pagan Egypt, the wearing of amulets. Plaques were worn round the neck depicting a deity known as Shed, or 'the saviour'.[68] He was called 'the great god, lord of heaven' and also 'lord of deserts'. He was represented as a hunter who pursued gazelles and lions in his chariot. He also destroyed snakes, scorpions and crocodiles. He was sometimes identified with the youthful Horus. In this case, he was represented as a divine child, with a lion and a gazelle, standing on the heads of two crocodiles and holding snakes and scorpions in his hands.

In the Coptic text of the *Dormition of the Virgin*, the appearance of the Saviour on a chariot followed the prayer of the Virgin for deliverance from the animal forms and other torments of *Amente*:

> Now when she had finished this prayer, we also said the Amen. Behold, there were thunderings and lightnings and the whole place was moved to its foundations. The Lord Jesus appeared in our midst, mounted upon a chariot of light, Moses being before him, with all the rest of the prophets, David the King and the righteous Kings. The whole place gave light like a fire. As we could not bear the fear, we fell down in the midst, we became like a dead man. But He, our Lord Jesus, called in His sweet voice: 'Greeting my Virgin Mother, greeting my holy apostles, greeting you virgins gathered in this place.' And suddenly the fear left us. We fell down, we worshipped Him. And He said to His Mother: 'I have heard the prayer. And the supplication has come into my presence upon my throne of my glory.'
>
> *Of the falling asleep of Mary*, II (Robinson, p. 102)

The prostration of the apostles with fear, the removal of their fear and the greeting of the Virgin by the Saviour were described in terms similar to those of the present quotations from the martyr stories. The purpose of the visitation of the Saviour, represented in the text on the *Dormition*, was the removal of the soul of the Virgin to heaven. In the present texts, the greeting was given to the martyr (1–8), who was commanded to take courage and strength (1, 2, 5, 9–18). In addition, the admission of the martyr to the community of heaven was signified by the action of the Saviour in embracing him (1, 13–18) or giving him (the Kiss of) Peace.

In the Graeco-Roman world, the kiss was used, both socially and ritually, in the worship of deities. The lips and beard of the statue of Herakles at Agrigentium were said, by Cicero,[69] to have been almost worn away by the kisses of the devout. The Kiss of Peace, in the early Church, was the means by which the Christian community greeted and gave recognition to one another. To 'give the Peace'[70] (*dare pacem*) was, in the early days of the Church, to perform a ritual act, implying admission to the circle of those ready to die rather than return to paganism. In the martyr cult, however, the Saviour was the figure fulfilling the wishes of the populace for salvation from fear, pain and, particularly, from the demonic experiences of death. The narrator's purpose in telling the story of the martyr was to provide evidence that this form of salvation was possible. In the present episodes, the martyr was shown receiving from an external source the guarantee that, under divine protection, he was invincible. As in the incubation cults, immortality and infallibility were here represented as belonging to a world separated from man.

3   Releasing

Eusebius, in his *History of the Church*, gave detailed descriptions of the persecutions of the martyrs from the time of Nero onwards. His writings were based on his own observations and on contemporary documents from which he quoted. The whole history was probably completed by A.D. 325 and therefore reflects his own attitude to these events together with that of other observers. What distinguished many of the descriptions, found in the work of Eusebius, from those of the present narratives, was their portrayal of the torments. In the majority of his accounts, the martyrs were said to have suffered their fate, with no suggestion that this was alleviated by divine liberation or deliverance. The martyrdom of St. James,[71] the martyrdoms at Vienne and Lyon,[72] the martyrdom of Origen and his pupils,[73] and martyrdoms under Decius and his successors,[74] and those under Diocletian,[75] even if allowance be made for the personal bias of the author, were accounts of objective events.

The tendency to relate the martyrdoms to Old Testament events, and particularly to those of the *Book of Daniel*, was seen in the account, from the Church of Smyrna, of the martyrdom of Polycarp. In the *Song of the Three Children* occurred the account of the transformation of the midst of the furnace to a moist wind:

> But the angel of the Lord came down into the furnace together with Azarias and his fellows, and he smote the flame of the fire out of the furnace;
> and made the midst of the furnace as if it had been a moist whistling wind, so that the fire touched them not at all, neither hurt nor troubled them.
>
> *Song of the Three Children*, 26, 27

Similarly, in the martyrdom of Polycarp, it was said that the flames made a ring round the martyr, so that his body was preserved:

> When he had offered up the Amen and completed his prayer, the men in charge lit the fire, and a great flame shot up. Then we saw a marvellous sight, we who were privileged to see it and were spared to tell the others what happened. The fire took the shape of a vaulted room,

like a ship's sail filled with wind, and made a wall round the martyr's body, which was in the middle not like burning flesh but like gold and silver refined in a furnace. Indeed, we were conscious of a wonderful fragrance, like a breath of frankincense or some other costly spice. At last, seeing that the body could not be consumed by the fire, the lawless people summoned a confector to come forward and drive home his sword. When he did so there came out a stream of blood that quenched the fire, so that the whole crowd was astonished.

Eusebius, History of the Church, IV.15.40

Like the martyrdom of Polycarp, the *Song of the Three Children* was perhaps the model for later narratives. In these, not only was the body of the saint preserved, but when the flames were removed from the martyr (Quotations 1, 2, 7, 9, 10–14, 18) and the fire became like cool dew or water (Quotations 1–4, 6, 7, 10–13, 16, 17), he was said to come forth uninjured.

In the descriptions of the martyrdoms in Palestine and Egypt,[76] a further parallel between the martyrdoms and the *Book of Daniel* appeared. The wild animals, to which they were thrown by their persecutors, were said to have refused to attack the martyrs. The subduing of the ferocity of animals and even its transformation to reverence was also depicted in the present narratives (24–27).

In the religions of antiquity, a close relation existed between pain and trance states (see Chapter I.III.2). Through ritual, pain was, on the one hand, a means of inducing hallucinatory states and thus of obtaining revelations. On the other hand, unavoidable pain or sickness could be made endurable by entering into states of trance. In the martyrdom of Isaiah, the prophet was depicted as oblivious of the pain to which he was subjected:

And Balchira spake thus to Isaiah: 'Say what I say unto thee and I will turn their heart, and I will compel Manesseh and the princes of Judah and the people and all Jerusalem to reverence thee.' And Isaiah answered and said: 'So far as I have utterance (I say): Damned and accursed be thou and all thy powers and all thy house. For thou canst not take (from me) aught save the skin of my body.' And they seized and sawed in sunder Isaiah, the son of Amoz, with a wooden saw. And Manesseh and Balchira and the false prophets and the princes and the people (and) all stood looking on. . . . And when Isaiah was being sawn in sunder, he neither cried aloud nor wept, but his lips spake with the Holy Spirit until he was sawn in twain.

Ascension of Isaiah, V.8–14 (Charles)

The ambiguity of the imagery relating to the overcoming of pain was discussed in connection with the desert ascetics (Chapter I.ɪɪɪ). That the martyrs, as a historical fact, endured pain to the point of death, was recorded in contemporary writings. Later accounts, however, depicted their experiences in terms appropriate to pre-Christian cults. The use of the imagery of a heavenly visitation enabled the narrator to ascribe the preservation of the martyr's body to divine intervention. Nevertheless, to show the miraculous removal of the source of pain was also to depict the martyr deprived of the experience for which he was being commemorated. Experience of the divine world could be, on the one hand, the experience in comparison with which pain was as nothing. On the other hand, by positing the removal of pain, the experience could be altered to the status of a dream. The miracle depicted, in the latter case, was not the fortitude of the martyr, but the preservation of his body.

The correspondence has already been noted of the imagery of fire and animal forms, in the martyr stories, to that of the demons of the after-life (p. 201). The claims made by the martyr cult, as exemplified in the promises made concerning rewards in heaven and earth (p. 182) far exceeded those of pagan cults. The ancient Egyptian religion provided men with ritual means to survive in the life after death. The ascetics, like their pagan predecessors, acknowledged that all must cross the River of Fire. The martyr cult claimed for its participants that these experiences would be transformed or obliterated altogether. Just as the fire and the wild beasts were prevented from harming the martyr, so through the ritual surrounding his commemoration, demonic experiences would be prevented from entering the consciousness of the congregation.

In certain miracles, said to have occurred at their shrines, the martyrs were shown as appearing in answer to prayer. Like the deities of the incubation cults, one of their functions was the exorcism of demons. The appearance of the latter as dragons and snakes has already been discussed (p. 157). In Quotation 29, the martyr was shown killing the dragon during his lifetime, helped by an archangel. Quotations 29–32 showed how the divine intervention, on which depended the overcoming of the dragon or demon, was effected by the martyr after his death. This type of miracle story upheld, on the one hand the appropriateness, for experience of the divine, of the circumstances of the incubation cult. On the other hand, exorcism of the demonic world, by invocation of the dead martyr, was shown as infallible. The sanctified dead of the Christian community were represented as a source of protection to the living.

209

4 *Restoring*

In the Hellenistic period, the increasing decadence of the ancient Egyptian religion involved the reintroduction of the archaic practices of earlier times (see Chapter II.II.1). Among these were the ritual killing and mummification of sacred animals.[77] The conservation, in this way, of hundreds of thousands of animal corpses is evidence of a widespread belief in the efficacy, for the living, of preserving even animal bodies after death. The keeping intact of the dead body was such an essential part of the pagan religion that mummification continued to be practised even after its prohibition in Christian times. The final disappearance of the custom probably took place after the Arab conquest in the seventh century.[78] The Egyptian funerary cult was the expression of a psychological attitude in which experience of the divine was a reality only insofar as it was physically embodied. In the case of the dead, the potential vehicle for the divine was the intact body or even the statue of the deceased.

On the advice of Augustine, Gregory Thaumaturgus and Gregory the Great, popular observances, if not 'absolutely evil' in themselves, were given a Christian form.[79] Features from local funerary customs and from the Graeco-Roman incubation cults thus appeared in stories of the martyrs. The widespread distribution of the cults of Serapis and Isis in Hellenistic times may have contributed to a general acceptance of Egyptian notions on the significance of the body after death. In texts originating in Egypt and elsewhere, appeared accounts of the miraculous restoration of the bodies of martyrs during their 'trials'. The deaths of the martyrs, as described by Eusebius and others, involved the dismemberment, decapitation, disembowelling and burning of their bodies. In the present narratives, whatever methods were used to destroy them, the bodies of the martyrs were restored and healed by divine intervention.

The ancient funerary ritual of Egypt established for the deceased a divine and universal significance. Only after the recitation of the proper formulae were the various parts of the body related to the regions of the universe. The relationship of the body to the divine world, in the imagination of the community, thus depended on the repetition of these ritual performances. In Christian times, the body of the martyr was regarded as the bearer of those powers by which, after death, he benefited those who commemorated him. In the imagination of this audience, the martyr story, recited periodically, invested his body with that same divine power which was said to have preserved it during life.

The fact that, in perhaps the majority of cases, the identity of the relic was not that of the martyr named, was irrelevant. Collective ritual attributed divine powers to the martyr's body as it had to the mummy in ancient Egypt. Whereas in pre-Christian times, the ritual had linked and thus 'subjected' the body to the phenomena of the universe, Christianity 'liberated' men from the rulership of the stars. In ancient Egypt, ritual had enabled men to regard the whole universe as divine. In Christian times, the same technique was used, but its application was limited to certain enshrined human remains.

The cult of Osiris, in ancient Egypt, commemorated the gathering together, by Isis, of the parts of his dead body, dismembered and scattered by Seth. Dismemberment and decapitation of the dead was practised in predynastic Egypt.[80] Possibly the story of the dismemberment and restoration of the body of Osiris preserved, in mythological form, these early funerary rituals. Separation of the joints of wrists, ankles, elbows, knees, shoulders and hips gave rise to the situation of the martyr depicted in Narrative 21 (see text pp. 46–47). His decapitation, described in Section V.i.2, Narrative 23, said to have been performed after death, would have left his body in fourteen pieces, the number into which the body of Osiris was divided.[81]

The signing of the body with the Cross as a protection against pagan assaults (Narratives 1–11, 29), emphasised the importance of the preservation of the body. It is noteworthy that, in the present-day Coptic Baptismal rites, the thirty-six sites of inunction include two aspects of both joints of shoulders, elbows, wrists, hips, knees and ankles,[82] the sites at which bodies were dismembered. Uniting of the limbs was described in Narratives 20, 22. The stereotyped formulae of healing (Narratives 6, 7, 9, 12–16, 18, 19, 23, 25, 26, 31–35, 36), touching or passing the hand over the body (3, 6, 12–19, 26, 29, 32–34), restoring the body (10, 24–31, 37), so that there was no injury upon the body (9, 16, 17, 20, 22, 25, 28, 29), were perhaps derived from pagan healing cults. Disembowelling, frequently described in the martyr stories, was a necessary prelude to mummification. Emphasis, in these stories, on the falling to the ground of bodily organs or blood (10, 21–23, 25–31) may be imagery once of ritual significance.

In the martyr stories, the influence of the Old Testament was also evident. The divine intervention occurred in answer to the martyr's prayer (8, 9, 12–16, 20, 22–24, 26, 28, 29, 32–34). The deity, who appeared in order to save the martyr, was represented as doing so for the sake of preserving the honour of his own name. Like the enemies of the God of Israel, the hegemon, duke or king, who persecuted the martyr, was put to shame (9, 13, 14, 24–25, 28, 47–50). Among the episodes demonstrating the victory of the deity was the standing up of the martyr, his body unharmed from the torments, in the presence of the hegemon (9, 19, 20, 22, 24). After the intervention of the deity, the martyr was said to rejoice (1, 8, 17, 18, 31, 36, 38, 39) like one risen from a feast (17, 38–40) or from drinking wine (43–46). His body was not only found to be whole (35, 36) but his face or body gave light or appeared red (35, 36, 41–43) or gave forth a sweet smell (35, 36). The significance of these last manifestations is discussed in Chapter V.III.1, 4. Alternatively, the body of the martyr was found untouched in the midst of the fire (35, 36; see also the martyrdom of Polycarp quoted on p. 208).

In ancient Egypt, restoration or preservation of the body was a ritual renewal of the relationship of man, as a physical entity, with the whole universe. Since the universe itself was regarded as divine, man attributed to his body a measure of that same divinity which he ascribed to the universe. In the martyr cult, as in Judaism, the sacred was ritually separated from the profane. The physical universe was regarded as belonging to the latter category. The martyr's body and shrine, like the Holy of Holies of the Tabernacle, was, for the worshippers, one of the few legitimate sources of divine manifestations.

5 Raising from the Dead

In the Apostolic Age, Christianity claimed, on the one hand, to achieve the liberation of men from the domination of Destiny, the powers attributed to the universe and to the physical body. On the other hand, the resurrection of the body was preached, implying a restoration of the physical creation to a new status. The time and manner of this resurrection was variously expressed as was the allocation of power in this transformed situation. The role of the individual as recipient or initiator of salvation was also differently represented, according to the source of the writings on the subject.

In the ancient religions of Egypt and Greece, the death and rebirth of gods was originally connected with the rising and setting of the heavenly bodies and with the succession of one season of the year by the next. Gods were put to death, mourned, buried or dismembered, and restored to life, as periodic ritual acts. The resurrection of a deity was as inevitable as his death. Nevertheless, misfortune or death were feared for those who neglected the cult of the gods. For the individual, death was thought to occur at the time appointed by Destiny. In the conversation of Abraham with Death, in the *Apocalypse of Abraham*, a Zodiac of deaths was represented, of which one was at the right time:

Then said Abraham: I beseech thee tell me: is there an untimely death? Death said: Verily, verily I say unto thee as God's truth there are seventy-two deaths. One is the just death that has its allotted time.

Testament of Abraham, XX (Box, p. 35)

In the Mystery religions, the individual underwent ritual experiences of 'death' and 'resurrection' and received revelations concerning his fate during sleep or trance. The awakening from this condition represented his rebirth or resurrection. The use of the imagery of awakening from sleep or death was frequently found in Christian narratives depicting miraculous cures (see Section III.1.4). The recalling to life of the Virgin, in the Coptic version of the *Dormition*, was perhaps a 'Christianised' version of such a ritual:

When the Lord had said these things over the coffin of stone, immediately it opened, for indeed it was shut like the ark of Noah, at the time when no one could open it except God, He who shut it at the time. Immediately the body of the chaste Virgin arose and embraced its own soul, like two brothers who have come forth from the strange country, and they became one with one another. Immediately the Singer David came into the midst at that hour. He struck his harp, saying: 'Mercy and truth are come forth to meet one another; righteousness and peace have saluted one another.' And when these things had happened, He went up to the heavens, blessing us.

Of the falling asleep of Mary, II (Robinson, p. 124)

Knowledge of the Mystery of the raising of the dead was said, in the *Pistis Sophia*, to give to the individual authority over demons and thus over sickness:

Now therefore, Maria, not only you, but every man who will complete the Mystery of the Raising of the Dead—this cures demons and every pain and every sickness, with the blind and with the lame, with the maimed, with the dumb, with the deaf, this I gave to you once— he who will perform a Mystery and complete it, afterwards when he asks for anything—poverty and riches, weakness and strength, disease and sound body, with every healing of the body and with raising of the dead, to cure the lame and the blind and the deaf and the dumb, with every sickness and every pain, in a word, he who will complete that mystery and ask anything which I have said, it will happen to him instantly.

Pistis Sophia, 256a–256b

In the gnostic sect which produced this text, knowledge of the Mysteries was said to be the means of achieving liberation from the rulership of Destiny or the Archons. It was not merely a method of knowing the future.

The release of the soul from domination by the body was said, by Plato, to be a condition attained through philosophy. The imagery of collecting and bringing together by the soul of its scattered members, much used by later writers, appeared in the *Phaedo*:

> And does not the purification consist in this which has been mentioned long ago in our discourse, in separating, so far as possible, the soul from the body, and teaching the soul the habit of collecting and bringing itself together from all parts of the body, and living, so far as it can, both now and hereafter, alone by itself, freed from the body as from fetters? ...
>
> Well, then, this is what we call death, is it not, a release and separation from the body?
>
> Plato, *Phaedo*, 67C, D

In using this same imagery, Porphyry laid stress on the process as one of inner unification and 'ascension' of the soul:

> If thou study to ascend into thyself, gathering from the body all thy scattered members which have been scattered into a multitude from the unity which up to a point held sway.
>
> Porphyry, *Epistle to Marcella*, 10 (Wilson, I, p. 275)

This image was also used by the writer of the apocryphal *Gospel of Philip*, quoted in the *Panarion* of Epiphanius, a polemic against fourth century heresies. In the gospel, the imagery of the 'ascent' was applied to the passage of the soul through the planetary spheres, to whose rulership the soul was not subject:

> The Lord revealed to me what the soul must say in its ascent to heaven, and how it must answer each of the powers above: 'I have recognized myself and gathered myself together from all sides and have not sown children to the Archon and have gathered the scattered members, and I know thee who thou art; for I belong to those from above.' And so it is set free.
>
> Epiphanius, *Panarion*, 26.13.2–3 (*Gospel of Philip*) (Wilson, I, p. 273)

The Judeo-Christian *Odes of Solomon* also described the liberation of the individual from bondage. Salvation was, however, said to be given from above:

> My arms I lifted up to the Most High, even to the grace of the Lord: because He had cast off my bonds from me: and my Helper had lifted

me up to His Grace and to His Salvation: and I put off darkness and clothed myself with light, and my soul acquired a body free from sorrow or affliction or pains.

Odes of Solomon, XXI.1–3

The individual was represented as the recipient of bodily renewal and freedom from pain and sickness:

My members were strengthened that they might not fall from His strength. Sicknesses removed from my body, and it stood to the Lord by His will.

Odes of Solomon, XVIII.2, 3

In certain Judeo-Christian apocrypha, the imagery of the separation of the soul from the body was used in describing the raising of the righteous to heaven after death. In the *Ascension of Isaiah*, the descent of the Messiah through the heavens and finally to Hades was said to be followed by the liberation of the righteous and their ascent with Him to heaven:

When He hath plundered the angel of death, He will ascend on the third day, and He will remain in this world 545 days. And then many of the righteous will ascend with Him, whose spirits do not receive their garments till the Lord Christ ascend and they ascend with him. Then indeed they will receive their garments and thrones and crowns, when He has ascended into the seventh heaven.

Ascension of Isaiah, IX.16–19 (Charles)

A similar gathering of the righteous at the Ascension was represented in the second century apocryphal *Epistle of the Apostles*:

When he had said this, and had finished his discourse with us, he said unto us again: Behold, on the third day and at the third hour he shall come which hath sent me, that I may depart with him. And as he so spake there was thunder and lightning and an earthquake, and the heavens parted asunder and there appeared a bright cloud which bore him up. And there came voices of many angels, rejoicing and singing praises and saying: 'Gather us, O priest, into the light of thy majesty.' And when he drew nigh to the firmament of heaven, we heard his voice saying unto us: 'Depart hence in peace.'

Epistle of the Apostles, 51 (PO.IX.Col.239)

Among the early Church Fathers, Irenaeus, following St. Paul, used the imagery of *Psalm* 67 (68),[83] in connection with the Descent into Hell and the Ascension. The 'leading of captivity captive' was, in some writings, applied to the liberation of the Old Testament saints and their elevation

215

to heaven. In Irenaeus, however, the 'captivity' referred to the rulership of the rebel angels (or archons) over the living:

> And when raised from the dead Christ was to ascend into heaven, as David says: The chariot of God is thousands and thousands of angels; the Lord is among them in Sinai, in the holy place. He ascends on high, leading the throng of captives; he hath given gifts to men. By 'captivity' the prophet means the destruction of the power of the rebel angels.
>
> <div align="right">Irenaeus, <i>Demonstrations</i>, 83</div>

The notion of the ascension of the Messiah as a second 'captivity' for the righteous was derived from Jewish Apocrypha.[84] This use of the imagery of the ascent of the soul after death, gathering its members, implied the dependence of man on salvation from without. A similar use of this same imagery was made in the *Odes of Solomon*. In certain *Odes*, written in the first person and referring to the liberation of His people by the Messiah, the 'captivity' and salvation was extended to the whole world:

> I was strengthened and made mighty and took the world captive; and it became to me for the praise of the Most High, and of God my Father. And the Gentiles were gathered together who were scattered abroad. . . . and they walked in life and were saved and became my people for ever.
>
> Odes of Solomon, X.4–8

(see also *Ode* XVII.8–14)

The Messianic salvation was also shown to include Hades and to involve the overthrowing of the dragon with seven heads (see p. 157), the gathering of the dead and the renewal of their bodies:

> He who brought me down from on high, also brought me up from the regions below; and He who gathers together the things that are betwixt is He also who cast me down: He who scattered my enemies and my adversaries: He who gave me authority over bonds that I might loose them; He that overthrew by my hands the dragon with seven heads: and thou hast set me over his roots that I might destroy his seed. Thou wast there and didst help me, and in every place thy name was blessed by me. Thy right hand destroyed his wicked poison; and thy hand levelled the way for those who believe in thee: and thou didst choose them from the graves and didst separate them from the dead. Thou didst take dead bones and thou didst cover them with bodies. They were motionless, and thou didst give them energy for life. Thy way was without corruption, and thy face brought thy world

to corruption: that everything might be dissolved and then renewed, and that the foundation for everything might be thy rock: and on it thou didst build thy Kingdom; and thou wast the dwelling place of the saints.

Odes of Solomon, XXII.1–12

In ancient times, for the philosopher who could free himself from dependence on the life of the senses, death was merely an extension of his way of life. This independence of the philosopher from the workings of Destiny was perhaps the basis of accounts of his power to heal and even to raise the dead. The *Life* of Apollonius of Tyana showed him as able to perform these feats.[85] Such power was generally attributed to the gods and to figures like Asclepius. The cult of these deities and deified healers was a means by which the populace hoped to circumvent Destiny. In the apocryphal *Acts of the Apostles*, accounts were given of the conflict of Christianity, as a religion of 'liberation', with pagan cults and individuals making similar claims. The raising of the dead was regarded, in the pre-Christian world, as the ultimate test of divine powers. Numerous instances were given in the apocryphal *Acts* that the apostles were able, not only to raise the dead, but even to ensure the death of their opponents. Each side accused the other of performing these feats 'only in appearance'.[86] These accounts followed the pattern of the deaths and resurrections enacted within the ancient cults, in which the imagination of the participants was controlled within the ritual. The liberation from Fate, claimed by the Mystery religions, was a subjective experience for the individual. The enactment of the death and resurrection of a god was a subjective rather than an objective event, in which the community shared. The description of the activities of the apostles, in terms derived from these cults, represented the triumph of pagan methods of experiencing the divine through external control of the imagination. The apostles appeared, not as individuals, but as saviour gods who, as dreams or hallucinations, restored the bodies of their worshippers.

The emphasis on bodily restoration was perhaps the outcome of the attempts of the opponents of Christianity to repudiate the Resurrection. Judeo-Christian apocryphal writings maintained that a physical resurrection would occur and that the earth would restore the bodies delivered into it. In the *Book of Baruch*, a future return of the dead to life was foretold, in order that they should be recognised by the living:

And He answered and said unto me: 'Hear Baruch, this word, and write in the remembrance of thy heart all that thou shalt learn. For the earth shall then assuredly restore the dead, (which it now receives,

217

in order to preserve them). It shall make no change in their form, but as it has received, so shall it restore them, and as I delivered them unto it, so also shall it raise them.

For then it will be necessary to show to the living that the dead have come to life again, and that those who had departed have returned (again). And it shall come to pass, when they have severally recognized those whom they now know, then judgment shall grow strong, and those things which before were spoken of shall come.

II Baruch, 50.1-2 (Charles)

Opponents of Christianity sought to destroy the bodies of saints and martyrs so that their bodies would not be able to rise again. Such an attitude was described by Eusebius, in connection with the martyrdoms at Vienne and Lyon:

Thus the martyrs' bodies, after six days' exposure to every kind of insult and to the open sky, were finally burnt to ashes and swept by these wicked men into the Rhône which flows near by, that not even a trace of them might be seen on the earth again. And this they did as if they could defeat God and rob the dead of their rebirth, 'in order' they said, 'that they might have no hope of resurrection—the belief that has led them to bring into this country a new foreign cult and treat torture with contempt, going willingly and cheerfully to their death. Now let us see if they will rise again, and if their god can help and save them from our hands.'

Eusebius, *History of the Church*, V.1.62, 63

In the present narratives, the indestructibility of the body of the martyr was demonstrated. The imagery of the scattered members of the soul was applied to the body, whose parts were gathered and restored by a Saviour who then ascended to heaven.

The imagery of the raising of the martyr from the dead, in the present Section, also included that of the Last Judgment. In the apocalyptic literature, destruction of the elemental spheres and of the heavenly luminaries, chaos and darkness were foretold (see p. 164ff.) as the prelude to the opening of the graves and the resurrection of the dead. The significance of these events is discussed in Chapter V.III.4. In the present narratives, the pit (1, 2, 3), the mountain or dunghill (5, 6, 7, 9, 10) and the cauldron (11–13) were the situations from which the bodily remains of the martyrs were gathered. The martyr's body, after rising from the dead, was thus represented as an anticipation of the form in which man would appear after the Last Judgment.

The body of the martyr, thus miraculously 'raised' or preserved, was regarded, by the early Church Fathers, as being able itself to raise the dead. The restorations to life which occurred at shrines of St. Stephen were described by Augustine.[87] The number of such accounts in martyr stories is perhaps a measure of the resistance of the pagan world to recognising divinity in the human individual who is subject to physical death. The martyrs who, as historic individuals, disregarded their own physical lives, were commemorated as if they were pagan deities, rising from the dead and restoring others to life.

III HEAVENLY SIGNS

1 Heavenly Light

Revelations in the ancient world were experienced, either by abstracting the attention from the sense world and disciplining the mind, or by ritually exercising the imagination and attributing divine qualities to the outer universe. In either case, the vision often appeared in the form of light. In the first category of experiences can be included those achieved by the methods described by Plato. By exercise of the intellect, the Absolute Good was perceived. The process was said to be comparable to the raising of the eyes to the light of the visible world:

And so we have at last arrived at the hymn of Dialectic.
This is that strain which is of the intellect only, but which the faculty of sight will nevertheless be found to imitate. When a person starts on the discovery of the Absolute by the light of reason only, without the assistance of the senses, and never desists until by pure intelligence he arrives at the perception of the Absolute Good, he at last finds himself at the end of the intellectual world, as in the case of sight at the end of the visible.
This power of elevating the highest principle in the soul to the contemplation of that which is best in existence, with which we compare the raising of that faculty which is the very light of the body to the sight of that which is brightest in the material and visible world—this power is given by the pursuit of the above mentioned arts.
Plato, Republic, VII.532

The means described by Plotinus, by which he attained to mystical union with the divine light, were similar to those of Plato. Beyond what was comprehensible to the intellect, was said to be the dimension in which the seer was united with the source of light:

By these methods one becomes, to self and all else, at once seen and seer; identical with Being and Divine Intellect and the entire living

219

All, we no longer see the Supreme as an external; we are near now, the next is That and It is close at hand, radiant above the Intellectual. Here we put aside all learning; disciplined to this pitch, established in beauty, but suddenly swept beyond it by the very crest of the wave of Intellect surging beneath, the quester is lifted and sees, never knowing how; the vision floods the eyes with light, but it is not a light showing some other thing, the light is itself the vision. No longer is there object seen and light to show it, no longer Intellect and objects of Intellection; this is the very Radiance that brought both into being.

Plotinus, Enneads, VI.7.36, The Good

Among early Christian writers, Augustine described how he practised methods similar to those of Plotinus, and attained to a mystical vision of light:

And, being by these books admonished to return into myself, I entered into the secret closet of my soul, guided by Thee; and this I could do because Thou wast my helper. I entered, and beheld with the mysterious eye of my soul the light that never changes, above the eye of my soul, above my intelligence. It was not the common light which all flesh can see, nor was it greater yet of the same kind, as if the light of day were to grow brighter and flood all space. It was not like this, but something altogether different from any earthly illumination. . . . Thus step by step was I led upwards, from bodies to the soul which perceives by means of the bodily senses, and thence to the soul's inward faculty, to which bodily sense reports external facts, and this belongs even to beasts, and thence again to the reasoning power, to whose judgment is referred the knowledge received by the bodily senses.

And when this power also within me found itself changeable, it lifted itself up to its own intelligence, and withdrew its thoughts from experience, abstracting itself from the contradictory throng of sensuous images, that it might find out what that light was wherein it was bathed. . . . And thus with the flash of one hurried glance, it attained to the vision of that which is. . . . But I could not sustain my gaze; my weakness was dashed back, and I was relegated to my ordinary experiences, bearing with me nothing but a loving remembrance.

Augustine, Confessions, VII.10.1/17.2, 3

In the second category of experiences, described above, fall those depicted by Iamblichos. These were probably achieved through the rituals of Hellenistic mystery and incubation cults. The divine unity which pervaded and controlled the universe was said to be perceptible as light:

> The light that is the object of perception is one, continuous and everywhere the same entirety; so that it is not possible for a part of it to be cut off by itself, or to be enclosed in a circle, or at any time to remove itself from the source of illumination. According to the same principles, therefore, the whole universe, being susceptible of division, is distinguished with reference to the one and indivisible light of the gods. In short, this light is one and the same everywhere, and is not only present, undivided, with all things that are capable of participating of it, but it, likewise, by an absolute power and by an infinite superiority, fills all things, as a cause, joins them together in itself, unites them everywhere with itself, and combines the ends with the beginnings. The whole heaven, including with it the universe imitating this, goes around in a circular revolution, unites all to itself, and leads the elements whirling in a circle; and all things being in one another, and borne toward one another, it holds them together and defines their equal proportions.
>
> Iamblichos, *The Egyptian Mysteries*, I.III (Wilder, p. 47)

The deities which presided over the various regions of the universe were said to be recognisable by means of their luminosity:

> In the (Epoptic) Vision the figures of the gods shine brilliantly; those of the archangels are awe-inspiring and yet gentle; those of the angels are milder; those of the demons are alarming. . . .
> In a like manner, let us explain also, in regard to the luminosity. The images of the gods glow with abundance of light, and those of the archangels are surpassing luminous. Those of the angels are resplendent with light, but the demons present the appearance of smouldering fire, and the half-gods a commingling from many sources.
>
> Iamblichos, *The Egyptian Mysteries*, II.v (Wilder, pp. 82; 86)

The divine light was said to be derived from without and to manifest not only through the gods, but in the heavenly bodies:

> There are also many other ways for bringing the Light; but they may all be reduced to one, namely: to its illumination in whatever way and through whatever instrumentalities the gods may choose to shine forth. Since not only the light is from without, and alone possesses everything subject to the will and intelligence of the gods, but, what is more important, it has a sacred irradiation derived not only under the aether on high but also from the air or from the moon or the sun, or some other celestial sphere, it is manifest from all these things that

such a mode of divination is unlimited, primary in operation, and worthy of the gods.

Iamblichos, *The Egyptian Mysteries*, III.viii (Wilder, p. 135)

The theophanies of the Old and New Testaments fell chiefly into the second of the above categories. The luminous qualities of angels were depicted in *Daniel* and *Revelation*.[88] The 'glory' of the environment, as a manifestation of the presence of the Deity, was described in *i Kings* and *ii Chronicles*[89]; similarly the light of the Heavenly Jerusalem was said to be of divine origin.[90] The beneficence of God was depicted as the shining of His face[91]; the shining of the divine countenance was also compared with the sun.[92] After receiving the divine inspiration, the face of Moses was said to shine.[93] The righteous and wise were compared to the firmament of stars in apocalyptic writings.[94] Similar imagery was used in *I Enoch*:

And all the righteous and elect before Him shall be strong as fiery lights, and their mouths shall be full of blessing.

I Enoch, 39.7b (Charles)

The Biblical writings were the model on which descriptions of divine light, in the stories of ascetics and martyrs, were based. Comparison was made of the faces of the ascetics and that of Moses (35, 37). Not only the face but the whole body was also said to undergo a fiery transformation (41, 67). The fire in these narratives appears to have been the image of light rather than that of heat. Fire was also used as an image of divine inspiration by later Syrian mystical writers (see p. 135). In this case, the 'condition' was depicted as a purely subjective experience, rather than one which the bystanders shared:

This condition is followed by another one, in which a man is clad with fire from the sole of his feet to the crown of his head, and when he looks at himself he will not be able to see any material body, but only the fire with which he is clad.

'Abdisho' Hazzaya, *Treatises* (Woodbrooke Studies, VII, p. 172)

Light was depicted as illuminating the environment, either at the time of a heavenly visitation, or as the result of the presence of a holy man. A holy man was recognised by means of manifestations of light (77–80). The light was often said to be such that it was impossible to look at it. The appearance of the Saviour to the martyr and the illumination of the whole place (18–29) was described in terms similar to those used in depicting the Descent to *Amente* (17).

The heavenly visitors, like the stellar deities of paganism, appeared to their worshippers as illuminated figures. They wore or carried garments or crowns of light. The Saviour was often described as a man or youth of light. The 'vehicles' in which the soul ascended to the heavenly realms were represented as wings, chariots or clouds of light.

2   Heavenly Fire

In Greek and Jewish writings generally, fire was the 'visible' sign of divine inspiration and indwelling. Possession by the deity involved obliteration of self-consciousness. In the writings of Iamblichos, describing the Hellenistic cults, the divine fire was said to be visible, both to the possessed individual and to the bystanders. The evocation was performed by the priests and the recipient of the divine fire was said to be completely dominated and controlled by it. The nature of the 'god' was discernible to the beholders by virtue of the quality of the luminosity manifested (see p. 221).

> The principal thing in the evoking of a spirit is that the spirit is seen coming down and entering into an individual, also its importance and kind, and he is mystically persuaded and governed by it. The form of fire is seen by the recipient before the receiving of the spirit, and sometimes, either when the god is descending or when he is withdrawing himself, it becomes visible to all the Beholders. From this manifestation the sign of the god which is the most genuine, the most potent, and most perfectly ordered, becomes known to a certainty; and it is not only proper to proclaim what is true in respect to certain matters, but also to exhibit the power or to complete the rite. . . .
> If the presence of the fire of the gods and an ineffable form of light without shall permeate the individual who is under control, fill him completely, have absolute dominion over him and encompass him from all sides so that he can put forth no energy of his own, what sense or mental effort or purpose of his own can he have who receives the divine fire? . . .
> Let such as these be then, the divine tokens of genuine inspiration from the gods.
> Iamblichos, *The Egyptian Mysteries*, III.vii (Wilder, pp. 116, 117)

In the Delphic oracle, also described by Iamblichos, inspiration was said to be associated with the physical act of breathing fiery fumes. These issued from below the shrine. Plutarch attributed the failure of the Delphic oracle to inconsistency, both in the quality of the vapour and in the 'disposition' of the prophetess.[95] According to Iamblichos, in performing her role as medium of the god, the prophetess herself was illuminated by the fiery mist:

The prophetess at Delphi, however, whether she gives oracles to human beings from a tenuous and fire-like spirit brought up from somewhere through an aperture, or vaticinates sitting in the inner shrine, upon the bronze chair with three feet or upon the four-footed chair sacred to the divinities, gives herself entirely to the divine spirit and is shined upon by the ray of the fire. In fact, when the fiery mist coming up from the aperture, dense and abundant, encompasses her on every side in a circle, she becomes filled by it with a divine luminance, and when she sits down in the seat of the god she comes into harmony with the unwavering oracular power of the divinity, and from these two preparatory operations she becomes entirely the medium of the god.

Iamblichos, *The Egyptian Mysteries*, III.vii (Wilder, p. 126)

In Judaism, fire was the 'visible' sign of communication between the prophet and the Deity. In the *Exodus* account, the burning bush, and the cloud, dark by day and luminous by night, which covered the tabernacle, were the situations in which Moses heard the voice of the Lord. Fire marked the occasion when the Deity announced to Moses His name in the words 'I am'.[96] The 'visible' evidence of the divine presence was the fiery cloud; its dwelling was between the cherubim of the tabernacle or temple, the religious centre of the people of Israel. The imagery of fire was, in the Old Testament, associated with that of darkness, smoke and cloud. A 'sleep' and a 'horror of great darkness' fell upon Abraham when he received his instructions.[97] Moses heard the words of God out of cloud and thick darkness.[98] The Lord dwelt in 'thick darkness'.[99] In the dark, the divine fire of the pillar of cloud was visible.[100]

Episodes in the lives of the ascetics contained imagery similar to that of pre-Christian times. The distinguishing of divine or demonic influences by virtue of the light emitted by their recipients, was described in V.iii.1 (Narratives 43, 44). Recognition of a god by similar observations was described by Iamblichos (see p. 223). Fire as an image of divine communication appeared in a number of the present narratives. The words of holy men were said to appear as fire or lightning (1–6). The outstretched hands of the ascetic in an attitude of prayer were described as lights or lamps of fire (8–13). The column, or pillar of fire, an image derived from the *Exodus* account, appeared to have various meanings. It represented the holy man who was 'perfect' (17); it appeared as a sign from heaven (15, 20, 21, 31); it stood for the prayers of the brethren (16); it represented divine guidance (14, 18, 19, 22). Fire as evidence of the divine presence was depicted in Narratives 7, 23–27; of divine wrath in Narratives 28–31.

The imagery of light and fire as a manifestation of the divine was appropriate to descriptions of pre-Christian cults. In these, within the context of the ritual, manifestations of light and fire were caused to 'appear' to the participants. States of possession and mystical states had in common the fact that full self-consciousness was not maintained. Their biographies ascribed to the ascetics and their experiences the characteristics of the theophanies of the ancient world. It was thus implied that the ascetics achieved the very condition from which they had striven to liberate themselves. Both light and fire were used to designate attainment by the holy men. It is possible to assume that the biographers themselves regarded the divine as a universal power by which the ascetics were inspired, rather than the expression of individual self-consciousness.

3   Heavenly Beauty

According to Plato, the memory retained by the soul of the beauty of the heavenly world enabled man, through sight, to distinguish beauty in earthly things:

So much, then in honour of memory, on account of which I have now spoken at some length, through yearning for the joys of that other time. But beauty, as I said before, shone in brilliance among those visions; and since we came to earth we have found it shining most clearly through the clearest of our senses; for sight is the sharpest of the physical senses, though wisdom is not seen by it, for wisdom would arouse terrible love, if such a clear image of it were granted as would come through sight, and the same is true of the other lovely realities; but beauty alone has this privilege, and therefore it is most clearly seen and loveliest.

Plato, *Phaedrus*, 250C, D

The Hellenistic mystery religions and incubation cults claimed to enable man to 're-enter' the heavenly world or to establish relations with its deities. Accounts based on initiation experiences emphasised the beauty of both face and dress of the heavenly visitors. Apuleius, in his *Metamorphoses*, described at length the appearance of Isis, who visited him during 'sleep':

Scarcely had I closed my eyes when lo, from the midst of the deep there arose that face divine to which even the gods must do reverence. Then a little at a time, slowly, her whole shining body emerged from the sea and came into full view. I would like to tell you all the wonder of this vision . . .

First, the tresses of her hair were long and thick, and streamed down softly, flowing and curling about her divine neck. On her head she wore as a crown many garlands of flowers, and in the middle of her forehead shone white and glowing a round disc like a mirror, or rather like the moon; on its right and left it was bound about with the furrowed coils of rising vipers, and above it were stalks of grain. Her tunic was of many colours, woven of the finest linen, now gleaming with snowy whiteness, now yellow like the crocus, now rosy-red like a flame. But what dazzled my eyes more than anything else was her cloak, for it was a deep black, glistening with sable sheen; . . . Here and there along its embroidered border, and also in its surface, were scattered sequins of sparkling stars, and in their midst the full moon of midmonth shone forth like a flame of fire. And all along the border of that gorgeous robe there was an unbroken garland of all kinds of flowers and fruits. . . .

Such was the vision, and of such majesty. Then, breathing forth all the blessed fragrance of happy Arabia, she deigned to address me with voice divine.

Apuleius, *Metamorphoses*, XI.3, 4 (Grant, pp. 137, 138)

To Iamblichos, importance lay in the recognition of the apparitions evoked during ceremonies. Thus the varying degrees of beauty of gods, archangels and angels were said by him to be distinguishable:

With these peculiarities there flashes out from the gods Beauty which seems inconceivable, holding the Beholders fixed with wonder, imparting to them an unutterable gladness, displaying itself to view with ineffable symmetry, and carrying off the palm from other forms of comeliness. The glorious views of the archangels have themselves very great beauty, but it is by no means ineffable and admirable as that of the gods. Those of the angels partake in a degree of the beauty which they receive from the archangels.

Iamblichos, *The Egyptian Mysteries*, II.v (Wilder, p. 83)

Jewish apocalyptic literature contained numerous references to the beauty of angels and archangels (see Quotation 2 from *II Enoch*, in Section III.iv.1). The imagery was partly derived from descriptions of the heavenly world in the prophetic writings. The appearance of the Archangel Jaoel (a name possibly substituted for that of Jahweh) was described in the *Apocalypse of Abraham*:

And I rose up and saw him who had grasped me by my right hand and set me upon my feet; and the appearance of his body was like sapphire, and the look of his countenance was like chrysolite, and the

226

hair of his head like snow, and the turban upon his head like the appearance of the rainbow, and the clothing of his garments like purple; and a golden sceptre was in his right hand.

Apocalypse of Abraham, XI (Box, p. 49)

The seers of the apocalyptic writings were also represented as seeing the Lord's face. Descriptions emphasised its great and terrible aspect rather than its beauty:

On the (tenth) Heaven, Aravoth, I saw the appearance of the Lord's face, like iron made to glow in fire, and brought out, emitting sparks, and it burns. Thus I saw the Lord's face, but the Lord's face is ineffable, marvellous and very awful, and very, very terrible. And who am I to tell of the Lord's unspeakable being, and of his very wonderful face? And I cannot tell the quantity of his many instructions, and various voices, the Lord's throne very great and not made with hands, nor the quantity of those standing round him, troops of cherubim and seraphim, not their incessant singing, not his immutable beauty, and who shall tell of the ineffable greatness of his glory.

II Enoch, 22.1–3 (Charles)

In the apocryphal writings, the Old Testament Patriarchs were recognised by their beauty. Radiant beauty and miraculous powers of speech, from birth, were ascribed to the infant Noah. The imagery, nevertheless, was that of a solar deity who shed light on his surroundings:

And after some days my son Methuselah took a wife for his son Lamech, and she became pregnant by him and bore a son. And his body was white as snow and red as the blooming of a rose, and the hair of his head and his long locks were white as wool, and his eyes beautiful. And when he opened his eyes he lighted up the whole house like the sun, and the whole house was very bright. And thereupon he arose in the hands of the mid-wife, opened his mouth, and conversed with the Lord of righteousness.

Fragment of the *Book of Noah*, 106, 1–3 (Charles)

The sun, moon and stars were the patterns of beauty to the ancient world. Solar imagery was the chief means of expressing both beauty and attainment, in Judaism and in the present texts. Beauty, in the Hellenistic world, as seen in the writings of Apuleius, was not only expressed in bodily features, but in dress and surroundings. The oriental monarch was also regarded as beautiful by virtue of the splendour of his robes and regalia and those of his subjects. The association between the Emperor and the sun has already been discussed (p. 120). Planetary deities were, in this imagery, represented as youthful warriors in the service of the king.

In certain of the present texts, emphasis was placed on the royal or military dress of the heavenly visitors (1–8). Here beauty was an expression of royalty. In Quotations 9–13, all extracts from the *Apocalypse of Paul*, it was represented that each of the Old Testament Patriarchs was beautiful in his appearance. As in the Jewish apocrypha, the beauty of the Patriarchs was here derived from their relationship to the Deity.

The ancient world was unwilling to recognise beauty co-existent with the decay and weakening of bodily powers. Some Christian writings presented the paradox of beauty in a context of physical decline (18). Generally, however, following the attitude seen in the *Life of Apollonius* and other biographies of philosphers, the physical benefits of austerity were set forth. Thus Narratives 14–16, from the *Life of Anthony*, presented the ascetic life as conducive to physical beauty. To the ancient world, physical beauty was an expression of the divine. The solar imagery was inadequate to express beauty which did not depend on physical qualities. The authors of the present texts were also hampered by their stereotyped vocabulary. It was impossible to express the new in forms which, for millenia, had resisted change.

4 Miraculous Events

The miraculous event, anticipated in the mythology and ritual of the ancient world, was the emergence of the self-conscious individual. Paradoxically, much of the imagery and many of the practices which concerned this event, in one way or another, precluded the possibility of its occurrence. Even more paradoxically, when some men had succeeded in achieving a measure of individual freedom, the value of their accomplishments was obscured by the traditional imagery with which these deeds were described. The narratives of the present Section illustrate this form of misrepresentation.

The relation of the ascetics to the life of the senses was discussed in Chapters I and II. In Narratives 1–4, the powers of the holy man to pass through the elements at will were described. On the one hand, such descriptions of a passage through fire, air, water and earth concerned the experiences of the soul in the 'life after death' (see Chapter III, p. 120), and were appropriate to the mystery cults. On the other hand, accounts of this kind were applicable to collective rituals involving trance states. When 'possessed' by the gods, men were said to be able to undergo painful experiences to which they were insensitive. Iam-

THE ESTABLISHMENT OF COMMEMORATIVE RITUAL

blichos described such states which were induced in the worshippers of Artemis and similar deities:

> Here I wish to show the tokens in these occurrences of those who are really possessed by the gods. For they have either placed their whole life at the disposal as a vehicle or organ for the inspiring gods, or they exchange the human for the divine life, or else they carry on their own life in reference to the divinity. They are not acting by sense, nor are they watchful as those whose senses are aroused to greater acuteness, nor do they attempt the study of the future, nor are they moved as those who are active from impulse. On the other hand, they do not understand themselves, either as they were formerly or in any other way; nor, in short, do they exercise their own intelligence for themselves, nor do they put forth any superior knowledge of their own. The chief token may be adduced as follows: Many, through the divine afflatus, are not burned when brought to the fire, nor when the fire touches them. Many, also, who are burned do not perceive it, because in this case they are not living the life of an animal. Some, also, who are pierced with spits do not feel it; and others who have been struck on the shoulders with axes, and others still whose arms are cut with knives, do not mind it at all. Indeed, their performances are not at all usual with human beings. For to those who are divinely possessed, inaccessible places become accessible: they are thrown into the fire; they go through fire; they pass through rivers like the holy maids in Kastabalis. From these examples it is shown that they who are enthusiasts do not have any thought of themselves, and that they do not live a human or an animal life so far as relates to sense or natural impulse, but that they exchange it for another more divine life by which they are inspired and by which they are held fast.
>
> Iamblichos, *The Egyptian Mysteries*, III.vii (Wilder, pp. 114, 115)

Not only the possessed individual, but also the bystanders experienced alterations of consciousness with regard to the relationships of bodies in space:

> From these diversities it follows that the distinctive signs denoting those who are inspired are of many kinds. Not only among them are the motions of the body and of specific parts, but likewise its perfect repose ... The body also is seen lifted up, or increased in size, or borne along raised up in the air, or there appear occurrences in relation to it the contrary of these.
>
> Iamblichos, *The Egyptian Mysteries*, III.vii (Wilder, pp. 115–116)

In all cases, these miraculous 'events' were subjective experiences and evidence, not of self-consciousness, but of its suppression.

The hand was a sign from heaven which, in Narratives 5–8, was said to have appeared to the holy men. In the Old Testament, the hand of God which fell upon the prophet[101] was an image of the compulsive power of divine inspiration. The prophet did not act or speak of his own volition, but by the constraint of the will of the Deity. The hand of God enabled the prophet to speak of events at a distance or to be in another place.[102] 'The hand', in prophetic writings, was synonymous with 'the Spirit'. The Spirit carried the prophet to Jerusalem,[103] to Babylon,[104] lifted him up[105]; the hand set him down on a high mountain.[106] The hand was experienced as a form of 'seizure'. The hand of God, as the means by which the soul, after death, was conveyed to heaven was generally recognised in Hellenistic religions. The epitaph of the Roman funerary cult 'dis manibus', was adopted by Christians. In Chapter III.III.3, the coming forth of the soul into the hands of the Deity or of His angels was discussed. The hand of God in all these accounts represented a link between man and the divine as an external power. As an individual experience, it could only refer to the post-mortem world or the trance state.

Perfume, in ancient Egypt and in the Hellenistic world generally, had a significance somewhat similar to that of light as a divine manifestation. In Egypt, perfumes in the form of oils and ointments were applied to the bodies of the living and the dead. As resins, they were of importance in preserving the bodies of the dead. They were depicted, on the walls of funerary chapels, being poured on the heads of those who banqueted in the heavenly world. Incense (from the Latin *incendere*) was the source of the perfume (*per fumum*) given off by an odoriferous substance when burnt. Such perfume was thought to create an atmosphere pleasant to the gods. Incense was among the many offerings made to the dead. In the Hellenistic Mystery cults, incense was valued for its power in stimulating the imagination, rather than the senses. Plutarch described the beneficial effects of incense in promoting the prophetic faculties exercised in dreams:

> The *Kuphi* is composed of sixteen ingredients. . . . The majority of the ingredients possessing aromatical properties, send out a sweet breath and salubrius exhalation, whereby, when the air is changed and the body excited in the proper manner, they (of themselves lull people) to sleep, and have a seductive tendency; . . . and the imaginative and prophetic part of dreams, they brighten up and render more clear, like as it were a mirror, to no less degree than do the tunes on

230

the lyre which the Pythagoreans used to play before going to sleep; thus charming down and doctoring the irrational and passionate portion of the soul.

Plutarch, On Isis and Osiris, LXXXI

Knowledge of the ingredients of incense was thus a means of gaining control of the imagination from without. A considerable body of doctrine surrounded the various substances and their astrological relationships.[107] Philo, in his commentary on *Numbers* 7.10, gave current views on the connections between four ingredients of incense and the four elements of the universe.[108] The gathering and mixing of the substances also involved rituals and invocations. Finally, the subjective effects of incense were induced in the participants of the cults through ritual 'fumigations'.

That in Judaism, a sweet smell was associated with trance experiences of the divine, is suggested by the reference to it in the *Ascension of Isaiah*:

And the vision which the holy Isaiah saw was not from this world but from the world which is hidden from the flesh.

And after Isaiah had seen this vision, he narrated it to Hezekiah, and to Josab his son and to the other prophets who had come. But the leaders and the eunuchs and the people did not hear but only Samna the scribe, and Îjôaqêm, and Asaph the recorder; for these also were doers of righteousness, and the sweet smell of the Spirit was upon them.

Ascension of Isaiah, VI.15–17 (Charles)

In the present Narratives 9–20, perfume appears to have also denoted experience of the divine. In Quotations 9–11, this was said to have occurred to those who were in the environment of the living saint. In the remainder of the quotations, the perfume was experienced by the bystanders at his death. Only at his own death was the holy man himself said to experience the perfume (15).

In Narratives 22–34, great disturbances were said to have accompanied the salvation of martyrs. In Narrative 22, the disturbance took place among the bystanders. In the other narratives, the elements of the universe were disturbed. The imagery of thunder, lightning, earthquake and darkness was that of the divine manifestation at Sinai. The imagery of cloud and darkness portrayed man's lack of self-consciousness at the time of apprehending the divine (see p. 12). Similar disturbances of the elements were foretold, in the apocalyptic literature, for the time of the Last Judgment. Man's resurrection, like the revelation on Sinai, was portrayed as an event in which he was a passive participant. This imagery, which was proper to Judaism, was adopted by Christian writers to depict the miraculous preservation of the martyr's body. It showed man as an obedient puppet, animated from without.

Narratives 35 and 36 contained similar features. In both, the vision seen was compared to the sun. In 36, a hind was said to have appeared on the horizon like the rising sun. Between the horns of the animal, in both accounts, a divine manifestation was seen. It is perhaps significant that, in ancient Egypt, one of the chief deities was Hathor, the divine cow, between whose horns appeared the solar disc. If this account be compared with the dream vision of Isis, given by Apuleius, in his *Metamorphoses* (see p. 226), certain similarities can be seen. In the latter, the body of the goddess was said to rise from the sea. The speech made by the Deity in the present narratives, in which, in the first person, He declared His identity and powers, was paralleled by that made by Isis to Lucius.[109] Such aretologies were preserved at the cult centres of the various deities (see V.ii.1). The *Oxyrhynchus Papyrus* XI, 1380, is another example of a list of the titles of Isis, this time in the form of an address to the goddess. In the present narratives, the whole event was the occasion of the call to martyrdom of the holy man. Like the accounts in Section V.i.1, the experience was described in the stereotyped imagery of the dream vision, whose pattern was derived from tradition. This imagery was adequate only to portray man acting under the compulsion of the 'external' divinities which he himself created.

CONCLUSION

The texts relating to the martyr cult suggest the importance of the role played by the early Church in relation to the control of human imagination. It should be emphasised that all that is here said in no sense implies criticism. At a time of widespread corruption and decadence, it appears unlikely that the Church could have done otherwise than to assume complete authority over human affairs and to exercise control over human faculties.

The martyr cult established, for its participants, the compulsive cycle of a new ritual. However, within the congregation of the Church, men were freed from the psychic domination of the divinities of the physical universe, a condition induced by pagan ritual. Control of the imagination was exercised by the authorities of the Church, in the name of a transcendant Deity. The demonic and heavenly worlds, as places of punishment or reward, were established in the life after death. Exorcism of the affairs of daily life from disturbing psychic associations was effected through the rituals of the liturgy and of the martyr cult. Thus man was effectively protected from the psychic aftermath of his abandonment of pagan ritual.

Whereas the mythology of paganism was concerned with the nature of the visible universe, the stories of the martyrs, like the Scriptures, were concerned with the human community and the individual in relation to it. Even if the part played, in the first four centuries, by the saints and martyrs was not clearly understood, within the Church it was not forgotten. After a lapse of nearly two millenia, it is perhaps possible to re-evaluate their achievements. Those who left their communities, who were conscious that the source of the divine was in themselves, who created a non-material dimension which they called Paradise and who knew that they were playing a historic role, do not appear to have been 'seers' in the sense accepted then—or even now. Seership, in the ancient world, precluded individual development. It is perhaps as pioneers, in this new sphere of achievement, that the saints and martyrs should be remembered. In spite of the obscurity of their biographies, it may be also legitimate to deduce that the divine, for the ascetics, was not a 'vision' of the universe. It was an experience, imaginatively conceived, of human life and human relationships.

POSTSCRIPT

Archaism in the Twentieth Century

There has been an increasingly rapid cultural interchange in this century between the so-called Christian world and members of non-Christian cultures. The extreme importance for all peoples of their cultural roots, both for themselves and as an enrichment of human social life, has been widely acknowledged and need merely be stated here. However, many non-Christian cultures have their origins in remote antiquity. None of them stresses the central importance, in social life, of the individual rather than the group. Many practise techniques, including the taking of drugs, for inducing dream or trance states.[1] For perhaps large numbers of groups who thus bind their members within the circle of their own religious or cultural rituals, the emergence of 'individuals' must necessarily be a gradual process. This important aspect of the subject is beyond the scope of this chapter, which is concerned with the significance of hallucinogenic techniques for the individual today, irrespective of his race or culture.

The 'modern' individual regards with fascination and envy the involvement in life which their use of the imagination gives to people of less sophisticated cultures. With or without special techniques, by virtue of their social ritual, they appear able to endow their 'vision' of the world with a vitality and significance apparent, not only to them but to a mere observer. The problem of the modern individual is the sterility of his imagination. He can mass-produce all the 'images' available to him from his own and other cultures. For him they provide no experience, either divine or demonic. Modern 'culture' has exorcised both angels and devils from the world without asking whether it was not possible that man's imagination put them there in the first place.

It seems relevant, in summing up, to look at general issues at the risk of over-simplifying them. The picture given above of the individual today perhaps accounts for the widespread increase of practices which reduce or obliterate individual self-consciousness. Of these, the taking of hallucinogenic drugs has become a serious social and medical problem during the last two decades. These aspects of drug-taking and similar techniques for altering consciousness cannot be ignored. It is, however, with their specific effects on the individual that this assessment

234

is concerned. It has been seen in the previous chapters how ritual techniques, employed by pre-Christian communities, created psycho-physiological cycles which bound the group to their environment. Such methods of psychic conditioning had an educational value in early societies, but precluded such individual self-consciousness as is known today. Individual self-consciousness was developed at the expense of losing a faculty of experiencing a relationship between the physiological processes of the human body and the workings of the 'universe'. This trance or dream 'vision' was collectively induced and had a negative side. The latter was a chaotic and overwhelming experience of the destructive potentialities of the human psyche. Fear of the latter kept members of the group obedient to the laws of their own culture.

Modern scientific and intellectual development prevents the individual of today from 'imagining' the universe as did the members of an archaic society. Early rituals were performed to ensure community life and survival; the latter depended on a right relation to the environment. The modern individual, even if he abolishes his normal self-consciousness, cannot do more than experience his own physiological processes. Even if this 'vision' is pleasant, it can have no objective significance in the sense that it relates him consciously to his fellow men or to the world. In addition, the human psyche, uncontrolled by relationship with others or by self-consciousness, is self-destructive. In the vicious circle produced by dependence on drug-taking or on ritual techniques, not only may the individual be unable to escape, but he may also lose his sense of individuality altogether. The techniques which were appropriate to ancient cultures are anachronistic today.

Conditions which, in the modern age, have been observed to be conducive to hallucinogenesis are those in which the subject is isolated and deprived of normal sensory rapport with his surroundings. Hallucinations have been reported among survivors from shipwrecks, explorers[2] and those subjected to special stresses in prison.[3] Recently, the effect of environment on the production of hallucinations has been studied under experimental conditions of isolation and sensory deprivation.[4] From studies carried out from the year 1951 onwards, two conclusions emerge which are relevant here. The hallucinatory experiences were invariably trivial[5] and there was evidence of enhanced suggestibility on the part of their subjects.[6] Nothing in their content supported the suggestion put forward by some workers that they were related to the experiences of the ancient 'mystics'.[7] Secondly, the experiments were found by a number of subjects to be extremely disturbing and alarming.[8] A number of workers suggested that subjects of unstable personality were the most liable to these negative experiences, and that ability to

235

endure the experimental conditions depended on a strong sense of personal identity.[9]

These results support the view that individual self-consciousness is a psychological attitude which can be 'disturbed', 'altered', if not obliterated, by physical, chemical and environmental means, and that its loss is intolerable to the normal person. Certain individuals, among whom are the psychically sick and the inmates of prisons, for reasons outside their control, have no choice but to submit to those in charge of their environment and medication. Drugs and techniques are known today which can be used for psychotherapeutic and other purposes to deprive human beings of their sense of individuality. Man, however primitive, in the process of evolving, has all the human potentialities within him. Modern man, deprived of his sense of individuality, shares his physiological processes with the animal world. The direction in which this authoritarian approach to the individual is tending cannot be ignored.

The content of dream and trance revelations today is merely an enhancement, by the 'imagination', of physiological experiences. No longer can it have a valid relationship to the 'universe'. Nevertheless, the increasing demands for such experiences are perhaps evidence of a desire, by individuals, to escape from the present-day situation, in which from all sides, the imagination is externally controlled. For the individual, freedom of speech and even freedom of action are not enough. What is necessary is liberation of his imagination from the illusion that he is not the author of its content and of the compulsions to which he subjects himself and others.

Today it is not necessary to go into the desert to experience the threat to the individual. Nearly two thousand years ago, the emergence of the individual from the community was a 'break-through' of far greater significance than any scientific achievement of modern times. However, it was not for their efforts to become individuals that the early saints were recognised. Today, regression to archaism and imitation of primitive societies is thought to be a solution to the problems of the individual. The question for modern man is surely whether, through human relationships and not by archaic techniques, he can imagine himself a member of a world community, and translate this 'vision' into practice.

The notion of man as the source of the divine does not appear to commend itself to the psychiatrists or to the priesthood. One reason perhaps is the moral responsibility involved. Nevertheless, it appears likely that the 'liberating' effect of this self-knowledge (properly understood) could be beyond anything given by present-day techniques for man's psychic liberation. That human physiology was the basis of the experiences by which man first apprehended the divine, appears from the ancient texts. The experience of the divine as an organic whole was and is valid for peoples at an early stage of human development. A new source of divine experience was found by the early ascetics. It is not, however, in modern times, necessary to imitate the ascetics in their practices of withdrawal and self-mortification. Modern individuals are already isolated from one another. Not further isolation, but rather a social relationship which does not involve submergence of individuality and a society created to promote the individual are appropriate today. It is possible that the only form of society that would achieve this is one on the model of a 'living organism'. That which was implicit in the visions of antiquity could, in this form, perhaps be a way of life today.

The ascetics created a new community in their imagination; their 'vision' was not realisable at that time. Only now is it possible for Mankind to be 'seen' as a whole. Today individuals can, if they so wish, 'see' one another without the constraints previously imposed on them by racial, national and religious groupings. Whether human beings now create a new society or annihilate themselves as a race, these events will previously have been enacted in their imagination. Paradise and Catastrophe were conceived in the mythology and ritual of the ancient world. Today only by the conscious use of the imagination can Mankind decide on its own future; this future depends on Mankind's 'vision' of itself. Only the individual can exercise his imagination consciously and only the individual can 'see' his own significance and that of others. Finally, it is suggested, only a social order imaginatively conceived by individuals can fulfil the world's potentialities and realise the 'visions' of the ancient seers.

NOTES ON CHAPTERS I–V

For the sake of non-specialist readers, references in the Chapter Notes are, where possible, given to translations, books or articles rather than to primary editions of texts.
(See p. 261 for Abbreviations used).

INTRODUCTION

1. 'Coming forth at daytime' was the Egyptian title for the whole *Book of the Dead.*
   'True of voice' was an epithet added to the names of dead persons, originally applied to Osiris and to Horus with reference to their victories over their opponents; see A. Gardiner, *Egyptian Grammar*, 1950, para. 55.

2. 'Repeating life' was an epithet bestowed on the deceased; see A. Gardiner, *op. cit.*, para. 55.

3. 'Ritual of the Divine Cult': for copies of the texts and scenes see A. M. Calverley and M. F. Brooke, *The Temple of King Sethos I at Abydos*, Vols. I, II, 1933–35. See also A. Moret, *Le Rituel du culte divin journalier en Egypte*, 1902. 'Ritual of the Funerary Cult': see N. de G. Davies, *The Tomb of Rekh-mi-Rē at Thebes*, New York Metropolitan Museum of Art, 1943, Vol. II.

4. 'May he live, be prosperous, be healthy' was an auspicious wish formula, for kings and honoured persons; see A. Gardiner, *op. cit.*, para. 55.

5. See J. Harrison, *Prologomena to the Study of Greek Religion*, 1903, Ch. I.

6. See J. Harrison, *op. cit.*, Ch. IX, X.

7. See J. Harrison, *op. cit.*, Ch. X.

8. See C. M. Bowra, *The Greek Experience*, 1957, Ch. 2.

9. See J. Lindblom, *Prophecy in Ancient Israel*, 1963, pp. 93–95.

10. See J. Lindblom, *op. cit.*, pp. 173–178.

11. *Amos* 8.11; *Mic.* 3.6, 7.

12. *i Sam.* 3.3; 28.6, 15.

13. *Ezek.* 7.26.

14. *Tos. Soṭah*, 13.2; *Sanhedrin*, 11a.
    See D. S. Russell, *The Method and Message of Jewish Apocalyptic*, 1964, pp. 80–84.

15. *Against Apion*, I.8(34–41).

16. See D. S. Russell, *op. cit.*, pp. 178–181.

17. See B. Gerhardsson, *Memory and Manuscript. Oral Tradition and Written Transmission in Rabbinic Judaism and Early Christianity*, 1961, Ch. 10.

238

18. See B. Gerhardsson, *op. cit.*, Ch. 11. See D. S. Russell, *op. cit.*, pp. 178–181.
19. *i Macc.* 14.41.
20. *Phaedrus*, 245A.
21. See D. S. Russell, *op. cit.*, pp. 48–54.
22. See D. S. Russell, *op. cit.*, pp. 127–139.
23. See D. S. Russell, *op. cit.*, pp. 109–118.
24. See D. S. Russell, *op. cit.*, pp. 140–147.
25. See D. S. Russell, *op. cit.*, pp. 142–145.
26. *In Ioannem. comm.* 13.46.

CHAPTER I

1. See A. J. Wensinck, *Legends of Eastern Saints, chiefly from Syriac sources*, II, 1913, pp. xxii–xxiv.
2. See O. Chadwick, *Western Asceticism*, 1958, p. 191.
3. See W. F. Albright, *From the Stone Age to Christianity*, 1940. Ch. I, D.2. The Transmission of Written Documents.
4. See R. T. Meyer, *Athanasius: The Life of Anthony*, 1950, Introduction, pp. 11–14.
5. See R. T. Meyer, *op. cit.*, p. 9; *Vit. Ant.* 72–80; 69.
6. The site of Nitria was elucidated by E. White in *The History of the Monasteries of Nitria and of Scetis*, 1932. The 'Mountain of Nitria', the site of the first settlement of Amun, *c.* 330 A.D., was on the edge of the Western desert, about nine miles south of the present town of Damanhûr (Hermopolis parva, Arabic El Barnugi). Near El Barnugi are natron lakes which were exploited in classical times. Forty miles south are more extensive lakes, known today as the Wadi 'N Natrun. This is the site of the 'Desert of Scetis' (until recently, mistakenly identified with Nitria) and here survive four monasteries today. A note on the site of the second Nitrian settlement, the 'Cells', was published by O. Toussoun in *Mémoires de la Société Royale d'Archéologie d'Alexandrie*, VII.II., 1935. This site, lying about twelve miles south of the first, was confirmed by A. Guillamont in *RA*, II, 1964, pp. 43–50. The settlement was a group of community buildings, of which the remains are being studied today. Scetis is the Greek form of the Coptic Shiet; both forms of this place name will be found among the present quotations, the source of the text being the determinant.
7. For the crossing of the desert as a journey of the soul for Philo and Origen, see Daniélou, *Les Figures du Christ dans l'Ancien Testament*, 1950, pp. 183–190.
8. *Deut.* 8.2.
9. 'No angelic office exists except as a reward of merit.' Origen, *Principia*, I.VIII.4. For the 'men of the Council' as 'princes in the company of angels', see Qumran *Hymns*, VI.10. For the monks who 'wrought and fulfilled the lives and deeds of angels', see E. A. W. Budge,

239

The Book of Paradise of Palladius, Vol. I, Ch. I. p. 128 (text p. 106) para. 1.

10. E. A. W. Budge, *The Book of the Dead*, 1898, Ch. CXXV. See p. 109.

11. See O. Chadwick, *op. cit.*, p. 192. There are over 260 Biblical quotations or allusions in the *Life of Anthony*. See 'Notes' in R. T. Meyer, *op. cit.*

12. See D. S. Russell, *The Method and Message of Jewish Apocalyptic*, 1964, pp. 195–202.

13. See J. Van Goudoever, *Biblical Calendars*, 1961, Ch. II.

14. See J. Van Goudoever, *op. cit.*, Ch. XI.

15. See J. Van Goudoever, *op. cit.*, Ch. VIII.

16. Origen, *On the 150 Psalms* (fragment).
    See J. Van Goudoever, *op. cit.*, p. 185.

17. See J. Van Goudoever, *op. cit.*, pp. 28–29.

18. J. Van Goudoever, *op. cit.*, p. 26.
    For the three seven-week fasting periods in Syrian solitary asceticism, see Dadisho', *On Solitude* (tr. A. Mingana. Woodbrooke Studies, VII, 1934, p. 78).

19. Clement. *Strom.* IV.22. Origen. *Hom. in Lev.* 10,11. Cassian, *Conf.* 18.4–6. (tr. O. Chadwick, *op. cit.*)
    For the superiority of solitary over community life, see Budge, *op. cit.*, Vol. II, Appendix 3, pp. 1002 ff. For the bad effects of community life, see *Vit. Ant.* 85.

20. See O. Chadwick, *op. cit.*, p. 191.
    For community life as preparation for withdrawal to solitary life, see Cassian, *Conf.* 18.4–6 (tr. O. Chadwick, *op. cit.*).

21. See O. Chadwick, *op. cit.*, p. 24.
    Cassian, *Conf.* 19.4–6 (tr. O. Chadwick, *op. cit*).
    For rejection of the idea of the solitary life as superior to community life, see Budge, *op. cit.*, Vol. II, Appendix, 102, p. 1072.

22. See O. Chadwick, *op. cit.*, pp. 26–30.
    The Rule of St. Benedict. (tr. O. Chadwick, *op. cit.*, pp. 291–337).
    For the merits of obedience to an elder, see *The Sayings of the Fathers*, I.9; XIV. 7, 18, 19 (tr. O. Chadwick, *op. cit*).

23. See C. A. Williams, *Oriental Affinities of the Legend of the Hairy Anchorite. I. Pre-Christian.* University of Illinois Studies in Language and Literature, X. 2, 1925.
    For absence of hair as evidence of asceticism, see *The Lausiac History of Palladius*, XVIII. 29 (tr. W. K. Lowther Clarke, 1918).

24. Herodotus. *Hist. II*, 83.

25. See J. Lacarrière, *The God-Possessed*, 1963, pp. 159–168.
    See also A.-J. Festugière, *Antioche Païenne et Chrétienne*, 1959, pp. 388–506.

26. Lucian, *The Syrian Goddess*, 1.49–50 (tr. F. C. Grant, Hellenistic Religions, 1953, pp. 116–120).
    Apuleius, *Metamorphoses*, VIII.27–28.

27. In ancient Egypt the body was depicted prone after death.

For standing as the posture of the athlete, see E. A. W. Budge, *op. cit.*, Vol. I. *The Sayings of the Fathers*, 163, p. 637.

28. E. A. W. Budge, *The Liturgy of Funerary Offerings*, 1909, pp. 64 ff.

For the formula of offerings used in the funerary cult from the Middle Kingdom onwards, see Gardiner, *Egyptian Grammar*, 1950. pp. 170–172; the king was said to give a favour to the god, so that the latter might give invocation offerings of bread, beer, oxen, fowl, alabaster and clothing, etc. to the 'soul' of the deceased person. The greater part of the food offerings made to the temples were distributed to the persons in charge of private funerary cults.

29. Herodotus, *Hist. II*, 38–40.

30. Council of Ancyra, A.D. 314.

31. See J. Lacarrière, *op. cit.*, pp. 31–32.

32. Meat and oil were the ingredients in the burnt sacrifice of the bull which was afterwards eaten; see Herodotus, *Hist. II*, 40.

The priests of ancient Egypt were said to abstain from meat; see Plutarch, *On Isis and Osiris*, V.

For abstinence from meat in ancient Egypt, see W. Robertson Smith, *The Religion of the Semites* (1889), 1959, Lect. VIII, pp. 301–302.

33. *Acts* 15.29; 21.25.

For meat eating as sacramental communion among Semites, see W. Robertson Smith, *op. cit.*, Lect. XI, p. 439.

34. The priests of ancient Egypt were said to abstain from wine; see Plutarch, *On Isis and Osiris*, VI.

35. For the orgiastic drinking of wine in Hellenistic society, see Philo, *On the Contemplative Life*, V.40–47. The Rule of Pachomius forbade wine; see L. Th. Lefort, 'Œuvres de S. Pachôme et de ses Disciples', *CSCO*, Vol. 160, 1960, pp. 19–20; 36. For examples of the designation of the Pharaoh as son of a divine mother, see *BAR*, IV, 251; as son of a divine father, see *BAR*, III, 400, 411; IV, 351.

36. *Num.* 6.2–5; *Jud.* 16.17; *i Sam.* 1.11.

37. For fasting on Wednesday and Friday, see *Didache*, 8.1; *Hermas. Sim.* 5.1.2.

For fasting before Easter, see R. Arbesmann, 'Fasting and Prophecy in Pagan and Christian Antiquity', Traditio. VII, 1949–51, pp. 42–44.

38. II.XXXVII; see R. Arbesmann, *op. cit.*, I. 2. 'Fasting in preparation for mantic activity', pp. 9–32.

39. The prophetess was said to fast for three days prior to giving an oracle; see Iamblichos, *The Egyptian Mysteries* (tr. A. Wilder), London, 1911, III.vii, p. 127.

See also Plutarch, *On the cessation of Oracles*, XXI.

40. Certain foods produced confused dreams, according to some authors. Plutarch cited beans; see *Quaestiones conviviales*, 734F.

41. *Ex.* 24.18; *Deut.* 9.9, 18, 25; 10.10;
i Kg. 19.8, 9.
Dan. 9.3; 10.2, 3.

42. *II Esdras*, 5.20; 6.31, 35; 9.23–25; 12.49–51.

43. *II Baruch*, 9.2; 12.5; 21.1; 47.2.

44. *Vit. Ad. et Ev.*, 6.1.

45. For Abaris, see Herodotus, IV.36.

    For Epimedes, see Diogenes Laertius, *De clarorum philosophorum vitis*, 1.10.114.

    For Pythagorus, see Porphyry, *Vita Pythagorae*, 34; *De Abstinentia*, 3.27.

CHAPTER II

1. For Anthony as an exponent of Neoplatonic views on asceticism and theological arguments for the refutation of Arianism, see *Vit. Ant.* 72–80, 69.

2. See A. Gardiner, *Egyptian Grammar*, 1950, pp. 5–6.

3. For an account of the Origenist controversy and of the influence of Evagrius on Rufinus, Palladius and John Cassian, see A. Guillaumont, Les '*Kephalaia Gnostica*' *d'Evagre le Pontique et l'histoire de l'Origénisme chez les Grecs et chez les Syriens*, 1962, pp. 69–80.

4. *Antirrheticos*, W. Frankenberg, *Euagrius Pontikus*, Berlin, 1912, pp. 472–585.

    For the association of the seven principal vices with seven devils in earlier writings, see *The Testament of Reuben*, III.3–6; for the designation of vices as demons, see *Hermas. Mand.* II.3; *Sim.* IX. 22.3.

    For the demons as vices in Cassian, see A. Guillaumont, *op. cit.*, p. 77.

5. See J. Harrison, *Prologomena to the Study of Greek Religion* (1903), 1955, p. 232.

6. See *The Epistle of Palladius to Lausus:* Syriac text tr. E. A. W. Budge, *The Book of Paradise*, 1904, Vol. I, p. 111.

7. *Vit. Ant.* 70, 71.

8. *Vit. Ant.* 84, 87. On prayer by the Pharaoh for the Nile flood, see G. Posener, *De la Divinité du Pharaon*, 1960, pp. 41, 54, 55, 59.

9. See Tertullian, *de Anima*.

10. *i Cor.* 14. 6–14.

11. For the influence of Evagrius on Syrian mysticism, see A. Guillaumont, *op. cit.*, pp. 196–332.

12. Withdrawal from the sight and sound of men often precluded such communications: see E. A. W. Budge, *op. cit.*, Vol. I, *Questions and Answers etc.*, 223(219), p. 883.

13. On study of the Scriptures among the Essenes, see Philo, *Every Virtuous Man is Free*, XII.80, 82; Josephus, *Jewish War*, II.VIII.6, 12.

14. On the exclusion of Montanists from the Church, see Eusebius, *History of the Church*, V.3.4.

15. For attitudes to the Montanists, see Eusebius, *op. cit.*, V.14–19; Tertullian, *de ieiunio adversus psychicos* 3, and *de Anima* 9.

16. For the letters and sermons of Shenute, see J. Leipoldt, *Sinuthi Archimandritae. Vita et Opera Omnia*, 1949–53.

    See also P. Du Bourguet, 'Diatribe de Chenouté contre le démon', *BSAC*, XVI, 1961–62, pp. 17–72.

17. For editions of the hymns of Ephraim, see C. Moss, *Catalogue of Syriac Printed Books and related literature*, British Museum, 1962.

18. For editions of some hymns of the Coptic Church, see De Lacy O'Leary, *The Difnar (Antiphonarium) of the Coptic Church*, 1926–1930.

19. Didymus, *de Trinitate*, 3.41.1. For the utterances of the Montanists, see H. Lietzmann, *A History of the Early Church*, Vol. II, 1961, p. 195.

20. For the Nubian conquest of Egypt and its effect on the Egyptian religion, see J. Černý, *Ancient Egyptian Religion*, 1951, pp. 131–133.

21. J. Černý, *op. cit.*, p. 144.

22. See J. Černý, *op. cit.*, pp. 142–143.

23. Herodotus, *Hist. II*, 42, 43.

24. See P. D. Scott-Moncrieff, *Paganism and Christianity in Egypt*, 1913, pp. 18–21.

25. See J. Černý, *op. cit.*, p. 140.

26. See Plutarch, *On Superstition*.

27. For consultation of the Apis Bull, see Pliny, *Natural History*, VIII.71; Amm. Marcellinus, XXII.14.
    See Erman, *ZÄ*, XXIX, 1891, for locating a burial place by means of a gazelle.
    For divination by the inspection of sacrificial victims, see Herodotus, *Hist. II*, 58.

28. For the expiation of offenses against the gods by the sacrificial offering of human beings or material property, see W. Robertson Smith, *The Religion of the Semites*, (1889), 1959 Lecture XI, pp. 396–398.

29. For the Canaanite gods as vindicators of the duties of kinship, see W. Robertson Smith, *op. cit.*, Lecture XI, p. 425.
    For ancestor worship and the cult of animals in the Old Testament, see E. Langton, *Good and Evil Spirits*, 1942, pp. 100–116.

30. For the relation of the sacrificial meal to kinship, see W. Robertson Smith, *op. cit.*, Lecture VIII, pp. 277–300. For the shedding of blood in making a covenant; for the eating of raw flesh and the drinking of blood, see W. Robertson Smith, *op. cit.*, Lecture IX, pp. 312–323.
    For the prohibition of eating blood in Jewish apocryphal literature, see *The Book of Jubilees*, 6.12; 21.18.

31. For discussion on the relationship seen by Origen between demons and the animals prohibited in *Lev. II*, that the latter served for divination among the Egyptians, see J. Daniélou, *Message Evangelique et Culture Hellenistique*, 1961, Ch. V, p. 400.

32. Clement, *Stromat*, VII, xviii. 109.

33. See E. Langton, *Essentials of Demonology*, 1949, p. 71.

34. For discussion on matrilineal descent in ancient Egypt, in Judaism and among the Claudian Emperors of Rome, see M. A. Murray, *The Splendour that was Egypt*, 1949, pp. 100–103; Appendix 2.
    For brother-sister marriage in Egypt, see J. Černý, *JEA*, **40**, 1954, pp. 23–29; for evidence of the continual breakup of the Egyptian family into small units, as against the formation of a tribe or family

clan, see J. Černý, *A Note on the Ancient Egyptian Family*, Studi in onori di Aristide Calderini e Roberto Paribeni, Vol. II, 1957, pp. 51–55.

35. 'Father of the god' was the designation of a category of priests. See J. Černý, *Ancient Egyptian Religion*, p. 116.

36. *Ex.* 34.15; *Lev.* 17.7; *Num.* 15.39; 25.1,2; *Jud.* 2.17; 8.27,33.

37. *Deut.* 12.31; 18.10; *ii Kg.* 16.3; 17.17; 21.6; 23.10; *Ps.* 106.(105).37. *Jer.* 32.35; *Ezek.* 20.26; 23.37.

38. *Lev.* 20.27.

39. *Is.* 42.17; *Wis.* 13.10; 15.16.

40. *Deut* 4.28; *Ps.* 115.(114).5–8; 135.16–18; *Is.* 44.18; *Wis.* 15.15.

41. *Deut.* 7.16; *Jud.* 2.3; *Ps.* 106.(105).36.

42. *Vit. Ant.* 5, 55.

43. *i Chr.* 21.1; *Job* 1.6; *Zech.* 3.1,2.

44. For discussion on the phenomena of demoniacal possession in the Gospels, see E. Langton, *op. cit.*, pp. 151–174.

45. *Deut.* 32.17.

46. For the Nubian as a hostile sorcerer in late Pharaonic demotic literature, see F. Ll. Griffith, *Stories of the High Priests of Memphis. The Second Tale of Khamuas*, II–VI. For the story of a satyr which attacked Ethiopian women, see Philostratus, *Life of Apollonius of Tyana*, VI, XXVII.

For the Ethiopian woman in the Apocryphal literature, see *The Testament of Joseph*, 3.1 ff.; *Acts of Peter*, 22. For the astrological sign of the Virgin as ruler of the regions of Meroë and Elephantine (Nubia), in Hermetic literature, see *Liber Hermetis*, pp. 21–23 (quoted A. -J. Festugière, *La Révélation d'Hermès Trismégiste*, 1950, Vol. 1, p. 117).

47. *Is.* 27.1; *Jer.* 51.34; *Ezek.* 29.3; *Rev.* 12.3, etc.

See also *III Baruch*, V.3, in which Hades is said to be the belly of the dragon (compare the extract from the *Pistis Sophia*, quoted p. 163).

48. For serpents with multiple heads in Egyptian funerary texts, see *The Book of what is in the Dēt (or Underworld) the fourth hour;* copies of the scenes and texts in P. Bucher, *Les Textes des Tombes de Thutmosis III et d'Aménophis II*, Vol. I, 1932; E. Lefébure, *Les Hypogées royaux de Thèbes*, 1886–9. See also *The Book of the Gates*, the ninth division of the *Dēt* in Ch. Maystre and A. Piankoff, *Le Livre des Portes*, Vol. I, 1946.

49. The centre of the cult was at Buto in Lower Egypt; for evidence that Buto was the capital of Lower Egypt in pre-dynastic times and that the name of the cobra deity, with that of the vulture of Upper Egypt, in the kings' titulary, signified the union of the 'two lands', see A. Gardiner, *Egypt of the Pharaohs*, 1961, p. 422.

50. In the Pyramid texts; *Pyr.* 388; 507–508. For the cult of the crocodile deity in Roman times, see J. Černý, *op. cit.*, p. 145.

51. See J. Černý, *op. cit.*, pp. 71–72.

52. Cassian, *Conferences*, X.2–5.

53. For examples elsewhere of this Jewish belief, see R. H. Charles, *Apocrypha and Pseudepigrapha of the Old Testament in English*, Vol. II, p. 17, note 28.

54. *Ps.* 7.(6).2; 17.(16).12; 22.(21).12, 13, 16, 20, 21; 35.(34).15, 21; 37.(36).12 56.(55).2; 59.(58).6, 14; 118.(117).11, 12.

55. See the tables of Biblical references at the end of editions of Coptic texts of lives of saints or martyrs for the numerical predominance of those from *Psalms*.

56. See Josephus, *Jewish War*, II, VIII.7. Compare the Rules of the Qumran sect: *Community Rule* V–IX; *Damascus Rule* IX–XIV.

57. *Mand.* VI.2.2–5.

58. *Community Rule* III.13–IV.1.

59. For exclusion from the Eucharist and the performance of penitential exercises, see Basil, *Epistolae*, CXCIX.22, CCXVII.56; Tertullian, *de Paenitentia*.

60. *Community Rule* VI.24–VII.25.

61. For translations of the Coptic, Syriac, Greek and other versions of the *Apocryphal Acts of the Apostles*, see R. McL. Wilson, *New Testament Apocrypha*, Vol. II, Ch. XIII.

62. For the falling of demons from a height: see *Vit. Ant.* 22 for the doctrine that the demons fell to earth; for the fall of a sorcerer, see *Acts of Peter* 32; for the fall of a temple and idols, see *Acts of John* 42; for the casting to earth of women possessed by demons, see *Acts of Thomas* 62 ff.

63. *i Sam.* 16.23.

64. See *Acts of John* 40.

65. For scourging as a means of exorcism and healing in the 14th and 15th centuries in Europe, see article, R. M. Jones: 'Flagellants' in *ERE*, Vol. IV, 1911.

CHAPTER III

1. For the relation of Egyptian oracles to festal events, see article J. Foucart, 'Festivals and Fasts (Egyptian)' in *ERE*, Vol. V, 1912; R. A. Parker, *A Saite Oracle Papyrus in the Brooklyn Museum*, III, 'The Oracle Texts', pp. 7–11; J. Černý in R. A. Parker, *op. cit.*, VI, 'Egyptian Oracles', pp. 35–48.

2. Herodotus, *Hist. II*, 63. For the warlike character of Egyptian festivals and the relation of the ritual journeys and battles to the calendar, see article J. Foucart, 'Calendar (Egyptian)', in *ERE*, Vol. III, 1910.

3. See *I Enoch*, 12–36; 72–78; 82; *II Enoch*, 4–33; etc.
For mention of the signs of the Zodiac, see *I Enoch*, 48.3; 72.13, 19; 75.3.

4. For angels as indication of the demotion of the gods of the heathen and the increasing transcendance of the God of Israel, see D. S. Russell, *The Method and Message of Jewish Apocalyptic*, 1964, pp. 235–237.

For the view that the dominance of the angelic hierarchies is the reward of their merit, see Origen, *Principia*, I.V.2.

5. For angels as stars, see *Job* 38.7. For the host of the height and the host of heaven, see *Is.* 24.21 and *Gen.* 2.1; *i Kg.* 17.6, etc. For the overthrowing of the sun, moon and stars, see *Joel* 2.31; 24.21, 23. *Is.* 34.4; For the hierarchy of angels, see *Zech.* 2.3,4. For angels as princes, see *Dan.* 10.13; 12.1.

6. See C. G. Jung, *The Integration of the Personality*, 1940, Ch. III.

7. For writings on the transformation of the Elements, see Cyril of Jerusalem, *Catecheses Mystagogicae*; Gregory of Nyssa, *Oratio Catech.* c. 37; John Chrysostom, *in Ioann. Hom.* 46.3; 47.1.

8. For the Monophysite controversy and the appeal by both sides to the Eucharist in support of their respective doctrines, see article J. H. Srawley, 'Eucharist (to end of Middle Ages) 3. The Eucharist in the later Patristic period, 5th–8th centuries', in *ERE*, Vol. V, 1912.

9. For the two developments in Eucharistic teaching: (1) that there was a distinction between the Elements and that which they signified, and (2) that complete identification occurred, see J. H. Srawley, *ibid.*

10. The Patriarch John, the personage to whom the questions of Theodore were addressed, held office at Alexandria from 681 to 689; see notes on the text by A. Van Lantschoot, *op. cit.*

11. See p. 63 for discussion on the effect on the Coptic monks of their lack of intellectual training.

12. The pronouncements of the Council of Chalcedon (461) were rejected by the Churches of Egypt and Palestine. Two of the participants in the controversy, to whom was attributed the correspondence quoted, were Acacius, Court Patriarch of Constantinople, and Petrus Mongus, Archbishop of Alexandria.

13. The 'Tome of Leon' was a letter from Pope Leo to Flavian of Constantinople (dated 449), on the 'nature' of the Second Person of the Trinity. Its content was subsequently confirmed by the Council of Chalcedon.

14. The 'putting to shame' of the Jews, by the demonstration of the superior powers of the Church or its saints, was a frequent theme of apocryphal literature. The focus of the controversy lay in the miraculous events claimed by the Church in connection with the Elements of the Eucharist and with the bodies of martyrs. See Chapter V, note 86, and pp. 217 ff.

15. Ancient Egyptian place names often contained the name of the deity of whose cult the particular places were centres. Thus Busiris was the Greek form of *Per-Asar*, the House of Osiris.

16. See H-C. Puech, *Le Manichéisme, son Fondateur, sa Doctrine*, 1949, pp. 85–91
For a description of Manichaean asceticism and its relation to Syrian monasticism, see A. Vööbus, *History of Asceticism in the Syrian Orient. I. The Origin of Asceticism. Early Monasticism in Persia. CSCO*, Vol. 184, Subsidia. 14, 1958, Ch. IV.

17. For the complexity of the Manichaean cosmology, see G. Widengren, *Mani and Manichaeism* (1961), 1965, Ch. IV.

18. See Augustine, *Reply to Faustus the Manichaean*, VI.3.

19. Eusebius, *History of the Church*, VI.8.5.

20. For the liver as the seat of divination, see Plato, *Timaeus*, 71, 72.A.B.; for the liver as the seat of wrath, see *The Testament of Napthhali*, 2.8; as the seat of fighting, see *The Testament of Reuben*, 3.4; for pain in the liver, due to envy, see *The Testament of Simeon*, 2.4; 4.1; *The Testament of Gad*, 5.11.

21. For the spleen as an organ to keep the liver clean, to remove impurities like a napkin, see Plato, *Timaeus*, 72.C.D.

22. According to the title of this text, the *Life* was narrated on the day of his commemoration (see Chapter V.1.6i).

23. See G. Foucart article 'Disease and Medicine (Egyptian)', *ERE*. Vol. IV, 1911.
    On the consultation of medical writings by the Pharaoh, see G. Posener, *De la Divinité du Pharaon*, 1960, pp. 70–72.

24. See the *Tetrabiblos* of Claudius Ptolemy (*c.* A.D. 100–178), III.11, 12; on Hermetic medicine, which was more Greek than Egyptian, see A.-J. Festugière, *La Révélation d'Hermès Trismégiste*, Vol. I, 1950, pp. 128–126.

25. *Gen.* 12.2; 13.14.15; 15.1 ff.; 17.4–8; 18.18; etc.

26. *Gen.* 16.1; *Gen.* 25.21; *Gen.* 29.31.

27. See Chapter II, Note 35. On the role of a god as father of the Pharaoh, see *BAR*, III, 534; on favours received from the gods relating to theogamy and the royal nativity and coronation, see *BAR*, II, 187–212; 215–242.

28. *BAR*, II, 187–212.

29. *BAR*, III, 297–414.

30. *Gen.* 6.1–3.

31. On cosmic events linking the order of the universe to the life of the Egyptian community, see Posener, *op. cit.*, pp. 56, 57.

32. *Lk.* 1.18–24; 26–37; *Protevanagelium of James*, 2–5; 11.

33. See 'Healings and Miracles at Epidaurus', Votive Tablet I, in F. C. Grant, *Hellenistic Religions*, 1953, p. 56.

34. *i Sam.* 1.11–28. *Gen.* 30.23; *Is.* 4.1; see *Lk.* 1.25.

35. *de Somn.* 141–142; *de Gigant.* 6–9.

36. Plutarch, *On the Cessation of Oracles*, XIII ff.

37. 550K.

38. *Phaedo*, 107D; *Republic*, 617D.

39. *Politicus*, 271D.

40. *Didache*; *Treatise of the Two Ways*, quoted in J. Daniélou, *Theology of Jewish Christianity*, 1964, p. 142.

41. See J. Daniélou, *Les Figures du Christ dans l'Ancien Testament 'Sacramentum Futuri'*, 1950.

42. For a threefold meaning in the Scripture, see Origen, *Principia*, IV.II.4–9.

43. See J. Janssen, *De traditioneele egyptische autobiografie vóór het Nieuwe Rijk*, 1946, I, pp. 46–47.
   On the public recognition of Thutmosis III by the god Amun, see J. H. Breasted, *A New Chapter in the Life of Thutmose III*, 1900, pp. 9 ff.

44. On the allocation, by the deified King Amenhotep I, of the site of a tomb 'through a writing', see A. M. Blackman, 'Hieratic ostraca, *Brit. Mus.* 5624', *JEA*, **12**, 1926, pp. 176–81.

45. See P. Fox, *Tutankhamun's Treasure*, 1951, Plate 26.

46. On the deified King Amenhotep I as the source of oracles on the Theban west bank, see article J. Černý in R. A. Parker (ed.) *A Saite Oracle Papyrus from Thebes in the Brooklyn Museum*, VI, 'Egyptian Oracles', 1962, pp. 41–43.

47. See Mustafa El-Amir, *A Family Archive from Thebes. Demotic Papyri in the Philadelphia and Cairo Museums from the Ptolemaic period*, 1959, Part II.iv, pp. 71–112.

48. See J. Černý, *Ancient Egyptian Religion*, 1952, pp. 76, 112, 116.

49. Palladius, *Lausiac History*, XI. 9.

50. See G. Horner, *The Statutes of the Apostles* (tr. of the Sahidic text), pp. 295–363.

51. See H. Scottas, *La Préservation de la Propriété Funéraire dans l'ancienne Egypte avec le recueil des formules d'imprécation*, 1913, Ch.I, II.
   For a promise of protection to his descendants by the deceased, with threats against those who contravened his decree, see *BAR*, IV, para. 795.

52. See Papyrus of Kerasher, *Brit. Mus.* No. 9995.
   See E. A. W. Budge, *The book of the Dead*, 1898, Introduction; A. Gardiner, *Egyptian Grammar*, 1950, p. 19.

53. The term 'Coffin Texts' is used for the invocations inscribed on the coffins of the nobles of Dynasties IX–XI. Some were used again in the Saite period. See A. de Buck, *The Egyptian Coffin Texts*, 3 vols., 1935–47.

54. On the dedication of organs of the body to deities, see S. A. B. Mercer, *The Religion of Ancient Egypt*, 1949, p. 70.

55. See Papyrus of Ani (*Brit. Mus.* No. 10470, sheets 3, 4).

56. See Papyrus of Ani (*Brit. Mus.* No. 10470, sheet 6).

57. See Mustafa El-Amir, *op. cit.*, 'The Cult of Ḥry.w and Ḥsy.w in the Theban Necropolis', pp. 126–131.

58. Herodotus, *Hist. II*, 90.

59. For the practice of keeping the mummified bodies of the dead in men's houses, see Herodotus, *Hist. II*, 86.

60. See Herodotus, *Hist.* II, 82.
   On proper names of the type 'God so and so said: He (or she) shall live', see J. Černý, 'Egyptian Oracles', 1962, p. 43.

61. *Gen.* 15.15; 47.30; 49.29; *Deut.* 31.16; *ii Sam.* 7.12; see *i Macc.* 2.70.

62. Compare *ii Kg.* 20.1–6; *Is.* 38.1–5.

63. See Papyrus of Ani (*Brit. Mus.* No. 10470, sheets 3, 4).
64. See the beginning of each 'testament' in the *Testaments of the Twelve Patriarchs*.
65. *ii Kg.* 2.7.
66. *Ascension of Isaiah*, VI.3.
67. See *I Enoch, II Enoch, II Baruch*.
68. See the *Sahidic Fragment III: On the Death of Joseph*, XXIII, in J. A. Robinson, *Coptic Apocryphal Gospels*. Texts and Studies, Vol. IV.2 (1896) 1967, p. 158.
69. Herodotus, *Hist. II*, 86.
70. Diodorus Siculus, *Bibliotheca*, I.91.5–6.
71. E. A. W. Budge, *The Mummy*, 1925, p. 216.
72. See Papyrus of Ani (*Brit. Mus.* No. 10470, Sheet 6).
73. Herodotus, *Hist. II*, 60, 63.
    On processional transportation of the god Amun, accompanied by singing women, see Strabo. C.814; Diodorus, 17.50.6–7.
74. See F. Cumont, *Astrology and Religion among the Greeks and Romans* (1912) 1960, Lecture I.
75. See F. Cumont, *op. cit.*, Lecture II.
76. See F. Cumont, *op. cit.*, Lecture III.
77. For the decans as the thirty-six constellations, or parts of such, which rose at particular hours of the night during the thirty-six periods of ten days constituting the Egyptian year, see A. Gardiner, *op. cit.*, 1950, p. 206. Periods, or decades, were named according to the calendar month in which they occurred: first, middle or last decade. Some of the names of the decans survived in Greek. See Ch. IV, Note 22. For the decans as 'those who rule over the ten' (degrees of the circle of the ecliptic), three decans for each zodiacal sign (30°), thirty-six decans for the whole circle (360°), and the relation of the decans to the solar year, see A.-J. Festugière, *Hermès Trismégiste*, III, 1954, 'Introduction', pp. xl–lxi; 'Fragment extrait de Stobée', VI, pp. 34–39.
    See also F. Cumont, *op. cit.*, Lecture IV.
78. See F. Cumont, *op. cit.*, Lecture III.
79. See F. Cumont, *op. cit.*, Lecture IV.
80. See F. Cumont, *op. cit.*, Lecture VI.
81. *Deut.* 10.14.
82. *i Kg.* 22.19.
83. *Deut.* 12.2.
84. *ii Kg.* 23. 4–20.
85. *IV Ezra*, 7.31, 50; *II Baruch*, 44.9–12; see also the Qumran texts: *The War Rule*, XVII, XVIII.
86. *Republic*, 617–619.
87. *Republic*, 614 ff.
88. For the Watchers as archangels, see *I Enoch*, 12.2, 3; 'who watch';

I Enoch, 20.1; 'who sleep not': *I Enoch*, 39.12, 13; 40.2; 61.12; 71.7; see also *Dan.* 4.13, 17, 23.

For the Watchers as fallen angels, see *I Enoch*, 1.5; 10.9; 12.4; 13.10; 14.1; 15.2; 16.1, 2; 91.15; as giants *II Enoch*, 18.1–9; *I Enoch*, 16.1; for the cause of the fall of the Watchers as fornication, see *Testament of Reuben*, 5.1–7; *I Enoch*, 19; 86.

For the comparison of 'they who watch by night' with angels called Watchers, see Clement. *Paed.* II.ix.79.

89. For the equivalence of stars and stellar gods with angels, see R. H. Charles, *The Apocrypha and Pseudepigrapha of the Old Testament in English* (1913), 1964, p. 589, n. 97; see also *IV Ezra*, 7.97, 98, 125; *I Enoch*, 39.7; 51.5; 104.2. See Chapter IV, p. 164.

For the circumpolar stars in ancient Egypt as 'those who can never set' and the stars which rise and set as 'those who can never become weary', and on the 'watch' as the term of service of the 'hour-priest' who served a monthly rota in the temple ('he who is in his month'), see J. Černý, *Ancient Egyptian Religion*, 1952, pp. 51, 117.

90. For sacrifices at the tomb in Greece on the third, ninth and thirtieth days after burial, see Plutarch, *Lyc.* 27; for the relation of the mourning ceremonies in Egypt to the processes of embalming and wrapping, see F. Ll. Griffith, *Stories of the High Priests of Memphis*, 1900, pp. 29–30.

91. For the suggestion that forty days represented the period of embalming only and that the whole process of mummification and wrapping occupied seventy days, see F. Ll. Griffith, *op. cit.*, pp. 29–30; also A. Lucas, *Ancient Egyptian Materials and Industries*, 4th ed., 1962, p. 299; for seventy days as the period of mummification, see Herodotus, *Hist. II*, 86.

92. The name of Osiris contains both the eye and the throne hieroglyphic signs, that of Isis, the throne alone.

For the relation of 'chariots', 'thrones' and 'rejoicing' to the aspects of the planets, see Ptolemy, *Tetrabíblos*, I.23.

93. See J. Černý, 'Egyptian Oracles', 1962, p. 37, Fig. 8 (King Haremhab in procession).

94. For the relation of the Ras Shamra texts to Judaism, see A. S. Kapelrud, *The Ras Shamra Discoveries and the Old Testament*, 1965.

95. *Ps.* 47(46); 93(92); 95(94)–99(98), etc. quoted by A. S. Kapelrud, *op. cit.*, p. 67, from S. Mowinckel, *Psalmenstudien*, Vol. II, *Das Thronbesteigungsfest Jahwäs und der Ursprung der Eschatologie Kristiania*, 1922.

96. See G. G. Scholem, *Major Trends in Jewish Mysticism*, 1941, Lecture II, 'Merkabah Mysticism and Jewish Gnosticism'.

97. For the relation of the Qumran cult to the solar calendar, see A. R. C. Leaney, *The Rule of Qumran and its Meaning*, 1966, pp. 75–107.

98. *Ex.* 18.25.

99. *Rev.* 21.17.

100. See Papyrus of Ani (*Brit. Mus.* No. 10470, sheet 35).

101. See R. Graves, *Greek Myths*, II, 1955, 133a.

102. See R. Graves, *op. cit.*, 123.1.

103. The mythology of Judaism emphasised the necessity for the destruction of the offspring of the union of the sons of God and women (*Gen.* 6.1–7).

104. *Ex.* 23.29, 30; 32.13; *Num.* 26.53; *Deut.* 4.38; 32.8, 9; *Jos.* 1.6; 14.9, etc.; *Heb.* 11.9, etc.

105. Philostratus, *The Life of Apollonius of Tyana*, Books III, VI.

CHAPTER IV

1. On the encroachment of priestly influence into life in the Twenty-first Dynasty, the appointment of officials and the settlement of judicial investigations by oracles, see A. Gardiner, 'The Gods of Thebes as Guarantors of Personal Property', *JEA*, **48**, 1962, pp. 57–69.

2. *Ex.* 18.21–27.

3. *Gorgias*, 523C.

4. Compare *The Book of the Dead*, Chapter CXXV. (Papyrus of Ani: *Brit. Mus.* No. 10470, sheet 30; Papyrus of Nu; *Brit. Mus.* No. 10477, sheet 22; Papyrus of Nebseni: *Brit. Mus.* No. 9900, sheet 30).

5. On two 'judgments', compare the journey of the soul between one incarnation and the next in Plato, *Phaedo*, 107D–108B (quoted p. 150) and the doctrine of the thousand years between the first and 'Last' judgments (see Chapter V.I.6.ii).

6. See D. S. Russell, *The Method and Message of Jewish Apocalyptic*, 1964, pp. 107–118.

7. *Testament of Levi*, 5.4; *Testament of Asher*, 2.10.

8. *I Enoch*. 81.1–3.

9. *II Enoch*, 22.12.

10. *Republic*, X.614.

11. *Apocalypse of Elias*, 12.

12. *Apocalypse of Elias*, 13.

13. The *Tê* represents the transliteration from the demotic script, *Dêt* (formerly read *Duat*) from the hieroglyphic; both designations referred to the region of the night journey of the sun and are synonymous with *Amente* (the West).

14. For reference to the placing of the right pupil under the pivot of the door of *Amente* as a form of punishment, see Togo Mina, *Le Martyre d'Apa Epima*, 1937, p. 71.

15. For commentary on the *Pistis Sophia*, made before the discovery of the Nag Hamadi texts (1948), see C. Schmidt, *Pistis Sophia*, 1925, pp. ix–xxxviii.

16. *Antimimon* is here translated as 'counterpart'; in ancient Egypt, one of the non-material parts of man was the *ka* or 'double'; it was to the *ka* that funerary services were performed.

17. For discussion on the *Midst* in Valentinian gnosticism, see C. A. Baynes, *A Coptic Gnostic Treatise (Bruce MS. 96)*, 1933, pp. 184–188.

18. On the Receivers (*paralemptores*) as powers concerned with the embodiment and release of souls, see C. A. Baynes, *op. cit.*, p. 105; on the three days spent by the soul after death seeing earthly places, see pp. 131–132.

19. For *Abbadon* as a term applied to *Sheol*, and related to the notion of destruction, see E. Langton, *Good and Evil Spirits*, 1942, p. 148.
   See also Qumran *Hymns*, III.4, 5. in G. Vermes, *The Dead Sea Scrolls in English*, 1962, p. 158.

20. *Job.* 26.6; 28.22; *Ps.* 88(87).11; *Pr.* 15.11.

21. *Rev.* 9.11.

22. See Chapter III, Note 77. In Pharaonic Egypt, the decans were those constellations which rose and set during each ten-day period; on the use of decan lists as 'star clocks' to determine the hours of the night throughout the year, see O. Neugebauer and R. A. Parker, *Brown Egyptological Studies, VI. Egyptian Astronomical Texts. III Decans, Planets, and Zodiacs*, 1969; Zodiacs were not found in Egypt prior to the Ptolemaic period, when decans became the designations of the ten-degree divisions of the ecliptic; see O. Neugebauer and R. A. Parker, *op. cit.*, pp. 4, 117.

23. For the relation of the three faces (*prosôpa*) of each planet to the decans, see A.-J. Festugière, *Hermès Trismégiste*, III, 1954, 'Introduction' p. xlvii; for the relation of the decans to the animal deities of Egypt, see pp. xlix–li; for the relation of the decans to demons, see 'Fragment de Stobée', VI. 10.
   See also Ptolemy, *Tetrabiblos*, I. 23.
   For the relation of decans to various parts and organs of the body and to the diseases of these parts, see A. -J. Festugière, *La Révélation d'Hermès Trismégiste*, 1950, Vol. I, pp. 128–143.

24. *Rev.* 12.3, 4. See p. 216.

25. For the animal representatives of various systems of decans, see A.-J. Festugière, *op. cit.*, pp. 128–143.

26. Book XI.

27. Book VI.

28. See F. Ll. Griffith, *Stories of the High Priests of Memphis*, 1900. *First Tale of Khamuas*, IV.9, 14, 20.

29. *I Enoch*, 104.7. See p. 185.

30. See J. Daniélou, *Les Figures du Christ dans l'ancien Testament*, 1950, pp. 9–12.

31. Origen, *Contra Celsum*, VI.22.

32. See *Book of the Dead*, Chapters XCIX, CXXV and CXLIV: Papyrus of Nu (*Brit. Mus.* No. 10477, sheets 21, 22, 24, 26), etc.

33. Chapter LXXVI concerned transformation of a man into whatever form he wishes; Chapters LXXVII–LXXXVIII concerned the making of other transformations.

34. *Apocalypse of Elias*, 6.

35. See Ch. Maystre and A. Piankoff, *Le Livre des Portes*, Vol. II, 1939–46,

pp. 163–165; see also E. A. W. Budge, *The Egyptian Heaven and Hell*, Vol. II, 1905, p. 303.

36. See C. Rabin, 'The Literary structure of the War Scroll', in *Essays on the Dead Sea Scrolls*, ed. C. Rabin and Y. Yadin, 1957.

   For the concept of a holy forty years war against the Gentiles, see J. van der Ploeg, *Le Rouleau de la guerre*, 1959, pp. 11–22.

37. On the Phlegrean fields as the site of Avernus and the river Styx, see R. F. Paget, *In the Footsteps of Orpheus*, 1967, Ch. I.

38. Book X.21.34.

   In this connection see also T. F. Glasson, *Greek influence in Jewish Eschatology*, 1961, pp. 12–19.

39. See F. Ll. Griffith, *Stories of the High Priests of Memphis. Second Tale of Khamuas*, I.34, II.1, 16–21.

40. For treasuries of souls in *Sheol*, see *II Baruch*, 21.23, 24.

41. For Baptism as the *sphragis*, which, like circumcision, incorporated a person into the people of God, see J. Daniélou, *The Theology of Jewish Christianity*, 1964, p. 329.

42. For the *Descensus* as a means of salvation of the Old Testament Patriarchs and for the descent of the Apostles in order to give Baptism to the Patriarchs in Hell, see J. Daniélou, *op. cit.*, pp. 233–239.

43. For the *Descensus* as a conflict with the Devil and for the doctrinal relation, in Judeo-Christian apocrypha, between death and Baptism, see J. Daniélou, *op. cit.*, pp. 239–248.

44. F. Ll. Griffith, *op. cit.*, pp. 16–40.

45. *Apocalypse of Elias*, 17, 18.

46. See O. H. E. KHS-Burmester, *The Egyptian or Coptic Church*, 1967, pp. 123, 124.

47. *Ps.* 74(73).13.

   For the prayers of exorcism of the Baptismal water and Chrism, see O. H. E. KHS-Burmester, 'The Baptismal Rite of the Coptic Church (a critical study)', *BSAC*, XI, 1945, pp. 27–46.

CHAPTER V

1. For the accusations made against Christians in North Africa, see Tertullian, *Apologeticum*.

2. Eusebius, *History of the Church*, VI.

3. For the Calendar of the Egyptian Church and the calculation of dates according to the Era of the Martyrs, see O. H. E. KHS-Burmester, *The Egyptian or Coptic Church*, 1967, p. 12.

4. Eusebius, *op. cit.*, VIII.

5. Eusebius, *op. cit.*, X.

6. For the Stoic cult of suicide in the first century A.D. and the Gymnosophistae (Brahmins) who set fire to themselves, see A. D. Nock, *Conversion*, 1933, Ch. XII; repr. 1963, pp. 197–201.

7. Eusebius, *op. cit.*, VI.41–43.

8. For the influence of Greek panegyric on the rhetoric of the Church Fathers, see H. Delehaye, *Les Passions des Martyrs et les Genres Littéraires*, 1966 (2nd ed.), pp. 134–169.

9. See H. Delehaye, *Les Origines du Culte des Martyrs*, 1933, p. 110.

10. H. Delehaye, *op. cit.*, p. 112.

11. H. Delehaye, *op. cit.*, p. 111.

12. H. Delehaye, *op. cit.*, p. 112.

13. H. Delehaye, *op. cit.*, p. 112.

14. H. Delehaye, *op. cit.*, p. 114.

15. H. Delehaye, *op. cit.*, p. 116.

16. H. Delehaye, *op. cit.*, pp. 116, 120.

17. H. Delehaye, *op. cit.*, p. 119.

18. *City of God*, XXII, VIII.

19. See H. Delehaye, *Cinq Leçons sur la Méthode Hagiographique*, 1934, p. 13; on the local character of the majority of Egyptian martyr cults, see J. Drescher, *Apa Mena*, 1946, pp. x–xi.

20. *Acts* 7.55–56.

21. See the *First and Second Tales of Khamua*, in F. Ll. Griffith, *Stories of the High Priests of Memphis*, 1900, pp. 16–40; 42–66; also *Tale of Anpu and Bata, Tale of the Doomed Prince*, in W. M. F. Petrie, *Egyptian Tales*. Second Series, 1985, pp. 13–27; 36–65.

22. *Iliad*, II ff,; *Aeneid*, IV.556–570; *Gen.* 15.1; *Deut.* 31.6–8; *Jos.* 1.5–9; *Acts* 23.11; 27.23–24, etc.

23. For formulae comparing the Pharaoh with Rē, see G. Posener, *De la divinité du Pharaon*, 1960, p. 8.

24. *IV Ezra*, 7.97.

25. *Testament of Levi*, 3.5–6.

26. On *Philanthropa*, or boons, granted by Ptolemaic emperors, as a result of which freedom from obligations or restoration of property was allowed to debtors and prisoners, see H. S. Smith, 'A Note on Amnesty', *JEA*, **54**, 1968, pp. 209–214.

27. For the deprivation of Egyptians of their lands in the Roman and Byzantine periods, and for the systems of taxation imposed, see H. I. Bell, *Egypt from Alexander the Great to the Arab conquest*, 1948, pp. 96–100, 117–125.

28. For *klêroi* as allotments of land and *dôreai* as grants of land to Greek and Egyptians in Ptolemaic times, see H. I. Bell, *op. cit.*, p. 45.

29. See *Ex.* 32.32.

30. For the imagery of the athletic contest in Stoic philosophy, see D. Epictetos, ii.18.22; iii.20.9; 16.22; for comparison of the *pneumata* in the body to the course of the horse race, see Philo, *God unchangeable* 35.

31. For the relation of the nomes of Egypt to the constellations of the Zodiac, see A.-J. Festugière, *La Révélation d'Hermès Trismégiste*, Vol. I, 1950, p. 117.

32. See J. Černý, *Ancient Egyptian Religion*, 1952, pp. 105, 106.

33. See J. Drescher, *op. cit.*, p. 99.
34. For pre-Christian imagery of death as a boat journey in Coptic times, see A. Badawy, 'Idéologie et formulaire paiens dans les épitaphes Coptes', *BSAC*, X, 1944, pp. 7–9.
35. For discussion on the possibility that the cult of Saint Menas took the place of a pagan centre of worship and pilgrimage, see J. Drescher, *op. cit.*, pp. xiii–xix.
36. See J. Drescher, *op. cit.*, pp. 141–142.
37. For a summary of the Arabic narrative of the Acts and Martyrdom of Julius of Aqfahs (Kbehes) from *Paris arabe*, 4788, see de Lacy O'Leary, *The Saints of Egypt*, 1937, pp. 174–175.
    See also H. Delehaye, *Les Passions des Martyrs et les Genres Littéraires* (1920), 1966, p. 222.
38. See E. A. W. Budge, *The Book of Opening the Mouth*, 1909, Vol. I, pp. 14–17.
39. See H. Delehaye, *Les Passions des Martyrs et les Genres Littéraires*, 1921, pp. 177–182.
40. *City of God*, XXII.VIII; *Confessions*, IX.VII. Quoted pp. 199–200.
41. For the account by Gregory of Nyanza, see H. Delehaye, *Les Origines du Culte des Martyrs*, 1933, p. 75.
42. See H. Delehaye, *op. cit.*, p. 78.
43. See H. Delehaye, *op. cit.*, pp. 80–83.
44. See H. Delehaye, *op. cit.*, pp. 84–85.
45. Compare the revelation, through an oracle, of the whereabouts of a hero's grave, Herodotus, *Hist. I*, 67, 68.
46. See 'Contracts of Hepzefi', *BAR*, 535–593.
47. The sixth century Gaianite heresy, a form of Docetism, denied the doctrine of the Incarnation; the term *Theotokos* designated the status of the Virgin as the 'Mother of God'.
48. The beneficial effects in the life after death, of writing or copying books for the Church, was expressed in the colophons regularly appended to such books; see A. Van Lantschoot, *Recueil de Colophons . . . Sahidiques*, Bibliothèque du Muséon, Tom. I, fasc. 1, 1929.
49. Originally a prayer band consisting of extracts from the Law of Moses, worn by Jews on the forehead or arm (*Matt.* 23.5), the Phylactery later took the form of a case containing inscribed parchment (the passages were *Ex.* 13.1–10; 11–16; *Deut.* 6.4–9; 11.13–21); on passages from the Scriptures used for exorcism, see M. Gaster article: 'Charms and Amulets (Jewish)' in *ERE*, Vol. III, 1910.
    On papyrus strips containing texts promising protection by the gods for the body, flesh and bones against disease, magicians and bad dreams, see J. Černý, 'Egyptian Oracles', 1962, pp. 39–40.
50. For the evolution, from the Old Kingdom onwards, of formulae of imprecation against desecration of the tomb, see H. Sottas, *La préservation de la Propriété Funéraire dans l'ancienne Egypte*, 1913, pp. 7–82.

51. For the combination, from the Middle Kingdom onwards, of the imprecatory formula with one promising rewards, see H. Sottas, *op. cit.*, pp. 67–82.

52. On the compiling of martyrologies and on the cult of saints on the basis of their names alone, see H. Delehaye, *Sanctus*, 1927, Ch. V, 'Les Saints qui n'ont jamais existé', pp. 208–232.

53. On the centres of the cult in the Orient see H. Delehaye, *Les Origines du Culte des Martyrs*, 1933, Ch. V, VI.

54. See note 46.

55. *Is.* 65.17–25; *Rev.* 20.4.

56. Pausanius, *Guide to Greece*, II (Corinth), 11.1–12.1 and 26.1–28.2 (Sanctuaries at Titane and Epidaurus).

57. See J. B. Hurry, *Imhotep*, 1928, pp. 105–111.

58. See F. C. Grant, *Hellenistic Religions*, 1953, pp. 55–58.
   For votive stelae relating to Imhotep, see J. B. Hurry, *op. cit.*, pp. 108–109.

59. On the healing oil from the shrine of St. Menas, see J. Drescher, *op. cit.*, p. xxi.

60. On the translation of the bodies of the saints to the site of the shrine of Isis, see H. Delehaye, 'Les saints d'Aboukir', *Anal. Boll.*, XXX, pp. 448–450; *Les Origines du Culte des Martyrs*, 1933, pp. 223–225. On the use, by Cyril of Alexandria of the name of the saint, *Kuros* (Cyrus) to replace *Kura*, the title of Isis, see Delehaye, *op. cit.*, p. 409.

61. On Chaldean and Etruscan haruspicy in the Roman empire, and on the use of engraved models of the liver, see G. Wissowa article: 'Divination (Roman)' in *ERE*, Vol. IV, 1911. See also Chapter III, Note 20.

62. For the imagery of attacks by animals in the Psalms, see Chapter II, Note 54; for the imagery of destruction by fire, see *Ps.* 11(10).6; 18(17).8; 21(20).9; 79(78).5; 80(79).15, 16; 106(105).18; 140(139).10; for the imagery of overwhelming waters, darkness, and the pit, see *Ps.* 7(6).15; 16(15).10; 18(17).4, 5; 30(29).2, 3; 42(41).7; 49(48).9.15; 55(54).15; 57(56).6; 69(68).1, 2, 15; 86(85).13; 88(87).4, 6, 17; 89(88).48; 103(102).3, 4; 119(118).85; 124(123).4, 5; 143(142).3, 7.

63. *Ps.* 74(73).10, 18, 22; 79(78).10–12; 89(88).50, 51.

64. For an address by a deity to the Pharaoh, in which the roles of both are defined by naming, see *BAR*, II.288; on reciprocity as the basis of the relationship between the Pharaoh and the gods, see G. Posener, *op. cit.*, p. 40.

65. See I. Abrahams article: 'Name of God (Jewish)', in *ERE*, Vol. I, IX, 1917.

66. *Ezek.* 20.41.

67. On martyrdom among the Essenes see Josephus, *Jewish War*, Book II, VIII.10; on the Alexandrian origin of *iv Maccabees* see H. Delehaye, *Les Passions des Martyrs*, 1921, p. 226, and R. H. Charles, *Apocrypha and Pseudepigrapha of the Old Testament*, 1913, p. 657; on *iv Maccabees* as a prototype of martyrdom stories, see H. Delehaye, *op. cit.*, p. 226.

68. See J. Černý, *Ancient Egyptian Religion*, 1952, p. 72.
    For a representation of Shed, see *Berlin* 4434 (reproduced in A. Erman, *Die Religion der Ägypter*, 1934, p. 310).

69. *In verrem actio secunda*, IV. xliii.94.

70. On the significance of the kiss in Roman and early Christian times, see A. E. Crawley article: 'Kissing. 5. The Kiss of Peace', in *ERE*, Vol. VII, 1914.

71. Eusebius, *History of the Church*, II.23. 4–17.

72. Eusebius, *op. cit.*, V.1. 4–51.

73. Eusebius, *op. cit.*, VI.54–5; 39.5.

74. Eusebius, *op. cit.* VI. 39–46; VII.

75. Eusebius, *op. cit.*, VIII.

76. Eusebius, *op. cit.*, VIII.7.

77. Herodotus, *Hist. II*, 39,40; 66–69.

78. See P. Scott Moncrieff, *Paganism and Christianity in Egypt*, 1913, p. 102.

79. See H. Thurston article: 'Saints and Martyrs (Christian)' in *ERE*, Vol. IX, 1920, p. 58.

80. *The Book of the Dead*, which incorporates earlier ritual, contains invocations against removal of the head (Chapters XLIII, CLIV). See Note 38.

81. Plutarch, *On Isis and Osiris*, XVIII.

82. See O. H. E. KHS-Burmester, *The Egyptian or Coptic Church*, 1967, pp. 123–124.

83. *Ps.* 68(67).18; *Eph.* 4.8.

84. See J. Daniélou, *The Theology of Jewish Christianity*, 1964, pp. 233–236.

85. *Life of Apollonius of Tyana*, IV, xlv. For the raising of the dead by Asclepiades, see Pliny, *Natural History*, VII.124; XXVI.15.

86. Eusebius, *History of the Church*, V.7.4; *Apocryphal Acts of the Apostles*: see *Acts of John*, 46, 47, 48–53, 73–83; *Acts of Peter*, 23–28; *Acts of Andrew*, 2, 7, 18, 19, 24; *Acts of Philip*, 1.1–5; *Acts of Paul*, 2; *Acts of Thomas*, 33.

87. *City of God*, XXII.vi. See p. 182.

88. *Dan.* 10.5–6; *Rev.* 10.1.

89. *i Kg.* 8.10; *ii Chr.* 5.13–14.

90. *Is.* 60.19–20; *Rev.* 21.23; 22.5.

91. *Ps.* 31(30).16; 80(79).19; 89(88).15; 119(118).135.

92. *Rev.* 1.16.

93. *Ex.* 34.29, 30, 35.

94. *Dan.* 12.3; *II Ezra*, 7.125.

95. *On the cessation of Oracles*, LI.

96. *Ex.* 3.2, 14.

97. *Gen.* 15.12.

98. *Ex.* 20.21; *Deut.* 5.22.

 99. *i Kg.* 8.12; *ii Chr.* 6.1.
100. *Ex.* 13.21–22, etc.
101. *i Kg.* 18.46; *ii Kg.* 3.15.
102. *Ezek.* 40.1, 2.
103. *Ezek.* 8.3.
104. *Ezek.* 11.24.
105. *Ezek.* 3.12, 14.
106. *Ezek.* 40.1, 2.
107. See Ptolemy, *Tetrabiblos*, IV.4, 178–179; on the relation of plants to decans, to the signs of the Zodiac and to the planets, see A.-J. Festugière, *op. cit.*, Vol. I, 1950, pp. 139–160.
108. *Who is the Heir?* XLI; *On the migration of Abraham*, VII, 179.181.
109. Apuleius, *Metamorphoses*, XI.5.

POSTSCRIPT

1. On the cultural value of hallucinations in primitive societies, see M. Eliade, *Archaic Techniques of Ecstasy*, tr. W. R. Trask, Payot, Paris 1951; Routledge and Kegan Paul, London 1964; E. H. Erikson, *Childhood and Society*, Chicago, 1950, pp. 150–153; A. F. C. Wallace, 'Cultural Determinants of Response to Hallucinatory Experience', *A.M.A. Archives of General Psychiatry*, I, 1959, pp. 58–69; E. A. Weinstein, 'Social Aspects of Hallucinations', in L. J. West (ed.) *Hallucinations*, New York, 1962, pp. 233–238.

    For the implication that, because hallucinogenic techniques are used for social purposes in primitive or decadent cultures, they are relevant in modern society, see A. Huxley, *The Doors of Perception*, 1954; F. Huxley in R. Crocket, R. A. Sandison and A. Walk (ed.), *The Hallucinogenic Drugs and their Psychotherapeutic Use*, Proceedings of the Quarterly Meeting of the Royal Medico-Psychological Association in London, February 1961, H. K. Lewis, London, 1963, p. 174; for the implication that, because techniques which increase suggestibility and disorganise brain function are just as effective in modern as in primitive societies, their use for therapeutic purposes is therefore justified, see W. Sargant: 'Witch Doctoring, Zar and Voodoo; their relation to modern psychiatric treatment', *Proc. R. Soc. Med.*, **60**, 1967, pp. 1055–60; 'Drugs and Human Behaviour', *The Advancement of Science*, **22**, 1966, pp. 681–687; 'The Physiology of Faith', *Brit. Journ. Psychiat.*, **115**, 1969, pp. 505–518.

2. See E. W. Anderson, 'Abnormal Mental States in Survivors with special reference to Collective Hallucinations', *Journal of the Royal Naval Medical Service*, **28**, 1942, pp. 361–377; E. Tiira, *Raft of Despair*, London, 1954; M. Critchley, 'The Idea of a Presence', *Acta Psychiatrica et Neurologica Scandinavica*, **30**, 1955, pp. 155–168.

3. See L. J. West, 'United States Air Force prisoners of the Chinese Communists', *GAP Symposium No. 4*, July 1957, p. 270.

    On psychosis induced by prolonged wakefulness, see J. T. Brauchi and L. J. West, 'Sleep Deprivation', *JAMA*, **171**, 1959, pp. 11–14.

4. On the experimental techniques whereby the 'information input' through the special senses is de-patterned or reduced, see W. H. Bexton, W. Heron and T. H. Scott, 'Effects of decreased variation in the sensory environment', *Canad. Journ. Psychol.*, **8**, 1954, pp. 70–76; J. C. Lilly, 'Mental effects of reduction of ordinary levels of physical stimuli on intact healthy persons', *Psychiat. Res. Rep. Amer. Psychiat. Ass.* **5**, 1956, pp. 1–9; L. Goldberger and R. R. Holt, 'Experimental interference with reality contact (perceptual isolation); method and group results', *Journ. Nerv. and Ment. Dis.*, **127**, No. 2, 1958, pp. 99–112; J. Vernon, *Inside the Black Room*, New York 1963, Part I.

5. For reports on the content of hallucinations experienced under experimental and other situations, see L. Goldberger and R. R. Holt, 'Experimental interference with reality contact (perceptual isolation); method and group results', *loc. cit.*, pp. 99–112; J. Vernon, T. E. McGill and H. Schiffman, 'Visual hallucinations during perceptual isolation', *Canad. Journ. Psychol.*, **12**, 1958, pp. 31–34; S. J. Freedman and M. Greenblatt, 'Studies in human isolation. II. Hallucinations and other cognitive findings', *United States Armed Forces Medical Journal*, **11**, 1960, pp. 1479–1497; S. J. Freedman, H. U. Grunebaum, F. A. Stare and M. Greenblatt, 'Imagery in sensory deprivation' in L. J. West (ed.), *Hallucinations*, New York, 1962, pp. 108–117; J. C. Pollard, L. Uhr and C. Wesley-Jackson, 'Studies in sensory deprivation', *A.M.A. Archives of General Psychiatry*, **5**, 1963, pp. 435–454; J. Vernon, *Inside the Black Room*, New York, 1963, Ch. XI.

6. On the increased degree of suggestibility found among subjects of hallucinatory experiences, see E. W. Anderson, *loc. cit.*, pp. 361–377; J. M. Schneck, 'Hypnotic hallucinatory behaviour', *Journ. Clin. and Exper. Hypnosis*, **I**, 1953, pp. 4–11; M. Critchley, *loc. cit.*, pp. 155–168. E. J. Kandal, T. I. Myers and D. B. Murphy, 'Influence of prior verbalisations and instructions on visual sensations reported under conditions of reduced sensory input', paper read before Amer. Psychol. Assoc., Washington D.C., August 1958; T. H. Scott, W. H. Bexton, W. Heron and B. K. Doane, 'Cognitive effects of perceptual isolation', *Canad. Journ. Psychol.*, **13**, 1959, pp. 200–209; J. C. Pollard, L. Uhr and C. Wesley-Jackson, *loc. cit.*, pp. 435–454; J. Vernon, *loc. cit.*, Ch. IV.

7. For the recommendation, by psychologists and others, of hallucinogenic drugs as a means, suitable in modern society, of attaining religious or mystical experience, see P. G. Stafford and B. H. Golightly, *LSD, the problem-solving Psychedelic*, Preface by H. Osmond, Introduction by D. Blewett and Afterword by S. Krippner, Tandem Books, New York, 1967, Ch. VI; W. Van Dusen, 'LSD and the enlightenment of Zen', quoted in P. G. Stafford and B. H. Golightly, *op. cit.*, p. 145; H. Smith, 'Do drugs have religious import?', *The Journal of Philosophy*, Vol. LXI, No. 17, Sept. 1964; R. E. L. Masters and J. Houston, *The Varieties of Psychedelic Experience*, Holt, Reinehart and Winston, 1966; R. Blum *et. al.*, *Utopiates, the Use and Users of LSD-26*, Atherton Press, New York, 1964; E. Dalton, 'Mysticism and General

Semantics', *ETC, A Review of General Semantics*, Vol. XXII, No. 4, 1965; W. W. Harman, 'The Issue of the Consciousness-Expanding Drugs', *Main Currents of Modern Thought*, Sept./Oct. 1963; C. Savage, D. Jackson and J. Terrill, 'LSD, Transcendence and the New Beginning', *Journ. Nerv. and Ment. Dis.*, **135**, No. 5, 1962.

8. On disturbing and catastrophic effects of hallucinatory experiences among primitive people, see Z. Gussow, 'A preliminary report of *kayak-angst* among the Eskimo of West Greenland; a study in sensory deprivation', *International Journal of Social Psychiatry*, **9**, 1963, pp. 18–26.

On disturbing and distressing experiences arising as a result of interference with customary relationships to the environment, see D. E. Cameron, 'Studies on senile nocturnal delirium', *Psychiat. Quart.*, Jan. 1941, pp. 1–7; H. Azima and F. J. Cramer-Azima, 'Studies in perceptual isolation', *Dis. Nerv. System* (Monograph Supplement) **18**, 1957, pp. 1–6; S. Smith and W. Lewty, 'Perceptual Isolation using a silent room', *Lancet*, ii, 1959, p. 342; S. J. Freedman and M. Greenblatt, *loc. cit.*, pp. 1479–1497; R. Vosberg, N. Fraser and J. Guehl, 'Imagery sequence in sensory deprivation', *A.M.A. Arch. Gen. Psychiat.*, **2**, 1960, pp. 356–357; D. E. Cameron, L. Levy, T. Ban and L. Rubenstein, 'Sensory deprivation; effects upon the functioning human in space systems', in B. E. Flaherty (ed.), *Psychophysiological aspects of space flight*, New York, 1961, pp. 225–236; J. Vernon, *loc. cit.*, Ch. XV.

9. On the factors involved among subjects who found experimental conditions of sensory deprivation intolerable, see J. Vernon, *loc. cit.*, pp. 164–183; see also J. Freedman and M. Greenblatt, *loc. cit.*, pp. 1490–1491; on affective disturbances and depersonalisation among experimental subjects, see L. Goldberger and R. R. Holt, *loc. cit.*, pp. 99–112.

ABBREVIATIONS

ANCL   *Ante-Nicene Christian Library*, Edinburgh.
BAR   Breasted, J. H. *Ancient Records of Egypt*, Chicago.
BSAC   *Bulletin de la Société d'Archéologie Copte*, Cairo.
CSCO   *Corpus Scriptorum Christianorum Orientalium*, Louvain.
DACL   *Dictionnaire d'Archéologie Chrétienne et de Liturgie*, Paris.
ERE   *Encyclopaedia of Religion and Ethics*, London.
JEA   *Journal of Egyptian Archaeology*, London.
PO   *Patrologia Orientalis*, Paris.
RA   *Revue Archéologique*, Paris.
RE   *Revue Egyptologique*, Paris.
ZÄ   *Zeitschrift für Ägyptische Sprache und Altertumskunde*, Leipzig.

ABBREVIATIONS

USED IN REFERENCES TO THE TEXTS
IN SECTIONS I–V

COPTIC TEXTS

Amélineau, E. Annales du Musée Guimet. Tome 17. Monuments pour servir a l'histoire de l'Egypte Chrétienne au IVᵉ siècle. Leroux, Paris 1889.

AM.TH.B. *Vie de Théodore, Disciple de Pakhome*, pp. 215–334.

Annales du Musée Guimet. Tome 25. Monuments pour servir a l'histoire de l'Egypte Chrétienne. Histoire des Monastères de la Basse Egypte. Leroux, Paris 1894.

AM.PAUL.B. *Vie de St. Paul*, pp. 1–14

AM.AP.ANT.B. *Apoththegmes sur Saint Antoine*, pp. 15–45.

AM.MAC.SC.B. *Vie de Macaire de Scete*, pp. 46–117.

AM.AP.MAC.B. *Apophthegmes sur Saint Macaire*, pp. 203–234.

AM.MAC.AL.B. *Vie de Macaire d'Alexandrie*, pp. 235–261.

AM.MA.DO.B. *Vie des Saints Maxime et Domèce*, pp. 262–315.

AM.JOH.K.B. *Vie de Jean Kolobes*, pp. 316–410.

Mémoires de l'Institut Egyptien. Tome II. Cairo 1889.

AM.PIS.KE.B. *Un Evêque de Keft au VIIᵉ siècle. Encomion par Abba Moise, Evêque de Keft, au sujet de Abba Pisentios, Evêque de cette même ville de Keft*, pp. 333–423.

Mémoires de la Mission Archéologique Française du Caire. Tome IV. Monuments pour servir a l'histoire de l'Egypte Chrétienne au IVᵉ et Vᵉ siècles. Leroux, Paris 1888.

AM.MAC.TK.B. *Panégyrique de Macaire de Tkou par Dioscore d'Alexandrie*, pp. 92–164.

AM.CYR.AL.B. *Sermon de St. Cyrille d'Alexandrie*, pp. 165–195.

Mémoires de la Mission Archéologique Française du Caire. Tome IV, 2ᵉ fasc. Monuments pour servir a l'histoire de l'Egypte Chrétienne au IVᵉ, VIᵉ et VIIᵉ siècles. Leroux, Paris 1895.

AM.JOH.LY.S. *Vie de Jean de Lycopolis*, pp. 605–665.

AM.MAN.S. *Vie de Manasse*, pp. 666–679.

AM.MO.S. *Vie de Moise*, pp. 680–706.

262

AM.MAT.P.S.	*Fragments de la Vie de Matthieu le Pauvre*, pp. 707–736.
AM.CO.ABR.S.	*Vie d'un Contemporain d'Abraham*, pp. 754–758.
AM.PAUL.T.S.	*Vie de Paul de Tamoueh*, pp. 759–769.
Balestri, I. et Hyvernat, H.	Corpus Scriptorum Christianorum Orientalium. Scriptores Coptici. Vol. 43. Acta Martyrum I (1924). Louvain 1947.
BA.HY.I.LAC.B.	*Martyrium Sancti Apa Lacaronis*, pp. 1–23.
BA.HY.I.ANAT.P.B.	*Martyrium Sancti Anatolii Persae*, pp. 24–33.
BA.HY.I.TH.O.B.	*Martyrium Sancti Theodori Orientalis*, pp. 34–62.
BA.HY.I.SA.PA.B.	*Martyrium Sancti Apa Serapionis de Panephosi*, pp. 63–88.
BA.HY.I.AP.B.	*Martyrium Sancti Apatil*, pp. 89–109.
BA.HY.I.PAP.B.	*Martyrium Sancti Apa Paphnuti*, pp. 110–119.
BA.HY.I.EPIM.B.	*Martyrium Sancti Apa Epime*, pp. 120–156.
BA.HY.I.TH.S.B.	*Martyrium Sancti Theodori Stratelates*, pp. 157–199.
BA.HY.I.AN.B.	*Martyrium Sancti Apa Anub*, pp. 200–241.
BA.HY.I.APOL.B.	*Martyrium Sancti Apa Apoli*, pp. 242–248.
	Corpus Scriptorum Christianorum Orientalium. Scriptores Coptici. Vol. 86. Acta Martyrum II. 1953.
BA.HY.II.IAC.P.B.	*Martyrium Sancti Iacobi Persae*, pp. 24–61.
BA.HY.II.POL.SM.B.	*Martyrium Sancti Polycarpi Smyrnae*, pp. 62–72.
BA.HY.II.IS.TI.B.	*Martyrium Sancti Isaaci Tiphrensis*, pp. 73–89.
BA.HY.II.T.A.T.S.B.	*Theodori Antiocheni Archiepiscopi oratio in laudem S. Theodori Orientalis et S. Theodori Stratelates*, pp. 90–156.
BA.HY.II.JOH.PH.B.	*Martyrium Sancti Johannes Phanidjoitani*, pp. 157–182.
BA.HY.II.GEO.DI.B.	*Theodoti Ancyrani oratio en laudem sancti Georgi Diospolitaeni*, pp. 183–269.
BA.HY.II.GEO.B.	*Martyrium Sancti Georgi*, pp. 270–310.
BA.HY.II.MIR.GEO.B.	*Miraculi Sancti Georgi*, pp. 311–360.
Budge, E. A. W.	Oriental Text Series I. London 1888.
BU.GEO.C.S.	*The Martyrdom and Miracles of Saint George of Cappadocia.*
	Coptic Apocrypha in the Dialect of Upper Egypt. London 1913.
BU.BART.R.S.	*The Book of the Resurrection by Bartholomew the Apostle*, pp. 1–48.
BU.AP.PIS.S.	*The Life of Bishop Pisentius by John the Elder*, pp. 75–127.
BU.CH.JOH.S.	*An Encomium on Saint John the Baptist by Saint John Chrysostom*, pp. 128–145.

263

Coptic Martyrdoms in the Dialect of Upper Egypt. London 1914.

BU.EUS.TH.S.   *The Life of Saints Eustathius and Theopiste and of their two children*, pp. 102–127.

BU.CYR.S.   *The Life of Apa Cyrus*, pp. 128–136.

BU.ON.S.   *The Life of Apa Onnophrius the Anchorite*, pp. 205–224.

BU.ABB.S.   *An Encomium by Timothy, Archbishop of Alexandria, on the history of the establishing of Abbaton, the Angel of Death*, pp. 225–249.

Miscellaneous Coptic Texts in the Dialect of Upper Egypt. London 1915.

BU.M.TIM.S.   *The Discourse which Saint Timothy, Archbishop of Alexandria, pronounced on the festival of the holy archangel Michael*, pp. 512–525.

BU.AP.PAUL.S.   *The Apocalypse of Paul*, pp. 534–574.

Chaine, M.   Revue de l'Orient Chrétien, 3ᵉ series. Tome VII (XXVII). Paris 1930.

CHA.MART.B.   *La Recension Copte de la Vie d'Abba Martyrianos de Cesarée*, pp. 140–180.

Publication de l'Institut Français d'Archéologie Orientale. Bibliothèque d'Etudes Coptes. Tome VI. Le Caire 1960.

CHA.AP.PA.S.   *Le Manuscrit de la Version Copte en Dialecte Sahidique des ' Apophthegmata Patrum'.*

Davis, M. H.   Patrologia Orientalis (ed. R. Graffin and F. Nau). Tome XIV, fasc. 2. Firmin-Didot, Paris 1919.

DAV.JOH.KH.B.   *The Life of Abba John Khame.*

De Lagarde, P.   Aegyptica. Göttingen 1883.

LA.MOR.JOS.B.   *de morte Iosephi*, pp. 1–37.

LA.DOR.MAR.B.   *de dormitione Mariae*, pp. 38–63.

Garitte, G.   Corpus Scriptorum Christianorum Orientalium. Scriptores Coptici. Vol. 177. Louvain 1949.

GAR.ANT.S.   *S. Antonii Vita. Versio Sahidici.*

Guidi, M. I.   Revue de l'Orient Chrétien. Vol. V. 1900.

GUI.DAN.B.   *Vie et Récits de l'Abbé Daniel de Scète (VIᵉ siècle)*, pp. 335–564.

Rendiconti della Reall. Accad. die Lincei, Cl. di Scienze Morali, etc. Ser. 5, t. 9. Rome 1900.

GUI.IS.B.   *Il Testamento di Isacco*, pp. 223–244.

Hyvernat, H.   Les Actes des Martyres de l'Egypte tirés des Manuscrits Coptes de la Bibliothèque Vaticane et du

	Musée Borgia. Vol. I, fasc. I–IV. Leroux, Paris 1886.
HY.EUSEB.B.	*Martyre de Saint Eusèbe*, pp. 1–39.
HY.MAC.AN.B.	*Martyre de Saint Macaire d'Antioche*, pp. 40–77.
HY.AP.IR.B.	*Martyre de Saint Apater et d'Irai sa soeur*, fasc. II, pp. 81–113.
HY.PI.AT.B.	*Martyre des Saints Piroou et Athom*, fasc. II, pp. 135–160; fasc. III, pp. 161–173.
HY.JE.SI.B.	*Martyre des Saints Jean et Siméon*, pp. 174–201.
HY.ARI.B.	*Martyre de Saint Apa Ari*, pp. 202–224.
HY.MACR.B.	*Martyre de Saint Macrobe*, fasc. III, pp. 225–240.
HY.PET.AL.B.	*Encomion de Saint Pierre d'Alexandrie par Abba Alexandre*, pp. 247–262.
HY.DID.B.	*Martyre d'Apa Didyme*, pp. 284–303.
HY.SAR.B.	*Martyre de Saint Sarapamon*, pp. 304–331.
Lefort, L. TH.	Corpus Scriptorum Christianorum Orientalium. Scriptores Coptici. Vol. 99 et 100. Louvain 1952 (1934).
LE.PAC.S.	*S. Pachomii Vitae. Sahidice Scriptae.*
	Corpus Scriptorum Christianorum Orientalium. Scriptores Coptici. Vol. 89. Louvain 1953 (1925).
LE.PAC.B.	*S. Pachomii Vita. Bohairice Scripta.*
Leipoldt, I.	Corpus Scriptorum Christianorum Orientalium. Scriptores Coptici. Series II. Vol. 41. Louvain 1946.
LEI.SIN.B.	*Sinuthi Archimandritae Vitae et Opera Omnia. Sinuthi Vita Bohairice.*
Porcher, E.	Patrologia Orientalis. Tome XI, fasc. 3. Firmin-Didot, Paris 1914.
POR.IS.B.	*Vie d'Isaac.* Patriarche d'Alexandrie de 686 à 689.
Robinson, J. F.	Texts and Studies. Vol. 4, no. 2. Coptic Apocryphal Gospels. Cambridge 1986. Kraus Reprint 1967.
ROB.MAR.S.	*Of the falling asleep of Mary*, II, pp. 71–127.
ROB.VIR.S.	*Of the life of the Virgin*, IIA; IV, pp. 14–16; 24–40.
Sobhy, G. P. G.	Bibliothèque d'Etudes Coptes. Tome I. Publications de l'Institut Français d'Archéologie Orientale. Le Caire 1919.
SOB.HEL.S.	*Le Martyre de Saint Hélias.*
Steindorff, G.	
ST.AP.EL.S.	*Die Apokalypse des Elias.* Leipzig 1899.

Till, W.

Koptische Heiligen und Martyrer Legenden. Orientalia Christiana Analecta 102. Erster Teil. Roma 1935.

TIL.I.NAH.S.   *Nahrow*, pp. 3–8.
TIL.I.WAN.S.   *Wanofre*, pp. 14–16.
TIL.I.HER.S.   *Heraklides*, pp. 34–36.
TIL.I.VIC.S.   *Viktor*, pp. 45–51.
TIL.I.PA.TH.S.   *Paese und Thekla*, pp. 71–84.
TIL.I.PAN.S.   *Panesnew*, pp. 94–101.
TIL.I.TIM.S.   *Timotheos*, pp. 112–119.
TIL.I.JOH.LY.S.   *Johannes von Lykopolis*, pp. 139–147.
TIL.II.MAT.A.S.   *Matthaeus der Arme*, Zweiter Teil, pp. 8–22.
TIL.II.PTOL.S.   *Ptolemaios*, pp. 28–38.

Togo Mina   Service des Antiquités de l'Egypte. Le Caire 1937.
MIN.EPIM.S.   *Le Martyre d'Apa Epima.*

Van Lantschoot, A.   Studi e Testi. Roma 1957.
VAN.L.Q.TH.S.   *Questions de Théodore.*

Worrell, W. H.   The Coptic Manuscripts in the Freer Collection. Macmillan, New York 1923.
WOR.GAB.S.   *A Homily on the Archangel Gabriel by Celestinus, Archbishop of Rome.*

SYRIAC TEXTS

Brockelmann, C.
BRO.EP.SY.   *Das Leben des heilige Ephraem des Syrers.* Syrische Grammatik, Chrestomathie, (Berlin 1899) Leipzig 1960, pp. 22–43.

Brooks, E. W.   Patrologia Orientalis (R. Graffin and F. Nau). John of Ephesus. Lives of the Eastern Saints.

Tome XVII. fasc. 1 Paris 1923.
BR.PAUL.SY.   *Life of Paul the Anchorite.* pp. 111–118.
BR.ZAC.SY.   *From the Convent of Zacharia.* pp. 273–274.
BR.THOM.SY.   *Thomas the Armenian.* pp. 297–298.

Tome XVIII, fasc. 4. Paris 1924.
BR.AM.SY.   *Of the Amidene convents*, pp. 607–623.
Tome XIX, fasc. 2. Paris 1925.
BR.ANTI.SY.   *Lives of two Antiochenes*, pp. 164–179.
BR.PRI.SY.   *Priscus*, pp. 179–185.
BR.JAM.SY.   *Spurious Life of James*, pp. 228–273.

Budge, E. A. W.
BU.II.PAL.SY.
BU.II.HIER.SY.   *The Book of Paradise (Lady Meux Manuscript No. 6): being the histories and sayings of the monks and ascetics of the Egyptian Desert by Palladius, Hieronymus and others.* London 1904.

Guillamont, A.	Patrologia Orientalis. Tome XXVIII, fasc. I. Paris 1958.
GU.EV.SY.	*Les six centuries des ' Kephalaia Gnostica' d'Evagre le Pontique.*
Kugener, M. A.	Patrologia Orientalis. Tome II, fasc. 1. 1907.
KUG.SEV.SY.	*Vie de Sévère par Zacharie le Scholastique.*
Look, A. E.	
LOOK.MAR.SY.	*The History of Abba Marcus of Mount Tharmaka.* Oxford 1929.
Macler, F.	
MAC.AZ.SY.	*Histoire de Saint Azazil.* Paris 1902.
Nau, F.	Patrologia Orientalis. Tome XI, fasc. 4. Paris 1916.
NAU.AMM.SY.	*Ammonas, Successeur de Saint Antoine*, pp. 393–504.
	Patrologia Orientalis. Tome V, fasc. 5. Paris 1910.
NAU.AAR.SY.	*Aaron de Sarog*, pp. 703–749.
NAU.ABR.SY.	*Abraham de la Haute Montagne*, pp. 767–773.
NAU.JE.PE.SY.	*Histoire de Jean le Petit, Hegoumène de Scète, au IVᵉ siècle.* Paris 1914.
NAU.JON.SY.	*Les Fils de Jonadab, Fils de Réchab et les Iles Fortunées* (Histoire de Zozime). Leroux, Paris 1899.

GREEK TEXTS

Festugière, A.-J.	Les Moines d'Orient. Editions du Cerf, Paris 1961–1964.
FE.II.DAN.G.	II. *Vie de Daniel le Stylite*, pp. 87–171.
FE.II.HYP.G.	II. *Vie d'Hypatios*, pp. 9–86.
FE.III/I.EUT.G.	III/I. *Vie de Saint Euthyme.*
FE.IV/I.HIS.G.	IV/I. *Historia Monachorum in Aegypto.*
Lowther Clarke, W. K.	Translations of Christian Literature. Series 1. New York 1918.
LO.PAL.G.	*The Lausiac History of Palladius.*
Wilson, R. McL.	Ed. English tr. Hennecke, E. New Testament Apocrypha. Vol. II. Lutterworth Press, London 1964.
WIL.II.THOM.G.	*Acts of Thomas*, pp. 425–531.

LATIN TEXTS

Chadwick, O.	Western Asceticism. Library of Christian Classics. Vol. XII. S.C.M. Press, London 1958.

CHA.SA.L.   *Sayings of the Fathers*, pp. 33–189.

Charles, R. H.   The Apocrypha and Pseudepigrapha of the Old Testament. Vol. II. Pseudepigrapha, Oxford 1913.

CH.AD.EV.L.   *Vita Adae et Evae*, pp. 123–154.

ETHIOPIC, SLAVONIC, HEBREW TEXTS

Charles, R. H.   The Apocrypha and Pseudepigrapha of the Old Testament. Vol. II. Pseudepigrapha, Oxford 1913.

CH.EN.I.E.   *The Book of Enoch (Enoch I)*, pp. 163–277.

CH.EN.II.SL.   *The Book of Secrets of Enoch (Enoch II)*, pp. 431–469.

Halper, B.   Post-Biblical Literature. The Jewish Publication Society of America, Philadelphia 1821.

MID.MOS.H.   *The Death of Moses*, from *Midrash Petirat Mosheh*, pp. 39–44.

Tisserant, E.   Documents pour l'étude de la Bible. Paris 1909.

TIS.ASC.IS.E.(G).   *Ascension d'Isie.* tr. de la version Ethiopienne. *Legende Grec*, pp. 217–226.

Wilson, R. McL.   New Testament Apocrypha. Vol. II. Lutterworth Press, London 1964. Ethiopic text tr. H. Duensing.

WIL.II.PET.G.(E).   *Apocalypse of Peter*, pp. 663–683.

Introduction to the Translated Texts

Translations in Sections I–V are extracts from Coptic literature on the saints and martyrs of the Christian Middle East, together with Jewish and Christian apocryphal writings. Greek, Latin, Syriac and other versions are given when these are either the only remaining sources, or when they show significant differences from the Coptic texts. The complete texts are not quoted, but only those parts which are relevant to the subject of visions or the cult of seership. Any omissions of textual matter, whether deliberate (in the case of irrelevant material), or unavoidable (in the case of imperfect originals), are indicated by brackets ( ).

A list of the texts and of the abbreviations used is found on pp. 262–268. All the quotations are drawn from translated editions of texts and are here given in English (or French). In the case of the Coptic and Syriac texts, the existing translations have been the basis for re-translation. The translations of the Greek, Latin, Slavonic, Ethiopic and Hebrew texts have been transcribed verbatim from the editions cited.

The system of abbreviations here used does not correspond to that of Crum's Dictionary or that of any other standard system. However, it enables those familiar with Coptic literature to identify the editor, the saint or his biographer and the dialect of the original text. The name of the editor is given first thus: GAR (Garitte); the volume number: I, II, etc.; the title or subject of the text: ANT (Life of Anthony); the original language or dialect of the text: S (Sahidic), B (Bohairic), A (Achimic), SY (Syriac), G (Greek), L (Latin), SL (Slavonic), E (Ethiopic), H (Hebrew); the page and line: 150.5 refers, in the case of translations from *Coptic* and *Syriac*, to the *original text*. Paragraph numbers are given last in brackets: (5). When the translation has been made from Greek, Latin, Slavonic, Ethiopic or Hebrew, the page number refers to that of the *translation* in the edition cited. Paragraph numbers are given last in Roman numerals: (X).

Interruptions of the text marked ( ) are of varying length. After long breaks in the narrative, the next line of the text is indicated thus *. At the end of the QUOTATION, two page and line references are given, the second of which corresponds to the page and line at which the text is resumed after the break.

The QUOTATIONS are arranged in five SECTIONS, numbered I–V, and are discussed in the CHAPTERS of the corresponding number. The SECTIONS are divided into SUB-SECTIONS, to which Roman and Arabic numerals are given; QUOTATIONS have Arabic numbers. The subject matter of the QUOTATIONS is summarised at the beginning of each SUB-SECTION under the heading: THEMES and EPISODES. The THEMES refer to those general features of the subject which run through some or all of the QUOTATIONS. The EPISODES are incidents or situations which constitute, or are contained in, the narratives. The various sub-divisions represent an attempt to classify, according to subject, texts which are mainly built up from separate narratives juxtaposed. The preservation of the sense of a QUOTATION sometimes necessitates the inclusion in it of material quoted elsewhere. The occasional repetition of some material nevertheless allows all the extracts quoted under a given heading to be reviewed simultaneously. The alternative method of presentation, using a system of cross-references, would have both lost clarity and inconvenienced the reader. The longest and most complete QUOTATIONS on any subject are usually given first. The SUB-SECTIONS exemplify different aspects of a subject and bring together relevant material from all the texts.

In the present translations of Coptic and Syriac texts, an attempt has been made to distinguish the original structure of the narratives. The writings are easily sub-divided into short 'word-groups'. (The divisions have no consistent relation to the punctuation marks in the text). On the basis of these word-groups which consist of phrases or complete sentences, *Coptic* and *Syriac* texts are presented in short lines. The grouping is somewhat arbitrary, but it may perhaps serve to identify the original literary units from which these writings were composed. That these literary units were interchangeable can be seen from the appearance in different contexts of single lines or sequences of lines. Those lines of the *Coptic* texts which recur in a number of narratives have been set in italics and these word-groups have been collected together under headings in their original Coptic form. It is thus possible, by classifying the word-groups according to subject matter, to see more clearly their relation to other and earlier traditions.

These Coptic word-groups, together with lists of selected words of special interest, are contained in the 'Supplementary Volume'. For non-specialist readers, however, the present volume is complete in itself.

SECTION I

Withdrawal from the Environment of the Senses

I THE ASCETIC WAY OF LIFE

1 ASCETIC PRACTICES

THEMES

The way of life including habitation, posture, diet, clothing, sleep and prayer; the duration of the ascetic life.
The mental powers acquired.
The expectation of death.
The practice of extreme self-discipline.

EPISODES

The description by an eye-witness of the way of life of an ascetic.
The repetition of a traditional story of the life of an ascetic.
The journey into the desert to visit an ascetic in order to see his way of life.
The description by an ascetic of his own way of life.

QUOTATIONS

1. Then when they proceeded a little way from that place
   that man met them and gave them salutation
   and Paul said to him: 'Our brother, explain to us thy way of life;
   for the day after tomorrow thou wilt go to God.'
   Abba Nopi said to them: ( )
   'Since the day wherein I confessed the name of Our Lord
   Jesus Christ, our Redeemer and God,
   no falsehood whatever has gone forth from my mouth on earth.
   I have never taken any earthly thing,
   for an angel has fed me daily with heavenly food.
   In my heart I have never had any other desire
   than that which is of God;
   and God has not hidden from me anything
   which is honourable and glorious.

I have never been deprived of or lacked the light of my eyes,
I have never slept in the daytime
and at night I have never rested from supplication to God,
but the angel of God has accompanied me at all times
and has shown me the power of the world that is to come.
Every request I have made, I have received from God straight away.
At all times I have seen the myriads of angels standing before God,
I have seen the companies of saints,
I have seen the congregations of the martyrs,
I have seen the triumphs of the men who mourn,
I have seen the way of life of the solitary monks
and the congregations of the righteous.
I have seen all created things praising God,
I have seen Satan delivered over to the fire,
I have also seen his angels being tormented,
I have also seen the righteous enjoying increasing happiness.'
When he had told us these things and many others like them,
he delivered up his soul on the third day.
And straightway the angels and the companies of the martyrs
  received it
and took it up to heaven
while we were seeing and hearing their praises.

BU.II.HIER.SY. 418.7

2. Le régime de saint Hypatios consistait en légumes secs, salade et
un peu de pain. Dans sa vieillesse il prenait un peu de vin. Il ne
mangeait jamais qu'a la neuvieme heure bien sonnée, et souvent
même il tardait encore au-delà. Durant le Carême, il ne mangeait
que tous les deux jours; il vivait alors en reclus, priant, chantant
l'office de Prime, Tierce, Sexte, None, Vêpres, Première Vigile,
Matines. ( ) Durant l'espace d'un jour et d'une nuit, en plus des
parties de l'office, il disait cent psaumes et cent oraisons, Il maintint
ce genre de vie jusqu'à sa mort, et il le laissa en héritage à ses
disciples. Jamais en sa vieillesse il ne relâcha en quelque point du
régime qu'il avait toujours conservé. De fait, il garda jusqu'au bout
sa bonne santé, son corps était resté solide. Et il avait la mine aussi
fleurie qu'homme à la table somptueuse. C'est qu'en verité les saints
ont un menu splendide, puisque, dans l'homme intérieur, ils
jouissent des mets divins et spirituels.

FE.II.HYP.G. 47(XXVI)

3. I met him when he was an old man seventy years of age.
And when he had lived fifteen years longer,

273

he departed from this world.
Now to the end of his life,
this holy man never put on either a linen tunic, or even a head
    covering.
And he never washed,
and he never ate flesh and he never enjoyed a full meal.
And thus through Divine Grace, his body shone.
And he possessed a healthy body,
while by the Grace of Christ he was strengthened,
so that those who beheld him, who did not know him,
would not be persuaded of his austerity.

BU.II.PAL.SY. 107.17

4. For the blessed Mar Ephraim, from when he began in asceticism
    until the end of his life, did not eat meat,
but only barley and pulse from time to time and herbs.
For his drink was water.
His body was dried up upon his bones like a hard clay pot.
And his garments were from many coloured rags of the dung-hill.
In stature he was small, his appearance was always mournful
and he did not give way to laughter at all.
And he was bald and beardless.

BRO.EP.SY. 41.22

5. The woman who turned to the Lord through repentance
    lived for twelve years in the monastery.
At all times she made obeisances.
She did not drink wine, or eat grapes, or any fruit.
Nor did she eat oil, or anoint her body with it.
Her food was bread with salt.
This is the way of life of that blessed woman
and these were her conflicts in the Lord.
She completed her course well, she died.
She was taken to the Lord
and He received her to Himself to His place of rest in heaven,
in the peace of God, Amen.

CHA.MART.B. 12.25

6. *He prayed twelve times in the day*
    and made twenty-four obeisances each time.
He did not sleep at all at night, until the light began.

274

Then he would take a little sleep for the sake of the body lest it perish
  quickly.
For many times he would not eat from Sabbath to Sabbath
and also he would spend the Forty Days of the Holy Pascha without
  eating bread,
but his food was edible herbs and soaked grain.

LEI.SIN.B. 13.15

7. And God had been with him until the completion of a hundred
   years.
   And he had fasted every day until sunset,
   offering up his sacrifices with those of his house for the salvation of
     his soul
   and spending half the day in his ascetic practices
   and half the night praying to God.
   And he did thus for many years.
   And he had spent forty days without eating three times every year.
   And neither drank wine, nor ate fruit,
   nor slept upon a sleeping place nor upon a couch.
   And he prayed to God.

GUI.IS.B. 231.5

8. For continually he fasts and prays, and eats only bread with salt,
   and his drink is water, and he wears one garment whether in fine
   weather or in foul (winter), and takes nothing from anyone, and
   what he has he gives to others.

WIL.II.THOM.G. 453

9. There is a mountain in Egypt called Pherme, which borders on the
   great desert of Scete. On this mountain dwell some five hundred
   men, devotees of asceticism. One of them, a man named Paul, had
   this manner of life: he touched no work and no business nor did he
   receive anything from any man, beyond what he ate. But his work
   and his asceticism consisted in ceaseless prayer. So he had three
   hundred set prayers and he collected as many pebbles at each prayer.

LO.PAL.G. 90(XX)

10. The monastic rule, as those who preceded us have taught us, is this:
    at all times we spend half the night in vigil,
    in meditation on the words of God.
    Otherwise many times, from evening until morning,
    we do much handwork, either rope or hair or palm fibre,

275

so that sleep does not trouble us
and for the need of sustenance of the body.
The remainder, which exceeds our need, we give to the poor.

LE.PAC.B. 9.3

11. Abba John the Short said: '( ) Keep God's commandment, ( ) in working with your own hands; in watching in the night; in hunger and thirst, in cold and nakedness, in labours; burying yourself in a tomb as though you were already dead, and every day feeling that death is upon you.'

CHA.SA.L. 38(I)

12. It was said of Apa Simeon, the Syrian,
that he spent more than sixty years standing upon a column.
He ate nothing of human food
and no man knew how he lived ( ).
One (of those who surrounded him) who was without blemish in his
life saw him
while he was standing before him on the top of the column.
And behold, an angel came from the East with food in his hand, which
is that of the angels,
and, when he had given to Apa Simeon,
he gave also of this very food to the other who was there.

CHA.AP.PA.S. 75.3(243)

13. Quand on eut enlevé le parapet, on trouva les genoux du saint collés à sa poitrine, ses cuisses à ses talons et à ses jambes, Et lorsqu'on voulut forcer ses membres à s'étendre, il fit un tel craquement des os que nous pensions qu'il éclaterait en morceaux. Néanmoins, une fois qu'on l'eut déposé, son corps apparut complètement intact, sauf que les pieds avaient été rongés par la gangrène et les vers qui les mangeaient. La masse des cheveux de sa tête était divisée en douze queues, chaque queue mesurant quatre coudées; pareillement aussi la masse de sa barbe était divisée en deux queues, chaque étant de trois coudées: ( ). On le revêtit d'une tunique de peau, comme il en avait coutume, et, lorsqu'on eut apporté et placé sur la colonne une planche, il y fut déposé.

FE.II.DAN.G. 163(XLVII)

14. L'ami du Christ Hypatios se fit construire une cellule toute petite, où il s'enfermait durant le Carême après avoir bouché la porte, avec du ciment. Il y avait une petite fenêtre dans la porte, et c'est par là

que tous les trois jours il reçevait son pain et qu'il conversait avec les visiteurs et les consolait. Quand il en sortait le saint jour de Pâcques, il apparaissait, d'après son visage, qu'il était un ange de Dieu rempli de grâce.

FE.II.HYP.G. 29(XIII)

15. 'Nous ne l'avons jamais surpris en train de manger ou de causer avec personne, sauf grande nécessité, en dehors du samedi et du dimanche. Nous ne l'avons jamais vu dormir étendu sur le côté, mais tantôt il prenait un peu de sommeil en restant assis, tantôt, saississant des deux mains une corde suspendue au toit dans un coin de sa cellule, il se laissait aller à un court somme à cause des besoins de nature, répétant peut-être le mot du grand Arsénios: 'Ici mauvais serviteur.'"

FE.III/i.EUT.G. 88(XXI)

16. Then this holy man told me about this maiden of Alexandria, whose name was Alexandra.
She left the city and shut herself in a certain tomb, until the end of her life.
She received her food and her necessities through a window and no man and no woman saw her face
and neither did she see the face of any man for twelve years. ( )
And she said to me: 'I am occupied with my prayers and with the work of my hands and I have no rest.
For the morning until the ninth hour, I weave linen and I recite the psalms and I pray,
and during the rest of the day I commemorate in my heart the holy fathers.
And I resolve in my thoughts the histories of all the prophets and apostles and martyrs.
And during the remaining hours, I work with my hands and I eat my bread
and by means of these things I am comforted,
whilst I await the end of my life in good hope.'

BU.II.PAL.SY. 115.12

17. He told me also of a maid-servant named Alexandra, who having left the city and shut herself in a tank, received the necessaries of life through an opening, seeing neither women nor men face to face for ten years. And in the tenth year she fell asleep having arrayed herself (for death). ( )

'When I said,' she continued, 'How then do you endure never meeting anyone, but struggling with accidie?' She replied: 'From early morn to the ninth hour I pray hour by hour, spinning flax the while. During the remaining hours I meditate on the holy patriarchs and prophets and apostles and martyrs. And having eaten my bread I remain in patience for the other hours, waiting for my end with cheerful hope.'

LO.PAL.G. 53(V)

18. I (Paphnute) walked in (to the desert),
I looked, I saw a man afar off, who was very fearful.
His hair was spread over his body like a leopard;
for he was naked, while leaves covered his male parts.
When he approached me, *I was afraid.*
I climbed on a mountain peak, lest perhaps he was a mountain ass.
When he came, he cast himself for a little in the shade of the mountain peak;
for he suffered greatly from inner afflictions, hunger and thirst. ( )
He raised his eyes to the mountain peak, he saw me,
he called: 'Come down to me, O holy man.
I also am a man of the mountain like thee. I am in this desert for my sins.'
He said to me: '*Thou art a companion of God also.'*
I sat again in his presence and I begged him to tell me his name.
He said to me: 'Onnophrius is my name
and behold, for sixty years I have been in the desert,
walking in the mountains like the animals.'

BU.ON.S. 209.34

19. *I walked to the desert,*
I found another cave with a man's footprints.
I rejoiced, I went into the cave.
I knocked, but no one answered me.
I went inside, no one was there.
I stood outside the cave and said:
'The servant of God should come to this place.'
When the day began to decline,
I saw some antelopes approaching and the servant of God coming with them,
naked, with his hair covering his indecency.
When he drew near to me, *he thought that I was a spirit.*
He stood to pray; for he was tempted many times by spirits.
I said to him: 'I am a man, O servant of God;
see my footsteps upon the earth

and feel me that I am flesh and blood.'
After saying: 'Amen,' he looked at me,
he was comforted, he took me into the cave.

CHA.AP.PA.S. 82.7(268)

20. Afterwards, *as the sun was setting I looked,*
I saw a herd of antelopes approaching from afar, with that brother in
their midst.
When he drew near me, *he was naked*
and his hair covered his indecency and it served as a garment to clothe
him.
When he reached me, *he was greatly afraid.*
He thought that I was a spirit.
He stood and prayed;
for many spirits tempted him.

BU.ON.S. 206.13

21. *We walked to the South of the mountain* Tereb,
until we came to the mountain of Rotashans in the South of Kos.
We found some antelopes in the depth of the valley, with a monk in
the midst. ( )
My father said to him: 'On what dost thou live as thou walkest with
these antelopes?'
He said: '*My food and that of these antelopes is one food;*
this is herbs of the field and these vegetables.'
My father said to him: ' *Dost thou not freeze in the Winter and burn*
in the Summer?'
He said to him: '*If it is Winter, I sleep in the midst of these antelopes*
and they keep me warm with their breath which is in their mouths.
If it is Summer, they gather together and stand
and give shade to me against the heat which troubles me.'

AM.PAUL.T.S. 761.14

22. And the holy old man Abba Macarius went forth *and he walked*
for four days
and he came upon a lake. He saw an island in its middle
and when he came to the island he looked *and behold, he saw some*
naked men,
their flesh being swollen and thickened by the air,
and their hair and nails were long, and of changed form.
When he saw them, he trembled, he said: 'They are spirits.'
They, when they saw he was afraid,
so that he did not descend for a little (while),

279

they greeted him in the name of the Lord.
He then, having received courage, spoke to them
and they said to him: 'What has happened to thee?
Whence art thou and what dost thou seek?'
He said to them: 'I have found that which I seek
and may the Lord not deprive me of that which is our blessing.'
And when he approached them, he seized them because perhaps they
    were spirits
and when he knew they were saintly men, he worshipped them.
Then they looked at him and he inquired of them about some matters.
They said to him: '*We are not in a monastery in the desert*
and we do not see a monk's robe ever,
like that which thou wearest,
but when a gathering happens in our midst, we come to this place.
Behold, it is a very long time since we came.
We have not met a man of this world, except thee;
for we go with one another in this mountain.
We see many animals which are of many kinds
and many times we meet the men of the mountains
and through the help of the Lord, nothing happens to injure us.
And in this way, as thou seest, we walk now naked.
In this way, on all occasions, *we do not suffer, either in Summer or*
    in Winter,'

AM.MAC.SC.B. 94.11

23. (Apa Macarius of Egypt said) *I went into the desert*
    and I found there a lake of water with an island in the middle of it;
    and beasts of the desert came to drink at that place.
    I saw, in their midst, two naked men
    and my body shook with fear, as I thought they were spirits.
    They, when they saw me, that I was afraid, they said to me: '*Do not*
        fear, we also are men.'
    I said to them: 'Whence are you and how did you come to this desert?'
    They said to me: '*We are from a monastery* and we agreed with one
        another.
    We came forth from the monastery now forty years ago.'
    One was an Egyptian, the other a Libyan. ( )
    I asked them: '*When it is Winter, are you not frozen*
    and when it is Summer, are bodies not burnt?'
    They said: '*The Lord has made for us this dispensation:*
    it is not freezing in the Winter, nor burning in the Summer.'

CHA.AP.PA.S. 74.15.(242)

24. When I had entered his cave, he said to me:
    'Behold, my son for ninety-five years I have been in this cave.
    My eyes have not seen a living thing,
    I have eaten no human bread,
    I have not worn clothing of (this) world.
    For thirty years I have been here in great distress
    from hunger, thirst, nakedness and conflict with devils,
    I even ate dust, my son, from hunger,
    I drank water from the sea from thirst.
    Thirty years of severe peril have passed over me.
    I have been in great tribulations.
    Sometimes myriads of demons who were in the sea
    lay in wait for me that they might drown me.
    Frequently they dragged me from here to the base of the mountain
    until there was no skin or flesh on my limbs.
    They shouted at me and kept saying:
    "Go away from our land and from our place.
    Not since our days has anyone else come here."
    And when I had endured patiently for thirty years
    through hunger, thirst, nakedness and conflicts with demons,
    then finally the mercy of God rested on me.
    He commanded my body and the hair grew
    until it weighted down my limbs with its weight.
    A continual supply of spiritual food from the Lord was sent to me.
    Angels descended and ascended in my presence.
    I saw the realms of the Kingdom
    and the habitations of the souls of the saints.
    I saw the blessedness which is promised to the righteous.
    I saw the Paradise of God.
    He showed me that tree from which Adam and Eve ate.
    I saw Enoch and Elijah in the Land of the Living.
    There was nothing which I sought from God which he did not show
        me.'

LOOK.MAR.SY. 9.11

25. He answered and said to me:
    'Brother Serapion, behold how God loves his saints.
    Every single day He sends me a fish but today,
    because of you, God has sent us two.
    Every day, my brother, God thus sends to me spiritual food and
        spiritual drink.
    For thirty years I was in this mountain,

eating dust from hunger and drinking foul water from the sea.
I went naked and barefoot until the skin was worn from off my
limbs
and my flesh was scorched by the sun
and I was prostrate upon the ground as dead.
Demons fought with me,
they were dragging me along the ground and torturing me.
And God permitted me to be persecuted by them for thirty years
while I was tormented by hunger, thirst and nakedness.
Moreover, I did not see a single animal or bird
which might have comforted me.
Behold I have been here ninety-five years today,
in which my eyes have not seen any of the creatures which God
created, except demons only.
And when that period of thirty years was finished
when I was in great perils of affliction,
God commanded my body and the hair grew until all my limbs were
covered.
And from that time the evil spirits were not able to touch me
and no hunger or thirst overpowered me
and I did not become sick or weak.
And behold, the allotted time of my life is completed
and God has sent thee that thou shouldst bury this poor body with
thy holy hands.'

LOOK.MAR.SY. 15.6

26. *We walked to the South to the Mountain of Pshgepoke.*
   We found a cave on the West side.
   My father knocked on the stone three times,
   according to the rule of the brotherhood of the monks,
   and immediately we heard a small voice saying: 'Bless me, my holy
   fathers.'
   And in this way he came forth, he opened the door to us.
   We bowed ourselves to him, and we embraced him.
   His body was very weak from hunger and thirst and he took us into
   the cave.
   We prayed, we sat, we spoke of the greatness of God.
   My father said to him: 'What is thy name?'
   He answered saying: 'Phib is my name
   and I am a man of Prgoush in the nome of Touko.'
   My father said to him: '*How many years is it since thou didst come*
   to this place?'

282

He said: '*It is eighteen years.*'
My father said to him: '*For how long dost thou remain in this place?*'
He said to him again: '*This is my dwelling in life and in death.*'
My father said to him: 'What dost thou eat or drink? Who serves thee?'
The holy man, Apa Phib answered: '*Since the time of my youth, when I came forth from my dwelling,*
until today, wherever I live, *when I have completed my Forty Days fast,*
every time I find a loaf and a jug of water placed in my presence.'

AM.PAUL.T.S. 763.1

2. DISCIPLESHIP

THEMES

The reverence of the disciple for the virtues of his master.
The obedience of the disciple to the commands of his master.
The influence of the master over his disciple.
The emulation by the disciple of his master and of others.

EPISODES

The reception by an old man of a disciple; the clothing of a monk.
The training of the disciple in ascetic practices.
The assignment of the disciple to a dwelling place.
The admonition and advice given to the disciple on his ascetic way of life.
The cure of illusions in the disciples.

QUOTATIONS

1. And a certain youth approached him
   and begged him to make him his disciple
   and when he received him, he caused him to dress himself
   in the manner in which he dressed.
   This was a sleeveless tunic and a short cloak
   and he placed a cowl upon his head
   and tied a loin-cloth upon his loins
   and he showed him the path
   and taught him the rules of the ascetic life.
   And he placed a hood upon his shoulders.

BU.II.HIER.SY. 409.23

2. Our father, Abba Amoi, was entrusted with the service in this matter by God,

since the day when he accepted our father, Abba John.
He did not cease to instruct him in the Law of the Lord
and to exercise him to receive the teaching of piety ( ),
or the psalmody and vigils,
or harsh, severe austerities,
or solitude and withdrawal,
or sleeping on the ground and renunciation,
or lowliness and silence,
or humility and purity,
or respect and simplicity
and his whole course of life which he completed,
keeping the counsel which he heard;
and especially to cause him to guard his senses in purity
and his heart from defilement of the passions
and to watch his mind, especially regarding fantasies.

AM.JOH.K.B. 332.14

3. Afterwards he shaved the head of John
and he placed the garments for clothing him before the two of them.
And they stood in prayer for three days and three nights,
without eating and without drinking,
but standing and praying upon the clothes.
Then on the third day the angel of the Lord came and stood before
   them.
And he made three crosses upon the garments
and he was removed from their presence.
And when it was morning, John put on the garments of monkhood
and he took upon himself the yoke,
in spiritual joy with watchfulness and diligence,
in order to tread the path of perfection.

NAU.JE.PE.SY. XV.4

4. And thus Abba John still trod the footsteps of these holy men
and because of this he was worthy to walk in their narrow paths,
which are remote from all falsehood.
And he went, abandoning his own will
and following the command of his master,
like Timothy following the Apostle Paul.
Since the first day that he was received by Abba Bamouyah, his
   master,
he did not cease from walking in the divine law.
Then he tested him

in order to teach him, by experience, the fear of God.
And he encouraged him in the practice of virtues,
by the recitation of psalms,
by the reading of holy books, by night and by day,
with fasts, with vigils, with prayers, with sweats,
with the conflicts and the labours which afflict the flesh and its
    strength,
with solitude and withdrawal from all men,
by sleeping on the ground
and by depriving (himself) of everything,
by keeping the silence
which is the chief of all the perfections,
without at all considering himself to be among men,
and by walking in all humility
and by abasing himself before all men,
in the simplicity of a heart which has no guile.
He thus restrained his thought from every side
by these excellent practices
and by means of them, he enlightened his mind,
in order to be diligent and to accept the commands which were
    imposed on him.

NAU.JE.PE.SY. XVI.4

5. Then the holy man, Abba John, went to the place of this tree,
   according to the command of his master
   and he made for himself there a cell in a cave,
   in order to add to his conflicts and his labour.
   And furthermore, he prepared himself in this cave a hole
   into which he descended constantly, in order not to be seen by men.
   And he spent a whole week in it,
   without bread and without water,
   nourished by the grace of God.
   And also he prepared for himself a garment of palm fibres,
   with which he clothed himself.
   When he rose, the brothers saw him in the likeness of a luminous
      column of fire.
   His fame was spoken in all the land and on all sides,
   so that a number of men gathered and dwelt near him.
   And thus, little by little, they united and came near him,
   without fear, from all sides.

NAU.JE.PE.SY. XXX.18

6. '*Seek the dwelling place of my father Teroti*
   and become a monk with him and wear the habit of the angels.'

   DAV.JOH.KH.B. 334.1

7. *I walked in the desert for six or seven miles,*
   I saw a cave, I turned into it
   because I saw there was a man within it.
   A great saint of God came forth,
   beautiful in appearance, with much grace in his face.
   When I saw him, I worshipped him.
   But he raised me. He embraced me.
   He said to me: 'Thou art Onnophrius, my fellow-worker in Christ.
   The Lord be with thee.
   Enter in and enjoy the good things to which he invites thee.'
   I went in, I sat before him for a few days.
   I learned of the edification of godliness from him,
   and he taught me the doings of the desert.
   When he saw that I knew the hidden conflict
   and the fears which are in the desert,
   he said to me: '*Rise, my son,*
   I will take thee to a desert place in the inner desert
   and thou shalt be in it alone for God,
   since the Lord God commands this for thee that thou shouldst be
      in the desert.'
   Immediately he rose, he walked with me into the desert for four days
      march.
   At the end of the fourth day we came to a small hut.
   He said: '*This is the place which the Lord assigns to thee, that thou*
      shouldst be in it.'
   He sat before me for a month until I knew the good thing,
   which was necessary for me to have.
   Afterwards he walked out *and we did not see each other for a year,*
   until the day when he died
   and I buried him, in the place where he was.

   BU.ON.S. 212.29

8. One day therefore, when I was sitting in the desert,
   according to my custom I began to meditate
   on the peaceful way of life of the brethren who were in the monas-
      tery.
   And I saw also the face of our holy father as if it were an image
   and his perfect and abundant love towards me

and how, in every way, he was anxious that I should not be separated
from him.
Since I was not persuaded through the divine revelation,
he bore witness beforehand concerning those things prepared to
happen to me.

BU.II.PAL.SY. 285.14

9. A brother came to Abba Ares and said: 'Tell me, what must I do
to be saved?' And the old man said: 'Go away, eat bread and salt
every evening for a whole year: and come back, and I will talk to
you.' So the brother went away and did so, and at the end of a year
came again to Abba Ares. ( ) This time Abba Ares said to the
brother: 'Go away, fast for a year, and eat every second day.'

CHA.SA.L. 149.(XIV)

10. The old man said: 'Go into your cell, and stay there fifty days without a break. Eat bread and salt once a day. At the end I will tell
you what to do next.' And he did so, and at the end came back to
the old man. The old man knew him for an earnest person, and told
him what sort of a person he ought to be in his cell. And the brother
went down to his cell, and for three days and nights he lay prone
upon the ground, in penitence before God.

CHA.SA.L. 153(XIV)

11. When he was eighteen years old
he learnt the psalms and he was trained in the recitation of the
Scriptures
in the presence of him who had baptised him.

BRO.EP.SY. 28.4

12. They said, concerning those who were in Scete,
that no pride was found among them,
because they surpassed one another in spiritual excellence.
They fasted, so that one ate every two days
and another every four days
and another every seven days.
Another would eat no bread and another would drink no water
and, to speak briefly, they were adorned with every spiritual
excellence.

BU.II.PAL.SY. 642.16

13. They were zealous in all their virtuous deeds of fortitude
and they were striving to outstrip one another

287

in their glorious and excellent ways of life.
And some of them possessed divine vision
and others virtues of asceticism.

BY.II.HIER.SU. 423.17

14. Thus, from the first hour of the night, or at most the second, no
    man in full health was to be found on his mat, or not lying on his
       face (   ),
    everyone thenceforth emulating and rivalling his neighbour.
    And though emulation in its nature is a deadly and destructive
       thing,
    there an emulation was seen which was beautiful and good and
       right,
    a thing that it is difficult for hearers to believe,
    that emulation ever was a good thing.

BR.AM.SY. 611.13

15. Many of the monks, therefore, after his death, tried to rival him by
    dwelling in his cell, but they could not complete a year, for the place
    is terrible and inconsolably dreary.

LO.PAL.G. 138(XXXIX)

16. She makes seven hundred prayers, and when I learned this, I
    despaired of myself, because I could not make more than three
    hundred.

LO.PAL.G. 90(XX)

17. This was the method of his asceticism. If ever he heard of any feat,
    he did the same thing perfectly.

LO.PAL.G. 77(XVIII)

18. Our saintly father, Abba John Kolobos, *as he was burning*
    with the fire of the Holy Spirit,
    desiring to resemble at all times the way of life of the powers above, (   )
    went forth to the desert.

AM.JOH.K.B. 354.7

19. There was a certain Abramius, an Egyptian by race, who lived a
    very rough and savage life in the wilderness. Afflicted in his mind
    by an untimely fancy, he went to the church and contended with
    the priests, saying: 'I have been ordained a priest by Christ this
    night, accept me as a celebrant.' The fathers removed him from the
    desert and led him to a less ascetic and calmer life and cured him of

288

his presumption, bringing this man, who had been deluded by the demon, to a knowledge of his own weakness.

LO.PAL.G. 157(LIII)

20. Macarius, knowing that he was the victim of illusion, went the next day to exhort him and said to him: 'Valens you are the victim of illusions. Stop it.' And when he would not listen to his exhortations, he retired.

So the demon, convinced that he was completely persuaded by his deception went away and disguised himself as the Saviour, and came by night in a vision of a thousand angels bearing lamps and a fiery wheel, in which it seemed that the Saviour appeared, and one came in front of the others and said: 'Christ has loved you because of your conduct and the freedom of your life and He has come to see you. So go out of the cell, do nothing else but look at His face from afar, stoop down and worship and then go to your cell.'

So he went out and saw them in ranks carrying lamps, and Antichrist about a stade away, and he fell down and worshipped. Then the next day again he became so mad that he entered into the church and before the assembled brotherhood said: 'I have no need of Communion, for I have seen the Christ today.' Then the fathers bound him and put him in irons for a year and so cured him, destroying his pride by their prayers and indifference and calmer mode of life. As it is said: 'Diseases are cured by their opposites.'

LO.PAL.G. 105(XXV)

21. When therefore (Abba Valens) had gone forth
and seen the ranks bearing lamps of fire
and Antichrist himself sitting upon a chariot of fire
and he was about one mile distant from him,
he fell down and worshipped him.
Then the next day (Abba Valens) was so far injured in his mind
that he spoke wildly as if he would enter the church
and say before all the brethren, when they were assembled:
'I have no need to partake of the Offering,
for this day I have seen the Christ.'
Then the fathers bound him
and put iron fetters upon him for about the period of one year.
They healed him thus and because he prayed continually.
And by various labours he was humbled.
And from the high opinion which he held about himself,
they brought him down and laid him low.

289

And they rooted out from him pride,
as it is said in some book that opposing illnesses are healed
by medicines which are contrary and opposite.

BU.II.PAL.SY. 165.13

22. Alors donc qu'il (le disciple Macaire) avait passé dix-huit ans au
monastère, le diable, incapable de trouver aucun moyen de le
dompter, finit par le trouver plus faible sur le point de l'humilité.
Il fit remonter dans sa mémoire toute la peine que lui avaient coutée
ses vertus, il lui présenta des visions ou il se montrait sous la figure
du Christ, et l'emmena enfin, captif, à de vaines opinions de lui-
même en lui mettant dans l'esprit ces pensées: 'Tu es plus juste que
tous. Tu as pratiqué l'ascèse plus que tous. Jésus t'aime, habite en
toi, et parle par ta bouche aux frères.' Quelque temps ayant passé,
Hypatios, avec quelques-uns des frères, reconnut a ses discours qu'il
s'égarait, et lui fit des remontrances. Mais Macaire ne voulut pas
l'écouter, il se moquait de tous, car il était possédé par la force
contraire du démon: et cela était arrivé à cause de son manque de
discernement. Il en vint donc à un tel dérangement d'esprit qu'il
injuriait librement saint Hypatios. ( ) Hypatios eut pitié de lui, et
pour que, dans cet égarement, il ne sortît pas du monastère, il lui
mit des fers qux pieds: ainsi, sous bonne garde, il rentrerait en
lui-même.

FE.II.HYP.G. 67(XLII)

23. His mind became so darkened that he too was afterwards put in
irons, since he was unwilling even to attend the mysteries—truth is
dear. He was excessively abstemious in his mode of life so that many
who knew him intimately declared that he frequently went three
months without eating, being content with the Communion of the
Mysteries and any wild herbs that might be found. And I too had an
experience of him when I went to Scete with the blessed Albanius.

LO.PAL.G. 106(XXVI)

II SELF-ISOLATION

1 PROLONGED SOLITUDE

THEMES

The practice of spending a life-time alone.
The occurrence of death in isolation.

290

The practice of associating with animals in solitude.
The withdrawal from the sight and sound of other men.
The maintenance of silence.

EPISODES

The meeting and questioning of solitary ascetics.
The meeting with ascetics who live with animals.
The finding of ascetics who have died in solitude.
The gathering of solitary ascetics together to celebrate the Eucharist.

QUOTATIONS

1. It was said that the blessed Sarah, the virgin,
   spent sixty years living above the river,
   without ever going out to see the river.

   CHA.AP.PA.S. 9.12(42)

2. *He spent nearly thirty years enclosed,*
   and he received all his needs through a window,
   by the hand of him who served him.

   TIL.I.JOH.LY.S. 141.6

3. I said to them: 'Whence are you and how did you come to this desert?'
   They said to me: '*We are from a monastery* and we agreed with one another.
   We came forth from the monastery now forty years ago.'

   CHA.AP.PA.S. 74.20(242)

4. For thirty years I was in this mountain, ( )
   while I was tormented by hunger, thirst and nakedness.
   Moreover, I did not see a single animal or bird which might have comforted me.

   LOOK.MAR.SY. 15.10

5. *He spent twenty years practising asceticism in this way by himself*
   never going out and not being seen many times by any man.

   GAR.ANT.S. 19.22

6. '*How many years is it since thou didst come to this place?*'
   He said: 'Behold, I am in this place eighteen years.'

   BU.CYR.S. 129.18

7. Apa Pamoun, 'he of the robe', this indeed being his name, said: 'O my beloved father, *behold, it is twenty years since I came to this place.*'

BU.CYR.S. 130.15

8. He told me also of a maid-servant named Alexandra, who, having left the city and shut herself in a tank, received the necessaries of life through an opening, seeing neither women nor men face to face for ten years. And in the tenth year she fell asleep, having arrayed herself (for death).

LO.PAL.G. 53(V)

9. *My father said to him*: '*How many years is it since thou didst come to this place?*'
He said: '*It is eighteen years.*'
My father said to him: '*For how long dost thou remain in this place?*'
He said to him again: '*This is my dwelling in life and death.*'

AM.PAUL.T.S. 763.9

10. *I thought once to go into the inner desert*
in case I should find one in there *who was a servant of the Lord Jesus Christ*
and I walked for four days.
I found a cave and I looked within it.
I saw a man sitting
and I knocked, according to the custom of the monks,
so that he should come forth and embrace me.
He did not move, for he was dead.
I did not delay, but I went in,
I seized his shoulder
and immediately he crumbled and became dust.
I looked and saw a tunic hanging up.
I seized it and it also dissolved to nothing.

CHA.AP.PA.S. 81.27(268)

11. (Apa Macarius of Egypt said): '*I went into the desert*
and I found there a lake of water with an island in the middle of it and beasts of the desert came to drink at that place.
I saw, in their midst, two naked men.'

CHA.AP.PA.S. 74.15(242)

12. They said to him: '*We are not in a monastery in the desert and we do not wear a monk's robe ever,*

292

like that which thou wearest,
but when a gathering happens in our midst, we come to this place.
Behold, it is a very long time since we came.
We have not met a man of this world, except thee, for we go with one another in this mountain.
We see many animals which are of many kinds and many times we meet the men of the mountains
and, through the help of the Lord, nothing happens to injure us.
And in this way, as thou seest, we walk now naked.
In this way, on all occasions, *we do not suffer, either in Summer or in Winter.'*

AM.MAC.SC.B. 95.9

13. *When morning came,* our father Apa Apollo also accompanied us South to the monastery.
He embraced us, he left us in peace.
We walked to the South to the mountain Tereb,
until we came to the mountain of Rotashans in the South of Kos.
We found some antelopes in the depth of the valley, with a monk in the midst.
My father made his way, he embraced him.
He said to him: 'What is thy name?'
He said: 'My name is Aphou. Remember me, my father, Apa Paul. May the Lord perfect me well.'
My father said to him: 'Behold, for how many years hast thou been in this place?'
He said: 'Behold, for forty five years.'
My father said to him: 'Who gave thee the monk's robe?'
He said: 'Apa Anthony of Shiet.'
My father said to him: 'On what dost thou live as thou walkest with these antelopes?'
He said: *'My food and that of these antelopes is one food,*
this is herbs of the field and these vegetables.'
My father said to him: 'Dost thou not freeze in the Winter and burn in the Summer?'
He said to him: 'If it is Winter, I sleep in the midst of these antelopes
and they keep me warm with their breath which is in their mouths.
If it is Summer they gather together and stand
and give shade to me against the heat which troubles me.'

AM.PAUL.T.S. 761.12

14. *I walked to the desert,*
I found another cave with a man's footprints. ( )

When the day began to decline,
I saw some antelopes approaching and the servant of God coming
  with them,
naked, with his hair covering his indecency.

CHA.AP.PA.S. 82.7(268)

15. Afterwards, *as the sun was setting I looked,*
  I saw a herd of antelopes approaching from afar,
  with that brother in their midst.

BU.ON.S. 206.13

16. *I looked, I saw a man afar off, who was very fearful.*
  His hair was spread over his body like a leopard; for he was naked
    while leaves covered his male parts. ( )
  He said to me: 'Onnophrius is my name
  and behold, for sixty years I have been in the desert,
  walking in the mountains like the animals.'

BU.ON.S. 210.1

17. For they dwelt in a desert place and their dwellings were remote
  and also they were separated, one from another,
  so that a man may not be known to his fellow
  and he may not be seen quickly nor his voice heard,
  but they live in a great silence and each one of them is secluded in
    his cell
  and only on Saturday and Sunday do they assemble in the church
    and meet one another.
  On many occasions numbers of them have been found dying in
    their inner chambers
  without having seen one another, except when assembled.
  Then some of them only assembled after three or four months
  and thus they were remote from one another.

BU.II.HIER.SY. 424.4

18. Ils habitent un lieu désert, et ils ont leurs cellules éloigneés l'une de
  l'autre, en sorte qu'aucun ne puisse être reconnu de loin par un
  autre, ni être vu dès le premier coup d'oeil, ni entendre un bruit de
  voix: bien plutôt ils vivent dans un profond silence, chacun en-
  fermé à part soi. C'est seulement le samedi et le dimanche qu'ils
  se rassemblaient dans les églises et se prenaient mutuellement à
  part. Beaucoup d'entre eux, souvent, étaient trouvés morts dans
  leurs cellules, de trois ou quatre jours, du fait qu'ils ne se voyaient

jamais les un les autres, sauf aux synaxes. Il y en avait parmi eux
qui venaient à la synaxe d'une distance de trois ou quatre milles,
tant ils sont grandement éloignés l'un de l'autre.

FE.IV/I.HIS.G. 111(XX)

19. Nous avons vu aussi un autre père non loin de la ville
    (d'Oxyrhynque) vers le désert, du nom de Théon, un saint
    homme qui, reclus solitaire dans une chambrette, avait
    pratiqué le silence depuis trente années.

FE.IV/I.HIS.G. 41(VI)

20. *They made their whole care to speak with no man*
    nor to visit any place except their dwelling and the church.

AM.MA.DO.B. 296.8

21. They said of Abba Agatho that for three years he kept a pebble in
    his mouth, to teach himself silence.

CHA.SA.L. 49(IV)

22. *He did not speak to anyone, nor did he open his mouth at all,*
    but he stood in silence, praying in his heart, doing his basket work.

AM.MAC.AL.B. 243.11

23. And he continued working ( )
    and he was in silence for twenty days.

BU.II.PAL.SY. 592.22

24. There was another in this same place whose name was Daniel. ( )
    His aim was not to speak at all except for matters of necessity.

CHA.AP.PA.S. 77.33(250)

25. For I lived with him for about a year in Bethlehem,
    when he was living beyond the Monastery of the Shepherds,
    which was beside it. ( )
    He told me one day:
    'When I was living by the side of Porphyrites,
    for one whole year I did not speak with a man
    and I did not hear the voice of a man speaking.'

BU.II.PAL.SY. 215.9

26. Among other things, he himself told me this one day: 'Living for a
    year in the Porphyrites district, the whole year I met no man, heard

295

no talk, touched no bread. I merely subsisted on a few dates and any wild herbs that I found. This happened one day. My food failing, I went out from the cave to go back to the world.'

LO.PAL.G. 125(XXXVI)

2 SELF-ENCLOSURE

THEMES

The practice of prolonged self-enclosure.
The use of devices to promote physical isolation in darkness and silence.

EPISODES

Self-enclosure in a tomb, fort, cave or hole in the ground.
The building of cells or huts for self-enclosure.
The use of different cells for different purposes.
The use of a window or the roof for communication with the outside world.

QUOTATIONS

1. In his early days, war against fornication and gluttony was his lot. He drove out these passions by shutting himself up and wearing irons, ( ) After persevering in this course for eighteen years, he sang the hymn of triumph to Christ. ( ) He abode in one monastery for forty years. ( ) Once when timidity attacked him, in order to get rid of it, he shut himself in a tomb for six years.

LO.PAL.G. 146(XLV)

2. *Many times he went forth from his dwelling*
and entered into tombs full of corpses
and spent the whole night, from evening until morning,
praying.

LE.PAC.B.12.9

3. *He went into some empty tombs which were at a distance from the*
village. ( )
He went into one of the tombs and the monk remained alone,
he having shut the door upon himself.

GAR.ANT.S. 12.25

4. This Elpidius had a disciple, by name Sisinnius. ( ) After dwelling with Elpidius six or seven years, finally he shut himself up in a tomb and continued for three years in a tomb, praying constantly, sitting

296

down neither by night nor day, neither lying down nor walking out.
He was counted worthy of a gift (of power) over demons.

LO.PAL.G. 156(XLIX)

5. When therefore he, Sisinnius, had passed some time with the holy
    man Elpidius, ( )
at length he shut himself in a tomb for three years.
And thus he endured there, that neither by night nor by day
did he sit or lie down.
And he never went out from it.

BU.II.PAL.SY. 229.18

6. *There were some tombs in the neighbourhood of the place in which the
    old man Apa Palamon dwelt.*
He went into one of the tombs.

LE.PAC.S. 111b.19

7. She left the city and shut herself in a certain tomb until the end of
    her life.
She received her food and her necessities through a window
and no man and no woman saw her face
and neither did she see the face of any man for twelve years.

BY.II.PAL.SY. 115.13

8. *He made his way to the mountain, he saw a deserted fort.*
And in the course of time it had become filled with reptiles from
    the river bank
and he dwelt in that place,
but those reptiles fled, as if they were pursued, and they retreated ( ).
He enclosed himself ( ).
And he remained in that place alone,
never going forth and never seeing anyone who came to him.
He spent a long time in this manner of asceticism.

GAR.ANT.S. 17.19

9. *When evening came he went down to a cellar in the deserted village*
    in which he dwelt.
He placed a brick beneath his feet *and he stretched out his hands.*
He prayed to God with tears all night, from evening until morning.

LE.PAC.S. 108b.22

10. When I had entered his cave, he said to me:
    'Behold, my son, for ninety-five years I have been in this cave.
My eyes have not seen a living thing.'

LOOK.MAR.SY. 9.11

11. And she said: '*Behold, for thirty-eight years I have been in this cave,* ( )
as a servant of Christ and I never saw a man until today;
for God has sent you to bury my body.'
And when she had said this she died.
The old men gave glory to God
and they buried her body and withdrew.

CHA.AP.PAS. 81.4(266)

12. In the caves of the Amorites around about Jericho ( ) there lived a certain Elpidius. ( ) He came and settled in one of the caves. He showed such self-discipline in his asceticism as to put all others in the shade. ( ) The story is told by his zealous disciples that he never turned (to gaze) towards the west because the mountain with its height dominated the door of the cave. Nor did he ever see the sun after the sixth hour, ( ) or even the stars in the west for twenty-five years. From the time he entered the cave he did not descend the mountain until he was buried.

LO.PAL.G. 154(XLVIII)

13. *I walked in the desert for six or seven miles,*
I saw a cave, I turned into it,
because I saw there was a man within it.

BU.ON.S. 212.29

14. *When our father, the holy John, dwelt in the cave,*
he meditated on the saving name of Our Lord Jesus Christ, our God,
with unceasing prayers, with secret petitions not to be spoken of.
For no man knew the fulness of the sufferings which he endured.

DAV.JOH.KH.B. 351.1

15. There is in this desert one of our brethren, whose name is John, ( )
and no man can find him at once,
because he wanders from place to place in the desert.
He once previously spent three years under a rock, standing and praying.

BU.II.HIER.SY. 397.20

16. Our father Abba John ( ) *built for himself a small grotto in which he could be quiet.* ( )
He built for himself a hidden place below the earth in the grotto
and he took himself there especially to remain with God.

AM.JOH.K.B. 351.2

17. Then the holy man, Abba John, went to the place of this tree, ( )
    and he made for himself there a cell in a cave ( ).
    And furthermore, he prepared for himself in this cave a hole into
        which he descended constantly,
    in order not to be seen by men.
    And he spent a whole week in it.

    NAU.JE.PE.SY. XXX.18

18. *He would stand in a low place, in which no man could see him.* ( )
    By chance a brother monk passed by him one day,
    he visited him in his hole.

    AM.PIS.KE.B. 335.7

19. *When he had completed these things,*
    he gave himself to prayer and fasting and seclusion.
    *He did not go forth from his hole ever, except at the time when he
        would fill his jug.*

    AM.PIS.KE.B. 344.7

20. And he (Thomas) thereupon made himself a small hut of planks
    and in it he carried out the great labour of his secret practices.

    BR.THOM.SY. 297.7

21. And after two days, two brothers came to him
    and the blessed man built for himself a place of retreat.

    NAU.ABR.SY. 769.14

22. And his master said to him: 'Seek a place for thyself
    and we will build a cell for thee and thou wilt become a hermit.'
    And he went and found himself a place,
    which was distant from his master about a hundred paces,
    and he made himself a cell.
    The old man said to that brother: '( )
    Only thou shouldst not go forth from thy cell until the Sabbath day
    and then thou shalt come to me.'

    BU.II.PAL.SY. 496.12

23. Having lived in various monasteries for five years, he retired by
    himself to the mountain of Lyco where he made himself three cells
    on the actual summit and went in and immured himself, ( )
    receiving the necessaries of life through a window from one who
    ministered to him. ( ) (He said) 'Forty years have I spent in the

299

cell. I have not seen the face of woman nor the appearance of money. I have seen no one chewing, nor has anyone seen me eating or drinking.'

LO.PAL.G. 120(XXXV)

24. *The holy John went to the Mountain of Siout.*
He withdrew to the holy place.
When he had built three treasuries of the monastery,
he made himself a hole in the mountain, he went in and slept.
When he had made three places, ( )
he spent thirty years enclosed
and he received all his needs through a window,
by the hand of him who served him.

TIL.I.JOH.LY.S. 140.26

25. It was said of one in Egypt whose name was Bané, ( )
that he spent fifteen years standing in a cell in which he was enclosed,
there being no light at all in it.

CHA.AP.PA.S. 75.28(244)

26. Then (Pachomius) commanded him to depart
and to seclude himself in a cell alone
and not to converse with men until his death.

BY.II.PAL.SY. 328.17

27. *His custom was, when he came to the days of the Holy Forty Days,*
that he would withdraw to a small dwelling outside the monastery
so that he would not meet any man.

POR.IS.B. 337.10

28. *It happened that during the Holy Forty Days of our salvation,*
the blessed Isaac went forth to the small dwelling according to his
custom.

POR.IS.B. 339.10

29. *I went into the cell which is in the inner desert,*
which has no door or window,
in which there is no light,
so that it is not possible for a man to find me.
And I stood upon the mat in the cell.

AM.MAC.AL.B. 245.4

30. *He had three cells in Shiet,*
    one in the great inner desert
    and one placed in the centre of the monastery in Shiet
    and one which is approached by men for a small desire.

    AM.MAC.AL.B. 251.13

31. Now the blessed man had four cells in the desert,
    one in Scete in the inner desert, and one in Aliboni
    and one in the 'cells' and one in the mountains of Nitria.
    (Two) of these were without windows
    so that he dwelt in them in darkness during the Forty Days fast,
    another was so narrow that he could not stretch out his legs,
    but another, in which he received those who came to him, was wide.

    BU.II.PAL.SY. 148.7

32. Now he had several cells in the desert: one in Scete, the great in-
    terior desert, and one in the Libyan desert, and one at the so-called
    Cellia, and one on Mount Nitria. Some of these are without win-
    dows, and in these he was said to sit during Lent in darkness.
    Another was too narrow for him to stretch out his feet in it. Another
    in which he met his visitors was more spacious.

    LO.PAL.G. 80(XVIII)

33. *It happened, one day, that our father, the prophet Apa Shenute, went*
    North to the mountain of Siout,
    to visit his fellow prophet Apa John, the holy anchorite,
    him who is called the Carpenter,
    who is shut in and enclosed in the desert in a small dwelling place
    and he speaks with those who come to him through a small window.

    LEI.SIN.B. 55.10

III SELF MORTIFICATION

1 FATIGUE AND WEAKENING OF THE BODY

THEMES

The punishing, crushing and mortifying of the body by hard labour.
The fatiguing of the body by prolonged prayer.
The weakening of the body by fatigue and lack of sleep.

EPISODES

The endurance by ascetics of fatigue when covering long distances on
    foot.

301

The carrying of heavy loads by ascetics in the desert during the hours of sleep.

The prolonged repetition by holy men of prayers under conditions of physical discomfort.

QUOTATIONS

1. When he said this he turned his face,
   he saw one who followed after him, counting the footsteps of his feet.
   He asked: 'Who art thou?'
   He said: 'I am an angel of the Lord
   who has been sent to count the footsteps of thy feet
   and to give thee thy reward.'
   When he heard this, *the old man was quiet of heart and he was more diligent.*
   He added another five miles to his distance in the desert.

   CHA.AP.PA.S. 10.2(46)

2. The saint wished to make his way by road, on foot, running well in the course ( )
   going forth from place to place, until he completed his course.
   And he passed sixty-five towns and villages before he finished.

   CHA.MART.B. 20.8

3. *He made many great fasts,*
   with prostrations without number, ( )
   and he would go forth in the evening, having changed his clothes, and he spent the evening drawing water in the path on which strangers passed.

   HY.AP.IR.B. 84.12

4. So he returned and from that hour practised asceticism more vehemently, ( ) accomplishing a great deal of work and completing fifty prayers (a day). Thus he mortified his body, but he still continued to burn and be troubled by dreams. ( ) So he suggested to himself yet another plan, and going out by night he would visit the cells of the older and more ascetic (monks) and taking their water-pots, secretly would fill them with water. For they fetch their water from a distance, some from two miles off, some five miles, others half a mile.

   LO.PAL.G. 88(XIX)

5. He went to his cell
   and he made a covenant before God

302

that he would not sleep the whole night, nor bend his knees.
And he dwelt in this cell for seven years.
And he remained standing the whole of each night with his eyes open
and he never closed them.
And afterwards he set himself other ascetic labours;
for he would go forth during the nights
and go to the cells of the old men
and take their water skins and fill them with water.

BU.II.PAL.SY. 268.14

6. *If sleep troubled them as they worked,*
   they changed to other hand-work *and put away the heaviness of sleep.*
   But if they saw that sleep continued to overcome them,
   they rose, they went forth to the mountain outside their dwelling
   and they transported sand in baskets from place to place,
   fatiguing their bodies so that they would be vigilant for prayer.

LE.PAC.S. 214b.25

7. So having lain there a long while, he got up, but when night came
   on they attacked him again, and having filled a two-bushel basket
   with sand and put it on his shoulders, he tramped about in the
   desert. Theosebius the Cosmetor, an Antiochian by race, met him
   and said to him: 'What are you carrying, father? Give me the
   burden and don't trouble yourself.' But he said to him 'I trouble
   my troubler. For he is insatiable and tempts me to go out.' So,
   having tramped about for a long time, he went into his cell, having
   punished his body.

LO.PAL.G. 84(XVIII)

8. *And when night came, the thoughts troubled him again.*
   He took a basket, he put into it two measures of sand,
   he carried it, he went round with it in the whole desert. ( )
   When he had prolonged going round in the desert
   he went into his cell, his body being crushed.

AM.MAC.AL.B. 252.15

9. Now the life of Dorotheus was one of very hard labour
   and his practices were severe and his food was meagre, ( )
   and all day, in the heat of the noonday,
   he went round in the desert by the side of the sea,
   while he collected stones with which he built cells.
   And he gave them to the brethren who were not able to build

303

and he finished one cell every year.
One day I said to the holy man:
'Father, why dost thou work thus in thine old age?
For thou wilt kill thy body in all this heat.'
And he said to me:
'I kill it lest it should kill me.' (   )
I never saw this man stretch out and lie down as (men) are wont
and he never slept upon a bed of palm leaves or anything else,
but he worked the whole night,
weaving baskets to provide his food for nourishment.

BU.II.PAL.SY. 110.13

10. All day long in the burning heat he would collect stones in the desert
by the sea and build with them continually and make cells, and then
he would retire in favour of those who could not build for themselves. Each year he completed one cell. And once when I said to
him: 'What do you mean, father, at your great age by trying to kill
your poor body in these heats?' And he answered thus: 'It kills me,
I kill it.' (   ) I never knew him stretch his legs and go to sleep on a
rush mat or on a bed. But he would sit up all night long and weave
ropes of palm-leaves to provide himself with food.

LO.PAL.G. 49(II)

11. And her asceticism was as follows. She (   ) assigned to herself a
part of the daily work of her own slave women, whom also she made
her fellow ascetics.

LO.PAL.G. 168(LXI)

12. *He was weak in his body because of the asceticisms which he practised.*

HY.AP.IR.B. 91.9

13. Abba Theodore said: 'The monk's body grows weak with eating
little bread.' But another elder said: 'It grows weaker with watching
in the night.'

CHA.SA.L. 51(IV)

14. One day a certain brother, who himself also attained such great
excellence,
that the period in which the whole of the sole of his foot was lying
and resting on the ground,
during the hour of service, was reckoned by him as sin.
'Behold, I have removed myself from fervour toward God.'
Thus it was impossible for anyone to see him (   ) without his eyes
being extended towards heaven,

304

his soul also being in this way drawn upward with his body,
so that whenever anyone observed the soles of his feet,
his heels were always raised and moving up and down,
so that in this way his soul was extended upwards
and at one moment he would stand upon the tips of his toes,
as if he were in the act of ascending
and at another moment when his toes were fatigued,
he would let his soles drop and again raise them and so in all the
    service.
Thus if barbarians came in among them, he would be unaware of
    them
and would not lower the gaze of his eyes from heaven.
Thus when he happened to be in front of me at the service,
I was amazed at the fervour of his soul before God,
since his hands also under his robe,
that is, the palms themselves were secretly extended.
And every part of him was being drawn upwards,
while not a sentence was allowed to pass out from his mouth,
without an expression of praise or thanksgiving between each sen-
    tence: 'Praise to thee Lord.'

BR.ZAC.SY. 273.7

2 PAIN

(i) SELF-INFLICTION OF PAIN

THEMES

The necessity of pain in the struggle for self-control.
The necessity of performing acts of endurance in secret.
The refusal to indulge in physical comfort.
The expression of sorrow by a life-time of mourning.

EPISODES

The application by ascetics of painful objects to the body for long periods
    of time.
The burning of the body by ascetics.
The discovery by bystanders of the injuries self-inflicted by ascetics.
The wearing by ascetics of irritant clothing.
The exposure of the body by ascetics to heat and cold by the discarding
    of clothing.
The description by ascetics of their sufferings in the desert.
The refusal by ascetics to bathe or anoint themselves.
The description of ascetics who wept continuously.

The affirmation by ascetics that their sufferings were relieved by divine intervention.

QUOTATIONS

1. He wore a tunic of hair and an iron belt upon his loins under his tunic.

NAU.ABR.SY. 770.2

2. In his early days, war against fornication and gluttony was his lot. He drove out these passions by ( ) wearing irons. ( ) Once when timidity attacked him, ( ) he shut himself in a tomb for six years.

LO.PAL.G. 146(XLV)

3. Or il arriva que, tandis qu'il priait au milieu de la nuit, alors que le quatrième jour (mercredi) commençait à luire, il entend une voix qui distinctement lui dit: 'Descends avec tes pères et ne sois pas dans le doute. Puis, de nouveau, accomplis en paix la course de ton ascèse.' Confiant donc dans l'encouragement du Seigneur, il réveille ses serviteurs. L'échelle une fois posée, ils montent et lui enlèvent les chaînes de fer qui le ceignent. Le saint descend avec peine en raison des tourments que lui causent ses pieds.

FE.II.DAN.G. 144(XXXVII)

4. *He practised his exercises chiefly in those deserts,*
   among the great thorn trees which surround them and the distant desert.
   If some spines entered into his feet,
   he would endure them without removing them,
   remembering the nails piercing the feet of our Lord Jesus upon the Cross.

LE.PAC.B. 16.23

5. They said, concerning a brother in the Paradise of Shiet in the olden days,
   that *he spent forty days standing in the sun before he came into the shelter.*
   When the sun set, he would stand upon a thornbush until the morrow.
   When the sun rose he would go and stand in it.

AM.PIS.KE.B. 339.2

6. He (Abba Martyrianus) filled his heart with His (God's) fear.
   He threw himself upon the rock in the presence of God.
   He wept greatly and, after he began to pray to God,

306

he rose, he took some twigs, he gathered them in, he piled them up,
he brought them up upon the rock.
He made a fire, he kindled them until there was a great fire.
He stood in the midst of the fire with the great heat upon his feet and
his whole body
so that gradually the fire overcame him to (the point of) death.
He came out of the fire.
His feet were destroyed through the great heat of the burning fire.
As he came forth from the fire, he cast himself upon the ground.

CHA.MART.B. 7.24

7. *The clothing which he wore*
was hair inside
and skin outside.

GAR.ANT.S. 54.2

8. *They wore garments of hair.*

LE.PAC.S. 105a.11

9. *And he wore a garment of hair.*

LE.PAC.S. 165b.27

10. Apa Isaac said: 'Our fathers and Apa Pambo used to *wear clothes*
which were torn and in rags and garments of palm fibre.
You now wear admirable clothes.
Go away. You have spoilt this place.'

CHA.AP.PA.S. 4.26(23)

11. Then the holy man, Abba John, went to the place of this tree, ( )
and he made for himself there a cell in a cave,
in order to add to his conflicts and his labour. ( )
And he also prepared for himself a garment of palm-fibres,
with which he clothed himself.

NAU.JE.PE.SY. XXX.18

12. Our father Abba John ( ) *practised great self-control*
and he increased his austerities and his exercises, ( )
with many supplications and unceasing prayers.
He made himself a garment of palm fibres and he wore it.

AM.JOH.K.B. 351.3

13. Our saintly father, Abba John Kolobos, ( ) *stripped off his clothes*;
he went forth to the desert.
He spent a week without eating or drinking.

AM.JOH.K.B. 354.13

14. They also said these words to us about him, that *in his youth*
   he spent a whole year without wearing clothes
   except for a rag of cloth
   bound upon his loins and his (private) parts.

AM.MAC.AL.B. 251.11

15. There was another monk, Sarapion, and he was surnamed Sindo-
   nite; for apart from a sindon, he never wore clothes. ( ) He was
   unable to remain calmly in the cell, not because he was distracted
   by material things, yet none the less he travelled up and down the
   world and perfected this type of asceticism.

LO.PAL.G. 127(XXXVII)

16. (It was said of Apa Dioscorus that) *concerning his sleep,*
   he was not used to have a mat under him, nor a skin nor anything of
       this kind,
   but he slept upon the ground only.

CHA.AP.PA.S. 78.29(254)

17. *A mat was sufficient for him to sleep upon*
   and many times he would sleep upon the ground alone.

GAR.ANT.S. 11.20

18. For thirty years ( ) I went naked and barefoot
   until the skin was worn from off my limbs
   and my flesh was scorched by the sun
   and I was prostrate upon the ground as dead. ( )
   And when that period of thirty years was finished,
   when I was in great perils of affliction,
   God commanded my body and the hair grew until all my limbs were
       covered.

LOOK.MAR.SY. 15.10

19. When I had entered his cave, he said to me,
   'Behold, my son, for ninety-five years I have been in this cave. ( )
   I have not worn clothing of (this) world.
   For thirty years I have been here in great distress
   from ( ) nakedness and conflicts with devils. ( )
   Thirty years of severe peril have passed over me. ( )
   Then finally the mercy of God rested upon me.
   He commanded my body and the hair grew
   until it weighted down my limbs with its weight.'

LOOK.MAR.SY. 9.11

20. *I had nothing, either clothing or bread food;*
my hair increased and my clothes were completely destroyed.
I covered the necessary place, covering it with my hair.

BU.ON.S. 208.14

21. And the holy old man Abba Macarius went forth *and he walked for*
four days
and he came upon a lake. He saw an island in its middle
and when he came to the island he looked *and behold he saw some*
naked men,
their flesh being swollen and thickened by the air,
and their hair and nails were long and of changed form.

AM.MAC.SC.B. 94.11

22. The blessed old man said to me: '*I suffered greatly many times from*
hunger and thirst
and from the fire outside by day and the great cold at night.
My flesh swelled in the dew of heaven.'

BU.ON.S. 213.27

23. *I saw a herd of antelopes approaching from afar, with that brother in*
their midst.
When he drew near me, *he was naked*
and his hair covered his indecency and it served as a garment to clothe
him.

BU.ON.S. 206.14

24. *I saw some antelopes approaching and the servant of God coming with*
them,
naked, with his hair covering his indecency.

CHA.AP.PA.S. 82.11(268)

25. *I looked, I saw a man afar off, who was very fearful.*
His hair was spread over his body like a leopard,
for he was naked, while leaves covered his male parts. ( )
When he came, he cast himself for a little in the shade of the
mountain peak,
for he suffered greatly from inner afflictions, hunger and thirst.

BU.ON.S. 210.1

26. I (Pambo) *approached* (*that brother*), *we embraced one another,*
we prayed, we sat down.

21   309

I said to him: '*My father, art thou not frozen in winter and faint in summer,*
wearing such a garment?'
Apa Pamoun, 'he of the robe', this indeed being his name, said:
'O my beloved father, *behold, it is twenty years since I came to this place.*
In this one garment I have kept warm in winter
and (in) a draught of air in summer.
And I assure thee that this suffices me until the day of my death.'

BU.CYR.S. 130.14

27. I asked them: '*When it is Winter, are you not frozen and when it is Summer, are your bodies not burnt?'*
They said: '*The Lord has made for us this dispensation;*
it is not freezing in the Winter, nor burning in the Summer.'

CHA.AP.PA.S. 74.31(242)

28. *My father said to him: ' Dost thou not freeze in the Winter and burn in the Summer?'*
He said to him: 'If it is Winter, I sleep in the midst of these antelopes
and they keep me warm with their breath which is in their mouths.
If it is Summer they gather together and stand
and give shade to me against the heat which troubles me.'

AM.PAUL.T.S. 762.8

29. *And until his death he did not bathe in water and he did not wash his feet at all apart from necessity.*

GAR.ANT.S. 54.4

30. *He would watch closely lest (anyone) should anoint himself with oil.*

GAR.ANT.S. 11.22

31. Now to the end of his life, this holy man never put on either a linen tunic
or even a head covering.
And he never washed.

BU.II.PAL.SY. 107.19

32. (Evagrius) tortured his body with vigils
and he never bathed, except on one day alone;
this was the eve of Easter, the Feast of the Great Resurrection of our Saviour of all, the Christ.
(Severus) imitated him ( ) and he also tortured his body by fasting.

He did not bathe for most of the year,
until it was the day on which he (Evagrius) did so.

KUG.SEV.SY. 56.10

33. In the third year he entered the desert. So he lived fourteen years in
the place they call Cellia. (   ) And he made a hundred prayers. (   )
And all night long he stood naked in the well, though it was winter,
so that his flesh was frozen. (   ) On another occasion (   ) for forty
days he did not enter under a roof, as he told us himself, so that his
body threw out ticks, like the bodies of irrational animals. (   ) And
he said: 'From the time that I took to the desert, I have not touched
(   ) a bath.'

LO.PAL.G. 136(XXXVIII)

34. And he said: 'From the time that I came to the desert
I have not used a bath.'

BU.II.PAL.SY. 279.13

35. *In this way his flesh wasted greatly*
and the tears were sweet like honey on his face,
so that his eyes were sunken like holes of walls and they were very
dark
because of the great flow of tears
which poured from his eyes at all times like water.

LEI.SIN.B. 13.23

36. Then (Pachomius) commanded him to depart and to seclude himself (   )
and to make two mats every day and never to cease from weeping.

BU.II.PAL.SY. 328.17

37. Quand il priait, Hypatios était continuellement touché de com-
ponction, il pleurait et criait si fort vers Dieu que nous, versant des
larmes, nous étions saisis de crainte sacrée.

FE.II.HYP.G. 48(XXVII)

38. And he remained with them for three days
and straightway he went forth from them and departed into the
desert. (   )
And he was there for three years in prayers and tears.
And after three years he returned to the Church (   ).
And he went forth and departed to the desert
and he was in the desert there for a further seven years.

BU.II.HIER.SY. 409.5

311

(ii) DISREGARD OF PAIN

THEMES

The ability to continue in prayer, meditation or work in spite of physical pain.

The disregard of the advice of bystanders.

The attempt to assume the condition of death during life.

EPISODES

The disregard by ascetics of the pain of their prolonged standing posture.

The exacerbation by ascetics of their sufferings by additional self-mortification.

The adoption by ascetics of excessively hot places for meditation.

The disregard by ascetics of the exudation of blood, sweat or pus from the body.

The disregard by ascetics of bodily emaciation.

QUOTATIONS

1. *They mortified themselves during their prayers.*
   They did not move their feet or their hands,
   which they held outstretched *so that sleep should not overcome them.*
   Against the demands of sleep
   they did not often bend the knee during the whole night.
   Their feet swelled from the fatigue due to the standing upon them all night.
   Likewise their hands were bathed with blood
   because they did not withdraw them at all from the multitude of mosquitoes which ate them.

   LE.PAC.S. 133b.4

2. *They went to hot places and prayed from evening until morning,*
   mortifying themselves during their prayers.
   They did not move their feet or their hands,
   which they held outstretched, *so that sleep should not overcome them.*
   It was against the demands of sleep
   that they did not often bend their knees during the whole night.
   Their feet used to swell from the fatigue due to their standing upon them all night.
   Likewise their hands were bathed with blood,
   because they did not withdraw them at all from the multitude of mosquitoes which ate them.

WITHDRAWAL FROM THE ENVIRONMENT OF THE SENSES

If it was necessary for them to sleep a little,
they would sit in the midst of the place in which they prayed
and they did not lean their backs against any wall.
And if they were doing a material work during the day
and if the sun rose above them and the great heat,
they did not change to another place,
unless they had finished the work with which they were occupied.

LE.PAC.S. 105a.13

3. He determined to dispense with sleep, and he told us how he did
not go under a roof for twenty days, that he might conquer sleep,
being burnt up by the sun's heat and shrivelled up with cold at night,
and he used to say this: 'Unless I had gone under a roof and got
some sleep, my brain would have dried up so as to drive me into
delirium for ever after. And I conquered so far as depended on me,
but I gave way so far as depended on my nature that had need of
sleep.'

LO.PAL.G. 78(XVIII)

4. Thus from the first hour of the night, or at most the second,
no man in full health was to be found on his mat,
or not lying on his face, with genuflexion and tearful prayer; ( )
(some) for the duration of a whole night and a day,
and others ranged in rows and standing on standing-posts
and others who were tied to the ceiling of the room by ropes and
    vine branches
and were suspending themselves by them in a standing posture all
    night,
having put them under their armpits;
and others who were sitting on seats and never falling completely
    on their sides,
old and young, strong and weak.

BR.AM.SY. 611.13

5. He showed such self-discipline in his asceticism as to put all others
in the shade. For during his twenty-five years' life there he ( )
would spend the nights standing up and singing psalms. ( ) Once
a scorpion stung this Elpidius as he sang psalms by night and we too
were singing with him. He trod it underfoot nor did he even move
from his standing position, despising the pain caused by the
scorpion.

LO.PAL.G. 155(XLVIII)

6. *It was also said of him that when he stood at prayer, he used to bend*
   the knee with great power, without interruption,
   as though (he formed) a ring,
   until the sweat of his body flowed down upon his feet like water,
   as though one should bathe oneself therein and wet one's whole body.
   For he made many thousand obeisances.

   DAV.JOH.KH.B. 340.14

7. The youth Pachomius saw the courage of the old man Abba
   Palamon.
   Many times he went forth from his dwelling
   and entered into tombs full of corpses
   and spent the whole night, from evening until morning,
   praying to the Lord Jesus,
   so that *the place on which he stood* became like mud
   because of the amount of sweat on his body.

   LE.PAC.B. 12.7

8. *He prayed thus to God all night* in these words,
   so that the brick on which he stood dissolved under him
   from the sweat which flowed down upon it.
   There was a great heat down in that place because it was Summer.
   And when morning came he ceased from praying.

   LE.PAC.S. 2.15

9. *When evening came,*
   he went down to a cellar in the deserted village in which he dwelt.
   He placed a brick beneath his feet and *he stretched out his hands.*
   He prayed to God with tears all night, from evening until morning. ( )
   And as he prayed thus to God all night in these words,
   the brick on which he stood dissolved under him
   with the sweat of his body which flowed down upon it.
   There was a great heat down in that place.

   LE.PAC.S. 108.b.22

10. There is in the desert one of our brethren, whose name is John, ( )
    and no man can find him at once,
    because he wanders from place to place in the desert.
    He once previously spent three years under a rock, standing and
      praying.
    And he never sat down at all, ( ).
    Then the legs of the blessed man burst open,

314

because of much standing upon them,
and pus and discharge flowed from them.

BU.II.HIER.SY. 397.20

11. (Concerning Apa Dioscorus) ( ). *When he first came to God, as servant,*
his bowels bled from the deprivations of his body and his feet were gangrenous.
He took no remedy for them at all, *nor did he tell any man,*
but he wrapped them in cloth rags until God sent death to him.
His disciples said to him once: 'Put a little heated saffron on them.'
But he did not listen at all.

CHA.AP.PA.S. 79.1(255)

12. His body was dried up upon his bones like a hard clay pot.
And his garments were from many coloured rags of the dung-hill.
In stature he was small,
his appearance was always mournful and he did not give way to laughter at all.
And he was bald and beardless.

BRO.EP.SY. 42.3

13. I have heard of a certain Julian in the region of Edessa, a very ascetic man, who wore away his flesh till it was so thin that he carried about only skin and bone.

LO.PAL.G. 142(XLII)

14. Eustathius ( ) followed so strenuously after the acquisition of impassibility
and he made his body so dry, by the labours of vigil and fasting,
that the sun could be seen between his ribs.
And it is also related of him ( )
that he never faced towards the West.

BU.II.PAL.SY. 229.2

15. Une fois donc qu'Hypatios était terriblement en butte à cette guerre (avec le démon), durant cinquante jours, malgré les chaleurs brûlantes, il ne but point, son ventre s'était entièrement durci et ses lèvres, par la sécheresse, avaient crevé.

FE.II.HYP.G. 21(V)

16. Abba Poemen said that a brother asked Abba Moses: 'How does a man mortify himself? Is it by his neighbour?' And he answered:

315

'Unless a man has it in his heart that he has been shut in a tomb for three years, he cannot attain to mortification.'

CHA.SA.L. 118(X)

17. *He* (Isaac) *went to the holy mountain of Shiet*
in which were choirs of the holy angels of God,
these being blessed monks, who crucify their flesh with the afflictions of virtue,
carrying at all times the death of Jesus in their bodies.

POR.IS.B. 312.6

18. At length he shut himself in a tomb for three years.
And thus he endured there, so that neither by night nor by day did he sit or lie down.
And he never went out from it.

BU.II.PAL.SY. 229.20

19. An old man made a resolution not to drink for forty days. And if ever he thirsted, he washed a vessel and filled it with water and hung it in front of his eyes. And when the brothers asked him why he was doing this he replied: 'So that if I do not taste what I long for and can see, my devotion will be greater and I shall be granted a greater reward by the Lord.'

CHA.SA.L. 59(IV)

20. Now this miracle is told of him, that he dug in the place where he lived and found some very bitter water. And, until he died, he remained there accepting the bitterness of the water in order to show his endurance.

LO.PAL.G. 138(XXXIX)

(iii) DEVICES FOR PREVENTING REST

THEMES

The practice of standing during the performance of ascetic exercises.
The practice of maintaining the standing posture for long periods of time.
The prevention of sleep by physical devices.
The repetition of prayers for long periods of time.
The repetition of great numbers of prayers in succession.
The practice of doing repetitive hand-work while standing at prayer.
The value of repetitive work for attaining mental concentration.

316

EPISODES

The spending of a life-time without moving from a standing position.
The spending of a number of days standing in prayer.
The immersion of the body in water in order to stand and pray.
The building of narrow enclosures within which sleep is impossible.
The spending of a life-time in unceasing prayer.
The practice of enumerating the prayers said daily.

QUOTATIONS

1. It was said of Apa Simeon the Syrian that *he spent more than sixty years standing upon a column.*

   CHA.AP.PA.S. 75.3(243)

2. It was said of one in Egypt whose name was Bané, who was in the Monastery of Houor,
   that he spent fifteen years standing in a cell in which he was enclosed.

   CHA.AP.PA.S. 75.28(244)

3. The righteous John *stood every night praying
   and he did not sleep until he had recited the whole Psalter
   and sometimes also the Acts.*

   HY.JE.SI.B. 181.18

4. It was said by Appa Besarion: '( )
   I spent forty nights standing in the midst of a spine thicket, without sleep.'

   CHA.AP.PA.S. 6.21(33)

5. *His custom was that he did not sit at all during Easter (week),
   but he would stand doing (his) handwork.*

   POR.IS.B. 341.5

6. He saw each man practising different ways of asceticism, ( ) standing all night but sitting down by day. So, having moistened palm-leaves in large numbers, he stood in a corner and until the forty days were completed and Easter had come, ( ) neither knelt down nor reclined ( ), speaking to no one and not opening his mouth, but standing in silence.

   LO.PAL.G. 81(XVIII)

7. *And he spent three days and three nights, without eating and without drinking,
   standing with our father Abba John upon the clothes, both praying.*

   AM.JOH.K.B. 330.12

317

8. And they stood in prayer for three days and three nights,
without eating and without drinking,
but standing and praying upon the clothes.

NAU.JE.PE.SY. XV.5

9. And Adam said to Eve: 'Thou canst not do so much as I, but do
only so much as thou hast strength for. For I will spend forty days
fasting, but do thou arise and go to the river Tigris and lift up a
stone and stand on it in the water up to thy neck in the deep of the
river. And let no speech proceed out of thy mouth, since we are
unworthy. ( ) And do thou stand in the water of the river thirty-
seven days. I will spend forty days in the water of Jordan, perchance
the Lord God will take pity on us.'
    And Eve walked to the river Tigris and did as Adam had told her.
Likewise Adam walked to the river Jordan and stood on a stone up
to his neck in the water.

CH.AD.EV.L. 135(VI)

10. Then the boy (Shenute) went down to the water *and he prayed to
    God,*
stretching out his hands to heaven.

LEI.SIN.B. 9.14

11. Shenute would go down to a cistern of water
which was at a little distance from the village.
It was the month of Tobi in those days.
And in this way he would stretch his hands forth and pray
while the water came to his neck.

LEI.SIN.B. 9.1

12. They said concerning Abba Sisoes, of Babylon,
that when he wished to conquer sleep,
he stood himself upon a steep precipice
and the angel of the Lord saved him from thence
and commanded him never to do thus again,
nor to entrust this tradition to another.

BU.II.PAL.SY. 460.21

13. *He forgot food and sleep*
because of the strong power of the wealth of the Holy Spirit which was
    in him.
He built himself a path from sharp stones which hung from the sides
and it was a cubit long and a cubit broad

318

*and when the law of nature constrained him he would take a small
    breath within it.*
In this way, if he sat, he would be roused by it.

AM.JOH.K.B. 371.8

14. *His disciple, obedient to his father,*
    stood upon his feet all the days which our father passed in Southern
        (Egypt),
    standing in the place where his father left him when he departed from
        him,
    showing endurance and directing the house,
    so that his body swelled like a pillar
    and the brethren besought him that he would sit a little and rest
        himself.
    (But he did not consent and *the brothers set some stones about him*
    and he remained standing in great obedience.

DAV.JOH.KH.B. 355.16

15. Now the blessed man had four cells in the desert,
    one in the inner desert, and one in Aliboni
    and one in the 'cells' and one in the Mountain of Nitria.
    Two of these were without windows
    so that he dwelt in them in darkness during the Forty Days fast.
    another was so narrow that he could not stretch out his legs,
    but another, in which he received those who came to him, was wide.

BU.II.PAL.SY. 148.7

16. *When our father, the holy John, dwelt in the cave,*
    he meditated on the saving name of Our Lord Jesus Christ, our God,
    with unceasing prayers, with secret petitions not to be spoken of;
    for no man knew the fulness of the sufferings which he endured.

DAV.JOH.KH.B. 351.1

17. When formerly the blessed man was in the inner desert, (   )
    he passed the whole time of his life in prayer and in praise.

BU.II.HIER.SY. 368.8

18. If he (Daniel) took a short time for sleep from vigil,
    he would fall while he spoke,
    prolonging his recitation.

CHA.AP.PA.S. 78.8(250)

319

19. He (Polycarp) *went forth to a field at a distance from the city.*
    He stood there without any others and did nothing at all,
    but by day and night he remained alone in prayers to the Lord.

    BA.HY.II.POL.SM.B. 64.8

20. His work and his asceticism consisted in ceaseless prayer. So he had
    three hundred set prayers and he collected as many pebbles and kept
    them in his lap and threw out of his lap one pebble at each prayer.

    LO.PAL.G. 90(XX)

21. He said to him: 'In a certain village there dwells a virgin who has
    lived the ascetic life for thirty years. ( ) But all the while ( ) she
    makes seven hundred prayers.'

    LO.PAL.G. 90(XX)

22. The holy Macarius answered him: 'I am now sixty years old, I make
    one hundred set prayers and produce my food by my own work.'

    LO.PAL.G. 91(XX)

23. *The rules of the services:*
    sixty times of prayer in the day and fifty in the night,
    apart from those which we are used to do occasionally
    so that we should not be liars,
    because we have been ordered to pray without ceasing.

    LE.PAC.B. 9.17

24. *They made prayers aloud, saying psalms six in succession with an*
    alleluia.

    AM.MA.DO.B. 296.13

25. *He stood in a corner of his cell, he plaited baskets until the forty days*
    were over,
    without sitting at all or eating bread or drinking water or bending
    the knee.

    AM.MAC.AL.B. 243.5

26. *Otherwise many times, from evening until morning,*
    we do much handwork, either rope or hair or palm fibre, so that sleep
    does not trouble us.

    LE.PAC.B. 9.6

27. He never lay upon his back until his departure in death,
    but he worked all day in the garden

and towards sunset he took food and went into his cell,
and, sitting on a chair in the middle of his cell,
he twisted ropes until the service of the night, (   )
repeating the Scriptures.

BU.II.PAL.SY. 335.20

28. His father said to him: '(   ) Take for thyself seven pairs of bread
      loaves
    and a few palm leaves, sufficient for forty days.' (   )
    And he took them and departed
    and he continued working and twisting dried palm leaves and plait-
      ing,
    and eating dry bread
    and he was in silence for twenty days.

BU.II.PAL.SY. 592.19

29. This man was (   ) a great elder,
    who for twenty years did not lie upon one or other of his sides,
    but slept upon the seat of his work.

BU.II.PAL.SY. 499.20

30. She replied: 'From early morning to the ninth hour I pray hour by
    hour, spinning flax the while. During the remaining hours I meditate
    on the holy patriarchs and prophets and apostles and martyrs. And
    (   ) I remain in patience for the other hours, waiting for my end
    with cheerful hope.'

LO.PAL.G. 53(V)

31. And she said to me:
    'I am occupied with my prayers and with the work of my hands and
      I have no rest.
    From morning until the ninth hour, I weave linen
    and I recite the psalms and I pray,
    and during the rest of the day I commemorate in my heart the holy
      fathers.
    And I resolve in my thoughts the histories of all the prophets and
      apostles and martyrs.
    And during the remaining hours, I work with my hands
    and I eat my bread and by means of these things I am comforted,
    whilst I await the end of my life in good hope.'

BU.II.PAL.SY. 116.10

32. They tell the story that on one occasion,
    when the blessed man Anthony was dwelling in the desert,

thoughts of depression of mind rose in him
and he was in great darkness of thought and he said to God:
'Lord, I wish to live and my thoughts will not permit me.
What shall I do in my afflictions to be saved?'
And he approached a little from where he was
and he saw a man in the likeness of the blessed man Anthony,
with his form, who was sitting and twisting ropes.
And he rose from his work and prayed
and afterwards he sat down and continued.
And again he stood up and prayed;
for he was an angel who had been sent from God
for the correction and admonition of the blessed man Anthony,
who afterwards heard him say to him: 'Do thou Anthony also do
    this and live.'
And when he heard these things, the blessed man had great joy
and afterwards he did thus and lived.

BU.II.PAL.SY. 465.17

33. *He saw one in the likeness of a man,*
    sitting weaving a basket and, as he rose from time to time from the
        hand-work,
    he prayed and then sat again working.

AM.AP.ANT.B. 31.3

IV   FOOD DEPRIVATION

1   RESTRICTION OF DIET

THEMES

The practice of never eating to satiety.
The practice of never eating until sunset.
The practice of abstaining from meat, wine, oil and fruit.
The practice of abstaining from cooked food.
The restriction of the diet to bread, salt, herbs and water.
The restriction of the diet to barley, pulse, herbs and water.
The restriction of the diet to bread, salt and water only.
The restriction of the diet to herbs and water only.
The restriction of the diet to dates and water only.
The practice of moderation in old age.

EPISODES

The restriction of the diet as a means of achieving self-control.
The bringing of bread to ascetics who remained in enclosed dwellings,

The partaking by ascetics of the same vegetable food as the animals with
which they lived.

The eating of one bunch of dates a month only from a date-palm which
produced twelve bunches of dates a year.

The eating of small quantities for the sake of others.

The bringing of cooked food and luxuries by disciples to ascetics in their
old age.

QUOTATIONS

1. (Evagrius) was a practising philosopher of our Lord Jesus Christ,
   seeing that he fasted every day ( ).
   And he abstained from eating meat,
   not because it is evil, as the Manichaeans say,
   but because abstaining from it one approaches to philosophy
   the more.

   KUG.SEV.SY. 56.8

2. Now to the end of his life, this holy man never ( ) ate flesh
   and he never enjoyed a full meal.

   BU.II.PAL.SY. 107.19

3. He used to eat (daily) six ounces of bread, and a bunch of herbs,
   and drink water in proportion.

   LO.PAL.G. 49(II)

4. His food was meagre, for his nourishment was dry bread. ( )
   He ate one small bread loaf, which weighed about six ounces, each
   day
   and one small bundle of green herbs.
   And he drank water by measure.

   BU.II.PAL.SY. 110.14

5. This then was the method of his asceticism. ( ) Having heard from
   some that the monks of Tabennesi, all through Lent, eat (only) food
   that has not been near the fire, he decided for seven years to eat
   nothing that had been through the fire, and, except for raw vegetables, if any such were found, and moistened pulse, he tasted nothing. Having practised this virtue to perfection, he heard about another
   man, that he ate a pound of bread. And having broken up his ration
   biscuit and put it into a vessel with a narrow mouth, he decided to
   eat just as much as his hand brought out. ( ) For three years he
   kept up this practice of asceticism, eating four or five ounces of
   bread and drinking as much water, and a pint of oil in the year.

   LO.PAL.G. 77(XVIII)

6. Abba Daniel said of him (Abba Arsenius): 'All the years he stayed
   with us, we gave him a little enough measure of food for the year.
   And every time we came to visit him, he shared it with us.'

   CHA.SA.L. 49(IV)

7. *For twenty-five days after the Saviour appeared to the blessed Apater,*
   he did not eat bread to satiety, or flesh,
   but tasted a little, because of those with whom he ate.

   HY.AP.IR.B. 84.10

8. *And she fasted daily until the days of the pregnancy were ended and*
   thus she gave birth to her son.

   HY.JE.SI.B. 176.10

9. His father said to him: '(   ) Take thyself for thyself seven pairs of
   bread loaves
   and a few palm leaves, sufficient for forty days.' (   )
   And he took them and departed.
   And he continued working and twisting dried palm leaves and plaiting,
   and eating dry bread.

   BU.II.PAL.SY. 592.19

10. So he returned and from that hour practised asceticism more
    vehemently and especially refrained from food, taking nothing
    except dry bread to the extent of twelve ounces.

    LO.PAL.G. 88(XIX)

11. Then (Pachomius) commanded him to (   ) eat once daily of bread
    and salt only
    and to drink water only, all the period of his life.

    BU.II.PAL.SY. 328.17

12. (Pachomius and his brother John) *both lived in extreme withdrawal.*
    They did not keep anything,
    apart from two loaves daily and a little salt.

    LE.PAC.S. 105a.5

13. For *he did not eat every day until evening when the sun set,*
    and also he did not eat to satiety and his food was bread and salt.

324

With these, his body became dry and his flesh adhered to his bones and he was very thin.

LEI.SIN.B. 12.21

14. *And when they looked inside his dwelling, they could not see anything except a few bread (loaves) and a little salt.*
They wondered at his endurance.

POR.IS.B. 338.1

15. The woman who turned to the Lord, ( )
she did not drink wine, or eat grapes, or any fruit,
nor did she eat oil, or anoint her body with it.
Her food was bread with salt.

CHA.MART.B. 12.25

16. (It was said of Apa Dioscorus that) concerning his food,
he tasted nothing, except bread and salt and water alone. ( )
he did not allow oil in the cell at all.

CHA.AP.PA.S. 78.28(254)

17. *He went into some empty tombs which were at a distance from the village.*
He remained there, *having commanded one to bring his bread* (at intervals of) many days.

GAR.ANT.S. 12.25

18. *He closed the door* and he laid by for himself loaves sufficient for six months. ( )
He enclosed himself and there was water there. ( )
He received his loaves through the roof twice a year.

GAR.ANT.S. 18.1

19. And she said: '*Behold for thirty-eight years I have been living in this cave on roots.*'

CHA.AP.PA.S. 81.4(266)

20. When formerly the blessed man was in the inner desert,
he ate roots and herbs and he drank water when he was able.

BU.II.HIER.SY. 368.8

21. In his early days, war against fornication and gluttony was his lot.
He drove away these passions by ( ) abstinence from corn, bread

and all things cooked by fire. (   ) He told us this: 'For thirty-two years I touched no fruit.'

LO.PAL.G. 146(XLV)

22. For the blessed Mar Ephraim, from when he began in asceticism
    until the end of his life,
did not eat meat, but only barley and pulse from time to time and
    herbs.
For his drink was water.

BRO.EP.SY. 41.22

23. And many of them did not eat bread or fruit,
but (God forbid) bitter herbs and vegetables crushed (in vinegar).

BU.II.HIER.SY. 419.23

24. *We found some antelopes in the depth of the valley, with a monk in
    the midst.* (   )
My father said to him: 'On what dost thou live as thou walkest with
    these antelopes?'
He said: '*My food and that of these antelopes is one food,
this is herbs of the field and these vegetables.*'

AM.PAUL.T.S. 761.15

25. I (Onnophrius) *went to the desert* (   ),
I found this well of water and this date palm and this cave.
*This date palm produces twelve bunches of dates every year, a bunch
    for every month.
This bunch of dates suffices me for the month.*

BU.ON.S. 208.8

26. *He said: 'Behold, I am in this place eighteen years
and I have eaten no food of this world,
but I live on the fruit of the trees.'*
For a date palm was growing outside his dwelling place,
*which produced twelve bunches, one bunch a month.
And he lived on its fruit.*

BU.CYR.S. 129.21

27. He laid down for himself absolutely not to taste either bread or
    wine,
unless necessity constrained him,
and thus he fed upon pulse and some fruit only,

326

sometimes from one week to the next and again on the first day of
the week
and sometimes every two or three days.

BR.THOM.SY. 297.9

28. *The brothers who served him*, they asked to serve him.
For many months *they brought him olives and cereal and oil*;
for he was an old man.

GAR.ANT.S. 57.20

29. Dans sa vieillesse il mangeait, vers le soir, trois onces de pain et
trois olives. Durant sa jeunesse, il était toujours resté à ne manger
qu'une fois la semaine.

FE.IV/I.HIS.G.45(VII)

30. So he lived fourteen years in the place they call Cellia, and he used
to eat a pound of bread and in three months a pint of oil, though he
was a man who had come from a luxurious and refined and volup-
tuous life. (   ) And he said: 'From the time that I took to the desert,
I have not touched lettuce, nor any other green vegetable, nor any
fruit, nor grapes, nor meat, (   ). And later, in the sixteenth year of
his life without cooked food, his flesh felt a need, owing to the
weakness of his stomach, to partake of (something that had been)
on the fire. He did not, however take bread even now, but, having
been fed on herbs or gruel or pulse for two years, in this regime he
died.

LO.PAL.G. 136(XXXVIII)

2 DAYS OF FASTING

THEMES

The practice of eating at intervals of two, three, four, or five days.
The practice of eating once a week on the Sabbath.
The practice of fasting for forty days before Easter.
The practice of prolonged fasting.

EPISODES

Individual habits concerning days of fasting.

QUOTATIONS

1. *Their food was bread with salt* at all times.
Since they entered the life of monkhood
they did not take flesh at all, or wine, or fish

327

*and they prolonged (their fast) two days in succession at all times
and they made prayers aloud, saying psalms six in succession, with
an alleluia.*

AM.MA.DO.B. 296.10

2. When he reached twelve years, *he gave himself great abstinences.
He did not eat food, except that which the monks ate.
He fasted until evening daily.
Sometimes he prolonged his fast for two days.*

LE.PAC.B. 33.25

3. (The brother who had sinned) was ( ) *fasting every second day.
And he ate nothing on the second day, but bread and salt alone
and he drank water from the well.*

LE.PAC.S. 165b.19

4. *He spent three days and he did not eat or drink
nor did he speak with us.*

BU.AP.PIS.S. 124.27

5. *And he spent three days and three nights, without eating and without
drinking,
standing with our father Abba John upon the clothes, both praying.*

AM.JOH.K.B. 330.12

6. And they stood in prayer for three days and three nights,
without eating and without drinking,
but standing and praying upon the clothes.

NAU.JE.PE.SY. XV.5

7. 'I tell thee furthermore, that *this is the fifth day in which I have not
tasted any food of this world
and I am satisfied, like one who ate and drank at evening.*'

TIL.II.PTOL.S. 35.24

8. He said to him: 'In a certain village there dwells a virgin who has
lived the ascetic life for thirty years. They have told me that, except
on Saturday and Sunday, she never eats, ( ) dragging out the long
weeks and eating at intervals of five days.'

LO.PAL.G. 90(XX)

9. And her asceticism was as follows. She ate every other day—to
begin with, after a five days intervals.

LO.PAL.G. 168(LXI)

10. For by reason of his excessive abstinence ( ) he was even suspected
    of being a phantom. For in Lent he would eat at intervals of five
    days and all the rest of the time every other day.

    LO.PAL.G. 143(XLIII)

11. They said concerning those who were in Scete, that ( )
    they fasted, so that one ate every two days
    and another every four days and another every seven days.
    Another would eat no bread and another would drink no water.

    BU.II.PAL.SY. 642.16

12. This man was ( ) a great elder ( ).
    Sometimes he ate once in two days and in four at times and in five
      at times
    and thus he passed twenty years.

    BU.II.PAL.SY. 499.20

13. Abba Joseph said to him:
    'When thou wast a youth didst thou not fast two days at a time,
      father?'
    The old man said to him:
    'And three days at a time and four days at a time
    and also a week.
    And all these things the fathers have tried by experience, like mighty
      ones.'

    BU.II.PAL.SY. 457.15

14. *He only ate once daily at sunset.*
    Many times he would delay till the second or fourth (day).
    His food was bread with salt and water.
    Concerning flesh and wine ( ) nothing of this nature was found among
      the zealous.

    GAR.ANT.S. 11.15

15. He (Abba Macarius) saw all the brothers; each one of them was
      doing different practices.
    Some prolonged (their fast) till evening daily,
    others prolonged (their fast) by two (days),
    others prolonged (their) fast, standing all night and sitting by day.

    AM.MAC.AL.B. 242.15

16. (The monastic rule): *the eating of oil, or drinking of wine or eating*
      of cooked food,

329

such things we do not know among ourselves at all.
At all times we fast until the evening, daily, in the days of Summer,
but in the days of Winter, every two or three days.

LE.PAC.B. 9.13

17. Ce père ne mangeait que deux fois la semaine, le dimanche et le
cinquième jour. Son régime était une petite bouillie de farine de
blé; il ne pouvait rien prendre d'autre, car l'habitude l'avait ainsi
façonné.

FE.IV/I.HIS.G. 99(XV)

18. For, during his twenty-five years' life there, he used to take food only
on Sunday and Saturday. (   ) To such a height of impassivity did
he attain in drying up his body, that the sun shone through his
bones.

LO.PAL.G. 155(XLVIII)

19. And he deprived himself of bread and of everything
and he nourished himself from roots and vegetables.
He fasted from Sunday to Sunday.

NAU.ABR.SY. 770.1

20. *It was said of another old man that he spent seventy weeks fasting,*
eating once a week.

CHA.AP.PA.S. 32.27(147)

21. They spoke concerning a certain elder
who fasted for seventy weeks and only ate each Sabbath.

BU.II.PAL.SY. 565.23

22. Souvant en effet, pour leur (les moines) montrer ce que doit être
l'ascèse, il ne mangeait que le dimanche, dans leur compagnie, ne
prenant d'ailleurs lui-même rien de plus que celles des herbes que
jaillissent spontanément du sol, ni pain tout ce temps-là, ni légumi-
neuses, ni aucun des fruits des arbres, ni rien de ce qu'on utilise
après cuisson.

FE.HIS.IV/I.G. 49(VIII)

23. *For they say of the holy Apa Kolouthus, (   ) the perfect one in all his*
works,
that at all times thou wouldst find him fasting and he prolonged his
fast by two days at a time. (   )

They also bore witness of the holy Apa Kolouthus, that *he prolonged his fast the whole week until the Sabbath.*

AM.PIS.KE.B. 338.5

24. My father would *prolong his fast three days at a time in the week. At other times, when his body was not weak, he fasted for the whole week.*

AM.PIS.KE.B. 399.11

25. *My father used to fast for three days at a time. At other times when his body was healed from illness he would fast the whole week.*

BU.AP.PIS.S. 98.22

26. *Thou shalt visit me every Sabbath and bring me a little food and water to drink for the maintenance of this body.*

AM.PIS.KE.B. 401.11

27. He (John) *spent seven days and seven nights thus without eating or drinking* or going on any road, sitting with long-suffering before the door (of Abba Amoi).

AM.JOH.K.B. 335.13

28. Our saintly father, Abba John Kolobos, ( ) *stripped off his clothes he went forth to the desert, He spent a week without eating or drinking.*

AM.JOH.K.B. 354.7

29. He (Abba Pachomius) did not receive him (Abba Macarius) either on the first day, or the second, until the seventh day, *while Abba Macarius became weak, as he remained without eating.*

AM.MAC.AL.B. 242.7

30. He prepared for himself in this cave a hole into which he descended constantly ( ), and he spent a whole week in it, without bread and without water, nourished by the grace of God.

NAU.JE.PE.SY. XXX.20

31. He was excessively abstemious in his mode of life so that many who knew him intimately declared that he frequently went three months without eating, being content with the Communion of the Mysteries

331

and any wild herbs that might be found. And I too had an experience of him when I went to Scete with the blessed Albanius. Scete was forty miles away from us. In the course of those forty miles, we ate twice and drank water three times, but he, without eating, went on foot (   ); yet we could not keep up with him as he walked.

LO.PAL.G. 106(XXVI)

32. *For many times he would not eat from Sabbath to Sabbath*
   and also he would spend the Forty days of the Holy Pascha without
      eating bread,
   but his food was edible herbs and soaked grain.

LEI.SIN.B. 13.19

33. It is also said, concerning our most saintly father,
   that many times he would not eat from Sabbath to Sabbath,
   but at other times he would not eat, except every forty days.

DAV.JOH.KH.B. 342.9

34. *My father then spent forty days and forty nights*
   without eating or drinking.

AM.PAUL.T.S. 767.5

35. He saw each man practising different ways of asceticism, one eating in the evening only, another every two days, another every five (   ). So (   ) until the forty days were completed and Easter had come, (   ) (he) ate no bread and drank no water, (   ) and, apart from a few cabbage leaves, took nothing and then only on Sunday that he might appear to eat.

LO.PAL.G. 81(XVIII)

36. The saint Aba Macarius answered, *he spoke to him in the power of*
      God,
   saying: '(   ) *Behold for twenty-one days nothing of this world has*
      entered my mouth.'

HY.MAC.AN.B. 68.1

37. (It was said of Apa Bané that) his early life was thus: (   )
   if he spent ten days (outside the monastery) (   )
   he did not eat or drink, until he returned to the monastery fasting.

CHA.AP.PA.S. 76.2(239)

3 HEAVENLY FOOD

THEMES

The supplying of heavenly food to replace earthly food.
The replacement of earthly food by the Eucharist.
The ability to live without earthly food.

EPISODES

The supplying from heaven of a loaf of bread and a jug of water.
The bringing by an angel of the fruits of the Tree of Life.
The bringing of the Eucharist by angels.
The bringing of fruit in a basket by an angel.
The supplying of a banquet on a table from heaven.
The bringing by angels of a continuous supply of heavenly food.

QUOTATIONS

1. It happened that *during the Forty Days of our salvation,*
   the blessed Isaac went forth to the small dwelling according to his
      custom.
   The brothers forgot to take bread to him.
   He spent the first day, and the second, and the third until the fifth day
      without eating.
   On the fifth day of his being without eating he looked and saw a large
      loaf of bread,
   placed in his presence.

   POR.IS.B. 339.10

2. My father said to him: 'What dost thou eat or drink? Who serves
      thee?'
   The holy man, Apa Phib answered: '*Since the time of my youth,*
   when I came forth from my house,
   until today, wherever I live,
   when I have completed my Forty Days fast,
   every time I find a bread (loaf) and a jug of water placed in my
      presence.'

   AM.PAUL.T.S. 763.12

3. He went forth from them and departed into the desert. (   )
   And when he had been for five weeks without bread,
   a man came to him carrying bread and water
   and he entreated him to taste and refresh himself.

333

And he was there for three years ( )
and he ate the roots of the wilderness and was nourished by them.
( )
And this blessed man was worthy of a great gift from heaven;
for regularly bread was found every Sunday in his pillow cloth.
And then when he had prayed and given thanks,
he ate and then he fasted again until the following Sunday with no
suffering.

BU.II.HIER.SY. 409.6

4. Voici encore ce qu'il nous dit sur le temps où il vint vivre en ermite dans ce lieu-ci: '( ) Un jour que nous avions manqué de pain, j'étais assis à midi au portail et, plein de tristesse, je m'endormis. Je vois alors un vieillard brillant qui vient à moi, me frappe du pied au côté et me dit: 'Tu te chagrines, Hypatios, de n'avoir de pains? Allons, lève-toi, ne sois pas triste. Car de ce jour, jamais le pain ne manquera sur la table, ni pour toi ni pour tes compagnons.'

FE.II.HYP.G. 32(XVII)

5. *Her food was brought to her by the angels of God from heaven.*
And she was serving in the Temple,
while the angels of God ministered to her.
And many times *they would bring her fruits from the Tree of Life,*
that she might eat of them with joy.

ROB.VIR.S. 14.21

6. There is in this desert one of our brethren, whose name is John ( ).
And from Sunday to Sunday, a certain priest brought him the
Sacrament
and nothing else did he taste. ( )
He went around in the desert and ate roots
and Sunday by Sunday he came to his place and partook of the
Holy Offering.

BU.II.HIER.SY. 397.20

7. I said to him: 'O my holy father, where do you celebrate the service
on the Sabbath and the Lord's day?'
He said to me: '*An angel of God,* O my holy father, *comes and serves*
me
on the Sabbath and the Lord's Day.
And to every one who is in the desert,
who lives for God and not to see men,
an angel comes and serves them.'

BU.ON.S. 214.19

8. When it was evening, he said to me:
    'Brother Serapion, is it not time to make an oblation of love?'
    I did not answer him a word.
    He arose and stretched out his hands to heaven and recited this
       psalm:
    'The Lord is my shepherd, I shall not want.'
    He turned to me and said: 'My son, He has prepared the table.'
    Thereupon I said to him: 'Excuse me, Abba.'
    And he said to me: 'Come, my son, let us enjoy what God has sent
       us.'
    And I marvelled and I was seized with dizziness,
    for there was no one inside the cave and there was nothing in it.
    When we entered within the cave I looked and saw a beautiful table
       prepared,
    with two chairs in place, bread, white as snow, beautiful choice
       fruits,
    two great fishes roasted with fire,
    fine vegetables, olives, dates and a large water pot filled with water.
    When we sat down he said to me: 'Say Grace, brother Serapion.'
    But I said to him: 'Excuse me, Abba.'
    And thereupon he said: 'Blessed is my Lord.'
    And I saw, as it were, a hand of fire,
    stretched out and it drew a cross upon that wall.
    And when we had eaten, he said: 'My son, remove from here.'
    And immediately that table was taken away.
    And in all my life I have never eaten food which was as pleasant and
       enjoyable as that,
    or drink as enjoyable as that.

                                          LOOK.MAR.SY. 14.3

9. Michael, the Archangel, brought to him a table.
    The blessed man ate.
    He placed bread of heaven upon the table of the widow
    which was filled with the most choice bread.

                                    BA.HY.II.GEO.DI.B. 230.6

10. Behold, Michael the Archangel came to him with a table
    which was full of all good things.
    The holy man ate and he received refreshment
    and the table was full of bread and all good things.

                                      BA.HY.II.GEO.B. 293.24

11. And once when they were in the cave they lacked bread
    and an angel in the form of a brother brought them food.

Another occasion was when ten of the brethren sought him.
After seven days of their fast they found him
and he commanded them to refresh themselves in his cave.
Then when they reminded him about the food, he said to them:
'God is able to prepare food for us in the desert.'
And immediately an angel of God in the form of a beautiful youth
stood
and knocked at the door while they were praying.
Then they opened the door and found the youth
carrying a great basket in which were bread and olives.
And they took it from him and they ate and gave thanks to God.
And the youth departed from them.
These and many other wonderful things were performed by the
blessed man Apellen.

BU.II.HIER.SY. 396.20

12. And, having walked all the day, with difficulty did I get two miles
from the cave. Well, looking round I saw a horseman with the appearance of a soldier, having on his head a helmet in the shape of a
tiara. And expecting him to be a soldier, I ran to the cave and found
(on the way) a basket of grapes and newly picked figs. I picked it up
and went to the cave over-joyed, and had that food as my comfort
for two months.

LO.PAL.G. 125(XXXVI)

13. He told me one day: ( )
'For one whole year ( ) I did not eat bread,
but the moistened pith of palm trees
and, if I found (them), wild herbs.
There was a time when these things failed me.
I was greatly afflicted and I went forth from the cave,
to go to the dwellings (of men).
And when I had travelled the whole day,
I was scarcely two miles distant from the cave.
And I turned backwards and I saw, as it were, a rider on horseback,
whose appearance resembled that of a soldier.
And there was on his head the likeness of a helmet.
And, as I thought that he was a Roman,
I returned to the cave
and I found outside it a basket of grapes and of newly ripened figs.'

BU.II.PAL.SY. 215.12

14. *Behold Michael, the Archangel, came to the holy man Helias.* ( )
    *And brought him fruits of the trees of Paradise so that he should eat
        of them.*
    For he had not eaten since the day that he was sent to sea with the
    animals.

    SOB.HEL.S. 33b.26

15. (It was said of Apa Bané) *that he did not eat human food* ( )
    until he completed his life course.

    CHA.AP.PA.S. 75.32(244)

16. Abba Nopi said to them: ( )
    'I have never taken any earthly thing;
    for an angel has fed me daily with heavenly food.'

    BU.II.HIER.SY. 418.10

17. 'Je sais un homme qui, au désert, n'a pris pendant dix ans aucun
    aliment terrestre: un ange, tous les trois jours, lui apportait une
    nourriture céleste, la lui mettait dans la bouche, et cela lui tenait
    lieu de nourriture et de boisson.'

    FE.IV/I.HIS.G. 32(II)

18. When God saw that *I endured in my good practice of fasting
    and that I was devoted to austerity,*
    he caused his holy angels to serve me with my daily food.
    He gives it to me in the evening, sustaining my body.

    BU.ON.S. 213.31

19. It was said of Apa Simeon, the Syrian, that *he spent more than sixty
        years standing upon a column.*
    He ate nothing of human food and no man knew how he lived. ( )
    One ( ) *who was without blemish in his life* saw him
    while he was standing before him on the top of the column.
    And behold, an angel came from East with food in his hand,
    which is that of the angels,
    and when he had given to Apa Simeon,
    he gave also of this very food to the other who was there

    CHA.AP.PA.S. 75.3(243)

20. When I had entered his cave, he said to me:
    'Behold, my son, for ninety-five years ( ) I have eaten no human
        bread.

337

For thirty years I have been here in great distress from hunger (and) thirst, ( )

I even ate dust, my son, from hunger, I drank water from the sea from thirst. ( )

And when I had endured patiently for thirty years through hunger (and) thirst, ( )

then finally the mercy of God rested on me. ( )

A continual supply of spiritual food from the Lord was sent to me.'

LOOK.MAR.SY. 9.11

21. He answered and said to me:

'Brother Serapion, behold how God loves His saints.

Every single day He sends me a fish but today, because of you, God has sent us two.

Every day, my brother, God thus sends to me spiritual food and spiritual drink.

For thirty years I was in this mountain,

eating dust from hunger and drinking foul water from the sea.'

LOOK.MAR.SY. 15.6

22. While the saint was saying these things,

behold Michael came forth from heaven. ( )

He brought some good things from heaven.

He ate and drank and his heart rejoiced.

MIN.EP.S. 27.15

V SLEEP DEPRIVATION

1 COMPLETE DEPRIVATION

THEMES

The practice of never sleeping.

The practice of snatching a few moments of sleep while standing upright.

The practice of never lying down, sitting or bending the knee.

The practice of ceaseless prayer.

EPISODES

The spending of a life-time without sleeping.

The prevention of sleep by ascetic labours.

QUOTATIONS

1. (It was said of Apa Bané) that *he did not sleep at all until he completed his life course.*

CHA.AP.PA.S. 75.32(243)

2. I never saw this man stretch out and lie down as (men) are wont.
   And he never slept upon a bed of palm leaves or anything else,
   but he worked the whole night,
   weaving baskets to provide his food for nourishment.

   BU.II.PAL.SY. 110.24

3. There is in this desert one of our brethren, whose name is John, ( )
   and he never sat down at all or slept,
   but he snatched a little sleep as he stood.

   BU.II.HIER.SY. 397.20

4. If he (Daniel) took a short time for sleep from vigil,
   he would fall while he spoke,
   prolonging his recitation.

   CHA.AP.PA.S. 78.8(250)

5. Further, they bear witness concerning him
   that *he did not sleep either by day or night,*
   except only for a brief slumber,
   leaning against the wall,
   after which he would arise quickly and would sing in this psalm.

   DAV.JOH.KH.B. 342.14

6. (I) ascertained that this had been his manner of life from youth and
   that he had never deliberately gone to sleep. Only when working or
   eating he closed his eyes overcome by sleep, so that often the piece
   of food fell from his mouth at the moment of eating, so great was
   his drowsiness. (He said): 'If you can persuade angels to sleep, you
   will also persuade the zealous man.'

   LO.PAL.G. 49(II)

7. He went to his cell
   and he made a covenant before God
   that he would not sleep the whole night, nor bend his knees.
   And he dwelt in this cell for seven years.
   And he remained standing the whole night with his eyes open
   and he never closed them.
   And afterwards he set himself other ascetic labours;
   for he would go forth during the nights
   and go to the cells of the old men
   and take their water skins and fill them with water.

   BU.II.PAL.SY. 268.14

339

8. For by reason of his excessive ( ) vigils he was even suspected of being a phantom. ( ) But his greatest act of asceticism was this. From evening until the time when the brotherhood began to assemble again in their house of prayer, he would continue on his feet singing psalms and praying, on the Mount of Olives, the Hill of the Ascension, whence Jesus was taken up. And whether it snowed or rained or there was white frost, he remained undaunted. ( ) Then he went away to his own cell before daybreak, so that of a truth the brethren often had to undress him and wring out his clothes as if after the wash, and put other clothes on him.

LO.PAL.G. 143(XLIII)

2 NIGHTS OF VIGIL

THEMES

The practice of spending the time from evening till morning in vigil.
The practice of spending the time of vigil in genuflexion and prostration.
The practice of taking sufficient sleep to preserve life.
The practice of fasting during the time spent in vigil.

EPISODES

The spending of a ritually prescribed number of nights in vigil.
The monastic rule of spending half the night in vigil.

QUOTATIONS

1. *Many times he would spend the night in vigil without sleep.*
   He did this, not once or twice, but many times.

GAR.ANT.S. 11.12

2. He went to a hidden place
   and he stretched his hands towards God during the whole night,
   while he prostrated himself before Him and begged Him to reveal His will.

NAU.JE.PE.SY. XIV.7

3. It was said by Apa Besarion: ( )
   '*I spent forty nights standing in the midst of a spine thicket, without sleep.*'

CHA.AP.PA.S. 6.21(33)

4. *They went to hot places and prayed from evening until morning.*

LE.PAC.S. 105a.13

5. *They* (Pachomius and his brother John) *went to hot places and prayed from evening until morning.*

LE.PAC.S. 133b.1

6. He went away to his cell and gave his word that he would not sleep all night nor bend his knees. So he remained in his cell for six years and every night he stood in the middle of his cell, praying and not closing his eyes.

LO.PAL.G. 89(XIX)

7. And they stood in prayer for three days and three nights,
without eating and without drinking,
but standing and praying upon the clothes.

NAU.JE.PE.SY. XV.5

8. And some of them did not sleep all night,
but, either sitting or standing, they continued in prayer until morning.

BU.II.HIER.SY. 420.1

9. Thus, from the first hour of the night, or at most the second,
no man in full health was to be found on his mat,
or not lying on his face, with genuflexion and tearful prayer, (   )
for the duration of a whole night and a day.

BR.AM.SY. 611.13

10. *Afterwards, when the sun had set a little,*
while they stood, they prayed
and they continued with the night of vigil,
blessing God and doing their handwork without ceasing.

LE.PAC.S. 214b.14

11. *He did not sleep at all at night, until the light began.*
Then he would take a little sleep for the sake of the body, lest it perish quickly.

LEI.SIN.B. 13.17

12. The monastic rule, as those who preceded us have taught us, is this:
at all times we spend half the night in vigil,
in meditation on the words of God.

LE.PAC.B. 9.3

13. Then (Pachomius) commanded him (   ) to keep vigil as long as possible.

BU.II.PAL.SY. 328.17

14. He worked all day in the garden
    and towards sunset he (   ) went into his cell,
    and, sitting on a chair in the middle of his cell,
    he twisted ropes until the service of the night.
    And thus it happened that he would snatch a little sleep,
    because of the need of his corporeal nature;
    and he slept while he was sitting (   ).
    And (   ) he was sitting in darkness and repeating the Scriptures.

BU.II.PAL.SY. 335.21

15. Abba Daniel said of Abba Arsenius that he used to spend all night
    watching. He would stay awake all night, and about dawn, when
    nature seemed to force him into sleep, he would say to sleep: 'Come,
    you wicked servant;' and he would snatch a little sleep still sitting,
    and at once rose up.
        Abba Arsenius said: 'An hour's sleep is enough for a monk, that
    is, if he is a fighter.'

CHA.SA.L. 48(IV)

SECTION II

The Establishment of a Non-Material Environment

I MENTAL POWERS

1 PRAYER AND MEDITATION

THEMES

The difficulties experienced in the effort to control thought.
The increase in the powers of the soul when the body is weakened.
The building of a world of thought.
The contemplation of the sufferings of the life after death.
The belief that the prayers of holy men affect human life and natural
  phenomena.
The certainty of the holy man that his prayer would be answered.
The answers to prayer given in the form of revelations.

EPISODES

The questioning of a holy man on ways of obtaining relief from trouble-
  some thoughts.
The hearing of a voice from heaven giving an answer to prayer.
The giving of signs from heaven as answers to prayer.

QUOTATIONS

1. They tell the story that on one occasion,
     when the blessed man Anthony was dwelling in the desert,
     thoughts of depression of mind rose in him
     and he was in great darkness of thought and he said to God:
     'Lord, I wish to live and my thoughts will not permit me.
     What shall I do in my afflictions to be saved?'

   BU.II.PAL.SY. 465.17

2. An old man was asked: '*Why, as I sit in my dwelling,*
     does my mind (heart) turn from side to side?'
     The old man answered: 'Because *thy outer senses are sick*:
     the sight, the hearing, the sense of smell, the speech.

344

If thou acquirest their working in purity,
the inner senses will be in peace and health.'

CHA.AP.PA.S. 2.19(5)

3. It was said of Abba Anthony that, *as he was sitting once in the desert,*
he was in stupefaction and affliction with the number of thoughts and he prayed to God.

AM.AP.ANT.B. 30.15

4. *He would say that the mental power of the soul increases when the sensations of the body are diminished.*

GAR.ANT.S. 12.3

5. Apa Daniel said: '*The more the body increases, the more the soul is weakened*
and the more the body is weakened, the more the soul increases.'

CHA.AP.PA.S. 12.14(54)

6. Abba Daniel said: 'If the body is strong, the soul withers. If the body withers, the soul is strong.' He also said: 'If the body is fat, the soul grows lean; if the body is lean, the soul grows fat.'

CHA.SA.L. 109(X)

7. *And when night came, the thoughts troubled him again.*
He took a basket, he put into it two measures of sand, he carried it.
He went round with it in the whole desert. (   )
He said: '*I am tiring him who troubles me,*
because indeed, unless I kill him, he brings me thoughts
(such as): "*Rise, go to a strange (place).*"'
When he had prolonged going round in the desert, he went into his cell,
his body being crushed.

AM.MAC.AL.B. 252.15

8. Abba Allois said: 'Unless a man say in his heart, Only I and God are in the world, he shall not find rest.' He also said: 'If a man wills, in one day he can come by the evening to a measure of divinity.'

CHA.SA.L. 132(XI)

9. Abba Evagrius said: 'While you sit in your cell, draw in your mind, and remember the day of your death, and then you will see your body mortifying. Think on the loss, feel the pain. Shrink from the

345

vanity of the world outside. Be retiring and careful to keep your vow of quiet, and you will not weaken. Remember the souls in hell. Meditate within on their condition, the bitter silence and the moaning, the fear and the strife, the waiting and the pain without relief, the tears that cannot cease to flow.

Weep and lament for the judgment of sinners, bring to life the grief they suffer; be afraid that you are hurrying towards the same condemnation.'

CHA.SA.L. 44(III)

10. Someone asked an old man: '*Why am I weary as I sit in my dwelling?*'

He answered: 'Because thou hast not yet considered the rest for which we hope,

or the punishment which is to come.

If thou hadst considered these with attention,

even if thy dwelling were filled with worms,

so that they reached to thy neck,

thou wouldst remain in their midst and endure them

and thou wouldst not be weary.'

CHA.AP.PA.S. 2.24(6)

11. The Mind which is freed from passions and sees the intellections of the beings, does not therefore truly receive the images which (come) through the senses. But it is as if another world was created by its science and it drew its thought to itself and it cast from itself the sensible world.

GU.EV.SY. 181.12(V)

12. In pure thought are imprinted a heaven splendid to see and a spacious region, in which are seen, as it were, the intellections of beings and the holy angels come to the presence of those who are worthy. And this vision which is imprinted, ill-will causes it to be seen obscurely, and anger, when it flares up, destroys it completely.

GU.EV.SY. 193.39(V)

13. The world which is built in thought is considered to be difficult to see by day because the Mind is drawn by the sense and by the sensible light which shines. But at night it is possible to see it when it is imprinted in light at the time of prayer.

GU.EV.SY. 195.42(V)

14. Thus at noon, the time when the brethren were wont to take food,
    the mind of this holy man was carried away, as it were in sleep,
    so that many of the brethren marvelled at his intention and his
        knowledge
    and they begged him many times to relate to them those things which
        he saw
    and entreated him to tell them concerning the wonder which had
        come upon him.
    But he was not persuaded.
    Then at last by the power of their love he was constrained
    and he answered and said to them:
    'My mind departed and was carried away by contemplation
    and I was caught up in the formation of a thought.
    And I was nourished with the food of glory,
    which is something impossible for me to describe.'

                                    BU.II.PAL.SY. 108.11

15. He (Polycarp) *went forth to a field at a distance from the city.*
    He stood there without any others and did nothing at all,
    but by day and night he remained alone in prayers to the Lord,
    these in which he begged and prayed,
    asking for peace for the Churches in the whole world.

                                    BA.HY.II.POL.SM.B. 64.8

16. It happened at the time that *our father Apa Shenute was in the cell*
        which is in the desert
    and he refrained from coming forth to the monastery,
    because he was praying concerning the waters of the river.

                                    LEI.SIN.B. 56.6

17. Il est pleinement évident pour tous ceux de là-bas que c'est par eux
    que le monde tient debout et à cause d'eux que le genre humain
    subsiste et garde quelque valeur aux yeux de Dieu.

                                    FE.IV/I.HIS.G. 8

18. Abba Dulas, the disciple of Abba Bessarion, said: 'I once went
    into the cell of my abba, and found him standing in prayer, with his
    hands stretched towards heaven. He stayed like that for fourteen
    days. At the end he called me and said: 'Follow me.' We went out
    and took our way through the desert. I grew thirsty, and said to
    him: 'Abba, I am thirsty.' He took off his cloak, and went away a

                                    347

stone's throw: and he prayed, and brought me the cloak full of water.

CHA.SA.L. 141(XII)

19. It was said of the blessed Abba Pisentius that he was speaking with the brothers, saying:
'Behold we perform services according to our powers,
we pray, we fast, but is God satisfied with us or not?
Now I will not cease from praying for His goodness
until I know whether He hears our prayers or not.' (   )
At the beginning of the fourteenth day, as he was standing praying
with all his attention firmly directed on high,
immediately a voice came to him saying:
'*Pisentius, thy prayer has been heard*
and that which thou hast requested from the Lord will happen to thee.
Thus a spring of water will rise at this place where thou art standing
and it will be a sign to all the generations to come after thee,
and it will be a source of healing to all who receive it in faith.'
And he was standing praying, the place opened below his feet;
it sent up water until his feet were drenched with water.

AM.PIS.KE.B. 413.7

20. And Cronius told this story also: 'In that night blessed Anthony told me this: "For a whole year I prayed that the place of the just and of sinners might be revealed to me. And I saw a tall giant reaching to the clouds, black, with his hands stretched up to heaven, and under him a lake as vast as the sea, and I saw souls flying like birds. And as many as flew over his hands and head were saved. But as many as were struck by his hands fell into the lake. Then came a voice to me saying: 'These souls of the righteous which thou seest flying, are the souls which are saved from Paradise. But the others are those which are drawn down to hell, having followed the desires of the flesh and revenge.'"'

LO.PAL.G. 95(XXI)

21. Vint de nouveau la voix, qui lui dit: 'Va, car tout ce que tu auras demandé à Dieu, tu l'obtiendras,'

FE.IV/I.HIS.G. 47(VIII)

22. Mais ce qu'il accomplissait par ses actes est plus grand encore; car tout ce qu'il demandait à Dieu dans ses prières lui était aussitôt accordé.

FE.IV/I.HIS.G. 51(VIII)

23. *His* (Daniel's) *memory and application were remarkable.*
    Of great gentleness, he was concerned over each word that he said
        with great accuracy.
    It was witnessed of him that, as he was meditating on Jeremiah the
        prophet,
    he struggled for a word, he remained distressed, wishing to know it
    because it would not be repeated unless he said it.
    At that moment the prophet answered him: 'I said it thus.'
CHA.AP.PA.S. 78.1(250)

24. They spoke concerning a certain elder
    who fasted for seventy weeks
    and only ate each Sabbath;
    and he asked from God that a word of Scripture should be given to
        him
    and it was not given.
    And he said these things to himself:
    'Behold I have laboured at all things and I have omitted nothing.
    I will arise and go to my brother and question him.'
    And when he shut the door,
    the angel of the Lord appeared to him and said to him: ( )
    'I was sent to make known to thee the word and to give thee rest.'
    And thus he informed him and caused him to rest and departed.
BU.II.PAL.SY. 565.23

25. Abba Nopi said to them: ( )
    'In my heart I have never had any other desire than that which is
        of God
    and God has not hidden from me any thing which is honourable or
        glorious.
    I have never been deprived of or lacked the light of my eyes,
    I have never slept in the daytime
    and at night I have never rested from supplication to God. ( )
    Every request I have received from God straight away.'
BU.II.HIER.SY. 418.10

26. He (Anthony) also had this favour;
    for, *as he sat alone on the mountain,*
    if a question to be solved came to him
    and he was at a loss about it,
    Providence would reveal it to him, as he prayed.
GAR.ANT.S. 71.25

27. 'Angels descended and ascended in my presence.
I saw the realms of the Kingdom
and the habitations of the souls of the righteous.
I saw the Paradise of God.
He showed me that tree from which Adam and Eve ate.
I saw Enoch and Elijah in the Land of the Living
There was nothing which I sought from God which He did not
show me.'

LOOK.MAR.SY. 11.4

28. *The old men ( ) knew that he was elevated in his life. ( )*
They said: 'Let us pray to God this week about this mystery
and we believe that God will reveal it to us.'
Immediately God heard him.

CHA.AP.PA.S. 40.8(175)

29. And the blessed Cyril, the Archbishop of Alexandria ( ) knew
that the old man was able to perform signs
and that everything which he asked Him, the Lord revealed to him. ( )
The old man, confident of his attitude, said with confidence:
'*Allow me three days*
and I will pray the Lord because of this.'

CHA.AP.PA.S. 41.23(176)

30. And when he had prayed for about three hours
and had entreated God much concerning this,
suddenly there was sent from heaven into his right hand
something like a letter, written on paper.

BU.II.PAL.SY. 334.4

2 ATTAINMENT

THEMES

The recognition of attainment in a holy man.
The designation of one who has attained as 'A Perfect One.'
The humility of those who have attained.
The heavenly manifestations consequent on attainment.

EPISODES

The revelation in answer to prayer of the spiritual status of a holy man.
The bodily appearance of a holy man as a sign of his attainment.
The visit of the fathers to test the spiritual status of a holy man.

QUOTATIONS

1. There were two hermits in the desert who were in equality with one
      another

   and they led a life of virtuous asceticism and exalted practices.

   Then it happened that one of them was called to be Archimandrite
      of a monastery of the brethren,

   but the other remained in the desert

   and he became perfected in asceticism.

   And he was found worthy by God of a gift

   and he healed those possessed of devils,

   and he knew beforehand things that would happen

   and he healed the sick.

   And when he who was Archimandrite heard these things,

   he decided in his mind that this hermit had attained these things
      suddenly.

   And he also became silent and ceased from conversation with men
      for three weeks

   and he besought God continually that He would show him how he
      performed these mighty things. (   )

   And an angel appeared to him and said to him: 'He dwells in

   and makes supplication to God by night and by day

   and his pain and his personal care are for our Lord,

   but thou hast care for many things and thou hast conversation with
      many.

   The consolation and encouragement of men are sufficient for
      thee.'

BU.II.PAL.SY. 433.20

2. When Abba Sisoes was about to die and the fathers were sitting in
      his presence,

   they saw that his face was shining like the sun;

   and he said to them immediately: 'Behold, Abba Anthony has
      come.'

   And again after a little time he said: 'Behold the company of pro-
      phets has come.'

   And his face shone again

   and he said: 'Behold the company of the apostles has come.'

   And again his face shone twice as much

   and he became suddenly like one who was speaking with somebody.

   And the old men who were seated entreated him and they said to
      him:

   'Show us with whom thou art speaking, our father.'

351

He then immediately said to them: 'Behold the angels came to take me away

and I besought them to leave me, that I should tarry a little and repent.'

And the old men said to him: 'Thou hast no need to repent, our father.'

The old man said to them: 'I am not sure in my soul that I have rightly begun to repent.'

And they all learned that the old man was perfect.

And again, suddenly, his face shone like the sun,

and all those seated were afraid,

and he said to them suddenly: 'See, see, behold, Our Lord has come

and He says: "Bring to me the chosen vessel which is in the desert."'

And immediately he delivered up his spirit and there was lightning and the whole place was filled with sweet perfume.

BU.II.PAL.SY. 643.13

3. Once one of the brethren went to the cell of Abba Arsenius in Scete

and he looked through the window

and he saw the old man standing up and all of him was like fire;

for that brother was worthy to see this which he saw.

And, when he knocked, the old man came forth to him

and he saw that brother marvelling at the sight which he saw

and he said to him: 'Is it a long time that thou hast knocked?

Perhaps thou hast seen something.'

And he said to him: 'No.'

And he spoke with him and dismissed him.

BU.II.PAL.SY. 608.22

4. A brother went to the cell of Apa Arsenius in Shiet

and he observed him through a window.

He saw the old man completely on fire.

The brother was worthy to see

and when he knocked, the old man came out.

He saw the brother who was in amazement, and he said to him:

'Thou didst delay to knock. Didst thou see anything?'

The brother said: 'No.'

And he spoke to him. He left him.

CHA.AP.PA.S. 39.4(174)

5. *And afterwards, behold I will appear to thee again and thou shalt become a perfect one.*

'I will manifest myself to thee, I will speak to thee, mouth to mouth,'
saith the Lord God.

AM.MAC.SC.B. 58.5

6. Once when Abba Zachariah was dwelling in Scete,
   there appeared to him a vision from God.
   And he rose and came to his father, Abba Kurion.
   And the old man was perfect
   and he did not seek to be celebrated for these things.
   And he rose up and smote him.

BU.II.PAL.SY. 687.21

7. Then his master went forth on Sunday,
   in order to go in the morning to the Church.
   And as he turned, he looked at the place in which was the holy man,
      John.
   He saw seven angels, shining with light,
   carrying seven crowns of light
   and they were flying above the head of the holy man, John,
   and they were crowning him, one after the other and rising up.
   When the old man saw this great and wonderful vision,
   he ran with great joy and he embraced Abba John with love
   and he gave him the holy and spiritual Peace,
   he received him and made him enter the cell.
   From thenceforward, from these things, he held him to be a father
      and an elder.

NAU.JE.PE.SY. XVIII.15

8. It was said concerning Abba John that, when he was asleep one day,
   it happened that an elder came to his cell for a (certain) reason, he
   saw an angel of the Lord standing above the head of Abba John,
      guarding him.
   Then when Abba John awoke from his sleep,
   he asked his disciple by the divine knowledge which he had, saying:
   'Perhaps someone came here while I was asleep?'
   Then he said: 'Yes my lord, a certain elder came here.'
   Then the holy man, John, knew that the elder who had come, had
      seen the angel,
   because he was perfect and he had reached the stature of Abba
      John.

NAU.JE.PE.SY. XLIII.4

353

9. Afterwards his father rose and he took two of the fathers with him
   and they went to his cell.
   While they were on the road, they said to one another:
   'Know this that if he recalls to us what the father has done to him,
   he is like one of us.
   If not, it is certain that he is perfect
   and more elevated than all of us.'
   When they arrived at his cell, from it there reached them a sweet
      smell
   and they heard the voices of angels who were praising God. ( )
   The holy man John was standing in their midst, praising God.
   Then the fathers were astonished
   and they stood considering the greatness of the vision.
   And after an hour they awoke as if from sleep,
   and they knocked on the door of the cell.
   And the holy man John, came forth immediately in their presence,
   while his face was shining in the likeness of a seraphim.
   Then these fathers began to speak conciliatory words to him
   to make him think again on what the elder had done to him. ( )
   Then the holy man remained with his face turned towards the ground
      and he was silent.
   Then his father said to him: 'What is this? Dost thou not answer
      me?'
   The holy man, as if by the inspiration of the Holy Spirit which was
      in him,
   answered in a humble voice and said:
   'Forgive me, my fathers, because I know nothing of what you tell
      me at all.'

   NAU.JE.PE.SY. XXII.1

10. For every petition which he asked of God was immediately granted
       to him.
    And visions also appeared to him: for once he saw his brother,
    who was older than him and who had also completed his life in the
       desert,
    and his ascetic practices were greater than his
    and for a long time he had lived with him in the desert.
    He saw, as if in a dream, that he was a fellow-assessor with the
       apostles
    and that God had caused him to be an inheritor of glory.
    And, as it were, he was begging and entreating God
    that He would bring about his departure speedily,

that he might rest with him in heaven and it was said to him by our
Redeemer:
'For a short time it is necessary that Apollo should live upon the
earth,
until many shall become perfect through emulation of his glorious
deeds;
for he is prepared to be given charge over a great population of
monks
and those who cultivate righteousness,
so that he may receive glory in accordance with his labours.'

BU.II.HIER.SY. 380.5

3 VISION

THEMES

The desire to keep the mind concentrated on the vision of heaven.
The vision of Paradise and the saints and the vision of Hell.
The effect of improper thoughts and actions on the vision of heaven.
The reluctance of holy men to tell their visions.

EPISODES

The interruption of meditation by demons.
The relating by a holy man of his visions of Paradise and Hell.
The appearance of signs from heaven revealing the spiritual status of
holy men.
The visit of a disciple to a holy man who was at that time receiving a
revelation.

QUOTATIONS

1. Then he (Macarius) said: 'Every practice and rule of life
   of self denial and fasting which I have desired,
   I have fulfilled.
   And there came to me this wish,
   that for only five days my mind should be with God in heaven,
   while I should be raised from the affliction of worldly thoughts.
   And when I had meditated on this, I shut the door of the courtyard
   and of the cell.
   And I constrained myself that I should not give an answer to any
   man.
   And I continued thus and I began on the second day of the week
   and I commanded my mind and I said to it:
   "Thou shalt not descend from heaven, for behold, there thou hast
   angels

and the chief of angels and all the hosts which are in heaven
and especially the good and gracious God, the Lord of all.
Thou shalt not come down from heaven."
And I continued and I was sufficient for this thing for two days and
   two nights.
And I constrained the Evil One thus,
so that he became a flame of fire
and he burnt everything which I had in my cell,
until even the mat upon which I stood blazed with fire
and I thought that I should be completely burnt.
At last the fear of the fire took hold of me,
my mind descended from heaven on the third day,
because I was not able to keep my mind thus collected
and I descended to the vision of the world and its affairs;
and this happened that I should not boast.'

BU.II.PAL.SY. 150.2

2. On another occasion he told us this story: 'Having perfected every
kind of life that I desired, then I had another desire. I desired to
keep my mind for five days only undistracted from (the contemplation of) God. And, having determined this, I barred the cell and
enclosure, so as not to have to answer to any man, and I took my
stand, beginning at the second hour. So I gave this commandment
to my mind: "Do not descend from heaven, there you have angels,
archangels, the powers on high, the God of all; do not descend below heaven."
And having lasted out two days and two nights, I exasperated the
demon so that he became a flame of fire and burned up all the
things in the cell, so that even the little mat on which I stood was
consumed with fire and I thought I was being all burned up.
Finally stricken with fear, I left off on the third day, being unable
to keep my mind free from distraction, but I descended to contemplation of the world lest vanity be imputed to me.'

LO.PAL.G. 82(XVIII)

3. '*I wished to spend five days*
with my heart concentrated on God at all times,
so that it pays no attention to anything in the path of this world.
As I promised this in my heart, *I went into the cell which is in the*
   inner desert,
which has no door or window,
in which there is no light,

356

so that it is not possible for a man to find me.
And I stood upon the mat in the cell
and I concentrated my thoughts, saying thus: 'Guard thyself, do
not come down from heaven.
Thou hast there the patriarchs and the prophets
and the archangels and the powers who are above
and the cherubim and the seraphim.
Join thyself to God the Father and the Only-Begotten Son and the
Holy Spirit,
the Consubstantial Trinity, God of the Gods, the King of all the
aeons.
Mount thyself upon the Cross of the Son, which is in heaven.
Do not come down from the place of victory."'
And he said: 'When I had spent two days and two nights,
the demons were maddened, so that they changed in a multitude of
phantasies.
Many times they were in the likenesses of lions attacking my feet with
their claws,
many times they were like serpents, twisting round my feet.
At last they became like a flame of fire
and they burnt everything which was in the cell and the mat on which
I stood.
They were all burnt, except my two sandals alone.
Then I thought that I should burn also ( )
and on the fourth day I was not able to fix my thoughts without
taking them down
and I came down into the sights and the cares of this human aeon.
For I have understood that, if I had succeeded until I completed
this task,
I would have destroyed my reason and suffered madness.
Because of this, I came to rest in my heart among the cares of this
world. ( )
I spent forty years in asceticism, I never suffered like these days.'

AM.MAC.AL.B. 245.2

4. Il raconta un jour aux frères que, revenant du désert, il avait été
enlevé, en vision, aux cieux et qu'il y avait vu toutes les bonnes
choses qui attendent les vrais moines, et que nul discours ne peut
rendre. Et il dit aussi qu'il avait été transporté corporellement au
paradis et qu'il y avait vu une foule de saints. Il avait goûté,
disait-il, aux fruits du paradis, et, de la réalité du fait, il donnait
une preuve: il avait rapporté en effet à ses disciples une figue

énorme, extraordinaire, remplie d'un riche parfum, et il leur montrait par là que son récit etait vrai.

FE.IV/I.HIS.G. 73(X)

5. And they said that many wonders were performed by him
and they testified about him
that, on many occasions, he walked upon the water.
And further, he was found in an upper room with the brothers,
having risen, although the doors were shut
and he came to them in the air, by the speed of the angels.
And they also said that everything which he asked from God, he
    was able (to do)
and at all times he was able to go wherever he wished, without
    trouble.
And the blessed man Petarpemotis once related to the brethren
how once he went forth from the desert
and he saw in his dream,
as if he had been taken up to heaven
and he saw there the good things, which had been prepared for the
    monks,
of which it is not possible to speak, nor could they be described by
    the mouths of men.
And he also said: 'I saw Paradise with the eyes of this body
and I saw there many multitudes of saints
and I tasted the fruits of Paradise.'

BU.II.HIER.SY. 413.4

6. Abbâ Anouph leur dit: 'Béni soit Dieu, qui m'a fait connaître cela à moi aussi, ainsi que votre visite et votre genre de vie.' Il dit alors les accomplissements de chacun, puis décrivit aussi les siens, en ces termes: 'Du jour où j'ai confessé le nom du Sauveur sur la terre, nul mensonge n'est sorti de ma bouche. Rien de terrestre ne m'a sustenté, car un ange me nourrit chaque jour de l'aliment céleste. Il n'est monté à mon coeur désir de rien d'autre que de Dieu. Dieu n'a rien caché des choses terrestres, qu'il ne me l'ait révélé. La lumière n'a cessé de briller a mes yeux. Je n'ai point dormi le jour, je ne me suis pas arrêté la nuit de chercher Dieu, un ange m'était toujours présent qui me désignait les puissances du monde. La lumière spirituelle en moi ne s'est jamais éteinte. Tout ce que j'ai demandé à mon Dieu, je l'ai aussitôt obtenu. J'ai vu souvent des myriades d'anges assistant Dieu; j'ai vu les chœurs des justes; j'ai vu les corporations des moines; j'ai vu la foule compacte des martyrs; j'ai vu l'office de tous ceux qui chantent la

louange de Dieu. J'ai vu Satan livré au feu; j'ai vu ses anges en
proie au châtiment; j'ai vu les justes jouissant d'une béatitude
éternelle.'

FE.IV/I.HIS.G. 79(XI)

7. And while the old man was sitting alone, he was rapt and was
shown a vision of a glorious place, and a throne in it, and on the
throne seven crowns. And he asked the angel who showed the
vision: 'Whose are those?' And he said: 'They are the crowns of
your disciple; God has given him this place and throne because of
his goodness; tonight he has been granted these seven crowns.'

CHA.SA.L. 95(VII)

8. It happened once that a certain heathen priest came to Scete
and he came to the cell of one of the brethren and passed the night
there.
And he saw the labours of his way of life and he marvelled and he
said to him:
'Do you labour thus and yet do not see visions from your God?'
That brother said to him: 'We do not see (visions).'
That priest said to him: 'When we serve as priests our God, he
hides nothing from us,
but he reveals to us his mysteries,
and you who have your labours of vigil and abstinence and silent
contemplation,
you say that you see nothing.
There are evil thoughts in your hearts and they separate you from
your God
and for this reason he does not reveal to you his mysteries.'
Then the brother went and informed the elders of the word(s) of
that priest
and they marvelled and said: 'It is thus;
for thoughts which are not pure separate a man from God.'

BU.II.PAL.SY. 618.4

9. One of the old men (   ) *saw his way of life and said to him:*
'*Do you not see anything through your God?*'
And he said to him: 'No.'
The priest said: 'We perform small liturgies *and the mysteries are
revealed to us.*
*And you do these kinds of works, nights of vigils and austerities and
solitude,*

and you say: "We have no evil thoughts in our hearts."
And (yet) that is what separates you from your God *so that he does
not reveal to you his mysteries.'*

CHA.AP.PA.S. 18.21(90)

10. *You, my brothers, seek after calmness at all times,
so that you can exercise yourselves to see those of heaven.*

TIL.I.JOH.LY.S. 139.14

11. One of the elders said: 'Once the fathers were sitting and speaking
on profitable matters
and there was in their midst one of the elders and he saw visions.
And he saw angels flying above them.
And when they came to another subject, the angels departed from
thence
and he saw pigs rolling about among them and wallowing in the mire.
And afterwards they began to speak on profitable things
and then the angels came again and they glorified God.'

BU.II.PAL.SY. 612.11

12. He said to his son: 'If thou hadst continued these forty days and
kept my commandment,
to thee it would be that thou wouldst have seen a vision of something
more excellent.'

BU.II.PAL.SY. 593.9

13. *Apa Isidorus said to him: 'Look to the East';
and he looked, he saw innumerable multitudes in glory.*

CHA.AP.PA.S. 45.25(184)

14. *It was revealed to Apa Anthony in the desert*
that there was one who resembled him in the city,
who was a physician by profession,
who gave most (of his money) to those in need
and he would spend the whole day saying the Trisagion with angels.

CHA.AP.PA.S. 39.1(172)

15. During all these things which the Saviour said to the holy Apa
Anub,
*He caused the eyes of Julius to be opened.
He saw the Saviour saying all these words to the holy Apa Anub.*

BA.HY.I.AN.B. 236.25

16. Apa Zacharias, the disciple of Apa Sylvanus, came once in to him.
    He found him in ecstasy
    with his hands outstretched to heaven;
    and he closed the door, he came out.
    He went in again at the sixth hour and the ninth. He found him
    again in this (state).
    When the tenth hour came, *he knocked and entered in.*
    He found him resting.
    He said to him: 'What hast thou today, my father?'
    He said to him: 'My son, I was sick today.'
    But he seized his feet, saying; 'I will not leave thee if thou dost not
    tell me what thou didst see.'
    The old man said to him: '*I was taken to heaven*
    and I saw the glory of God,
    and I stood there till now and I was released now.'

    > CHA.AP.PA.S. 50.8(193)

17. On another occasion there came to him (Abba Sylvanus) his dis-
    ciple Zachariah
    and found him in a trance of prayer,
    and his hands were raised to heaven.
    And he went forth and closed the door,
    and he came again at the ninth hour
    and found him thus, and again at the tenth hour he found him thus.
    He knocked and entered and found him in (a state of) silence.
    And he said to him: 'What hast thou today, our father?'
    Then he said to him: 'My son I lost my strength.'
    Then he laid hold of his feet, saying: 'I will not leave thee
    until thou dost tell me what thou hast seen.'
    The old man said to him: 'Swear to me that thou wilt not reveal
    (this) to any man
    until I go forth from the body and I will tell thee.'
    And he entreated him and the old man said to him: 'I was snatched
    up into heaven
    and I saw the glory of God and just now I was dismissed.'

    > BU.II.PAL.SY. 674.4

18. While Abba Sylvanus was sitting
    and the brethren were in his presence
    he (was) in a trance which was from the presence of God
    and he fell upon his face
    and after a long time, when he arose, he wept

and the brethren entreated him and they said to him:
'What hast thou, our father?'
But he held his peace
and they continued to persuade and constrained him to tell them.
And he answered and said to them:
'I have just been snatched away to the place of judgment of God
and I saw many from our order, (namely) Christians,
who were going to punishment and many from the world going to
    the Kingdom.'
And the old man mourned and did not wish to go forth from his
    cell.
And he covered his face with his cloak, saying:
'Why should I seek to see the light of a time in which there is no
    profit?'

BU.II.PAL.SY. 673.19

19. They said of Abba Sisois that, unless he soon lowered his hands
when he stood up to pray, his mind was snatched up into the
heavenly places. So if he happened to be praying with another
brother, he quickly lowered his hands and ended the prayer, so that
his mind should not be rapt or remain in prayer too long for his
brother.

CHA.SA.L. 143(XII)

20. One day a certain hermit, who saw (things) in the spirit,
descended to the town to buy food.

BRO.EP.SY. 31.12

21. And he (Thomas) thereupon made himself a small hut of planks
and in it he carried out the great labour of his secret practices,
while he laid down for himself absolutely not to taste either bread
    or wine, ( )
so that he was granted the gift of secret vision.

BR.THOM.SY. 297.7

22. And some of them possessed divine vision
and others, virtues of asceticism.

BU.II.HIER.SY. 423.19

23. They said that one of the elders asked God
that he might see the fathers.
And he saw them with the exception of Abba Anthony.

362

He said to him who showed him: 'Where is Abba Anthony?'
He said to him: 'Wherever God is, there is Anthony.'

BU.II.PAL.SY. 628.21

24. Tabennesi is a place (   ), in which there lived a certain Pachomius, one of those who have lived in the straight way, so that he was counted worthy both of prophecies and angelic visions.

LO.PAL.G. 112(XXXII)

25. And there was also another solitary monk in a distant part of the desert. (   )
He was girded with compassion all his days;
and he excelled greatly in prayers
and in praises and in numbers of visions.
And spiritual revelations were manifested to him so exactly,
some of them in visions and some in dreams,
that he was able to walk in the footsteps of those without bodies.

BU.II.HIER.SY. 361.7

26. So great a knowledge had he of the Holy Scriptures and the divine precepts that even at the very meals of the brethren he would have periods of absent-mindedness and remain silent. And, being urged to tell the details of his ecstasy, he would say: 'I went away in thought on a journey, seized by contemplation.' For my part I often knew him weep at table and, when I asked the cause of the tears, I heard him say: 'I shrink from partaking of irrational food, being myself rational and destined to live in a paradise of delight owing to the power given us by Christ.'

LO.PAL.G. 47(I)

27. 'Rise, therefore, from sleep and go upon thy way in peace
and take good heed of those things which thou has heard and those
that have been said to thee; (   )
and see that thou dost not say anything of this vision, which thou hast
seen, for a time.'

AM.MAC.SC.B. 58.3

4   GIFTS

(i) PROPHECY

THEMES

The granting to a holy man of the gift of prophecy.
The prediction of the future destruction of monastic and church life.

The prediction of the future sufferings of Christians.

The prediction of the future decay or spread of the teachings.

The prediction of the future punishments of the Christians in the next life.

The prediction of future events in the world.

The knowledge of events at a distance.

EPISODES

The appearance, growing from the tongue, of a vine which filled the earth.

The distress to a holy man caused by the sight of Christians undergoing punishment after death.

The distress caused to a holy man by the sight of the future assaults against the Church.

The inability to cross a river of a monk without wings of fire.

The revelation of future events in answer to prayer.

QUOTATIONS

1. It was said concerning Abba Jean, the holy man,
   that he was elevated to the place of future and secret things
   and he revealed those which are hidden from men
   and with a prophetic eye he saw everything from afar.
   What would happen, he spoke of in parables on the future, and what would come.
   He pronounced and spoke many powerful words
   from the books inspired by God and from his pure intelligence.

   NAU.JE.PE.SY. XLIV.11

2. Having completed thirty years thus immured (   ), he was counted worthy of the gift of predictions.

   LO.PAL.G. 120(XXXV)

3. *And he (John) was worthy of this gift of grace,*
   that he knew things which were ordained to happen before they happened.

   TIL.I.JOH.LY.S. 141.9

4. (Our holy father) bore witness beforehand
   concerning those things prepared to happen to me.

   BU.II.PAL.SY. 285.19

5. To one of his disciples he made known by prophecy
   that which would happen to him after eighteen years;
   and what he said came to him.

BU.II.PAL.SY. 279.11

6. Il accomplissait un très grand nombre de miracles et passait chez
   ces gens-là pour prophète.

FE.IV/I.HIS.G. 41(VI)

7. Nous avons vu aussi dans le désert d'Antinooupolis, métropole de
   la Thébaïde, un autre vieillard, du nom d'Elie, agé maintenant de
   cent dix ans; l'esprit du prophète Elie était, disait-on, reposé sur
   lui. Il etait célèbre pour avoir passé soixante-dix ans dans ce
   terrible désert.

FE.IV/I.HIS.G. 44(VII)

8. After three days, before they were completed,
   a vision appeared to him at night as he prayed,
   so that he saw his garment which he was wearing burning at once
   as if it was being burnt by a fire.
   And when he rose quickly he told the vision to those who were near
       him.
   He first foretold to them what would happen to him
   and he told them with firmness that *the end of his life would be by
       fire, for the sake of Christ.*

BA.HY.II.POL.SM.B. 64.14

9. And when we had prayed, we sat and we spoke of the glory of the
       progress according to God,
   together with the way of life which is good
   and the establishment of the practice which is in Shiet.
   And after this, Abba Macarius answered, he said: 'My brothers,
   one of you seven will end (life) in the field of martyrdom
   and another seven brethren will end (life) similarly with him.'

AM.VER.MAC.B. 187.1

10. When the blessed Ephraim was a young boy,
    he saw in a dream or a vision
    a grape vine growing in his tongue.
    And it grew, it filled the whole earth under the heaven,
    its fruits being very good; and all the birds of heaven came, they
        ate its fruit.

And what was eaten from the grape vine would cause it to increase
the more abundantly.

CHA.AP.PA.S. 42.6(177)

11. It is said concerning him (Ephraim), that when he was young,
he saw a dream, that is to say, a vision,
wherein a vine grew in his tongue and it increased in size
and it filled everything beneath the heavens
and it bore bunches of grapes abundantly.
And all the birds of the heavens came and ate from its fruit.
And while they were eating,
the grape bunches increased in number and size.

BU.II.PAL.SY. 225.23

12. For this story was told concerning the holy Mar Ephraim, that when
he was a small boy,
he saw a dream, that is to say, a vision,
which men relate and which is also written in his testament,
that there was a vine shoot in his tongue
and it grew and it filled with itself everything beneath the heavens.
And it bore clusters of grapes in abundance.
And the birds of the air came and ate
and its clusters of grapes became increasingly more.

BRO.EP.SY. 29.14

13. *For many times, as he* (Anthony) *was sitting upon the mountain,*
he would know what was happening in Egypt,
and he would tell the Bishop Sarapion, as he was with him in the
mountain.
It happened one day, *as he was sitting working,*
he was in an ecstasy and he groaned greatly while he was seeing the
vision.
After some time he turned to the brothers, groaning, and he was
afraid.
He rose, he prayed.
He knelt down and (as) the old man rose he was weeping.
Those who were with him were shaken and they feared greatly.
They asked him to tell them what he had seen,
and they constrained him by force until he told them what he had
seen.
He said to them in great sorrow: 'My sons, it is preferable to me to
die

366

before those things happen which I saw.'
They asked him further to tell them.
He wept, he said to them: 'Wrath will strike the Church
and she will be given into the hands of men who are like beasts.
For I saw the Church, with mules standing in her,
surrounding her on all sides and kicking those that were in that
    place,
like the beasts as they leap and run wild.
You surely felt when I groaned.
*I heard a voice saying: "*My altar will be desecrated."'
The God-loving old man saw these things.
After two years, the Arians assaulted the Church, they robbed her,
they stole the vessels that were in her by force.
They caused the heathen to take them away.
They compelled multitudes of those who work to hold services
    there.

GAR.ANT.S. 87.23

14. *Now, when the multitude who were gathered to him had heard these*
    things,
  they cried together in a loud voice. ( )
  Then the God-loving old man became silent,
  he drew up the robe, he covered his face. ( )
  But the angel of his father came to him,
  he took him up to the heavens.
  And in fear and consternation he saw a multitude
  divided to this side and that,
  after the manner of the last day,
  and it was a great consternation to see them.

GUI.IS.B. 235.18

15. Abba Silvanus was sitting one day among the brethren, and was
    seized into a rapture of mind, and fell upon his face. And after a
    while he rose up and lamented. And the brothers asked him:
    'What is the matter, Father?' But he was silent and wept. When
    they pressed him for an answer, he said to them: 'I was taken before
    the Judgment seat, and I saw many of our cloth going down to
    torment, and many of the world going into the Kingdom.' And the
    old man grieved and would not leave his cell: and if he was forced
    to go out, he covered his face with his shawl and said: 'Why should
    I have to see the light of this world, wherein nothing is profitable?'

CHA.SA.L. 46(III)

16. And he answered and said to them:
'I have just been snatched away to the place of Judgment of God
and I saw many from our order, (namely) Christians, who were
going to punishment
and many from the world going to the Kingdom.' ( )
And he covered his face with his cloak, saying:
'Why should I seek the light of a time in which there is no profit?'

BU.II.PAL.SY. 673.23

17. Apa John told that *one of the old men saw in a vision*
three monks standing on the shore of the sea
and a voice came to them on the bank saying:
'*Take wings of fire and come to me.*'
And two of them took wings, they flew until they reached the other
bank.
But the other remained behind weeping and crying out.
At last he was given wings,
but they were not of fire but *weak and powerless*,
and he flew with difficulty, plunging and rising up
and with great difficulty he reached the bank.
This is also the way of this generation.
Even if they have received wings, they are not of fire
and they just receive ones *which are weak and powerless*.

CHA.AP.PA.S. 43.11(180)

18. Abba John said that one of the elders saw in a vision,
while he was in a trance.
And behold, three monks were standing by the shore of a lake
and a voice from heaven came to them from the other side,
which said; 'Take for yourselves wings of fire and come to me.'
And two of them took wings of fire and flew to the other side,
as it was told them.
Then the other one remained behind
and he wept much and cried out;
and at last wings were given to him also.
They were not of fire, like those of his fellows
but they were weak and feeble.
And with great labour, while sinking and rising with no small
exertions, he reached the shore.
And thus also this generation, it takes wings
and they are not powerful ones of fire,
but by necessity, it takes weak and feeble ones.

BU.II.PAL.SY. 626.14

19. Then it was revealed to the holy man, Abba John,
    by the Holy Spirit which dwelt in him,
    in a remarkable mystery
    and he saw with his eyes lighted by his intelligence,
    the age in which the holy fathers lived
    together with the fulness and the perfection,
    the zeal and the strong faith which they possessed.
    And, as if in a prophecy, he looked and he saw the faintness
    and the negligence and the spiritual disgust
    of those who would come after them in the last age.
    He thought of a comparison for this
    and he said, as he signified that it was himself:
    'An old man saw three monks who were standing at a crossing
    place of the sea
    and a voice was heard by them coming from the other side saying:
    "Each take two wings of fire for yourselves and cross over to me."
    Two of them did so and they made the crossing
    and reached him who called them,
    The other remained complaining and crying alone, agitated and
        afflicted.
    At last he was given wings
    but they were not of fire and they were very weak and they had no
        power,
    and after great dangers, sometimes immersed and sometimes
        rising,
    at last with great difficulty he was able to make the crossing.
    Thus it is with this last generation.
    They will not pass with wings of fire in the manner of the holy
        fathers.'

                              NAU.JE.PE.SY. XXIV.11

20. Nous avons donc vu dans le territoire de Lyco en Thébaïde le grand
    et bienheureux Jean, homme vraiment saint et vertueux, qui, par
    ses opérations, se montra manifestement à tous doué du don de pro-
    phétie. Il annonçait d'avance au très pieux empereur Théodose tout
    ce qui devait, par la volonté de Dieu, arriver au monde et il lui
    prédisait derechef ce qui en devait résulter.

                              FE.IV/HIS.G. 9(I)

21. Our father Pachomius was once with the brethren during the harvest
        of rushes,
    when they were coming to the boat one day all laden with rushes,

walking behind our father Pachomius, meditating.
And when they came to the middle of the road,
our father Pachomius looked up to heaven, he saw a great vision.
Afterwards he cast away his burden of rushes with the brothers,
　　they stood praying.
The man of God stood amazed at the great sight of the glorious vision
　　which he had seen
and he cast himself upon his face, he wept for a long time
while the brothers also shed many tears in great weeping.
When he rose after his prostration upon the earth, the brethren
　　asked him:
'Say to us, what thou hast seen, O our father.'
He sat, he spoke with them in the words of God, and he said to them:
'*I saw the whole gathering of the congregation in great distress.*
Some were surrounded by a great flame and were not able to cross.
Others were in the midst of thorns while spines pierced them,
and there was no means for them to come forth.
Others were at the bottom of a high cliff, suffering and afflicted
and unable to go up because of the painful steepness of the cliff.
And they were unable to jump in the river
because of the crocodiles which waited for them.
Now my sons, woe is me, *because after my death these things will*
　　happen to the brothers.'

LE.PAC.S. 232.11

22. Our father Pachomius was once with the brethren at the harvest of
　　the rushes
　　and, when they were coming to the boat one day, they were all
　　　laden with rushes,
　　walking after our father Pachomius, meditating on the holy Scrip-
　　　tures.
　　And, when he reached the middle of the path,
　　he looked up to heaven, he saw a great vision.
　　Afterwards he cast away his burden of rushes with the brothers.
　　　They stood, they prayed.
　　The man of God Pachomius, *as he stood,*
　　he was amazed at the great sight of the fearful vision which he saw.
　　And he cast himself on his face, he stood weeping for a long time.
　　The brothers also wept with him with a great weeping.
　　When he rose from his prostration on the ground the brothers
　　　asked him:
　　'Tell us what thou hast seen, our father.'

He then sat. He spoke with them with the words of God. And he said
  to them:
'*I saw the whole gathering of the congregation in great distress.*
Some were surrounded by a great flame of fire, unable to cross over.
Others were in the midst of thorns, with spines piercing them,
with no means to come forth.
Others were at the bottom of a great deep pit
where they were suffering and afflicted
and they could not come up because of the height of that cliff.
And they were not able to cast themselves into the river
because of the crocodiles which awaited them.
Now my sons, woe is me because *I think that after my death*
all these things will happen to the brethren.'
Then he rose, he prayed, he picked up his burden of rushes.
The brethren also carried their loads,
meditating, until they come to the boat.

LE.PAC.B. 66.20

23. And it happened that when it was necessary that Apa Pachomius
    and the brothers with him should return to the boat, ( )
    he looked with his eyes, he saw a fearful vision.
    For he looked, and behold, some of the brothers were in the mouths of
      wild beasts,
    others were in the mouths of crocodiles
    and others were in the midst of a fire.
    Others were at the bottom of cliffs wishing to come up and unable.
    And they cried out in this affliction saying: 'Help us.'
    When he saw them all in this great affliction,
    he cast away the burden of reeds which he was carrying in the middle
      of the road,
    he stood there, he stretched out his hands,
    he cried out with a great voice, he prayed,
    beseeching God about them,
    And it happened that, when each of the brothers came up to him
      laden,
    they threw away their burdens and prayed,
    and they remained thus, praying until evening ( ).
    (He said that *what*) *he saw would happen to the brothers after his*
      death.

LE.PAC.S. 56a.23

24. For you remember in the time when he was with us,
    the manner in which it was revealed to him by the Lord

all those things which have happened to us today, before they hap-
    pened,
how the Lord opened his eyes in a vision so that he saw most of the
    brothers,
some in the mouths of crocodiles,
others in a fire,
and some in the mouths of beasts,
and others about to be wrecked in the middle of the river,
calling out and seeking for help.
And immediately he stood,
he prayed for the salvation of those he saw in danger.

LE.PAC.S. 275.25

25. Then he saw an endless congregation of brethren
    who were travelling in a deep and gloomy valley
    and many came to ascend from the valley and they were not able.
    And many met one another face to face and did not recognise (each
        other)
    because of the great intensity of the darkness.
    And there were many who fell down from exhaustion
    and others who cried out with lamenting voices.
    And a few of them with difficulty and toil were able to ascend from
        that valley,
    and when they had risen up, immediately the light met them.
    And when they came to the light, they praised God greatly.

BU.II.PAL.SY. 316.4

26. *It was said of a great old man of Shiet*
    that at the time when the brethren were building,
    he would go forth rejoicing and he would lay the foundations
    and would not withdraw until he had finished.
    He went forth once to build a cell,
    He was very sorrowful and the brothers said to him:
    'Why art thou sorrowful and troubled, O father?'
    He said: 'My sons, this place will be desecrated;
    for I saw a fire burning in Shiet
    and the brothers were taking palm branches and they beat upon it,
    they extinguished it ( ) and the fire relit for the third time
    and it filled the whole of Shiet and they were not able to extinguish
        it.
    Because of this I am sorrowful and troubled.'

CHA.AP.PA.S. 51.8(198)

27. They said concerning a great elder who lived in Scete,
    that whenever the brethren were building cells in Scete,
    he would go out and lay the foundation
    and he did not depart until it was completed.
    On one occasion when he went forth to build
    he was greatly afflicted and grieved
    and the brethren said to him: 'Why art thou thus sad and sorry
       Abba?'
    Then he said to them: 'My sons this place will be laid waste
    for I have seen a fire kindled in Scete,
    and the brethren took palm branches and beat upon it until they
       extinguished it.
    And again it broke out and the brethren took palm branches and
       extinguished it.
    And then it broke out a third time and it filled all Scete
    and thenceforth the brethren were not able to extinguish it.
    For this reason I am grieved and sad.'

                                        BU.II.PAL.SY. 666.3

28. As the brethren were sitting before him (? Apa Moses), he said to
       them:
    'Behold, the barbarians are coming to Shiet today. Rise and flee.'
    They said to him: 'Thou, dost thou not flee?'
    He said to them: '*Behold, for all these years I have beheld this day,*
    so that the word of Christ should be fulfilled when He said: "All
       those who take the sword will perish by the sword."'
    They said to him: 'We also, we will not flee, but we will die with
       thee.'
    He said to them: 'This is not my affair, let each one behold whether
       he remains.'
    They were seven brothers, and he said to them:
    'Behold, the barbarians *approach the door.*'
    They entered in, they killed them.
    But one of them was afraid, he went under some baskets
    *and he saw seven crowns descending from heaven with which the seven
       were crowned.*

                                        CHA.AP.PA.S. 46.4(186)

29. Once when the brethren were sitting with Abba Moses,
    he said to them: 'Behold, this day the barbarians have come to
       Scete;
    but rise up and flee.'

They said to him: 'Wilt thou thyself not flee, father?'
He said to them: 'For many years I have been expecting this day
would be,
so that the command might be fulfilled of our Saviour who said:
"They who take the sword will perish by the sword."'
They said to him: 'Therefore we will not flee but we will die with
thee.'
He said to them: 'It does not concern me that this is your desire.
Let every man see to himself, as it is written.'
There were there seven brethren
and after a little he said to them: 'Behold, the barbarians have
drawn near the door.'
Then the barbarians entered and they slew them.
One of them was afraid and he fled among the palm leaves.
And he saw seven crowns descending and crowning the heads of
those who had been slain.

BU.II.PAL.SY. 629.9

30. When evening came, the Bishop said to Isaac, his disciple:
'*Let us pray together this evening.*
Perhaps the Lord God will reveal to us what will happen to this man.'
And while the two were standing praying,
behold, the whole place then became light
and the old man was not able to bear the light.
He fell upon the ground.
The holy man Isaac was motionless
until he saw the light of the Lord with courage.
The angel told him what things would happen to the man.

POR.IS.B. 335.13

31. *It happened that night that the Lord revealed to the Archbishop:*
'Send tomorrow to Athanasius, the Chartulary, saying:
"If thou believest in Christ who has established me over His Holy
Church,
then the Lord will give the grace of healing to thy son."'
When the holy man had recovered from the vision, he called his
disciples saying:
'Is there a bishop in this place?'
He said: 'Yes, there are Abba Georgius and Abba Gregorius
with Abba Piamot, the Bishop of Damietta.'
The Patriarch, having called the bishops, *told them what he saw in*
the vision. ( )

374

'What I say to you, do with confidence before all.
It is Saint Mark the Evangelist who commands you.'

POR.IS.B. 369.14

32. De fait un jour, comme il devait y avoir une famine, il se vit, la
nuit, distribuant des pains aux pauvres, et il vit l'ange de Dieu, qui
l'assistait toujours, lui dire: 'Fais des provisions, abbâ. Il va y
avoir une famine, et il faut que tu puisses alors donner aux gens.'

FE.II.HYP.G. 54(XXXI)

33. Comme il était près d'approcher la ville, saint Hypatios voit en
vision que, dans la sainte église de la dite capitale, certain laïcs
installent Nestorius sur le trône. Aussitôt une voix prononce:
'Trois ans et une demi-année, puis arrachez l'ivraie.' ( ) De ce
moment donc, Hypatios se mit à dire à certaines gens et aux frères:
'J'ai des craintes, mes enfants, pour celui qui doit devenir évêque,
car j'ai vu à son sujet qu'il suivra des voies obliques en égard à la
foi, et qu'il ne régnera que trois ans et demi.'

FE.II.HYP.G. 55(XXXII)

34. On the revelation which he (Abba Pachomius) received on the
settlement (Katastasis) of the brethren:
And when he went into the monastery,
he found the brethren gathered together for prayer
and he joined with them and completed the prayer.
And when the brethren went forth to eat,
he remained alone in the building
that he might complete the prayers of the congregation according
to custom.
And he shut the door and prayed to God
that he might know concerning the settlements that would afterwards come to the brethren.
When he had prolonged his prayer from the tenth hour
until they struck (the boards to summon) the brethren to the service
of the night,
while he was praying until midnight,
suddenly a vision appeared to him from heaven,
which informed him concerning the settlements of the brethren
which would follow,
and that they would live thus rightly in Christ,
and the increase of monasteries which was prepared to take place.

BU.II.PAL.SY. 315.16

35. And this blessed man Didymus himself told me this story:
   'At one time I was suffering because of the wretched Emperor
      Julian.
   Then one day, when it was evening
   and I had eaten nothing from this anxiety,
   while I was sitting upon my mat, I sank into a short sleep
   and a marvellous thing fell upon me.
   And behold, I saw there were white horses galloping
   and their riders were dressed in white
   and they were crying out, saying:
   "Tell Didymus that on this day, at the seventh hour, Julian died.
   Rise therefore and eat and send the report to Athanasius, the
      Bishop,
   so that he may know and rejoice also."
   and I wrote down the day and the hour and the month
   and it was found that it had happened as it was told me in the
      vision.'

BU.II.PAL.SY. 115.3

(ii) MEMORY

THEMES

The ability to learn part or all of the Scriptures by heart.
The recitation by heart of the Scriptures.

EPISODES

The repetition by heart of the Scriptures as part of ascetic training.
The astonishment caused to the hearers by the power of memory of a
   holy man.

QUOTATIONS

1. He practised great detachment from possessions and, being well-
   educated, knew all the Scriptures by heart.

LO.PAL.G. 127(XXXVII)

2. There was another in this same place whose name was Daniel, *a*
   great ascetic and discerner.
   He knew by heart the whole Scripture, the New and Old Testaments,
   with all the Canons and episcopal treatises.
   His aim was not to speak at all except for matters of necessity ( ).
   It was witnessed of him that he recited ten thousand verses by heart
   every day.

CHA.AP.PA.S. 77.30(250)

THE ESTABLISHMENT OF A NON-MATERIAL ENVIRONMENT

3. And ( ) straightway he went forth from them and departed into
the desert. ( )
And he was there for three years in prayers and tears. ( )
And after three years he returned to the Church
and repeated before the fathers the belief and all the doctrine of the
Church.
And although he had never learned letters, he could repeat the
Scriptures by heart.
Then the elders marvelled at him, how he reached the degree of
asceticism,
and enlightened him with speech and also learning.

BU.II.HIER.SY. 409.6

4. This holy Macarius told me the following—for he was a priest: 'I
noticed at the time of distributing the Mysteries that it was never I
who gave the Oblation to Marcus, the ascetic, but an angel used to
give it him from the altar. I saw only the knuckle of the donor's
hand.' Now this Marcus was a young man, who learned by heart the
Old and New Testaments, exceedingly meek and continent, beyond
all others.

LO.PAL.G. 85(XVIII)

5. Macarius, the priest, told us: 'I gave heed,
at the time that I was giving the Holy Offering to (Mark), the
Mourner.
I never gave the Offering to him, but an angel gave to him from the
altar.
I alone saw that it was the palm of the hand of the angel giving to
him.
For this (Mark) was a young man
and he repeated by heart the New and the Old Testaments.
And he was meek beyond measure
and he was purer than most in body and in thought.'

BU.II.PAL.SY. 242.14

6. (He) said by heart fifteen psalms, then the long psalm then the
Epistle to the Hebrews, then Isaiah and part of Jeremiah, then Luke
the Evangelist, then the Proverbs.

LO.PAL.G. 107(XXVI)

7. *The righteous John stood every night praying*
and he did not sleep until he had recited the whole Psalter
and sometimes also the Acts.

HY.JE.SI.B. 181.18

8. *After he learnt the Psalter by heart,*
   he began the twelve Minor Prophets
   and in twelve days, he had memorised them, taking one a day.
   He also learnt by heart the holy Gospel of John.

   AM.PIS.KE.B. 343.10

9. He would not place it (a stone) down
   until he had said the whole Psalter by heart,

   AM.PIS.KE.B. 335.9

10. *It was said of him (Bishop Pisentius of Coptos),*
    that when he first became a monk he learnt the Psalter by heart.

    AM.PIS.KE.B. 335.4

11. When he was eighteen years old he learnt the Psalms
    and he was trained in the recitation of the Scriptures
    in the presence of him who had baptised him.

    BRO.EP.SY. 28.4

12. *The young boy stood as he had been commanded,*
    he repeated by heart the gift of grace of God, the four Gospels, with-
       out a verse missing,
    so that the bishop and the clerics with him were made to be astonished.

    AM.MO.S. 683.11

13. *At the age of ten years he knew (by heart) the whole Psalter*
    with the fourteen Epistles of Paul and the Acts of our fathers, the
       Apostles.
    He knew them all by heart.
    He was fulfilled in the grace of God.

    HY.JE.SI.B. 178.20

(iii) THE GIFT OF TONGUES

THEMES

The ability of a holy man to speak and read foreign languages.
The power to speak as a result of inspiration.

EPISODES

The gift of a written document giving the power to speak.
The appearance of the words of an inspired speaker as birds, flashes of
   lightning or a spring of water.

QUOTATIONS

1. Then (Pachomius) left him and went to pray by himself
   and he stretched out his hands to heaven and he prayed to God
      saying:

THE ESTABLISHMENT OF A NON-MATERIAL ENVIRONMENT

'Lord Almighty, who sustainest all,
if I am not able to benefit the sons of men ( )
(grant) that I may know their languages.'
And when he had prayed for about three hours
and had entreated God much concerning this,
suddenly there was sent from heaven into his right hand
something like a letter, written on paper.
And when he read it he learned immediately to speak all languages.
And he sent up praise to the Father and to the Son and to the Holy
    Spirit.

BU.II.PAL.SY. 333.21

2. Ce père avait été instruit par don céleste dans les trois langues, il
pouvait lire le grec, le latin et l'égyptien, comme nous l'avons
appris non seulement de beaucoup, mais de lui-même. En effet,
lorsqu'il eut reconnu que nous étions étrangers, il écrivait sur une
tablette quelques mots de reconnaissance à Dieu à notre sujet.

FE.IV/I.HIS.G. 42(VI)

3. Il avait d'abord été illettré: mais, quand il fut venu du désert au
pays habité, une grâce lui fut donnée du ciel et il récitait par cœur
les Ecritures. De fait, les frères lui ayant un jour tendu un livre, il
se mit dès lors à lire, comme s'il avait su ses lettres.

FE.IV/I.HIS.G. 31(II)

4. *Now when the multitude heard that the man of God was seeing visions,
they gathered to him from all countries and from every place,*
to hear his living teachings,
knowing that it was a spirit of God speaking within him.

GUI.IS.B. 231.15

5. *Then one of the holy men, in a dream, saw troops of angels
coming down from heaven, through the command of God,
having in their hands rolls, which were a book, written inside and
    outside,*
saying to one another: 'Who is worthy to work with this?'
Some said this one, others that one. ( )
At last they said: '*There is no one who is able to work with this
    except Ephraim.*'
The old man who saw the vision saw that they gave the roll to Ephraim.
And he rose in the morning, *he found Ephraim teaching*

*and when he heard him, it was like a bubbling spring coming forth
    from his mouth.*
And the old man who saw the vision
knew that what came forth from his lips belonged to the Holy Spirit.

CHA.AP.PA.S. 42.11(178)

6. It happened further one day, *while our father Pachomius was praying
    in a place alone,*
    he saw in a vison as if all the brethren were standing in the service,
    while Our Lord was sitting upon a throne,
    speaking to them in the words of the Gospels,
    and the words which He spoke and their interpretation,
    he heard them as He was speaking them with His mouth,
    in the vision which he saw.
    And afterwards, *when he wished to speak to the brethren on the word
        of God,*
    *he would stand in the place where he saw the Lord sitting and speak-
        ing them.*
    And it happened that, *when he spoke to tell them the words*
    which he had heard, with their interpretation,
    a great flash of light came in the words,
    so that all the brethren were like men drunk with wine. ( )
    And they saw the words coming forth from his mouth
    like birds of gold, silver and precious stones,
    which flew over the brethren in secret
    and went into the ears of many of those who listened well.

LE.PAC.S. 156b.3

7. *As he was praying one day in a place alone, our father Pachomius
    fell into an ecstasy,*
    as if all the brethren were standing in the service
    while our Lord was sitting upon a throne which was raised,
    speaking with them with parables of the Holy Gospel.
    And the words which He spoke, with their explanation,
    he heard them as He was saying them with His mouth,
    in the vision which he saw (that) day.
    And since that day *when our father Pachomius wished to speak with
        the brethren in the words of God,*
    *he would stand in the place where he saw the Lord sitting speaking
        with the brethren.*
    It happened again *when he was speaking,*

380

telling them the words which he had heard from the Lord with their explanation,

a great flash of lightning happened in the words, which flashed forth light,

so that all the brethren were afraid because of the words of our father Pachomius,

which were like flashes of lightning coming forth from his mouth.

LE.PAC.B. 95.20

(iv) THE GIFT OF KNOWLEDGE AND WISDOM

THEMES

The power of influencing events.
The power of healing.

QUOTATIONS

1. And the elder who was always at the side of the door said
   that all who dwelt within were so holy that they performed signs
   and that it was impossible that one of them should fall into sickness
   before the day of his departure from the world;
   but when the end of one of them was coming,
   he foretold it and informed them all and he lay down and died.

   BU.II.HIER.SY. 407.1

2. And when that period of thirty years was finished,
   when I was in great perils of affliction,
   God commanded my body and the hair grew (   ).
   And from that time the evil spirits were not able to touch me
   and no hunger or thirst overpowered me and I did not become sick
   or weak.

   LOOK.MAR.SY. 16.6

3. And he (Evagrius) wrote during the year only the value of what he
   ate—for he wrote the Oxyrhynchus characters excellently. So in the
   course of fifteen years, having purified his mind to the utmost, he
   was counted worthy of the gift of knowledge and wisdom and the
   discerning of spirits. (   ) Shortly before his death he told us: 'For
   three years I have not been troubled by fleshly desires.'

   LO.PAL.G. 136(XXXVIII)

4. *And great miracles will happen through thee in thy life,*
   in my name. Thou shalt heal those that are sick,

381

thou shalt cause the blind to see,
thou shalt raise the dead.

HY.MAC.AN.B. 41.14

5. To this saint, O my beloved one, *God gave the grace of the gift of healing in many ways.*

POR.IS.B. 356.7

6. I have heard of a certain Julian in the region of Edessa, a very ascetic man. ( ) At the very end of his life he was counted worthy of the honour of the gift of healing.

LO.PAL.G. 14(XLII)

7. Il avait reçu aussi, comme autre don, celui de chasser les démons, en sorte qu'on lui présentait en grand nombre, même malgré eux, les possédés, qui proclamaient ses mérites. Il ne cessait non plus d'accomplir les autres sortes de guérisons, si bien que, des moines s'étant rassemblés de tous côtés auprès de lui, il y en avait là ensemble jusqu'à des milliers.

FE.IV/I.HIS.G. 31(II)

8. The other (hermit) remained in the desert
and he became perfected in asceticism.
And he was found worthy by God of a gift
and he healed those possessed of devils.
And he knew beforehand things that would happen
and he healed the sick.

BU.II.PAL.SY. 433.24

9. When therefore he, Sisinnius, had passed some time with the holy man Elpidius
and had striven in the godly way of life
for a period of six or seven years,
at length he shut himself in a tomb for three years. ( )
And this man was held worthy to have the gift of authority over devils.

BU.II.PAL.SY. 229.18

10. Finally he shut himself up in a tomb. ( ) He was counted worthy of a gift (of power) over demons.

LO.PAL.G. 156(XLIX)

11. And the holy Basileus said to him: 'It is good that thou hast come,
    O father of the desert, who chasest away devils;
    for what is thy labour, O father, and why has thou come to see a
       sinful man?
    May the Lord give thee the reward for thy trouble.'

BRO.EP.SY. 35.8

II DEMONIC VISITS

1 FORMS

THEMES

The Devil as Christ, as an archangel, as an angel.
The Devil in the form of a woman.
The Devil as a Nubian, a tall black figure, a black boy.
The Devil as a dragon.
The Devil in changing forms.
The hearing of demonic voices.

EPISODES

The appearance of angels to delude ascetics.
The appearance of Christ and angels to test the humility of ascetics.
The appearance of nude women at the time of eating.
The appearance of women at the doors of ascetics' cells, wishing to
    enter.
The appearance of a Nubian who threatens and attacks.
The appearance of a Nubian woman as the personification of fornication.
The appearance of a black boy to delude ascetics.
The appearance of a small Nubian as the personification of pride.
The appearance of a dragon attempting to terrify and overthrow.
The appearance by the Devil in one form after another.
The appearance of terrifying fantasies of changing forms: women,
    monks, beggars, Nubians, soldiers, animal forms, reptiles.

QUOTATIONS

1. *In the middle of the night*
   the holy man Apa Lacaron rose, he prayed ( ).
   As the blessed Apa Lacaron finished praying,
   the Devil, in the form of an angel of God, came to the saint.
   He said: 'Thou hast multiplied thy prayers in the presence of God.
   He has sent me to thee to strengthen thee.'

BA.HY.I.LAC.B. 10.16

2. *The Devil changed himself into the form of an angel of light.*
   He appeared to one of the brothers and said to him:
   '*I am Gabriel, I have been sent to thee.*'
   He said to him: 'Thou hast been sent to another brother; for I am
   not worthy.'
   Immediately he became invisible.

   CHA.AP.PA.S. 32.5(143)

3. The old men said: 'In truth, *if an angel appears to thee, do not
   receive him*,
   but humble thyself and say: "*I am not worthy to see the angel*, as
   I have lived in sin."'

   CHA.AP.PA.S. 32.10(144)

4. To one of the elders
   Satan appeared in the form of an angel of light and said:
   'I, even I, am Gabriel, who have been sent to thee.'
   Then he said to him: 'Hast thou not been sent to another, for I am
   a sinner?'
   Then when he heard, he was not seen again.
   And the old man said: 'If, in truth, an angel appears to thee,
   say: "(What hast thou to do) with me in my presence; for I am not
   worthy."'

   BU.II.PAL.SY. 624.19

5. A brother was sitting quietly in his cell, and demons wanted to
   seduce him in the guise of angels. And they stirred him up to go
   out to the congregation in church, and they showed him a light.
   But he went to an old man and said: 'Abba, angels come to me with
   light, and stir me to go to the congregation.' And the old man
   said to him: 'Heed them not, my son: they are demons. When they
   come to stir you out, say: "I go when I want, and I do not listen to
   you."'

   CHA.SA.L. 126(X)

6. Sur ces entrefaites, Hypatios vit dans sa cellule l'Ennemi du bien
   sous l'aspect d'un être resplendissant qui dit: 'Pourquoi m'as tu
   enlevé cet homme, Hypatios?'

   FE.II.HYP.G. 31(XV)

7. He reached such a pitch of arrogance, that he was deceived by
   demons. For by deceiving him little by little they induced him to be
   very proud, supposing that angels met him.

   LO.PAL.G. 104(XXV)

8. So the demon, convinced that he was completely persuaded by his deception went away and disguised himself as the Saviour, and came by night in a vision of a thousand angels, bearing lamps and a fiery wheel, in which it seemed that the Saviour appeared, and one came in front of the others and said: 'Christ has loved you because of your conduct and the freedom of your life and He has come to see you. So go out of the cell, do nothing else but look at his face from afar, stoop down and worship and then go to your cell.' So he went out and saw them in ranks carrying lamps, and Antichrist about a stade away, and he fell down and worshipped.

LO.PAL.G. 105(XXV)

9. *And the Devil took the form of a woman in the night.*
   He adopted all shapes in (different) forms
   in order to tempt Anthony.
   He thought of Christ in his heart
   and of the spiritual vision.

GAR.ANT.S. 8.18

10. Many times, when he was sitting about to eat his bread,
    they (the demons) would come to him in the forms of nude women
    and sit, in order to eat with him also.
    The man of God would shut his eyes and his heart,
    until they were destroyed and brought to nought.
    He prayed to the Lord that he would take sleep from him,
    so that he would not sleep until he had conquered those who fought
        with him,
    as it is written: 'I shall not rest until my enemies are destroyed.'

LE.PAC.B. 21.17

11. Once when (Pachomius) and Theodore, whom he loved,
    were walking through the monastery at night,
    they suddenly saw a great phantom full of much deceit;
    and that which appeared was in the form of a woman.
    And its beauty was indescribable,
    so that no man could tell the beauty,
    or the form or the appearance present in that phantom.
    Thus Theodore, who looked at that phantom,
    was greatly troubled and his face changed.
    And when the blessed man saw this, that he was afraid,
    he said to him: 'Take courage in the Lord, Theodore and do not
        fear,'

385

And when he had said these things to him,
he commanded him to pray with him,
so that this astonishing phantom be driven away from them.
And while they were praying,
it came nearer to them with boldness
and their prayer did not drive it away.
And when it and the company of devils which ran before it drew
near,
it came towards them and spoke to them.

BU.II.PAL.SY. 329.25

12. (A brother) after a few days was in his dwelling, in a state of great
pride,
when the demon, who first tempted him to be proud, saw (him).
*Then he took the form of a beautiful woman, he knocked at the door
of the dwelling, that he should receive him within.*
He came forth in haste, he opened the door.
And the demon in the form of a woman said to him:
'I beg thee my lord, father, to have mercy on me and receive me
until morning, ( )'
he was not able to distinguish that he should not receive her to him,
but he received her.
He took her into his dwelling place rejoicing greatly. ( )
*Suddenly the demon overturned him and tormented him greatly till
the morrow.*

LE.PAC.B. 14.12

13. It happened to me yesterday ( ) *I looked, I saw a great Nubian,
tall, with his eyes emitting flames of fire into my face.*
He stood before me saying: 'I have laboured to ensnare thee, my
lawless one.
Behold, for three years I have set snares for thee by day and by
night.' ( )
And when he said these things, he seized my two feet,
he cast me down into the oven.
I was burned completely, ( )
I did not know whether I was alive or dead, because I had entered
into death.
And in that night *I saw the holy Archangel Gabriel.*
He came to me, he made the sign of the Cross over me,
he healed me,
he departed up to heaven in a robe of light.

WOR.GAB.S. 237.7

14. *I* (Ezekiel the monk) *walked with him* (*the man summoning him to his father*) *in the whole desert.*
I spent the first day and the second.
As we walked, I said to him: 'Have we not reached that place?'
He said: 'No.'
We came to the third day walking in the desert.
I said to him again: 'Have we not yet reached it?'
He said: 'Behold, we are approaching it.'
As he was speaking to me he was changed, he became a tall Nubian,
whose eyes were filled with blood, whose whole body was full of spines,
who smelt like a he-goat.
He said to me: 'Dost thou not follow me, O Ezekiel?'
I said: 'No.' ( )
Then he jumped upon me like a wild lion wishing to kill me.

AM.PAUL.T.S. 765.11

15. And he saw the likeness of a Nubian,
who stood and gnashed his teeth at him.
And he ran quickly from his great fear
and he came to his master and he knocked hastily, saying: '( )
I beg thee my father, I saw a black Nubian upon my bed when I came to lie down.'

BU.II.PAL.SY. 496.23

16. And he looked and behold the work of fornication came and approached him
and he stood before him in the likeness of a Nubian woman, whose smell was very foul.
And he was not able to endure the foul smell of fornication and he drove her away from his presence.
She said to him: 'In the hearts of men I have a sweet and pleasant smell,
but because of thy obedience and labour, God has not allowed me to lead thee astray,
but I have made thee acquainted with the foulness of my smell.'

BU.II.PAL.SY. 592.24

17. *One day he* (Satan) *knocked at the door of the monastery and, when I came forth,*
I saw one who was black and very tall.

GAR.ANT.S. 47.21

18. *Finally when the dragon was not able to overcome Anthony*
    he raged and gnashed his teeth against him. ( )
    He appeared to him in a fantasy in the form of a small black boy,
    He was like one prone to fall.

                                                        GAR.ANT.S. 9.6

19. *He appeared to the Saint Theodore in the form of a Nubian of the*
        desert,
    he stood on the top of the mountain in great shamelessness,
    he said to Saint Theodore: 'O Theodore, dost thou know who I
        am? ( )
    Behold, thou hast overcome me three times.'

                                                 BA.HY.II.T.A.T.S.B. 153.6

20. On me pose, dit-il (Paul), tout proche du saint tombeau et aussitôt,
    revenu à moi-même, je prie avec larmes le saint père de me délivrer
    du démon qui m'afflige et de me purifier de ses atteintes. La nuit
    donc où vous m'avez vu louer Dieu à l'église, environ la cinquième
    heure de la nuit, je priais avec larmes et gémissements, et j'entre
    comme en extase, j'ai une vision, c'était comme si j'étais en lieu
    plein de gloire et redoutable, dont on ne saurait décrire la gloire,
    il me semblait avoir sur la tête une cuculle de laine noire qui,
    selon le mot de l'Ecriture, ( ) était un instrument épineux avec
    des crins qui me piquaient brutalement et me causaient d'horribles
    tortures. J'ouvris la bouche et dis: 'Aie pitié de moi, saint père
    Euthyme, et délivre moi du tourment qui m'accable.' Aussitôt
    je vois le saint resplendissant de lumière, blanc de poil, de la
    taille d'un nain, avec une longue barbe, le visage rond, les yeux
    porteurs de joie, vêtu d'un manteau tirant sur le noir plus court
    que le colobium, tenant de la main un bâton. Il me dit: 'Pourquoi
    m'importuner? Que veux-tu que je te fasse?' Quand je lui eus dit
    avec crainte: ( ) alors avec un frémissement de colère, le saint se
    saisit de la cuculle noire et l'arracha avec peine de ma tête. Elle
    m'apparut dans sa main comme un petit Ethiopien dont les regards
    lançaient du feu. Et, ayant baissé les yeux, je vois à terre devant
    lui un gouffre extrêmement profond et épouvantable; c'est dans ce
    gouffre que le saint précipita l'Ethiopien; puis tourné vers moi,
    il me dit; 'Vois, tu as été guéri. Ne pèche plus, mais veille sur toi-
    même, de peur qu'il ne t'arrive un malheur pire.'

                                                 FE.III/I.EUT.G. 128/130(L)

21. He lived for forty years in the inner desert,
    where he practised the works of perfection.

At the end he heard, as it were, the voice of God, which said to him:
  'Apollo ( )
Now do thou go quickly to the desert,
to the place which is near to the dwellings of men,
that thou mayest beget for me a holy people
who shall be exalted by (their) good works.'
Then Apollo made answer and said: 'Lord, take thou away from
  me pride,
lest I become exalted over the brotherhood and I lose all its good.'
Then the divine voice spoke to him again:
'Place thy hand upon thy neck and whatever thou layest hold
  upon,
(take it) down and bury it in the dust.'
Then he quickly laid his hand upon his neck
and took hold of a small Nubian
and buried him in the dust.
And he cried out and said: 'I am the spirit of pride.'
And again the voice came to him and said:
'Go, and everything that thou shalt ask from thy God shall be
  given to thee.'

BU.HIER.SẎ. 376.18

22. Alors qu'il s'était retiré du monde a l'âge de quinze ans, et qu'il
avait passé quarante années au désert, où il avait pratiqué stricte-
ment toute espèce de vertu, il lui sembla entendre, après cela, une
voix de Dieu qui lui disait; 'Apollô, Apollô, ( ) Va vers le pays
habité: car tu m'engendreras un peuple qui me soit propre, zélé
pour les bonnes oeuvres.' ( ) Il répondit: 'Eloigne de moi,
Maître, la jactance.' ( ) La voix divine à nouveau lui dit: 'Met-toi
la main au cou, tu prendras la jactance et l'enterreras dans le sable.'
Il se mit bien vite la main au cou, y empoigne un petit Ethiopien
et l'enterra dans le sable, qui criait et disait: 'Je suis le démon de
l'orgueil.'

FE.IV/I.HIS.G. 47(VIII)

23. *Many times, as he was holding his services,*
the demons took the form of dragons of serpents
which stretched their heads to one another and went towards
  our father in envy and fearful deceit,
But he was not troubled by them
nor did he cease from praying to God until he had finished his service.
And he scarcely turned his face to them,

but by lowering his eyes, he said to them:
'Do not lead astray, *O demons, withdraw yourselves.*
You are in error with your Father the Devil.
It is Christ who drives you away.'

AM.MAT.P.S. 710.15

24. Souvent, durant son temps de réclusion, bien des secrets lui
étaient révélés. ( ) Ainsi par example, touchant un frère qui
venait d'arriver, ( ) le père l'avait vu entièrement encirclé par un
serpent qui s'inclinait vers la bouche du frère.

FE.II.HYP.G. 30(XIV)

25. *While the blessed man was standing praying one day,*
the Devil took the form of a great dragon.
He went below his cell,
he began to dig, wishing to overthrow him.
The blessed man, when he had finished his prayer,
he looked out of the window,
he said to him: '( ) As for me, thy fantasies do not frighten me,
because *I have the Lord Jesus Christ who helps me* ( )'.
When he had heard these things from the saint,
he made himself like smoke,
he ran forth from him,
saying: 'Thou sayest these things to me, O Martyrius.
Behold I return to thee quickly.
I shall not delay away from thee.
I shall bring upon thee a great passion which is very strong
and I will bring thee down from thy great glory,
because indeed thou hast given me much trouble.'
Having said this be became invisible to him.

CHA.MART.B. 3.1

26. *While the King* (Erodianus, King of India) *was asleep that night,*
behold, the Devil went in to him
in the form of a great black dragon with five heads,
he being very terrifying.
When the King saw him, he was disturbed, he cried out:
'*Who art thou whom I see thus in this form, with this terrifying*
shape?'
The dragon answered: '*I am the Devil, the enemy of the Christians.*
Why hast thou allowed Helias, this Christian magician, to destroy
thy gods? ( )'

390

When he had said this, the dragon led astray the King's heart,
he made a flame of fire as he disappeared.

SOB.HEL.S. 21a.11

27. (A woman) *was sitting at midday in her house.*
The Devil rose in the form of a man begging alms.
He went to the house of the woman, he knocked as if he were
    asking alms from her.
The woman called him in, saying: 'Sit thyself, my father,
until the necessary things come and I give to thee that which thou
    wishest.'
But he, the wicked demon, he began to change his form in her presence,
    little by little.
The God-loving woman realised that he was the Devil.
Immediately she cried out saying: '*God of the saint Theodore, help*
    me in my time of need.'
Immediately, the wicked demon changed,
he became like a Nubian, with an animal's face.
He jumped upon the woman, he strangled her. (   )
As he was strangling her, *behold, the saint Theodore stood above her*
    in great glory.
The Devil, when he saw him, was afraid.
He changed his form and took the appearance of a righteous man.
The saint Theodore said to him: '*Who art thou in this manner, O thou*
    unclean one? (   )'
The Devil said to him: 'I adjure thee in Christ, O my lord, that
    thou dost not destroy me before my time;
for thou hast already killed my great power,
who was my instrument and dwelling place, namely the great
    dragon.'
When he had said these things to him, (   )
he became invisible.
But the saint Theodore *blessed the woman, he gave her courage,*
he became invisible to her.

BA.HY.I.TH.S.B. 187.25

28. If they (the demons) are not able to deceive the soul in what is
    manifest, through unclean pleasure,
    they arise again against it in other forms
    and make fantasies which are fearful,
    as they change their form and resemble women and wild animals

391

and reptiles and forms of bodies and crowds of soldiers. ( )
They are very daring and without shame.
If they are overcome in this form, they will rise again in another.
They are wont to distinguish (events) also, saying what will happen
after some days.
They appear tall, so that they reach the roof, and broad in their form.

GAR.ANT.S. 29.19

29. *And they are prepared to change (their forms);*
many times they act like those who sing psalms in darkness
and they say verses from the Scriptures.
It happens also that, as we recite, they also say what we have
recited.
Some times also, when we are asleep, they rouse us to pray.
These things they do many times, hardly allowing us to sleep.
Sometimes also, they simulate monks,
speaking hypocritically as if they were servants of God,
so that they will deceive us with these likenesses.
Afterwards we follow them where they please.
But it is not necessary to pay attention to them.

GAR.ANT.S. 32.10

30. *For the ascetic practices and services which he* (Matthew) *did by*
day and night
were not small,
as he cast himself upon the ground many times.
He was in danger from his suffering ( )
from *the afflictions of the demons who rose against him by day and*
night.
For he saw them face to face in visions,
they being in a multitude of forms before him.

AM.MAT.P.S. 710.4

31. Of the things which he (Abba Pachomius) heard said in the air by
the devils
as he was journeying in the desert to his monastery.

BU.II.PAL.SY. 311.1

32. *I* (Pachomius) *heard one day a demon, who was sad, say to another*
demon:
'These days I am round a man who is difficult in everything which
he does.

The moment I send an evil thought into him,
he will rise immediately and pray and weep to the Lord.
And I burn and flee.'
And the other demon said also: 'Everything which I counsel to
    him with whom I dwell,
he does immediately and even more.'

LE.PAC.B. 68.17

33. They related concerning Abba Pachomius and said that on many
    occasions
he heard the devils repeating many different evil things,
some of which would come upon the brethren.
First he heard one of them say: 'I am opposing a man who is
    constantly against me,
and every time when I approach to sow thoughts in his mind,
    immediately he turns to prayer and I depart from his presence
    burning.' And another devil said: 'I am with a man who is easy
    to persuade
and whatever I counsel him to do, he hears me and acts,
and I love him greatly.'

BU.II.PAL.SY. 530.6

34. And as they were praying
they heard the (daughters of) the voices of the devils from the air
and the sounds of armour and of horses and of many horsemen.
And they also heard the voices of the devils,
who were saying to one another: 'You shall not have mercy upon
    them.'
And they said again: 'O unfortunate hermits, why do you stand
    against us?
If we acted against you, not one of you could be found on the face
    of the earth.
We will not leave you or withdraw from you.'

BU.II.PAL.SY. 684.8

35. On one occasion a certain hermit saw a devil
who was calling to his fellow to come with him
and between the two of them that they should wake a certain
    hermit for service
and by this means to lead him to mistake thereby that angels had
    appeared to him.

393

And he heard the voice of the other one who made answer to his
   fellow, saying:
'I cannot do this; for once I woke him
and he stood up and defeated me with a severe defeat,
while he sang psalms and prayed.'

BU.II.PAL.SY. 464.12

2   THE DEVIL AS DEITY

THEMES

The Devil as father to Diocletian.
The Devil as guardian of a pagan sanctuary.

EPISODES

The granting to Diocletian of favours in return for worship.
The giving of commands to set up temples and columns for the worship
   of pagan gods.
The granting of victory in battle in return for the honouring of pagan
   gods.

QUOTATIONS

1. *After a hundred days, Satan manifested himself ( )*
    wearing royal purple as ornament,
    in a terrifying fantasy.
    He said to Agrippidus: 'Dost thou know who I am?'
    Agrippidus answered: 'Who art thou, my lord, who art in this great
       glory?'
    The Devil said to him: 'I am he who has raised thee ( )
    if thou wilt obey me, *I will give the favour to thee of the Kingdom*
       of the Romans.
    I will make thee King in my place,
    because it is I who give the kingdoms to all the kings of the earth
       and they are my servants.
    But I will make thee my son so that thou art not an orphan.'
    Agrippidus said to him: 'That which thou commandest me, I am
       prepared to do.'
    He said to him: 'First then I desire that thou worshippest me.'
    And immediately Agrippidus did this; *with zeal he threw himself*
       down, he worshipped him.
    Agrippidus said to him further: '*Who art thou, my lord?*'
    He said to him: 'I am the great Demoniacus.'
    Having said this to him, he became invisible to him.

BA.HY.I.TH.O.B. 36.24

2. *The Devil appeared to him in the night.*
He said to him: 'My son Agrippidus, thou hast seen that thy
  father has made thee King.
Do my will in those things which I will tell thee
and thou shalt see greater things than these.'
The King said to him: 'All things which thou commandest me,
I am prepared to do and to fulfil, since *I am thy son.*'
Immediately he hastened to prostrate himself.
He said to him: '(   )
My name and thine are one,'
BA.HY.I.TH.O.B. 38.14

3. *His father, Demoniacus, stood on his right hand* and spoke to him.
BA.HY.I.TH.O.B. 39.12

4. Immediately Demoniacus, the father of Diocletian,
who was the Devil, the father of all wickedness, the enemy of truth,
made his way to Diocletian the King, as he was seated.
And he was clothed like an Egyptian.
He said to him: 'My son Agrippidus, behold, I have caused thy
  brother to sit as King with thee.' (   )
As he was about to eat, *he saw Demoniacus, his father,*
reclining with him, face to face like a man, with his friend.
He rose immediately, he prostrated himself,
he worshipped him and kissed his breast.
He said to him: 'Diocletian, my beloved son,
go on foot and approach the throne of the kingdom,
and seize the hand of thy brother, Maximinian.
Kiss his mouth and bring him to me that I show to you what is in
  my heart.'
Immediately Diocletian arose, according to the command of his
  father, the Devil.
He brought his brother in to him as he was in the eating place.
He embraced him.
Then they both worshipped his feet.
Afterwards they mounted with their father, they ate with him.
He made them to be kings together without jealousy (   )
They then promised to erect for him statues and columns.
For this he gave them power, he withdrew.
BA.HY.I.TH.O.B. 41.10

5. *At midnight, behold, Saklabaoth, he who disturbs heaven and earth,*
  appeared to them (Diocletian and Maximinian) *in the form of a*
  nobleman (   ).

Sataniel then said to them: 'In the morning set up temples and columns of gold and silver.

Worship them on my behalf and offer sacrifices to them and raise up frankincense for them.'

BA.HY.I.TH.O.B. 44.17

6. The holy man, Mar Azazail, answered and said to the King: 'Who are thy gods?' The King said to the holy man: 'My gods are merciful and it is they who do good to men. If thou turnest to them, they will receive thee and they will not bear anger against one who approaches them. And also I and the priests will pray and beseech them to forgive thee thine offence. They are the seventy-two gods.'

MAC.AZ.SY. 11.19

7. *Then the Devil appeared to Diocletian, he said to him: 'My son Agrippida,*
I know seventy ancient gods which men have left.
Henceforward, O my son Agrippida, build statues of gold,
set them up in thy presence
and I will cause the gods to go secretly and dwell in them.
And I will make thee strong to overcome in battle.'

BA.HY.II.T.A.T.S.B. 142.26

8. He (Diocletian) spoke with his nobles, saying: 'Hear me, my friends.'
They said: 'Speak, our Lord King.'
He said to them: 'I love you, my friends, hear me.'
They said: 'May our Lord speak, his servants hear.'
He said to them: 'You know that the King does not lie.
As I was asleep this night, Apollo, the great god, came in to me with these other seventy gods.
They spoke to me in a sweet tongue.
They said to me: "*Behold, we have honoured thee, we have given thee victory in the battle.*
Do thou also honour us in thy kingdom."
What, therefore, shall we say to them?'

MIN.EPIM.S. 1.15

9. He (Diocletian) said to them (the nobles): 'You know that the King does not tell lies.
For it happened that I was asleep during this night.
Apollo, the great god, came in to me with the seventy gods.

They said: "*Behold, we have honoured thee, we have given thee victory in battle.*

Do thou also honour us in thy kingdom."

Now, therefore, what do you wish me to do for them?'

HY.DID.B. 284.3

10. The (people) prostrated themselves before our father, Apa Moses, because an evil demon, called Bes, had gone into the temple which is to the North of the monastery.

And he would come forth and strike those who passed.

Some among those whom he struck became blind in one eye,

in others their hands withered,

others he made lame in their feet,

in others he caused their faces to be twisted,

others he made deaf and dumb.

For many saw him jumping down in the temple

changing himself into many forms. (   )

The holy man, Apa Moses, took seven brothers, strong in the faith (   ) and also myself, this sinner.

He took us, he entered at evening time.

The holy man said to us: 'Pray continuously, let us beseech God.'

When we began to pray, *the place shook before us*

and a great voice appeared there to us, like lightning and thunder.

Our father said: 'Do not fear, they are fantasies of demons.'

We saw great power, *we endured and we remained in prayer.*

At midnight the demon cried out (   ).

Some times we heard the voice of multitudes who ran upon us

and did not draw near to us at all.

Sometimes also the place in which we were standing would shake,

as if it would fall upon us.

And one of us fell upon his face because he knew our danger.

(*But our father seized us and raised us* saying: '*Do not fear but have courage. You will see the glory of God.*' (Zoega. p. 534)).

AM.MO.S. 689.2

11. Il parcourut chaque coin du temple, y faisant génuflexion et prière.

Quand la nuit fut tombée, voici que des pierres, dit-on, étaient jetées contre lui et qu'il y eut le bruit d'une multitude qui faisait entendre des grondements et des clameurs, mais il n'en persévérait pas moins dans la prière. Il passa ainsi la première nuit, puis la seconde. Durant la troisième, le sommeil triompha une fois de lui, car il n'était qu'un homme qui porte un corps. Alors il se présenta à lui une foule de spectres, comme d'êtres gigantesques, dont les uns disaient: 'Qui t'a poussé à habiter ici, malheureux? Tu veux donc périr misérablement? Allons, tirons-le dehors et jetons-le dans le courant.' D'autres, qui portaient, semblait-il, d'énormes pierres, se tenaient près de sa tête comme s'ils la voulaient écraser. A son réveil, l'athlète du Christ parcourut de nouveau les coins du temple en priant et psalmodiant et il déclarait aux mauvais esprits: 'Partez d'ici sans quoi c'est brûlés par la puissance de la Croix que vous prendrez la fruite.' Mais eux n'en faisaient que plus de tapage et de hurlement. Alors, plein de mépris pour eux et tenant comme entièrement non avenues leurs clameurs, il bouche la porte du temple et ne laisse qu'une petite fenêtre, à travers laquelle il conversait avec ceux qui montaient vers lui.

FE.II.DAN.G. 102(IX)

12. When he (father of Ephraim) had finished praying,
    according to his custom, before his idols,
    the unclean Devil began to speak,
    saying to the priest: 'For many years I have known thee,
    that thou art the guardian of this sanctuary
    and thy petition regarding thy son I am not able to receive.
    Because just as it is not possible for the heaven to be the earth,
    thus also it is not possible for me that any portion or pleasure
        should be in him.
    But if thou art wishing to fulfil my pleasure,
    drive him to go from thy house
    and chastise him from my neighbourhood.
    For this, thy son, I know that he is destined to be a persecutor of
        the gods.'
    And immediately his father went forth and said to him:
    'Rise and depart whither thou wilt.'

BRO.EP.SY. 24.11

3. MODE OF ACTIVITY

THEMES

The attempt to distract the ascetic from prayer.
The attempt to prevent the ascetic from resting.
The attempt to give the ascetic a distaste for his cell.
The attempt to tempt the ascetic to follow.

The attempt to terrify the ascetic by personal attack.
The attempt to cause the death of the ascetic.

EPISODES

The appearance of demons performing useless activities.
The appearance of demons mocking the ascetic.
The appearance of silver in the path of the ascetic.
The appearance of demons surrounding the mouth of the ascetic like flies.
The appearance of demons as animals or pagan creatures tempting the ascetic in the desert.
The demonic assault upon the ascetic by multitudes causing audible tumult.
The demonic assault upon the ascetic by wild animals and reptiles encircling him.
The demonic assault with painful blows upon the ascetic to the point of death.

QUOTATIONS

1. He once went to visit (Apa Abraham).
   The Devil gathered some demons in his path.
   They were crying out much, they stood in his path at (the distance of) the flight of an arrow.
   For it was evening and those ones raised a great piece of wood, crying out to one another, ( )
   and they bound it with a great rope.
   They did this for no other (reason) except *that the holy man should cease praying and look at them.*
   He did not look at them at all.
   But he bent his face down, meditating on the Gospel of John.
   I walked with him that night.
   When he had passed them a little, *I turned my face back,*
   I saw them giving cries like (dogs).
   They fled in great shame.

   AM.CO.ABR.S. 756.2

2. When the evildoers saw that they were not able to tempt him,
   they brought an object in the form of a leaf of a tree,
   with long ropes which were thick,
   as if they were a crowd of men doing very strenuous labour.
   They acted as if they had attached the rope to a large stone
   to drag it and remove it to another place.

All these things they did, making loud cries
so that he should see them and smile,
so that they would overcome him.
Immediately he stretched out his hands, he prayed, groaning,
until they dissolved away and became invisible to him.

LE.PAC.B. 21.7

3. *It happened many times as he was praying,*
   when he was about to bend the knee,
   that he would see before him the likeness of a pit in a fantasy,
   so that he would be afraid and not pray to the Lord.
   But he knew the wiles of him who tempts. ( )
   And he put the demons to shame.

LE.PAC.B. 20.11

4. As he would be going to work
   (the demons) *would walk in front of him in two rows,*
   like soldiers in front of a commander,
   saying to one another: 'Make way for the man of God,'
   wishing to tempt him to look at them.
   But he, the man of God, through the hope which he had in God,
      did not look at them
   but he mocked them as useless.
   And suddenly they would become invisible to him.

LE.PAC.B. 20.18

5. *There were some tombs in the neighbourhood of the place in which*
      the old man Apa Palamon dwelt.
   He went into one of the tombs.
   He prayed and immediately demons appeared to him
   in that place below in the tomb.
   They walked before him in two rows, as it is done in front of rulers.
   And one of them was in the form of a herald in their midst
   and he cried out, saying: 'Make way.'

LE.PAC.S. 111b.19

6. Then when the holy old man was journeying to his monastery
   and he was by the side of the desert which is called 'Ammon',
   there rose against him legions of devils
   and thronged him both on his right hand and on his left.
   And others ran in front of him saying:
   'Behold the blessed man of God.'

BU.II.PAL.SY. 311.3

7. Moi-même, une nuit, les démons m'ont harcelé ainsi d'illusions; ils ne me permirent ni de prier ni de dormir, toute la nuit ils me présentaient des fantômes. Le matin, s'étant jetés a mes pieds, ils me dirent par raillerie: 'Pardonne-nous, abbâ, de ce que nous t'avons causé du trouble la nuit.' Moi je leur dis: 'Loin de moi, vous tous artisans d'iniquité, ( ) car vous n'induirez pas en tentation le serviteur de Dieu.'

FE.IV/I.HIS.G. 26(I)

8. *They deceived me many times at night,*
   they would not let me rest,
   they brought me fantasies all night.
   And when morning came, they would appear to me, mocking me,
   saying: 'Forgive us, father because we have troubled thee all night.'
   Then I would say to them: 'Remove yourselves.'

TIL.I.JOH.LY.S. 139.5

9. The Enemy saw his zeal. He wished to put a stumbling block upon his way.
   He cast a large silver disc in his way in a fantasy.
   He (Anthony) knew the plans of the hater of goodness.
   He stood, he looked at the disc.
   He knew that a work of the Devil was in it and he said: 'Whence does this disc come in this desert? ( )
   Thou wilt not cause me to stumble with this, O Devil, but this will be destruction to thee.'
   As Anthony said these things, that thing vanished in smoke.

GAR.ANT.S. 16.19

10. *Afterwards, as he walked upon the road, he saw gold,*
    not in a phantasy, but in truth.
    Whether it was the Enemy who taught him, or a higher power training (him) ( ) neither did he tell us, nor do we know; ( )
    he turned, he ran like one would run from a fire,
    so that he did not approach it at all.

GAR.ANT.S. 17.10

11. *As he was sitting working one day,*
    one of the demons took the form of a cock.
    It crowed in his face
    but he shut his eyes.
    He did not look at it, nor was he afraid at all.

LE.PAC.B. 21.3

12. Having been mocked at the outset by the demon who mocks all men and deceives them, he seemed to feel a distaste (accidie) for his first cell and went off and built another nearer a village. ( ) Three or four months after, the demon came by night, holding a whip of oxhide like the executioners, and having the appearance of a ragged soldier, and began cracking his whip. Then the blessed Nathanael answered and said: 'Who are you who do such things in my dwelling?' The demon answered: 'I am he who drove you from that cell. I have come to chase you out of this too.' Knowing that he was the victim of an illusion, he returned again to the first cell, and, in a period of thirty-seven years in all, did not cross the threshold, having a quarrel with the demon; who showed him such wonders, trying to force him out, as it impossible to relate.

LO.PAL.G. 71(XVI)

13. *The elder* (brother) *roused the younger. They rose,*
they girded themselves.
I saw them.
They did not see me.
They stretched out their hands to heaven.
And I saw the demons coming upon the younger like flies.
And they came upon his eyes and mouth.
And I saw an angel of the Lord, with a sword of fire in his hand,
guarding him, chasing after the demons.
They were not able to approach the elder at all.

AM.MA.DO.B. 298.14

14. *The elder* (brother) *roused the younger, they rose, they girded*
themselves.
They stretched their hands up to heaven.
I saw them. They did not see me.
And I saw the demons coming upon the younger like flies flying,
Some went upon his eyes and his mouth.
And I saw an angel of the Lord, with a sword in his hand,
guarding him, chasing after the demons.
But they were not able to approach the elder.

AM.AP.MAC.B. 210.11

15. *The elder* (brother) *roused the younger, they rose, they girded*
themselves.
and they stretched out their hands to heaven.
I saw them, but they did not see me.
And I saw the demons fly upon the younger like flies.

402

Some were settling upon his mouth, others upon his eyes,
and I saw an angel of the Lord, with a sword of fire in his hand,
guarding him, chasing the demons away from him.
They were not able to approach the elder.

CHA.AP.PA.S. 72.11(239)

16. By chance, as he became old and weak, the demons wished to test
      him
    and they left him sitting in the court
    and when the sun was about to set, he bowed his head as if to sleep.
    They came beside the door from outside and, as they formed a
      crowd, *they took the shape of beggars,*
    they knocked, they asked: 'Give us alms.' ( )
    Then they threw stones.
    They struck upon the door and again he took no notice of them.
    At last they took stones, they threw (them) into the court,
    and while the Lord protected him, none of the stones approached
      him,
    but he stood, he cast himself on the couch to sleep.

AM.MAC.SC.B. 99.7

17. It was said of an old man that *he prayed to see demons.*
    And it was revealed to him that it is not necessary to see them.
    The old man begged saying: 'O Lord, thou hast power to protect me
      with thy grace.'
    And God opened his eyes, he saw them like honey bees surrounding
      the man,
    grinding their teeth over him and the angel of God rebuked them.

CHA.AP.PA.S. 52.17(204)

18. La diable donc crée pour lui le mirage d'une chamelle de bàt
    errant par le désert avec toutes les provisions nécessaires. Elle
    voit Macaire et vient s'asseoir devant lui. Mais le saint avait
    compris que c'était un phantasme, ce qu'elle était bien: il se
    dressa en prière, et la chamelle, aussitôt, fut engloutie dans le sol.

FE.IV/I.HIS.G. 116(XXI)

19. *Then he took the form of a herd of camels* which were with their
      young in the desert,
    wishing to deceive the holy man, the saint Theodore.
    He saw the herd of camels.
    He and his soldiers pursued them but they were not able to reach
      them but he made his way after them.

403

Then a number of his soldiers were tired and also the horses.
They were dry with thirst. They were not able to walk nor were the
horses.
After this, he stood upon the mountain, he looked at them.
Behold, a voice came to him from heaven saying:
'Theodore, son of John, thou man of Egypt,
cease from pursuing in the desert with thy soldiers,
for it is the Tempter who tempts thee.'

BA.HY.II.T.A.T.S.B. 116.19

20. He (Abba Anthony) saw a man like two,
    one half was a man, the other half was a horse.
    This is what the wise men call a centaur. ( )
    The blessed old man walked, proceeding along the road.
    The blessed Abba Anthony marvelled.
    That animal ran forth before his face till he came to a broad place.
    He was the Devil, who had changed his form to a centaur.
    And Abba Anthony marvelled, as he said:
    '*How has he changed himself to this animal and appeared?*'
    After he went on a little, *he saw a man who resembled him,*
    who was a homunculus and he was standing upon a stone
    and there were horns upon his head, (on) his forehead.
    When Abba Anthony saw him ( ) *he said to him: 'Who art thou*
        whom I see?'
    He answered him: 'I am a dead man and I am in this desert.
    I am one of those whom the heathen call satyr.
    For *these are those who tempt the souls of the Greeks*
    until they become followers of demons.'

AM.PAUL.B. 4.3

21. After a few days, he was working;
    for he took care to exert himself.
    One stood before the door, he drew out the plait on which he was
        working;
    for he was plaiting baskets to give to those who came to him,
    in exchange for what they brought him.
    When he rose he saw an animal with the face of a man,
    while his limbs and feet and hooves were like those of an ass.
    When Anthony saw him, he crossed himself.
    He said to him: 'I am the servant of Christ,
    if you have been sent to me, behold here I am.'
    But the animal and the demons with it fled
    in such speed that they fell dead.

404

The death of the animal was the fall of the wicked beasts and
  demons,
which were doing everything to bring Anthony forth from the desert,
but they were not able.

GAR.ANT.S. 59.5

22. *Those who served him, among those who knew him,*
  because he would not let them enter, would remain outside.
  They would spend days and nights before the door
  and they would hear a tumult,
  as if a great multitude were within
  and they heard voices shouting and many weak voices crying out,
    saying:
  'Depart from what is ours. Why dost thou dwell in this desert?
  Thou wilt not be able to withstand our snares.'
  The men who were outside thought at first that men were within,
  who had entered in to him by means of ladders.
  But they looked through holes,
  they could not see anyting.
  Then they knew, in truth, that those were demons.
  But he when he heard them, did not pay attention to them (the
    demons).
  Anthony came before the door.
  He begged the men to withdraw themselves and not to fear, saying:
  '*This is the way the demons act in these forms of fantasies which*
    frighten.
  But cross yourselves and go courageously
  and leave these to humiliate themselves alone.'
  They departed, strengthened by the sign of the Cross.

GAR.ANT.S. 18.11

23. *How many sufferings he endured.* (   )
  We know these things through those who served him.
  For they heard, in that place, tumults and many voices and the
    sound of weapons.
  At night they saw the mountain full of sparks of fire.
  They saw him, as if he was fighting with some he was seeing
  and he was praying against them.
  To those who served him, he would give more encouragement.
  Truly he was worthy of wonder, that, alone as he was in this desert,
    he was not afraid of the demons and the many wild animals in that
    place.

GAR.ANT.S. 57.24

24. And he went and arrived at the cave
and near it, at about half a furrow's length, he set up a cross.
And he brought stones and he traced the plan of a small oratory
and he knelt there in prayer
and he passed the night in the place.
And during the night shapes of basilisks and fearful shapes of every kind
gathered together against him.
And the more constancy he, on his side, showed,
the more the gruff voices and grievous exhalations increased,
just as if great serpents had arrived and were coming
and as if their breath were striking against the clothes of the blessed man
in order to drive him away.
But he was thus constant in prayer
all that night and all the day and again another night also.
And next behold the sound of boulders
being uprooted above the blessed man
and they were broken and fell upon him from the rock above
and they came and reached him.
And thus they passed him as he was kneeling at his prayer, not having the power to touch him.
And thus he passed seven days and nights in that place in such conflicts.

BR.PAUL.SY. 112.8

25. And from that time I remained settled in the cave,
while they (the demons) used to display to me foul visions
many fearful shapes, strange to the sight of men.
And thereupon they would speak with me with speech like men.
And further they even took the shapes of men
and they came and they pretended to entreat me to come out
and to go with them to their houses,
for the purpose (as they said) of visiting the sick.
And again they often came and cried: 'Flee, flee.
Behold, the land is full of Huns.'
And Huns appeared to me in various fearful shapes,
riding on horses, with swords drawn and flashing.
And behold, they came to the door, crying in barbaric language
and in an excited state and with arrows fitted to their bows.

BR.PAUL.SY. 114.12

26. *As the saint prayed,*
    behold, the whole company of demons came down to the cave upon
        the rock
    in the form of a troop of horses engaged in fighting one another.
    Others came before the door,
    they made balls of fire which they cast inside the cave,
    and suddenly they would vanish.
    The saint Macarius sang psalms with fortitude.

AM.MAC.SC.B. 81.11

27. *When the evil demons saw his perfection,*
    they armed against him in troops and in hosts of darkness,
    thinking to bring him down from the height of virtue
    and attacking his mind with evil thoughts unceasingly by day and
        night,
    and terrifying him with phantom forms.
    But the righteous man pursued them with the holy sign of the Cross.
    And when God saw his great endurance, He gave him rest from all
        thoughts.

DAV.JOH.KH.B. 351.6

28. The holy man saw a cave in which was no one
    and he heard the sound of a great tumult.
    And the holy man said to the angel:
    'What is the sound of this great tumult?'
    The angel said to him: 'These are the demons which thou hast
        caused to depart from the land of Syria.
    Their chief is he who was in the house of Gabriel. Their number is
        three thousand and thirty-nine, a regiment and a half,
    which thou hast expelled from all the land of the Syrians.
    Now God has given thee power against them to expel them from
        here and to scatter them.'

NAU.AAR.SY. 721.13

29. *That evening, he* (the Devil) *came with these deceptions,*
    so that the whole place seemed to be shaking,
    as if the four walls were being burst,
    with demons entering in through them.
    They had the forms of animals and reptiles in a fantasy.
    And immediately that place was filled with phantoms,
    in the form of lions and bears and leopards
    and bulls and serpents and asps with wolves.

407

And each one made its way towards him,
with a great noise according to its kind.
The lions roared, wanting to spring on him,
the bull appeared to be about to gore him,
the serpent crawled and did not reach him,
and the wolf made his way.
All these appeared with one another
and the noise of their voices was very terrifying.
But Anthony, beaten by them, felt a great pain in his body.
In his soul, he was more alert
and he stayed prostrate, strong without fear.
He groaned because of the pain in his body,
but his mind was firm and he mocked them.

GAR.ANT.S. 14.16

30. The Devil observed Anthony.
    As David says in the Psalms: 'He gnashed his teeth against him.'
    Anthony was comforted by the Saviour,
    who saved him from the works of the Enemy and his many deceits.
    As Anthony was keeping vigil in the night
    the Enemy sent wild animals against him
    and all the hyenas which are in that desert.
    They came forth from their holes,
    they surrounded him like a circle.
    Each one opened his mouth at him threatening to bite him.
    But he knew the craft of the Enemy.
    He said to them all: 'If you have been given authority over me,
    I am prepared that you should eat me,
    but if the demons are they who have sent you,
    do not remain in this place but withdraw;
    for I am the servant of Christ.'
    When Anthony said this, they fled,
    as if his words followed them like a whip.

GAR.ANT.S. 58.12

31. The demons saw the work of piety and the number of souls whom
    the saint (Macarius) helped,
    especially that he brought them as gifts to God,
    so that they should follow Him.
    They were greatly angered and *they came upon him at midday as he*
    was sitting alone
    and they all surrounded him like dogs.

They leapt upon his face and they tore his flesh without mercy,
so that his whole body was like a bruise.

AM.MAC.SC.B. 88.4

32. He was beaten with innumerable stripes by the devils,
and he learned by experience much about their cunning.

BU.II.PAL.SY. 279.10

33. 'Demons fought with me,
they were dragging me along the ground and torturing me.
and God permitted me to be persecuted by them for thirty years. ( )
And from that time the evil spirits were not able to touch me.'

LOOK.MAR.SY. 15.14

34. 'I have been in great tribulations.
Sometimes myriads of demons who were in the sea
lay in wait for me that they might drown me.
Frequently they dragged me from here to the base of the mountain
until there was no skin or flesh left on my limbs.
They shouted at me and kept saying:
"Go away from our land and from our place.
Not since our days has anyone else come here."'

LOOK.MAR.SY. 10.5

35. One night he went to fill the (water-skins with) water, according to
his wont.
As soon as he had bent down over the spring,
immediately the devil smote him a blow upon his loins,
as with a stick.
And they departed and left him half dead.
And he understood who had done this thing to him.

BU.II.PAL.SY. 268.21

36. *He (the Enemy) came at night with a multitude of demons,*
he beat him with great blows,
so that he was left lying prostrate without power to speak, from the
pain of the blows.

GAR.ANT.S. 13.5

37. On many occasions the devils beat this man
and they brought many illnesses upon him
so that he was not able to stand beside the altar
nor even to offer up the Offering,
but an angel came and took him by the hand

and he straightway was strengthened.
And he made him stand up healed before the altar.
Then the brethren saw the scars of his beatings and they marvelled.

BU.II.HIER.SY. 427.20

38. One night the demon watched for him, having lost his patience, and as he stooped down at the well, gave him a blow with a cudgel across the loins and left him (apparently) dead, with no perception of what he had suffered or from whom. ( ) And for a year he was so ill that with difficulty did his body and soul recover strength.

LO.PAL.G. 89(XIX)

39. And when those devils had remained with him a long time
and had done nothing, as they were speaking,
these wicked and evil devils laid hold of him
and smote him with severe blows
and wounded his whole body and tore him cruelly
and they left him with little life remaining in him.
Then he lay groaning in the place in which they left him
and he was not able to turn and depart to another place.
And after a little time, when his breath came to him,
the members of his house and helpers who were near him
went forth in grief to seek him.
And when they found him, they learned from him the cause of the
    wounds
and they begged him to go with them to his house.
Then this youth did not yield to their many and urgent entreaties.
And again on another night, those devils made to come upon him
    wounds
which were more numerous and more severe than before.
And to the entreaty of those helpers who were near him
that he would depart from that district
he would not agree, but he said to them:
'It is better for me to die than to live with the blemishes of this
    world.'
Then on the third night in a short time,
from the many blows of the devils,
he departed from this present life;
for without mercy they fell upon him
and they smote him with blows upon the former blows
and thus they injured him until he struggled for breath.

BU.II.HIER.SY. 360.1

DISCERNING SPIRITS: DISPELLING EVIL

1. RECOGNITION

THEMES

The recognition of fantasies by their effect on the emotions.
The recognition of demons by their effect on thought.
The recognition of spirits by their behaviour.
The necessity for courage in the discernment of spirits.
The necessity for self-preparation in order to attain the power of
    distinguishing spirits.
The discerning of spirits as a gift.

EPISODES

The ability of certain ascetics to distinguish spirits.
The advising of disciples on methods of discerning spirits.

QUOTATIONS

1. If they (the demons) come to you at night and wish to tell you what
        will happen,
    or they say: 'We are angels',
    do not listen to them; for they are lying.
    If they praise your austerities and call you blessed,
    do not listen to them, but cross yourselves and your dwellings and
        pray.
    And you will see them disappear in shame.
    For they are powerless and afraid of the Cross of Christ,
    because he stripped them naked by it and condemned them.
    If they stand shamelessly dancing and changing their appearance
        in fantasies,
    do not fear or attend to them as if they were good.
    For it is easy to know and to distinguish the presence of the evil ones
        from them that are good, when God gives grace.
    For it is possible to know them in this:
    the vision of the holy ones does not disturb, nor do they cry out,
    nor will one hear their voice.
    They will be quiet and gentle, so that joy and consolation of that soul
        immediately appear.
    For the Lord is with them, who is the consolation and the whole
        light,
    so that we see those who appear.

411

If some fear as men, *when they see the vision of the glorious and good beings,*
those who appear take away that fear with love. ( )
For their fear is not weakness of the soul,
but to give the knowledge of the glorified ones who have come to them.
Such then is the vision of the Holy Ones.

GAR.ANT.S. 41.15

2. For we have the sign wherein not to fear.
   When a fantasy appears to someone,
   let him not fall down before it in weakness,
   but whatever it is, let him ask it first courageously:
   'Who art thou, or where hast thou come from?'
   If it be a holy vision that is revealed to thee, it will reassure thee,
   and thy fear will change to joy.
   But if it is one from the Devil,
   immediately it will become weak, as it sees thy pure heart.
   For this is a sign of calmness for a man to ask:
   'Who art thou or whence dost thou come?'

GAR.ANT.S. 50.1

3. When he (Pachomius) brought him (the man of Alexandria) to the brothers,
   he gave him ascetic exercises and fasts to do,
   so that he should be able to live.
   He commanded him to fast until evening daily
   without fat and not to eat any cooked food or any food.
   He said to him further: 'If thou shouldest be sick at some time,
   do not believe that it is an illness,
   unless thou tellest me,
   and we examine it, whether it is an illness from God or from the demons of evil. ( )
   If we know that it is an illness according to God,
   I will command the brethren to care for thee until thou art recovered.'

LE.PAC.S. 173.15

4. The brethren came to Abba Anthony,
   that he should tell them about the fantasies which they saw,
   whether they were real or from devils. ( )
   They said to him: 'And how does the Abba know that our ass has died?'

412

Abba Anthony said to them: 'The devils showed me.'
Therefore they said to him: 'We also have come to question thee,
because we have seen fantasies and often they have been real
and we wish to know whether we have erred.'
And the old man showed them
that these things are from the devils which cannot be inquired into.

BU.II.PAL.SY. 632.23

5. *And* (the Lord) *gave him a sign that he might distinguish (spirits)*
from one another. ( )
And the ministers of the enemy were never able to lead him astray. ( )
If it was an unclean spirit which was appearing before him, then his
body emitted fear,
but *if it was an angel of light, the limbs of his body would pain him*
and his thoughts would not disappear at all in his heart.
And through the gift of God, he would know them and separate them
from one another and rebuke the evil.
He would receive the words of the angels of God
and these words which were sent to him,
he would examine them,
whether they were in accordance with the Scriptures or not.

LE.PAC.S. 13b.19

6. Many times they (the demons) wished to deceive him (Pachomius).
They would appear to him in multitudes of forms and, through the gift
which the Lord had given him,
he recognised them and he rebuked them in His name.

LE.PAC.S. 17a.2

7. *A great matter in the ascetic practice of Anthony*
was that he had the gift of distinguishing spirits. ( )
For he knew what moved within him
and he knew the intention of each of them to him.
Not only was he, Anthony, not deceived by them
but he would teach others who fought against them as they disturbed
them in their thoughts,
how they might have power over their designs,
telling them of the wiles of those that worked within them.
Each one of those that came to him was enabled to prevail
if he was trained by him.

GAR.ANT.S. 94.3

8. (Abba Amoi taught Abba John) *especially concerning the (distinction between) phantasies of the revelation of the spirit (and) either visions or revelations, to act with true discernment.*

AM.JOH.K.B. 333.10

9. One day *as he* (Pachomius) *was sitting working on a mat, a demon appeared to him.*
He took the form in which the Lord appeared to him, saying to him from a distance: 'Greeting.'
And when he (Pachomius) saw him, he considered in his heart what kind this was.
Then he discerned in himself that *behold, he was meditating according to (his) custom*
and when the demon saw the meditations, he began to take them out of his heart.
He said to himself: 'Why now am I not thinking?
Now my thoughts have disappeared.'
Immediately he leaped up, he stood according to what the Lord put in his heart,
he seized the hand of the phantom of the demon.
He breathed immediately into its face.
It became dark.
The hand of the demon disappeared little by little from his hand like smoke.
When that one had disappeared he (Pachomius) *stood, he prayed to God.*

LE.PAC.S. 15b.3

10. *The fantasies of the evil ones disturb and trouble through noises and loud voices and cries.* ( )
Then immediately there appear in the soul, from them, fear, confusion and disturbance of thought,
hatred (of asceticism) sadness, memory of relatives, fear of death, and after these the desire for evil, indifference to virtue, hatred of asceticism.
When, therefore, you see some revealed to you, do not fear.
If the fear is removed, immediately joy appears to you in its place,
with rejoicing and rest and calmness of thought in the heart,
with the love of God. Be courageous and pray. ( )
If visions appear to you with great disturbance of soul,
with threat of death and what comes after, ( )
know that the visit is from the wicked.

GAR.ANT.S. 42.21

414

11. First we know this, that the demons are not called demons because
      they were created thus.
God forbid; for God did not create anything (evil) ever,
but they also were created good.
When they fell from the thought of heaven,
thenceforward they have rolled upon the earth.
They have deceived the pagans with fantasies,
but they are envious of us Christians.
They move all things in the way
so that we should not go up to heaven, in order that we may not enter
the place from which they fell.
Hence the need of great austerities and great prayers,
so that gradually we shall receive an advancement,
and a gift of grace and of distinguishing spirits
and be able to know which of them are a little wicked and which are
more wicked
and what is the interest of each
and in what things and how each of them is overcome and cast out.

GAR.ANT.S. 28.8

2   DISTINGUISHING GOOD AND EVIL IN FELLOW-MEN

THEMES

The ability to recognise subjects of speech and attitudes of mind in
    fellow-men.
The ability to recognise the way of life of those partaking of the Euchar-
    ist.
The recognition by angels of the worth of men.

EPISODES

The appearance of angels or pigs according to the subjects of speech of
    men.
The appearance of honey, bread, or excrement as food of men, according
    to their attitudes of mind.
The appearance of the faces of those entering and leaving the church
    as either lighted or in darkness.
The distinguishing by angels of the worth of those partaking of the
    Eucharist.
The admonition by angels of those misbehaving at the celebration of
    the Eucharist.
The giving or withholding of the Sacrament by angels in accordance
    with the worth of the participants.

QUOTATIONS

1. One said that, as the old men were sitting once speaking profitably,
there was one among them who saw visions.
He saw the angels giving glory and singing to them.
But when other talk came between them the angels withdrew
and pigs came in their midst, full of evil smell, and defiled them.
When they returned to speaking profitably,
the angels came again and gave glory to them.

CHA.AP.PA.S. 50.30(196)

2. *Some monks came forth from their cells.*
They gathered in one place and they were moved to speak
of asceticism and the service of God and of the necessity of pleasing
God.
As they were speaking thus, *two angels appeared to some of the*
old men among them,
with scapularies in their hands,
giving glory to each one who was speaking of the Kingdom of God.
And those who saw the vision were silent.
On the morrow they gathered at that place,
they were moved to speak of one of the brothers who had sinned
and they blamed (him)
and there appeared to the first old men a pig full of evil smell and
all impurity.
Those who saw the vision, when they knew the sin which was committed,
they told the brothers of the glory from the angels and the form of
the pig.

CHA.AP.PA.S. 54.1(208)

3. One of the elders said: 'Once the fathers were sitting and speaking
on profitable matters
and there was in their midst one of the elders and he saw visions
and he saw angels flying above them.
And when they came to another subject, the angels departed thence
and he saw pigs rolling about them and wallowing in the mire.
And afterwards they began to speak on profitable things and then
the angels came again and they glorified God.'

BU.II.PAL.SY. 612.11

4. There was a certain great elder who saw visions
and he happened to be eating with the company of the brethren,

416

and while they were eating, the old man saw in the spirit,
as he was sitting at the table,
that some of the brethren were eating honey, others bread, and
others dung,
and he wondered at these within himself.
And he made supplication and he entreated from God
and said: 'Lord reveal to me this mystery.
Since this food is one, why, when these are laid upon the table,
are they various and thus are seen to be eating differently,
some of the brothers honey, some of them bread and some of them
dung?'
And a voice came to him from above, saying:
'Those who are eating honey are those who eat with fear
and with trembling and with spiritual joy ( ).
Those who eat bread are those who confess and receive the grace
of God for these things, ( )
Those who eat dung are those who complain.'

BU.II.PAL.SY. 528.15

5. *There was a great old man who was a seer*
and it happened that he was eating with a number of brothers,
and as they ate, *the old man saw, through the spirit.*
He saw among those sitting at the table
some who were eating honey,
some who were eating bread,
some who were eating excrement.
And he marvelled in his heart, he prayed to God,
saying: 'O Lord, reveal to me this mystery; for this one and the same
food is placed before them all,
and in the eating, it is changed and appears thus;
some are eating honey, some bread, some excrement.'
A voice came to him from on high.

CHA.AP.PA.S. 62.12(215)

6. After they had spoken with one another *they went into the church
of God*
to perform the appointed service.
Apa Paul said: '*I looked at each one of those that entered to see in
what state were the souls that went in.*'
For he had this gift from God, to see how each one was,
in the way that we see the faces of one another.
All those who entered *had joyful faces and their looks were glad,*
so that the angel of each one rejoiced with him.

417

Then he saw one who was black whose whole body was dark,
while demons enclosed him on all sides to seize him
and they drew him towards themselves, putting a muzzle on his nose.
His holy angel, who followed him at a distance, was greatly dis-
tressed.
Paul then wept and he struck his breast with his hand many times.
He sat before the church, *he wept greatly over that which was*
thus revealed to him. ( )
He sat outside in silence and wept greatly over what was revealed
to him.
When they had finished, they left the church, they all came forth.
Again Paul noticed each one, knowing in what way he had entered.
He saw him whom he had previously seen black and in darkness
with his whole body giving light as he came forth from the church.
His face was shining, giving light.
The demons followed at a distance from him.
The holy angel which accompanied him rejoiced
and was glad and was in great joy over the man.

CHA.AP.PA.S. 47.18(191)

7. The blessed man Paul the Simple, ( )
related to the fathers the following matter:
'I once went to a certain monastery that I might visit the brethren ( )';
they went to the holy church of God that they might ( )
perform the service. ( )
And the blessed Paul looked at and examined each one of them
(seeing) by this means how the soul entered;
for he had the gift which had been given to him by God,
so that he saw the soul of every man and he knew how it was,
in the manner that we look at the faces of one another.
And he saw that everyone who was entering was glorious in the
appearance of (his) soul,
and lighted in (his) face
and that the angel of each one was rejoicing in him.
And he saw one whose face was in sickness and affliction
and whose whole body was in darkness
and that devils had hold of him by each of his hands
and that they were lifting him up and dragging him towards them
and that they had put a ring in his nose
and that his holy angel was a long way from him
and that he followed after him grieving and sorrowful over him. ( )

418

Then after a short time when the service was ended
and they were all coming forth,
then Paul examined each one of them (that he might see)
in what manner came out those whom he had seen entering,
whether with the appearance with which they entered, or whether
    with another.
And then he saw that man whom he saw entering,
whose whole body, before he entered the church, was in darkness,
when he came forth from the church, (he saw) his face lighted and
    his body white
and the devils were afar off
and his holy angel was close to him and walked with him.
And he (Paul) was glad and rejoiced greatly over that man.

                                      BU.II.PAL.SY. 298.8

8. After those who approached the holy Mysteries had received the
    holy and fearful Offering,
he saw the souls through their faces, to what sins each of them was
    subject.
And he saw the face of sinners like charcoal,
he saw some of them whose faces were burning and their eyes red,
    full of blood.
Others among them had their faces lighted and their garments were
    white.
Others while they were partaking in the body of the Lord *were*
    on fire and burning.
Some became like the light which entered their mouths and caused
    their whole body to be lighted. ( )
But these two women came, of whom they had spoken to the bishop,
    for whom he had thus prayed.
And he saw them also about to approach to partake of the Holy
    Mysteries of Christ
and their faces gave light and were dignified and their garments were
    white.
And when they also received the Holy Mysteries of Christ,
they became illuminated with light.
When (the bishop) *turned again to beseech God to know the things*
    which had been revealed to him ( )
an angel of God stood before him.
He commanded him to question him on each one.
Immediately the holy bishop, concerning those two women, ( ) said
    to the angel:

'How, when they partook of the Mystery of Christ, *did their faces
    give light*
and their clothes appear white and their bearing elevated?'
The angel answered: 'Because they repented of those things which
    they had done.'

CHA.AP.PA.S. 58.7(211)

9. Les pères m'ont rapporté que l'illuminé Euthyme avait reçu aussi
de Dieu la grâce que voici: d'après l'aspect du corps visible, il
discernait les mouvements de l'âme et savait dire contre quelles
tentations chacun avait à lutter, de quelles il se rendait mâitre,
par quelles il était vaincu. De même aussi, quand il offrait le saint
sacrifice, il voyait très souvent les anges accomplir avec lui la
liturgie, et il racontait en privé à ses disciples: 'Très souvent, au
moment de distribuer aux frères les divins mystères (de l'Eucharistie), j'en ai vu, parmi ceux qui s'approchaient, qui étaient illuminés
par la communion, et d'autres qui par elle étaient condamnés et
de quelque façon cadavérisés parce qu'ils étaient indignes de la
divine lumière.'

FE.III/I.EUT.G. 100(XIX)

10. Nous avons vu là un prêtre, homme saint et d'une rare humilité,
que jouissait constamment de visions: il se nommait Piammônâs.
Ce prêtre un jour, alors qu'il offrait à Dieu le sacrifice, vit un ange
debout à la droite de l'autel, qui notait les frères qui s'approchaient
de l'Eucharistie et inscrivait leurs noms dans un livre. Comme certains frères n'étaient pas venus à la synaxe, il vit qu'on biffait leurs
noms: ces frères, après treize jours, moururent. Les démons torturai-
ent souvent ce prêtre, et ils l'avaient rendu si faible, qu'il ne pouvait
se tenir debout a l'autel ni offrir le sacrifice. Mais un ange vint qui,
lui ayant pris la main, le remplit sur-le-champ de force et le remit
sain et sauf à l'autel. Quand les frères virent la trace de ses tortures,
ils en furent frappés de stupeur.

FE.IV/I.HIS.G. 128(XXV)

11. But one day, while he was offering the Oblation,
    an Arab man, who had recently been baptised was present there.
    And he saw that fire came down from heaven
    and tongues of flame were hovering over the Oblation
    and hosts of angels with their heads bowed before the divine
        sacrifice.

And he saw that whoever received the Oblation,
they wrote his name in the Book of Life.
And that barbarian believed and praised God.

BR.JAM.SY. 265.2

12. And when this man was offering to God the service,
he saw an angel standing at the right hand of the altar.
And he wrote down and engraved in a book
the names of the brothers who offered up the Sacrament.
And he saw that the names of those who did not come to the con
gregation were erased
and that after three days these died.

BU.II.HIER.SY. 427.16

13. (He said): 'At the time when I mount the throne, *I see the sinners
thus*
with angels fleeing from them because of their evil smell.
I see also the righteous clothed in light in the service
while their faces are bright like light
and like the sun giving rays of light.
As the angels run toward them, they embrace them with joy
because of the sweet smell of their practices.
When I see these things I weep and I groan, because of the separation
of these from those others.
Believe me, O God-loving people, that *as I stood upon the altar
one day.*
I saw the sinners coming towards the altar *with sad faces,*
like darkness, while their angels followed them weeping,
and there were boards of wood in the hands of the angels like tablets
and they were holding them out to the Saviour upon the altar
saying:
"These are the sins of the men which they have committed yesterday
and last night.
They are not pure to receive thy blessed body and blood."
And I heard a voice above the altar rebuking me greatly, saying:
"Macarius, why dost thou not teach the people, so that they cease
their sins before they die?"'

AM.MAC.TK.B. 107.5

14. Once a hermit fell ill. ( ) And the Lord sent his angel to minister
to him. After the angel had ministered to him for a week, the
fathers remembered him and said to each other: 'Let us go and see

whether the old man is ill.' ( ) And he said: 'For a month I was ill and no one visited me. Now for a week an angel of the Lord has ministered to me, but he went away the moment you arrived.' And with these words, he peacefully died.

CHA.SA.L. 95(VII)

15. It was said of him, that at the sacred time
    when he was standing at the altar, making the Offering,
    he saw the Holy Spirit descending,
    who made of the bread, the body and of the wine, the blood.
    God also revealed to him that he should know those
    who were worthy to partake of the divine Sacraments and those who were not worthy.
    Then he saw again the angel of the Lord, standing in the midst of
        the monks,
    holding a sharp spear of fire.
    He was angry and enraged against those who talked and whispered
        among themselves.
    and who thought of things not proper to that sacred time.
    He wished to let fall his spear upon them and to transfix them,
    but by the supplication and the prayer
    which he made secretly to God for them,
    he averted the anger from them,
    while he hoped that they would turn towards the Lord
    and would do penance for their wickedness.
    He also saw those who stood in fear and trembling and attentive-
        ness,
    while they were silent and applying themselves to the divine words
    and were free from wicked and terrestrial thoughts.
    And for the God-loving, (he saw the angels) overshadowing them
        and protecting them.
    And he also saw the light which went forth from the splendour of the
        face of the Lord,
    from the interior of the Holy Sanctuary,
    and entered into the hearts of those who were worthy among the
        brothers.

NAU.JE.PE.SY. LVI.9

16. Every time that our all-holy, saintly father, John, accomplished
        the Holy Sacrament,
    he was worthy to see the presence of the Holy Spirit upon the altar,
    turning the bread to the body and the chalice to the nature of blood.
    It was also revealed to him

422

who were worthy to receive from the Holy Mysteries
and who were not worthy,
so that they also were revealed to him through God.
When all the people were gathered while he was making the offering,
as he began to give them from the Holy Mysteries,
he looked out among the brethren
and he saw an angel of the Lord standing in their midst
with a sword grasped in his hand.
And if there is one among the brethren
who speaks or thinks of matters which are unfitting,
the angel threatens him,
wishing to strike upon him with the sword in his hand.

AM.JOH.K.B. 381.7

17. My father Macarius said to me: 'I observed, *at the time of* (*the*
    celebration of) *the Mysteries,*
    I did not give the Sacrament to Mark, the ascetic, once,
    but when he came to receive, I saw an angel
    giving the Sacrament to him in his hands.'
    Abba Macarius was a priest of the Church.

AM.MAC.AL.B. 253.10

18. Macarius, the priest, told us: 'I gave heed, at the time that I was
    giving the Holy Offering, to Mark the Mourner.
    I never gave the Offering to him,
    but an angel gave to him from the altar.
    I alone saw that it was the palm of the hand of the angel giving to
    him.'

BU.II.PAL.SY. 242.14

19. The holy Macarius told me the following—for he was a priest; 'I
    noticed at the time of distributing the Mysteries that it was never I
    who gave the Oblation to Marcus, the ascetic, but an angel used to
    give it him from the altar. I saw only the knuckle of the donor's
    hand.'

LO.PAL.G. 85(XVIII)

20. While we were distributing the Holy Offering,
    the priests received and then the deacons.
    And when the deacons began to receive,
    God gave a revelation to the holy man.
    He saw one of the deacons of the clergy,
    as he came to receive this Holy Mystery,

423

the body and the blood of Christ,
he saw the angel of the Offering stretch forth his hand.
He took the Mystery from the hand of the deacon,
he placed it upon the table.

LE.PAC.S. 347b.10

21. *He was worthy to see many times the Son of the Living God upon the*
    holy altar.
    giving to those who were worthy by the hand of the Archbishop.
    It happened one day a man came to partake of the Holy Mysteries
     of our Lord Jesus Christ
    and when the Archbishop stretched forth his hand to give to him,
    forthwith he saw the hand of the Son of God restraining his hand
    so that he could not give to him, saying to him:
    'Archbishop, do not give to him; for he is not worthy to partake of
     my holy body.'

HY.PET.AL.B. 254.20

22. *For many times the Lord opened their* (Pachomius and Theodore) *eyes*
    and they saw the angel of God, within the Sanctuary, upon the altar,
    giving the Holy Mystery to the men who were worthy,
    through the hand of him who served, either a priest or a bishop.
    If one was not worthy, or was unclean, and he approached to par-
     take of the Holy Mysteries,
    the angel would withdraw his hand, so that the priest alone gave to him.

LE.PAC.B. 93.25

23. *Many times the Lord opened their* (Pachomius and Theodore) *eyes.*
    They saw the angel of the Lord
    in the Sanctuary upon the altar,
    giving the Sacrament to the man who was worthy,
    through the hand of him who was serving, either bishop or priest.
    But if one who was unworthy or impure approached the altar to
     partake,
    the angel would withdraw his hand from him
    and the cleric alone gave to that one.

LE.PAC.S. 154a.32

3 POSSESSION AND THE CASTING OUT OF DEVILS

THEMES

The effects of demonic possession.
The use of violence in the casting out of demons.

424

THE ESTABLISHMENT OF A NON-MATERIAL ENVIRONMENT

The use of words in the casting out of demons.
The forms taken by the Devil and demons after their expulsion.

EPISODES

The casting out of a demon from a demoniac at the sanctuary of a saint.
The casting out by ascetics of demons causing delusions.
The disappearance of expelled demons in the form of fire or smoke.
The departure of demons by running away.

QUOTATIONS

1. The man who had been a demoniac answered saying:
   '*Allow me, my holy father, to tell thee the things which I saw.*
   Since my youth a demon was with me until today
   and I never saw him with my eyes, except today.
   And when he was about to come upon me, at *times I saw a fire in
   my presence,*
   I would be disturbed and fall down upon the ground.
   I knew nothing until the demon left me and men came and stood me
   up.
   It happend to me that, when he came upon me this time,
   I became unconscious, I saw the saint George.
   He came into the Sanctuary,
   He took my hand,
   he encouraged me.
   *I saw that demon this time with my eyes, in the form of a man in my
   presence,*
   while the saint George gave him a great chastisement.
   He seized him, he dragged him up the column until he reached the
   top
   and he gave great pain to him.
   At last the demon cried out with a loud voice, swearing oaths,
   saying: "I will leave this man, I will not return to him ever."
   I saw the saint George, he took the demon,
   he raised him up, he cast him down upon the paving;
   and the demon gave a great sound from his nose, he departed and left.
   For my part I knew that I was healed in my body,
   I slept and rested.
   I did not see anyone until this lame man came and saw me
   and as I opened my eyes, I saw the saint George.
   He took my hands,
   he put them round the neck of the lame man,
   he signed to me to hold him well. (   )

He signed to me,
I released his neck, he rose, he departed running.
And the saint George went to heaven
as I looked after him.'

BA.HY.II.MIR.GEO.B. 324.26

2. The holy old man, Abba Palamon, and Pachomius, when they saw
    his great humiliation,
they wept with great sorrow and they grasped him,
and they wept together.
That demon threw him down again upon the earth and tormented him
    more.
But they stood over him *and they prayed to the Lord for him with*
    tears
until his mind was restored to him and he stood up in their presence,
and they began to grasp him to take him into a place alone,
until the Lord gave to him the grace of healing from that unclean
    spirit.
But he, *through the power of the demon which was with him,*
he seized a large (piece of) wood and was about to kill the two.
They were not able to grasp him
and immediately he ran to the north by the mountain until he reached
    Achmin,
and alone he cast himself into the furnace of the bath and was
    burned miserably.

LE.PAC.B. 15.13

3. And one day the Devil stood in the likeness of a priest
    and urged him to receive communion from him:
    'Away, thou who art full of deceit
    and father of all falsehood and enemy of all righteousness.
    Wilt thou never cease to lead astray the souls of Christians?
    And dost thou also dare to trample upon the Holy Mysteries?'
    Then he (the Devil) said to him:
    'A little more and I had prevailed over thee in thy fall;
    for thus I have led astray another man
    and driven him out of his mind and made him mad.
    And when many holy men made supplication on his behalf in prayer,
    then he returned to his senses.'
    And when he had said these things to him, the Devil departed from
    him.

BU.II.HIER.SY. 398.4

4. And I constrained the Evil One thus,
   so that he became a flame of fire
   and he burnt everything which I had in my cell,
   until even the mat upon which I stood blazed with fire
   and I thought that I should be completely burnt.

   BU.II.PAL.SY. 150.22

5. And having lasted out two days and two nights, I exasperated the
   demon so that he became a flame of fire and burned up all the things
   in the cell, so that even the little mat on which I stood was consumed
   with fire and I thought I was being all burned up.

   LO.PAL.G. 82(XVIII)

6. And he said: '*They appear on many occasions, in the form in which*
        God revealed the Devil to Job,
   saying: "His eyes are like the morning star.
   Lamps of fire come forth from his mouth,
   worms of fire come forth from his mouth.
   Smoke of a furnace, burning with coals of fire,
   these are the fires of his soul.
   A flame of fire comes forth from his mouth."'

   GAR.ANT.S. 30.12

7. *And we will see the false work of the demons as smoke*,
   while they flee from us and do not pursue us.
   For they are very weak, ( )
   looking ahead at all times to the fire which is prepared for them.

   GAR.ANT.S. 49.24

8. *It happened that, when the blessed Helias finished praying, behold*,
        Michael the Archangel came to him.
   He beat all the demons, he cast them forth on the mountain.
   And the Devil became a flame of fire and departed.

   SOB.HEL.S. 44a.2

9. *It happened one day, while my father was sitting in the monastery*,
   behold, the Devil with a crowd of demons came in to him
   and he spoke with my father with great threats and evil (words).
   My father, when he saw the Devil, he knew (him).
   Immediately, he jumped up and overpowered him
   and seized him and cast him upon the ground
   and placed his foot upon him.

427

And he called to the brothers who were near him: 'Take the rest
which follow him.'
And suddenly they dissolved like smoke.

LEI.SIN.B. 36.27

4 DISPELLING EVIL

THEMES

The means used by the ascetics to conquer the Devil.
The causing of the Devil to depart and to become invisible.

EPISODES

The expelling of the Devil by blowing, by making the sign of the Cross.
The defeating of the Devil by humility.
The dispelling of demons by prayer, meditation, reading the Scriptures.
The dispelling of the Devil by speaking the name of Christ.
Confining the Devil within a circle traced on the ground.

QUOTATIONS

1. *The devil took the form of an old man, ( )*
   the boy blew into his face
   and immediately he became invisible.

LE.PAC.B. 3.2

2. But Satan, the hater of good things, on seeing the two co-sponsors
   going, in earnestness and in divine love, to be blessed by the holy
       man,
   showed them an apparition,
   in order that they might not come again to the presence of the holy
       man.
   And when they reached the door of his cell in the monastery,
   they saw that a girl, beautiful to look at, came out from his presence,
       merry and laughing.
   And when that presbyter saw her, he said to his co-sponsor:
   'See to whom you are urging me to come and be blessed.'
   For he was scandalised. ( )
   Then he (the holy man) commanded them to pray
   and he himself, having knelt down, continued entreating God,
   who wishes for the life of men,
   by his secret power to force the demon,
   who had appeared to these men in the form of a woman,
   to come and appear in the same form which they had seen.
   And suddenly that woman stood among them, mourning.

And the blessed man asked them: 'Is this the woman whom you
  saw?'
And they said: 'It is she in truth.'
And while they still supposed that it was a woman clad in flesh,
the holy man breathed upon her and made the sign of the Cross and
  said:
'Go to perdition, evil demon, and be not a stumbling block to
  believers.'
And as he spoke, the woman became like smoke
and vanished from them.

BR.JAM.SY. 249.9

3. *It happened one evening that the Devil, envious of his patience in afflic-*
    tions, passed over him,
  and threw down the jug, so that it was in two halves ( ).
  And Apater took the broken parts, he signed them with the form of
    holy Cross.
  It was joined immediately like brass, *as before.*

HY.AP.IR.B. 85.3

4. But one must by no means fear their fantasies;
  for they are nothing and go to destruction quickly,
  especially if one surrounds oneself with a wall
  through faith and the sign of the Cross.

GAR.ANT.S. 29.25

5. And every day the demons stoned him to oblige him to leave this
    cave.
  The holy man did not leave, but God gave him power against these
    demons.
  And he went forth from his cave, he set up a cross.
  And he prayed there all day and he begged God to give him victory.
  And on the second day he proceeded further and he made an oratory
  and he raised up another cross and the demons were seized with fear.
  On the third day he proceeded further again and set up a cross.
  He prayed and entered into the cave in which were the demons.
  He made them go forth and depart thence, like straw before the
    wind.
  And he made them go up the mountain, which is above the monas-
    tery.
  And the holy man set up three crosses on three hills
  in the name of the Father and the Son and the Holy Spirit.

And he halted them by the power of the victorious Cross
and he said to them: 'You have not the power to trouble in any way
the men who are in the limits of my monastery,
either by night or by day.'
And their chief turned and said to the holy man:
'Thou hast sent us from Syria and we came and we dwelt in this cave
and behold, thou dost send us from here.'

NAU.AAR.SY. 722.10

6. Once when Apa Macarius was walking on the edge of the marsh,
      carrying palm leaves,
   behold, the Devil met him in his path with a sickle in his hand.
   And he wished to overthrow him, but he was not able and he said to
      him:
   'My injury from thee is great, because I am powerless against thee.
   For behold, everything which thou dost, I do them also. ( )
   There is one thing in which thou dost surpass me. ( )
   It is thy humility.'

CHA.AP.PA.S. 24.4(102)

7. As Apa Macarius was passing once from the marsh to his cell,
      carrying palm leaves,
   the Devil met him upon the path with a sickle and he turned to strike
      him,
   but he was not able and he said to him:
   'Oh, thou art strong, Macarius, because it is not possible for me
      to prevail over thee.
   Behold, what thou dost, I also do it. ( )
   Because of thy humility, it is not possible for me to
      prevail over thee.'

AM.VER.MAC.B. 119.14

8. They said concerning Abba Macarius
   that on one occasion, when he was passing along a road,
   Satan met him and he was holding a sickle in his hand
   and wished to wound him and, when he was not able,
   he said to him: 'Macarius, I am driven from thee by a great force
   and I am not able to overcome thee.
   Behold, everything which thou doest, I do also.
   Thou dost fast but I never eat.
   Thou dost keep vigil, but I never sleep.
   But there is one practice alone in which thou dost surpass me.'

430

Macarius said to him: 'What is that?'
Then he said: 'It is thy humility;
for because of it I am not able to conquer thee.'
Then he spread out his hands in prayer
and then that Devil was not seen further.

BU.II.PAL.SY. 562.12

9. Abba Macarius was once going from the wood to his cell
and he was carrying palm leaves.
And Satan met him on the road, carrying a sickle.
And when he sought to wound him, he (Satan) was afraid
and fell down and worshipped the blessed man.
Then the old man fled thence and he related to the brethren every-
thing which had happened.
And they heard, they glorified God.

BU.II.PAL.SY. 624.6

10. On one occasion a devil took a knife
and stood over Abba Macarius and wished to cut off his foot.
And when he was unable because of his humility, he answered and
said to him:
'Everything which you possess we also possess.
But only in humility are you superior to us.
And (thus) you conquer us.'

BU.II.PAL.SY. 562.21

11. 'Quiconque donc, mes enfants', nous dit-il, 'veut chasser les démons doit commencer par asservir ses passions. De quelque passion
en effet qu'on se soit rendu maître, de cette passion aussi on chasse
le démon. Il vous faut peu à peu vaincre les passions, pour que,
de ces passions, vous chassiez les démons. Il y a un démon attaché
a la gourmandise: une fois donc que vous aurez triomphé de la
gourmandise, vous chasserez aussi le démon de ce vice.'

FE.IV/I.HIS.G. 99(XV)

12. There was a certain brother who lived in great seclusion
and while he was sleeping at night,
the devils in the form of angels wished to lead him astray
and roused him for the service and they showed him a light.
And he went to a certain old man and said to him:
'Father, the angels came to me with a light and woke me for the
service.'

431

And the old man said to him: 'Listen not to them my son; for they
  are devils.
But if they come to wake thee, say to them:
"When I wish to rise, I rise. But to you I will not listen."'

BU.II.PAL.SY. 511.9

13. *Anthony felt that the Lord had saved him and, as he breathed freely,*
   he felt that he was relieved from his suffering.
   He asked him who had manifested himself, saying:
   'Where wast thou? Why didst thou not appear to me, from the
      beginning, to heal me?'
   A voice came then to him, saying:
   'I was in this place, but *I waited to see thee fight.*
   Because thou didst endure and wast not overcome,
   I will be thy help at all times and I will make thee renowned in all
      places.'
   When he heard these things, he (Anthony) rose, he prayed
   and he was more powerful so that he felt the strength which had come
      to his body.

GAR.ANT.S. 16.1

14. *But Anthony, beaten by them, felt a great pain in his body.*
   In his soul, he was more alert and he stayed prostrate, strong without
      fear.
   He groaned because of the pain in his body.
   But his mind was firm and it was as if he mocked them.

GAR.ANT.S. 15.3

15. As he was walking on the road,
   the Devil brought a multitude of demons against him
   in the form of dogs which wished to kill him.
   The boy raised his eyes to heaven. He wept.
   Immediately they were scattered.

LE.PAC.B. 2.23

16. *Some times they (the demons) would shake his dwelling*
   to make him fear that it would fall upon him.
   Immediately he would open his mouth
   saying: 'Our God is our refuge and our power.'

LE.PAC.B. 20.26

17. *Many times they blessed me*
   and they cursed me in the name of the Lord.
   Many times they told me about the water of the river,

432

and I would say to them: 'What is your concern with this?'
They would surround me like soldiers.
Sometimes also they would fill the house with horses and reptiles and I
   would recite psalms ( ).
And at the prayer these were cast down by the Lord.
It happened one day that *they came in the dark with a phantom of*
   light in their hands, saying:
'We have come to make light for thee, O Anthony.'
But I shut my eyes, I prayed,
and immediately the light was quenched.
They came again once like singers of psalms and they spoke from
   the Scriptures,
but I, like one deaf, I did not hear.
One day *they shook my monastery but I was not shaken in my mind.*
They came again clapping, hissing and whistling,
but I prayed, I recited psalms, they began to weep and mourn.

GAR.ANT.S. 45.16

18. They said concerning Abba Theodore that when he dwelt in Scete
    a certain devil came and wished to enter into his presence.
    And he perceived him, that he wished to enter,
    and he bound him outside his cell.
    And then another devil came to enter and he also bound him.
    And in addition a third devil came
    and he found these bound before the door
    and he said to them: 'Why do you stand here outside?'
    They said to him: 'He who dwells within will not allow us to enter.'
    And he disobeyed, despising him, and he presumed to enter.
    Then when the old man saw, he also bound him.
    And as they all feared the prayers of the old man,
    they entreated him and they said: 'Release us.'
    The old man then accepted their petition
    and released them and said: 'Go.'
    And thus they departed, being ashamed.

BU.II.PAL.SY. 691.8

19. (An old man) said: '*I saw a brother meditating within his cell in a*
      monastery,
    and behold, a demon stood outside the door of the cell.
    While the brother was meditating, he was not able to enter into the
      cell.
    When he finished, the demon went in.'

CHA.AP.PA.S. 52.13(203)

20. *But I cried out: 'My Father, help me.'*
Immediately my father heard my voice, asking him to come to me.
He rose immediately. He came to me through God.
When my father approached him, *the Devil immediately changed.*
He took the form of a monk bearing a skin and a small bundle of palm leaves.
He came before my father, he prostrated himself at his feet,
according to the rule of the brethren of monkhood.
Immediately my father drew a line around him (so that) he could not move from side to side,
because he knew he was the Devil.
And he seized him. He tied his hands and feet.
He rolled him down into a valley.
We left him. We walked.

AM.PAUL.T.S. 766.9

21. L'un des frères, désireux d'être sauvé, lui demanda la permission de vivre avec lui au désert. Il répondit qu'il ne pourrait supporter les tentations des démons, mais l'autre dans son excessive émulation, promettait de tout supporter. Le père le reçut donc et l'invita à demeurer dans une autre grotte. Survinrent la nuit les démons, qui cherchaient à étrangler le frère après l'avoir harcelé de pensées impures. Il sortit en courant, et rapporta à abbâ Hellê ce qui lui était arrivé. Hellê traça alors une ligne autour du lieu, puis il ordonna au frère d'y rester désormais sans crainte.

FE.IV/I.HIS.G. 84(XI)

22. *I asked him: 'Who art thou?'*
He said: 'I am Satan.'
I said to him: 'And what art thou doing in this place?'
He said to me: 'Why do the monks and the Christians find fault with me
and why do they curse me at all times? ( )
For I have become weak; ( )
for I have no place at this time, henceforth. ( )
Let them mind themselves and not curse me without cause.' ( )
'When the Christ came he made thee powerless
and he cast thee down and stripped thee naked.' (I said)
When he heard the name of Christ,
he could not bear it, but immediately he became invisible.

GAR.ANT.S. 47.23

23. They said of an old man that *he sat in his cell, waging his contest.*
He saw the demons in a vision. He mocked them.
The Devil saw that he himself was being defeated by the old man
and *he came, he manifested himself to him, saying: 'I am the Christ.'*
When the old man saw him, he closed his eyes.
The Devil said to him: 'Why hast thou closed thy eyes? I am the
Christ.'
The old man said: 'I do not wish to see the Christ here.'
When the devil heard this, he became invisible.

CHA.AP.PA.S. 32.13(145)

24. They said concerning a certain elder
that when he was sitting in his cell and striving in the conflict,
he saw devils face to face.
And he treated them with contempt
and despised them through his antagonism.
Then when Satan saw that he was being overcome by the old man
he appeared to him in the likeness of a man
and said to him: 'I am Christ.'
And when the old man saw, he closed his eyes and he mocked him.
Satan said to him: 'Why dost thou close thine eyes? I, even I, am
Christ.'
And the old man answered and said to him: 'I do not wish to see
Christ here.'
And when Satan heard these things,
he departed from his presence and was not seen again.

BU.II.PAL.SY. 626.6

25. The demons said to another old man, whom they wished to lead
astray:
'Dost thou wish to see the Christ?'
He then said to them: 'You are anathema with him who you say is
the Christ.' ( )
And immediately they became invisible.

CHA.AP.PA.S. 32.21(143)

26. *As he was asleep at night (one day at mid-day),*
three demons came and said to Abba Macarius:
'*We are saints, rise so that we pray.'*
As he sat up, he said to them: '*Go to the Darkness, the place where*
there will be weeping.' ( )
Then he cursed them in the name of the Lord

435

and as they approached, *they began to shake him and the mat
  beneath him,*
and as he cried out: 'My Lord Jesus, help me.'
Suddenly, they became like smoke, and disappeared.

AM.MAC.SC.B. 92.15

27. Et je sais, touchant le même homme, que les démons vinrent à
lui en grande pompe, faisant parader devant lui des armées d'anges,
un char de feu, une nombreuse garde, comme si un roi venait le
visiter, qui lui disait: 'Tu as mené à bien toutes les vertus, mon
ami, maintenant, adore-moi, et je t'enlèverai au ciel comme
Elie.' Le moine se dit en son esprit: 'Chaque jour j'adore mon Roi
et mon Sauveur, et si celui-ci était mon roi, il ne demanderait pas
cela.' A peine eut-il déclaré au démon sa pensée: 'Mon Roi,
c'est le Christ, que j'adore sans cesse: toi, tu n'es pas mon roi,'
que le démon disparut aussitôt. Tout cela donc, il nous le racontait
comme à propos d'un autre, car il voulait cacher ses propres
mérites. Mais les pères qui vivaient avec lui disaient qu'il avait eu
lui-même cette vision.

FE.IV/I.HIS.G. 32(II)

28. *The holy man Apa Lacaron knew that he was the Devil.*
He said: 'Take thyself away from me, O Satan, thou minister of
  lawlessness.
Thou hast no part among the servants of Christ, the Son of the
  Living God.'
When the Devil heard the name of Christ,
he became like a flame of fire, he withdrew from him.

BA.HY.I.LAC.B. 10.28

SECTION III

The Representation of a Non-Material World

1 HEAVENLY VISITATIONS

1 PERSONAL APPEARANCE TO ASCETICS

THEMES

The practice of heavenly visitors of greeting, embracing, healing, and giving power and consolation.
The practice of ascetics of speaking face to face with heavenly visitors.
The participation of heavenly visitors in the life of the ascetics.

EPISODES

The visits of disciples to holy men while heavenly visitors are present.
The visits of prophets to assist in the celebration of the liturgy.
The visits of prophets during the meditation of monks.
The appearance of Christ to assist at the burial of an ascetic.
The appearance of relatives as a summons to the heavenly life.

QUOTATIONS

1. *It happened one day,*
    as our Saviour was sitting with my father Shenute, speaking with him,
    I Besa, his disciple entered wishing to meet him.
    Immediately the Saviour withdrew Himself.
    As I went in, I received the blessing of my father.
    Then I asked him: ' My holy father, who is this who was speaking with thee
    and as I entered he withdrew himself?'
    My father the prophet said to me: '*The Lord Jesus Christ is He who just now finished speaking with me of some mysteries.*'
    I said: 'I have also wished to see Him, and that He should bless me.'
    My father said to me: 'Thou art not able to see Him,
    because thou art a young boy'. ( )
    I said to him again, weeping: ' My father, I beg thee,
    let thy mercy raise me that I be made worthy to see Him also.'

438

My father said to me: 'When thou reachest the sixth hour tomorrow
come in.
Thou wilt find me sitting down with Him.
Look, but do not speak at all.'
It happened on the morrow,
I went according to the command of my father
and I struck the ring, according to the custom, so that I should
enter in and receive (their) blessing *and immediately the Lord
withdrew Himself.*
I wept, saying: '*Indeed I am not worthy to see the Lord in the flesh*'.
My father said to me: 'He will satisfy thy heart, my son Besa, and
will cause thee to hear His sweet voice.'
And beyond my merits, I heard Him speaking with my father that
once
and I have been thankful to Him all the days of my life.

LEI.SIN.B. 19.6

2. It happened once that *our father Apa Shenute was in the cell which
is in the desert*
and he refrained from coming forth to the monastery,
because *he was praying concerning the waters of the rivers in those
days.*
And he commanded us, saying: 'Let no one come into the desert.'
( )
Apa Joseph, the notary of our father ( )
went up to our father to the cell which is in the desert.
As he approached the cell, he heard him,
as if he were speaking with men and he was afraid to approach him.
After a little while our father called out:
'Joseph, come in. Do not stand outside.'
And so he went in, he received his blessing.
My father said to him: '*Why didst thou come to the desert,
and not open the door of the cell and enter in?*'
He answered with humility: 'I thought to myself that rulers of the
city had come up to thee
and were speaking with thee.
Because of this I did not enter, my father.'
Our father, Apa Shenute answered, he said to him:
'*Joseph, Shenute does not speak with men in the desert,
but I speak either with the angels or else the prophets or the apostles
or the martyrs.*
Only thou didst lose a great blessing today, O Joseph.

For the twelve apostles rose just now from this place
having come to visit me and they withdrew.
Believe me, that it was they who were speaking with me just now.'

LEI.SIN.B. 56.6

3. *It is also said of our holy father, that as he stood singing psalms with*
    the brethren at night,
    our father Athanasius, the Apostolic, appeared to him.
    He said to him: '*Peace be to thee, thou good and faithful servant of*
        God.
    Peace to all thy sons and to those that obey thy rules.
    The sweet smell of thy prayers has mounted up to the presence of God
    as a remembrance of thee for ever.
    Thy name shall endure for all generations.'
    Having said these things to him, Abba Athanasius hid himself from
        him.

DAV.JOH.KH.B. 353.3

4. A brother was sent to visit him (Abba Pisentius).
    Since he had left the brothers,
    the Lord had been sending the holy men to visit (Abba Pisentius) *to*
        give him courage.
    By the design of God, when the brother monk reached him,
    there was with him Elijah, the prophet.
    Then the brother monk stood knocking and calling out before him:
        'Bless me.'
    When Elijah, the Tishbite, saw the brother knocking,
    he wished to withdraw.
    The holy man Abba Pisentius grasped him, saying: 'I beseech you,
        my father, do not depart and leave me,
    but stay with me a little longer and comfort me.'
    The brother monk, when he saw that no one answered him,
    he made his way in,
    he found the holy men, the blessed Elijah the Tishbite,
    with the blessed Abba Pisentius who was lying sick.
    When the brother entered, he received the blessing of both.
    When he stood to pray, he was not able to raise up his eyes
    to look in the face of the blessed Elijah,
    because of the many rays of light which came from his face like
        lightning.
    The holy man Abba Pisentius said to the brother with a face full of
        joy:

440

'My brother, is it the rule that thou shouldst make thy way in
    without permission?
If it was a ruler of this world,
wouldst thou have been able to go in without permission?'
The brother monk answered: 'Forgive me, I have sinned.
As I spent time before the door knocking,
I thought that thou wast weak and unable to rise to open to me.
Because of this I made my way in to visit thee.'
When the brother monk said this as he prostrated himself, Elijah
    the Tishbite said to Apa Pisentius:
'*It is an ordinance of God,*
Indeed this brother is worthy to be embraced by us and to receive our
    blessing together.'
When Elijah, the prophet, had said this, he withdrew from them.
Then the brother monk asked the holy man: '*Whence is this man*
    with the long hair,
surrounded by such great glory?
Truly I have never seen one like him, full of glory and gentleness.
And now, when I seized his hands, I worshipped them,
a great power was in my body. I ceased to be weak
and I rejoiced like one who had risen from a feast.
If I say that this man is from this mountain,
I have never seen him in it and I have never seen any one
growing hair as he, with his appearance.'
The blessed Abba Pisentius answered, he said to the brother:
'*I conjure thee to guard the mystery I will tell thee.'*

AM.PIS.KE.B. 353.9

5. The brother, when he did not answer him,
    he made his way in without announcing himself at all,
    he found the two holy men seated.
    Apa Pisentius was lying and the holy man Elijah was sitting beside
        him,
    paying him a visit.
    When the brother went in, he received a blessing from both.
    He stood, he was unable to look into the face of the prophet Elijah,
    because of the rays of light which flashed from his face like lightning.
    ( )
    The holy man Apa Pisentius was vexed with the brother, he said to
        him:
    'Is this the rule of the brethren, to make thy way in without per-
        mission?

441

If this were a ruler thou wouldst not be able to go into him without
being announced to him.'
The brother answered: 'Forgive me, my father, I have sinned.
Behold, I waited a long time before the door, knocking.
I thought that perhaps thou wast sick and unable to rise.
Because of this I made my way in to visit thee.'
The prophet answered: '*This is the ordinance of God.*
Indeed he is worthy of our embrace, because of his conduct which is
good.
God has not deprived him of it.'
When the prophet had said this he withdrew.
When he had withdrawn, the brother said to Apa Pisentius:
'*Whence comes this brother who has much hair and with such grace
surrounding him?*
Truly I have never seen any one so gentle and filled with light.
And I say to thee, my brother, that at the moment that I grasped
his hands and kissed them,
*a great power came into my body, I ceased to be powerless, I became
strong indeed.*
I felt happy like one who has been in a wine shop.
If I say that he is from this mountain, *I have never seen any one like
him in our province,*
and I have never seen anyone with so much hair.'
And Apa Pisentius said to the brother: 'As I speak,
wilt thou keep this word as a mystery and not reveal it.'

BU.AP.PIS.S. 80.14

6. *It happened one day, our Lord Jesus Christ came to our father Apa
Shenute,*
He spoke with him thus, saying:
'Thy fellow ascetics who are in the desert have wished to see thy sons
and behold, they will come to thee tonight.'
And when He had said this, He withdrew Himself.
Then our father the prophet, Apa Shenute gathered the elder sons
and 'the men of the house' to the monastery,
he spoke to them thus: 'Some monks are coming to us tonight
and when they come into your midst,
see that not one of you or the brothers speaks with them,
but bow down your heads to them and receive their blessing,
because *they are truly holy men.*'
Therefore it happened that the hour of the gathering at night was
struck for meditation;

for it was winter and thus they sat before the brazier reciting by
heart at night.

Behold our father Apa Shenute entered and three monks walked with
him in great glory,

When the brothers saw them they all rose,

they prostrated themselves and received their blessing.

Those holy men then withdrew

and our holy father the prophet Apa Shenute walked with them.

And when morning came, they gathered to him, they asked him,
saying:

'Our father, *who were these glorious men who came to us last*
night?

For we have never seen any like them

walking with dignity and modesty with vestments of glory.

They are not changeable (as in) life but they are like angels of God.'

Our father, Apa Shenute, answered, he said to us: 'Go and give
glory to God for the gift which has come to us.

Believe me, these holy men who came in to you last night,

these were John the Baptist, with Elijah the Tishbite, and Elisha,

these great prophets who desired to see your work and asked
God.

Behold, he sent them to you.'

LEI.SIN.B. 54.3

7. It happened one day when the summons to the service was being
struck at the evening hour

and when the brethren were gathered to the church,

that another one came behind them, wearing a king's robe

and very beautiful in his appearance.

Immediately our holy father and prophet, Apa Shenute saw him,

he approached him, and as he met him, he spoke to him with a great
voice and he grasped his hand,

he took him up to the place of meditation of the brethren in the
church.

Then that one performed the meditation with great sweetness and
reverence

and all those who heard him enjoyed his speech

and his recitation and his goodly modesty.

And when he had finished meditating he made his way into the sanc-
tuary,

he became invisible.

Then some among the brethren complained, saying:

I

'Our father did not find one of us to perform the meditation but this
  layman whom he brought up,
he meditated for the brethren.'
When our father, the prophet Apa Shenute knew
that the brethren murmured and were disturbed by this,
he revealed the mystery to them, openly, saying to them:
'Believe me, my brethren, this man who came up to perform the
  meditation to us now,
this was the holy prophet David, the Son of Jesse,
who desired to perform the meditation in your church.
And behold, the Lord has favoured us with these great blessings.'

LEI.SIN.B. 44.21

8. All the people entered the shrine
   and they began to celebrate the feast, that is, the dedication of this
     church.
   And in the middle of the night, suddenly a great light shone in the
     church
   and there was shed a sweet and fragrant smell
   and the empty lamps themselves which were hanging there were
     lighted,
   and also a light appeared above the city.
   Therefore all the people believed in the benediction of the arrival of
     the holy men,
   especially as they came and appeared face to face with the Patriarch
     and he was blessed by them.
   And all those of this congregation who were worthy, had the favour
     of seeing them.
   And they assisted the Patriarch in the dedication of the church.
   And their vision was known to the bishops, the priests.
   And the brothers who were present and all the people, with one
   voice, gave praise to God.
   Afterwards the Patriarch approached and administered the Sacra-
     ments to the congregation.
   And signs and wonders without number were seen that day in the
     church.
   And many sick were cured,
   the lamps remained lighted seven days and seven nights, without
     oil and without water.
   And the light and the sweet smell remained for a long time in the
     church.

NAU.JE.PE.SY. LXI.5

9. *It happened one day as our father the prophet, Apa Shenute was walking with the great prophet Jeremiah,*
   in the spirit or in the body, the Lord knows.
   Then he came upon a brother sleeping, with his garment covering him
   and he had been meditating on the word of Jeremiah, the prophet.
   Then the prophet Jeremiah stood over that brother who was sleeping during his meditation
   and he wept, until his tears fell down upon that brother as he slept.
   And immediately my father roused the brother saying: 'Rouse thyself quickly.'
   And when he had risen, he asked, saying to him:
   'Dost thou know whence are these drops of water which fell on thee?'
   The brother answered: 'No but I thought that the sky was raining.'
   My father said to him openly: 'Believe me, my son,
   these drops of water which fell upon thee are the tears of the prophet Jeremiah.
   For he was standing over thee, weeping,
   at the time when thou wast meditating his words, saying them without fervour of heart.'

   LEI.SIN.B. 46.12

10. *Our holy father was once walking with the prophet Ezekiel*
    and a brother was sitting on one side apart,
    meditating on the words of the prophet.
    And the holy prophet Ezekiel approached, he stood over him.
    The brother, who was meditating, did not know,
    and our father, Apa Shenute, said to the prophet Ezekiel:
    'Come, let us sit, do not fatigue thyself standing.'
    The prophet said to him: 'Leave me for a time,
    I will not pass this brother, because indeed he meditates earnestly on my words.'
    There was another brother sitting in a corner,
    meditating on the twelve Minor Prophets
    and at the moment when he meditated on each one,
    our father Apa Shenute saw the prophet, on whom he was meditating,
    stand before the brother until he finished meditating.
    Afterwards he went, he sat with our father Apa Shenute and the prophet Ezekiel
    and they sat beside one another. And when that brother finished the eleventh Minor Prophet

he came to the last, namely Malachi.
He began to fall asleep, like a man of flesh.
His slumber was heavy for a little while,
because he had spent the whole night in vigil, meditating.
And the holy prophet Malachi did not pass him, he stood over him.
Then the prophet Ezekiel said to our father Shenute: 'Take the
    trouble to rouse the brother
so that he finishes the words of our brother Malachi,
so that he comes also and sits down with us.'
Our father went, he roused him saying: 'Rise my son,
and allow the great man to stop fatiguing himself on thy account
so that he joins his brothers.'
And thus he rose, he finished.
Then the prophet embraced his fellow prophets, they departed from
    (our father).

LEI.SIN.B. 47.4

11. *It happened one day that he* (Pisentius) *was meditating on the twelve*
    Minor Prophets.
    A brother was passing him as he was beginning the first of the Minor
        Prophets, namely Hosea,
    and when he heard him reading with piety,
    he sat outside his dwelling for a little, giving ear to him.
    And the brother looked in by the light of the door of his dwelling
    and saw how he worked; he was meditating,
    while the prophet Hosea stood before him.
    And when he finished, *he embraced him,*
    he returned to the height to Christ giving light like the sun. ( )
    The brother saw each of the twelve prophets in turn,
    as he meditated on him, come and stand before him until he finished,
    embrace him and withdraw.

AM.PIS.K.B. 349.6

12. Immediately two angels of God stood in his presence
    and with them was a Youth whose face was ineffable
    and whose appearance was indescribable.
    And on his head was placed a crown of thorns.
    And the angels caused Pachomius to stand up and they said to
        him:
    'Because thou hast asked God to send to thee His mercy,
    behold this is His mercy, the Lord of Glory, Jesus Christ,'

BU.II.PAL.SY. 317.15

13. The King said to him: '*When thou didst enter in to me,*
who were these who walked with thee?
I saw two men walking with thee,
while a great light surrounded thee and them, such as I have never seen.
If they had not disappeared I should have died then with fear.'
Then the holy Archbishop said to the King:
'*These two men whom thou didst see are disciples of Christ,*
the King of Kings, He through whom kings are made.
These ones, whom thou hast seen, walk with me at all times.'

POR.IS.B. 383.18

14. *He* (Apa Cyrus) *said to me* (Apa Pambo):
Christ must come to this place today according to His custom,
that I may kiss Him, mouth to mouth.
As he was saying this, behold, Christ opened the door of the cave,
He entered in, and immediately the door opened of itself.
And when He came in, ( ) I, the least of men, *saw the Christ make*
His way towards that brother,
He kissed him mouth to mouth, as a brother who has come from afar
and met his friend.
I, Pambo, the least of men, *was not worthy that He should kiss me*
at that time,
but He went forth from us, we did not know where He went.
I thought that He was a brother monk.
I said to him (Cyrus): '( )
Who is this brother monk who came in and *he kissed thee and I was*
not worthy that he should kiss me?'
He said to me: 'Didst thou not know him?'
I said to him: 'No my father. How should I know him?'
He said to me: '*This is the Lord of those of heaven and those of*
earth.
This is the Son of Mary the Holy Virgin.
This is He who fills the desert and is with all those who call on Him.'

BU.CYR.S. 133.24

15. *It happened, one day, that our father, the prophet Apa Shenoute,*
went North to the Mountain of Siout,
to visit his fellow prophet Apa John, the holy anchorite,
who is called the Carpenter,
who is shut in and enclosed in the desert in a small dwelling place
and he speaks with those who come to him through a small window.
And there are some martyrs lying on the North of the mountain of
Siout,

their bodies being buried by the road.
Whenever he went North on the road,
the martyrs there used to come out to meet him, before he ap-
    proached the road by which they lay
and they spoke with him *and embraced him, saying*:
'*It is good that thou hast come, beloved of God,*'
and then they walked with him, greeting him, for more than a mile
    in great joy,
consoling him with great praise.
And many times again he has spoken with our Lord Jesus Christ,
    mouth to mouth.
Sometimes also has he spoken with the prophets.
Sometimes have the apostles appeared to him, speaking with him.
All the holy men have spoken with him, consoling him.
Sometimes have the angels appeared to him, telling him things
    necessary to say
or those that he should console or those he should rebuke.

LEI.SIN.B. 55.10

16. Il avait en outre des visions de révélation. Par exemple, il vit son
frère aîné qui était mort lui aussi au désert après y avoir fait preuve
d'une ascèse plus éminente que la sienne: il avait longtemps vécu
lui-même en compagnie de ce frère au désert. Il le voyait donc en
songe, qui était assis sur un trône à côté des Apôtres et lui avait
légué en héritage ses vertus, et comment il intercédait pour lui
(Apollô), suppliant Dieu de le faire passer bien vite à l'autre vie et
de lui assurer le repos avec lui dans les cieux, cependant que le
Sauveur lui disait: 'Il me doit encore un peu de temps sur la terre
en vue de l'achèvement, ( ) afin qu'il acquière auprès de Dieu le
crédit que méritent ses fatigues.'

FE.IV/I.HIS.G. 51.VIII

17. *I (Apater) saw a vision, since my father Basilides died* for the name of
Christ.
I saw myself as if I was not asleep. ( )
I have never seen (clothes) *in all the place, like those of my father*
    Basilides.

HY.AP.IR.B. 80.12

18. *The saints stretched out their hands, they prayed* saying:
'*Lord God Almighty, fulfil for us our request*
that thou shouldst cause us to see our parents in the flesh
before we pass out of this world.'

448

Even as they prayed, behold, earthquakes happened and darkness,
so that the crowds who were walking with them became like dead
  men. ( )
They appeared to Apater. They embraced him with his sister.
Apa Victor said to Apater: 'O my beloved brother,
why art thou sorrowful because thou hast separated from thy parents?
Art thou not better than I? But bless my Lord Jesus Christ.
Come and be in the Heavenly Jerusalem with us, with our holy family.
Blessed are we because we have left behind the kingdoms of this
transitory world for the glory of our Lord Jesus Christ.
And our Lord Jesus Christ has given us the Heavenly Kingdom for
  ever.'

HY.AP.IR.B. 110.13

19. '*It happened to me, as I lay last night, that I (Ira) raised my eyes,*
    I saw my father Basilides, and thou didst come walking after him
      on his right.
    A woman walked with you, in great glory.
    My father said to me: "Ira my daughter."
    He was as if he had not died.
    I ran towards him, wishing to embrace him.
    He said to me: "*Thou art not worthy to kiss me now,*
    but if thou wilt be obedient to me and thy brother,
    not only wilt thou kiss my mouth,
    but thou wilt kiss the mouth of the Lord of All, my Lord Jesus Christ."
    I said to him: "I have not been disobedient to my brother ever."
    And he took my hand, he put in in thine,
    he said to thee: "*Behold, I give my daughter into thy hands.*
    Do not leave her because she is a trust and a heritage."
    I said to him: "*Who is that young girl who walks with thee, who is*
      very beautiful?"
    She said to me: "*I am Ira of Tamoy.*"
    I jumped up from the vision.
    I have not told my mother or my sister until I told thee first,
    because *thou art he to whom I was given in the vision.*'

HY.AP.IR.B. 86.2

2 APPEARANCE AT THE EUCHARIST

THEME

The ability of holy men to see visions during the celebration of the
  Eucharist.

THE CULT OF THE SEER IN THE ANCIENT MIDDLE EAST

EPISODES

The appearance of Christ, the Virgin Mary and angels at the Eucharist.
The appearance of light and fire on the altar.

QUOTATIONS

1. It was also said of our holy father John, that all things which the
      brethren did
   whether (acts of) virtue or otherwise,
   he would see them in secret.
   For this reason, his name was renowned everywhere.
   O who is able to tell the number
   of the visions and the mysteries and the revelations which he saw at
      times.
   For many times he would see the glory of the Lord upon the altar like
      a fire
   and he would hear the angels singing the Trisagion at the time of the
      Holy Offering.
   It was also said of our holy father John that many times the holy
      Theotokos Mary,
   she who bore for us our Lord Jesus Christ, our true King, gave him
      peace and consoled him.

   DAV.JOH.KH.B. 343.12

2. *Every time when he was about to mount upon the altar to make the*
      Offering,
   from the time when he was about to begin to make to Holy Offering,
   his eyes would pour with tears until he completed the service.
   And when he reached the time when the Holy Spirit came upon the
      altar,
   he would see the Holy Spirit coming upon the Offering,
   changing the bread and the chalice into the divine body of Christ.
   When the saint saw this great vision, fear would seize him, with joy.
   Immediately his face would give forth rays of light,
   so that everyone marvelled saying:
   'God has made us worthy of a saint of such holiness.'

   POR.IS.B. 356.8

3. *He was a wise teacher to all in the fear of Jesus Christ*
   and a great blessing happened through him
   and the Saviour appeared to him, speaking with him.
   And He told him mysteries
   and every time he was about to make the Offering upon the altar,

450

he saw an angel of God standing on the right side of the altar guarding it.

HY.ARI.B. 203.13

4. The priest said: 'I have heard in many places that at the time when the Oblation is about to be offered up, the Son of God comes down with all his ranks and stands upon the altar until they have finished giving Communion to all the people.'

VAN.L.Q.T.S. 44.9

5. The holy man, Apa Martyrus, said to our father the prophet Apa Shenute:
'Dost thou wish, my father, that the cantor should stop singing, for behold, the people and brethren have received the blessing?'
My father answered him saying: 'What is it to thee? *Let him sing, for behold, a chorus of angels surrounds him, making the responses and behold the prophet David stands beside him,*
giving him the words which are right for him to say.'

LEI.SIN.B. 46.2

6. There was a priest serving upon that altar at that time, making the holy Offering, whose name was Silas.
And his eyes were opened. He saw the Lord upon the altar, with His blessed Mother and the angelic host.

AM.MAC.TK.B. 127.14

7. After these things they honoured our holy father (John), they consecrated him priest against his will.
As he mounted upon the altar, he began to make the Holy Offering,
a glory of the Lord appeared upon the altar like a fire.
When our holy father saw this sight, he gave glory to God.

DAV.JOH.KH.B. 354.9

8. One day he (Pisentius) looked, he saw the priest spit phlegm from his mouth, within the Sanctuary,
while the Holy Mysteries were spread out.
Immediately he had him called to himself to a place in which he was quiet.
The holy man Abba Pisentius said to the priest:
'My son, what is this thing which thou hast dared to do, spitting in the holy place?
And tell me what thou hast said in thy prayer.
Dost thou not know that *myriads of angels and archangels and cherubim and seraphim*

451

stand before thee upon the Sanctuary,
singing with sweet voices in one chant? (   )
Dost thou not know who they are, which are standing?'

AM.PIS.K.B. 369.5

9. It happened once, when our father was holding a service,
that the King was passing with his multitude.
He came outside the door of the church.
He looked within, he saw the Archbishop standing before the altar,
while a fire surrounded him
and a light power was behind him, fortifying him.
When the King saw this great vision, he was amazed
and he said to one of those who accompanied him:
'Go and call the Archbishop to me.'
He wished to know about the power which surrounded him,
who it was who spoke to him in the path on which he stood.
And when he wished to send the man within,
the King saw the power coming forth towards him.
Fear seized him. He fled quickly with those who were with him.
None saw the vision except the King alone.
When he returned to his house, he lay down from fear,
he became like a dead man, he was not able to speak for that day.
The chartularies came, *they entered in to visit him.*
They found him lying sick from fear.
When they enquired of him the cause of this illness,
he revealed to them the matter which his eyes saw.
And when they heard they marvelled, they gave glory to God.
He sent one of them, he called the Archbishop.
When he came to him, he questioned him saying:
'*At the time when thou wast standing before the altar,*
with whom wast thou speaking at that moment?
Who was it whom I saw standing beside thee,
a being of light and fire?'
The holy Archbishop answered, he said to the King:
'*I was speaking with my God.'*
The Archbishop was not ignorant of the power
which stood at all times with him when he mounted upon the altar.
(   )
The King said further: '*Each time when thou dost approach the altar,*
dost thou see thy God?'
The Archbishop replied: 'Yes.'

POR.IS.B. 363.17

452

10. *And again when* (Theodore) *came to the place of the door of the Sanctuary,*
    he looked within, he saw in the vision
    the place where the feet (stood) in the form in which there was manifested ( )
    (*He was not*) *able to look in his face because of the great light which flashed in his presence.*
    One of the angels who were standing by him said:
    'Why dost thou not pray the brothers repeatedly not to neglect the service at the hour of prayer?'

    LE.PAC.S. 281b.20

11. *It happened one day, as our father Theodore was lying asleep,*
    an angel roused him, saying to him:
    '*Rise quickly and go to the church. Behold, the Lord is there.*'
    He rose, he went in obedience to the voice which had come to him. ( )
    And when he came to the place of the door of the church,
    he looked in, he saw a vision
    and in the place of its feet, in the form in which it appeared to him,
    it was like a sapphire stone which gave light.
    And he was unable to look into its face,
    because of the great light which flashed lightning in his presence without ceasing.

    LE.PAC.B. 162.27

3 INTERPRETATION OF DOCTRINE

THEMES

The settling of doctrinal disputes by obtaining the answer from heaven.
The revelation to holy men of the meaning of their visions.

EPISODES

The transformation of the Eucharist bread and wine into flesh and blood
The giving of an interpretation by an angel or by a voice from heaven.

QUOTATIONS

1. *A certain one in Shiet was very elevated in his practice,*
   but he was simple in his faith
   and he was differing because of his simplicity.
   And he would say that the bread, which we receive upon the altar,
   is not the body of Christ in nature, but its form.
   Two old men heard that he spoke these words
   and they knew that he was elevated in his life.

30 453

They knew that he said this in simplicity and lack of knowledge,
and they came to him (   ).
They said: '*Let us pray to God this week about this mystery*
and we believe that God will reveal it to us.' (   )
Immediately God heard them.
When the week was completed, they went to the church on Sunday.
They all three sat upon that same seat, with the old man in their
midst.
Their inner eyes were opened
and when the bread was placed upon the holy table,
it appeared to the three alone as a small child
and when the priest stretched forth his hand to take the bread and
cut it,
behold, an angel came from heaven with a knife in his hand.
He cut the small child, he poured his blood into the chalice.
When the priest broke the bread into pieces
the angel also divided the small child in fragments.
And when they advanced to partake of the holy things,
the old man received a fragment full of blood.
And when he saw, he was afraid, he cried out:
'O Lord I believe that the bread is thy body and the chalice thy
blood.'
And immediately the flesh which was in his hand became bread,
according to the glory of the Mystery.
He put it into his mouth and partook, thanking the Lord.

CHA.AP.PA.S. 40.4(175)

2. Abba Daniel Parnaya, the disciple of Abba Arsenius, spoke concerning a man from Scete
and he said that he was one of great labours,
but he was simple in the faith.
And in ignorance, he considered and said that this bread, which we
receive,
is not truly the body of Christ, but the likeness of His body. (   )
And this old man said: 'While I am not persuaded by this matter,
I will not listen.'
Then they said to him: 'Let us pray to God for the whole week on
this mystery
and we believe that He will reveal it to us.'
And the old man received this answer with great joy
and each man went to his cell. (   )
And God heard the entreaty of the two fathers

and when the week was ended, they came to the church
and the three of them sat down by themselves on one seat.
And the old man was sitting between them
and He opened the eyes of their understanding.
And when it was the time of the Mysteries,
and the bread was laid upon the Holy Table,
there appeared to the three of them, as it were, a child upon the
    Table.
And when the priest stretched out his hand to break the bread,
behold the angel of the Lord descended from heaven and a knife was
    in his hand
and he sacrificed the child and strained its blood into a cup.
And when the priest broke off small portions from the bread,
the old man drew near to partake of the Holy Offering
and living flesh was given to him smeared with blood.
And when he saw, he was afraid and he cried out with a loud voice
and he said: 'I believe, Lord, that the bread is thy body and the
    cup is thy blood.'
And immediately, the flesh that was in his hand was bread,
in the likeness of the Mystery.
And he took it and gave thanks to God.
And these old men said to him: 'God knows the nature of men
and that it is not possible to eat living flesh
and for this reason he turns His body to bread and His blood to
    wine,
for those who receive Him in faith.'

BU.II.PAL.SY. 621.11

3. It was said concerning Abba Macarius that ( )
the Lord of Glory sent a Cherubim.
He showed him the way into this mountain and he placed his hand
    like a measure on his chest.
And Abba Macarius said to him: 'What is this?'
The Cherubim said to him: 'I have measured thy heart.'
Abba Macarius said to him: '*What is the interpretation of this
    saying?*'
The Cherubim said to him: 'The name of thy heart will be given to
    this mountain,
this one which thy Lord has given thee as an inheritance.'

AM.VER.MAC.B. 118.3

4. *As he* (Theodore) *was sitting in a place alone
reciting from the Book of the Twelve (Minor) Prophets,*

455

when he reached Micah, the prophet,
an angel of the Lord appeared to him and questioned him on this passage which is written in Micah:
'Like water which comes down from its source'
And he said to him: '*What is its interpretation, dost thou think?*'
While he was considering, in order to understand it, the angel answered him:
'Why, O Theodore, dost thou not understand its meaning?
Is it not manifest that it is the water of the river which comes down from Paradise.'
And when the angel had said this, immediately he ceased to see him.

LE.PAC.S. 197.13

5. Apa Daniel has told of a great old man who lived in a part of Egypt, who in simplicity said that Melchisedek was Christ, the Son of God. And the blessed Cyril, the Archbishop of Alexandria, was told about him and he sent for him.
As he knew that the old man was able to perform signs
and that everything which he asked Him, the Lord revealed to him,
and that he spoke this word in simplicity, ( )
(he said) 'Because of this I have sent for thee,
so that *thou shouldst pray to God that He reveal to thee concerning this.*'
The old man, confident of his attitude, said with confidence:
'Allow me three days
and I will pray the Lord about this and I will tell thee who he is.'
Then he went, he prayed to God about this word
and after three days, he came to the Archbishop
and he said: 'Melchisedek is a man.'
The Archbishop said to him: 'How dost thou know?'
He said: '*God has revealed to me the face of all the patriarchs,*
each one of them passing by from Adam to Melchisedek.
And the angel told me: "This one is Melchisedek and be sure that this is he."'
And he departed proclaiming by himself: 'Melchisedek is a man.'
And the blessed Cyril rejoiced greatly.

CHA.AP.PA.S. 41.20(176)

6. He (the angel) turned and came to him for the second time:
'The house which the man built, how many stories has it?'
He was not able to give (the) reply to him.

456

Then he turned again for the third time to him, he said to him:
'The house which the man built, how many stories has it?'
When he said to him: 'It has ten stories,' the angel smiled, he
  departed.
When Apa told us, we asked him: 'Give us its explanation.'
He said to us: 'The man is God,
the ten stories of the house are the seven heavens
with the Firmament and the earth and Amente.'
He said to us: 'If I had been ignorant the third time to find what to
  say to him,
the ignorance would not have left the brethren for ever.'
We said to him: 'Thou hast saved us and our seed for ever.'

LE.PAC.S. 263.5

7. *Then a voice came from heaven saying:*
   '*Anthony, these souls which thou hast seen being cast down by his
   hands,*
   these indeed are the souls of sinners who are dragged down to Amente.'

AM.AP.ANT.B. 32.3

8. *A voice came to Anthony saying:*
   '*Understand what thou art seeing.*'
   And when his mind was opened
   he knew that this was the taking upwards of souls which he had seen.

GAR.ANT.S. 72.17

9. *He prayed, wishing to know whom he had seen.*
   And immediately a voice came to him.

GAR.ANT.S. 66.4

4 HEALING

THEMES

The removal from holy men of the physical causes of their sufferings.
The giving of power, the restoration of health and strength.

EPISODES

The castration of holy men by angels.
The performance of operations to relieve painful disease.
The healing of blindness.
The healing of illness of demonic origin.

QUOTATIONS

1. And when it was evening, he slept in the desert.
   And as he related, three angels came to him
   and they took hold of him, saying to him: 'Why didst thou go forth
      from the nunnery?'
   And he related to them the matter and he said to them:
   'I was afraid, lest I should cause harm to them and to my soul
      also.'
   They said to him: 'If now we make thee to be free from this passion,
   do thou go and take care of their (affairs).' ( )
   Then they laid hold of him by his hands and his feet
   and one of them took a razor and cut off his testicles,
   not in truth, but as in an illusion and in appearance.
   He thought therefore in the vision that it was as if he was healed.
   According to what men say, they asked him therefore:
   'Dost thou feel that thou hast been helped?'
   He said to them: 'I am greatly relieved from the trouble.'

   BU.II.PAL.SY. 178.5

2. When evening had come, he fell asleep in the desert and three
   angels came to him ( ) and caught hold of him and said:
   'Why then did you leave the monastery of the women?' He explained
   the matter to them: 'Because I was afraid I might harm both them
   and myself.' They said to him: 'Then if we relieve you of the
   passion, will you go and care for them?' ( ) He agreed to this.
   Then one of them seized his hands, and another his feet, and a
   third taking a razor unmanned him, not in reality but in appearance.
   So he seemed to himself to have been cured, so to say, in the trance.
   They asked him: 'Do you feel any benefit?' He said to them: 'I feel
   greatly lightened and am persuaded that I am relieved of my
   passion.'

   LO.PAL.G. 109(XXIX)

3. *I suffered greatly because of the pain that was upon me. I looked,*
   I saw a very glorious man standing before me.
   He said to me: 'Where art thou suffering?'
   My strength came to me a little, I said to him: '*My Lord, I am*
      suffering in my liver.'
   He said to me: 'Show me the place where thou art suffering.'
   I showed him my liver which was diseased.
   He stretched forth his hand to me while his fingers were laid upon one
      another.

   458

He divided my side like a sword.
And he brought forth my liver,
he showed me the sores which were upon it.
He scraped them, he put their pus in a cloth.
He returned my liver to its place again.
And he made smooth my body with his hands.
He joined the places which he had divided from one another.
He said to me: '*Behold thou hast been healed.*
Do not return to committing sin lest a worse evil than this happen
    to thee.
But become a servant of the Lord from now forever.'
Since that day all that is within me is healed
and I have ceased to suffer with my liver.
I exist in this desert place without trouble.
He showed me the linen with the pus upon it.

BU.ON.S. 208.26

4. *After four days I* (Paphnute) *suffered,*
   I stretched out my hands to heaven. I prayed
   and behold, the man who first came to me, came again to me.
   He gave power to me as before.

BU.ON.S. 209.30

5. '*My spleen was tormenting me greatly.*
   I begged my Lord, Jesus Christ.
   He gave me the Grace of the healing of my body.
   And concerning this man whom thou hast seen, he is Elijah, the Tish-
      bite,
   he who was taken up to heaven on a chariot of fire,
   but I beg thee my God-loving brother
   not to tell to any man until the day of my death.'
   When the brother heard this from the old man, he rejoiced greatly
   and he did not reveal the word until the Lord visited him.

AM.PIS.KE.B. 357.11

6. '*My spleen was tormenting me greatly,*
   I begged the Lord yesterday to give me the grace of healing.
   When He saw my weakness and lack of helpers,
   He sent one of the holy men to me.
   He granted my body healing.
   And I say to thee that this man, from whom thou didst receive a
      blessing,

459

is Elijah the Tishbite, he of the Mount Carmel,
he who was taken up to heaven in a chariot of fire and earthquake.
I beg thee, my God-loving brother, do not reveal the mystery to any
man until the day of my visitation.'

BU.AP.PIS.S. 82.1

7. I (a man blind in both eyes) prayed the holy Archangel Gabriel.
   In that moment I felt a man's hand come down upon my face.
   It made the sign of the Cross on my eyes
   and immediately I saw and I heard a voice saying to me:
   'Behold, I have granted the light of thine eyes, as thou didst beseech
      me.'

WOR.GAB.S. 189.1

8. *And in that night I saw the holy Archangel Gabriel.*
   He came to me, he made the sign of the Cross over me,
   he healed me,
   he departed up to heaven in a robe of light.

WOR.GAB.S. 239.7

9. And when I cast myself upon the ground as dead,
   behold these two brethren, whom I had seen in my dream
   when I was in the cell of Abba John,
   came and stood over me. And they said to me:
   'Now wast thou not waiting for us to go with thee?
   Arise by the strength of Our Lord.'
   When I arose I saw one of them looking at the ground
   and he turned to me and said:
   'Dost thou need a drink of water?'
   I said to him: 'Yes, Abba.'
   He showed me a root called 'qamus' and he said to me:
   'Eat this root and proceed by the strength of Our Lord.'
   When I ate a little of it, immediately I sweated as if I had been
      rinsed with water.
   My soul was strengthened and my face became joyful,
   my limbs were lightened and I was like one who never travelled by
      road.
   They showed me the road by which I should go to the saint.

LOOK.MAR.SY. 4.8

10. *My father spent forty days and forty nights*
    without eating or drinking,
    sitting upon a brick within the dwelling place,
    looking at a mirror in a window.

460

And he did not shut his eyes for these forty days
until they burst and poured forth blood upon the ground.
The holy Archangel Michael came forth from heaven
at the hour on the Lord's day,
at the completion of the Forty Days.
He signed him with the Cross,
he ended all his afflictions.
His eyes were thus restored.
Michael went to the heavens in glory.

AM.PAUL.T.S. 767.5

11. Then the legs of the blessed man burst open,
    because of much standing upon them
    and pus and discharge flowed from them.
    Then the angel (of the Lord) drew near to him and said to him:
    'The Lord be thy meat and the Holy Spirit thy drink.
    Truly, for thee, it is sufficient henceforth to have this spiritual food.'
    And after healing him, he caused him to pass from that place.

BU.II.HIER.SY. 398.13

12. On many occasions the devils beat this man
    and they brought many illnesses upon him
    so that he was not able to stand beside the altar
    nor even to offer up the Offering,
    but an angel came and took him by the hand
    and he straightway was strengthened.
    And he made him stand up healed before the altar.

BU.II.HIER.SY. 427.21

13. *It happened that night that the Lord revealed to the Archbishop:*
    'Send tomorrow to Athanasius, the Chartulary, saying:
    "If thou believest in Christ who has established me over His Holy
        Church,
    then the Lord will give the grace of healing to thy son."'

POR.IS.B. 359.14

5 THE FORETELLING OF THE BIRTH
OF HOLY MEN

THEMES

The seeing of a vision in answer to prayer.
The hearing of the prophecy concerning the future life of the child to be
    conceived.
The recounting of the vision.

EPISODES

The announcement in answer to prayer that a holy man would be born.

The conception of a holy man announced to sterile parents.

The answer to the prayers of sterile wives given at the shrines of holy men.

QUOTATIONS

1. The God-loving Moses (whose wife was sterile) *spread out his hands* (on the feast of John the Baptist), *he prayed* saying:
  'God hear me, I am a miserable sinner, give me a successor
  that I may call him by the name of thy forerunner John.
  I pray thee my Lord, hear me and *do not let me die without son, lest my memory perish.'* ( )
  Having said these things, he went up to his sleeping place and he slept.
  At midnight he saw in a vision a man of light as if he were standing in his presence,
  with much hair and a beard growing thickly,
  with a girdle of skin binding his loins
  and his face gave light greatly.
  When Moses saw him he was amazed and he feared.
  The man of light said to him: 'Dost thou know who I am?'
  He said: 'No, my Lord.'
  The man of light said to him:
  '*I am John*, the son of Zacharias, and my mother is Elizabeth,
  the kinswoman of Mary, the mother of Jesus, the Christ.
  Thou hast prayed this evening that thou shouldst see a son of thine,
      ( )
  Behold, there will be born to thee a son this year
  and he will be filled with the grace of the Holy Spirit,
  he will be a chosen one of the Lord and God will bless him.
  Men will give glory to him
  and he will manifest the name of the Lord at a time of persecution.'
  When he had seen these things,
  he woke up from the vision and when his heart was restored,
  he said: 'Truly, it was John, the Baptist, whom I saw.'
  And he stood praying until the light dawned.
  After this, Helena, his wife, became pregnant
  and she fasted daily until the days of her pregnancy were ended
  and thus she gave birth to her son
  and there was a great light in the house in which he was born.

HY.JE.SI.B. 175.1

2. *At night, as the blessed John* (father of Theodore Stratelates) *was*
   confined and lying in irons,
   weeping in distress,
   behold, a light shone upon him,
   he heard a voice saying: 'John, John, cease weeping.'
   He answered, saying: 'My Lord, I am weeping because they have
   seized me by force,
   taking me to a strange land,
   wishing to deprive me of the land of my fathers.'
   The voice said to him: '*Do not weep because of the land of thy fathers,*
   for it is necessary that thy seed dwell upon it for ever.
   The place in which thou art confined will be a dwelling place for his
   body for ever.
   He will guide the ships that sail.
   He will persecute the demons and the dragons which are upon the
   earth. ( )
   Therefore, O John, do not weep for the land of thy fathers
   and do not fear the battle.
   Thy sword will not shed blood and no wound will touch thy body.'
   The blessed John, his heart fortified, ceased from weeping,
   but he wondered: 'How will my seed inhabit my land?
   I have never taken a wife nor begotten sons.'

   BA.HY.II.T.A.T.S.B. 106.24

3. *He* (*John, father of Theodore.*) *lay that night weeping,*
   Behold, a man of light stood above him.
   He said to him: 'John why dost thou weep for Theodore thy son?'
   The blessed John said to him: '*Who art thou, my Lord, who art in*
   such great glory?'
   The man of light said to him:
   '*I am he who appeared to thee* in the winepress,
   I told thee what would happen to thee.
   Do not fear now since I am with thee in all thy troubles.' ( )
   The man of light said to him: 'Save thy soul from destruction
   In so far as she (his mother) has set thee free,
   withdraw thyself to thy land, for the sake of the disposition of thy
   body. ( )'
   The blessed John rose on the same night,
   he withdrew, no one knew where he went.

   BA.HY.II.T.A.T.S.B. 111.22

4. *In the following night, behold, she* (Sophia, the childless wife of
   Theodosius who had prayed at the shrine of Saint Peter and Saint
   Paul) *saw a vision,*

463

she told her husband, she said: '*Two men stood in my presence,*
in splendid clothes of the form of our father the Patriarch.
When I saw them, I was greatly afraid.
They said to me: "*Do not fear, we are they in whose shrine thou didst*
petition God yesterday, Peter and Paul.
We took the petition up to His presence,
He heard it and He had mercy on thee, O woman of faith.
Tomorrow rise, go to the Archbishop so that he may pray for thee
and thy petition will be fulfilled soon."
Behold those things which I have seen, I have told them to thy
holiness.
If, therefore, the matter please thee, I will go to the Archbishop.'

HY.PET.AL.B. 250.4

5. Or la bienheureuse Dionysia, après plusieurs années de vie commune
avec son mari, était stérile et n'enfantait pas. Aussi les parents,
dans un profond découragement, passaient-ils de longues heures à
prier Dieu instamment qu'il leur fût donné un enfant. Etant donc
allés à la chapelle, voisine de la ville, du glorieux et victorieux
martyr Polyeucte, ils y persévérèrent plusieurs jours dans la prière,
comme l'a rapporté le récit des Anciens qui me fut transmis, et une
nuit, tandis qu'ils priaient seuls, une vision leur apparaît qui leur
dit: 'Courage, courage, voici que Dieu vous a accordé un enfant
dont le nom sera pris à l'euthymie (bon courage), parce que, à
l'occasion de sa naissance, Celui qui vous l'accorde donnera euthymie à ses églises.' Après avoir noté l'heure de la vision, ils s'en retour-
nèrent dans leur maison, et, ayant reconnu d'après le temps de la
grossesse que les paroles de la vision s'étaient réalisées, dès le moment
de sa naissance ils nommèrent l'enfant Euthyme et promirent de
l'offrir à Dieu.

FE.III/I.EUT.G. 59(II)

Comme sa mère était stérile et en subissait le reproche de son
époux et de sa parenté, un jour, au milieu de la nuit en cachette de
son mari, elle sortit et, levant les mains au ciel, pria. ( ) Sur ce,
elle pleure amèrement, se brise le coeur en maints gémissements,
puis rentre auprès de son époux. Or, s'étant couchée à ses côtés,
elle voit dans un songe nocturne deux grands disques lumineux qui
descendent du ciel et se tiennent près d'elle. Une fois levée, elle
raconte la chose à son mari. ( ) Et après un délai de peu de jours,
elle conçut le saint homme.

FE.II.DAN.G. 94(II)

II HEAVENLY COMMUNICATIONS

1 THE RECOGNITION OF A HOLY MAN

THEMES

The visitation by Christ, in glory, as a youth, as a child.
The visitation by the Virgin Mary.
The visitation by a prophet, an apostle, a patriarch, a saint.
The hearing of a voice from heaven.

EPISODES

The recognition of a holy man in his youth by the seeing of signs and
   visions.
The recognition of a holy man by the hearing of a voice from heaven.
The recognition of a holy man by the sight of angels in his presence.
The rôle of angels in protecting holy men.
The recognition of the significance for the whole world of the holy man.

QUOTATIONS

1. *That night the bishop saw a vision.*
   When day came he told it to the clerics of the city
   and these also told it to the clerics of their villages.
   He said: 'I saw in a vision last night the youth Moses,
   wearing a monk's robe, with a multitude of monks standing with
      (him). ( )
   Behold, one made his way to me, he said: " *Dost thou recognise this*
      one standing in the middle of these two?"
   I answered: "He is Moses."
   He said to me: "Dost thou know him?"
   I said to him: "Yes."
   He said again to me: " *Who are these other two monks who are*
      standing on each side of him?"
   I answered: "I do not know them."
   He said to me: "Thou hast spoken the truth; for thou dost not know
      them but I will tell thee ( ):
   this youth whom thou seest, will also be the father of a multitude of
      monks
   and a multitude of men will be saved by his teaching."'

   AM.MO.S. 684.3

2. When he (Isaac) came to Shiet he dwelt in the monastery of Abba
   Zacharias of blessed memory, ( ),

a holy man, one who saw visions.

When the old man Abba Zacharias saw the holy youth coming towards him, *the Lord opened his eyes.*

He saw the sign of a Cross above his head.

And when he saw this incredible sign, he wondered greatly, he cried out, saying:

'Just as thy works are made great, O Lord, thy thoughts are dug deep.'

And as the holy old man Abba Zacharias was considering in himself what would happen to this youth,

suddenly he was blessed by an angel of the Lord who said to him:

'*Behold the Lord has given thee a great and holy favour, which is this youth* who has come to thee.

For he will be a shepherd of the sheep of Christ and Patriarch of the bishops.'

POR.IS.B. 312.15

3. As the three, Apa Pgoul, Apa Shenute and Apa Pshoi were walking together,

   a voice came to them from heaven saying:

   '*It is ordained that Shenute be Archimandrite of the whole world today.*'

   Apa Pgoul said to Apa Pshoi: 'My brother Pshoi, *didst thou also hear this voice which came from heaven now?*'

   Apa Pshoi said to Apa Pgoul: 'Yes.'

LEI.SIN.B. 11.28

4. My father said to him: 'Truly thou shouldst be called Apa Aphou of the antelopes.'

   Immediately a voice came to us: 'This is his name for all generations of the earth.'

   We marvelled at what happened. Quickly *we embraced him, we came out.*

AM.PAUL.T.S. 762.12

5. And therefore he humbly besought God
   that He would reveal to him in what manner was the great Basileus.
   One day, there overcame him amazement and alarm
   and he saw a column of fire standing before the holy altar,
   whose head reached up to heaven
   and there cried out from heaven (a voice) and said:

466

THE REPRESENTATION OF A NON-MATERIAL WORLD

'Ephraim, Ephraim, just as thou seest this column of fire,
thus is the great Basileus.'

BRO.EP.SY. 32.2

6. At eventide, when the sun was setting,
   behold those two blessed ones, whom I saw with Abba John, came
     to me and said to me:
   'Truly you have buried a body today
   of whom this world was not worthy.
   Arise, let us go in the cool of the night
   because you will not be able, in the day time, to go in this desert.'
   I went with them until dawn.
   When it was dawn they said to me:
   'Go in peace and pray for us.'

LOOK.MAR.SY. 21.11

7. It was also said of him (Isaac) *that many times,*
   as he slept, he would see a Cherubim of light,
   coming and clothing him with his wings,
   until he rose from sleep
   and he would then see him going up to heaven.

POR.IS.B. 323.5

8. It was said of him
   that when he penetrated these perfections and sublime things,
   God appointed for him two Cherubim
   who guarded him ceaselessly and directed him spiritually,
   so that all the hidden and secret things of the Holy Spirit were
     revealed to him.
   And this was given to him because of the purity of his heart.
   The Cherubim urged one another
   that they should shade him with their wings and one said to the
     other:
   'Let me shade the elect one of the Lord Sabaoth.'

NAU.JE.PE.SY. LVI.3

9. As our father Abba John was asleep one day,
   an old man came to his cell
   and he saw an angel of the Lord above our father Abba John, watching
     over him.
   When Abba John rose from sleep
   he said: 'Yes, a certain old man came here.'

467

And Abba John knew that the old man had seen the angel
because *that old man also reached the stature of our father, Abba John.*

AM.JOH.K.B. 365.15

10. He saw an angel of the Lord,
standing above the head of Abba John guarding him.

NAU.JE.PE.SY. XLIII.5

11. *When I* (Apa Onnophrius) *came out of my monastery,*
I looked, I saw a light in my presence.
I was afraid, I thought in my heart to turn back to the place
in which I was at first, to remain as I was.
When he knew that I was afraid, he said to me:
' *Do not fear, I am the angel who dwells with thee,*
who has walked with thee since thy youth.
This task which the Lord has ordained for thee, thou must fulfil.'

BU.ON.S. 212.21

The saint said to him: '(   )
Behold I see two angels standing by thee,
one is that of light, one that of darkness.'

HY.AP.IR.B. 109.5

12. *Then he saw one whose whole body was dark.* (   )
His holy angel, who followed him at a distance, was greatly dis-
tressed. (   )
He saw him whom he had previously seen in black and darkness. (   )
The holy angel which accompanied him was rejoicing
and was glad and was in great joy over the man.

CHA.AP.PA.S. 47.25(191)

13. And he saw that everyone who was entering was glorious in the
appearance of (his) soul, (   )
and that the angel of each one was rejoicing in him. (   )
And then he saw that man whom he saw entering, (   )
when he came forth from the church (   )
(he saw) his holy angel was close to him and walked with him.

BU.II.PAL.SY. 298.17

14. It happened that Theodore rose in the night
and passed through the monastery to survey the brethren
and he stood in a place and prayed.
Immediately an ecstasy came upon him.

He looked, he saw and it was as if all the brethren were lying like
sheep asleep
and an angel lay on his side in their midst, guarding them.
When Theodore saw him he rose to meet him and and he beckoned
to him.
He cast into his heart at that moment the question which he
wished to ask him,
before the word was in his mouth.
And he said to him: 'Who is it who watches over the brethren,
(is it) I or thou?'
And immediately Theodore was troubled. He returned to his place
and said: 'We are indeed only the semblance,
for the true shepherd, who guards us, is the angel of the
Lord.'
*The appearance of the costume of that angel as he stood was like a
soldier,*
equipped with a sticharion. At that moment he was not wearing
his chlamis.
And his sticharion, which he was wearing, was of the type of a
'paragaudis',
his 'medals' were very beautiful and all shining with light,
his belt was a palm's breadth in width and was very red and gave
flashes of *lightning.*

LE.PAC.S. 154b.33

15. Theodore rose once in the night
and he passed through the monastery watching over the brethren.
He stood in a place and prayed.
As he prayed, an ecstasy came upon him,
he saw in a vision, as if all the brethren were sleeping like sheep,
while an angel in their midst guarded them.
Theodore, when he saw him, he rose to meet him and he beckoned
to him
and he put into his heart the word which he wished to say to him,
before he said it with his mouth.
And he said to him: 'Who is it who watches over the brethren, is it
thou or I?'
And immediately Theodore was troubled and he returned to his
place, saying: 'Truly, we are the semblance alone.
In reality, the angels are the shepherds for us, we are the sheep of
the reasoning flock of Christ and it is they who guard us from the
evil snares of the enemy.'

The appearance of the costume of that angel resembled the form of
a soldier of the king,
with a sword of fire in his hand and he gave much light.
And he wore a sticharion; for at that moment he did not wear his
chlamis but on him was the sticharion.
There were great medals on the sticharion, all giving light and very
beautiful.
The width of his belt was a palm's breadth, it was very red, giving
flashes of lightning.

LE.PAC.B. 94.9

16. *I* (Macarius) *saw an angel of the Lord,*
    with a sword of fire in his hand,
    guarding him (*the younger stranger*), *chasing the demons away from*
    him.

CHA.AP.PA.S. 712.16(239)

17. *I* (Macarius) *saw an angel of the Lord, with a sword of fire in his hand,*
    guarding him (*the younger stranger*), *chasing after the demons.*

AM.MA.DO.B. 299.1

18. *I* (Macarius) *saw an angel of the Lord with a sword in his hand,*
    guarding him (*the younger stranger*), *chasing the demons from him.*

AM.AP.MAC.B. 210.15

19. When they (Abba Amoi and two elders) reached the dwelling place
    of Abba John,
    they smelt a very choice perfume from it.
    They also heard the chorus of angels,
    chanting and singing hymns to God in the dwelling place of *Abba*
    John ( ).
    And also our father Abba John was singing in their midst.
    The holy old men were amazed for a long time
    with true feeling, at the sight of this thing.
    At last when they recovered, they knocked at the door of Abba John.
    After a long time, when he came forth,
    they saw his face giving light like that of an angel of God.

AM.JOH.K.B. 341.2

20. When they arrived at his cell,
    from it there reached them a sweet smell
    and they heard the voices of angels who were praising God ( ).
    The holy man John was standing in their midst, praising God.

THE REPRESENTATION OF A NON-MATERIAL WORLD

Then the fathers were astonished
and they stood considering the greatness of the vision.
And after an hour they awoke as if from sleep,
and they knocked on the door of the cell.
And the holy man John came forth immediately in their presence,
while his face was shining in the likeness of a seraphim.

NAU.JE.PE.SY. XXII.6

21. *He looked towards Abba John. Behold, he saw seven holy angels,*
wearing bright robes in great glory and carrying seven crowns,
giving forth flashes of lightning above our holy father Abba John
and placing them upon his head, one after the other, filling him with
great joy.

AM.JOH.K.B. 336.7

22. And as he turned, he looked at the place in which was the holy man,
John.
He saw seven angels, shining with light,
carrying seven crowns of light
and they were flying above the head of the holy man, John,
and they were crowning him,
one after the other was rising up.

NAU.JE.PE.SY. XVIII.16

23. *And the wife of the King saw great gatherings of angels*
occupying the room with the holy man, the Archbishop.
And she saw a great light like burning lamps.
They were wearing white clothes
and the holy Patriarch Isaac was in their midst.
They sang to God all night, according to the custom of the Christians.
And when the morning light came, she told the King what she had seen.

POR.IS.B. 367.3

24. The holy man Paul, the chief of the disciples of Mar Anthony,
looked into the heavens and saw a couch which was spread with
great splendour
and three angels who were carrying three lamps
standing before that couch and a crown of glory which was laid upon
it.
And when he had seen all this glory, he said:
'This is only for my father Anthony.'
And a voice came to him from heaven, saying to him:

'It is not for thy father Anthony but for Thaisis, the harlot.'
And in the early morning the holy man Paul related the vision which
he had seen.

BU.II.PAL,SY. 176.8

25. *He saw the Son of God with His angels surrounding Him,*
each with a crown in his hand.

HY.MAC.AN.B. 60.10

2 THE CALL TO THE ASCETIC LIFE

The call to a solitary life.
The indication of the site in which the holy man should make his
    dwelling place.
The giving of the garment of office.

QUOTATIONS

1. *One day therefore, as he was preparing to receive the holy Sacraments*
    according to his custom,
   alone in his cell
   and also as he was about to stand at the altar according to his prac-
    tice,
   he looked to his right side
   and behold, he saw there a Cherubim with six wings and many eyes.
   And when Abba Macarius began to look at him wondering who he
       was,
   then through the brightness and the light of his glory,
   he fell upon his face.
   And Abba Macarius was like a dead man
   and when he had spent a short time lying upon the ground,
   the Cherubim grasped him and gave him power and raised him.
   And when he had recovered, he said to him. '( )
   Complete, therefore, the liturgy with which thou art entrusted,
   this which thou hast begun, and receive from the Holy Mys-
       teries, ( )
   and prepare thyself in the coming night to go forth from this place
       quickly.
   And thou shalt dwell in a place of which thou hast been told by the
    Lord already.'

AM.MAC.SC.B. 72.5

2. *On the following night, when he rose to perform the service, according*
    to his custom,
   behold, the whole place was made light as the hour of noon, in the
    days of Summer.

*And Abba Macarius knew by the agreement that it was the Cherubim
   who had come to him.*
That power spent a little while before it spoke with Abba Macarius,
   lest he be troubled.
Then at last he said to him:
'Rise, *gird thyself with power from God, He who gives power to thee,
   and follow after me to the road which was first told to thee by the
   Lord.*'
And thus he left behind everything in the cell,
he went forth rejoicing, being preceded by the Cherubim or rather
   by the power of God.
And after two days they came into the mountain
and they went round this side and that, *as though searching upon the
   mountain.*
*Then Abba Macarius said to him: 'I beg thee, my Lord, show me the
   place where I will be*
because I know nothing indeed upon this road.'
The Cherubim said to him: 'This district is that of thy choice.
Behold the place lies before thee. Only be discerning and take that
   which is profitable.
Only beware of evil spirits and wicked snares.'

AM.MAC.SC.B. 74.15

3. *He (Anthony) had received from the brethren a few loaves*
   and he sat upon the bank of the river.
   He looked in case a boat should pass which he might board and
      go to that place.
   As he was thinking of these things, a voice came to him from heaven,
      saying:
   'O Anthony, where art thou going from here?'
   He was not troubled at all but ( ) he answered thus:
   'Because the crowds do not allow me to withdraw or be at peace,
   because of this I wish to go to the South of Egypt ( )'
   The voice said to him: ( )
   '*If thou wishest in truth to be at peace, go to the inner desert.*'
   Anthony said: 'And who will show me the way there?'
   And immediately He showed him some Saracens who were going
      that way.

GAR.ANT.S. 55.7

4. Neuf années s'étaient écoulées qu'étant tombé un jour comme en
   extase, le serviteur de Dieu voit une immense colonne de nuée

473

dressée en face de lui, et le saint et bienheureux Syméon debout
au sommet de la colonne, ainsi que deux hommes de belle apparence
vêtus de blanc debout au sommet près de Syméon. Et il entend
la voix du saint et bienheureux Syméon qui lui dit: 'Viens à moi,
Daniel.' Lui de répondre: 'Père, père, comment pourrai-je monter
à cette hauteur?' Le saint alors dit aux jeunes gens debout près
de lui: 'Descendez et amenez-le moi.' Ils descendirent et l'amenèrent
près de Syméon et il se tint là. Alors Syméon l'embrassa et lui donna
le saint baiser, puis, à l'invitation de certains autres et sous leur
escorte, il fut emporté vers les hauteus, ayant abandonné Daniel sur
la colonne avec les deux hommes. Or, tandis que saint Daniel
le regardait qui montait vers le ciel, il entendit la voix de saint
Syméon: 'Tiens-toi ferme, conduis-toi en homme.' Cependant,
par l'effet de cette voix terrible et de sa frayeur—car c'était comme
un tonnerre éclatant à ses oreilles—il était tombé en pâmoison.
Revenu à lui-même, il raconta la chose à ses voisins. Ils dirent eux
aussi au saint: 'Il te faut monter sur une colonne, reprendre le
genre de vie de saint Syméon et être fortifié par les anges.' Le bienheureux répondit: 'Que le vouloir de Dieu mon mâitre s'accomplisse
sur son serviteur.'

FE.II.DAN.G. 105(XII)

5. While he was meditating thus, an angel of God descended from the
   heaven in his presence
   and said to him: 'Greeting to thee, thou elect of God, Mar Aaron,
   rightly hast thou thought of no longer dwelling on this mountain,
   but in the place which is commanded to thee.
   Thou hast dwelt here this time because of the wonders
   which God has done through thy hands,
   so that God should be glorified through thee,
   so that this mountain, which is blessed by thy holy footsteps,
   should become a place of refuge and salvation
   for all those who seek and who come and who take refuge in thy
   holy prayers
   and are concerned for the salvation of their souls.
   But now rise, depart from here wherever thou dost wish.'
   The holy man said to him: 'My lord, I do not know where I should
   go.'
   The angel said to him: 'Follow me.'
   And he descended to the great River Euphrates and they both
   walked upon the waters.
   And the angel led him for nine hours and when they reached the cave,

the holy man saw a cave in which was no one
and he heard the sound of a great tumult.
And the holy man said to the angel:
'What is the sound of this great tumult?'
The angel said to him: 'These are the demons which thou hast
    caused to depart from the land of Syria.
Their chief is he who was in the house of Gabriel.
Their number is three thousand and thirty-nine, a regiment and a
    half,
which thou hast expelled from all the land of the Syrians.
Now God has given thee power against them to expel them from
    here and to scatter them.
And this place will be thy dwelling and a place of refuge
for those who come for thee to thy presence and who walk in thy
    footsteps.
And the name of thy Lord will be glorified because of thee
in this place until the end.'

NAU.AAR.SY. 721.4

6. *An angel of the Lord appeared to the blessed John.*
   He said to him: 'John, dost thou know who I am?
   I am the angel who appeared to thee in the holy desert.
   I said to thee, *rise and walk to the south*
   to the desert of Siout, thy city,
   because it will have need of thee soon.'

AM.JOH.LY.S. 655.3

7. *As he* (Abba Amoi) *prayed with many tears that he might obtain his*
   request.
   As the passing of the night approached,
   behold, an angel of the Lord stood beside him and spoke to him thus:
   'Abba Amoi, *it is the Lord who commands thee: accept this brother*
     to thyself with joy because it is I who have sent him.
   Especially because his horn will be exalted in glory
   and his fruit will be to me a sweet smell, which is received in my
     presence for all generations.'
   When the angel had said these things, he became invisible to him.
   When morning came, the holy man Abba Amoi came to our father
     Abba John.
   He instructed him in the word of God ( ),
   he shaved his head and he laid down the monk's garments
   and *he spent three days and three nights, without eating and without*
     drinking,

475

standing with our father Abba John upon the clothes, both praying.
At the end of the three days and the three nights,
behold an angel of the Lord stood before them
and, with the sign of the Cross of Salvation,
he sealed the clothes three times and he became invisible from them.
When morning came, he put the clothes upon our father Abba John,
he received him to himself with spiritual joy.

AM.JOH.K.B. 329.13

8. And they stood in prayer for three days and three nights. ( )
   Then on the third day the angel of the Lord came and stood before
   them.
   And he made three crosses upon the garments
   and he was removed from their presence.

NAU.JE.PE.SY. XV.5

9. When evening came that day, Apa Pgoul slept in a place alone.
   The small boy Shenute also placed himself in a place alone.
   Apa Pgoul raised his eyes to heaven.
   He saw an angel of the Lord watching over the small boy, Shenute,
     as he was asleep
   and the angel said to Apa Pgoul:
   'When thou risest in the morning, *put the robe which thou shalt find*
     by thee on the small boy Shenute.
   For *the robe of Elijah the Tishbite, the Lord has sent to thee,*
   that thou shouldst place it upon him.'

LEI.SIN.B. 11.4

3 THE CALL TO FOUND A MONASTERY OR CHURCH

The designation of the place in which to build.
The prophecy of the growth of a new community, of the multiplication
of a new race of men.
The prophecy of the future memorial to the name of the holy man as a
founder.

QUOTATIONS

1. After these things, *it happened that one evening*
   while our most saintly father John was standing praying,
   he saw an angel of the Lord standing in glory in his presence.
   He said to him: '*Peace be with thee, O servant of God,*
   when thou riseth in the morning, come forth from this place

and go to the neighbourhood of the great light, Abba John.

Go to the West, far from all the dwellings and build a dwelling there and live in it.

The Lord God says these things: "*I will give thee an inheritance in that place.*

I will gather to thee many people and thou shalt lead them to the angelic work.

And thou shalt be to them a leader and the saviour of their souls.

And there shall be for thee a holy community and it will be called by thy name.

Thy name will be famous in the whole world."

The Lord will give thee an inheritance in these deserts,

because thou hast walked in the footprints of those who have become famous on this mountain.

They were the leaders of those who were in the desert,

namely the great Abba Macarius, and Abba John, and Abba Pishoi, and Maximus and Dometius.

And since thou has striven after their likeness,

thou shalt be with them in the same place of rest in the Kingdom of the Heavens.

And I will visit thee according to the commandment of the Lord.

And thy name will be called John Khame until thou has fulfilled all the wish of the Lord.'

When he had said these things *the angel went forth from him and appeared to his spiritual father*

and told him all these things.

But when morning came our righteous father rose, he went to our holy father Abba Teroti,

he told him those things which had been said to him.

DAV.JOH.KH.B. 337.15

2. *Then it happened on the holy night of the Lord's Day,*
while he stood performing his Office,
the Holy Theotokos Maria came to him in great and ineffable glory
and multitudes of angels accompanied her.
He fell upon his face through fear.
The Theotokos raised him, she said to him:
'*Peace be unto thee John, thou beloved of my Son Jesus and His Good Father and the Holy Spirit.*
Have courage and be strong and thou shalt become a mighty man, having great endurance,
fighting against the hostile spirits which contend with thee.

Behold, I am with thee until thou shalt overcome them all and their evil
*   dispositions*
and fulfil all the will of my Son.
Further I will establish my covenant with thee and I will ensure my
    mercy to thee,
since I will be in this place with thee because I love it.
It will become for thee a holy community
and there will be for thee multitudes of sons.
And they will call it by thy name and build a church in thy community
and call it by my name.
The blessing of my Son and His peace and His protection will be in thy
*   community.*
The angels will visit thy monastery and will watch over thy sons (   ).
I will bless their ministration and their handiwork
and they shall inherit life eternal with thee in the Kingdom of Heaven.'
And she gave to him three gold solidi having upon them the sign of
    the Cross. (   )
When she had said these things to him she gave him Peace
and she filled him with power.
She was hidden from him in great glory.

DAV.JOH.KH.B. 344.8

3. The *youth Pachomius strove to imitate him in all the works with*
    which he clothed himself.
And it happened one day, he made his way into that desert,
according to his custom, among many dense thorn trees.
And he walked under the impulse of the spirit for a distance of about
    ten miles,
until he reached a deserted village upon the river, (called) Tabennesi
and the idea came into his mind
to enter in there and to make a few prayers.
He followed that which moved him to do thus
and, as he entered into that place,
he stretched forth his hands, he prayed to the Lord Jesus Christ,
to tell him what was His pleasure.
As he prolonged his prayer *a voice came to him from heaven,*
saying: 'Pachomius, Pachomius, strive, dwell in this place and build
*   a monastery.*
For multitudes of men will come to thee to become monks under thee,
and find profit for their souls.'
And immediately, he (Pachomius) returned to his father, the old
    man, Abba Palamon,

and he told him what he had heard. ( ) He said to him: '( )
Now my son, *rise and let us go to the South
and build for thee the small dwelling.*'

LE.PAC.B. 18.6

4. ( ) a deserted village by the river, whose name was Tabennesi.
And when he knew that this was the place,
it came into his heart to go into that house and make a few prayers
and he followed that which moved him to this place.
*And when he had gone into that place,
he stood, he stretched forth his hands, he prayed to the Lord.*
When he had prolonged his prayer, *a voice came to him from heaven,
saying: 'Pachomius, Pachomius.'* He replied: 'Behold, here I am.'
The voice cried out the second time: '*Strive and dwell in this place
and build a monastery.
For many will come to thee to become monks with thee
and to profit their souls.*'
And when he ceased praying,
he returned immediately to the old man (Apa Palamon).

LE.PAC.S. 100b.4

5. And then the brothers increased in number in the monastery of
Tabennesi,
he (Pachomius) saw that they were overcrowded.
He remained praying to God about this matter
and he was told in a vision: 'Rise and go to the North
to the deserted village to thy north which is called Pbou
*and establish for thyself a monastery in that place
so that it will be for thee a foundation and a glorious name for ever.*'

LE.PAC.S. 228.14

6. *After some time, he* (Pachomius) *was told in a vision
to establish another monastery in the South.
He rose, he took the brothers.*
He went South to the district of Sne to a place called Phnoum.

LE.PAC.S. 230.1

7. *Behold, the Cherubim appeared to him* (Macarius) *and said to him:
'Behold, this is the place which the Lord has prepared for thee.
Rise now, follow me and I will show thee the road
on which thou wilt fulfil thyself till thy end.*'
And as he followed after him, *he brought him to the top of the rock*

479

to the South side of the marsh and on the West side of the well, above
   the valley.
And he said to him: 'Build thyself a dwelling place here in this place
   and build a church,
because indeed a great people will be in this place after a time.'

AM.MAC.SC.B. 88.13

8. And at the end he heard, as it were, the voice of God, which said
   to him:
   'Apollo, I am about to destroy the wisdom of the wise men of Egypt
     by thy hands
   and I will deprive the fools of the people of the knowledge which is
     not knowledge.
   And thou shalt destroy for me also with them the wise men of
     Babylon
   and wipe out all its service of devils.
   And do thou go quickly to the desert,
   to the place which is near to the dwellings of men,
   that thou mayest beget for me a holy people who shall be exalted by
     (their) good works.'

BU.II.HIER.SY. 376.19

9. And while he was there, he fell into a short sleep
   and he saw an angel in the form of a man,
   who said to him: ( )
   'Serve the cause of the angels before Christ the King
   and thou shalt receive from Him this power and authority.'
   And immediately he heard, he received from him with gladness.
   And he who had appeared to him in the likeness of an angel
   showed him a congregation of monks
   and commanded that he should have authority over them.

BU.II.HIER.SY. 408.13

10. *It happened, as he was lying down one evening, he dozed for a short*
    while.
   God wished to summon him into the holy and angelic life of monkhood.
   It happened that an angel of the Lord appeared to him as he slept.
   He said to him: 'Manasseh, Manasseh.'
   He said to him: 'Who art thou, in this form, my Lord?'
   The angel said to him: 'I am the angel of the Lord
   whom He has sent to speak with thee when He saw thy desire for Him.
   Now, *if thou dost wish to wear the holy garment of monkhood,*

this which thou hast desired, with withdrawal and especially
    asceticism,
rise and leave behind thee thy father and thy brothers
and go to the land of Egypt and be a monk in the community of the
    holy father Pachomius.
They will receive thee with love and thou wilt be a monk in that place.
Thy name will be very great.
Thou wilt spend a short time in that place while the Lord is with thee.
Afterwards thou wilt move from that place by the will of God
and thou wilt dwell in a mountain to the West opposite a village
    called Perpe. ( )
Thou shalt be in that place.
Thou shalt do great miracles like the apostles.
Thou shalt heal the sick, thou shalt cast (out) demons.
Thou shalt build a dwelling in that place and a church
as many souls will be saved through thee.
No man will be able to attack thee because of the power of God which
    is in thee. Behold I have spoken to thee.'
Thus far the vision,
and the angel left him.

AM.MAN.S. 666.1

11. *It happened when my father stood praying at the hour of dawn,*
    as he was performing his services, the angel of the Lord appeared to
    him.
He said to him: 'Manasseh, *I give peace to thee from God and His*
    angels.
Well done, O athlete of Christ, who hast fought in the stadium of thy
    Lord.
How therefore there is laid up for thee the crown of righteousness,
which the Lord will give thee on that day.
Now, therefore, when thou risest in the morning,
behold ten virgins will come to thee who are out of the one com-
    munity of Apa Pachomius.
Receive them to thyself and build them a nunnery and a church
and establish them in the fear of the Lord and the laws of the holy
    men.
This is the word which he has spoken to thee since the beginning:
"Do not reject any who shall come to thee, either man or woman,
not only these alone but all who shalt come to thee wishing to
    become monks.
Receive them to thee and put the habit upon them

481

and instruct them in the commandments and the regulations of the
  Lord." '

AM.MAN.S. 676.6

12. Comme il parlait ainsi, le vénérable Euthyme lui apparaît marchant
sur les eaux. Fidus fut pris de terreur, mais le vénérable Euthyme
lui dit: 'N'aie pas peur. Je suis Euthyme le serviteur de Dieu.
Sache que ton voyage n'est pas agréable à Dieu. ( ) Va à ma laure
et bâtis un coenobion au lieu où tu as édifié ma sépulture. ( )' A
ces paroles Fidus promit au saint d'agir ainsi. ( ) Le vénérable
Euthyme le recouvrit de son manteau et le congédia en paix. Or
Fiduis fut enlevé dans les airs à la manière, je pense, d'Habacuc et,
comme en un clin d'œil, il se trouva sur le rivage et à la ville sainte
dans un état de totale inconscience.

FE.III/I.EUT.G. 117(XLIII)

13. (The angel said:) 'For indeed *he will be a righteous man, and a chosen
    one,*
    no one will arise after him in all the land who resembles him.
    He will build a monastery
    *and he will be a consolation and shelter to all those who will go to
        his sanctuary*
    and his church will remain for generations to come.'

LEI.SIN.B. 11.13

14. To him as he sat in his cave, an angel appeared and said:
    'You have successfully ordered your own life. So it is superfluous
    to remain sitting in your cave. Up! Go out and collect all the young
    monks and dwell with them and according to the model which I now
    give you, so legislate for them.' And he gave him a brass tablet.

LO.PAL.G. 112(XXXII)

15. *In the time before the church was built,*
    *the Lord Jesus Christ appeared to our father Apa Shenute and said
        to him:*
    '*Rise and lay out the church and the foundation of the monastery and
        build a shrine in my name and thine.*'
    My father Apa Shenute said to the Lord: 'My Lord, where will I
        find something to spend on the shrine and to build it?'
    The Saviour said to him: '*Rise, go into the dwelling place which is in
        the desert.*
    That which thou wilt find upon the road, pick it up and spend it on
        the shrine.

482

And perhaps thou thinkest that it is a work of the devil.
No, but *this is the manner in which thou wilt build the church and the monastery according to my will.*
I, the Lord, have spoken.'
Then our father rose, he went into the inner desert and he prayed there all night.
When he came forth from the desert in the morning, he found a small bottle, a hand's breadth in length,
he stretched out his hand, he took it, he came to the monastery.
And then the Lord Jesus came to our father, they walked together.
They laid out the foundations of the monastery.

LEI.SIN.B. 21.8

16. When the blessed man was at a short distance from the monastery
he knelt in prayer and said:
'O God, lead me and direct me where it pleases thy will,
because I have loved thee alone above all.'
He took a path and arrived at the top of the mountain.
He found there a beautiful place with a field, in which was a spring of water.
When evening arrived, he performed the service,
he gathered roots for himself, he fed and he slept.
God appeared to him and said to him:
'Abraham, I have prepared this place for thee,
prosper in it and work to receive the incorruptible crown.
For it will happen that thy name will be proclaimed by all the world
and that I will perform, by thy hands, signs and wonders.
Rise, gird thy loins like a strong man
and build a monastery here.
For I have prepared disciples to come to thee.
Have courage and be strong and I will be with thee.'

NAU.ABR.SY. 769.5

17. *Then because of fatigue, the youth Macarius also slumbered and slept.*
And that night he found himself as if in a vision and a man stood above him,
in a garment giving forth flashes of lightning and it was variegated of many colours
and he spoke with him, saying:
'Rise and look down upon the circle of this rock and this valley in its midst.

483

Look, what dost thou see?'
'And as I looked,' he said, 'I spoke to him who spoke with me:
"I see nothing, except the beginning of the marsh, which is on the
    West of the valley
and the other mountain which surrounds it, I see also."
And he said to me: this is what God has said:
"This land I will give to thee and thou shalt be in it and thy fruit
    will grow
and thy seed will increase and thou shalt beget spiritual sons
and rulers will be nourished from thy breast and these will be placed
    in authority over peoples."'

AM.MAC.SC.B. 57.1

18. Then when he arrived at a great age,
    an angel appeared to him in a dream in the desert and said:
    'Thou shalt become a great race and wilt be in authority over many
        people
    and those who will be saved through thee will be ten myriads
    and thou shalt be ruler in a new world over all those who are in the
        world.
    Thou shalt continue in life and thou shalt not fear.'
    He said to him: 'Thou shalt never completely lack what is suitable
        for thee for thy nourishment,
    whenever thou shalt cry to God,
    until the day of thy departure in death.'

BU.II.HIER.SY. 368.11

19. Quand il fut parvenu désormais à la complète vieillesse, un ange
    lui apparut en songe au désert, qui lui dit: 'Tu deviendras une grande
    nation et l'on te confiera la charge d'un grand peuple. Dix myriades
    seront les gens sauvés par toi. Car autant tu en auras gagnés ici-bas,
    autant seront dans le monde à venir ceux de qui tu seras le chef.
    Et ne sois jamais dans le doute', lui dit l'ange, 'car les ressources
    nécéssaires ne te manqueront jamais jusqu'à la fin, toutes les fois
    que tu auras invoqué Dieu.'

FE.IV/I.HIS.G. 30(II)

20. *He remembered what he had seen, through the Lord,*
    in the vision on the day when he was instructed to become Christian,
    how they had seen in that vision,
    the dew of heaven which came down upon him,
    then it gathered together, it formed a drop of honey in his hand,
    it fell upon the earth;

and he was told in the vision:
'Take care about this event, because it will be fulfilled for thee after
a time.'
And afterwards he was told by the Spirit that this drop of honey
which gathered in his hand and fell upon the earth,
these are all the favours which have happened to thee from the Lord and
will also happen to thy brethren.

LE.PAC.S. 72a.12

21. *In the night on which he was baptised*
he saw a dream, as if he saw the dew of heaven coming down upon
his head.
Afterwards it gathered into a lump of honey in his right hand.
And even as he looked down upon it,
it fell upon the earth.
It spread upon the face of the whole earth.
And even as he was doubtful in his mind, a voice came to him from
heaven:
'Know this, Pachomius, for *it will happen to thee after some time.*'

LE.PAC.B. 6.17

22. (Pachomius) *and his brother went into a deserted village, namely*
Tabennesi, the place to which they had retired.
And that evening, after they had finished praying according to their
custom,
he (Pachomius) *sat on one side alone, at a little distance from his*
brother,
grieving and troubled concerning the will of God that he should
know it.
While it was yet dark, *behold, a man of light stood in his presence.*
He said to him: 'Why art thou sad and suffering?'
He answered, saying: 'I seek the will of God.'
He said to him: 'Dost thou truly wish the will of God?'
He said to him: 'Yes.'
He answered him: *'The will of God is the service of the race of man to*
reconcile them with him.'
He answered, as if indignant: 'I am seeking the will of God, thou
tellest me to serve men.'
That one answered three times: *'The will of God is the service of men,*
to summon them to him.'
And afterwards he ceased to see him.

LE.PAC.S. 107a.1

23. *As he* (Pachomius) *was sitting alone one day in a place,*
    gathering a few reeds for his handwork,
    while he kept vigil once in that place,
    according to his custom,
    an angel of the Lord appeared to him and said to him three times:
    'Pachomius, Pachomius, *it is the will of the Lord that thou servest*
        the race of men
    and that thou reconcilest them to Him.'
    When the angel of the Lord had gone
    our father Pachomius stood, he reflected;
    '*This matter is from our Lord.*'
    And when he finished gathering his few reeds, he went back to his
        monastery.

                                                    LE.PAC.B. 21.28

4   CALL TO THE MINISTRY

The giving of the keys of the ministry.
The appearance of a column of fire as a sign to undertake the ministry.
The giving of instructions concerning the ministry.
The hearing of a voice from heaven.

QUOTATIONS

1. *And God opened the eyes of the old man*
   when he recovered from sleep
   and behold, he saw a choir of monks surrounding Abba Macarius
       as he slept.
   And the old man saw that they were all white
   and all growing the likeness of wings upon their shoulders,
   after the manner of eagles.
   And he heard a voice saying: '*Rise Macarius, take care of the ministry,*
   for the time has come. Arise, go,
   because it is indeed I who send thee.'

                                                    AM.MAC.SC.B. 63.5

2. The holy man, Apa Pisentius, answered: 'Before the clergy came to
   my unworthy self, I slept a little.
   A voice came to me three times, saying: "Pisentius, Pisentius,
   Pisentius,
   behold the Ordinance of the Church.
   They come to thee, do not refuse the Ordinance.
   Which has been entrusted to thee from my chief apostle. Arise and
       follow them.

Do not leave the Church to be a widow."
When I had heard these things, the clergy called to me, I came forth,
    I followed them,'

BU.AP.PIS.S. 93.7

3. After this, *our holy father was told by the angel which dwelt with
        him to go to the South* (Egypt),
    for the salvation of some multitudes of souls together
    in the manner of our father Abba John and our father Abba Pshoi,
        the great light-bearers.
    Our holy father called one among his brethren, namely our father
        Shenute, his successor.
    He said to him: 'I have been summoned, my son, by the Lord, to a
        ministry.
    Behold I give the brethren into thy hand.
    Do thou stand in this place giving directions to the brethren until I
        return to thee.'

DAV.JOH.KH.B. 354.15

4. It is said in the Book of Paradise of Shiet on Salvation,
    that the brothers took Theodore by force, they appointed him
        deacon.
    The brothers begged him, saying: 'Allow it,
    because thou wilt not do service upon the altar,
    except to hold the chalice with the priest.' ( )
    Then he prayed to God saying: 'O Lord reveal to me this matter ( ).'
    And the Lord opened his eyes,
    he saw a column of fire resting upon the earth, reaching up to heaven.
    A voice came to him from heaven, saying:
    'If thou wilt be like this column of fire then proceed,
    perform the liturgy of this altar.'
    When Theodore saw this vision, he retired from the altar until the day
        of his death.

AM.PIS.KE.B. 362.11

5. They said concerning Abba Theodore that, when he was a deacon
        in Scete,
    he did not wish to take upon himself the ministrations
    and he fled to many places
    and the old men came to him saying to him: 'Thou shalt not forsake
        thy place.'
    Abba Theodore said to them: 'Allow me that I request from God

487

and if he persuades me I will stand in my place.'

And when he besought God, he said:

'If it be thy will, my Lord, that I should remain, persuade me.'

And there appeared to him a pillar of fire from earth to heaven

and a voice said to him: 'If thou art able to be like this pillar, go and minister.'

Then when he heard these things he again did not take on himself to minister.

And when he came to the church the brethren fell down before him and entreated him.

BU.II.PAL.SY. 678.5

6. Afterwards he (Theodore) prayed to the Lord concerning the hegumens of the congregations,

that He should tell him what to do with them.

And the Lord heard this prayer and revealed to him.

Behold, there came upon him an ecstasy and a vision.

He saw the form of our father Pachomius,

wearing a white garment like snow

and two angels of the Lord gave much light ( )

'*The garment which I saw on him in the vision was like royal purple and shone as lightning.*'

After causing him to see such great glory,

He told him the disposition of the elders of the congregation, designating each one by name,

and the congregation to which he would be assigned as hegumen.

And He recommended that each one of them should not be placed in the monastery as before,

but that he should be in a new one, so that they should be detached.

LE.PAC.B. 157.21

7. *As he stood praying, he saw a great vision.*

Behold, three angels came to him in the form of monks bearing white stoles,

and they were beautiful in their appearance and keys were in their hands.

And they said to him three times: 'Pisentius, Pisentius, Pisentius.'

He said: 'Bless me my fathers, I am the worthless servant

who will in a short time be destroyed and perish in the tomb.'

They said to him: 'The Lord has sent us to thee to give to thee the keys of the Church.

Now, therefore, receive these to thyself in thy hands,

The Lord entrusts them to thee for guarding his Church,
this which He acquired with His own blood.'

AM.PIS.KE.B. 361.4

8. As Theodore was sitting inside his cell one day in his first year,
plaiting rope and meditating
on those of the Holy Scriptures which he knew by heart,
he would rise from time to time
as his heart prompted him, to pray.
And when he was sitting meditating,
the cell in which he was, became light.
He was greatly disturbed.
Behold two angels, taking the forms of men giving light, appeared to
   him.
He was afraid. He ran. He came forth from his cell.
He ran up on the roof because he had not seen a vision before.
And when he reached the roof they (the angels) also came, ( )
they removed the fear from him so that he did not fear
and the taller of them said to him: 'Stretch forth thy hand, O
   Theodore.'
He held out (his hands) in the manner of those about to partake of
   the Holy Mysteries
and the angel gave into his hands many keys.
When he had received them he held them in his right hand.
While he was yet in amazement about this matter, he looked.
Suddenly he was unable to see the angels.
He looked also at his hand. He could not see any keys.
This vision he did not tell to our father Pachomius, being ashamed
because many times he heard him say: 'I was given keys secretly.'

LE.PAC.B. 37.2

9. After four years, *Pachomius saw the vision which he had seen at first,*
when the dew of heaven came down upon him
and fell and it filled the face of the whole earth.
And he also saw some keys being given to him in secret.
When the morning came he told the holy man Abba Palamon
of the vision which he had seen.
But he (Palamon) was greatly disturbed saying:
'There is a great meaning in the interpretation of this word, O my
   son Pachomius, but let the Lord's will be done.'

LE.PAC.B. 12.15

5 ADMONITION

Reproof of neglectful practices.
Advice on ascetic life.
Appointment of a successor.
Call to visit a holy man.

QUOTATIONS

1. And when he descended to a certain valley,
   an angel of the Lord appeared to him and said to him:
   'Ephraim, why dost thou flee?'
   He then said: 'My Lord, in order to sit in peace
   and to flee from the tumult of the world.'
   The angel said to him: 'See that it is not fulfilled in thee what they
      are saying,
   that Ephraim flees from me like a young calf
   whose shoulder rebels against the yoke.'
   Then he wept and said: 'My lord, I am weak and not worthy.'
   The angel said to him: 'O man, a man does not light a lamp
   and place it under a bushel,
   but upon a lampstand, so that all men may see its light.'
   And when he had spoken much with him,
   he then became invisible to him.

   BRO.EP.SY. 30.11

   It was said of Abba Anthony that it was once revealed to him
      concerning a virgin who fell into sin.
   *He rose, he took his staff of palm that was in his hand, he began to walk
      the way to the monastery,* ( )
   behold Christ the King of Glory appeared to him, the only Compas-
      sionate One. ( )
   The Saviour said to him with a face of mercy and a smile of grace:
   'Anthony, is there a reason for this great journey of thine hither?'

   AM.AP.ANT.B. 33.4

2. And after four months,
   as our father Pachomius was praying and beseeching, as he did daily,
      so that repentance should happen to him who had fallen,
   he saw an angel in a vision, according to the command of the Lord.
   And a voice came to him from him:
   'This man for whom thou art praying, that repentance should hap-
      pen to him,
   is he ignorant?

490

THE REPRESENTATION OF A NON-MATERIAL WORLD

Hast thou not many times taught him concerning the salvation of his
   soul
that he should not fall into the snares of the devil?
Did that one not teach others not to sin?
Now therefore his cutting off has happened, separate him from
   thyself.'

LE.PAC.S. 166.1

3. *And as he* (Pachomius) *was still praying, an angel of the Lord appeared*
   to him,
   being very terrifying, with a sword of fire held drawn in his hand
   and he said to our father Pachomius:
   '*Even as God erased his name from the Book of Life*
   do thou also cast them forth from among the brethren,' ( )
   When morning came, he put secular dress upon them and he said to
   them:
   'Go and act according to the clothes whose practices you have done.'

LE.PAC.B. 150.13

4. It happened that evening that the old man (who complained at
   having to clean the wells) *saw a vision.*
   He saw an angel of the Lord in their midst crying out among them,
   saying:
   'Receive the Holy Spirit to yourselves,
   for you do not do the work of men but *you do the work of the servants*
   of God.'
   He saw him also looking at himself saying:
   'O complaining and faithless old man, receive for thyself the
   spirit of disbelief.'
   And it happened in the morning,
   when the brothers were in the service praying,
   he came into their midst, he cried out saying:
   'Pray for me, that the Lord remove from me the spirit of disbelief.'

LE.PAC.S. 54b.20

5. *That evening he* (the brother who objected to cleaning wells) *saw*
   himself in a vision,
   as if he were above that well.
   He looked down into it, he saw a man who was glorious in his light
   in the midst of the brothers who were working joyfully,

491

and he was saying to them: 'Receive the spirit of obedience and power

but thou, old man, receive the spirit of disbelief towards the holy men.'

LE.PAC.B. 66.11

6. They told of a hermit who lived in a monastery of the brotherhood
that although he kept many vigils and prayed,
he was neglectful about communal prayer.
And one night there appeared to him
a glorious pillar of bright light from the meeting place of the brothers
and it reached to heaven.
And he also saw, as it were, a small spark round about the pillar,
and sometimes it shone and sometimes it was extinguished.
And while he was wondering at the vision,
it was explained to him by God and He said:
'The pillar which thou seest is the prayers from many
and they rise up to God and minister to Him.
And this spark is the prayers of those who dwell in the congregation
and despise the appointed services of the brotherhood.
And thou also, if thou dost wish to live,
fulfil with thy brethren those things that are customary
and then, if thou wishest and thou art able, those things that are apart.'
Then he related all these things before the brotherhood and they glorified God.

BU.I.PAL.SY. 630; BEDJAN. VII.121

7. Or, dans la nuit, le vénérable Euthyme apparaît au bienheureux Hélias et lui dit 'Que font-là ces chevaux aujourd'hui?' Sur sa réponse ( ), Euthyme le gourmande en ces termes: 'Pourquoi avez-vous négligé de prier Dieu, hommes de peu de foi? La main du Seigneur ne peut-elle vous donner de l'eau?' ( ) Hélias se lève, rapporte sa vision au bienheureux Fidus et à tous les autres et renvoie les chevaux à leurs monastères. Quand donc le soleil se fut levé, il monta au ciel un nuage, une forte pluie se répandit autour du monastère.

FE.III/1.EUT.G. 119(XLIV)

8. Our father, the prophet Apa Shenute was performing his services at night

and when he had finished the service,
he slept for a little while.
He saw a vision from the Lord thus:
he saw a man full of great glory standing in his presence.
There was a sweet smell coming from his mouth.
His face gave forth rays of light, like the sun.
The old man said to him: 'Who art thou, my Lord, who art thus, with
*   such great glory surrounding thee?'*
The man of light answered, saying: 'I am Paul, the Apostle of Christ.
*   ( )*
Behold the Lord has sent me to thee to console thee
for those things thou hast done to the hungry and needy.'
And thus he stood speaking with him until the hour of the assembly in
*   the church at night.*
Then he held out to him a loaf. He gave it to him.
The old man took it, he bound it in his pallium.
The apostle said to him: 'Take this bread ( ).
For a multitude of holy men have blessed this bread and also *our*
    Lord Jesus Christ blessed it and signed it with the Cross.
Be of good courage now, be strong and do not fear.
The peace of God remain with thee for ever.'
And then he embraced him, he departed from him.

LEI.SIN.B. 61.9

9. He suffered greatly saying: 'I have suffered today.'
   A voice came to him from heaven saying:
   'Apater, O man worthy of love, do not be discouraged, I am with thee
   *   in all thy suffering.'*

HY.AP.IR.B. 84.17

10. *A voice came to him saying:*
    'I was in this place, but I wanted to see thee fight.
    Because thou didst endure and wast not overcome.
    I will be thy help at all times
    and I will make thee renowned in all places.'

GAR.ANT.S. 16.5

11. *It was said of Abba Anthony that, as he was sitting once in the desert,*
    he was in stupefaction and affliction with the number of thoughts
    and he prayed to God, saying:
    'My Lord, I wish to be delivered.
    The thoughts do not leave me.

493

What shall I do in this plight or how shall I be saved?'
And, as he stood a little while outside on the mountain,
he saw one in the likeness of a man,
sitting weaving a basket and as he rose from time to time from the
handwork,
he prayed and then he sat again working.
And it was an angel of the Lord, whom He sent as an encouragement
to Anthony
and a strength against evil despondency.
He heard him saying to him: 'Do thus and thou shalt be delivered.'
When he heard, he was in great joy.
He received strength and he did thus all the days of his life.

AM.AP.ANT.B. 30.15

12. And he approached a little from where he was
    and he saw a man in the likeness of the blessed man Anthony,
    with his form, who was sitting and plaiting ropes.
    And he rose from his work and prayed,
    and afterwards he sat down and continued.
    And again he stood up and prayed, for he was an angel who had
        been sent from God
    for the correction and admonition of the blessed man Anthony,
    who afterwards heard him say to him: 'Do thou Anthony also do
        this and live.'
    And when he heard these things, the blessed man had great joy
    and afterwards he did thus and lived.

BU.II.PAL.SY. 465.21

13. It happened that a month after his father died,
    he (Isaac) was in great affliction
    because of his separation from this world of vanity.
    And the holy Archbishop Abba John prayed to God
    to reveal to him who would be worthy to follow him and to rule the
        the Church.
    He was informed through a vision telling him:
    'Send to Shiet to the monastery of Abba Zacharias for Isaac,
    the monk and ascetic: he will be thy successor.'

POR.IS.B. 346.11

14. And while he was standing in prayer he wept,
    he looked in the sky and he saw an angel of the Lord standing before
        him,

who said to him: 'Abba Bamouyah,
God tells thee to receive this young man with great joy and exultation,
because it is I who have sent him to thy presence
and he will raise his horn in glory and a sweet perfume,
acceptable before me, will mount from his fruits
till the last generation.'
When the angel had finished these words,
he passed from before the eyes of the old man.

NAU.JE.PE.SY. XIV.12

15. Then the Christ appeared to the blessed man and said to him:
   'Abraham, Abraham, thy works have pleased God.
   Rise, go to the city of Samosata.
   There is there a young man whose name is Barsoma.
   Take him with thee, because he is a chosen vessel for me.'
   Then the blessed man entrusted the brothers with the divine grace
      and departed.

NAU.ABR.SY. 771.4

16. As the holy old man Agabus was about to die, we asked him:
   'Our holy father, speak a word to us, that we may live by it after
      thee.'
   He said to us: '*This night, as I was standing up on this rock, to the*
      South,
   I saw as it were a monk standing in my presence, who was tall,
   wearing a black striped garment, with a hood upon his head, with
      crosses upon it,
   with a staff of date palm in his hand, with a cross.
   When I saw him, I was afraid.
   He approached me, he embraced me
   and he said to me: "Dost thou know who I am?"
   I said to him: "No, my holy father."
   He said to me: "*I am Macarius, the Egyptian,*
   who am come to summon thy sons to take them with me to Egypt."
   I said to him: "Wilt thou not take me with them, my father."
   He said to me: "No,
   but *I tell thee that after three more days thou wilt die and go to the*
      Lord
   and the king will send for his sons to take them to Constantinople.
   Therefore, bid them, that they come to Egypt to be under me,
   for it is God who has summoned them to me as sons.

495

Behold, I have spoken to thee.'
And when he had said these things, he became invisible to me.'

AM.MA.DO.B. 268.10

17. What I will tell is outside reason, but it is not possible for me to
    hide it.
    It happened to me during last night as I was wakeful because of
    illness
    and as I was able to stand I said some few psalms.
    When I had finished the small service according to my strength, (   )
    suddenly the King, the Lord of Glory appeared to me
    and he said to me: 'Greeting, thou good waterer of the spiritual
    garden.
    Entrust the garden to Petrus, the priest, that he water it
    and come, rest thyself with thy fathers.'

HY.PET.AL.B. 256.2

18. The blessed Serapion related to us
    when he was in the inner land, which is in the inner desert of Egypt:
    'I saw in a dream while I was asleep with Abba John, the great elder,
    that two brethren, monks, came
    and they were blessed by Abba John.
    And they said: "Who is that who sleeps here?"
    And he said to them: "Abba Serapion."
    One said to his comrade: "Arise, let us go and be blessed by him."
    And Abba John said to them: "He just came in from the desert and
       he is very tired.
    Let him rest a little."
    They said: "It is now some time that he has been labouring to
       weariness within this desert
    and he has not gone to Abba Marcus, who is in the mountain of
       Tharmaka.
    For he has no equal among all the monks who dwell in this desert.
    He is a hundred and thirty years old
    and for ninety years no man has seen him.
    And forty days from now,
    the fathers who are in the Land of Life are coming
    and they will fetch him to their abode."
    And when the two brethren had said these things, I Serapion awoke.
    And I saw that there was no one with Abba John.
    And I said to him: "Thus I saw in my dream, Abba."
    And he said to me: "Truly this was indeed a dream from God.

And I do not know where this mountain is."
And I said to him: "Pray for me."
And when he had prayed I bade him farewell and I was blessed by
    him.
And I travelled to Alexandria.
And I was twelve days (journey) from there.
And from the stupefaction of that vision which I had seen,
I took no food for (several) days.'

LOOK.MAR.SY. 1.2

19. One night I saw the angels of God descending to that saint
    and they were singing praises and saying:
    'Blessed art thou and good is thy soul, Abba Marcus.
    Behold, we have brought Serapion, whom thy soul desired to see.
    Another man from the race of men thou has not desired to see.'
    When I heard these things I was in great fear
    and I proceeded towards that sight, to the cave of Abba Marcus.
    And when the angels went to heaven,
    I approached the door of the cave.

LOOK.MAR.SY. 6.1

20. It happened in the time of Apa Pambo the priest of the Church of
    Shiet. ( )
    A vision appeared to him saying: 'Rise and go toward the ocean.
    Thou wilt find a great anchorite,
    the sandal of one of his feet the whole world is not worthy to unloose.'
    He, the blessed Apa Pambo,
    rose, he walked into the mountain,
    through the power of God which was within him, as with the blessed
        Anthony.

BU.CYR.S. 128.12

21. *He saw at night in a vision, as he was standing praying, a man of light.*
    The man of light spoke to him saying:
    'Do not be neglectful of the ministry which is assigned to thee
        by the Lord God.
    When thou risest on the morrow,
    go to Shiet to the desert of our father Abba Macarius
    and seek the dwelling place of my father Teroti
    and become a monk with him and wear the habit of the angels.'

DAV.JOH.KH.B. 333.13

III. THE DEATH OF A HOLY MAN

1. DEATH FORETOLD

THEMES

The ability of a holy man to foretell his own death.
The foretelling of his death to a holy man by an angel.
The foretelling of his death to a holy man by the fathers of the Church.
The request for burial by an ascetic, foretelling his own death.

EPISODES

The visit of an angel or of the fathers of the Church during the illness
of a holy man.
The instruction to the holy man to make his preparations for death.
The enabling of a dying man to see his future fate in heaven.
The burial of an ascetic in the desert; the wrapping of the body; the
disposal of the body.

QUOTATIONS

1. And the elder (   ) said that it was impossible
   that one of them should fall into sickness
   before the day of his departure from the world,
   but when the end of one of them was coming,
   he foretold it and informed them all
   and he lay down and died.

BU.II.HIER.SY. 407.1

2. Le prêtre qui demeurait constamment au portail (du monastère)
   nous dit que les moines de l'intérieur étaient si saints qu'ils pouvaient
   tous accomplir des miracles, et qu'aucun d'eux n'était jamais
   tombé malade avant de mourir: quand venait, pour chacun d'eux,
   l'heure du passage, il annonçait d'avance à tous, puis, s'étant
   couché, s'endormait.

FE.IV/1.HIS.G. 103(XVII)

3. *He was undergoing severe ascetic disciplines*
   and while he was there, *it was revealed to him through an angel of
   the Lord*
   *saying: 'The days of thy removal from the world are approaching
   when thou shalt go to Him whom thou lovest, the Christ.*
   That day was the first of the month of Pashons.'

GUI.DAN.B. 550.18

498

4. Now when the angel had said these things,
   he rose above the sleeping place of our father Isaac,
   he withdrew, while our father Isaac watched after him.
   And he was astonished at the revelation which he had seen
   and he said: 'I shall not see the daylight before they seek for me.'

   GUI.IS.B. 228.22

5. Outre les autres charismes que posséda le vénérable Euthyme, il lui fut donné aussi de savoir à l'avance le jour de sa dormition et ce qui devait advenir à sa laure.

   FE.III/1.EUT.G. 111(XXXIX)

6. Si grande fut la grâce de prophétie accordée à ce saint homme que, trois mois avant sa dormition, il nous prédit qu'au bout de ce peu de jours il devrait quitter le corps et se rendre près du Seigneur. A partir de ce moment, avec tous ceux qui allaient et venaient auprès de lui, il ne s'entretenait pas seulement des choses présentes, mais il leur annonçait par don de prescience les évènements futurs, les fortifiant par des paroles de bon conseil; d'autre part, il prescrivait à ses compagnons habituels et à nous la manière dont il faudrait descendre de la colonne son précieux corps.

   FE.II.DAN.G. 159(XLV)

7. Après que, cet homme aussi, Paphnuce l'eut envoyé d'avance au ciel, désormais il n'eut plus lui-même de goût à vivre, car il ne pouvait plus s'exercer à l'ascèse. Un ange alors se présenta à lui, qui lui dit: 'Viens maintenant toi aussi, bienheureux, aux tabernacles éternels de Dieu. Car voici déjà arrivés les prophètes, qui vont t'accueillir dans leurs chœurs. Je ne te l'ai pas divulgué plus tôt, de peur que tu n'en tires orgueil et ne perdes la récompense.' Il ne survécut qu'un sul jour. A la suite d'une révélation, des prêtres étaient allés le voir; il leur raconta tout, puis rendit l'âme. Les prêtres le virent clairement monter au ciel, parmi des chœurs de justes et d'anges qui chantaient Dieu.

   FE.IV/1.HIS.G. 96(XIV)

8. 'He (Abba Marcus) has no equal among all the monks who dwell in this desert.
   He is a hundred and thirty years old
   and for ninety years no man has seen him.
   And forty days from now,
   the fathers who are in the Land of Life are coming

   499

and they will fetch him to their abode.'
And when the two brethren had said these things,
I Serapion awoke.

LOOK.MAR.SY. 1.11

9. *When he became weak in his body,* the God-fearing servant ( )
   remained with him.
   As he was lying down, our father was wakeful in the night,
   especially because of the pain of the increasing illness.
   As they said, *the great Anthony and Abba Didjoi the Great, with
   Abba Macarius and Abba Amoi came in to him*
   and they gave courage to our father in many things, consoling him. ( )
   *And they said to him: 'Take courage in the Lord and be strong and
   prepare thyself,*
   for we will come for thee on the morning of the Lord's day
   and we will take thee with us to the life of eternity
   according to the command of the Lord.'
   When the holy men had said these things to our father
   they blessed him and they became invisible to him.

AM.JOH.K.B. 399.10

10. The faithful man, of whom we have spoken, was constantly near
    him
    and increased his benefits since he was ill.
    One night when he was awake and attentive upon his watch,
    he saw the master of the house coming.
    While he (John) was prostrated by his illness,
    suddenly Abba Anthony entered in to his presence,
    with Abba Macarius, the great and Abba Bamouyah, father of the
    holy man Abba John.
    They gave him Peace and comforted him and consoled him
    and fortified his mind with their spiritual words,
    and with the hope of new life and of the joy which was prepared for
    him.
    Then the fathers who were near him heard when it was said to him:
    'Rejoice and exult and let thy heart be fortified in God.
    And be ready, because in the night, this Sabbath,
    we shall come to thee to take thee with us
    to the good and blessed life, according to the command of Our
    Lord.'
    And the fathers went from his presence.

NAU.JE.PE.SY. LXIX.13

11. *Again the weakness overcame him and when he went to the cave
     alone he lay down.*
    It was then the seventh hour.
    And thus he thought in his heart, according to his custom,
    of his passing away,
    and of his meeting with God
    and of the sentence which would come forth upon him at that time
    and the place to which he would be taken.
    *Behold there appeared to him two saints shining greatly in glory and
      splendour,*
    while their faces were full of joy.
    And when the old man saw them he was silent
    and meanwhile *one of them said to him: ' Dost thou not know who I
      am?'*
    And when he had gazed at him
    he was not able to recognise him properly
    because of the greatness of the light in which they were.
    And after a short time he said to him who spoke with him:
    'According to me, thou art my father Abba Anthony.'
    And the holy Abba Anthony said to him:
    ' Dost thou not know this other, who he is?'
    And then he was silent, because he never answered hastily.
    He said to him: *'This is our brother Pachomius,*
    the father of the monks of Tabennesi,
    for indeed we have been sent to summon thee.
    Therefore make thy preparation, for indeed yet another nine days and
    thou wilt lay down the garment of skin and thou wilt be amongst us.
    And raise thine eyes and see the road which has been prepared for thee,
    so that thou shouldst receive joy and come forth with ease.'
    And thus the holy men withdrew from him.

    AM.MAC.SC.B. 107.6

12. My father answered: 'In truth, another five days have been given
     to me from the third hour today. (   )
    Before I spoke to thee, an ecstasy came upon me.
    A man of light came and stood before me.
    He said to me: "Pisentius, Pisentius, Pisentius," three times.
    "Prepare thyself, for there remain to thee in this world another five
      days and thou shalt come to me."
    And when he had said these things to me, he withdrew himself.
    Now behold I shall go the presence of all my fathers (   ).'
    But let us turn ourselves to his laying down of the body.

    33   501

For he spent three days and he did not eat or drink,
nor did he speak with us,
nor did he turn himself from side to side.
But he lay stretched out like a dead man
in the place of the great cell.
In the evening (   ) he called out: 'John.' I answered: 'Bless me.'
He said to me: 'I have reached my departure,
and I shall complete my course at the hour when the sun will set
  tomorrow. (   )
Take care, do thou not let any man take my body away
from the place which I cause to be dug for me.
And these three days which I have spent without speaking with you,
I was standing in the presence of God.
And he made my account from the ninth hour yesterday.'

BU.AP.PIS.S. 123.26

13. It happened when God wished to remove him from this place of
    sojourn
    to take him to the Land of the Living ones,
    the dwelling place of the patriarchs and the prophets and the
      apostles, (   )
    he saw a vision (   ).
    He said to me:
    'Before I spoke with thee an ecstasy fell upon me.
    I saw a multitude of orthodox bishops giving light like the sun,
    standing in this courtyard, singing to God,
    while Peter and Paul were standing in their midst.
    I cast myself upon my face.
    I worshipped them.
    Peter took my hand, he stood me up.
    He said to me: " Dost thou know who I am?"
    I said to him: "No my Lord."
    He answered: "I am Simon Peter and the Apostle of Jesus Christ,
    My brother whom thou seest is Paul and these are thy fellow bishops.
    We have been sent by our master Christ to summon thee to ourselves,
    so that thou shouldst prepare thy affairs for thy road to come forth
      from this life (   )
    and that thou shouldst come before us.
    For the time approaches."'

AM.PIS.KE.B. 415.6

14. Now it happened that *when the days of our father Isaac, the Patriarch*
    approached

(the time) that he should come forth from the body,
God, the merciful, sent to him the great holy Archangel, Michael,
whom He had sent to Abraham, his father, at the hour of day-
    light ( ).
He said to him:
'Greeting my son, thou chosen one of God and the son of his beloved
    one.'
Now the God-loving and righteous old man *our father Isaac was*
    accustomed to speak daily with the holy angels,
He turned down his face,
he saw him taking the likeness of father Abraham.
He opened his mouth, he lifted up his voice,
he cried out in great joy and exultation:
'I have seen thy face like him who has seen God.'
The angel said: 'Make provision for thyself, my beloved Isaac,
because I have been sent for thee from the Living God,
to take thee to the heavens to thy father Abraham and
that thou mayest keep festival with all the Holy Ones,
for thy father Abraham is looking out for thee
and he will come for thee himself.'

GUI.IS.B. 225.13

15. After all these things, *our father Apa Matthaius rose, he went forth*
    to the desert ( ).
Afterwards he came down, he went into his dwelling place.
We rose then, we went to him that we should receive blessing from
    his holiness.
When we had sat for a short time before him, he spoke with us
    saying:
'It happened to me last night,
when I had performed my service and completed my prayers,
I slept for a short time upon the small bench
on which I sit when doing my handwork.
I saw, in ecstasy, two monks
standing before me in great glory.
They said to me: "Rise, come quickly to meet the fathers of the
    schema,
Anthony, and Pachomius, and Theodore and our father Apa Moses
and also the elder and prophet Apa Shenute. ( )"*
They all came, they embraced me.
They said to me: "*It is good that thou has come to us to our gathering*
and that thou wilt come with us to the Heavenly Jerusalem."

503

I saw a great gate and a wall surrounding, I should say that
the wall and the door and the gate were inlaid with gold and stones of
    all colours.
When I approached the gate I heard a voice saying:
"*Open the door of the gate so that Matthaius may enter in,*
so that the elders may settle his account for they have been sent for
    him."
And I entered in, in fear and trembling.
I saw a great walk, so that I should say in my heart, it would be one
    or two miles (long)
and great multitudes of thrones extended on each side
and multitudes of monks were sitting upon their thrones in glory.
Then I said to those who stood with me:
"*Who are these, thus sitting on their thrones?*"
They said: "All these whom thou seest they are the fathers of the
    world
archbishops and priests and bishops, in short,
the fathers of monasteries and their sons of the schema (   ).
Look and see these four persons who are within these gates upon the
    thrones and know them."
And he pointed his finger at each one saying:
"*This is Anthony, this is Pachomius, this is Theodore and Petronius.*
This is Apa Shenute, of the monastery of Atribe, this is Apa Macarius
    of the monastery of Shiet.
These are the law givers of this multitude of monks."
Then I was in fear and trembling,
I stood I fell and worshipped them upon the ground.
One of those who was standing and appeared like a notarius,
with a pen in his hand, said:
"*Matthaius, rise quickly and go to thy monastery* and bring thy books
and sit and give account of thy monastery. (   )
These will be required of thee on the seventh day of this month" (   )
Then I rose up from the vision (   );
my time approaches that I should go to my place of rest.'

AM.MAT.P.B. 732.4

16. After all these things, *our father Apa Matthaius rose.*
    He went up to the desert (   ).
    Afterwards he came down to the monastery.
    We then rose to hasten to him to receive his blessing.
    When we entered in to him in the place where he was we sat a short
        while before him.

THE REPRESENTATION OF A NON-MATERIAL WORLD

He spoke with us, saying:
'It happened last night after I had made my service.
I completed my prayers.
I sat for a short while upon the small bench.
As I was sitting upon it doing my small handwork
I saw in an ecstasy, two brother monks
standing above me in great glory.
They answered and said to me: " Rise, come quickly to meet the fathers
    of the schema
Anthony and Pachomius and Theodore and our father Apa Moses
and the holy elder and prophet Apa Shenute the Archimandrite." ( )
They said to me:
"*It is good that thou shouldst come to our congregation*
and that thou comest with us to the Heavenly Jerusalem."
Then I saw a great tower and a very high wall, as I should say.
This wall with its door and this gate are ornamented with gold and
    precious stones of all colours.
When we came to the gate I heard a voice saying:
"*Open the gate that Matthaius may come in,*
that the elders may settle his account, for it is they who were sent for
    him until he came."
I then entered in fear and trembling.
I saw a great walk, as I should say in my heart,
it would be two or three miles long.
On its North side and its South side grew all fragrant trees
and other trees were bearing fruits in great abundance.
From end to end of the walk stretched a great multitude of thrones,
with great multitudes of monks sitting upon them in great glory.
I said to him who walked with me: " Who are these who are sitting
    upon their thrones?"
He answered, he said to me: " All those whom thou seest,
these are the fathers of the world and the fathers also of the monas-
    teries,
with their sons of the schema ( ).
Look and see these six great personages who are beyond thee
within upon these thrones of glory, and learn them."
And he pointed out each one of them to me.
He showed them saying: "*This is Anthony, this is Pachomius, and*
    Petronius and Theodore.
This is Apa Shenute of the monastery of Atribe. This is
    Macarius of Shiet.
These are the law-givers of this whole multitude of monks."

505

Then I stood up in fear and trembling and I prostrated myself.
I worshipped them upon the earth.
One of these who were standing, who had the appearance of a
  notary, with a pen in his hand, said to me:
"Matthaius, *arise and go to thy monastery*
and bring thy books and sit and give account of thy monastery. ( )
For they will send for thee on the seventh day of the month." ( )
Then I awoke from the vision.'

TIL.II.MAT.A.S. 20.3

17. *And we spent the whole night praying to God until the morning.*
    When the morning came,
    I saw his face which had changed and turned to become like
    another man.
    He became altogether like a fire and his form terrified me greatly.
    He said to me: 'Do not fear, my brother Paphnute.
    For the Lord has sent thee to take care of my body, and to bury it.
    For on this day I shall complete my course
    and I shall go to the place of rest for ever.'

BU.ONS. 215.34

18. 'And behold, the allotted time of my life is completed
    and God has sent thee
    that thou shouldst bury this poor body with thy holy hands.'

LOOK.MAR.SY. 16.10

19. *But I removed my tunic which I wore.*
    I used half as a shroud.
    The other half I wrapped it round me so that I would not be left
      naked.
    I placed his body down a cleft in a rock.
    I heard the voice of a multitude of angels rejoicing and saying
      'Alleluia.'
    I made my prayer over him. I rolled many stones upon him.
    I stood, I prayed a second time.

BU.ON.S. 217.28

20. *But I stripped off my robe*
    I used half of it as a shroud,
    in the other half I wrapped mysei fiest I remain naked.
    I placed his body down in the cleft in the rock.
    I heard the voices of a multitude of angels rejoicing and singing
      'Alleluia, Amen.'

506

I said my prayer over him. I rolled over him a great pile of stones.
I stood, I prayed a second time.

TIL.I.WAN.S. 15.11

21. Then the old man fell upon his body and wept with great and bitter
grief.
He wrapped him in an old garment with respect and reverence
and he placed him on one side in the corner of the cave.

NAU.JE.PE.SY. LXXII.6

22. When we had heard these things,
we hastened, *we wrapped his holy body.*
We laid him in an ornamented coffin and we buried him.

LEI.SIN.B. 76.5

23. After these things I was at a loss what to do with the body of the
blessed man,
and in what manner I should wrap it, and where I should put it.
The Saviour came forth from the door of the cave.
He shut the door. The Saviour put his hand upon the door of the
cave.
It pressed upon the body of the blessed man.
It was to him a place of safety until the Day of Judgment.

BU.CYR.S. 136.5

2.   THE LAST WORDS

THEMES

The gathering of the brethren of the holy man to his deathbed.
The overcoming of the fear of death.

EPISODES

The summons of the brethren to the bedside of the holy man.
The request by the holy man for the prayers of his brethren for the
safety of his soul after death.
The desire of the brethren to hear the last admonitions and teachings of
the holy man.
The appointment of his successor by the holy man.
The participation in the Eucharist by the brethren at the deathbed of
of the holy man.
The blessing of the bystanders by the holy man.

507

QUOTATIONS

1. When the holy old man rose, he gathered the brethren who were at the tower,
   he said to them: 'The days of my death are approaching.'
   Immediately he lay down. He became ill. (   )
   Then his disciple returned, he greeted him and he was not able to answer him.
   The disciple said: 'My holy father what is the matter with thee today?'
   He answered and said to him: 'My son, my tongue is twisted in me today.
   The sinews of my body are decaying
   and those that grind begin to cease so that the dust will return to dust again
   and it is God who knows where this unfortunate soul will go.'
   His disciple said to him: 'My father art thou afraid,
   thou a perfect one of such greatness?'
   He said to him: 'My son, if Abraham and Isaac and Jacob
   came into my presence, and said to me "Thou art a justified one"
   I would not believe it. (   )
   Moses who spoke with God (face to face),
   the prophets and all the holy men were afraid at this hour,
   even if they were justified ones.
   And this hour is painful to all men who are upon earth. (   )
   O my son, the road on which I shall travel I have never travelled,
   the messengers who come to fetch me, I have never seen their faces,
   the ministers who come to fetch me have changing faces
   and they do not receive gifts and they do not forgive.
   Nor are they ashamed before my white hairs, for it is their work to which they are appointed.'
   Having said these things, the blessed Daniel the younger, the second prophet of his generation,
   he turned his face to the East,
   he said to his disciple: 'Approach me, my son, for the hour draws near to me,
   I am weak with age.'
   He clasped his two hands, he placed them before his eyes
   saying: '*My Lord Jesus Christ, the beloved of my soul,*
   I give my spirit into thy hands.'
   When he had said this he gave his spirit in to the hands of the Lord.

GUI.DAN.B. 550.23

THE REPRESENTATION OF A NON-MATERIAL WORLD

2. (Sisinnius, the eunuch) *lay down, he was sick with the sickness of death.* ( )
And he prayed to God and the saint Theodore that He would have mercy on him at his meeting with Him.
Sisinnius, the eunuch, then sent for me, he said to me:
'My father, have the goodness to *come to me and visit me, because I am ill today.*'
I rose, I went to him with the holy men, Apa Shenute and Apa Victor.
When we visited, we sat, he said to us:
'*Remember me, O my holy fathers,*
that the Lord God may have mercy on my wretched soul, in my meeting with Him.'
We gave courage to him, saying: '*God is compassionate, He* will give thee thy reward.'

AM.CYR.AL.B. 178.4

3. He said to me: '( ) *I am sick today. Have the goodness to pray for me until I pass the way of fear and trembling.*'
I said to him: 'My beloved father, art thou also afraid
after the many ascetic practices which thou has borne in the world?'
He said to me: '( ) According to the indication to us by many witnesses,
there is a river of fire flowing before the judge.
And that river, every one must cross, whether righteous or sinner.
It is necessary that thou shouldst pray for me until I pass that way of fear.'

BU.CYR.S. 134.28

4. When this Abba Agatho was on his death-bed, he remained motionless for three days with his eyes open. The brothers shook him, saying: 'Abba, where are you?' And he said: 'I am standing in the presence of God's judgment.' They said to him: 'Are you afraid?' And he said: 'Mostly I have worked as much as I could to keep the commandments of God. But I am a man, and I do not know whether my works will be pleasing in God's sight.' ( ) When they still wished to ask him to speak, he said to them: 'Of your charity do not talk to me, for I am busy.' And at the words, he breathed forth his spirit with joy. And they saw him welcoming his spirit as a man greets his dear friends.

CHA.SA.L. 131(XI)

5. Abba Besarion said when he was dying: 'A monk ought to be all eye, like the Cherubim and Seraphim.'

> CHA.SA.L. 132(XI)

6. As the holy old man Agabus was about to die, we asked him: 'Our holy father, speak a word to us, that we may live by it after thee.'

> AM.MA.DO.B. 268.10

7. *Now when the multitude heard that the man of God had seen visions*
   they gathered to him from all countries and from every place
   to hear his living teachings,
   knowing that it was a spirit of God speaking within him.

> GUI.IS.B. 231.15

8. Our father Isaac said to Jacob: '*My beloved son,*
   keep this commandment which I give into thy hand today.
   Keep strict watch over thyself.
   Do not do harm to the likeness of God,
   for that which thou shalt do to the likeness of man, thou hast done to the likeness of God
   and God will do thus to thee in the hour when thou shalt meet Him.
   This is the Beginning and the End.'

> GUI.IS.B. 242.16

9. Trois jours avant sa dormition, au milieu de la nuit, il fut jugé digne de contempler tous les saints qui s'étaient rendus agréables à Dieu. Ceux-ci vinrent auprès de lui et, l'ayant salué, l'engagèrent à célébrer le divin et auguste sacrifice. De fait, les deux frères qui se trouvaient présents reçurent la faveur d'entendre les paroles liturgiques et d'y faire les réponses habituelles. Aussitôt qu'il eut achevé la liturgie de Dieu, réveillé de son extase et revenu à lui-même, il demanda qu'on lui portât la sainte communion; cela fait, quand il eut communié en premier, nous aussi, tous, en ce même moment du milieu de la nuit, nous participâmes aux saints mystères, tout comme s'il avait accompli lui-même la sainte anaphore.

> FE.II.DAN.G. 162(XLVI)

10. Comme il parlait ainsi, nous étions tous figés sur place et nous pleurions, voyant bien qu'il souhaitait de mourir. Il fut malade cinq jours. Le sixième jour, qui était un dimanche, il dit: 'Appelez les frères, pour que je leur donne la communion.' Il était déjà entré en extase, et, tandis qu'il donnait la communion—un autre lui soutenait

la main,—il entonna à demi-voix le psaume: 'Venez, exultons devant le Seigneur.' Les frères chantaient aussi, et, tout en recevant la communion de sa main, ils pleuraient tous, car ils comprenaient que cette exultation était en vérité celle des anges qui l'accueillaient au ciel, et que c'est pour cela qu'il chantait 'Venez, exultons devant le Seigneur.' Il voyait en effet comme des évêques et des amis intimes venir à lui et le prendre; dans l'extase où il se trouvait, il recevait du Président des eulogies, il lui semblait qu'il voulait les donner à d'autres et personne ne paraissait pour les recevoir, et le Président les reprenait à nouveau. En fait tous, amis, moines, clercs, s'étant rassemblés vinrent recevoir de lui des eulogies. Il les bénit tous, et, après les avoir salués, il s'endormit dans la paix et vint s'adjoindre aux saints Pères du ciel. Il laissait une communauté qui s'élevait à cinquante frères. Il les avait confiés à un successeur, pour qu'il les dirigeât.

FE.II.HYP.G. 79(LI)

3.   THE FETCHING OF THE SOUL

THEMES

The fetching of the soul by Christ, the archangels, angels, apostles, fathers of the Church.
The coming forth of the soul from the body.
The spectators as witnesses of the entry to heaven of the holy man.

EPISODES

The appearance, to the holy man, of Christ, the apostles, and the fathers of the Church to fetch his soul.
The identification, by the holy man, of those sent to fetch him; his joy at his reception.
The taking away of speech, the refusal of food prior to death.
The fetching of the soul by angels; their wrapping of the soul in a cloth.
The carrying of the soul by angels; their singing until they reach heaven.
The sending of David with his harp to bring forth the soul without pain.
The conveying of the souls of martyrs to heaven by angels; by Christ in His chariot.
The giving, to the souls of martyrs, of crowns, stoles, robes.
The ability of ascetics to see the souls conveyed to heaven, and to hear the voices of the angels.

QUOTATIONS

1. On the holy day of the Feast of the Epiphany, the feast of Tobi, *the blessed Maximus began to lie down ill.*

511

A great fever seized him.

When the illness increased he said:

'Have the goodness to call to me our father Abba Macarius.' I went I called him.

After the sun set he said to us: 'What is the hour?'

We told him: 'It is the end of the day.'

He said to us: '*Yet a little while and I will go to my place of rest.*'

When night came our father Abba Macarius said to us: 'Light the lamp.' And we lit it.

Then the mind of the blessed Maximus was taken up to heaven and he said: '( )

Save me from the powers of darkness of the air of spirits.' ( )

After this he was silent for a short time and then he said:

'Rouse yourselves, let us go forth.

Behold the apostles and the prophets have come to remove me from this.'

Then he was silent.

After a short time the holy man Abba Macarius saw the company of the holy men coming for him.

The blessed Macarius rose. He stood in silence.

When I saw that the lamp burned low,

I said to the old man Abba Macarius: 'Dost thou wish me to make the lamp better?' ( )

He answered: 'Be silent, my son,

for it is not the time to speak, but rather a time for silence.'

And the blessed Maximus spoke with one of the holy men,

asking him the name of the saints who surrounded him,

but we did not know what he said. But the spirit-bearing Abba Macarius told us:

'*They were telling him the names of the saints who are around him.*'

And his soul, when it had enjoyed the presence of the holy men,

suddenly it leapt forth from the body with joy.

This is the manner in which this blessed man died in peace

and went to rest with all the holy men

AM.MA.DO.B. 305.10

2. When Abba Sisoes was about to die

and the fathers were sitting in his presence,

they saw that his face was shining like the sun

and he said to them immediately: 'Behold, Abba Anthony has come.'

And again after a little time he said: 'Behold, the company of the prophets has come.'

And his face shone again and he said: 'Behold the company of the apostles has come.'

And again his face shone twice as much

and he became suddenly like one who was speaking with somebody.

And the old men who were seated entreated him and they said to him: 'Show us with whom thou art speaking, our father.'

He then immediately said to them: 'Behold the angels came to take me away

and I besought them to leave me, that I should tarry a little and repent.'

And the old men said to him: 'Thou hast no need to repent, our father,'

The old man said to them: 'I am not sure in my soul that I have rightly begun to repent.'

And they all learned that the old man was perfect.

And again, suddenly, his face shone like the sun, and all those seated were afraid

and he said to them suddenly: 'See, see, behold, Our Lord has come

and He says: "Bring to me the chosen vessel which is in the desert".'

And immediately he delivered up his spirit

and there was lightning

and the whole place was filled with sweet perfume.

BU.II.PAL.SY. 643.13

3. When the morning ( ) came, *our father lay sick.*

Then we went to him to visit him and we begged him that he would take a little food.

But he said to us: '*As the Lord lives, I will not eat, nor will I drink, nor will I taste any food of this earth,*

until I meet my holy fathers Anthony, and Pachomius.

I have given account of the manner in which I was able to complete my monk's life.'

At the hour of dawn, ( ) he smiled saying: '*Greeting at your coming Anthony and Pachomius,*

Welcome, thou of the small congregation, thou noble abbot Apa Shenute, thou honoured Archimandrite of the monastery of Atribe.

I come with you to the Heavenly Jerusalem in joy. ( )'

As he said these things and we all heard him,

he signed him(self) in the name of the Father and the Son and the Holy Spirit.
He opened his mouth.
He gave his spirit into the hands of God in peace.

AM.MAT.P.S. 736.1

4. When our father Theodore had said these things to us,
the man of God opened his mouth,
he gave up his spirit in great quietude and without trouble ( ) in peace.
Then a great fear came at that hour, with a sweet smell.

AM.TH.B. 285.3

5. Then to the blessed man Abraham, there were gathered sixty brothers.
Then through the Holy Spirit,
his disciple Stephen, he who wrote this story
and who was also worthy of the episcopal appointment,
saw three eagles descending from heaven
and gathering in the monastery of the blessed man,
while another eagle went forth from the monastery to meet them and they mounted to heaven.
These three eagles were Simeon and Thomas and John,
perfected ones, who were sent by God for the death of the holy man.
After seven days, while he was praying,
these three blessed ones came to him
and they remained speaking with him until the middle of the night.
And the blessed man answered and he said to his disciples:
'Remain in peace and pray for me.'
Then there appeared to his disciples, Stephen and Leon, a great light
and celestial powers filled the air
and the sound of singing and the celestial services.
And his soul was like a column of light in their midst.
His disciples approached and closed his eyes, weeping.

NAU.ABR.SY. 772.4

6. And when he lay down upon the mat according to his custom,
then he was not able to rise because of the severity of the illness
because he was afflicted by the fever.
Then, little by little, he lost power
and during the eighth or ninth night since he fell ill. ( )
Behold the Cherubim, that one which had remained with him since the beginning,

514

came with a great multitude of companies of bodiless ones.
And he said to him: 'Hasten thee, come forth for all these stand
    waiting for thee.'
And he said in a great voice:
'*My Lord Jesus, the beloved of my soul, receive my spirit to thyself.'*
And thus he died.

AM.MAC.SC.B. 109.3

7. *When they brought the body of Apa Macarius to the martyrion,*
    they placed it upon the coffin of the saints.
    A small boy in his twelfth year, who was dumb, *had his eyes opened.*
    At that moment he saw the saints John the Baptist with Elijah, the
        prophet,
    embracing the holy man, Abba Macarius, greeting him like brothers.
    And the mouth of the small boy was opened in that moment, he spoke,
    and when he took the hand of his father *he cried out,*
    saying: 'My father, I saw two men of light welcoming this man who
        was killed,
    saying to him: "*It is good that thou hast come, our brother,*
    come and rest thyself with us."'
    When his father heard these things, he cried out in a great voice,
    saying: 'The God of this Egyptian elder,
    who was martyred in the name of our Lord Jesus Christ our Saviour,
        is the only God.' (   )
    He said to them: 'I saw the first of them,
    he had a great beard with much hair which came down upon his
        shoulders.
    And the other one was bald and bare of face and he was tall.'
    And they knew that the man with much hair upon him was John the
        Baptist
    and he who had not much hair upon him was Elijah the prophet.

AM.MAC.TK.B. 158.9

8. On était arrivé désormais au saint départ même de Daniel quand
    un homme tourmenté par un esprit impur poussa soudain un cri
    devant toute la foule, annonçant la venue des saints auprès du
    saint homme, nommant chacun d'eux et disant: 'Il y a grande joie
    au ciel à cette heure. Car les saints anges sont venus prendre avec
    eux le saint, et il est venu en outre les nobles et glorieuses armées des
    prophètes et des apôtres, des martyrs et des saints. Ils me fouettent
    et demain, à la troisième heure, ils me chasseront de cette tente.
    Quand le saint prendra son départ vers les cieux et que sa sainte

dépouille sera mise en terre, je m'en irai.' C'est ce qui arriva. Notre illustre père Daniel mourut le lendemain, un samedi, à la troisième heure ( ) et à l'instant même de sa mort il accomplit un miracle, en ce que l'homme fut guéri de son esprit impur.

FE.II.DAN.G. 162(XLVI)

9. On the Friday, our father sent the God-loving servant to Egypt, ( )
so that no one would be able to be with him
as he was about to leave the body.
At the hour of cock crow on the holy Lord's Day,
behold, there came multitudes of the angelic companies
with the host of all the Holy Ones, through God,
in glory and splendour of the Lord,
in order to remove their fellow minister.
When our father saw the light of their glory ( )
especially because of their glory and the light of the presence of the
*   Lord of All,*
he, our father prostrated himself upon his face ( ).
In that moment he gave his spirit into the hands of the Lord ( )
in the peace of God,
and he was in his seventieth year according to what was said.
And he was placed in the midst of those holy companies
as they led his blessed soul to the height to the Lord of Glory,
with sweet hymns of the joy of the holy spirit by the holy company,
so that he would be under the protection of the right hand of the
    Most High for ever,
in the light of the Living Ones who are in the Land of Immortality. ( )
God received him. In the time of his visitation
he was found giving light,
as his soul was pleasing to the Lord, according to the word of
    wisdom,
and also in his translation he appeared before him
as one who was fulfilled in an unblemished life
and an old age which is good and undefiled ( ).
When the God-loving servant was yet on his way to the moun-
    tain ( )
according as he had been told,
he heard hymns of the Holy Ones as they were singing above him.
He looked high in the air, he saw the ranks of the angels.
He saw the (saints) also, in rank upon rank, in great glory
and our father in their midst, with a wonderful appearance.
And he saw one, who was great in size, above them all,

giving light like the sun,
as he addressed praise to our father,
while the whole population of the holy ones answered him.
And that holy servant was in a trance in the perception of this vision
for a long time.
And at the same time he desired especially to know who was this
great light bearer
who led this multitude
and who was praising our father;
the angel of the Lord came to him in that moment.
He said to him: '( ) *All these that thou seest are the heavenly ranks*
with the holy company whom the Lord has sent for his servant John,
to take him forth from the prison of this life, which is full of
afflictions,
to give to him the inheritance in the places of rest which are in the
Heavenly Jerusalem.
And this great man who leads them all, shining in glory,
this is the great Anthony, and this other who is behind him is the
great Pachomius.
This other one is Abba Macarius the great spirit-bearer,
with the rest of these others after them, who resemble them.'
The angel pointed his finger to each one of them,
all these holy ones, ( ) saying to him:
'And thou also O good follower, O blessed one,
thou also hast attained the glory and the splendour through the Lord
and his saints.'
And when the angel had said these things he became invisible to him.
When that God-loving servant went to the cave,
he found our thrice blessed father, Abba John
prostrated upon his knees,
and at the same time upon his face, as if he was worshipping the
Lord.
And there spread a marvellous perfume from his holy relic.
And he also worshipped upon his holy body, groaning and weeping.

AM.JOH.K.B. 400.7

10. When the day of Friday arrived, the holy man, Abba John called
the man who served him,
he sent him to the city on a pretext,
so that no man should be near him at his departure (in death).
When it was the night of Sunday, at cock-crow,
the fathers came with the multitude of angels,

with honour and glory, to meet the holy man John,

according to their promise to fetch this holy soul of the servant of
  God.

When the blessed man saw them shining with this glory and this
  light,

while a fragrant and everlasting perfume rose from them,

with great joy he prostrated himself before them.

And at that moment, he delivered up his soul into the hands of the
  Living God

and he fell asleep in peace on Sunday. (   )

The life of the holy man, Abba John was seventy years.

His soul departed in the midst of these saints and angels,

until it reached the heights above,

under the protection of the right hand of the Lord,

in the presence of the Light which does not pass away

and of the Life which does not cease,

to the place of which it was worthy,

because God has tested it like gold in the fire.

And it mounted pure and shining, like good ointment without stain.

Then the old man who served him came forth from the city

to go to the old man, Abba John and to see his state

because he knew that he was ill.

And when he reached a certain place,

he heard the praise of the angels and the voices of the saints.

And he raised his eyes to heaven and he saw hosts of angels

and multitudes of saints, rank upon rank, who were singing and
  praising.

And the holy man, Abba John, shining with light, was among them.

Then a tall man of great stature,

glorious and shining in the likeness of the sun,

was in their midst and he was praising the holy man, Abba John.

Then when that man saw the wonder which had appeared,

he was amazed and he took thought

and desired to know what was the meaning of this great vision.

By the command of the Lord, an angel was sent to him who said to
  him:

'Since thou dost desire to know this mystery for thy benefit and
  that of many,

listen well to what I shall show thee.

These are the angels of God, with the multitudes of saints,

who have been sent (by God) to fetch, from this world, the soul of
  the blessed man, Abba John,

that it should inherit life and rest in the Heavenly Jerusalem.
And the man who was praising John,
who was tall in his stature, was Abba Anthony the great.
And after him was Abba Pachomius and Abba Macarius,
with the rest of the fathers who resemble them.'
And the angel indicated to him, as if with the finger, to which one
    he indicated,
until he knew them all well and he said to him:
'Thou has seen these fathers.
We wish to glorify John with them
and with them to make him heir to the Kingdom of Heaven,
because he has laboured like them when he was in the world
and he has walked in their path.
And thou also who hast served him,
thou art blessed to have been worthy of the favour
and the honour of God and of those who please Him.'
After this the angel was removed from him
and the man went to the monastery of the holy man, Abba John,
    and entered his cave.
He found him kneeling, with his head bent before the Lord,
like a man who prays and worships before God.
From his holy body there spread a sweet and fragrant perfume.
Then the man fell upon his body and wept with great and bitter
    grief.

NAU.JE.PE.SY. LXX.3

11. *On the next day he began to be ill.*
    And when evening came on the eighth day of the month of Epep, his
        spirit was taken to the height.
    He spent three days and three nights without speaking with anyone.
    On the night of the twelfth day of the month of Epep he called:
        'John.'
    I said to him: 'Bless me my holy father.' He said to me: 'I seek thee
        because *my time approaches*
    and God will seek me at the hour of evening tomorrow, (   )
    And these three days which I have spent without speaking with
        man,
    I was standing in the presence of Christ, God.
    And he made my account from the ninth hour yesterday (   )'
    I said: '(   ) *Behold for three days thou hast not tasted anything.'*
    He answered: '*I will not taste any food of this world until I break*
        my fast with the Lord Jesus Christ, my King.'

After this he said: 'Holy martyr of Christ God, Ignatius the God-
    bearing, *be with me*
until I cross the River of Fire which runs before Christ,
because great is the terror of that place.'
I said to him: 'My Lord father, after all these sufferings,
these fasts and these prayers and these nights of vigil
which thou hast endured for the sake of God,
hast thou also fear before that River of Fire?' (   )
And he said nothing to any man.
When morning came the whole place filled with men inside and
    outside.
He spent the whole of that day like one anointing himself with oil.
At last he spoke these words:
'Behold, I have kept the commandment of the Lord
and I have made my preparation.'
And thus he opened his mouth,
he gave up the spirit into the hands of God,
at the hour of sunset.

AM.PIS.KE.B. 419.1

12. When the morning (   ) came, he laboured greatly in the illness.
    In the sixth hour of the day I said to him: 'My father what hast
        thou thus?'
He said to me: 'Woe is me because the way is long.
How long a time shall I spend as I travel to God?
There are on the road terrors and strong powers.
Woe is me until I meet the Lord.'
When he had said these things he was silent,
he was in a trance for half an hour.
Suddenly he cried out saying: 'Have the goodness to bless me my
    holy fathers.
Come sit in my presence in your ranks.'
He said further: 'Behold the patriarchs have come, with the prophets.
Behold the apostles, with the archbishops.
Behold the archimandrites have come, with all the holy men.'
He said further: 'My father Apa Pshoi, my father Apa Anthony,
    my father Apa Pachomius,
take my hand that I may rise
and worship him whom my soul loves,
for behold, he has come for me with his angels.'
At that moment a great perfume appeared.
Then he gave up his spirit into the hands of God (   ).

520

And behold voices came in the monastery,
we heard voices which were sweet,
crying out above his holy body
uttering hymns and psalms and spiritual odes,
in company upon company,
speaking thus: 'Peace to thee, Shenute, with thy meeting God.
Those of the heavens rejoice with thee today, ( )
beloved of Christ, the brother of all the Holy Ones.
We all rejoice with thee. ( )
Behold the gates of the heavens have opened for thee,
that thou shouldst enter in joy within them.'

LEI.SIN.B. 75.1

13. And thus he prayed, he said the prayer of the gospel,
he opened his mouth, he gave up his spirit,
like one falling asleep. ( )
While I was weeping over him,
behold, Christ opened the door of the cave, He came in,
He stood over the body of the blessed Apa Cyrus,
He wept over him. ( )
I saw the tears of Christ which fell upon the body of the blessed Apa
* Cyrus.*
Then Christ turned to me saying: 'Withdraw thyself outside the
  door of the cave.'
When I came outside *I saw a multitude of angels and archangels*
* and apostles*
and all the righteous who were all gathered standing up.
One of them, who was bald, walked towards me.
He said to me: 'Dost thou know me, who I am?'
I said to him: 'No my Lord.'
He said to me: 'Hear while I tell thee.
I am Cephas, he who was given the name Petrus.' ( )
When the blessed Apa Shenute went to rest yesterday,
he received the soul of the blessed Apa Cyrus
with Apa Shenute the Archimandrite in the places of rest. ( )
The Saviour went up to heaven with his angels.
Then I walked, I came forth to the brethren.

BU.CYR.S. 135.12

14. 'Brother Serapion, this day is the greatest of all the days of my life.
  Today, my brother, my soul will reach that desirable dwelling and
    will enter and find rest

521

in those spiritual habitations with the souls of the righteous.
Today this weak body will find rest from pains and sicknesses.
Today I will reach that abode of life.'
When he had said these things,
that cave was filled with light which was brighter than the dazzling
    rays of the sun
and I was aflame with the brilliance and the fragrant odour of the
    incense.
He held my hand and raised me up saying:
'Come in peace, Ministers of the Living God.
Behold, Gabriel and Michael are standing outside.
Let us go out to them.'
And he sealed that cave with the sign of the Cross
and he said: 'Remain in peace, O temple which sheltered me in
    exile.
In you I will leave this body
which was sheltered in you during life, until the Resurrection.'

LOOK.MAR.SY. 18.1

15. *And at the moment when the man is about to give up his spirit,*
    one stands beside his head and one beside his feet
    and they have the form of men who anoint him with oil with their
        hands
    until they bring forth his soul.
    The other one holds out a great spiritual cloth and receives the soul
        upon it.
    And the soul of the holy man is found to be beautiful and white like
        milk and snow.
    And *after the soul has come forth from the body upon the cloth,*
    one of the angels takes the two corners of the cloth at the back
    and the other one takes those in front,
    as men on earth raise the body.
    And the other angel walks in front singing (psalms)
    in a language which no one understands,
    not even those who see visions,
    our father Pachomius and Theodore, *they only heard the other*
        two angels saying 'Alleluia.'
    And thus they proceed with it through the air towards the East.
    They do not walk like men who walk on their feet,
    but they glide in their walk like water which flows,
    because they are spirits.

LE.PAC.S. 152a.5

THE REPRESENTATION OF A NON-MATERIAL WORLD

16. *And at the moment when the man is about to give up his spirit,*
   one stands beside his head and one beside his feet
   and they have the form of men who anoint him with oil with their
      hands
   until they bring forth his soul.
   The other one holds out a great spiritual cloth and receives it
      upon it
   and the soul of the holy man is found to be beautiful and white like
      milk and snow.
   And *after the soul has come forth from the body upon the cloth,*
   one of the angels takes the two corners of the cloth at the back
   and the other one takes those in front,
   as men of the earth raise the body.
   And the other angel walks in front singing (psalms)
   in a language no one understands,
   not even those who see visions, our father Pachomius and Theodore.
   They only heard the other two angels saying 'Alleluia.'
   And thus they proceed with it through the air to the East.
   They do not walk like men who tread upon their feet,
   but they glide in their walk like water which flows
   because they are spirits.

LE.PAC.S. 243b.24

17. *And at the moment when the man is about to give up his spirit, one*
      of the angels stands beside his head and one beside his feet
   and they have the form of men who anoint him with oil with their
      hands
   until his soul comes forth from his body.
   The other one holds out a great spiritual cloth and receives the soul
      upon it in glory.
   And the soul of the holy man is found to be beautiful in its appearance
      and white like snow.
   And *after the soul has come forth from the body upon the cloth,*
   one of the angels takes the two corners of the cloth at the back
   and the other takes those in front,
   as men of the earth raise the body.
   And the other angel sings (psalms) in front of it,
   in a language which no one understands,
   not even those who see visions, our father Pachomius and Theodore,
   they do not know their chant.
   They only hear the angel crying out, saying: 'Alleluia.'
   And thus they proceed with the soul in the air towards the East.

They do not walk like men who walk upon their feet
but they glide in their walk like water which flows
because they are spirits.

LE.PAC.B. 88.14

18. *He took the soul of my father Joseph, he brought it forth from
    the body at the hour of sunrise* (   ).
    All the days of the life of my beloved father Joseph made a hundred
        and eleven years.
    Michael seized the two corners of a glorious silken cloth,
    Gabriel took the other two corners.
    They embraced the soul of my beloved father Joseph.
    They placed it down on the cloth.
    None of those who sat beside him knew that he had died, even
        Mary my mother.
    *And I caused Michael and Gabriel to guard the soul of my beloved
    father Joseph* because of the robbers on the roads.
    *And I caused the bodiless angels to remain singing hymns before it
    until they reached the heavens to my good Father.*

TIL.JOS.Z.S. 278.29

19. *Now I will turn to the going forth from the body of my father Joseph,
        the righteous old man.*
    When he gave up his spirit I greeted it.
    The angels took his soul,
    they placed it in cloths of silken material.
    And I entered in, I sat beside him.
    No man knew that he had died amongst those who were sitting
        round him.
    And I caused Michael with Gabriel to watch his soul
    because of the powers which were upon the road,
    and the angels sang before it,
    until they gave it to my good father.

LA.MOR.JOS.B. 27.8

20. He found a man, who was a stranger, lying sick, and no man looked
        to him. (   )
    At the moment that he was about to die,
    *the brother saw Michael and Gabriel coming, wishing to fetch his
        soul.*
    One sat on the right of him and the other on the left.
    They remained begging the soul to come forth from the body
    but it did not wish to come forth.

13

Michael said to Gabriel: 'Let us take this soul and go.'
Gabriel said to him: 'God has said:
"Do not hurt it bringing it forth by force."
Now therefore it is not possible for me to bring it forth by force.'
Michael cried out, saying: 'O God what dost thou wish done to this
    soul
which does not wish to come forth?'
A voice came to him:
'Behold, I will send David with his harp
and all the psalmists of Jerusalem,
so that it hears their beautiful voices and comes forth.'
And immediately they all came down, they surrounded it
and sang hymns to the soul.
It came forth, it sat in the hand of Michael
and was taken up with joy.

CHA.AP.PA.S. 61.13(212)

21. After these things, when that brother entered the city,
    he saw a certain brother who was a stranger,
    who was lying sick in the market place and he had no man as his
        helper.
    And he remained with him for one day
    and at the time when his soul was departing,
    that brother saw Gabriel and Michael who were coming for his soul.
    And they sat one on his right hand and one on his left
    and they stayed there entreating his soul and wishing to carry it
        away.
    Then when his soul did not wish to leave his body,
    Gabriel said to Michael: 'Rise, take his soul now that we may depart.'
    Michael said to him: 'We were commanded by Our Lord
    to bring it forth without pain and without suffering.
    Therefore we cannot constrain it with violence.'
    Michael then cried out with a loud voice saying:
    'What dost thou command concerning this soul
    which will not be persuaded to come forth?'
    And a voice came to him saying:
    'Behold I am sending David and his harp and all those who sing
        with him,
    so that when it hears the sweetness of their (daughters of) voices
        it will come forth.'
    And they descended and surrounded it and as they were singing
        psalms,

it leapt and came forth.
And it rejoiced in the hands of Michael
and it was taken up with gladness.

BU.II.PAL.SY. 614.23

22. '*At the time when they came for me in order to separate my soul
   from my body,*
   a great and mighty angel came
   with a cloth of linen
   *and also multitudes of angels all girt with golden bands upon their
   loins*
   with sweet perfumes.
   That angel is called "Michael the Angel of Compassion".
   They all stood over me, their faces smiling at me.
   *And Michael signed my mouth in the name of the Father, and the Son
   and the Holy Spirit.*
   And at that moment my soul sprang forth from my body,
   it alighted upon the hand of Michael.
   He wrapped it in the linen cloth,
   they proceeded with it up to heaven
   singing hymns (until we) reached the River of Fire.'

BU.BART.R.S. 35.6

23. When they (Pachomius and Theodore) reached that place,
   they went in to him who was sick. ( )
   And while they spoke with one another,
   before (the brother) gave up his spirit,
   the eyes of our father Pachomius and Theodore were opened.
   They saw the angels who had come to fetch it,
   *giving baptism to it in secret before they brought it forth from the
   body.*

LE.PAC.S. 241a.18

24. When they (Pachomius and Theodore) reached that place (monastery of Thmoushons),
   they went in to the brother who was sick. ( )
   While they were speaking with one another
   before he (the brother) gave up his spirit,
   the eyes of our father Pachomius and Theodore were opened,
   they saw the angels who had come to fetch it,
   giving it baptism in secret before it came forth from the body.

LE.PAC.B. 87.3

526

25. At that moment Moses arose and sanctified himself, as do the Seraphim. The Holy One came down from the highest heaven of heavens to take the soul of Moses, and with Him were three ministering angels, Michael, Gabriel, and Zagzagel. Michael arranged Moses' bed, and Gabriel spread a garment of fine linen at his head; Zagzagel was at his feet. Michael stood at one side, and Gabriel at the other. The Holy One then said to Moses: 'Moses, close thine eye-lids, one upon the other.' Moses did as he was commanded. At that moment the Holy One summoned the soul from Moses' body, and said unto her: 'My daughter, one hundred and twenty years have I appointed for thee to be in Moses' body; the time to depart has now arrived. Come thou forth, tarry not.' The soul said unto Him; 'Lord of the universe, I know that Thou art the God of all the spirits, and that all the souls, the souls of the living and the dead, are delivered into Thy hands, and that Thou didst create and fashion me, and put me into Moses' body for one hundred and twenty years. Now is there in the world a body purer than that of Moses, upon which there never was any pollution, nor worm and maggot? Therefore I love it, and desire not to depart from it.' But the Holy One said: 'O soul, come forth, tarry not. I shall bring thee up to the highest heaven of heavens, and cause thee to dwell under My Throne of Glory near the Cherubim, Seraphim, and hosts of other angels.' The soul then said: 'O Lord of the universe, when from Thy Shekinah in heaven there came down two angels, Uzzah and Azzael, they covered the daughters of the earth, and corrupted their way upon the earth so that Thou didst suspend them between heaven and earth. But the son of Amram has not come in unto his wife from the day Thou didst reveal Thyself unto him in the bush, as it is written. I implore Thee, let me remain in Moses' body.'
At that moment the Holy One kissed him, and took away his soul with a kiss. God wept, and cried, as it were.

MID.MOS.H. 42

26. It happened then in the seventh month since *the Virgin, the holy Theotokos, Maria, went forth from the body*,
namely the month of Mesore,
that we rose on the fifteenth day of this month,
we gathered together at the tomb in which was the body of the Virgin,
the other virgins also being with us.
We spent all the night keeping watch,
and we sang and we offered up incense,

while the lamps burned in the hands of the virgins.
Then at the time of the light on this same night,
which is the morning of the sixteenth day of the month of Mesore,
there came to us in the place in which we were,
our Lord Jesus Christ in great glory. He said to us:
'*Peace be with you all, my holy apostles,*
the Peace of my Father I give to you.'
Then we prostrated ourselves, we worshipped Him and He blessed
* us all.* (   )
While our Saviour was speaking with us, we heard hymns in the height.
Immediately we looked, we saw a great chariot of light.
It came, it stood in our midst,
while Cherubims were drawing it.
The holy Virgin Maria was sitting upon it
and she was giving light ten thousand times more than the sun and
* the moon.*
Then we were in fear, we fell upon our faces, we worshipped her.
And she stretched out her hand towards us all, she blessed us, she gave
* us Peace.*
Again we worshipped her, being in great joy and exultation.
And she told us great mysteries which are hidden,
these which it is not lawful to reveal because of disbelieving men.
Then the Lord called into the tomb,
He raised the body of His Virgin mother,
He put her soul into her body again.
And we saw it living in the body as it was with us formerly, when it
  was wearing flesh.
And our Saviour stretched out His hand,
He mounted her upon the chariot with Himself. (   )
And when our Saviour had said these things to us,
He spent all that day with us with His Virgin mother.
Afterwards He gave us Peace, He went up to the heavens in glory,
the angels singing before Him.

LA.DOR.MAR.B. 60.11

27. *And the Lord received his soul in His own hand*
    and He embraced it
    and He wrapped it in royal purple
    and He went up to the height with it.
    And the whole Firmament was full of holy angels and the chorus of the
    * holy ones*
    and they were singing hymns before him

until He gave him as a gift to His good Father with the Holy Spirit.
And He put on him his stole of light
and a diadem of choice gold and it was studded with a precious stone,
and there were seven crowns upon it
and they were plaited with blossoms of the Tree of Life.
And He wrote his name with the First-Born for ever.
And He caused the whole flock of heaven and the companies of the
*   Holy Ones*
to seat Him upon the throne
and to make festival with him in the Heavenly Jerusalem.

BA.HY.II.GEO.DI.B. 257.25

28. *When the saint had said these things*
    in the ardour of his heart, behold the Lord Jesus Christ appeared to
    *   him*
    saying: 'Come now up to heaven and rest thyself
    in the dwelling place which I have prepared for thee in the Kingdom
    *   of my Father in the heavens.' (   )*
    The Lord Jesus received his blessed soul,
    He kissed it, He took it up to the heavens.
    He gave it as a gift to His good Father with the Holy Spirit.

BA.HY.II.GEO.B. 310.1

29. *While Apa Epima was saying these words,*
    behold the Lord Jesus came forth from heaven
    mounted upon a chariot of light.
    The whole Firmament was filled with angels.
    They came forth before the soul of Apa Epima. (   )
    The Lord Jesus took the soul of Apa Epima.
    He embraced it,
    He mounted it with Himself upon the chariot.
    He took it up to heaven.
    He made him sit upon his throne of glory.
    He placed on his head the imperishable crown of eternity.

MIN.EPIM.S. 33.16

30. *When He had said these things,*
    the Lord brought forth from his body his soul
    which was white like snow.
    He greeted it, he mounted it upon the chariot with Himself.
    He took it up to the heavens
    while the Seraphim went before it with His holy angels.
    He granted to him the good things of His Kingdom,

529

and all the requests which our father asked from the Lord,
He granted them to him as a covenant for ever.
This is the coming forth from the body of our lord and father, (   )
being a hundred and eighty years old.

GUI.IS.B. 242.23

31. *At that moment he gave the spirit into the hands of the Lord*
and the Saviour gave his soul into the hands of Michael the Archangel.
He guarded it.
He took it up to the heavens with him.

BA.HY.I.TH.O.B. 60.25

32. *Behold, he saw the Saviour with Michael*
with the soul of the Anatolian in their hands.
He fell upon his face. (   )
He caused Michael to take him so that he raised him.
And they took the soul of the Anatolian up to heaven.

BA.HY.II.T.A.T.S.B. 144.10

33. *He completed his good course. (   )*
There was a great light in that place.
The whole place spread perfume
because of the number of angels who had come for the soul of the
    blessed Apa Lacaron.
The Saviour received his soul into the heavens with Himself
and His angels who followed Him.
And the whole chorus of Holy Ones came forth to meet him,
they embraced him until he was taken to the City of our Lord and
    our God and our Saviour, Jesus Christ.

BA.HY.I.LAC.B. 22.21

34. *In that hour he gave his Spirit into the hands of the Lord in peace*
and the whole road was filled with fragrance
and a multitude of holy men were standing watching the soul of the
    saint Theodore.
as it was brought up to heaven to the place of rest of the Righteous
    with all the Holy Ones.

BA.HY.I.TH.S.B. 180.5

35. *And Michael with Gabriel received his soul.*
And the Saviour embraced it,
He took it up to the heavens in glory.

BA.HY.I.APOL.B. 247.14

530

36. The hegemon was angered against them. *He gave the sentence*
that they should be burned in fire
and they were taken to a desert place;
a pit was digged and filled with fire.
They were cast into it, and completed their martyrdom.
Apa Paphnute stood at a distance from them. *He saw the angels of*
God
standing over the fire,
receiving the souls of each and giving them to one another,
bringing them up to the aeons of the Firmament.
And the forty (martyrs) were burned on that day
and they completed their martyrdom.
They received the imperishable crown in the Heavenly Jerusalem,
the City of the Righteous.

BA.HY.I.PAP.B. 118.3

37. Then the saints were killed without mercy
and those who died first, *the angels brought before the altar in the*
presence of the Lord
and put crowns upon them according to their rank.
Then the Saviour would embrace them and the Holy Virgin Maria
said to the Saviour:
'My Lord and my God and my Son, behold I have offered up for
thee incense upon thy altar,
so that today be glorified for thee and thy good Father and the
Holy Spirit for ever.'

AM.MAC.TK.B. 128.9

38. *Symachus, the executioner, leapt up,*
he removed the heads of the rest of the holy men.
The whole Firmament filled with angels.
They came forth to meet them.
They carried their souls, they wrapped them in linen cloths.
They were like doves of light coming forth from their nests.
They took them up, they sat them upon their thrones,
they placed upon their heads the imperishable crown
while the saint Apa Epima looked up after them.

MIN.EPIM.S. 26.5

39. From the third hour of the day until now *I have been seeing the*
angels standing in the air
putting crowns on the martyrs of my Lord, Jesus Christ.

BA.HY.I.AN.B. 212.2

40. *The soldiers drew their swords,*
    they removed the head of the saintly martyrs.
    Behold Michael the Archangel received their souls
    he brought them to our Saviour.
    He embraced them.
    He put upon each of them three crowns,
    one for their martyrdom,
    one for their exile,
    one for their chastity.
    He brought them up with him into His Kingdom
    while the angels sang before them.

                                          HY.PI.AT.B. 170.13

41. Then the barbarians entered and slew them.
    One of them was afraid and he fled among the palm leaves.
    And he saw seven crowns descending
    and crowning the heads of those who had been slain.

                                          BU.II.PAL.SY. 629.18

42. *Behold a multitude of angels came down from the sky*
    with crowns of light in their hands.
    They greeted the souls of the holy martyrs,
    they placed the crowns of light upon them,
    they brought them up rejoicing to Him whom they loved, our Lord
        Jesus Christ.

                                          HY.MACR.B. 244.15

43. *And the Lord received his blessed soul,*
    He embraced it,
    He placed it on the stole of the Archangel Michael.
    And He took it up to heaven with Him,
    He put a crown on him
    in unspeakable glory in His Kingdom.

                                          BA.HY.I.EPIM.B. 154.4

44. It happened *when the hegemon had given the sentence to Apa*
        Koluthos,
    the priest and man of Antinoe,
    he sent to the prison, *he brought the blessed Apater to give the*
        sentence to him.
    While he prayed, he saw multitudes of martyrs among those who had
        died,

putting crowns upon them in the air.
They cried out to him in the air,
saying: '*Our beloved general of Christ, be strong,*
for the conflict approaches thee.'
When the saint saw them, he prayed to the Lord: 'Let this hour come.'
And the soldiers trembled, hearing the martyrs speaking with one
 another.

HY.AP.IR.B. 108.6

45. They sought the hegemon.
 They found him sitting on the Bema,
 giving judgment to a martyr whose name was Apa Êsi, a man of
  Psamaom of Gimenteti.
 The eyes of the saint were opened.
 He saw the angel of God standing in the air,
 putting a crown upon the martyrs,
 they were filled with the Holy Spirit.

HY.PI.AT.B. 164.14

46. *This is the manner in which he completed his martyrdom.*
 He went up to heaven in glory, he received the imperishable crown
  in peace. Amen.

SOB.HEL.S. 65b.16

47. *At that moment there came forth from heaven a great chorus of*
  angels, without number.
 They approached immediately, they carried away the body of the
  Virgin,
 mounted upon the body of our holy fathers, the apostles.
 My father Peter and my father John *looked after her as they flew*
  with her to the heavens,
 while thousands of thousands and myriads of myriads of angels
  without number were singing to her.
 And we did not cease standing and looking after the body of the
  Virgin,
 until they were hidden with it in the air.

ROB.MAR.S. 80.12

48. *The angels and all the holy ones came forth to meet him.*
 They embraced him and they sang odes and alleluias
 until they took him to the City of Christ.

SOB.HEL.S. 65a.11

49. *When the Lord had finished saying these things,*
He took the soul of the saint Theodore, He removed it with Him
up to the heavens,
while the angels sang before Him.

BA.HY.I.TH.O.B. 61.14

50. *He signed himself with the Cross three times with his hand.*
In that moment he opened his mouth,
he gave up his spirit ( )
at the tenth hour of the day.
And there was a great fear at that hour and that place shook three
times.
And many old men who used many times to see visions said:
'We saw multitudes of angels, in troops one after another, watching
him.
Afterwards they sang hymns before him with great joy
until they brought him to his place of rest,
so that the place where he rested,
spread forth perfume for many days.'

LE.PAC.S. 95.1

51. *When he had finished saying these things he rose,*
he stood, he prayed to God with groans and tears.
Afterwards he lay down on the earth
until he completed his course in peace.
He gave up his spirit into the hands of God ( ).
And I heard the voices of angels, singing hymns before the blessed
Apa Wanofre ( ).
And there was great joy at his meeting with God.

TIL.I.WAN.S. 15.2

52. *When he had finished saying these things, he rose,*
he prayed to God with many groans and with tears.
Afterwards he lay down upon the ground.
He completed his divine ministry.
And he gave up his spirit into the hand of God ( ).
And I heard voices of angels singing hymns before the blessed Apa
Onnophrius.
And there was great joy in his meeting with God.

BU.ON.S. 217.20

53. Symachus leapt up,
he killed the rest of the holy men.

And the Firmament filled with angels
coming forth to meet the holy men, rejoicing with them,
until they received their souls and wrapped them in linen cloths.
The blessed Apa Epima was looking up at them all, as they were
  praising God
and giving glory to Our Lord Jesus Christ.

BA.HY.I.EPIM.B. 146.13

54. *Raphael received his soul.*
   He embraced it.
   He wrapped it in a cloth of linen.
   He took it up to heaven in Glory.

HY.EUS.B. 38.15

55. *Orion the Cursor raised his eyes to the sky,*
   he saw a great chorus of angels, singing before the soul of the saint,
     Apa Sarapamon,
   wrapped in a linen cloth
   and he watched them until they reached up to the heavens.

HY.SAR.B. 330.5

56. *One day as* (Anthony) *was sitting on the mountain*
   he looked and saw one whom they were carrying in the air,
   while great joy was with those who came to meet him.
   Anthony marvelled and he blessed this chorus.
   He prayed, wishing to know whom he had seen.
   And immediately a voice came to him
   saying: 'This is the soul of Amoun, the monk from the mountain of
     Nitria.
   He indeed has been an ascetic from his youth until his old age.'

GAR.ANT.S. 65.25

57. Avant Macaire, il y avait eu en Nitrie un certain moine, du nom
   d'Amoûn, dont Antoine vit l'âme enlevée au ciel. Cet Amoûn fut
   le premier des moines à occuper la Nitrie. ( ) Lorsqu'ils furent
   arrivés chez Antoine, celui-ci tout le premier dit à Amoûn: 'Dieu
   m'a fait bien des révélations à ton sujet et il m'a annoncé ta mort;
   je me suis donc senti poussé à te faire venir jusqu'à moi' ( ) Et
   quand Amoûn se fut èteint seul en sa grotte, Antoine vit son âme
   enlevée au ciel par des anges.

FE.IV/1.HIS.G. 120/122(XXII)

58. *It happened that when the third hour came,*
    he (Anthony) *saw the company of angels on the way,*
    with ranks of the prophets and the apostles
    with Apa Paul shining in their midst like snow,
    as he proceeded with them up to heaven.

AM.PAUL.B. 11.3

59. Then it happened that the stranger died and the old man saw
    divine visions

    and he saw multitudes of angels bearing his soul in triumph until
    it reached heaven.

BU.II.PAL.SY. 612.22

60. *His blessed brother Dometius lay sick.* There seized him a great
    fever.

    When the great Abba Macarius saw that he was sick, he said to me:
    'Sit, my son and attend the brother until thou dost receive his
    blessing.'
    Then I kissed his feet saying to him: 'Pray for me my holy father.'
    On the next day the saint Dometius was worse in the illness
    and when he reached the third night ( ) I said to him:
    'Dost thou wish that I call our father Abba Macarius?'
    He said: 'Yes.'
    Then I went, I called him and while I was walking with him on the
    road,
    he stood for a long time looking towards the cave.
    He turned towards the East. ( )
    He was watching the company of the saints who were leading the
    blessed soul of the Saint Dometius.
    He looked up to heaven, he sighed and wept ( ). He said to me:
    'Come, my son, for the saint Dometius is at rest.'
    When we came into the cave, *we found him sitting, leaning against*
    the wall,
    with his two hands stretched up to heaven, having died thus ( ).
    We took his holy body, we laid it down upon the kolobion. ( )
    The holy Abba Macarius bore witness: '*The companies which came*
    for the soul of the elder,
    these were also those which came for the soul of his brother,
    he being with them also.'

AM.MA.DO.B. 307.12

61. And while he (Father Pachomius) was still there,
    he heard that a certain brother, from that monastery

which is called in Greek Beth Raya, ( )

was sick: 'And he wishes to see thee and to be blessed by thee
before he dies.'

When the man of God heard these things, he rose up, he departed
on the journey.

When he was about two miles from the monastery

the man of God heard a holy (daughter of a) voice in the air.

He raised his eyes

and he saw the soul of the brother who was sick with the holy
angels,

and being carried up to a blessed and divine life.

Meanwhile the brethren who were accompanying him did not see or
hear anything.

And when he had stood there and looked for a long time to the
East,

they said to him: 'Why dost thou stand, O father?

Let us go quickly that we may reach him while he is alive.'

Then he said to them: 'We will not reach him there,

for I have just seen him ascending to Everlasting Life.

Depart therefore, my sons to your monastery.'

Then when those brethren entreated him

concerning the manner he had seen the soul of the brother who had
died,

he said to them: 'In some form.'

BU.II.PAL.SY. 310.5

62. *Theodore heard in the air the voices of angels*
singing psalms with a sweet chant and beautiful feeling.
Immediately he rose, he went, he told our father Pachomius. And
he said to him:
'*It is a good soul which has gone forth from the body*
and is being carried above us.
And we have been given the favour that we have heard those that
bless God bearing it.'
And as they were speaking with one another,
they looked above them to the height of an eagle's flight.
They saw him who had received the visitation and they knew who he
was.

LE.PAC.S. 154a.1

63. It happened one day, as Theodore was sitting in a part of the place
of worship,

he heard the voice of some angels singing psalms in the air
with sweet psalmody.

Immediately he rose, he went to our father Pachomius, he said to him:

'*A justified soul which has come forth from the body*
is being taken with them up above us.

And we also have been given the favour that we hear those that bless God bearing it.'

And as they spoke with one another,
they looked above them,
they saw him who had received this visitation and they recognised him who he was.

LE.PAC.B. 93.15

64. As our father Theodore and the brothers one day were in a place outside the monastery working,
    as they worked, fear came over them.
    When he saw that they were afraid, our father Theodore signed to them,
    saying: 'Let us pray to the Lord.' *And when they had prayed,*
    he looked up to heaven,
    he saw a soul over which the angels of God were singing psalms
    as they took it to its place of rest.
    After such a vision of these things,
    he turned to the brothers.

LE.PAC.B. 160.3

65. Telle fut la narration d'Anouph, et il dit encore bien d'autres choses, pendant trois jours: après quoi il rendit l'âme. Des anges aussitôt l'accueillirent, avec des chœurs de martyrs, et la conduisirent au ciel: les autres pères voyaient la chose, et ils entendaient les hymnes.

FE.IV/1.HIS.G. 80(XI)

IV. JOURNEY TO PARADISE

1. THE SEPARATION OF THE SOUL FROM THE BODY

THEMES

The taking of the soul during sleep to Paradise.
The taking of the soul during martyrdom to see the rewards of heaven.
The taking of the soul to heaven and the returning of the soul to the body.

The taking of the soul to heaven during the celebration of the Eucharist.
The taking of the souls of desert ascetics to heaven.

EPISODES

The appearance of a tall figure, man of light, angel during sleep.
The appearance of the Saviour during martyrdom.
The appearance of angels to the desert ascetics.
The taking of the soul to heaven by an accompanying angel.

QUOTATIONS

1. When night came,
   sleep was heavy upon me.
   *At that moment someone, tall in stature and terrifying in face, stood
   above me.*
   And he terrified me by his appearance.
   With his angry look and hostile voice, he asked me
   saying: 'Tell me, thou, what is the nature of the thoughts of thy
   heart?'
   I, through fear of his face and form,
   I did not dare to look at him.
   He cried out with a loud voice
   commanding me to tell the projects which I planned in my
   heart. ( )
   Then he said to me: 'Come and see both thy father and thy mother,
   but the life which thou dost wish, choose it this time.'
   He took my hand, he dragged me.
   He took me to a great field
   in which were many gardens and trees of all kinds,
   whose beauty is beyond all words.
   He took me into the holy place
   and my father met me, he embraced me, he kissed my mouth
   saying: 'My daughter, be among the good.'
   Then I clasped him, begging that he would keep me with him.
   But he said: 'It is not possible now. ( )'
   As I begged him that I might remain together with him,
   he who had brought me to that place dragged me in his grasp.
   saying: 'Come and see thy mother also *who is being burnt in the fire,*
   so that thou mayest know which is the good and useful life and
   choose it.'

   CH.AP.PA.S. 56.4(210)

2. At that time, he said, when my hundred and sixty-fifth year was
   completed, I begat my son Mathusal. After this too I lived two
   hundred years and completed of all the years of my life three

539

hundred and sixty-five years. On the first day of the first month I was in my house alone and was resting on my couch and slept. And when I was asleep, great distress came up into my heart, and I was weeping with my eyes in sleep, and I could not understand what this distress was, or what would happen to me. And there appeared to me two men, exceeding big, so that I never saw such on earth; their faces were shining like the sun, their eyes too were like a burning light, and from their lips was fire coming forth with clothing and singing of various kinds in appearance purple, their wings were brighter than gold, their hands whiter than snow. They were standing at the head of my couch and began to call me by my name. And I arose from my sleep and saw clearly those two men standing in front of me; And I saluted them and was seized with fear and the appearance of my face was changed from terror, and those men said to me: 'Have courage, Enoch, do not fear: the eternal God sent us to thee and lo, thou shalt today ascend with us into heaven, and thou shalt tell thy sons and all thy household all that they shall do without thee on earth in thy house, and let no one seek thee till the Lord return thee to them.'

CH.EN.II.SL. 431.A(1)

3. Après cela, le roi Ezéchias ayant fait venir dans le palais le saint prophète Isaie, celui-ci entra chez lui, et le grand prophète Isaie, s'étant assis sur le divan du roi, fut en extase, et sa pensée fut ravie de ce monde.

Et lorsque cela eut lieu, Sômnas, l'historiographe, se mit à dire que le saint Isaie était mort. Alors le roi Ezéchias entra et, lui prenant la main, il reconnut qu'il n'était pas mort mais qu'il avait été ravi, c'est-à-dire qu'il était ailleurs (?), par ce que le souffle de vie était en lui.

Et il passa ainsi dans son extase, étendu sur le divan du roi trois jours et trois nuits.

Et lorsque le grand prophète Isaie eut vu dans les cieux les œuvres extraordinaires, inconcevables et incroyables de Dieu qui aime l'homme, la gloire du Père et du Fils Bien-Aimé et de l'Esprit, et l'ordre des saints anges et leur disposition en chœurs, et qu'il eut entendu les paroles ineffables et mystérieuses de Dieu, son âme retourna dans son corps.

Et, ceci passé, le grand Isaie convoqua son fils Yasoum et Sômnas, le scribe, et le roi Ezéchias, et tous les assistants qui étaient dignes d'entendre ce que le saint prophète Isaie avait vu.

TIS.ASC.IS.G. 219(II)

4. Et Isaie raconta la vision qu'il avait vue à Ezéchias et à Yôsâb, son fils, et à Michée et aux autres prophètes.

Et elle était ceci: 'Lorsque j'eus prophétisé selon le témoignage que vous avez entendu, je vis un ange glorieux, et il n'était pas selon la gloire des anges que j'avais toujours vus, mais il avait une grande gloire et une dignité (telle) que je ne puis décrire la splendeur de cet ange.

Et je vis lorsqu'il me prit par la main et je lui dis: 'Qui es-tu, et quel est ton nom? Et où me fais-tu monter?' car le pouvoir de m'entretenir avec lui m'avait été donné.

Et il me dit: 'Lorsque je t'aurai fait faire une ascension, et que je t'aurai fait voir la vision pour laquelle j'ai été envoyé, alors tu comprendras qui je suis, mais tu ne connaîtras pas mon nom,

parce que tu dois revenir dans cette chair. Mais là où je te ferai monter, tu verras, car j'ai été envoyé pour cela.'

Et je me réjouis parce qu'il m'avait parlé avec douceur.

Et il me dit: 'T'es-tu réjoui parce que je t'ai parlé doucement?' Et il dit: 'Celui qui est plus grand que moi, tu verras qu'il parlera doucement et paisiblement avec toi.

Et tu verras aussi le Père de celui qui est plus grand, car j'ai été envoyé du septième ciel afin de t'expliquer tout cela.'

TIS.ASC.IS.E. 142(VII)

5. The hegemon, when he heard these things, caused the saint to be
    raised upon the hermetarion *and tortured*
until his flesh and his blood fell scattered upon the ground.
The saint raised his eyes to heaven. He prayed in his heart ( ).
In that hour behold Suriel, the angel, came down from heaven.
He took the soul of the blessed Eusebius up to the heavens.
He showed it the firmaments of heaven.
And he took him (Eusebius) *he showed him his house and his throne*
    and his crown
as a consolation in great glory.
And further he showed him the house of all his kinsfolk, one by one
    and his father Basilides.
He showed him his house which was very great,
with all these dwellings surrounding it.
He took him further, he showed him the Paradise of Joy
and he returned his soul to his body.
He healed the wounds which he had received.
He gave Peace to him,
he departed up to heaven.

541

The executioners ceased from torturing him, they said to the hegemon: '*We are weary of torturing him, he does not feel at all.*'

HY.EUS.B. 33.8

6. It happened when they had set sail,
   behold, Michael came down from heaven with a cloud of light.
   He went down into the hold of the boat. He released the Saint Helias.
   He mounted him upon the cloud of light, he took him up to heaven.
   He saw all the holy men, he embraced them, they gave him joy.
   He took him up to the Third Heaven
   and also to Paradise in the midst of which is the Tree of Life.
   Then he took him into the Promised Land.
   He saw that its earth was white like pure silver
   and that many trees were growing, bearing exceedingly good fruits.
   Then he was taken to the City of Christ and twelve walls surrounded that city.
   Then he was shown a large house like a royal palace built within the wall,
   of the extent of sixteen sitiohe, *built entirely of gold and pearls,* and a hundred cubits in height.
   Its roof was built of precious stones which shone more than the sun.
   Michael said to him: 'Holy Helias, this is thy house built of gold and pearls.'
   When the holy man, Helias, heard these things, he rejoiced greatly.

SOB.HEL.S. 54b.6

7. And he commanded that he be hung on the hermetarion and that he be tortured. ( )
   They said: 'He does not know that he is being tortured at all.'
   Apa Macarius had his heart taken up to heaven.
   He was told the mysteries of the Kingdom of the Heavens.
   And all the holy men embraced him.
   Abel made his way to him.
   He embraced him
   and he said to him: 'Greeting to thee, O my brother, Apa Macarius. ( )
   The Lord ( ) has opened the Door of Paradise to me.'
   All the holy men made their way to him, they embraced him,
   and they gave courage to him saying: 'O blessing upon thee, O Apa Macarius ( ).'
   But the saint Apa Macarius jumped up from the vision, ( )

He stood up before the count. He said to him: 'Shame on thee, O minister of the Devil.'

HY.MAC.AN.B. 47.10

8. *The Saint Apater was praying strenuously to the Lord about his sister.*
Behold Michael, the Archangel, came down from heaven.
He took her to the Heavenly Jerusalem,
he showed her her house and her crown and her throne with that of her brother.

HY.AP.IR.B. 105.4

9. He suffered greatly for his body began to be divided apart.
Then the holy martyr raised his eyes up to heaven he prayed
thus saying: '( ) *I am a stranger and altogether a sojourner like all my fathers.* ( )
do not be distant from me,
and do not allow me to die until I put to shame this impious one ( ).'
As he said these things, the Lord Jesus appeared to him at that moment.
He said to him: 'Be strong, O holy martyr, beloved of my good father,
come to me that I may show thee thy crown.
Afterwards thou wilt return to the tribunal to contend for my name and put to shame this impious hegemon.'
The Saviour took the holy man up to heaven.
He showed him the Firmament of heaven.
He embraced him with all the holy men
and He showed him his throne with his crown and his stole of glory,
and all the holy men said to him with one voice:
'Be strong, O holy martyr, O athlete of the King, Christ,
thou wilt receive the imperishable crown of martyrdom
and inherit the good things of the Kingdom of Heaven.'
It happened after the Lord showed him all these things,
He brought him down to the earth. ( )
He took the limbs of the holy man, he united them together
and he raised him again. No evil was upon him at all.
The Lord then said to him: '*Peace to thee, go and put to shame the impious hegemon*
while the whole multitude watches thee.'
Then he rose up, he stood up before the hegemon and the whole multitude. ( )

He said: ( ) *'The Lord Christ, my God, took my limbs,*
He united them to one another, He raised me,
He sent me to thee so that I should put thee to shame, with thy
   impious kings.'

BA.HY.I.LAC.B. 13.22

10. *It happened once that he fell ill and he suffered so much*
   that the messengers who were sent for him, brought forth his soul
      and he died.
   Afterwards he was brought to the other aeon.
   When he reached the Gate of Life,
   a command came forth from God that he should be returned to his
      body again.
   And he, when he learned this, he was sad for he did not wish to return
      to his body again,
   when he saw the light of that air that it was marvellous and beautiful,
   so that there is no way of speaking of it because of its glory.
   And when he was sad, there looked down upon him
   a man who was standing above the gate.
   And the face of that man, because of his glory,
   gave light in the manner of a great picture,
   and the appearance of his body was altogether lighted.
   And this man said to him: 'Go my son and return to thy body,
   because thou hast another small martyrdom in the world.'
   When he heard these words he rejoiced greatly
   because he had a great wish *to become a martyr for the name of the*
      Lord.
   The angels who rejoiced with him told him:
   'The man with whom thou speakest is Paul, the Apostle.'
   At that moment, when he was brought to the place in which his body
      was,
   the soul looked down on its body
   and behold, it was dead.
   Then it took place that when the soul approached the body,
   all the members of the body were secretly opened.
   The soul rested in its place again
   and he lived again.

LE.PAC.S. 17a.16

11. Et comme il me conduisait au septième ciel, j'entendis une autre
   voix me dire: 'Affermis-toi, Isaie, fils d'Amos'. Et aussitôt l'Esprit
   qui parle en moi, me fortifia.

THE REPRESENTATION OF A NON-MATERIAL WORLD

Et je vis là tous les justes depuis Adam: le juste Abel et le juste Seth, le juste Iareth et le juste Hénoch, et tous ceux qui sont nés de ces justes.

Et je vis qu'ils adoraient, et je tombai moi aussi avec eux et j'adorai et je me relevai sur mes pieds.

Et lorsqu'ils eurent rendu l'adoration qui est due, le Seigneur s'assit à droite, et, m'appelant, il me dit: 'Ecoute, Isaie fils d'Amos, et sache qu'aucun des hommes n'est monté ici, et que personne autre devant retourner dans le vêtement de la chair n'a vu ce que tu as vu.'

Et ensuite, il me donna un livre dans les mains, et il me dit: 'Reçois ceci et lis (la réponse) à ce que tu méditais dans le troisième ciel, en montant ici, et sache que rien n'échappe des actions qui se font en ce monde, mauvaises ou bonnes.'

Et je pris le livre et je lus, et voici: en lui était le registre complet de tous les hommes de siècle en siècle, des bons et des méchants, et jusque de leurs pensées.

Et ayant lu le livre, je dis: 'Vraiment, Seigneur, rien n'est caché ici de ce qui se fait en ce monde.'

Et ensuite le Seigneur me parla ainsi: 'Retourne derechef, dans le vêtement de ta chair, car il faut que tu accomplisses le temps de ta vie dans le monde corruptible.'

Et moi, je le priai en disant: 'Seigneur, ne me renvoie pas dans ce monde vain.' Mais répondant de nouveau, il me dit: 'Va là. Car le temps de ta vie n'est pas encore rempli.'

Et je tombai à ses pieds en (le) priant de ne pas me renvoyer dans le monde. Et le Seigneur ajoutant encore (une parole) me dit: 'Pourquoi pleures-tu, Isaie, voici ta place, voici ton trône, voici ta couronne, et voici tous tes vêtements que je t'ai préparés.

Car tu dois monter ici, après avoir consommé le martyre par le lot du bois, car les méchants te scieront avec une scie de bois, et ils te partageront en deux de la tête aux pieds.'

TIS.ASC.IS.G. 222(II)

12. *When night fell, we celebrated the evening service according to custom*
    and we said the Amen, ( )
    and one of the bishops, our fathers, was taken in a vision up to heaven.
    And he saw mysteries which were very great.
    And it is not right that any man of the earth should speak of them.
    He said: 'I saw myself in the presence of the throne of the Father.
    I saw thousands of thousands and myriads of myriads singing to the
        holy consubstantial Trinity.

I saw all the saints coming according to their ranks.
And they were worshipping God and were giving glory to him.
And they were blessing him and were asking their petitions.
Afterwards they all stood in rows
and no man on earth could tell the glory and the greatness
of splendour in which they appeared.
And I saw one coming forth from within the Veil
who resembled a king.
And he was wearing a golden diadem with seven crowns upon it.
And he was riding a white horse
and he gave light many times more than the Sun.
He was armed with swords and weapons and kingly things,
in short there was no measure to his kingly regalia
and when he came forth a great multitude followed after him,
on this side and that of him.
And I saw all the saints worshipping him.
Then I was amazed and I wished to know who he was.
I looked to his right hand.
I saw a monk standing with wings like an angel of God
and he was wearing a kingly crown and garments.
Nothing in the kingdoms of the world resembled them.
And there was a staff of gold in his right hand
and his face was filled with joy and a great glory surrounded him.
And I begged him *saying: "My father, I beg thee, tell me who thou*
   art, who art in such great glory."
And then he embraced me and he said to me: "I am Paul, the man of
   Tamma. ( )
All souls who shall come forth from the body, either justified or
   sinners,
have all their works made manifest on a spiritual tablet. ( )
Then when it pleased the Lord Jesus Christ to give me rest, I, his
   servant whom he visited,
I came forth from this world. ( )
He brought me into His City
and I saw this one whom now thou also seest.
And he had this kingly diadem with seven crowns upon it.
I saw it. I read the writings which were written on it:
   This is George of Melos, the man of Diospolis. ( )
And I saw all the saints worshipping him. ( )"
*While the holy one spoke with me,
the soldier of God, the saint, George, came to me,
while his face gave light.

He embraced me, he filled me with joy and gladness
and he said to me: "*If thou goest to thy city of Ankara, build me a house there, so that I come and be with thee,*
because *it is another five or six months before thou comest to me in this Holy City.*"
When he had said these things to me, I rose immediately from the vision.'
The king with the twelve bishops, *when they saw the face of the Bishop which was giving light,*
knew that he had seen a vision.

BA.HY.II.GEO.DI.B. 263.15; *267.3

13. I said to him: 'O my holy father, where do you celebrate the service on the Sabbath and the Lord's Day?'
He said to me: '*An angel of God, O my holy father,*
comes and serves me on the Sabbath and the Lord's Day.
And to every one who is in the desert, who lives for God and not to see men,
there comes an angel and serves them. And he consoles them.
If they wish then to see men *they are taken to the heavens*
so that they see all the saints. And they embrace them
so that their hearts receive light and they rejoice and are glad with God in the good things which are there.
When they see them they are consoled
and they forget that they received sufferings at all.
Afterwards they are returned to their bodies.
And they remain consoled for a long time.
When they turn to the other aeon through the joy which they saw,
they do not remember that the world exists.'

BU.ON.S. 214.19

14. After these things *he was again taken to Paradise,*
the Lord knows in what manner,
as the apostle says 'Whether in the body, or out of the body, I know not; it is God who knows;
and it is thus that this man was taken to the Third Heaven
and heard secret words which it is not fitting to repeat.'
And thus also when our Father Pachomius was taken to that place,
he saw the cities of the Holy Ones whose buildings it is not possible to describe,
with their ornaments and good things which the Lord has prepared(   ).
The air of the aeon was very temperate

and its aspect was without limits.
The trees giving fruit and the vines produced spiritual food and they
   were indestructable. (   )
Every tree which grows and all plants which grow in the Paradise,
   their fruit does not fail.
They have a great strong perfume and it is not possible for men to
   bear that perfume without perishing,
unless the Lord gives them power.
And that aeon is above the earth and outside the Firmament.
That land is very far above the mountains.
And the light-givers which give light in this Firmament upon the
   earth, they are not those which give light to that aeon,
but the Lord is He who lights it as said by Isaiah. (   )
*There is there neither day nor night,
but it is an abundant and imperishable light which gives light to that
   aeon.
Its frontiers are so great that this world is nothing beside it.
A little way outside the Paradise there are very many fruit-giving trees
with vines, not at all like those of this world. (   )
**And that aeon has great and profound darkness surrounding it,
   full of invisible wild beasts,
   so that no one is able to go there *unless an angel of God takes him*
      to that place.

LE.PAC.S. 19b.2; *22a.12; **23a.11

15. It happened at this same time, *when they (the two monks) had died*
   and when our father Pachomius was taken to another aeon. (   )
   our father Pachomius was walking with the angel who instructed him
      on the beauty of the other aeon, (   )
   And he showed him its spiritual gardens and their fruits which are
      indestructable.
   And he showed him all its dwellings and the construction with which
      they were built,
   and their indescribable beauty, filled with the glory of the Lord.
   When he had showed him all its dwellings,
   the man of God rejoiced over him with great joy.
   Afterwards when they were outside the Paradise of Joy, at a small
      distance,
   they saw the old ascetic in a place of scorching heat
   and attached like a dog to a tree bearing fruit,
   and living on its fruit, without having the power to leave that tree.

LE.PAC.S. 86.6

2. THE EXPERIENCES OF SOULS IN THE LIFE AFTER DEATH

THEMES

The request of a holy man to be shown the fate of souls after death.
The journeys of the soul in the company of angels.
The viewing by the soul of the places of the righteous and the wicked.
The presentation of the soul to the Lord.

EPISODES

The showing by the accompanying angel to the soul of the whole of creation.
The showing by the accompanying angel to the soul of the holy places of heaven.
The showing by the accompanying angel to the soul of the places of torment.
The taking to the Lord of the soul as a gift.
The entry of the soul into the place of rest or of torment.

QUOTATIONS

1. Next the Revelation of Aba Marcus of the Mountain of Tarmaqa which was shown to him by God concerning the Souls of Men.

   And God commanded and the angels conducted me and showed me the Land of Delight and the dwellings of the souls of the Righteous. And I saw the Tree, that from which Adam and Eve ate and were put to shame. And I saw the Paradise of God and I saw Enoch and Elias in the Land of the Living. Not one thing did I ask from God which He did not show me.

   One day a thought concerning the souls of men rose in my heart ( ) concerning the manner in which the angels conduct them when they are released from the body, and in what abodes dwell the souls of the Righteous and those who had believed, and then where were the souls of the wicked and (those) who had not believed; whether indeed those that believed went to the Kingdom and those who were wicked to the torment of Gehenna. And upon this thought I meditated, I rose and I prayed before God from evening till morning, myself, all night, and I besought Him concerning this matter to reveal it to me.

   And at the ninth hour of the night, He sent to me two angels, clothed in light, and their light shone in all the cave and their breath exhaled fragrance like perfumes. And they approached me and gave me greeting and said to me: 'Peace be with thee, Marcus, friend of Christ.' ( )

Then I glorified God and I said: '( ) Now sons of Light, tell me, according to the word of Our Lord, how the souls of men are conducted and where they go when they depart from the body.'

Then they answered and said to me: 'Hear O servant of God how the souls of the Righteous are conducted, those who confessed the Christ, and partook of His body and His blood and were signed with the seal of Baptism. Thus the soul which is not defiled with sin and which is worthy of rest, with it go gentle and merciful angels. It sees the whole of creation which is visible, from end to end and rejoices in the air for three days.

'And when the Oblation is offered on the third (day), it is raised to heaven before the throne of Christ. And the angels worship and the soul also worships with them. And then a (daughter of a) voice is heard (saying): "Conduct this soul and show it all the places of the torments of the sinners and let it return in six days." And then, according to the command of God, the angels conduct it and show it all the places of torment and all the pits (containing) the servants of iniquity, as far as the outer darkness. And it sees the wicked standing in the torments and those who did not believe in Christ. It trembles and it is in great fear. And the angels say to it: "Thou art happy, O soul who had believed in Christ." And then it is strengthened and rejoices and is glad, that it has escaped from such torments, and it has confidence in the mercy of the Lord.

'And when the Oblation is offered on the ninth day it is standing on the tribunal of Christ. And then comes the order from God: "Let the soul go to the Place of Rest."

'But the soul of the sinner, defiled by the sins of the world, because of its obedience to the demons, the angels also conduct it and it stands before the tribunal of Christ and the angels worship, the soul also with them. And an order goes forth from God and the angels conduct it and show it the Paradise of Delights and the dwellings of the saints and the Garden of Light and the Kingdom of Heaven and the Land of the Living which keeps those who practise virtue. And the angels say: "Woe to thee, soul disinherited of these good things because of thy obedience to sin." ( ) And then the angels conduct this soul and it stands before the tribunal of Christ. And an order goes forth from God: "Let this soul which has not ceased from her practices go to the Place of Torment, according as its works deserve, until the Day of Retribution." ( )'

THE REPRESENTATION OF A NON-MATERIAL WORLD

And when they had said these things, they gave me Peace and they departed from my presence and mounted to heaven. I then, when I had heard these things from the angels, I glorified God for all His Providence.

VAN.L.MAR.SY.(MUS.63) 181

2. Discourse of consolation or revelation of Aba Macarius, head of the Monastery of Egypt, concerning souls: how they are removed from bodies.

My friends, the disciple of this holy man informed us, saying: he asked God to reveal and show to him this mystery of the going forth of the soul from the body. And on a certain day when he and his disciple were in the desert praying, suddenly two angels came from the sky and gave greeting to the holy man and led him forth, walking with him in the empty desert, praising and glorifying God. ( )

He then made to them an obeisance and said: 'By our Lord, explain to me this mystery of the removal of the soul from the body.'

Then they said to him: '( ) When we are commanded to descend to take a certain soul, we come, and when we have taken it from the body in which it dwells, we leave it in this air three days while it consoles the people of its house and the body from which it has gone forth. And when on its (the soul's) account the Offering on the third day is made in memory of the day on which Our Lord rose from the grave, according to this institution and tradition which the Holy Church keeps, then we carry it up before Our Lord and we conduct it whither He commands. But for the souls of heathens and unbelievers, these who do not affirm Our Lord Jesus, it is not thus. ( )'

Then Aba Macarius said: 'What now also is this tradition that on the third day and on the ninth, on the thirtieth and on the fortieth, the Oblation is offered in the Church to God for the soul of the deceased. For what reason is it carried on and what use is it there for the soul when it has departed?'

The angels answered him: 'Hear, O Macarius, blessed of God, ( ) on the third day of the departure of the man, during the offering, the soul receives encouragement and consolation while it is informed by the angel who has taken it that prayer, and Oblations are offered on its behalf to God in the Church, and from this come confidence and hope to it.

'The soul is thus left for two days with the angels, those who have removed it, to travel with them and to go everywhere it wishes.

551

If it has a desire for its body, it goes for a time by the body in the tomb, for a time by familiar associations as it was accustomed. And thus these three days pass while it flies and circles and seeks those who love it as a bird (seeks) its nest. In this way also a virtuous soul goes to those places where it had the custom to practise righteousness.

'On the third day, then, Christ, He who rose from the tomb and was saved on the third day, He who is the God exalted over all, commands every Christian soul to mount to heaven. Rightly, therefore, the Holy Church keeps the tradition everywhere of offering prayer and Oblation to the God of all, on the third day on behalf of the soul. In this way, after the soul has worshipped God, an order goes forth from Him about it, that it should be shown all the various tabernacles of the saints, also the excellence and the delights of Paradise. And when the soul has seen these things and learnt of them for another six days, it admires, is astonished and glorifies God, He the fashioner and preparer of these things. And when it sees them it is changed and forgets the affliction which it has because of her separation from the body. ( )

'Then after it has seen, during these six days, all the joy of the righteous and beauty and splendour of Paradise, it then again mounts to worship God. The Church rightly keeps this law of performing prayer and Oblation on the ninth day in memory of those who have died. And after this second adoration, an order then goes forth from the Lord of all about it, that it should descend to Sheol and that it be shown the judgments and the torments there and those foul and dark places prepared for the impious and wicked who are weeping and gnashing their teeth. And when the soul has circled and spent thirty days in these places, it is afraid and weeps and is in great alarm lest in one of these places it be tormented, kept until the coming of the Day of Judgment.

'And on the fortieth day again the soul is taken up to worship before the Lord. Then according to its works the Judge of All orders that it should go to the place of safe keeping (lit. prison) and there on the fortieth day the soul inherits the place according as it is worthy of it. And rightly, the Church keeps this custom, of celebrating the memory of those who have died, on the fortieth day.

'And these things are made known to thee, O blessed man, concerning those souls who have received Holy Baptism and who are Christians.

'Concerning those souls who have not the seal of Baptism, it is not thus. But to all punishments and cruel torments, the angels take them, chastising them cruelly and beating them, crying out, saying: "( ) You will inherit the fire and the eternal darkness with the demons, those which you have worshipped like gods during your life in the world".'

And when the angels had said these things, they gave Peace to the servant of God and mounted to heaven. And Aba Macarius and we went on our way, praising and glorifying our God.

VAN.L.MAR.SY.(MUS.63) 168

3. *They (the angels) proceed with it to the height*
   so that it (the soul) sees the world from one extremity to the other,
   and that it sees the whole creation and gives glory to the Lord.
   Afterwards it is instructed about its place of rest,
   according to the ordinance of the Lord,
   so that when it enters into its place of rest by virtue of its works,
   it may know of all the torments from which it has been saved. ( )
   Afterwards it is brought to the feet of the Man of God, who has given it life
   and nourished it in the law of the Lord.
   He in his turn takes it to the feet of the Lord who has created it, as a gift.
   And afterwards he (the deceased) proclaims and blesses ( ).
   And afterwards he is taken to his place of rest
   which is ordained for him by the Lord according to the measure of his works.
   At the moment when he is about to appear before the Lord,
   it is permitted to him to approach or to keep at a distance according to his merit.
   For every one who is worthy of life certainly sings and blesses the Lord
   before going to his place of rest.
   And at the time when they bless, (each) one sees whom he blesses, according to the measure of his purity.

LE.PAC.S. 152b.33

4. *They (the angels) proceed with it to the height*
   so that it (the soul) sees the world from one extremity to the other,
   and that it sees the whole creation and gives glory to the Lord.
   Afterwards it is instructed about its place of rest,
   according to the ordinance of the Lord,
   so that after it has entered into its place of rest by virtue of its works,
   it knows of all the torments from which it has been saved. ( )

553

Afterwards it is brought to the feet of the Man who has given it life
and nourished it in the law of the Lord.
He, in his turn, takes it to the feet of the Lord, who has created it,
    as a gift.
And afterwards he (the deceased man) proclaims and blesses, (   )
And afterwards he is taken to his place of rest,
which is ordained for him by the Lord, according to the measure
    of his works.
At the moment when he is about to appear before the Lord,
it is permitted to him to approach or to keep at a distance, accor-
    ding to his merit.
For everyone who is worthy of life certainly sings and blesses the
    Lord before going to his place of rest.
And at the time when they bless, (each) one sees Him whom he
    blesses,
according to his worth and his purity.
And according to the worth of each one who will rest among those
    who have pleased the Lord,
the Holy Ones come forth in their glory to meet them upon chariots
    with horses
but the chariots and horses are spiritual.
Some of them go forth to the Gates of Life to meet and embrace them
    as if they were their sons.
Others go forth to them according to their merit.
And some approach them as they sit, before they rise and embrace
    them.
Others are not worthy to be embraced by the Holy Ones,
but they only inherit the Life according to their inferiority.
As they go forth to meet them the Righteous Ones bring (crowns).

LE.PAC.S. 245a.15

5. *They (the angels) were proceeding with it to the height*
    so that it (the soul) might see the world from one extremity to the
        other
    and see the whole creation and give glory to God who made it.
    Afterwards it is told of its place of rest according to the command
        of the Lord,
    so that when it is caused to enter its place of rest by virtue of its
        good works which it has done,
    it knows the punishments from which it has been saved. (   )
    And afterwards it is brought to the feet of the Man of God,
    He who taught it the fear of the Lord and nourished it in His law,

and in his turn, he takes it to the feet of the Lord, as a gift.
Then it manifestly blesses the Lord. (   )
And afterwards he (the deceased) is taken to the place of rest which is
    ordained
for him by the Lord.
For according to the measure of the works which he has done,
he is given the permission to approach or to remain distant,
according to the worth of the good works which he has done upon
    the earth.
For everyone who is worthy of eternal life certainly sings and blesses
    the Lord until he goes to his place of rest
which the Lord has prepared for him;
(each) one sees the Lord and blesses him (   ).
And according to the worth of each one who rests among those who
    have pleased God,
the Holy Ones come forth in glory to meet him according to the
    command of the Lord.
Some of them go forth towards them to the Gates of Life and they
    embrace them.
Some go forth before them at a distance according to their merit.
Others are approached before they rise and greet them.
Others are not worthy at all that the holy ones should greet them,
but only that they should inherit the Life according to the measure of
their inferiority.
As they go forth to meet them, the Righteous Ones bring crowns.

LE.PAC.B. 89.9

3. THE CITY AND THRONES OF HEAVEN

THEMES

The journey through the places of heaven accompanied by an archangel,
    angel.
The journey to the Third Heaven, the Seventh Heaven.

EPISODES

The seeing of the twelve thrones of the apostles, the multitudes of
    thrones, the Throne of Fire.
The seeing of the twelve walls, the twelve rivers which surround the City.
The seeing of the Veil, the Tabernacle, the Altar within the City.
The hearing of the voice of the Lord.
The hearing of those of heaven praising the Lord.
The designation of the places of heaven by the accompanying angel.

THE CULT OF THE SEER IN THE ANCIENT MIDDLE EAST

QUOTATIONS

1. *Michael set me down from his hand (upon the River of Fire).*
   I went into it as if (it were) a small canal of water. ( )
   Michael (gave light to me until we crossed over.)
   After we had crossed over it we proceeded up to heaven.
   He took me upon the Acherusian Lake, he immersed me in it three times.
   Afterwards a voice (came) forth from the height saying:
   'O ye angels who bear good news,
   take this soul to the places of immortality
   and Paradise of the celestial life,
   so that it sees the places of the apostles with their crowns and their thrones.'
   And in that moment Michael took me to the place called 'The Tabernacle of the Father'.
   And I saw your twelve thrones of pearl, of light,
   and your twelve crowns inlaid with precious stones and topazes and emeralds
   which were giving light to the whole City of Christ.
   I also saw twelve white stoles which were laid upon the thrones of mercy.
   And there were also twelve trees which were laden with fruit at all times.
   And they gave shade to each one of the thrones.
   And there were twelve eagles with men's faces, covering them with their wings,
   one eagle to each throne.
   And the names of the twelve apostles were written, (one) upon each of the thrones.
   And there were twelve veils, (one) drawn over each throne,
   while there was a diadem of precious stones spread over the thrones above each.
   And a thousand angels (sang hymns) before each throne. ( )
   I said to Michael the Archangel: 'For whom are these twelve thrones?' ( )
   (And Michael answered, he said to me: 'These are the) twelve
   thrones of the twelve saints, the disciples,
   they who followed Jesus the Son of God in the world.
   For this reason God has appointed these thousands of angels to sing hymns to them
   until they complete their course
   and come and sit upon them,

556

as kings with the Son of God in his Kingdom.'
I answered, I said to Michael: '*My Lord, show me the throne of my*
*   father*
because I am not able to read the writings which are written upon
    the thrones.'
Michael took me to the midst of the thrones,
he showed it to me. (   ) I wished to sit upon it. He stopped me,
    saying: (   )
'It is not permitted for any one of flesh and blood to sit upon
    these thrones, except His apostles alone.' (   )
And the thousand angels blessed me with a great blessing of
*   heaven.* (   )
Michael took my soul.
He placed it in my body again.
I rose up alive, I have spoken to thee now.

BU.BART.R.S. 35.21

2. *I then saw thrones of gold*
   which were set about in various places,
   with diadems of glory
   placed at the top of the thrones.
   I looked, I saw the twelfth wall.
   I saw rows of thrones
   of whose glory I am not able to tell.
   I said to the angel: '*My Lord, who are they who will sit in this*
      place upon the thrones?'
   The angel said: 'They who (   ) make themselves foolish for the
      sake of God.'

BU.AP.PAUL.S. 536.3

3. *After all these things*
   I was carried off in a cloud
   I was taken to the Third Heaven. (   )
   I saw the angel who was walking with me change his form.
   He burned with heat like a flame
   and at that moment a voice came to me saying: '*Paul, thou beloved*
      of God,
   do not reveal to any man
   the things which thou wilt see in this place.
   For those things which thou shalt see are unspeakable (in) words.'
   I looked I saw a seal hanging (   ).
   And seven eagles of light were standing on the right side of the altar
   and seven on its left,

557

and they sang hymns in a choir of blessing to the Father.
And myriads upon myriads of angels stood in His presence.
And thousands of thousands of angels were surrounding Him saying:
'Honoured is thy name and splendid is thy glory, O Lord.'
And the Cherubim and the Seraphim said 'Amen'.
When I saw them, I Paul, trembled in all my limbs.
I fell down upon my face.
Behold the angel who walked with me
made his way to me, he raised me saying:
'Do not be afraid O Paul thou beloved of God.
Rise up now and follow me and I will show thee thy place.'
The angel who walked with me took me to Paradise.
I saw a multitude of men, who were walking and rejoicing, singing
  psalms, blessing God.
And they were exceedingly compassionate.
And their faces gave light
seven times more than the sun.
And the hair of their heads was like white wool.
There was a multitude of glorious thrones in that place.
And the glory of each one of them was different.
And each one exceeded the next in glory.
At the moment that I reached them
they cried out 'Blessed art thou O Paul.'

BU.AP.PAUL.S. 567.28

4. *The angel said to me:*
  'This is the holy land of the Lord
  and these men are all the prophets
  who will be in this place until the Day of Judgment ( ).
  And thine own throne also will be in this place.
  And it is necessary that thou shouldst see thy throne and thy house
  before thou goest down to the world.
  And in every place in which thou shalt preach this Apocalypse in all
    the world,
  there will be many who will hear and repent
  and will not come to the punishments and the torments which thou
    hast seen.'
  Then I, when I had heard these things from the angel who walked
    with me,
  I said to him: '( ) *Show me now my throne which is in this place.'*
  The angel took me to a tabernacle of light.
  He showed me a throne of glory and two angels were singing hymns to it.

*I said to the angel: 'My Lord, whose is this throne which is in such
        great glory*
and who are these angels who are singing hymns to it?'
He said to me: 'This is thy throne, O Paul.
*And these two angels are Uriel and Suriel who are singing hymns to
        thy throne.*
*Dost thou not know, O Paul, that thy name is renowned in the midst
        of the angels*
who are without number?'

BU.AP.PAUL.S. 568.30

5. '*After these things, the angel took me up to the heavens.*
   I saw my father Abraham, I worshipped him
   and he greeted me with all the Holy Ones.
   They were all gathered, they honoured me because of my father.
   They walked with me, they took me to the Veil of the Father.
   *I cast myself down, I worshipped Him with my father with all the
        Holy Ones.*
   We all sang a hymn to Him. (   )
   *The Father spoke to Michael out of the Holy Place saying:
   "*Michael, my faithful steward, call a multitude of angels and all
        the Holy Ones.*"
   And the Lord, our God, mounted upon the chariot of the Cherubim,
   *while the Seraphim went before him with the angels and all the Holy
        Ones.*'
   When he had said all these things Jacob went in to his father Isaac.
   He kissed his mouth, weeping.
   Our father Isaac touched him, giving him a sign
   by the winking of his eyes that he should be silent.

GUI.IS.B. 238.20, *241.23

6. 'My father Agathon has told me that within the heaven are numerous circular steps like a throne of fire. If thou reachest the first
   step, thou wilt find others (higher); if thou reachest the second,
   thou shalt find others much higher than these; in short, each one is
   higher than the other until thou reachest to God. He alone is
   raised above them all, while they all surround Him like a throne of
   fire. As He said: "No one goes up to heaven except Him who came
   forth from heaven."'

VAN.L.Q.T.S. 43.3

7. *Those who were in the City came forth before me in great joy.*
   I saw the City of Christ which gave light

559

seven times more than the sun.
It was built entirely of gold.
There were twelve walls of precious stones surrounding the City
and there were towers built within each wall.
And the circumference of each wall was one hundred stadia.
I said to the angel: 'My Lord how great is the stadium of God?'
The angel said to me: 'The stadium makes one day's journey.' ( )
And there are four rivers surrounding it.
On the West of the City is a River of Honey,
that on the Southern side of the City is a River of Milk.
On the East of the City is a River of Wine.
To the North of the City is a River of Oil.
I said to the Angel: 'What are these rivers which surround the City?'
The angel answered. He said to me: 'The four rivers which surround
   this City
resemble the four rivers which are upon the earth.
That which flows with honey resembles the Phison.
That which flows with milk resembles the Euphrates.
That which flows with wine resembles the Geon (Gihon).
That which flows with oil resembles the Tigris.'

BU.AP.PAUL.S. 564.7

8. *He (the angel) took me within to the middle of the City, to the*
   twelfth wall.
   I found it to be the most excellent of them all.
   There was great glory in that wall
   so that no man of flesh would be able to tell of the glory and the
   splendour of that wall.
   Then I said to the angel: 'My Lord, is there not a place in this
   which is more excellent than all?'
   The angel said to me: '( ) Behold the second wall is more excellent
   than the first,
   and the third wall is more excellent than the second,
   all excel the others (which precede them) up to the twelfth wall.'

BU.AP.PAUL.S. 535.21

9. *'And further I will take thee and show thee thy throne and thy crown*
   and that of thy brethren, the apostles.'
   The angel took me before the Veil
   in the holy land.
   I saw a throne spread out
   and a stole above the throne

which emitted beauty (lit. joy) in ineffable splendour.
There were mosaics of marble above the throne.
I answered, I said to the angel: 'My Lord, what is the dwelling of
  my brethren, my fellow-apostles?'
The angel took me before the Veil.
I saw a multitude of thrones and a multitude of angels,
singing psalms and giving glory to God.
I saw a multitude of garments and a multitude of crowns
laid out before the throne
and a sweet smell was spread abroad in that place.
The angel said to me: 'This is the place of thy brethren, thy fellow
  apostles.'
And I also saw a man wearing a white garment
with a lyre in his hand
and standing on the right side of the Veil.
And he was singing and playing upon his lyre
and the angels made answer to him.
I answered, I said to the angel: 'Who is this, my Lord?'
He said to me: 'This is David who sings psalms.'
And in the holy land, I saw a place inlaid with precious stones of
  sapphire
and that land was white like snow.
There was a multitude of crowns and a multitude of thrones.
And those who were in that place were all wearing scapularies and
  head dresses.
And a multitude of angels were singing hymns to them.
I said to the angel: 'Who are these?'
He said to me: 'These are the martyrs ( ). They will receive great
  honours.'
Then they made their way to me,
they kissed my mouth,
they said to me: 'Blessed art thou, Paul.'

BU.AP.PAUL.S. 571.16

10. Then again *I, Paul, saw a great altar in the middle of the City,*
  which was very high
  and there was a man standing before the altar
  and his face gave light like the sun,
  and there was a harp of gold in his hand,
  with a psalter of gold.

He was crying out 'Alleluia'.
Those who were upon the gate and those who were upon the tower
were all answering him: 'Alleluia'.
And the foundations of the City were shaken.
I said to the angel: 'My Lord, who in such wise is this power?'
The angel answered, he said to me:
'This is David, the father of Christ, according to the flesh.
Since this is the Heavenly Jerusalem,
when the God Christ appears in His Kingdom,
it is David the King who will sing psalms,
so that the Righteous ones may answer him: "Allelluia".'
I said to the angel: '*My Lord, why is it David who sings psalms but
   not all the Righteous Ones?*'
He said to me: '*As the Christ our Lord sits on the right hand of the
   Father in the heavens,*
It is David who sings psalms to Him in the Seventh Heaven,
according to the pattern which is done upon earth. ( )
Without David the prophet, it is not possible to offer up a sacrifice
   in any place.
He sings psalms over the flesh of Christ and the holy blood,
according to the pattern which is done in heaven.'

BU.AP.PAUL.S. 536.21

4. THE FOUNDATIONS OF HEAVEN: THE PARADISE OF THE THIRD HEAVEN: THE EARTHLY PARADISE

THEMES

The viewing of the foundations of heaven.
The identifying by the Saviour or the accompanying angel of the places
   of heaven.
The viewing of the beauty and the fruitfulness of the Paradise of the
   Third Heaven.
The granting of a view of the Earthly Paradise.

EPISODES

The viewing of the Ocean which surrounds the world; the ether and
   clouds; the course of the sun, moon and luminaries; the mountains
   and deeps; the mouths of all the rivers.
The walking in the Paradise of the Third Heaven; the seeing of the
   rivers flowing with milk and honey.
The seeing of the light and whiteness of the land.

THE REPRESENTATION OF A NON-MATERIAL WORLD

The dialogue with the Saviour and the accompanying angel on the dimensions of the trees and vines.

The enumerating of the trees and plants of the Paradise; the giving forth of perfume by the plants.

The enumerating of the walls and the columns of Paradise.

The seeing of the Paradise of Eden: the four rivers, the Tree of Knowledge of Good and Evil which pours forth water.

The transporting of the ascetic to the Earthly Paradise.

The meeting of the ascetic with the holy men of the Paradise; their explanations of their way of life.

The seeing of the trees of the Earthly Paradise whose roots pour forth water.

QUOTATIONS

1. *Then I went with the angel.*
   He took me to the place of setting of the sun.
   I found the foundations of the heaven
   established on the River of Water.
   I said to the angel: 'What is the River of Water
   on which this heaven is established?'
   He said to me: 'This is the Ocean.
   This is the river which goes round the whole world.'

   BU.AP.PAUL.S. 538.2

2. *He brought me forth from this gate, he took me to the second gate,*
   he brought me forth upon the Firmament.
   He took me to the place of the rising of the sun.
   I looked, I saw the foundations of the heaven were above a River of
   Water,
   and that the River of Water encircled the whole earth.
   I said to the angel: 'My Lord what is that River of Water
   which surrounds this whole world?'
   He said to me: 'This is the river Oceanos.'

   BU.AP.PAUL.S. 561.25

3. Of Enoch's assumption: how the angels took him into the first heaven. It came to pass, when Enoch had told his sons, that the angels took him on to their wings and bore him up on to the first heaven and placed him on the clouds. And there I looked and again I looked higher, and saw the ether, and they placed me on the first heaven and showed me a very great Sea, greater than the earthly sea.

   CH.EN.II.SL. 432.A(3)

4. And they took and brought me to a place in which those who were there were like flaming fire, and when they wished, they appeared as men. And they brought me to the place of darkness, and to a mountain the point of whose summit reached to heaven.

And I saw the places of the luminaries and the treasuries of the stars and of the thunder, and in the uttermost depths where were a fiery bow and arrows and their quiver, and a fiery sword, and all the lightnings.

And they took me to the living waters, and to the fire of the west, which receives every setting of the sun.

And I came to a river of fire in which the fire flows like water and discharges itself into the great sea towards the west.

And I saw great rivers and came to the great river and to the great darkness, and went to the place where no flesh walks.

I saw the mountains of the darkness of winter and the place whence all the waters of the deep flow.

I saw the mouths of all the rivers of the earth and the mouth of the deep.

CH.EN.I.E. 199(17)

5. And thence I went to another place, and he showed me in the west another great and high mountain (and) of hard rock.

(G) And there were four hollow places in it, deep and very smooth: three of them were dark and one bright; and there was a fountain of water in its midst. And I said: 'How smooth are these hollow places and dark to view.'

Then Raphael answered, one of the holy angels who was with me, and said unto me: 'These hollow places have been created for this very purpose, that the spirits of the souls of the dead should assemble therein, yea that all the souls of the children of men should assemble there.'

CH.EN.I.E. 202(22)

6. *I looked forth on that land.*
I saw a river flowing with milk and honey.
On both sides of the river
were growing trees which bore fruit.
I looked to the Eastern side, I found every creation of God in that
place.
I saw palm trees growing in that place,
different in form from one another.
Some of them were thirty cubits in height,

some twenty and some ten.
The land on which they grew was seven times whiter than silver.
From the root of each tree up to its top
there were ten thousand branches multiplied by ten thousand
  clusters.
There were ten thousand clusters upon each branch.
There were ten thousand dates in each cluster.
And thus it was also with the vines.
There were ten thousand branches on the vine.
And (ten thousand) bunches of grapes on each branch.
There were ten thousand grapes in each bunch.
All the other trees were in tens of thousands.
And their fruit was in proportion.

BU.AP.PAUL.S. 562.15

7. It happened that when the Good Saviour had said these things to us
   we rejoiced exceedingly at the great honours
   which God had bestowed upon John the Baptist.
   He said to us also: 'Come and I will show you
   the Paradise of the Third Heaven.'
   And he caused us to walk among the scented plants of that place
   which all gave fruit according to their kind
   and they spread forth perfume
   and the fruit trees also according to their kind
   with all the trees which are in that place.
   They all give fruit according to their kind
   from their roots to their crowns,
   the scented plants and cinnamon and amomum and mastic and vine
     branches
   which spread forth perfume, each one choice and fresh.
   Thomas said to the Saviour: '*My Lord behold thou hast taught us
     all the trees*
   which smell sweet which are in Paradise:
   the fruit trees and the palm trees.
   Teach us now how many bunches of dates to each palm tree
   and how many dates to a tree and to a bunch
   and how many bunches of grapes to a vine.'
   The Saviour said: *I will hide nothing from you of what you have
     sought to know.*
   Concerning the vine about which you have asked,
   to each bunch there are ten thousand grapes upon it
   and each grape will produce six liquid measures.

Concerning the date palms in Paradise
there are ten thousand dates to a bunch
and their length is the height of a man.
Likewise the fig trees have ten thousand figs to a branch.
And if three men were to eat one fig they would be satisfied.
One ear of corn of Paradise has ten thousand grains to the ear
and four measures of wheat to each.
The citrus trees likewise also, to each tree they have ten thousand
    (seeds)
and are exceedingly tall and the apple and the ivy-bearing trees
    are of the same measure
with ten thousand (fruits) to a branch,
and if three men were to eat of one they would be satisfied.
These are the good things which I have prepared
for all those who will commemorate my beloved one,
my kinsman John, upon the earth. (   )
These are the things which God has prepared for those that love Him
and those that love John His companion and kinsman.
This is he whom none have surpassed.
No one has attained his honour in heaven or upon the earth.
This is he who became worthy to baptise the Son of God with his
holy hands.'

BU.CH.JOH.S. 141.26

8. *I found that it was the light of the sun which gave light to that land.*
   And that land was seven times brighter than silver.
   And I said to the angel: 'What is this place?'
   He said to me: 'This is the Land of the Inheritance. (   )
   When the souls of the Righteous come forth from the body
   and they meet God,
   they are placed in this land.'
   I said to the angel: 'Shall this land be manifest after a time?'
   The angel answered, he said to me: 'When the Christ appears in
       His Kingdom,
   this land also will appear above this like a breath of dew.'

BU.AP.PAUL.S. 561.33

9. *The angel who walked with me took me,*
   he showed me a multitude of tall trees
   and a multitude of men surrounding the trees.
   And their garments were glorious.
   They all cried out to me:

THE REPRESENTATION OF A NON-MATERIAL WORLD

'Greeting Paul, thou beloved of God and men.'
They all embraced me.
I said to the angel: 'My Lord who are these?'
*The angel said to me: 'These are all the plants which thou hast
    planted in the world.'*
The angel took me, he said to me:
'Come that I may cause thee to see the Paradise of Heaven,
with thy throne and thy crown.'
I saw the Paradise and it was exceedingly wonderful.
There were three walls surrounding the Paradise of Heaven, two of silver
and a wall of gold in the middle of the two walls of silver,
one within the other.
Each wall was fifty and twenty and two cubits in height.
There was a curved course within each wall,
from the East to the West and from the North to the South.
And the Paradise was two hundred and forty thousand and four
    hundred reed measures each side.
There were two hundred and forty thousand strong columns within it
and each column was seventy-two cubits in height.
There were eighteen hundred different kinds of fruit trees in it,
there were two thousand magnificent plants within it;
there were forty-five kinds of scented herbs in it;
there were twelve cypress trees in it;
a wall of stone of the colour of leek surrounded it;
there were twelve hundred golden lamps within it;
there were sixteen pillars of silver and marble surrounding it;
and its entrance was a door;
there were three eagles on the right of the door
and three on the left of the door.
And all the Paradise was lighted with the colour of the sky
as at the hour of midday
with no darkness in it.
But it was the light of God which was in it at all times
making it completely light.
*The Paradise spread forth the perfume of fruit trees at the hour of
    morning*
and it spread forth the perfume of myrrh at the hour of midday,
and when the sun sets
*the perfume of all the trees which are in Paradise is spread forth
    until the night of the world is past.*
The bases of the columns were planted with malabathrum and
    storax (plants),

while their heads were hung with branches of almond and they were
one hundred and forty thousand and eight hundred in number.
And precious stones were inlaid within them.
And all the trees of Paradise sang hymns to God three times daily,
at the hour of dawn, at the hour of midday and the hour of evening.
And they all cried out blessing God, three times. (   )
And the Paradise cried out blessing God.

BU.AP.PAUL.S. 569.23

10. And thence I went towards the east, into the midst of the mountain
range of the desert, and I saw a wilderness and it was solitary, full
of trees and plants.

And water gushed forth from above.

Rushing like a copious watercourse (which flowed) towards the
north-west it caused clouds and dew to ascend on every side.

And thence I went to another place in the desert, and approached
to the east of this mountain range.

And there I saw aromatic trees exhaling the fragrance of frankincense and myrrh, and the trees also were similar to the almond
tree.

And beyond these, I went afar to the east, and I saw another
place, a valley (full) of water.

And therein there was a tree, the colour (?) of fragrant trees such
as the mastic.

And on the sides of those valleys I saw fragrant cinnamon.
And beyond these I proceeded to the east.

And I saw other mountains, and amongst them were groves of
trees, and there flowed forth from them nectar, which is named
sarara and galbanum.

And beyond these mountains I saw another mountain to the east
of the ends of the earth, whereon were aloe trees, and all the trees
were full of stacte, being like almond trees.

And when one burnt it, it smelt sweeter than any fragrant odour.

CH.EN.I.E. 206(28–31)

11. And after these fragrant odours, as I looked towards the north
over the mountains I saw seven mountains full of choice nard and
fragrant trees and cinnamon and pepper.

And thence I went over the summits of all these mountains, (   )
far towards the east of the earth, and passed over the angel Zotîêl.

And I came to the Garden of Righteousness, and saw beyond
those trees many large trees growing there and of goodly fragrance,

large, very beautiful and glorious, and the tree of wisdom whereof they eat and know wisdom.

That tree is in height like the fir, and its leaves are like (those of) the Carob tree: and its fruit is like the clusters of the vine, very beautiful; and the fragrance of the tree penetrates afar.

Then I said: 'How beautiful is the tree, and how attractive is its look.'

Then Raphael, the holy angel who was with me, answered me, and said: 'This is the tree of wisdom, of which thy father old (in years) and thy aged mother, who were before thee, have eaten, and they learnt wisdom and their eyes were opened, and they knew that they were naked and they were driven out of the garden.'

CH.EN.I.E. 207(32)

12. Of the assumption of Enoch to the third heaven.

And those men took me thence, and led me up on to the third heaven, and placed me there; and I looked downwards, and saw the produce of these places, such as has never been known for goodness. And I saw all the sweet-flowering trees and beheld their fruits, which were sweet-smelling, and all the foods borne by them bubbling with fragrant exhalation. And in the midst of the trees that of life, in that place whereon the Lord rests, when He goes up into paradise; and this tree is of ineffable goodness and fragrance, and adorned more than every existing thing; and on all sides it is in form gold-looking and vermilion and fire-like and covers all, and it has produce from all fruits. Its root is in the garden at the earth's end. ( ) And two springs come out which send forth oil and wine, and they separate into four parts, and go round with quiet course, and go down into the paradise of Eden, ( ) And thence they go forth along the earth and have a revolution to their circle even as other elements. And here there is no unfruitful tree, and every place is blessed. And there are three hundred angels very bright, who keep the garden, and with incessant sweet singing and never-silent voices serve the Lord throughout all days and hours.

CH.EN.II.SL. 433.A(8)

13. Then at that moment *Our Saviour commanded.*
He brought down a cloud of light.
He mounted upon (it) and he commanded us the apostles
and we mounted upon the cloud with Him.
He brought us up to the First Heaven,
afterwards to the Second Heaven.

569

Then He passed by the Third Heaven
and He did not allow us to enter into it.
But He took us to the Fourth Heaven,
and the Fifth, and the Sixth and the Seventh.
And He did not allow us to go in.
After He had shown us all these things,
He then brought us into the Third Heaven.
We marvelled at its beauty and its fruitfulness and its great glory.
And we saw John the Baptist, with Zacharias his father and Elizabeth
  his mother,
garbed in great glory,
wearing huge precious stones and many coloured stones.
Our Saviour caused us to stand in the presence of John.
He caused John to stand in our midst,
and also Zacharias on his right and Elizabeth his mother on his left.
Then He caused us, the apostles, to stand in order, from Peter our
  father to Matthias.
Our Saviour walked before us, He showed us the whole heaven,
He showed us the good things and the joys
which are prepared within it.

BU.CH.JOH.S. 138.8

14. *Then I walked with the angel.*
  He carried me off in the spirit.
  He took me to Paradise.
  The angel said to me: 'O Paul, thou seest the place to which I shall
    take thee.
  Paradise is in that place,
  the place in which Adam and his wife transgressed.'
  When I approached Paradise
  I saw the beginning of the four rivers in that place.
  The angel beckoned to me saying:
  '*This is Phison which surrounds the whole land of Eueilat* (Havilah).
  (*This is) Geon* (Gihon) *which surrounds all the land of the peoples*
    of Kush.
  This is Tigris which flows towards the (land of) the Assyrians.
  This is Euphrates which flows towards Mesopotamia.'
  At the moment I entered Paradise
  I saw a tree growing
  and its root poured forth water as a spring.
  And it gave water to the four sources of the four rivers.
  And the Spirit of God blew upon the tree

and when the water flowed, the Spirit cried out.

I said to the angel: 'My Lord what tree is this which pours forth water?'

The angel answered, ( ): 'At the time when God had not yet created heaven and the earth,

there was nothing except water alone.

And the Spirit of God used to come upon the waters.

When God made the heaven and the earth,

the Spirit was first upon the water.

It was also upon the tree.

When the Spirit breathed (upon it) the water flowed.'

He (the angel) seized my hand,

he took me to the middle of Paradise.

He showed me the Tree of Knowledge of Good and Evil.

He said to me: 'This is the tree through which Death came into the world.

This is the tree of which Adam ate

until Death came to every man.'

He showed me another tree growing in the middle of Paradise.

He said to me: 'This is the Tree of Life.'

And there was a Cherubim with a sword of fire guarding it,

when I stood to look at the glory of the Tree of Life.

BU.AP.PAUL.S. 550.16

15. And as we prayed, suddenly there appeared two men, standing before the Lord, on whom we were not able to look. For there went forth from their countenance a ray, as of the sun, and their raiment was shining, such as the eye of men never saw. For no mouth can describe nor heart conceive the glory with which they were clad nor the beauty of their countenance. And when we saw them we were astonished, for their bodies were whiter than any snow and redder than any rose. But the redness of them was mingled with the whiteness, and I simply cannot describe their beauty. For their hair was curled and charmingly suited their faces and their shoulders like some garland woven of blossom of nard and various coloured flowers or like a rainbow in the air: so beautifully formed was their appearance. When we saw their beauty, we were astonished before them, for they had appeared suddenly.

*And I approached the Lord and said, 'Who are these?' He said to me, 'These are your righteous brethren whose form ye did desire to see. (Ethiopic: These are Moses and Elias)' And I said to him, 'And where are all the righteous, and what is the nature of that world in which these are who possess such glory?' And the Lord showed me a widely extensive place outside this world, all gleaming with light, and the air there flooded by the rays of the sun, and the earth itself budding with flowers which fade not, and full of spices and plants which blossom gloriously and fade not and bear blessed fruit. So great was the fragrance of the flowers that it was borne thence even unto us. The inhabitants of that place were clad with the shining raiment of angels and their raiment was suitable to their place of habitation. Angels walked there amongst them. All who dwell there had an equal glory, and with one voice they praised God the Lord, rejoicing in that place. The Lord said unto us, 'This is the place of your high-priests (brothers?), the righteous men.'

WIL.II.PET.G. 680; *681

16. There was a certain admirable and excellent man who dwelt in the desert forty years and he did not eat bread and he did not drink wine and he did not see the faces of men. And his name was Zosimos. And he besought God by night and by day that He would show to him where those holy men, the sons of Jonadab, who were withdrawn from the world in the days of Jeremiah the prophet, lived and where He caused them to inhabit. And the Lord saw the zeal of the holy man Zosimos concerning these holy men. And then God answered his prayer and granted his request. And one day, while he prayed (a voice came to him) and an angel came to him and answered and said to him: 'Zosimos, man of God, I have been sent to thee from the Height to be a guide to thee and to show to thee the path on which thou shouldst go in order to see these holy men, according as thou has requested from the Lord. Nevertheless, be not glorified in thine eyes, that for forty years thou hast not eaten bread, nor drunk wine, nor seen the faces of men, but (only) the faces of angels. Now approach.'

NAU.JON.SY. 7.4

17. And suddenly there appeared two trees on the shore of the great sea whose like I had never seen and they were beautiful and very glorious. And then one of the trees bowed down and I was grasped in its branches securely. And it straightened towards the height and it took me and carried me in its top carefully towards the cloud. And the other tree also bowed down towards it. And it bent its head from there and conveyed me to the one from the other side. And it cast me gently within it. And thus I crossed the great ocean

and the cloud by the Providence of God. And I remained in the place three days. And there did not cease from my mouth the praise of God. Then I rose and journeyed through that land which was in the middle of the sea, which was desirable and beautiful and filled with splendid trees which bore desirable and fragrant fruits. And it was a great and wide island and there were no hills or high places in it. And it was ornamented with flowers and full of many delightful perfumes.

NAU.JON.SY. 9.9

18. As I was considering the beauty of this land, I approached a little and I saw a man who was sitting naked. And I feared when I saw him and I said: 'Peace to thee my brother.' Then he made answer to me and said: 'Go in peace and blessing be upon thee, for I know that thou art a man of God, for if not, thou wouldst not have been able to come here.' And again he asked me: 'Dost thou come from the world of vanity?' Then I said to him: 'Truly I have come from the world of vanity in order to see you. But tell me, why are you naked?' Then he said to me: 'It is thou who art naked and thou dost not know, because thy clothing is corruptible, but my clothing is not corruptible. And if thou dost wish to see me, come and behold the height of heaven.' And I looked up, I saw his face like the face of an angel and my eyes were obscured with fear. And I fell upon the earth. And then he approached me and took my hands.

NAU.JON.SY. 10.7

19. This land resembled the Paradise of God. And these holy men resembled Adam and Eve before they fell, for they fasted from the ninth hour to the ninth and their needs were satisfied by the fruits of those trees. Waters flowed from the roots of the trees which were sweet like honey. And each one drank his fill and when they had eaten they did not flow, for they flowed at the ninth hour only.

NAU.JON.SY. 12.7

20. Une autre fois, après un long jeûne et de longues prières il demanda à Dieu que lui fût montré le paradis que Jannès et Jambrès avaient jadis planté au désert d'Egypte dans le désir de créer une copie du vrai Paradis. Comme il avait donc erré trois semaines à travers le désert, et que, passant tout ce temps sans nourriture, il s'était désormais évanoui, un ange le déposa près du lieu. Or il y avait des démons qui, de toute part, gardaient les entrées du paradis

et ne l'y laissaient pas pénétrer: C'était en outre un terrain immense, d'énormes dimensions. Cependant, après avoir prié, il s'enhardit à entrer, et trouva dedans deux saints hommes, qui eux aussi étaient venus là de la même manière il y avait déjà longtemps. Ils firent une prière et s'embrassèrent mutuellement, tout réjouis de se trouver ensemble. Sur ce, ils lui lavèrent les pieds et lui offrirent des fruits du paradis. Il y goûta en rendant grâces à Dieu, plein d'admiration pour la grosseur de ces fruits et leurs mille couleurs variées. Et ils ne cessaient de se dire l'un à l'autre: 'Comme il serait beau que tous les moines fussent ici.' 'Il y avait' dit-il, 'au milieu du paradis, trois sources abondantes, jaillies de l'abîme, qui l'arrosaient, et des arbres immenses chargés de fruits, qui portaient toute espèce possible de fruits sous le ciel.' Macaire resta sept jours auprès d'eux, puis il leur demanda de rentrer au pays habité et de ramener avec lui les moines. Ces saints hommes lui répondirent que c'était impossible: le désert était vaste et s'étendait au loin, et il y avait beaucoup de démons qui, dans tout le désert, égaraient et tuaient les moines, de sorte que, souvent déjà, bien des gens qui avaient voulu venir avaient péri.

FE.IV/1.HIS.G. 116(XXI)

21. I said to the angel of the Lord: 'Is there no darkness in this place or night?' He said to me: 'No, because (in) the place in which are the Righteous and the Holy Ones, in that place is no darkness, but they are in the light at all times.'

ST.AP.EL.A. 36.2(2)

SECTION IV

SECTION IV

The Representation of Negative Experiences

I DEATH AND JUDGMENT

1 THE DEATH OF THE WICKED

THEMES

The fetching of the souls of the wicked by pitiless angels, black horses, the Keeper of Sheol, the Ruler of Tartarus.

The refusal to give rest or compassion to the souls of the wicked.

The conveying of the souls of the wicked to heaven by the powers of darkness.

The separation of the wicked from the righteous.

EPISODES

The tormenting of the soul at the time of death.

The drawing forth of the soul by a hook or three-pronged spear.

The seizing of the souls by a tall monster in the air; their descent to torment below.

The appearance of the powers of darkness with animal faces and weapons; their attacks on the souls in the air.

QUOTATIONS

1. *When he had seen the bringing forth from the body of the (soul of) the*
   justified
   he asked further how, for the soul of a sinner,
   was the bringing forth from the body.
   And the angel said to him: 'The Lord will satisfy thy heart in all things.
   If it is a soul which is evil in its conduct,
   at the time of its visitation,
   two pitiless angels come to fetch it.
   When a man approaches death,
   so that he is not able to recognise men,
   one of the pitiless angels stands beside his head and the other beside
   his feet

576

and thus they stand beating him until his miserable soul is about to
    come up.
Then they put in his mouth a curved object like a hook
and they draw up from the body his unfortunate soul,
and it is found to be black and in darkness.
Then they bind it to the tail of a spiritual horse,
because it also is a spirit,
and thus they take it and cast it to the torments
or to the bottom of Amente
according to the measure of its deeds.'

LE.PAC.B. 91.22

2. (He said) '*I wish to see the soul of a righteous man and sinner come*
    forth from the body.'
God did not wish to disappoint him in his wish. ( )
There was a man there whose name outside was that of a great
    anchorite.
He was ill, he awaited his hour.
The brother looked, he saw a multitude of torches and candles
and they were prepared. ( )
The moment of death approached.
The brother looked, he saw the ruler of Tartarus of Amente coming
with a three-pointed spear of fire in his hand.
He heard a voice saying: 'As this soul gave me no rest for one mo-
    ment
do not give it any rest as thou bringest it forth from the body.'
He plunged his spear of fire down into his heart for about an hour,
    torturing him,
he brought forth his soul.

CHA.AP.PA.S. 60.28(212)

3. A certain man who dwelt in a monastery who had gained renown
   and concerning whom a report had gone forth
   that he was a hermit of virtue
   and this man was severely ill
   and was waiting for his hour of death. ( )
   Then when the time came that he should end,
   that brother looked and he saw and behold the Keeper of Sheol
       entered
   with a three-pronged fork of fire in his hand.
   And he heard a voice which spoke thus, saying:
   'His soul gave me no rest, even for one moment

577

and thou shalt not show compassion to him
when thou takest away his soul.'

BU.II.PAL.SY. 614.8

4. A cette nouvelle, le clairvoyant s'en va en hâte pour recevoir la
   bénédiction de ce prétendu saint. Lorsqu'il fut proche de sa de-
   meure, il voit un grand appareil de cierges, et une foule énorme de
   clercs, de laïques et jusqu'à l'évêque lui-même, qui demeuraient au
   chevet du malade pour lui rendre les derniers devoirs. Etant donc
   entré chez lui, il le trouva respirant encore, et, l'ayant considéré
   des yeux de l'esprit, il voit le Tartare des Enfers avec un trident de
   feu, qui avait enfoncé son trident dans le cœur du moine, et, à
   grande torture, cherchait à lui arracher l'âme. Et il entendit une
   voix venir du ciel qui disait : 'De même que l'âme de cet homme n'a
   pas cessé un seul jour de me torturer, de même, toi non plus, ne
   cesse pas de le torturer et de lui arracher l'âme.'

FE.III/1.EUT.G. 92(XXIV)

5. They said concerning a certain old man,
   that he once went to one of the cities to sell his handiwork.
   And by chance he sat before the door of the court of a rich man
   who was approaching death
   and who was coming near to his end.
   And as he sat, he looked, he saw black horses with their black riders
   and they were very terrifying.
   And they held in their hands staffs of fire.
   Thus when they came to the door of the court,
   they stood their horses outside
   and they entered both together.
   And when the sick man saw them,
   he cried out with a mighty voice saying: 'Lord, help me.'
   Those who had been sent to him said:
   'Since the sun has set upon thee, thou has come to call to mind God.
   Why didst thou not seek Him while it was day?
   Now there is for thee not a portion of hope of consolation.'
   Then they took away his soul and departed.

BU.II.PAL.SY. 615.14

6. *As he sat, the old man looked he saw black horses and those that rode*
   them were also black, fearful,
   with a staff of fire in the hand of each.
   They reached the porch of the house.

578

They left their horses outside the house.
They entered in, each one with haste.
*The sick man saw them, he called, he cried out in a loud voice: 'Lord
   help me.'*
Those who came to fetch him answered saying:
'At the hour when the sun has set for thee thou hast sought after the
   Lord.
Why hast thou not sought after God until this day?
For now there is no part nor hope nor consolation for thee.'

CHA.AP.PA.S. 61.30(213)

7. It happened one day as he was about to eat
   when he rose to pray, it was the ninth hour,
   he knew that he was being taken in his spirit only,
   and the wonder was greater, that he stood seeing his own self
   as if he were outside himself,
   and some guided him to the air.
   And other very evil and bitter ones stood in the air,
   wishing to seize him,
   so that he should not pass by and over them.
   Those who guided him wished to resist them,
   those evil ones questioned them about him,
   so that they would know whether he was in their hands or he was
      liable to give account to them. (   )
   Then when those that accused him had no power to stand against
      him or to blame him,
   at that moment the way was free for him, they were not able to
      seize him,
   but immediately he saw himself standing as before as Anthony engaged
      in prayer.

GAR.ANT.S. 70.10

8. Afterwards he spoke one day, with some who came to him,
   about the course of life of the soul
   and concerning its dwelling,
   or in what kind of place it would be hereafter.
   The following night one called to him from heaven,
   saying: 'Anthony come forth and see.'
   (He went out) for he knew whose calls to obey.
   He looked up, he saw a monstrous form,
   very hateful in its appearance, and fearful,
   standing reaching to the clouds.

579

Some were going up having wings.
And that being was stretching forth his hand.
Some he stopped, others flew above him and rose up.
And at these the monster gnashed his teeth.
He rejoiced over those which fell beneath him.
A voice came to Anthony saying:
'Understand what thou art seeing.'
And when his mind was opened
he knew that this was the taking upwards of souls which he had seen.
And that monster standing was the enemy,
the envier of the faithful.
And he seized those who were guilty and liable to him.
And he prevented them so that even if they pass him,
their passage within is not without trouble and care.
But those who did not obey him,
he was not able to seize, but they were going up over him.

GAR.ANT.S. 72.3

9. Abba Anthony said: 'I spent a whole year praying to God
that he would reveal to me the way of the justified and the way of the
   sinners.
I saw one who was tall like a giant
standing who reached to the clouds.
And his hands stretched out below the sky
and below him was a lake which was wide like the sea.
I also saw souls which were flying like birds,
and all those which flew above his hands and above his head were
   saved
and all those which were caught in his hands and which he struck
fell down into the lake of fire which burned.
Then a voice came to me from heaven
saying: "Anthony, these souls whom thou hast seen being cast down
   by his hands,
these indeed are the souls of sinners who are dragged down to
Amente.

AM.AP.ANT.B. 31.11

10. In that night blessed Anthony told me thus:
'For a whole year I prayed that the place of the just and of sinners
   might be revealed to me.
And I saw a tall giant reaching to the clouds, black,
with his hands stretched up to heaven,
and under him a lake as vast as the sea,

580

and I saw souls flying like birds.
And as many as flew over his hands and head were saved.
But as many as were struck by his hands fell into the lake.
Then came a voice to me saying:
"These souls of the righteous, which thou seest flying,
are the souls which are saved for Paradise.
But the others are those which are drawn to hell, having followed
the desires of the flesh and revenge."

LO.PAL.G. 95(XXI)

11. He said to me: 'Let us kneel in prayer, my brethren.'
When we knelt in prayer, I heard a voice which said:
'Spread out your wings and bear (him) away.'
And when I heard these things, I rose and looked upward
and I saw his soul being borne by angels.
It was clothed in a white stole
and they were ministering to it and going up with it.
The veil of this air was drawn back
and I saw the guard of demons, standing ready.
And I heard a voice which said:
'Flee, children of darkness, from before the light.'
His soul was detained a moment and one of the evil spirits raised his
   voice and cried:
'Lead and go after the confounder of demons.'
And when his soul passed by all the hosts of demons,
immediately I saw, as it were, a likeness of a hand of fire
which was stretched out to him and I did not see him again.

LOOK.MAR.SY. 20.11

12. When night came
sleep was heavy upon me.
*At that moment someone, tall in stature and terrifying in face, stood
   above me.*
And he terrified me by his appearance.
With his angry look and hostile voice, he asked me
saying: 'Tell me, thou, what is the nature of the thoughts of thy
   heart?'
I, through fear of his face and form,
I did not dare to look at him.

CHA.AP.PA.S. 56.4(210)

13. *At the appointed moment, the powers will take it up to heaven*
(and inflict) suffering upon suffering. (   )

And the powers of darkness, some with faces of lions
wearing breastplates of iron burning with fire,
with slaughtering swords in their hands,
some with faces of bulls with hands like those of men,
with great horns of fire upon their foreheads,
with spears in their hands, piercing the souls of sinners, with them;
some with faces of bears
while their eyes shoot forth fire
to the four sides
and there is fury in their faces
and they have great iron knives in their hands,
prepared to torment the bodies of the wicked
before (the souls) come forth from the body,
tormenting them during the struggle of death.
Some have faces of dragons
with smoke coming forth from their mouths with fumes of fire,
with saw edged hooks in their hands
with which they torment these souls.
Some have faces of ibises
with tails like scorpions
and they are prepared to bite the souls
tormenting them without mercy.
Some have faces of asses
wearing black breastplates,
with spikes of fire in their hands and they ensnare the souls in fury.
Some have faces of crocodiles with great knives in their hands,
and they secretly cut off the limbs of the soul.
Some have faces of wild beasts
with tongues of fire outside their mouths
and teeth of iron.
These ( ) the souls when they have chewed them in their mouths.
And they swallow them for a time.
Afterwards they vomit them forth.

BU.AP.PAUL.S. 556.20

14. When I saw these things I was afraid. I said to that angel who walked with me: 'Who are these who are thus?' He said to me: 'These are the servants of the whole creation. These are they who are wont to go for the souls of impious men and bring them and lay them in this place. They are wont to spend three days circling with them in the air until they take them and cast them to eternal punishment.'

I said: 'I beg thee, O Lord, do not give them authority to come for me.' The angel said: 'Do not fear, I will not allow them to come for thee, because thou art a Holy One in the presence of the Lord. I will not allow them to come for thee, because the Lord the Almighty has sent me to thee because thou art holy in His presence.' Then he beckoned to them, they then withdrew themselves back, they departed from me.

ST.AP.EL.A. 42.4(5)

2   ABBATON, THE ANGEL OF DEATH

THEMES

The setting up of Abbaton.
The experience of those about to die; the fear of death.
The effect of the presence of Christ at death.

EPISODES

The appointment of the Angel Mouriel as the Angel of Death; the designation of his attributes and his relation to mankind.
The seeing, by those about to die, of the powers of darkness; the decans with changing faces.
The entrance of Death to fetch the soul
The rebuking by Christ of the powers of darkness.

QUOTATIONS

1. Concerning the setting up of Abbaton, the Angel of Death,
   when our holy fathers the apostles asked the Saviour concerning him,
   so that they might preach him to all mankind, (   )
   the Saviour did not wish to disappoint them. (   )
   He informed them saying: 'The day on which my Father appointed him, (   )
   He made him king over the whole creation which he had created,
   because of the transgression of Adam and Eve.' (   )
   God made him fearful and terrifying as he comes after all souls
   until they give up their spirits in misery.

   BU.ABB.S. 225.5

2. My Father said to Mouriel the Angel:
   'Behold, the man whom I made in my likeness
   has transgressed the commandment which I gave him.
   He has eaten from the tree.

583

He has brought a great injury upon all mankind.
For this reason I shall make thee king over him
for it is thou who didst bring him to me on this day. ( )
Thy name shall be fearful in the mouth of everyone.
They shall call thee Abbaton, the Angel of Death.
Thy likeness and thy image shall be to all souls as an accusation with
*   anger and threatening*
until they give up their spirits.
Thy eyes and thy face will be like the wheels of fire
which raise waves upon waves before me.
The noise of thy nostrils shall be like the sound of the lake of flame
which burns with fire and sulphur.
The noise of the roar of thy lips shall be like the sound of the seven
*   thunders*
which will speak with their tongues.
Thy head shall be like a great pillar of fire which reaches from heaven
*   downwards.*
Thy teeth shall be half a cubit in length outside thy mouth.
The digits of thy hands and of thy feet shall be like sharp reaping
*   knives.*
Seven heads will be above thy head
and they will change their appearance and their forms.
And their teeth will be outside their mouths two palms in length
and they will look to the four sides of the earth.
Thou wilt be suspended in the midst
and thou shalt sit upon a throne of fire.
Thine eyes shall be looking at those below the earth, down to those
    in the water.
None shall be hidden from thee under heaven,
from end to end of the earth, from the North to the South,
from the East to the West
in the whole of the creation which I have created.
Not one of them shall give up his spirit alone but all will see thee.
Thou shalt be compassionate neither to small nor to great.
Thou shalt bear away all without sparing (any).
Powers shall be before thee
and thou shalt send them after every soul.
And they will remain causing terror to them
as they change their forms.
When the period of their lives is completed,
thou shalt appear and they shall see thee.
When they see thy face their souls will not remain in them for one hour

without giving up their spirits.
Thou shalt remain thus as king over them
until the fixed time which I have appointed for the world shall be
    completed.'

BU.ABB.S. 240.33

3. I have seen a multitude of men about to die asking from the men
    who surround them what is the hour.
This is because God commanded the light of their eyes and it was
    withdrawn.
Others cast about upon their couches, turning from side to side,
because of the changing faces which they see
and the fear of death which approached them,
thinking they will flee from the hands of the powers who have come
    for them
but they will not be able to flee from them
because their strength has left them and their souls groan on all sides:
'Alas, we do not see our fathers and our brothers and friends.'
When they come to die they do not wish to go and leave behind them
    this great light.
If they should see all these changing images they are terrified,
in that hour (they see) these faces of lions and of dragons and of birds
    and these changing faces.
In that hour (a man's) eyes turn to his wife and his son
and he does not wish to depart and leave them.
And they are troubled for the unfortunate soul.
No one knows its troubles except itself alone,
nor is anyone able to help it in the stress which lies upon it.
And the great death rattle arises from the throat like a saw,
which saws into him who is dying like wood which is sawn up.

AM.CYR.AL.B. 169.5

4. *Then I (Christ) looked to the South to the door.*
I saw Death, he came and following after him Amente,
who has been his counsellor and the wicked devil from the beginning.
A multitude of decans with changing faces followed after him
all wearing breastplates of fire, they being without number,
with sulphur and smoke of fire coming from their mouths.
My father Joseph looked, he saw those who had come for him,
they being full of great rage, as they are wont to be full of passion and
    anger
against all souls of men which come forth from the body,

585

especially sinners, if they find a sign of their own upon them. ( )
The soul of my father Joseph wished to come forth in great distress
and it sought for a place in which to hide and could not find a place.
When I saw the great trouble which met the soul of my father Joseph
and that he watched forms which were changing greatly, a fearful
    thing to see,
I rose then, *I rebuked those that were agents of the devil*
and the troops which followed him.
They fled in great shame. ( )
When Death saw *that I had rebuked the powers of darkness which*
    followed him and I cast them forth ( )
Death was afraid. He fled, he hid himself behind the door. ( )
I said a prayer to my Father,
while Mary my beloved mother made responses after me in the language
    of those of heaven.
When I had said the Amen,
immediately, behold Michael and Gabriel and the chorus of angels
    came forth from heaven.
They came and stood over the body of my father Joseph.
And then the death rattle and the distressed breathing overcame him
    fast
and I knew that the bitter time had come.
And he remained in travail like one who gives birth. ( )
Fear would not allow Death to approach the body of my beloved
    father Joseph to separate him,
because he looked in, he saw me sitting beside his head holding his
    temples. ( )
And then I said to him '*O thou who camest forth from the places of*
    the South,
go in now and fulfil that which my Father commanded thee,
but guard him like the light of thine eye,
because he is my father according to the flesh ( ).'
Then Abbaton entered in.

                                    TIL.JOS.Z.S. 277.1

5. *Then I looked towards the South, I saw Death.*
   He came before the house, while Amente followed after him,
   he who is his instrument with the devil,
   while there was a multitude of decans following him, wearing garments
   of fire;
   they were without number,
   while smoke and sulphur came forth from their mouths.

THE REPRESENTATION OF NEGATIVE EXPERIENCES

Then my father Joseph looked, he saw those who came for him,
full of anger towards him,
in the manner in which they are wont to burn with anger in their faces
towards every soul which comes forth from the body,
especially the sinners, in whom they will find a little of their
  own.
When the good old man saw them, Death being with them,
his eyes shed tears.
In that moment the soul of my father Joseph was torn with great
  groaning,
as it sought for a way of hiding in order to be saved.
When I saw the groaning of my father Joseph, because *he saw powers*
which he had never seen,
I rose immediately, *I rebuked the devil and all those with him.*
Then they went in shame and in great confusion.
And no man among those who sat around my father Joseph knew,
not even Maria, my mother,
concerning all the fearful hosts which come after the souls of men.
Then when Death saw that *I rebuked the powers of darkness,*
and that I sent them forth, and none of the powers had power over him,
he was afraid.
Then I rose immediately, I offered up a prayer to my Father,
Him of the many mercies, and I spoke saying:
'My Father and the Father of all mercies, the Father of Truth,
the Eye which sees, the Ear which hears,
Hear thy beloved Son, even Me, as I pray to thee, concerning the
  work of thy hands,
even my father Joseph,
that thou wilt send to me a great choir of angels with Michael, the
  steward of goodness,
and Gabriel, the bearer of good news of the Light,
that they may go with the soul of my father Joseph,
until it passes the seven aeons of darkness,
and also that it should not pass through the narrow ways,
these in which it is fearful to walk,
and it is a great fear to see the powers which are set over them,
while the River of Fire flows there, like the waves of the sea.
And be merciful to the soul of my father Joseph as he comes up to thy
  holy hands,
because this is the hour in which he has need of mercy.'
I say to you, my honoured brethren and my blessed apostles,
that every man who was born into this world,

who has known good and evil, who has spent all time attached to the
    things of his eyes,
has need of the mercy of my Good Father *when he comes to the hour*
    of death,
with the passing of the passage way, with the fearful tribunal,
and the making a defence.

LA.MOR.JOS.B. 23.7

6. Then in a moment and the twinkling of an eye, *he appeared,*
    whose name is bitter among all men, Death.
It happened that *when she saw him with her eyes, her soul leapt forth*
    from her body,
upon the bosom of her beloved Son, in the place where He was
    sitting,
for indeed He was sitting before us in the place which God the
    Logos occupied,
and He fills the Heaven and the Earth.
It happened that *when He took hold of the soul of His virgin mother,*
for it was white like snow,
He embraced it, He wrapped it in linen cloths,
He gave it into the hands of Michael, the holy Archangel,
He mounted it upon his wings of light,
until He provided for its holy body. ( )
Then David, the holy psalmist, struck his spiritual harp, he cried out
    saying:
'*Honoured indeed in the presence of the Lord is the death of his Holy*
    Ones.
Rejoice, O Maria, thou mother of Christ, the King of Kings.
This is the day on which are fulfilled the prophecies
which I spoke concerning thee, thou true Queen.'

LA.DOR.MAR.B. 55.22

7. *It happened when the Holy Virgin had said the Amen,*
    she mounted upon the linen cloths and the spices.
She turned her face to the East, she signed herself in the name
of the Father and the Son and the Holy Spirit,
she lay down.
And at that moment the Lord came to her,
mounted upon the Chariots of the Cherubim, while the angels went
    before Him.
He came, He stood before her.

He said to her: '*Fear not Death,* O my mother, while all life is before thee.

It is necessary for thee to see him with thine eyes alone.

Unless I command him, he will not be able to come to thee.'

And thus the King (   ) commanded him, saying:

'*Come thou who comest from the store-house of the South in the hidden place.*'

And immediately when the Virgin saw him her soul leapt into the arms of her Son.

He covered her with the heavenly garments.

It happened when she had given her spirit into the hands of God,

the apostles laid their hands on her eyes.

She slept a good sleep in the night, (   )

in the Peace of God, Amen.

ROB.VIR.S. 40.2

3   THE MEETING WITH THOSE OF HEAVEN

THEMES

The meeting with the Virgin, the patriarchs, the prophets, the martyrs, the saints and brethren.

The identification of those of heaven by the accompanying angel.

The greeting, embracing and blessing by those of Heaven.

EPISODES

The coming from afar of those who approach.

The coming forth of the Righteous to embrace.

The finding of those of heaven within the gates.

The recognition of the beauty of those of heaven.

QUOTATIONS

1. *I saw the Virgin coming,*
   with three angels singing hymns to her.
   I answered, *I said to the angel:* '*Who is this, my Lord?*'
   He said to me: '*This is Maria, the mother of our Lord Jesus Christ*
   who is in this great glory.'
   And when she had approached me,
   she said to me: '*Greeting Paul, thou beloved one of God.*
   Greeting Paul, beloved by angels and men.
   Greeting Paul, who was a herald of the Truth
   in heaven and upon the earth.'

BU.AP.PAUL.S. 551.16

2. *And while the Virgin was speaking with me,*
   behold three other (men) came from afar
   and they were very beautiful in their appearance,
   and their angels were singing hymns to them.
   I said to the angel: 'Who are these my Lord who rejoiced with me
      when they saw me?'
   (The angel) said (to me): 'Dost thou not recognize them O Paul?'
   I said 'No my Lord'.
   (The angel) said to me: 'These are the fathers of the people, Abraham
      and Isaac and Jacob.'
   Immediately when they saw me they embraced me,
   they said to me: 'Greeting, Paul thou beloved of God and Man.'

   BU.AP.PAUL.S. 552.23

3. *While these ones were speaking*
   I looked afar, I saw twelve others coming.
   I said to the angel: 'Who are these, my Lord?'
   He said to me: 'These are the patriarchs.'
   Immediately they reached me they embraced me
   and they said to me: 'Greeting Paul, thou beloved of God and men.
   God has not disappointed us.
   But He has caused us to see thee in the flesh,
   before thou hast come forth from the body.'
   And each one repeated his name to me from Reuben to Benjamin.

   BU.AP.PAUL.S. 553.10

4. *While this man was speaking with me*
   I looked afar off, I saw another one
   whose angel was singing to him.
   I said to the angel: 'Who is this
   who is beautiful in his appearance?'
   He said to me: 'Dost thou not know this (man)?'
   I said to him: 'No my Lord.' *He said to me: 'This is Moses the*
      Law-giver,
   to whom God gave the Law.'
   And when he reached me he embraced me.
   He wept. I said to him: 'Why art thou weeping? I have heard that
   thou art the most compassionate of all men who are upon the earth.'

   BU.AP.PAUL.S. 553.26

5. *While this one was speaking, behold another twelve came from afar.*
   And when they reached me they said to me:

'Thou art Paul, the beloved of God.
Truly thou hast received glory in heaven and upon earth.'
I said to them: 'Who are you?'
They said: 'We are the prophets.'

BU.AP.PAUL.S. 554.20

6. While these were speaking with me,
   another one came to me
   who was very beautiful in his appearance.
   I said to the angel: 'Who is this my Lord, who when he saw me, he
   *   rejoiced?'*
   The angel said to me: 'This is Lot (   ).'
   And when he reached me he said as he embraced me:
   'Blessed art thou Paul and blessed is thy generation.'
   He said to me: 'I am Lot,'

BU.AP.PAUL.S. 555.5

7. While this one was speaking with me
   I saw another coming from afar
   who was very beautiful.
   And his face gave light and he was smiling,
   while the angels sang hymns to him.
   I said to the angel: 'Does an angel walk with each one of the Right-
   *   eous?'*
   He said to me: 'Their angels all sing hymns to them
   and they never leave them at any time.'
   And when he reached me he greeted me, he said to me:
   'Thou art honoured O Paul, thou beloved of God and men.
   I am Job.'

BU.AP.PAUL.S. 555.23

8. *While this one was speaking,*
   Enoch also came,
   he greeted me,
   he said: *'Because of the suffering which a man receives for the sake*
   *   of God,*
   God will not afflict him when he goes forth from the world.'
   While this one was speaking with me, behold two others came together.
   And another one walked behind them and was calling to them:
   'Stand (still) for me so that I may come and see Paul, the beloved of
   *   God,*
   Who has been cast up for us so that *we see him while he is in the*
   *   body.'*

I said to the angel: 'Who are these?'
He said to me: 'This is Zacharias and John his son.'
I said to the angel: 'Who is this other one who runs behind them?'
He said: 'This is Abel, whom Cain slew.'
And they greeted me, they said to me: 'Blessed art thou O Paul who
art upright in all thy works.'

BU.AP.PAUL.S. 566.25

9. *And the Righteous and all the angels surrounded me*
and they rejoiced with me (because) they had seen me in the flesh.
I looked, I saw another one who was taller than them all,
who was very beautiful.
I said to the angel: 'Who is this my Lord?'
He said to me: 'This is Adam, the father of you all.'
When he reached me he embraced me with joy,
he said to me: 'Be strong, O Paul, thou beloved of God.'

BU.AP.PAUL.S. 567.16

10. *He took me also to the River of Milk*
which is to the South of the City.
I found all the little children whom Herod killed because of the name
of Christ.
They all embraced me. ( )
He (the angel) took me to the River of Wine.
which is to the East of the City.
I found Abraham and Isaac and Jacob
and they embraced me.
I said to the angel: 'Who are these?'
He said to me: 'All men who love strangers, when they go forth from
the body,
they go to the foot of God and worship Him
and He gives them into the hand of Michael
and he takes them into the City.
And all the Righteous ones embrace them on the road saying: "( )
Come and inherit the City of the Lord our God."
Each of them finds men *like themselves in the City of Christ Jesus,*
Jerusalem, according to their works.'

BU.AP.PAUL.S. 534.20

11. *Then I went with the angel,*
he took me to the Third Heaven.
He stood me by a gate.

I saw that the gate was entirely of gold.
I saw two columns of gold before the gate
and there were plaques of gold upon the columns full of writing.
The angel turned to me, he said to me: ' Blessed art thou O Paul when
    thou shalt be taken within this gate.
It is not given to all to go within it. (   )'
I said to the angel: ' Who are those (whose names are) written on the
    plaques?'
He said: ' These are the names of all the Righteous
who serve God with their whole heart.'
I said to the angel: ' My Lord are their names in heaven
before they indeed come forth from this world?'
The angel answered, he said to me: 'Not only are their names alone
    in heaven, but the form also
of those who serve God with their whole heart.
And the angels recognise him,
that this is a man who serves God with his whole heart,
before he comes forth from the world.'
And immediately the gate was opened.
Behold an old man, whose face gave light like the sun,
approached me saying: ' Greeting Paul, beloved of God.'
And he smiled and kissed me.
Afterwards he ceased to smile, he wept, (   )
saying: 'I am distressed because of this name "Man" (   )'.
I said to the angel: ' Who is this my Lord?'
The angel answered, he said to me: ' This is Enoch, the Scribe of
    Righteousness.'
At that moment in which I entered that place I saw also Helias.
He came, he embraced me, he smiled.
Afterwards he also ceased to smile, he wept.

BU.AP.PAUL.S. 560.16

12. *And the angel led me to the River of Honey*
    which is to the West of the City.
    I found Isaiah within the gate
    with Jeremiah and Ezekiel and Amos and Micah
    and the Lesser and the Greater Prophets.
    They embraced me within the City.
    I said to the angel: ' Who are these, my Lord?'
    He said to me: ' This is the road of the prophets.
    Every man (   ) when he comes forth from the body
    he goes to the feet of God and worships Him.

He is given into the hand of Michael
and taken into this City
so that the prophets embrace him.'

BU.AP.PAUL.S. 566.3

13. *After these things, the angel took me up to the heavens.*
I saw my father Abraham, I worshipped him
and he greeted me with all the Holy Ones.
They were all gathered, they honoured me because of my father.

GUI.IS.B. 238.20

14. And he raised me up into the seventh heaven, and I saw there a wonderful light and angels innumerable.

And there I saw all the righteous from the time of Adam.

And there I saw the holy Abel and all the righteous.

And there I saw Enoch and all who were with him, stript of the garments of the flesh, and I saw them in their garments of the upper world, and they were like angels, standing there in great glory.

CH.ASC.IS.E. 60(IX)

II AMENTE

1 THE TORMENTS

THEMES

The journeying with the accompanying angel to the North of the Paradise of Delight; beyond the Ocean.

The identifying by the angel of the places and punishments of Amente.

EPISODES

The describing of the darkness, smoke, oppressiveness, evil smell, of Amente.

The seeing of the pits, lakes, cisterns, rivers, canals, valleys, houses, wheels of fire.

The enumeration of the dimensions of the places of torment.

The seeing of places of snow and ice; pitch and sulphur; excrement.

The seeing of animal forms, animal faces; those attacked by animals; those eaten by animals.

The seeing of souls in the torments; immersed in the pits, rivers; weeping.

The tormenting of the souls by the pitiless angels; the seeing of angels with whips, spears, knives of fire in their hands.

The seeing of the Angel of Tartarus, Abtelmolochus, who is set over
   the punishments.
The destruction of the memory of those cast into the pit.

QUOTATIONS

1. *It happened one day*
   that the Lord sent a vision to our father Pachomius
   and as he looked he saw the form of Amente which was dark and
      oppressive.
   And there was a column standing in the centre
   and there were voices within on all sides, crying out
   and saying: 'Behold the light here beside us.'
   The men who were in that place were groping
   because great was the darkness and oppression there
   and it was very fearful.
   It happened also when they heard: 'Behold the light by us.'
   that they ran there seeking the light and wishing to see it.
   While they were running forwards, they would hear another voice
      behind them:
   'Behold the light is here.'
   And they would turn back immediately,
   because of the voices which they heard, seeking after the light.
   He also saw in the vision some who were in the darkness as if going
      round a column,
   thinking they were going forwards and approaching the light.
   They did not know that is was a column round which they
      went.
   And he looked, he saw the whole community of the congregation in
      that place
   walking one by one,
   holding one another lest they go astray,
   because of the great darkness there.
   Those who led them *had a small light lighting them like the light of a*
      lamp
   and four men alone of the brothers saw that light.
   All the rest saw no light at all.
   Our father Pachomius watched the manner in which they
      walked.
   When one ceased to hold the one in front of him,
   he would stray in the darkness with all those who followed him. (   )
   The small light which led the brothers
   led them until they reached a great air-hole,

with a great light above it,
they came up out of it.

LE.PAC.B. 130.27

2. Of how Enoch was taken on to the second heaven.

And those men took me and led me up on to the heaven, and showed me darkness, greater than earthly darkness, and there I saw prisoners hanging, watching, awaiting the great and boundless judgment, and these angels were dark-looking, more than earthly darkness, and incessantly making weeping through all hours, and I said to the men who were with me: 'Wherefore are these incessantly tortured?' They answered me: 'These are God's apostates, who obeyed not God's commands, but took counsel with their own will, and turned away with their prince, who also is fastened on the fifth heaven.'

CH.EN.II.SL. 433.A(7)

3. Here they showed Enoch the terrible place and various tortures.

And those two men led me up to the Northern side, and showed me there a very terrible place, and there were all manner of tortures in that place: cruel darkness and unillumined gloom, and there is no light there, but murky fire constantly flameth forth, and there is a fiery river coming forth, and that whole place is everywhere fire, and everywhere there is frost and ice, thirst and shivering, while the bonds are very cruel, and the angels fearful and merciless, bearing angry weapons, merciless torture, and I said: 'Woe, woe, how very terrible is this place,' and those men said to me: 'This place, O Enoch, is prepared for those who dishonour God, ( ) for all these is prepared this place amongst these, for eternal inheritance.'

CH.EN.II.SL. 435.A(10)

4. *It happened one day that, by the command of the Lord,*
our father Pachomius was taken so that he should visit the punishments
and tortures with which men are tormented.
Whether he was taken in the body or out of the body,
as has been said before, God knows.
When he was taken, he was brought to the North of the Paradise of
    Delight,
far from this world and the Firmament.
He saw rivers, canals and valleys full of fire
in which were the souls of sinners being tormented.
And while he walked with the angel, he was inspecting the punish-
    ments. ( )

They groaned bitterly *and they were not able to cry out with their voices because of their weakness.* (   )

And the souls who were being tormented were without number, being very numerous.

He saw also pits and cisterns full of fire, their heat being very great. (   )

*the angels who were in charge of these torments

were in great joy and gladness. (   )

They also rejoiced because the Lord has created them pitiless

so that they have no pity at all for the souls of the impious. (   )

And if the souls beg them for mercy, they are full of anger and torment them.

LEC.PAC.S. 158b.32; *161a.11

5. *It happened one day that by the command of God,*

> *our father Pachomius was taken away to see the punishments and tortures*

with which the sons of men are tormented.

Whether in the body or out of the body he was removed, God knows.

When he was taken to the North of the Paradise of Joy

far from this world and the Firmament,

he saw rivers and canals and cisterns filled with fire

in which the souls of sinners were being tormented.

And while he walked with the angel, looking at the punishments,

he saw those, above whom he came, suffering more than those he had seen at first.

Tormenting angels, of terrifying appearance, were in charge of them.

And there were whips of fire in their hands. (   )

They groaned with difficulty, they were not able to cry out with their voices because of their weakness. (   )

The souls which were being tormented were without number, and very many.

He saw also pits and cisterns filled with fire, their fire being great in its heat. (   )

The tormenting angels were in great joy and gladness. (   )

They also rejoiced thus because the Lord has created them pitiless (   ).

As he walked a little further on he saw a multitude of souls of all ages, without number,

driven in confusion by the tormenting angels without pity.

And when he asked again about them from the angel who walked with him,

the angel said to him: 'These are the souls of the sinners

who have died today in the whole world
and they are assigned to one or other of the punishments according to
their worth.'
When he walked with the angel towards the West, with the angel
who walked with him and showed him the punishments,
he saw a door below which was over the gate of Amente.
Amente itself was very deep and dark and gave heat like a fire.
For that place is the prison of the Lord.
And whenever men were brought and cast down into it, they cried out
loudly ( ).
Then they were not able to speak at all,
because of the heat and the great darkness of that place.
And they did not recognise one another
because of the darkness and the constraint which prevails over them.
As he walked further to the South side of the West
he saw further severe punishments in that place
like those he had seen before on the North side
in which were souls who were being tormented.
He was also shown a form of a large house of stones
of which the length and breadth and height were very great.
That house was filled with fire

LE.PAC.B. 97.10

6. *And when I came beyond the Ocean*
I saw nothing in that place
except sorrow and groaning and sorrow of heart
and obscurity and darkness and mist and destruction.
Then I ( ) looked, I saw a great field of scorching heat,
terrifying to behold.
And it was pitted and dug with holes.
There was a pit dug to a depth of a hundred cubits,
there was a pit dug to a depth of fifty cubits,
there was a pit dug to a depth of thirty cubits,
there was a pit dug to a depth of twenty cubits.
There was a pit dug down to the boundaries of the abyss.
There was a pit which was full of dragons,
there was a pit which was full of ice,
there was a pit which was full of pitch and sulphur
which boiled up, like a cauldron,
and a lump was hurled up to the height of thirty cubits.
There was a pit which was filled with worms
which stank greatly.

THE REPRESENTATION OF NEGATIVE EXPERIENCES

There was a pit which was filled with waters which were fearful.
There was a pit which was filled with fire,
whose flame was of the colour of the leek.
There was a pit whose smoke went up to the Firmament.
There was a pit over which were a hundred decans. (   )
I saw a great River of Fire throwing up many waves.
There was a multitude of men and women submerged in it.
Some were submerged to their knees,
others to their waists,
some to their lips,
others to their hair.

BU.AP.PAUL.S. 538.8

7. *To the West also of this River of Fire*
   there was (a place) of various punishments,
   which was filled with men and women.
   And the River of Fire flowed over them. (   )
   I saw pits which went down for thrice ten thousand cubits,
   (filled with) souls upon souls,
   generations upon generations.
   For they were all groaning and weeping,
   saying: 'Have mercy upon us O Lord.'
   But no mercy at all was (given) to them.

BU.AP.PAUL.S. 539.17

8. *Then I looked upon the River of Fire.*
   I saw an old man who was brought, dragging him
   and he was immersed to his knees.
   The angel Abtelmolochus came with a great spear of fire
   which had three prongs.
   He brought forth his entrails through his mouth. (   )
   I saw an old man whom four Angels of Wrath were also bringing,
      running with him.
   They immersed him to his knees in the River of Fire
   while flashes of fire struck his face
   like whirl-winds.
   He was not allowed to say 'Have mercy upon me' at all. (   )
   And again I looked to my side, at the River of Fire.
   I saw another man who was immersed to his knees,
   while his hands were stained with blood
   and worms crept out of his mouth and nostrils.
   And he groaned and wept.

BU.AP.PAUL.S. 540.8

9. *I looked again to my side upon the River of Fire.*
I saw one whom they were bringing with them.
They immersed him in the River of Fire to his lips.
A pitiless angel came with a knife of fire.
He cut off his tongue and his lips little by little.
Then I groaned and I wept. ( )
Then again I looked, I saw pits by the River of Fire.
There were men and women immersed within them.
And the worms were eating them
and they were groaning and weeping.
But I wept and I groaned. ( )
Again ( ) *I looked to another place of scorching heat which was very*
far off.
There were other men and women in it gnawing their tongues.

BU.AP.PAUL.S. 541.14

10. *I looked again, I saw men and women with their hands and their feet*
cut off
down in a place of ice.
And worms were eating them.
I groaned and I wept.

BU.AP.PAUL.S. 542.32

11. *I looked again I saw others* ( ) *and their tongues were dry with thirst*
and they were not allowed to drink.
There were fruits from trees set before them
and they were not allowed to eat of them. ( )
I saw other men and other women ( ) *and great torches of fire burned*
before their faces,
and dragon-serpents wound round their bodies devouring them. ( )
I ( ) *saw again other men and other women* pierced with spits of fire.
They were wearing black garments
and they were blind
and they were going down into a single pit which was filled with fire. ( )
I also saw some other men and other women stretched upon spits of
fire
while wild beasts of prey were eating their entrails.
They were not allowed to say 'Have mercy on us' at all.
The angel who was over the punishments, Abtelmolochus, rebuked them.

BU.AP.PAUL.S. 543.6

12. *I looked again I saw (other) men and other women wearing pieces of*
sack cloth

THE REPRESENTATION OF NEGATIVE EXPERIENCES

filled with sulphur and pitch.
And serpents of fire were coiled round their necks
and their hands and their feet.
And pitiless angels were dragging them,
having horns of fire upon their heads,
and they pierced them.

BU.AP.PAUL.S. 544.25

13. *Then he took me to the West of all the punishments.*
He took me above the Pit of the Abyss.
I found it sealed with seven seals of fire.
The angel who walked with me said
to him who was over the Pit of the Abyss:
'Open the Pit so that Paul the beloved of God may see it,
for he is permitted to see everything which he seeks
which exists in the punishments.' ( )
Immediately he uncovered the Pit of the Abyss.
A great evil-smelling smoke rose up from the Pit ( ).
I looked down into it.
I found it bringing forth lumps of fire
which were burning on all sides.
And one man with difficulty scarcely went down into it.
The angel said to me: 'When a man is cast down into this Pit
and its mouth is sealed,
the memory of him never comes up to the presence
of the Father and the Son and the Holy Spirit with all the angels.'

BU.AP.PAUL.S. 545.33

14. *And each worm was of the length of one cubit*
and it had two heads.
I saw (other) men and other women who were in cold and ice,
with gnashing of teeth.
I said to the angel: 'My Lord who are these who are in these places of
suffering?' ( )
'Is there no heat in this place?' ( )
The angel said to me: 'If seven suns were to rise upon them
they would not become warm because of the ice which is upon them.'

BU.AP.PAUL.S. 546.25

15. *Now when the multitude who were gathered to him had heard these*
things,
they cried out all together in a loud voice. ( )

THE CULT OF THE SEER IN THE ANCIENT MIDDLE EAST

Then the God-loving old man became silent,
he drew up the robe, he covered his face. ( )
But the Angel of his father came to him, he took him up to the heavens.
And in fear and consternation he saw multitudes divided to this side
    and that
after the manner of the Last Day
and it was a great consternation to see them.
Some had faces of camels, others had faces of lions
and hyenas and leopards,
others had faces of dogs, others had one eye. ( )
And behold they brought one after whom they were pursuing. ( )
The lions advanced to him, they tore him in halves,
they rent him limb from limb,
they chewed him, they swallowed him,
afterwards they cast him up
and he became like himself again.
And they who came after the lions did thus again (to him).
In short they gave him into the hands of one another.
Each one would chew him and swallow him
and cast him up
and he became himself again each time. ( )
The angel said to me: '( ) *Behold, he was given into the hands of*
    five tormentors.
They spend a year tormenting him each for an hour at a time. ( )'
The angel said to me again: '( ) *There are seventy thousand tor-*
    mentors there. ( )'
He led me further to a River of Fire,
I saw that it was in waves, its waves being thirty cubits high.
And its sound was like the thunder of heaven.
I saw a multitude of souls immersed in it nine cubits (deep),
they who were in that river were crying out and weeping with a loud
    voice and great groans.
(The river) did not afflict the righteous, but the sinners.
These it burnt, knowing them
because of the great evil smell which surrounds them.
I saw the Pit of the Abyss whose smoke rose exceedingly high.
I saw a multitude of men who were cast down therein,
crying out and weeping, each one with his groaning.
The angel said to me: 'Look down and see these others.' ( )
He said to me: '*These who are plunged down into the cold,* ( )
they are afflicted greatly.'
I saw another pit, filled with worms which do not sleep and snakes,

while men were immersed in it,
crying out and weeping.
I saw further Abtelmolochus, him who is set over the punishments
and he was completely on fire,
striking the tormentors of Amente,
saying to them: 'Strike them, that they may know that God exists.'
I saw further another pit, completely of fire
and there was a multitude of men in it,
crying out and weeping, every one with his groaning.

GUI.IS.B. 235.18

16. (   ) *a lake which was very fearful,*
and that lake was in the midst of lakes
and the depth and the breadth were greater than that of all the pits.
I heard many voices within it
which were like the sound of many waters.
I asked the angel who walked with me:
'My Lord what is the purpose of this pit which I have seen?
There comes up from it a great smoke of fire
so that the flaming smoke goes up for a distance of three hundred
   stadia.
I have seen lions of fire (leaping)
with dragons of fire,
with snakes, with basilisks, the bear of fire and the worm which does
   not sleep, leaping in it,
in the form of female serpents,
and the wheel of fire in which thousands and tens of thousands of fiery
   lightnings were leaping
and coming down to the chaos of Tartarus which burns with fire.'
The angel said to me: '(   ) *Thou has seen the punishment*
which is more terrifying than all punishments.'

BU.M.TIM.S. 513.23

17. There came to me then a great angel, with a trumpet of gold in his
hand, he blew it up to heaven, the heaven opened from the place of
rising of the sun to its place of setting, from the north to the south.

   I saw the sea which I had seen below in Amente, its waves rose up
as far as the clouds. I saw all the souls who were immersed in it.
I saw some who were bound with their hands to their necks, who
were fettered hand and foot.

   I said: 'Who are these?' He said to me: 'These are they who are
wont to (corrupt). They give gold and silver to them until they cause
the souls of men to stray.' (   )

Then I also saw others, on whom was their hair. I said: 'Are there hair and bodies in this place?' He said: 'Yes. The Lord is wont to give bodies and hair to them as he pleases.'

ST.AP.EL.A. 58.14(14)

18. And she began to say: 'A man received me, hateful of countenance, entirely black, and his clothing exceedingly dirty. And he led me to a place in which there were many chasms, and much ill odour and a hateful vapour was given off thence. And he made me look down into each chasm, and I saw in the (first) chasm a flaming fire, and wheels of fire were running (hither and) thither, and souls were hung upon those wheels, dashed against each other. And there was a cry there and a very great lamentation, but there was none to deliver. And that man said to me: "These souls are kindred to thee, and in the days of reckoning they were delivered for punishment and destruction. And then (when the chastisement of each is ended) others are brought in their stead, and likewise these to another (chasm)."'

WIL.II.THOM.G. 473

19. But I saw also another place, opposite that one, very gloomy; and this was the place of punishment, and those who were punished there and the angels who punished had dark raiment, clothed according to the air of the place.

And some there were there hanging by their tongues: these were those who had blasphemed the way of righteousness: and under them was laid fire, blazing and tormenting them. And there was a great lake full of burning mire in which were fixed certain men who had turned away from righteousness, and tormenting angels were placed over them.

WIL.II.PET.G. 672

20. And there were also others there: women hanging by their hair over that boiling mire. These were they who had adorned themselves for adultery. (   )

And I saw the murderers and their accessories cast into a gorge full of venomous reptiles and tormented by those beasts and thus writhing in that torture, and worms oppressed them like dark clouds.

WIL.II.PET.G. 673

21. And near that place I saw another gorge in which the discharge and excrement of the tortured ran down and became like a lake. And

there sat women and the discharge came up to their throats; and opposite them sat many children, who were born prematurely, weeping.

WIL.II.PET.G. 674

2 THE REMISSION OF PUNISHMENTS

THEMES

The receiving of a remission by those in Amente who were worthy to see Christ when He was in this world.

The receiving of a remission by those in Amente as a result of the intervention of the Archangel Michael.

The receiving of a remission by those in Amente as a result of prayers of holy men.

The receiving of a remission of punishment by pagans in Amente as a result of baptism by holy men.

The bringing by Christ to those in Amente of a remission on the Lord's Day and on the Fifty Days after Easter.

EPISODES

The finding and raising from the dead of a corpse, a skull, who speaks of his experiences in Amente.

The interceding by Michael for those in Amente; the raising of those in Amente by Michael upon his wing.

The finding and raising from the dead of the corpses of pagans; their baptism by holy men.

QUOTATIONS

1. *It happened then while our father Apa Shenute was walking in the desert,*
   behold the Lord Jesus appeared to him,
   He spoke with him.
   As they were walking with one another
   they came upon a dead man who was cast out upon the mountain.
   Our father Apa Shenute cast himself down,
   he worshipped the Lord, saying: 'My Lord and my God,
   behold for many years now I have passed this dead man,
   I did not know his province or who he is, cast out in this place.'
   Then our Lord, Jesus Christ moved the dead man with His foot,
   saying: 'I say to thee, O dead man, be restored, rise up
   and *tell my servant Shenute who thou art, in this state.'*
   And at that moment the dead man rose,
   like one rising from sleep.

When he saw the Lord, he knew Him, he worshipped Him. ( )
The dead man answered, '( ) I was working with some men. *We
    rose.*
We came to the South ( ).
At the end of a few days *I became ill, I died;*
they brought me to this place,
they cast me forth because I was not related to them.'
My father Apa Shenute said to him: '*Did the Saviour come into the
    world at that time?*'
He said 'Yes, the news spread, coming to the South to us,
through those who passed, that a woman came to the city of Schmoun
with a small son in her arms.
Everything which He said came to pass,
He would raise the dead,
He would cast out demons,
He would cause the lame to walk,
He would make the deaf to hear,
He would make the dumb to speak,
He would cause the lepers to be cleansed. ( )'
When the dead man had said these things he cast himself down,
he worshipped the Saviour, and he begged Him
saying: '*Let thy mercy be upon me*
that thou dost not allow me to be cast again to the punishments. ( )'
The Lord said to him: '*Because thou wast worthy*
to see me in this world with my servant Shenute
I will give thee a small respite.
Therefore sleep now
*and the mercy be to thee that thou rest until the day of the Judgment
    of Truth.*'
At that moment the dead man fell asleep as he had been before.
The Saviour took the hand of my father Apa Shenute.
He walked with him to the cell which is in the desert.
And they were speaking together of great mysteries.
Afterwards He went up to the heavens
while the angels sang hymns before Him.

LEI.SIN.B. 66.29

2. It happened one day that my father and I were in the mountain of
    Gemi.
    My father said to me: 'John my son *rise and follow me*
    and I will show thee the place where I will make my retreat,
    so that thou shalt visit me every Sabbath

THE REPRESENTATION OF NEGATIVE EXPERIENCES

and bring me a little food and a little water to drink
for the maintenance of this body.'
My father rose, he walked ahead of me
meditating on the holy Scriptures inspired by God.
When we had walked about three miles as it seemed to me
we came upon an entrance which was in the form of a door-way
    widely open.
When we went into that place we found it was in the form of carved
    stone
and there were six columns rising from the rock, ( )
and there were the bodies of many corpses laid within it ( ).
*I then sat and listened to my father
while the corpse spoke with him.
My father said to the corpse: 'From what province art thou?'
He said: 'I am from the city of Ermant.'
My father said to him: 'Who is thy father?'
He said: 'Agricolaos is my father and Eustathia is my mother.'
My father said to him: 'Whom do they worship?'
He said: 'They worship him who is in the waters, namely Poseidon.'
My father said to him: '*Didst thou not hear before thou didst die*
that Christ came to the world?'
He said: 'No my father, but my parents were Greek. ( )
It happened to me, *when I came to the necessity of death,*
the first to come were the Cosmocrators who surrounded me.
They told all the evil things which I had done
and they said to me: "*Let (thy gods) come and save thee now*
from the punishments into which thou wilt be cast."
They had spears of iron in their hands
with points of iron which were sharp like spears.
They pierced my ribs with them
as they gnashed their teeth at me.
After a little time my eyes opened,
I saw Death hanging in the air in many forms.
At that moment the pitiless angels brought my wretched soul out of my
    body.
They bound it below a black spirit-horse,
they dragged me to the West ( ).
O my lord father *I was given into the hands of so many pitiless tor-*
    mentors
who changed shape with one another.
O how many wild animals I saw on the way.
O how many powers of torment.

THE CULT OF THE SEER IN THE ANCIENT MIDDLE EAST

When I was cast to the outer darkness,
I saw a great place which was more than two hundred cubits deep,
and it was filled with reptiles.
Each one of them had seven heads
and their bodies were all like scorpions.
There were some great worms in that place
which were very large and terrifying to see,
with teeth in (its) mouth in the form of iron tusks.
They took me and cast me down to that worm,
which never ceased from eating me at all times,
while all the wild beasts surrounded it,
it filled its mouth,
while all the animals which surrounded me also filled their mouths.'
My father said to him: 'Since thou died until today
wast thou not given any rest
or did they leave thee a little time without troubling thee?'
The corpse said: 'Yes my father,
they are wont to have mercy on all those in punishment on the Sabbath
 and the Lord's day.
When the Lord's day is ended they cast us again to the punishments
 as we were,
lest we forget our years which we spent on the earth.
When we have forgotten the pain of these punishments they cast us
 into others which are worse.
But when thou didst pray for me,
immediately the Lord commanded those who were beating me,
they drew from my mouth the hook of iron which was in my mouth.
They released me.
I came to thee.
Behold I have told thee those things which I have received in
 there.
O my Lord and father, *pray for me that they give me a little rest,*
and that they do not take me there again.'
My father said to him: 'The Lord is compassionate, he will show
 mercy to thee.
Return and sleep until the day of the Resurrection of the People
so that thou wilt also rise with all those who rise.' ( )
I saw the corpse with my eyes lie down to rest in his place as he was
 before.
Then I, when I saw these things, marvelled greatly and gave glory to
 God.

                                   AM.PIS.KE.B. 401.9; *406.10

THE REPRESENTATION OF NEGATIVE EXPERIENCES

3. *At that moment the holy Apa Macarius cried out* (to the dead man)

*saying: 'In the name of the Father and the Son and the Holy Spirit,
 rise and stand.'*

And immediately his wrappings fell off him *and he rose,*

he walked, alive while everyone watched him.

When he saw the saint Apa Macarius

he cast himself down at his feet, he worshipped him,

*he said to him: 'O blessed art thou, O thou holy one, Apa Maca-
 rius. (   )*

Thou has saved a sinful soul from Amente today.

By thy salvation, O our lord Apa Macarius

these six hours which I have spent *since I left the body* were worse
 for me

than my whole time which I spent upon the earth.

O my Lord, *I am indeed a man who worshipped idols*

and *as I was about to die there came after me decans*

with faces and forms changing into one another.

Some had faces of wild beasts,

some had faces of dragons, some had faces of lions,

some had faces of crocodiles, some had faces of bears.

And they tore my soul out of my body with great mercilessness.

They ran with it upon a great River of Fire.

They plunged me in it four hundred cubits

and they took me,

they stood me in the presence of the Judge of Truth.

And I heard a judgment which came forth from Him

saying: "*Remove this soul from me* which has made these demons
 into gods for itself

and it has denied God who made it.

Let it know now that God is in the highest."

After these things they ran with me to a place of darkness,

in which there was no light,

they cast me into the frost and the grinding of teeth.

I saw in that place the worm which does not sleep,

whose head was like a crocodile,

with all the reptiles around him.

They cast the souls in front of him.

When he had filled his mouth with them,

he caused all the wild beasts to eat also

and they tore us but we did not die.

Afterwards they removed me from that place

to take me to Amente for ever.
As they were dragging me, I heard a voice behind me
saying: "Return him,
verily, he must be returned to the earth again
because of the prayers of the saint Apa Macarius the Anatolian."
They brought my soul again
and they put it into my body.
Behold, what happened to me in Amente I have told thee,
   O my lord and father.
Now I beg thee, let thy mercy reach me; give me the seal of the
   Christians
so that I be not cast to those punishments again.'

HY.MAC.AN.B. 55.13

4. It was said of Apa Macarius
   that as he was once walking in the desert
   he found a skull. He moved it with his staff.
   It spoke.
   The old man said to him; 'Who art thou ?'
   He said to him: 'I am the Chief Priest of the Greeks who were in this
      place.
   And thou art Macarius the bearer of the Spirit.
   Every time that thou art compassionate towards those in the
      punishments they have a little respite.'
   Apa Macarius said to him: 'How great is the respite?'
   He said: 'As far as heaven is from the earth
   is the distance that the fire is below us and above us.
   While we stand in the midst of the fire,
   it is not possible for each one to see the face of him who is before
      him,
   but back is joined to back.
   At the time when thou dost pray for us,
   in part does each one see the face of his neighbour.'
   The old man listened. (   )
   After this the old man took the skull, he dug in the earth.
   He buried it and departed.

CHA.AP.PA.S. 66.5(226)

5. It was said of Abba Macarius, the Great,
   that once as he was walking in the mountain
   he saw a head of a dead man upon the mountain.
   He moved the head. It answered him.

610

The old man said to it: 'Who art thou who speakest to me thus?'
The skull said to him: 'I was a Greek in the time of the heathens,
I was released to speak with thee.'
The old man said: 'And I, who am I?'
The skull said to him: 'Thou art Abba Macarius, the spirit-bearing
one.'
The old man said to him: 'Art thou at rest or art thou in torment?'
The skull said to him: 'I am in the torments.' The old man said to
him: 'How are the torments?'
The skull said to him: 'As heaven is high over the earth,
in the same way *a River of Fire is above our heads boiling*
and it is below us throwing up waves below our feet.
We stand in the midst of it,
and no face sees a face before it,
but our backs are joined to one another.
At the time then, when a great prayer is made for us,
a little respite is given to us.'
The old man said to him: 'What is the respite?'
The skull said to him: 'For the twinkling of an eye we see the face
of one another.'
When the old man heard this he cried out, he wept.

AM.AP.MAC.B. 225.9

6. And the Archangel Michael has acted in this manner
since the Resurrection of Our Saviour to this day.
And moreover he will not cease to do this on every twelfth day of
Paone
until the consummation of this aeon.
Afterwards he takes them to (their) places,
each one according to his merit.
Then Michael goes within the Veil on the same day
and casts himself down at the feet of the Father and worships Him.
And he does not rise up until the Father has received his supplication
and has provided for the means of life for men and beasts
and for the water of the river.
For the angels who are over the powers of the earth
are all gathered together on the twelfth day of Paone outside the Veil
until the Archangel Michael comes forth
from inside the Veil.
At the moment that they see his face
and the manner of robes which the Father of Goodness has put
upon him,

immediately the angels who are over the affairs of the earth
know what ( ) will happen upon the earth.
(They know) by the manner of robes which Michael is wearing.
And the angels rejoice with great joy,
on behalf of all mankind, upon whom God the Father has had
compassion
through the supplications of the merciful Michael
and he has provided their means of life
and has caused the rising (of the river) to happen for men and beasts.

BU.M.TIM.S. 518.3

7. *I saw the heavens opening.*
I saw Michael the Archangel of the Covenant.
He came forth from heaven
with all the host of angels.
All the angels prostrated themselves upon their faces.
All those who were in the punishments saw them and they wept.
They said to him: '*Have mercy upon us, O Archangel of the Cove-*
nant ( ).
The world is at peace because of thee O Michael.'

BU.AP.PAUL.S. 547.11

8. *Then Michael with myriads of angels prostrated himself in the*
presence of God
saying: '*Have mercy upon thy Creation.*
Have mercy upon thine Image.
Have mercy upon the sons of Adam.'
I looked, I saw the heaven shake like a tree which is moved by the
wind.
And when they had cast themselves down before the throne of God,
I saw the Four and Twenty Elders and the Four Beasts
as they cast themselves down.
I saw the Altar and the Veil
as they cast themselves down.
I heard a voice. ( ) *I saw heaven opened.*
The Son of God came forth from heaven
with a diadem upon his head.
Those in the punishments saw him.
They cried out saying: '*Have mercy on us, O Son of the Living God.*
Thou hast given rest to those of heaven and those upon earth.
Give rest to us also,
since from the time when we saw thee, respite has reached us.'

612

At that moment the voice of the Son of God went forth
among all (those undergoing) punishments.

BU.AP.PAUL.S. 548.19

' *Because of my goodness*
and because I rose from the dead,
I will give you the Lord's day as a (day of) rest every week
and the Fifty Days which follow the (day of) Resurrection
whereon I rose from the dead.'

BU.AP.PAUL.S. 549.22

9. 'The wheel of fire which thou seest hanging down, falling upon the
   sinners which are in it,
   submerging them for three hundred days,
   scarcely would a man be able to adhere inside it.
   Afterwards (they are returned again down as on a wheel in the third
   year.)
   All (those to suffer) punishments are bound to it
   and the path of all leads to that pit. (   )
   Thou shalt see today a great wonder
   from the Archangel Michael and his great favour.'
   While I was talking to him, *behold Michael the Archangel came forth*
   from the heavens,
   seated upon the chariot of the Cherubim.
   The angels sang hymns before him
   while all the Righteous followed after him,
   with the patriarchs and all the prophets.
   They were robed in great splendour and great glory.
   with palm branches in their hands
   and sweet smelling branches
   singing hymns and psalms before him.
   He came (and stood) above the punishments.
   Immediately the flames (were extinguished) (   ).
   All the wild animals which were in them (   ) they became invisible.
   Immediately the Archangel Michael lowered his right wing.
   A crowd of souls came up upon it, whose number could not be told,
   from the arm of the compassionate Archangel to the tip of his wing,
   and he brought them up from the punishments,
   he poured them out upon the earth.
   He filled twelve arouras of land (with them).
   Then the Powerful One, Michael, lowered down his wing again.
   He raised a larger number of souls than the first time,
   he brought them up.

Afterwards all the Cherubim and Seraphim and Righteous who had
   come forth and followed him,
bowed down to him.
They begged him who is filled with all compassion, to lower down
(his wing) again the third time.
And Michael *brought up a greater number of souls.*
He saved them from unending punishments. (   )
Michael brought them to the presence of the Father of Goodness.
All the souls worshipped him.
At that hour Michael the Archangel took them to the everlasting rest.

BU.M.TIM.S. 514.12

10. *When He (Christ) had risen from the dead,*
   it was Michael who suffered with Him
   before the door of the tomb and down to Amente.
   Again it was Michael who bound Beliar by the command of his Lord,
   and it was Michael who brought to the Saviour all the captive souls
   over whom the Devil had tyrannised.
   Because of this, *Our Saviour went up to the Father with the captive*
      souls.
   After the Resurrection, the Father rejoiced over his beloved Son,
   He embraced Him,
   He granted to Him the power to judge the living and the dead.
   To Him belongs the power of the Godhead from these aeons for
      ever.
   Then the Son of Goodness, Jesus the Christ, arrayed Michael
   with great glory which was beyond words
   and greater than (the glory which He had bestowed upon him)
   when He established him as ruler over the Kingdom of the Heavens.

BU.M.TIM.S. 516.8

11. *When the Archangel Michael comes forth from the Veil of the Father,*
   all the ranks of the heavens,
   from Adam his creation,
   are gathered to him,
   singing hymns and psalms before the Archangel Michael,
   in the way that thou hast seen them (   ),
   until he comes to all the punishments.
   In that hour the road to all the punishments is opened,
   to the great punishment which is very deep and very fearful.
   And all the souls which are in the punishments gather together in this
      one pit every year,

according to the mercies of God the Father.
And the Commander-in-Chief Michael comes above the punishments
and he lowers down his right wing three times
and brings up a multitude of souls
and discharges them upon the earth.
And (each) time *he fills his wing with souls in this manner*
their number makes two hundred times ten thousand and nine
  times ten thousand and half of ten thousand and eight hundred
  and seventy.

BU.M.TIM.S. 516.28

12. And the three Kings went immediately to the entrance of the tomb.
They opened the door of the tomb.
They could not find any bones of the dead within it.
They gathered the dust from the bones which they found.
They brought it to the saint George.
Then the saint, George, cast himself upon his knees.
He prayed for the duration of an hour.
When he completed the Amen
there was a great disturbance with fiery lightning
and those bones became lighted
and suddenly five men and nine women and ten children came forth
  from them.
When the Kings saw what had happened, they were astonished.
Then the Kings called one of those who had risen from the dead.
They said to him: 'What is thy name?'
He who had risen from the dead answered,
saying: 'My name is Isoubên.'
The King said to him: 'Behold, how many years is it since thou died?'
(He said) 'Behold, more than two hundred years.'
The King said to him: '*In that time had Christ come to the world or not?*'
He who rose from the dead said to him:
'I do not remember nor did I hear whether he came.'
Dadianus said to him: 'In what god didst thou believe?'
He who rose said: '( ) I believed in one who was called Apollo,
a stupid, deaf, dumb and blind one.
When I left behind me the evil life I lived,
I was living on the roads which lead to the River of Fire
until I came to it. There was there the worm who does not sleep. ( )
Every man who shall exist upon the earth and acknowledge Him
  who was crucified, namely Christ, ( )
when he is removed from this evil world ( )

615

on the Lord's Day he is given rest
because indeed the Lord Jesus saw the punishments on the Lord's Day.
But even on the Lord's Day we are not given rest at all
because we did not acknowledge His Lordship while we were on
    earth.' ( )
The King answered he said: 'Is your heart forgiven after this long
    time of two hundred years?'
He who was raised from the dead looked at the martyr of Christ, the
    saint George,
he said to him: 'My lord, thou martyr of Christ,
we beg thee, give us the holy baptism of Christ
so that we are not cast again to the punishments in which we were.'
When the saint George saw their faith he gave a blow upon the earth.
Water gushed up
and he baptised them in the name of the Father and the Son and the
    Holy Spirit.
He said to them: 'Go in peace to Paradise'
and immediately they became invisible and were not to be seen.

BA.HY.II.GEO.B. 289.25

13. King Rakilloe and King Dadianus and King Dionysius of Egypt
    rose, *they opened the stone coffins.*
They brought up the bones of the dead which were rotten.
They said to him: 'O George, the bones have perished from the
    long time
and the bones have become dust.'
The justified one said: 'Bring me their dust.'
In this way the three Kings caused the servants
to bring the bones and their dust which they found.
And they brought them.
They placed them before the saint George.
The blessed one bent his knees, he made petitions to God.
At that moment a great earthquake happened with thunder and
    lightning.
A spirit of the Lord came on the earth in the bones and the dust
and five men and nine women and a small boy came forth.
A great fear came to the Kings and the crowd who were with them
because of the wonder which had happened.
They were troubled together.
The Kings called to one who had risen from the dead.
They said to him: 'What is thy name?'
He said to them: 'Boes is the name which I have.'

And the King said to him: 'Behold how many years (is it) since thou died?'
He answered: 'Behold four hundred years.'
They said to him: 'In thy time had Christ already come to the world?'
He said to them: 'No.'
They said to him: 'What god dost thou serve?'
He said to them: 'I serve the god Apollo,
the deaf and blind and soulless idol.
*It happened that when I died I was cast into the River of Unquenchable
    Fire*
which is beneath the Abyss and which devours without mercy,
and I was cast into it.
*Behold for four hundred and thirty years I have remained in its deep
    waves,*
while Apollo the idol was placed with me in it.
Then after a time, *Jesus the Son of the Living God came down to Amente*
and a Cross of light followed above Him.
The whole of Amente became lighted.
He brought all the captive souls up with Him.
And to the rest of those undergoing punishment,
when the day of the Lord comes, *God looks upon the punishments and
    he gives rest.*
*But we, the worshippers of idols were not given rest at all, at any
    time.'* (   )
The justified one (   ) gave a blow upon the ground,
there appeared a spring of water which was very white.
And they all received baptism in it from James the holy Apostle, the
    brother of John,
in the name of the Father and the Son and the Holy Spirit.
The saint George caused them to return to the coffin to rest.
They were perfected in peace.
They were removed to the Paradise of Joy
through the prayer of the saint, George.

BA.HY.II.GEO.DI.B. 226.3

14. When the holy martyr (George) saw his (the magician Athanasius')
        faith,
    he gave a blow with his foot upon the earth
    and a spring of water sprang up, which was full of very choice perfume.
    And the blessed man prayed in secret.
    Thomas the Apostle came.
    He baptised Athanasius, the magician in the name of the Father
        and the Son and the Holy Spirit.

617

He received absolution from his sins.
The Apostle gave Peace to them secretly.
He departed from them.

BA.HY.II.GEO.DI.B. 211.3

15. *We walked in the mountain,*
    we found a rock tomb,
    full of corpses of worshippers of idols only.
    When the holy men reached them they stood up.
    He prayed over them,
    they all rose up alive, making six hundred men and fifty-four women.
    The holy men said to them: ' What is your trouble?'
    One of them answered. He said: 'Hear me, O holy men,
    while I tell you our sins and our impieties.
    For we are one tribe.
    We worship a wild beast whose name is the wolf.
    We are concerned with him at all times.
    We offer up for him as sacrifices young children of three years.
    He gave us strength saying: "Do for me thus"
    and other things more evil than these, of which I do not wish to
        speak.
    Now therefore my holy fathers, let your mercy establish us
    and do you baptise us like the Christians.
    Because great distress is upon us.'

AM.PAUL.T.S. 768.6

16. '*Be seated in this place O my brother* (Pambo) *at this time*
    and thou shalt see great marvels.
    For it was the night of the Lord's Day that day,
    and when the daybreak of the Lord's Day was spreading,
    I heard voices crying out:' ( )
    He said to me: 'Do not fear my son.
    The Lord has come down to the punishments,
    He has commanded the tormentors who are over the souls
    to let them rest because today is the Lord's Day
    and the Resurrection of the Lord.'

BU.CYR.S. 133.16

3 PURIFICATION AFTER DEATH

THEMES

The crossing of the River of Fire.
The washing in the Acherusian Lake.
The immersion in the Lake of Fire.

618

EPISODES

The Boat of Gold as the means of crossing the River of Fire.

The oars and lamps of the Boat of Gold as the means of ferrying souls over the River of Fire; the lighting of souls on the roads of darkness.

The entry into the City of the Holy Ones after washing in the Acherusian Lake.

The boat of gold as the means of crossing the Acherusian Lake.

Purification in Heaven achieved by immersion in the Lake of Fire.

QUOTATIONS

1. 'Amen I say to thee, *all men who shall commemorate thee upon the earth*, my kinsman John,
   I will not show Amente to them for ever, nor its punishments,
   as far as the River of Fire,
   over which all men shall cross whether righteous or sinner.
   Behold this further favour I will give to thee, the ferry of this River of Fire which is the boat of gold.
   Those who will commemorate thee upon the earth,
   thou shalt ferry them in it on that River of Fire.'
   We, the Apostles, said to Him:
   '*Our Lord, how many stadia is the sea of that River of Fire? (   )*'
   Our Saviour said to us: 'I will inform you of its dimension
   and the dimension of the boat of gold
   which I have given to my beloved John.
   The extent of the river is thirty waves from bank to bank.
   And from the waves to the waves it is thirty stadia to each wave.
   And I give the boat of gold to John my kinsman
   for the crossing of the River of Fire,
   so that he may transport in it those who shall perform his commemoration upon earth,
   even to a small fragment of bread and a cup of cold water.
   And when they come to the end of the waves, I am wont to baptise them in the River of Fire.
   When all those who perform the commemoration of John shall come to be baptised,
   the River of Fire becomes like the water of a bath
   and like a tepid water in their presence,
   to the extent that a man will only wet himself in the River of Fire.
   Because of this, *all men who will perform thy commemoration upon* the *earth*, O John my companion and my kinsman,
   whether with an offering, or first fruits or any gift
   which they will give to thy shrine

in memory of thy holy name,
I command thee to transport them on the River of Fire,
in the boat of gold which I have bestowed upon thee.
And thou shalt take them into the Third Heaven
that they may enjoy themselves among the good things
which are prepared
and which endure for ever.'

BU.CH.JOH.S. 140.8

2. Peter spoke to the Saviour again saying: '*Our Lord and Our God,*
show us what is the purpose of these oars and these lamps.'
The Saviour said: 'There is a lamp to (each) oar
and there are seven holes to (each) lamp,
seven holes which are burning and give light.
Every man who will light the lamp of the shrine of the saint John, or
before his image,
will be ferried across the River of Fire in the golden boat
which I have bestowed upon my beloved one, John.
These lamps shall burn before them,
giving light to them until they have passed over the roads of darkness
and are taken into the Third Heaven,
which I have given as a favour to my beloved John,
and they inherit the good things within it for ever.'
When the good Saviour had said these things,
He mounted upon the cloud,
He commanded that we should mount with Him,
He brought us down, He set us upon the Mount of Olives.
He stood, He prayed with us,
He said to us: 'Peace be with you.'
And when He had said these things to us
He went up to the heavens in great glory while the angels sang hymns
to Him.

BU.CH.JOH.S. 143.11

3. '*Let the torturers of Amente flee from me,*
with the changing faces which I do not know,
these which trouble the soul.
Let the River of Fire which surges
cease in my presence till I cross it.
Let all the evil powers flee.'

BA.HY.I.AN.B. 240.2

620

4. *And he took me to the Eastern side of the River of Good Things.*
I looked, I saw the river of which the water was much whiter than
   milk.
I said again to the angel: 'My Lord, what is this?'
He said to me: 'This is the Acherusian Lake.
The City of the Holy Ones,
this which the Father built for his Only Begotten Son, Jesus Christ,
lies to the East of all these.
It has not been given every man to enter therein.
For this reason the Acherusian Lake has been placed on the
   road. ( )
A man ( ) *when he comes forth from the body,*
he first worships God.
And he is delivered into the hand of Michael
and he washes him in the Acherusian Lake,
and he is taken into the city' ( )
I blessed God because of the things I had seen.
The angel said to me: 'Follow thou after me Paul, and I will take thee
   into the City of Christ.'
I came upon the Acherusian Lake.
He mounted me in a boat of gold, taking a mast of silver, ( )
while precious stones were set in it.
There were three thousand angels who were steering it.
Then the angels sang hymns to me.
I was taken into the City of Christ.

BU.AP.PAUL.S. 563.18

5. *Then he brought me forth from the city*
in the midst of the trees
and from the Acherusian Lake.
He brought me forth from the Land of Good Things
upon the River of Milk and Honey.
He brought me forth upon the Ocean,
this which supports the heaven.
He took me up to the heaven.
The angel said to me: '( ) Dost thou know where thou art now?'
I said to him: 'Yes, my Lord.'
He answered saying to me: 'Follow (me) now
and I will show thee where they take the souls of the wicked and the
   sinners
when they die.'

BU.AP.PAUL.S. 537.26

6. *At the time when they came for me in order to separate my soul from my body,*
   a great and mighty angel came with a cloth of linen
   and also multitudes of angels all girt with golden bands upon their loins
   with sweet perfumes.
   That angel is called 'Michael the Angel of Compassion'.
   They all stood over me, their faces smiling at me.
   And Michael signed my mouth in the name of the Father, and the Son and the Holy Spirit.
   And at that moment my soul sprang forth from my body,
   it alighted upon the hand of Michael.
   He wrapped it in the linen cloth,
   they proceeded with it up to heaven
   singing hymns (until we) reached the River of Fire.
   Michael set me down from his hand (upon it),
   I went into it as if (it were) a small canal of water. ( )
   Michael gave light to me until we crossed over.
   After we had crossed over it we proceeded up to heaven.
   He took me upon the Acherusian Lake, he immersed me in it three times.
   Afterwards a voice (came) forth from the height saying:
   '*O ye angels who bear good news, take this soul*
   to the places of immortality and Paradise of the celestial life,'

   BU.BART.R.S. 35.6

7. And when the hour of dawn came,
   he said: 'I have seen a pathway established upon the earth like a ladder
   and its top reached up to the vaults of the sky.
   I saw,' said Theodore, 'a youth
   with an unearthly face,
   as if he was in his twentieth year,
   sitting at the top of the staircase of the seat.
   And his glory was very great. *And very great faces surrounded his throne.*
   On his right they were like a face of a lion and of a bull,
   on his left like a face of an eagle and of a man.
   And they had many wings hiding their faces.
   And the wheel was like (four) saws, two upon two, turning like a whirlwind
   And after this I looked again, *I saw a great tent upon the summit* of the seat.

622

THE REPRESENTATION OF NEGATIVE EXPERIENCES

I was not told the mystery of the seat and the tent,
but they said to me: "*Thus far is the vision.*"
He who sat upon the seat said to me: "Theodore, dost thou wish
    to be my son?"
I said to him: "Who art thou thus, that I see in great glory?
Tell me, O my Lord, who thou art that I may speak thy word to my
    brother, Leontius.
Tell me, my Lord, for I fear the enemy, for he is a hater of men."
The Saviour said to me: ( ) "*I am the First Logos of God, the Father.*
    ( )
I am the God of all flesh."
I, Theodore, said in the presence of Him who spoke with me:
"*I am thy servant, my Lord, I am also the son of thy maidservant.*" ( )
The Saviour spoke to me saying: "If in truth, O Theodore, it pleases
    thee to become my son,
then cast thyself down into this Lake of Fire so that thou become
    purified." ( )
And those who were standing near him suspended me, ( )
by the hair of my head,
they immersed me three times,
they set me upon my feet,
they clothed my body with a pure garment.
Immediately I moved freely in His presence,
in the manner of those who stood in His presence
ready to do those things which came forth from His mouth.'

BA.HY.I.TH.O.B. 47.9

SECTION V

SECTION V

The Establishment of Commemorative Ritual

I THE MARTYR CULT

1 MARTYRDOM FORETOLD

THEMES

The foretelling of martyrdom by Christ, an archangel, angel, man of light, voice from heaven.
The call to enter the conflict.

EPISODES

The receiving of the call at night; during sleep; during torment.
The foretelling that death would take place several times; that raising from the dead would take place.
The foretelling of the trials that would take place.
The foretelling that the soul would be fetched; received as a pledge.
The foretelling that the completion of the trials would take place within a short time.
The foretelling of the place of martyrdom; the manner of burial.

QUOTATIONS

  1. When he lay down to sleep,
     as he was thinking of these things, *a voice came to him,*
     saying: 'Helias, Helias.' He said: 'Behold me, O Lord.
     Who art thou who calls me?' ( )
     The voice came to him a second time,
     saying: 'My chosen one, Helias, ( )
     open thine eyes and know who I am.
     I am Jesus the sweet smell of incense of the Father.
     I am Jesus, the true physician,
     who cures all illnesses and heals those who suffer.
     I am Jesus, the sweet scent of the true vine of the Good Father.
     I am Jesus, the joy of the waters of the Lake of Acheron.
     I am Jesus, the unloosable bond of the aeons.

626

I am Jesus, who helps all those who believe in him with their whole heart.'
When the holy Helias heard these things,
he raised his eyes,
he saw Jesus mounted upon the chariot of Cherubim
with Michael, the Archangel on His right hand and the holy Soterichos on His left
with a robe of glory upon Him such as no king of this earth would be able to wear.
When the holy Helias saw these things he prostrated himself in the presence of the Lord, ( )
And at that moment Jesus raised him,
saying to him: 'Arise my chosen one, Helias,
I am Jesus who doth help thee.
Amen, I say to thee that I will grant thee my kingdom.
For behold, I have already written thy name in the Book of Life.
For I know that thou wilt receive many afflictions for my name.
But do not fear.
They will not prevail against thee,
because I am with thee in every place to which thou shalt be taken.
I will give power to thee, until thou dost complete thy course. ( )
I am with thee and I will fill thee with the Holy Spirit.
And I will give thee power so that my name be glorified through thee.
Rise therefore now.
Come embrace thy fellow Soterichos, whom thou hast prayed to see.'
When the Saviour had said these things,
He gave him Peace,
He went up to the heavens in glory,
while the holy Helias looked after Him.
Then a great fragrance spread in the room in which the holy Helias was lying.

SOB.HEL.S. 8b.19

2. *It happened when the blessed Apa Epime was sleeping in his house,*
he saw a youth of light standing above him.
He stirred his right side.
When the saint Apa Epime woke, he roused him,
he saw a man of light standing above him.
He was troubled.
And he said to him: *'Epime, open thy eyes so that thou mayest know who I am.*
I am Jesus Christ, He whose star gave light in the East.

627

I am Jesus the Christ, He whose star the wise men saw and they worshipped Him. ( )
I am Jesus Christ the crown of martyrs.
It is necessary for thee to receive a multitude of sufferings for my name.
And I shall cause thy name to become famous in the whole world.
Rise go to the hegemon and manifest my name.
Do not fear for I am with thee.
The Peace of my Father which He gave to me as I came forth from Him,
I shall also give it to thee.'
When the Saviour has said these things to him,
He signed him with the Cross,
lest any torture should touch his body.
He went up to heaven
while he looked after Him.

BA.HY.I.EPIM.B. 126.4

3. *The blessed Apa Epima was sleeping one day in his house*
   when behold, a youth of light stood above him.
   He was troubled.
   He said to him: '*Epima, Epima open thy eyes and know who I am.*
   I am Jesus Christ, whose star gave light in the East.
   I am Jesus, whose star the wise men saw.
   I am Jesus, whom the angels proclaimed to the shepherds. ( )
   I am Jesus, who became a martyr under Pontius Pilate.
   I am Jesus, the crown of martyrs,
   the judge of those who fight well.
   The Peace my Father gave to me as I came to the world, I also give to thee.
   Why therefore dost thou dwell here neglectful,
   while the fight spreads
   and crowns are given freely?
   Behold, I have already prepared for thee a dwelling in heaven
   and an imperishable crown for ever.
   There is a great fight set for thee tomorrow in the city of Pemjê.
   Thy death will be on the eighth day of the month of Epep.'

MIN.EPIM.S. 5.11

4. *At the eleventh hour of the night,*
   as the holy Apa Didymus was sleeping in his room,
   behold a man of light stood over him.
   He said to him in a sweet voice:

628

'Greeting, O noble Apa Didymus, thou warrior of Christ,
Peace be to thee.
Why dost thou dwell thus, neglectful, adding day to day.
Arise go to Augustamnike.
Behold the battle spreads
so that thou mayest receive thy crown freely.
For thy crown is already prepared in the heavens
and all the Holy Ones will rejoice over thee and thy contest
for the name of Christ against this impious hegemon.
Therefore rise now and do not be neglectful.
The Peace of my Lord, Jesus Christ be with thee, Amen.'
When he had said these things to him,
the man of light went up to the heavens in great glory.

HY.DID.B. 288.7

5. *Behold Christ sent his angel to the saint Theodore, the General,*
   saying: 'Rise and go to the city of the kingdom
   so that thou seest the martyrdom of thy comrade the Anatolian.'
   ( )
   Behold, he saw the Saviour with Michael
   with the soul of the Anatolian in his hands.
   He fell upon his face.
   The Saviour sent Michael, the Archangel, he took him, he stood him
   up.
   The Saviour said to him: 'O chosen one, Theodore, there is also a
   wonderful contest appointed for thee ( )
   before thou dost become a martyr like thy comrade the Anatolian.
   Now therefore rejoice, because thy soul will be taken to the place
   where the soul of the Anatolian will be taken,
   when thou hast completed (thy course).'

BA.HY.II.T.A.T.S.B. 143.27

6. *That night Raphael, the angel, appeared to him,*
   he said to him: 'Greeting Paese, thou man worthy of love.'
   When he saw the Archangel, he prostrated himself, he worshipped him.
   He raised him
   and his face gave light like the sun.
   The holy men saw the light,
   they were afraid, they worshipped the Archangel.
   He said to them: *'Peace be with you.'*
   Raphael blessed them, saying: *'May the power of the Lord bless you,*
   so that you put to shame the enemy and that the name of God receive
   Glory. ( )

And further, the Duke will send for thee tomorrow to the tribunal. ( )
I will be in front of thee so that the fire does not touch thee at all.
Take power and become a man of might,
*because thy martyrdom under the impious Duke will be for seven
months.'*
The blessed Apa Paese said: 'Give power to me, O my lord father
and I will give my body to the tortures of the court of justice.'
The angel embraced him,
he went up to the heavens.

TIL.I.PA.TH.S. 75.10

7. Arianus, the hegemon, commanded that he be hung from a Persea
tree. ( )
A great thunder came and lightning flashed in the heights
so that the edges of the altar were filled with fire
and a great disturbance took place,
so that the hegemon became afraid and his retinue and all his body
trembled with fear.
*And in that hour Michael and Gabriel and the whole army of angels
came forth from heaven,*
*singing hymns to the Saviour who appeared upon the branches of the
Persea tree.*
He said to Apa Timotheus: '*Endure and do not fear,*
I am Jesus who works all these miracles with thee. ( )
for it is I who am with you in all places to which you will go
until I shall give you my kingdom.
*Behold O Timotheus, a great trial will take place through thee today
in the city,*
so that all the multitude may believe in my name through thee.'
*When the Saviour had said these things, He signed Apa Timotheus and
his daughter with the Cross, with His fingers.*
He withdrew to heaven.
*And at that moment, Apa Timotheus was released from the Persea
tree.*

TIL.I.TIM.S. 114.20

8. It happened on one of the days in which he was in battle,
as he was sleeping in the night while his soldiers surrounded him,
behold our Lord Jesus Christ stood above him.
He stirred his side.
He said to him: 'Arise,

why art thou asleep, while the battle spreads abroad?'
When he rose up from sleep and he saw the Lord,
he was very afraid and he was troubled.
The good Saviour said to him: 'Dost thou know who I am?'
The blessed man said to Him: 'No, my Lord,
I beg thee to tell me who thou art, who art in this great glory.
For truly when I see thee, I am in great fear, O my Lord.'
The Lord said to him: 'I am Jesus, thy true king,
why dost thou fight on behalf of a king who will die?
Rise, go and do battle for my name,
that thou mayest receive the unfading crown in my Kingdom in the
   heavens. (   )
Now this is the time that thou shouldst manifest my name in the
   presence of the impious king.
Thou wilt receive many afflictions for my name.
Then take courage. Do not fear,
I am with thee in all thy troubles.
Rise, go first to Euchetos, the city, and kill this dragon whom they
   serve,
who destroys the souls of the Christians, who belong to me.'
When the Saviour had said these things to him,
He gave him His Peace,
He went up to the heavens in glory with His holy angels.

BA.HY.I.TH.S.B. 158.20

9. *The saint Apatil enclosed himself in a place alone*
   and he prayed to God with tears continuously (   ).
   When he had finished his service according to his custom,
   he fell asleep for a short while
   and thus Christ appeared to him in a vision
   in the form of a beautiful youth giving light greatly.
   And He said to him: 'Why dost thou sleep while the conflict spreads?
   Rise, fight for my name
   so that thou mayest receive the unfading crown from me.
   And when thou hast completed well the good fight of the faith,
   I will take thee and offer thee to my Father as a gift
   and thus thou wilt be in unspeakable joy.
   Do not fear the torments,
   for I will be with thee in all thy afflictions which thou wilt receive for
      my name,
   therefore be a mighty fighter.'
   When the Saviour had said these things

he ceased to see Him.
And immediately morning came.

BA.HY.I.AP.B. 92.4

10. *In the third night then*
when the holy man was with wounds, the Lord Jesus came to him in the
*   prison with His holy angels.*
And the prison was filled with light.
Christ said to him: 'George, behold I command thee, stand upon thy
*   feet healed.'*
And in that moment he rose up uninjured.
The Lord embraced him
and he passed His hand over his whole body.
He filled him with courage.
He said to him: 'Rise and depart to these impious kings and put them
*   and their impious gods to shame.*
Take courage, do not fear, I am with thee at all times.
I say to thee, O my beloved George, that there is joy in heaven at
*   thy endurance*
and the angels have rejoiced over thy good fight.
Behold, now for another seven years thou wilt receive these torments
*   from the impious kings.*
And thou shalt die three times.
I myself will come with the holy angels and I will receive thy soul
and I will give thee rest in the bosom of Abraham,
with Isaac and Jacob, in the Paradise of Joy.'
When the Lord had said these things to him
and He had given him Peace,
He departed up to heaven in glory,
while he looked after Him.

BA.HY.II.GEO.DI.B. 217.18

11. *That night the Lord appeared to the saint, George,*
He said to him, '*Be strong and have courage, my beloved George.*
It is I who give power to thee
so that thou shouldst bear all these afflictions which are brought upon
*   thee.*
I swear by myself with my holy angels, that there is not one among
*   those born of women*
greater than John, the Baptist.
After him, none will rise like thee.
Behold, I have granted thee to overcome seventy kings.

632

That which thou shalt say, will happen to them.
But thou wilt die three times and I will raise thee.
The fourth time, I myself will come upon the clouds,
I will take my pledge which I have entrusted to thee in thy holy dwelling.
Take courage, do not fear,
for it is I who remain with thee.'
And when He had embraced him,
He went up to heaven in great glory with the holy angels.

BA.HY.II.GEO.B. 275.19

12. *The Saint suffered greatly in this torment*
   and he said: '*My Lord Christ, the Son of the Living God,*
   remember me and do not forsake me.'
   And at that moment our Lord Jesus Christ appeared to him
   and He said to him: 'Greeting to thee, O my chosen one, Apa Macar-
       ius,
   my Peace be with thee,
   for I am He who has chosen thee like Victor, the son of Romanos.
   And the crown which he bore I will grant to thee also.
   For I am Jesus Christ, the Son of the Living God,
   who have come to bring good news to thee.
   Do not fear, thou wilt receive great afflictions for my name
   and I am He who will save thee from them all. (   )
   I will cause Michael to minister to thee
   for thou shalt die twice and I will raise thee.
   But the third time,
   I will come for thy soul and I will fetch it
   and cause it to rest with Abraham and Isaac and Jacob, thy fellow
       inheritors
   in the places of the Kingdom of Immortality.
   For thou wilt appear before three tribunals.
   Do not fear, I am with thee
   and I will save thee from them all.'
   And He passed His hands over his whole body,
   He healed him,
   He departed up to heaven in glory.

HY.MAC.AN.B. 41.4

13. *It happened that in the middle of the night*
   an angel of light appeared to him in the prison.
   And there was a great earthquake, so that the town moved to its
       foundations.

And behold, the Lord came into the prison,
with myriads of His holy angels
and the whole place was filled with very choice perfume.
And the Lord called to him thus, saying: 'My beloved George,
rise from thy sleep, thou art saved,
there is no injury upon thee.'
He jumped up immediately without harm in his body at all,
but he was like one who had risen from a king's feast.
And he cast himself down, he worshipped the Lord.
Thus He took hold of him,
He raised him and He embraced him
and He passed His hand upon his whole body,
He filled him with power
and He said to him: '*Take courage and be strong, my beloved one,*
I am with thee until thou dost put to shame these impious kings.
I swear by myself to thee, O George, my beloved,
just as no one has risen of those born of women greater than John,
    the Baptist,
so there is none among the martyrs who resembles thee
and no one who will be like thee for ever.
Behold, thou wilt spend seven years being tortured by these seventy
    impious kings.
Thou wilt do many miracles
and thou wilt die three times and I will raise thee.
And the fourth time I will come to thee upon a cloud of light
with the hosts of the Firmament and the prophets and the apostles, the
    holy martyrs
and I will receive the pledge which I entrusted to thee.'
When He ceased saying these things
the Saviour gave him Peace
and He filled him with joy entirely.
He departed up to the heavens with His angels,
while the blessed man was looking after Him.
And the justified one rejoiced greatly, praising God until the morning
    broke,
because of the things which the Lord had told him.

BA.HY.II.GEO.DI.B. 206.12

14. *The Lord appeared to him that night saying:*
    '*Be strong my chosen one, George and take courage.*
    Do not give way, for I am with thee.
    A great joy exists for thee in heaven as a result of thy conflict.

634

Behold, thou hast died once, I have raised thee.
Thou wilt die yet another twice and I will raise thee again.
On the fourth occasion, I myself will come in clouds
and receive the pledge which I have entrusted to thy body.
It is I who will give power to thy holy body
and I will cause thee to rest with Abraham and Isaac and Jacob.
Do not be faint-hearted.
I remain with thee
for thy martyrdom will be in the presence of these seventy kings,
these in whose presence thou shalt bear witness concerning me.
Thou wilt spend seven years enduring torture for my name.
Take courage, do not be faint-hearted.'
When the Lord had addressed him,
He went up to the heavens with His holy angels,
while the valiant martyr of Christ watched Him.
And he remained in vigil until the light broke
rejoicing in the gladness which the Lord gave him.

BA.HY.II.GEO.B. 284.5

15. *The Lord appeared to him that night.*
    He said to him: 'Be strong George, for I am with thee.
    Behold thou hast died the first time and I have raised thee.
    The fourth time, I will come to thee upon the clouds,
    I will receive the pledge which I entrusted to thee,
    namely thy body and thy soul.
    For thy martyrdom will be honoured in the kingdoms for seven years.
    Now be strong and do not give up.'
    And the Lord embraced him,
    He went up to the heavens with his angels.

BU.GEO.C.S. 183.14

16. The soldiers did to him according to the command of the hegemon.
    The holy man Apa Lacaron prayed as he was hanging on the pillar,
        saying thus:
    'My Lord Jesus Christ, the first martyr
    who alone art the Lord of the Aeons in thy divine power.
    Do thou send me thy holy angel to help me.'
    As the holy man, Apa Lacaron, said these things,
    behold an angel of the Lord stood above him.
    He released him from the pillar.
    He placed him down.
    He stood him up without any blemish.

635

The angel said to him: '*Be strong and be a man of might, O athlete of Christ.*

For the completion of thy course approaches.'
When he had said these things to him,
the angel of the Lord embraced him,
He departed up to heaven,
while the saint looked after him.

BA.HY.I.LAC.B. 18.11

17. They went and did according as the impious king commanded them.

   And they threw and cast him down (the pit)
   and let fall his head first and he fell upon the nape of his neck.
   God who always preserves those who cry to him in truth,
   sent an angel to his help in the middle of the night.
   And the dark pit was filled with light more powerful than the sun.
   He consoled him and encouraged him and strengthened him.
   And he passed his hand over his body, and he healed his wounds.
   And this place was filled with a sweet smell more pleasant and agreeable than spices.
   And the angel of the Lord said to him: 'O Azazail, victorious martyr,
   do not be angry that they cast thee into the dark pit.
   Thou hast this prepared, that instead of this darkness,
   thou shalt enjoy the light of eternity in the Kingdom of Heaven.
   And concerning the prayer which thou hast prayed to thy Lord
   that He should grant thee that thou shouldst suffer more torments,
   there remain to thee a few more torments and afflictions to endure.
   And then thou wilt depart to Christ, thy Lord,
   to be glad and rejoice in the resting place of the heavenly light
   with the holy martyrs, thy fellows, who watch thee and wait for thee.
   And Christ thy Lord has spoken to thee thus:
   that He is with thee and He will not leave thee.
   He will help thee and give thee victory
   against this tyrannical and unjust king.
   Behold, I have healed thy wounds,
   and thou remainest without pain or sickness,
   without trouble or torment.
   So now put him to shame, and do not tremble or fear him,
   because I am with thee and I will not leave thee.'

MAC.AZ.SY. 17(32/33)

18. *While he remained in prison,*
    on that night the holy man was keeping watch
    and he made great petitions up to God for the whole world.
    The Lord Jesus Christ appeared to him in unspeakable glory.
    And he said to him: '*Greeting my chosen one, Macrobius,*
    thou good shepherd of the spiritual flock.
    Take courage and be strong.
    Do not fear, for indeed I am with thee
    to save thee from all thy afflictions.
    For there is yet a little time before thou dost receive the crown of
        immortality
    and rest thyself with all the Holy Ones.'
    When the Saviour had said these things,
    He gave him Peace
    and thus He departed from him in great glory.
    The saint Abba Macrobius was in great joy in the prison when he had
        seen the Lord.

    HY.MACR.B. 233.3

19. And this man said to him;
    'Go my son, and return to thy body,
    because thou hast another small martyrdom in the world.'

    LE.PAC.S.18a.21

20. *While the blessed man was praying, God sent the Archangel to him,*
    He quenched the power of the fire.
    He brought him up.
    There was no injury upon him at all.
    And he said to him: '*Be courageous and let thy heart be strong,*
    for yet a little (while) and thou shalt complete thy course.'

    BA.HY.I.ANAT.P.B. 28.1

21. *Further, while he was walking in the city, behold the Lord Jesus came*
        forth from heaven towards him.
    He said to him: '*Be strong, O Helias, my beloved. Thy martyrdom*
        approaches.
    Behold, thou has seen what a number of good things are prepared
    for those that will believe in me with their whole hearts.
    I am Jesus, the good news of all the aeons.
    Behold I bring good news to thee also today.
    Thou, my beloved, when they take thee to Media,
    Eutuchodoros, the King of Media will kill thee.
    Then thou shalt complete thy course at his hands.'

    SOB.HEL.S. 56a.8

22. As he was saying these things,
    behold Gabriel the Archangel came down from heaven,
    he caused the fire to be quenched under them,
    he gave the hand to the holy men,
    he brought them up.
    He said to them: 'Now go and reprove the impious one,
    that he may know that the power of God prevails over all things (   ).
    And *behold I am with you until you complete your course.*
    Be long-suffering, O beloved ones of the Lord,
    even if many days remain until you complete your course.
    I will come again to you. (   )'
    When he had said these things he disappeared from them.

                                                        TIL.I.TIM.S. 112.18

23. When the saints were taken to the prison,
    they stood and prayed all that night until the (day) light came,
        saying:
    'Our Lord and Master, we beg of thy goodness that thou wilt be
        with us
    and *give courage to us until we shame this wicked man with his*
        unclean idols.'
    While the saints were standing praying a voice came to them from
        heaven, saying:
    '*Be of good courage, O my chosen ones, Pirow and Athom,*
    I am with you until you complete your contest.'

                                                        HY.PI.AT.B. 139.10

24. 'And thy body will be in the monastery of Tchinouote, (   ) for a long
        time.
    After that time thy body will be brought to thy house (   ).
    Thou wilt be taken to Alexandria
    and thou wilt be heard in that place.
    And great miracles will happen through thee in that place.
    Afterwards thou wilt be brought back to the land of Egypt
    and thy death will be in that place in a province which is not thine.
    I have appointed for thee Julius, the helper,
    the historiographer and man of Kbehes,
    so that he should take care of thee in that place
    and that he should write all thy undertakings,
    and take them into his house and place them there,
    until the time that my Father wishes them to appear.
    Afterwards he will appoint his servants for thee,

                                638

so that they be attached to thee until the fulfilment of thy course,
so that thy body be placed safely and duly buried. ( )
And do thou die in glory in exile ( ).
And on the day when my Father wishes the bringing of thy body
back to thy house and the placing of it there
I will cause a sign to appear so that they believe in thee. ( )
But tell Julius to command his servants to whom he will give thy
    body,
saying: "*Take good care of it and place it in the shrine where my
    body will be placed.*"
When the Saviour had said these things to the saint Apa Epima,
He signed his body with the Cross,
lest torments prevail against him.
He embraced him,
He went up to heaven
while the saint looked after Him.

MIN.EPIM.S. 5.24

25. *When the saint Apa Anub had completed the Amen,*
    behold, the Lord Jesus Christ came to him,
    mounted upon a chariot of light,
    with Michael on His right and Gabriel on His left side.
    He said to him: ' Be strong, O my beloved Apa Anub.
    Do not fear, I am thy Lord, I am with thee.
    Do not be afraid.
    Behold, I have appointed for thee Michael, the Archangel,
    to stand and give power to thee.
    I am Jesus thy King
    He for whose holy name thou receivest these afflictions.
    I say to thee, O my beloved Apa Anub,
    that this hegemon will become a martyr, with a multitude of souls,
        through thee.
    Thou wilt be tortured twice in this place,
    Michael will stand with thee to give power to thee
    lest anything evil prevail over thee.
    And thou wilt be taken to Alexandria to Armenius, the count.
    Thou wilt die in that place.
    I will appoint for thee Julius, the man of Kbehes, the historiog-
        rapher,
    that he should bury thy body and take thee to thy village.'

BA.HY.I.AN.B. 215.28

26. *And in that moment Michael came down from heaven with Gabriel.*
They went to him, they embraced him,
they said to him: '*Be strong, Saint Helias, no one will be able to do thee harm.*
For we were sent to thee that we should guide thy boat
until we have taken thee to the country of Kounthia.
For there is a great strife prepared for thee in that place.'
While the angels were speaking to him,
while one sat at the front of the boat and one at the back,
at that moment they came to the boundary of Kounthia,
and the angels of the Lord embraced him.
They went up to heaven in glory and in the peace of God. Amen.

SOB.HEL.S. 28a.1

27. *As the saints were standing,*
Behold Gabriel the Archangel appeared to them.
The whole place was lighted.
The angel said to them: '*Greeting, O chosen ones of Christ,*
be strong and take courage,
for the Lord has sent me to you,
so that I should tell you everything which will happen to you.
For it is necessary for you that you receive many afflictions from this impious hegemon.
You will prevail against him through Him who gives power to you, the Christ.
You will perform many miracles in the midst of this city ( ).
Seek a faithful man, make him guardian of the body of the holy martyr, the saint Apa Anoya,
to put water in his vessel and to light his lamp.
For a time will come that they will make your house a church
and spiritual offerings will be offered up in it
to the glory of our Lord Jesus Christ for ever, Amen.
Afterwards go you to Psariom
that you may complete your course in that place,
that you receive the crown of life from our Lord Jesus Christ.'
When the angel had said these things,
he gave Peace to them,
he departed up to the heavens.

HY.PI.AT.B. 152.4

28. As the blessed Apa Sarapion was speaking with the brethren,
behold the Saviour stood in their midst.

He embraced them,
He gave them all Peace.
He said to Apa Sarapion: 'My beloved Sarapion, I know that thou
  has done all my will.
Behold, thy sentence will be pronounced
and thou wilt be taken to thy village
and thy head will be removed.
But do not fear, my beloved,
for behold, I am with thee,
giving power to thee in all the places in which thou wilt go.
For I have already prepared three crowns for thee,
one because of the sufferings
which thou hast received for my name in the town of Antinoe from
  Arianus the hegemon,
another because of thy village which thou hast left behind
and to which thou hast become a stranger
with thy many goods and all thy possessions which thou hast put
  aside for my name,
another because of thy martyrdom which thou wilt complete.'

BA.HY.I.SA.PA.B. 84.5

29. *He endured all that day until evening came*
   and when the night came he rose, he stretched forth his hands, he
     prayed saying: '( )
   Send to me thy Angel of Light, that he give me power at the shedding
     of my blood.'
   As the holy Apa Anub still prayed, behold Michael, the Archangel,
     came forth from the sky.
   The whole place gave light like the sun.
   Immediately the young boy fell upon his face before him and he was
     like one dead.
   And Michael raised him, he stood him up, he encouraged him saying:
   '*Hail to thee O virtuous youth Anub, hail to thee from God,*
   O man worthy of love, have courage and be strong.
   I am Michael, the Commander-in-Chief of the power of the heavens.
   The Lord has sent me to thee so that I should give power to thee in the
     contest.
   When thou risest in the morning, go to the hegemon, proclaim the
     name of Christ.
   They will torture thee for three days in this place.
   I will give thee power.
   I will heal thy body

and they will take thee to the South to Athribe,
They will torture thee and thou wilt put to shame Satan and his evil
  demons.
I will be with thee in all places to which thou wilt go.'
When he had said these things to him,
Michael the Archangel gave Peace to him.
He went up to the heavens in glory,
while the holy man looked after him.

BA.HY.I.AN.B. 205.15

30. *Immediately behold, Michael, the Archangel came forth from heaven,*
    together with Suriel and Raphael.
    They took the limbs of his body.
    They united them to one another.
    And they blew into the face of the justified one.
    He rose uninjured.
    Suriel said to him: '*Be strong, O athlete who striveth well,*
    have courage, we are with thee giving thee power
    until thou dost put to shame the impious one with his idols.
    Behold, they will take thee to the city of Alexandria to Armenius,
      the Count,
    and he will torture thee.
    We will come to thee and heal thee.
    Afterwards he will pass sentence upon thee
    and remove thy head in that place.
    And Julius the man of Kbehes will bury thy body.
    He will take thee to thy village.'

BA.HY.I.AN.B. 221.16

2 REWARDS IN HEAVEN

THEMES

The receiving of crowns, thrones, diadems.
The keeping of the Festival with the Holy Ones in the Heavenly Jerusa-
  lem; the Wedding Feast of the Lord.
The partaking of the endless Offering to the Church of the Firstborn in
  the Heavenly Jerusalem.
The writing of the martyr's names on tablets in the Church of the
  Firstborn.
The writing of the martyr's names in the Book of Life.
The ruling over the Land of the Inheritance; the inheriting of the King-
  dom.

The rejoicing with the Holy Ones; the receiving of the applause of the Holy Ones.

EPISODES

The promising to the martyr of rewards in return for his sufferings.
The promising of rewards to the martyr at the moment of death.

QUOTATIONS

1. *Now it happened that when the days of our father Isaac, the Patriarch approached*
   (the time) that he should come forth from the body,
   God, the merciful, sent to him the great holy Archangel Michael,
   whom He had sent to Abraham, his father, at the hour of day-light ( ).
   He said to him:
   'Greeting my son, the chosen one of God and His beloved Son.'
   Now the God-loving and righteous old man, our father Isaac,
   was accustomed to speak with the holy angels.
   He turned down his face,
   he saw him that he had taken the likeness of his father Abraham.
   He opened his mouth, he lifted up his voice, he cried out in great joy and exultation:
   'I have seen thy face like him who has seen God.'
   The angel said: 'Make provision for thyself, my beloved Isaac,
   because I have been sent for thee from the Living God,
   to take thee to the heavens to thy father Abraham,
   and that thou mayest keep festival with all the Holy Ones,
   for thy father Abraham is looking out for thee
   and he will come for thee himself.
   But behold thy throne, it is prepared for thee in the heavens,
   beside thy father Abraham, thee with thy beloved son Jacob.
   You will be (there) and your inheritance will be exalted
   above that of all those who are in the Kingdom of the heavens
   in the Glory of the Father and the Son and the Holy Spirit,
   for you will be called by this name to all generations:
   "Patriarch and Father of all the World."'
   Then the God-loving old man, our father Isaac, answered and said
   to the angel: '( )
   Art thou not my father Abraham?'
   The angel said: 'My beloved Isaac, *I am the angel who ministers to thy father Abraham.'*

                                                      GUI.IS.B. 225.13

2. *When he said the Amen,*
   the Firmament was completely filled with the angels of the height
   and our Lord Jesus Christ came to him
   and He was seated upon the Cherubim and the Seraphim,
   and the choir of the prophets and the patriarchs and the apostles
   and the martyrs and all the Holy Ones sang hymns to him,
   with all the ranks of the heavens.
   And the soldiers who walked with the blessed man all fell asleep and
      were like the dead.
   The Lord said to the blessed George: '*Greeting, thou who art mine,*
      George,
   greeting, my beloved and that of my angels,
   greeting, thou fighter of the Kingdom of the Heavens.
   Blessed art thou today, O my beloved George.
   I have prepared for thee seven crowns of glory,
   in the hands of my Father who will place them on thy head on this day.
   Blessed art thou, O my beloved George,
   for there is prepared for thee a royal diadem
   and it is decorated with gold and pearls
   and I will place it on thy head with my hands today.
   Blessed art thou, O my beloved George,
   for there is prepared for thee a great throne
   which is tall and decorated with beauty
   in very choice gold with a precious stone of great value
   and thou wilt be seated upon it today in the heavens above
   through the Holy Spirit.
   Blessed art thou, O my beloved George,
   because the Gates of Pearl of the Tabernacles of Light are open to
      thee,
   that thou mayest enter into the presence of the Holy Trinity without
      hindrance.'

BA.HY.II.GEO.DI.B. 252.8

3. *The saint Apa Anub stretched forth his hands in the midst of the fire*
   saying: 'Hear me my Lord Jesus Christ,
   I am thy servant and the son of thy handmaid.
   Hear my voice now in the midst of this fire. (   )
   Send to me thy angel to give power to me
   for thine is the glory for ever, Amen.'
   At that moment, behold, the Saviour came forth from heaven,
   with Michael on His right side and Gabriel on His left,
   while the Cherubim and the Seraphim drew His chariot.

At that moment the flame of the fire ceased and was extinguished
and became like a breath of cool dew.
He commanded Michael to bring up the justified one, Apa Anub and
he was uninjured.
The Saviour said to him: '*Take courage, O thou who art mine, Apa*
 Anub,
my fighter in the battles.
Be strong, I am with thee,
I am Jesus thy King.
Behold the time of thy death has come, O Apa Anub, my beloved.
I have risen,
I have come to thee to tell thee of thy crown of light.
Behold, three crowns have I prepared for thee,
to place them on thy head,
one for thy exile,
one for thy blood which thou hast shed,
the other one for all the afflictions
which thou hast received for my name, O my chosen one, Apa Anub.'

BA.HY.I.AN.B. 235.4

4. *That night the Lord appeared to him.*
 *He said to him: '*Be strong of heart, O Lacaron,
 for I am the Lord, Jesus Christ.
 Be strong and have courage.
 I am with thee in all thy afflictions which will happen to thee.
 I swear by myself that thou wilt make festival
 with all the Holy Ones of the house in the Heavenly Jerusalem.
 And thy name will receive glory upon the whole earth
 and thy martyrdom will be famous in the whole world.
 Be strong and have courage.'
 Thus the Saviour embraced him,
 He gave him Peace,
 He departed up to heaven in glory, with His holy angels.
 The blessed Apa Lacaron kept vigil for the whole night until the light
 dawned,
 being strengthened in heart with the joy which the Lord had granted
 him.

BA.HY.I.LAC.B. 4.3

5. *In the middle of the night,*
 while the holy men were in the prison,
 behold, our Lord Jesus Christ came down from heaven,

with Michael on His right side and Gabriel on His left side.
The whole prison was greatly lighted.
The good Saviour answered, he said to them:
'Greeting my chosen ones in the hour of greeting,
greeting my holy martyrs. Be strong and take power,
I am the Lord for whose name you receive these afflictions.
I am Jesus, who has sent His angel.
He has saved you, He has taken you down from the hermetarion.'
As our Lord Jesus Christ was saying these things
the saints took courage,
the chains which bound them were loosed, the stones fell down from them,
they cast themselves down forthwith at the feet of our Lord Jesus, they worshipped Him.
He embraced them,
He said to them: 'Take courage and fight in the contest
so that you may wear the crown given by my Father.
For it is necessary for you to receive many afflictions for my name from this impious one.
I will send to you Gabriel, the Archangel, to save you from all your sufferings. (   )
Thou, O my beloved Athom, do thou take courage and be strong,
I know that thou art a determined one,
thou art firm in thy state of mind, long-suffering with these impious ones
until thou dost receive the unfading crown in my Kingdom for ever.'
When the Saviour had said these things to them,
He gave them Peace,
He departed up to the heavens,
while the holy men looked after Him.

HY.PI.AT.B. 144.13

6. At that moment, behold the archangel Michael came down from heaven,
he embraced them all one by one.
He turned to the Saint Apa Sarapion.
He said to him: 'Greeting, O best man of Christ the King.
I say to thee, O thou beloved of God, Apa Sarapion
that there is a multitude of justified ones
who will applaud the great glory which will appear for thee,
for indeed thy fragrance has spread forth in the Heavenly Jerusalem (   ).

646

For a number of miracles will happen because of thee
and thou wilt confound Arianus and his unclean idols.'
The blessed man said to Michael, the Archangel:
'I beg thee, my Lord, that thou wilt give strength to me
until I complete my course.'
And thus the Archangel Michael stretched forth his right hand over the
*   body of the blessed Apa Sarapion, saying:*
'No torments will be able to prevail over thy body. ( )
A great gift will be manifest in this town because of thee.'
After this Michael turned to the crowd of holy men, he said to them:
'Take courage, let your hearts be strong
for this time tomorrow the hegemon will pronounce sentence on you.
I will come to you with a multitude of angels to remove your souls up
*   to the heavens*
so that each one of you receive his throne and his crown.'
After this Michael embraced them.
He gave them Peace.
He went up to the heavens in glory.
The blessed Apa Sarapion continued to give encouragement
to the brother martyrs from the holy Scriptures
until the dawn rose.

BA.HY.I.SA.PA.B. 74.11

7. *In the middle of the night*
    an angel of the Lord appeared to him.
    The whole house became greatly lighted.
    The angel said to him: *'Greeting, Abba Isaac,*
    the Lord be with thee.'
    The blessed man said to him: 'Thy blessing be with me.'
    He brought him outside his house,
    he said to him: 'Endure and thou wilt receive the imperishable crown.
    For I say to thee, (they are) thy crown and thy throne in the heavens.
    Do not fear, I remain with thee
    until thou completest thy martyrdom.
    Thou wilt receive many afflictions for the name of Christ,
    but take courage and I will come and give power to thee.'
    When he had said these things, the angel departed up to the heavens.

BA.HY.II.IS.TI.B. 74.21

8. *In the middle of the night the Lord with His holy angels came into the*
    prison.
    He passed His hand over his whole body.
    He healed him.

647

He stood him up.
He said to him: '*Take courage O my beloved holy, strong one.*
I am with thee with my good Father and the Holy Spirit.
For the day approaches on which thou shalt receive the diadem of the
Kingdom and the unfading crown for ever and ever.'
When the Lord had said these things to him, He embraced him
and He filled him completely with power.
He departed up to heaven in glory and splendour.

BA.HY.II.GEO.DI.B. 235.13

9. When he went forth in the hour of morning according to his custom,
   he knew nothing.
   Michael, the Archangel, appeared to him,
   he said to him: '*Greeting, Paphnute, thou soldier of Christ.*'
   Apa Paphnute also greeted him: 'Hail.'
   The Archangel said to him: '*Thy dwelling, which thou has been*
   building since thy childhood,
   walk with me and I will cause thee to complete its roof.
   Go into thy cell, gird thyself with thy girdle and put on the vestment of
   service
   because I have come today to summon thee to the wedding chamber
   of thy Lord in this place
   so that thou mayest remain in the company of thy Lord. ( )
   But take courage. Do not fear,
   for I am Michael, the Archangel, he who was with thy fathers.
   I will be with thee also.
   The Lord will give power to thee until thou dost put to shame Arianus
   and his (idols) made by hand.'
   And when he had heard these things from the Archangel,
   Apa Paphnute made his way into his cell.
   He girded himself with his girdle and he put on his service vestment
   namely his pallium with his lention
   and he walked rejoicing like one going to a feast.
   And the angel took his hand, he spoke with him,
   telling him of the mysteries of heaven until they came forth upon the
   river.
   Immediately they arrived upon the bank,
   Michael told him all things which would happen to him.
   And he embraced him.
   He went up to heaven
   while his eyes followed him.

BA.HY.I.PAP.B. 110.16

10. *When night came he prayed,* ( )
    '*Let me be worthy to see a consolation tonight,*
    because this is the first night that I have dealings with thy holy men
    and I shall know that thou wilt give power to me
    until I receive thy imperishable crown.'
    While the saint Apa Pteleme was praying until the (middle) of the
        night,
    behold, he saw a vision
    as if Apa Paphnute stood with Apa Dorotheus, the Light,
    and the Saviour was in their midst.
    Apa Paphnute said to him: '*Blessing upon thee, my son Pteleme,*
    for great is thy lot and the day on which thou wast born,
    until thou wast worthy of this great gift which will be assigned to
        thee.'
    The saint Apa Paphnute said to him: 'O Pteleme,
    thy father Nestorius will celebrate thy birthday before the Holy Ones
        in heaven.'
    Apa Pteleme said to the Holy Ones: '*Who is this other one who is in*
        your midst
    and of whom I am not worthy that he should speak with me?
    For I see that he is more glorious than you.'
    Apa Paphnute said to him: 'Thou art not yet worthy to speak with
        him.
    When thou hast received thy crown of martyrdom,
    he will appear to thee and speak with thee at all times.'
    Then Apa Pteleme perceived that it was the Lord Jesus Christ.
    He hastened to fall upon his face.
    He worshipped Him, he said: 'Forgive me, my Lord Jesus Christ.'
    He said to him: '*My peace be with thee, O my chosen one Pteleme,*
    who hast done the will of my Father, who is in the heavens.'
    At that moment He gave him Peace,
    He departed up to heaven.
    Immediately the blessed Apa Pteleme heard voices from heaven.
    He jumped up under the impulse of the vision,
    while his whole body was bathed in sweat,
    as if his flesh was unharmed,
    he found the light coming forth.

                                        TIL.II.PTOL.S. 29.28

11. The wicked custodians took the holy man Azazail while little life
        was in him
    and they cast him into prison.

And the angel of the Lord descended beside him and said to him:
'Peace be with thee, Azazail, chosen martyr of the Lord,
truly thou hast suffered greatly for Him.
And thou hast borne many torments for love of Him.
Behold, He expects thee in His presence,
that thou shouldst rejoice with Him in His Kingdom
with all His saints who have loved and have done His will.
Behold the garden (of Paradise) is prepared for thee.
And the Table of Life is kept for thee.
And He has sent me to thee to heal thy wounds and stripes,
so that thou shouldst go again and put to shame the impious and
    godless king,
whose empire will be destroyed in a short time,
and who will perish and go to Gehenna,
which is waiting and ready for him,
in which he will be punished.
And know that after ten days, He will call for thee
that thou shouldst receive the crown of martyrdom.
But rise and pray for the earth and its inhabitants
and for the Church and her sons.
And pray for peace and quiet,
because all that thou shalt ask from Christ thy Lord, He will give
    thee.'

MAC.AZ.SY. 25(53)

12. *As he was praying on these things,*
    behold, a great light shone in the place in which he was enclosed.
    And he saw a chorus of saints
    with the Lord Jesus Christ in their midst
    and the Lord said to him: 'Be strong and take power, O valiant
        athlete.
    Behold I am with thee, giving power to thee
    in the great stadium in which thou dost stand
    until thou dost receive the crown of thy confession.
    For behold, thou wilt receive further great afflictions for my name
    until thou dost complete thy contest.
    But after a short time thou wilt rejoice with me upon my table
    in my Kingdom which is in the heavens
    and I will cause thy name to be famous in all places
    as far as the land of Egypt, the place in which thy body will lie.
    After a time, they will build for thee a martyrion in that place
    as a memorial for thee, in which great miracles and marvels will happen

650

to everyone who will ask me in thy name.'
And the chorus of saints made their way,
they drew out all the spikes from his body
and he was healed.
Immediately his whole body was whole,
he sang psalms. (   )
Then the Lord departed up from him
and again he sang psalms.

BA.HY.II.IAC.P.B. 33.21

13. *It happened one night,*
   as the holy Saint Basilides was standing keeping vigil
   and making his prayers, according to his custom,
   behold, the good Saviour appeared in the form of a beautiful youth.
   He said to him: *'Greeting my chosen one, Basilides;*
   greeting, O strong athlete in the contests,
   greeting, thou for whom is built thy house in the Heavenly Jerusalem
   the City of all the Righteous;
   greeting, thou whose name is written on the diptych
   in the Church of the First-Born which is in the heavens,
   together with the name of Eusebius thy son and Macarius and all thy
      relatives,
   thou who art called the father of the martyrs.'
   Basilides said to Him: 'Tell me who thou art my Lord,
   who art in such great glory.'
   The Saviour said to him: 'I am Jesus Christ,
   whom thou dost serve and to whom thou art servant.
   Behold, my Father has already written thy name
   with Eusebius and Macarius, thy sons, and all thy relatives
   on the diptych of the Church of the First-Born. (   )'
   When the Saviour had said these things to him,
   He filled him with power,
   He gave him Peace,
   He departed up to heaven in glory.

HY.EUS.B. 1.16

14. They cast him down into the hold of the ship.
   They sailed with him while he was below in the hold of the ship.
   He was distressed. The blessed man wept, saying: (   )
   'Be with me wherever I shall go, because I shall be taken to a place
      which I do not know, (   )'
   When the Saint Apa Epima had said these things,

651

his prayer was effective at the throne of God.
His prayer entered into the ears of the Lord Sabaoth.
The Lord Jesus came mounted upon a cloud of light,
with Michael at His right side and Gabriel on His left,
while a multitude of angels sang hymns to him.
He stood in the air above the boat.
He said to the Saint Apa Epima: 'Greeting at the time of greeting.
Courage at the time of courage.
I am Jesus (   ).
Do not fear, my chosen one, Epima,
for I am with thee, wherever thou shalt be taken.
I shall give thee thy reward according to thy sufferings.
I shall cause thee to sit upon thy throne
with my saints in my Kingdom.
I shall give thee an honoured name.
I shall cause thee to partake of the endless offering
in the Church of the First-Born in the Heavenly Jerusalem.
Do not fear, my chosen one Epima.
My peace be with thee in all places, Amen.'
When the Saviour had said these things
He went up to the heavens in great glory,
while the angels sang hymns to Him.
And the blessed man's heart rejoiced because he had seen the Lord.

MIN.EPIM.S. 12.16

15. As they said these things,
     behold, our Lord, Jesus Christ came forth from heaven,
     sitting upon a chariot of light,
     with Michael on His right side and Gabriel on His left side,
     while myriads of angels sang hymns to Him.
     He said to the holy men: *'Greeting in the time of greeting, my chosen*
          holy martyrs.
     For your names are already written among the chorus of martyrs
     in the Church of the First-Born by my Good Father.'

HY.PI.AT.B. 169.7

16. *Abraham said to the Lord: 'My Lord, remember my son. (   )'*
     The Lord said to him: *'My power shall be with him*
     and he will be glorified in my name
     and he will rule over the Land of the Inheritance
     and the Enemy will not gain advantage over him.'

GUI.IS.B. 242.10

17. Michael said to him: '*Be strong, O holy man Helias, strong man, athlete,*
contestant who receives the crown,
our fellow-inheritor with Jesus Christ.
Amen, I say to thee, thy throne is already prepared
in the Seventh Heaven at the right hand of Christ.
Do not fear. I will attach myself to thee to help thee
in all places to which thou shalt be taken.'
And when the angel of the Lord said this to him,
he went up to heaven in glory.

SOB.HEL.S. 34a.22

18. *Then he* (Koulkyanus, the hegemon) *took him with Arianus, he proceeded to the South.*
The blessed man was cast into the hold of the ship.
Behold the Saviour appeared to him in the hold of the ship.
When the blessed man saw Him, he cast himself down, he worshipped Him,
saying: '*Remember me, O Lord and give power to me until I complete my course.*'
The Lord said to him: '*Do not fear, I will not forsake thee,*
thee and those who resemble thee
until you become inheritors of the Kingdom.'
Saying these things,
He gave him Peace,
He went up to the heavens.

BA.HY.II.IS.TI.B. 80.5

19. *In the middle of the night,*
behold, the Good Saviour appeared to them,
mounted on a chariot of light,
with Michael on His right side and Gabriel on His left.
And the whole place gave light
seven times more than the sun.
And the Saviour caused the holy Archangel Michael to touch them and rouse them.
When they awakened from sleep they saw the light which surrounded them.
They were afraid and they were disturbed.
The Good Saviour took them,
He removed the fear from them
and He said to them: '*Do not fear, O soldiers of my Good Father and the Holy Spirit,*

653

I am Jesus, the Son of the Living God.'
Then they cast themselves down, they all worshipped Him.
He said to them: 'Do not fear, I am with you,
*giving power to you and saving you in all the battles which come upon
    you.*
I am also He who has guarded you since your youth until today.
*Amen, I say to you that my Father has already written your names in
    the Book of Life*
and your houses have already been built in the Heavenly Jerusalem
the City of all the Holy Ones.
Now the time has come that you should go to your houses
and see the faces of your brothers
*and that you should complete the service which has been assigned to
    you,*
*so that you receive the indestructible crowns in the Kingdom of the
    Heavens*
and that you should feast with me for ever and ever, ( )
for the time has come that I should take you to the heavens with me
and that you should rest in Eternal Life.'
When the Good Saviour had said these things to them,
He embraced them,
He gave them Peace,
He departed up to the heavens
as they looked after Him.

HY.EUS.B. 9.9

20. *In the night of the holy Lord's Day,*
    behold our Saviour, Jesus came to him
    and the whole room became light.
    Apater leapt up when he saw the light.
    He said: '*My Lord Jesus Christ, I recognise the glory of thy Godhead,
        my Lord, who hast come to me.'*
    A voice came to him from the light,
    saying: '*Greeting Apater, man worthy of love.*
    Behold, the time of sowing is past. Now is the time for reaping.
    Now therefore rise. ( ) Be strong and have courage, O Apater.
    For my Father has already written your names in the Book of Life.'
    When the Saviour had said these things to him,
    He became invisible to him.

HY.AP.IR.B. 88.1

21. The saint Theodore was taken to the foot of the Persea tree accord-
    ing to the command of the kings

in order that he be hung upon it. ( )
In the middle of the night, behold the Devil stood in his presence. ( )
Theodore said:
'As He who was crucified lives, I will give thee a stab with a spear
  for every nail which pierces in my body.'
Immediately he wept, he fled in shame.
At the hour of daylight the Lord came to him
with the Archangel Michael at His right hand and with Gabriel on
  His left hand.
He said to him: 'Greeting Theodore, my beloved,
dost thou wish me to give thee rest from all thy afflictions? ( )'
He said: 'Yes my Lord.'
At that moment he gave the spirit into the hands of the Lord
and the Saviour gave his soul into the hands of Michael the Archangel.
He guarded it.
He took it up to the heavens with him.
He made him second general.
He placed him on his right hand,
Leontius also on the right of Gabriel, Panikyris also on his left.
This is the manner in which the Lord disposed them in the heavens.

BA.HY.I.TH.O.B. 60.3

22. *As they were saying these things as they were praying, they heard a*
    voice from heaven saying:
    '*As you have been strong athletes in this life,*
    and you have endured many trials, now do not fear.
    Come up to this place in peace
    and receive the imperishable crown
    and enjoy yourselves in the good things which have been prepared for
      you for ever and ever,
    in place of the afflictions which you have received
    and the trials you have endured for a short time.'
    When the holy ones heard these things they gave themselves up with
      joy.
    The soldiers cast them into the brass machine.

BU.EUS.TH.S. 126.7

23. *Thus also was the saint Iakobus, the servant of God,*
    while his head alone was standing with his chest and his belly
    and all his limbs were scattered on the ground in his presence
    and half of his body was dead beneath him. ( )
    And in that hour he saw the Lord Jesus Christ standing above him,

655

saying to him: 'Blessing on thee
because thou hast received affliction for a short time in this place.
Come now and inherit the life eternal
and the good things which are prepared for thee, these which last for ever.
Raise thy eyes up and see the throne which is prepared for thee,
and behold thy crown in the hand of Michael the Archangel.
And all the First-Born whom Herod killed, they come forth before thee
singing psalms to thee, with all the Holy Ones
until thou art brought into the presence of my Father, ( )
so that thou mayest rejoice with all the Holy Ones who have been in this aeon,
namely Abel and Noah and Abraham and Isaac and Jacob and Moses and the rest.'
When our Saviour had said these things *he went up to the heavens in glory.*
And as soon as he gave up his spirit,
one of his companions removed the head of the holy noble martyr, the saint Iakobus.
He went to his rest in peace
having received the crown of the confession

BA.HY.II.IAC.P.B. 47.23; *49.13

3   THE BOAT JOURNEY

THEME

The taking of the martyr to the place appointed for him for death or burial.

EPISODES

The taking of the martyr by boat to his place of execution.
The casting of the martyr into the hold of the boat.
The announcement of the place at which the execution should take place.
The care of the body of the martyr after death.
The taking of the body of the martyr by boat to the South.
The landing of the boat at the place appointed for the burial of the body.

QUOTATIONS

1. The hegemon and the duke mounted on the ship with some groups of soldiers who went with them.
   They spread the sail of the ship.
   They proceeded to the South by the river,

656

until they came to the boundaries of the city of Hnes.
When they reached the landing stage of a village which was called
  Penamoun,
on the West side of the river,
the wind left them.
The boat was moored to the bank with the holy man.
The angel of the Lord stirred the holy Apa Epima,
he said to him: 'Prepare thyself, O athlete of Christ, for thy fight
  approaches.
For this is the place which the Lord has prepared for thee,
that thou shouldst complete the course in it.'
There was a camp in that place in which was the tribune, ( )
they brought some oxen in order to go up to the temple and worship
  the unclean gods.
At that moment the oxen stopped.
They would not walk to one side or the other.
The saint Apa Epima said to them: '*As God lives,*
you will not pass this place before you give to me my sentence,
for this is the place for my course which has been assigned to me.'

MIN.EPIM.S. 30.12

2. The hegemon and the duke mounted the ship with a group of sol-
     diers.
   They proceeded to the South
   until they reached the city of Hnes.
   When they reached a village called (Penamoun) on the west side of
     the river,
   the wind left the ship.
   They reached the bank with the holy man
   and an angel of the Lord stirred the side of Apa Epime.
   He said to him: 'Prepare thyself, O athlete of Christ the King,
   for thy crown and thy conflict approach.
   This is the path which the Lord has prepared for thee
   in which to complete thy holy profession (of faith).'
   The hegemon and the duke spent three days waiting in that place
   because of the tempestuousness of the winds.
   Afterwards they were told: 'There is a temple to the West of the
     city with some gods within.
   Rise, let us go there and worship them.'
   There was a camp in it with the tribune set up over it. ( )
   The hegemon sent to bring to him some oxen

that they should go to the temple and worship the gods.
At that moment the oxen stopped and were not able to walk at all.
The saint Apa Epime said to them: '*As the Lord Jesus Christ lives,*
you will not pass this road until you pronounce my sentence,
because this is the road which the Lord has appointed for me
that I should complete on it my course.'

BA.HY.I.EPIM.B. 149.14

3. *Behold a great marvel and a great miracle happened through God,*
   so that a great thunder came from the sky.
   And the hegemon was troubled with all his company,
   so that the oxen stood still and would not walk under them.
   When Philea, the orator and man of Ashmun, saw what had
      happened (   )
   he said (   ): 'Now therefore, behold, he has stopped the oxen and
      he does not allow them to walk before us.
   See what thou wilt do to him, so that he will allow us to proceed.'

TIL.I.TIM.S. 118.15

4. *After these things, they mounted him on the ship,*
   they proceeded to the South
   until they reached a village which was called Chetnoufi.
   The saint Apa Macarius made many great prayers,
   by day and night.
   Then while he was praying one night,
   Michael, the holy Archangel, appeared to him.
   He said to him: 'Macarius, do not fear,
   for the crown of thy martyrdom approaches.
   This is the place which the Lord has appointed for thee
   in which thy holy body is to be placed.
   And He will not allow anything good to lack to it,
   because of thy body which He has consigned to it.'

HY.MAC.AN.B. 66.1

5. While the blessed Apater prayed,
   for he was weak in his body because of the asceticism which he
      practised,
   behold the place in which he stood all became light.
   He saw a hand beckoning him in the light.
   He walked after it.
   He came forth to waken his sister.
   The Saviour did not allow him, saying: 'Do not disturb her now.'

And he came forth troubled because of the voice, as he followed after
  it.
The Saviour said to him: 'Obey me.'
Rise and go to the South of Egypt, thou and thy sister,
because my Father has already blessed that road.
Walk upon the banks of the river.
After five days, thou wilt reach Terenouthi.
Cross the river, *walk to the South in that place.*
Thou shalt go to the Camp of Babylon
and seek after Apokrajon, the monk and man of Nebou.
It is he who will teach thee the good fight.
Afterwards thou wilt go South to a village called Tchinilah, near to
  the town of Shmoun,
the place where I was guest, with Mary my mother and Joseph.
Do not be sad, because I also became a stranger, I your Lord. ( )
I will cause a multitude of angels to attend on (thy body)
because thou hast renounced all things for my name.
Go in peace. My peace be with you.
To the village in which your bodies will be laid, no trouble or danger
  will come to that village.'

HY.AP.IR.B. 91.9

6. When they rose in the morning, they looked each way. ( )
   As they were considering, a voice came from heaven
   saying: 'O Sarapion, my beloved, this is not the village at which you
     landed,
   but *this is thy village, the place in which thy body will be laid.*
   In the shrine, in which thy body will be laid,
   I will cause my blessing and my peace to be.
   I will cause many cures to happen to every one who will come to thy
     shrine.
   I will make a great feast day of benediction
   to take place in the shrine in which thy body will be laid, ( )
   apart from (that on) the day on which thou wilt complete thy martyr-
     dom.'

BA.HY.I.SA.PA.B. 87.3

7. *And in that hour they boarded the blessed Apa Anub on the ship.*
   They proceeded to the South with him.
   The saint, Apa Anub, prayed in the hold of the ship,
   saying: '( ) *I saw thy angels, my Lord, putting crowns on thy holy*
     martyrs.

659

Do thou give power to me, O my Lord Jesus Christ, until thy will con-
cerning me is fulfilled.
Thou knowest me, O my Lord, that I am a stranger,
being taken to a strange country, which is far from my village.
I have no man to follow me,
neither father nor mother to bury my body,
neither relatives nor villagers to take my bones to my village. ( )'
And he did not cease from beseeching, as he prayed until the middle
of the night.
In the middle of the night,
behold, the Archangel Michael came to him in the hold of the ship.
He caused the whole ship to give light in the night, as if it were the
day.
He said to him: 'Greeting, thou beloved one of God, Apa Anub.
Greeting to all who have believed through thee.
Take courage, Do not be faint-hearted,
for indeed, I will grant all thy requests, ( )
until thou shalt receive the unfading crown.'
Immediately he gave him Peace,
he departed up to the heavens in glory.

BA.HY.I.AN.B. 224.28

8. They put irons on his feet, *they cast him into the hold of the ship,*
   they sailed with him to the North of Alexandria.
   The blessed Apa Epime was distressed, he raised his eyes to heaven
   saying: 'My Lord Jesus Christ, be to me a help in all paths on which
   I shall be taken.'
   When he had said these things,
   behold, our Lord, Jesus Christ came to him,
   mounted on a cloud of light,
   with Michael on His right side and Gabriel on His left side.
   The Saviour answered, He said to Apa Epime:
   'Greeting, my chosen one Epime,
   be strong and have courage,
   for I am with thee in all places to which thou shalt be taken.
   I am Jesus, thy King, ( )
   I will cause thy name to be famous in the whole world.
   I will cause great signs and cures to happen through thee.
   I will cause the peoples to come forth in all places to worship over thy
   holy body.'
   When the Saviour had said these things
   He went up to the heavens in glory.

The blessed Apa Epime, when he had seen the Lord, his heart rejoiced.

BA.HY.I.EPIM.B. 133.19

9. He was given into the hands of four soldiers
   and they brought him to the river
   and they cast him into the hold of the ship,
   bound hand and foot.
   And behold, our Lord, Jesus Christ came down from heaven,
   mounted on a cloud of light.
   He stood above the ship,
   He said to the Saint: '*Greeting, thou who art mine, Apa Didymus.*
   Be strong, O noble one, I am Jesus thy King,
   do not fear, I am with thee in all places to which thou wilt go.
   I will give thee glory which is wonderful upon the earth.
   I will cause thee to partake of the endless offering.'
   And He gave him Peace, He went up to heaven in great glory.

HY.DID.B. 296.13

10. The saint Apa Epima smiled at Julius
    and said: '(   ) *There is one thing which I ask of thee*
    because I am in a strange land,
    I have no man to care for me
    in this place when my sentence is pronounced.
    I wish that thou shouldst care for my body
    and that thou shouldst send it to my burial place
    with my fathers and all my kinsmen,
    for my God has said to me: "*Thy body will spend a long time in that place.*"
    But do thou command the men to whom thou shalt give my body,
    saying: "Do not tell anyone upon the road on which you will travel that it is a martyr,"
    otherwise they will remove it from them
    and will not allow them to take it to the shrine
    which God has prepared for me.
    If thou wilt do this favour for me,
    I also will receive grace for thee from my God, Christ Jesus.'
    Julius said to him: 'I am prepared to do this thing,
    since last night I was commanded in a vision from an angel of God that I should do this.
    And I will write thy memorials.
    I will take them to my house and place them there,

*so that thy blessing and thy peace will remain
in my house and my whole seed
for all the generations of the earth.
But I beg thee, that thou wilt remember me and all my house
in the places to which thou wilt go.'*
The saint, *Apa Epima opened his mouth, he blessed Julius*
saying: '*My Lord Jesus will bless thee with the blessing of His mouth,
He will bless thy heavenly house which is not made with hands, in
heaven
And neither famine nor pestilence will happen in thy house upon earth,
and thy descendants for three or four generations will not see the
judgment of Amente.
Thou wilt be numbered among the choir of martyrs of Jesus Christ,
Amen.'*

MIN.EPIM.S. 16.15

11. The saint Apa Epime smiled, he said to Julius: ( )
    '*There is a favour which I ask of thee,
    that thou shouldst care for my body
    when sentence is pronounced upon me,
    and that thou shouldst take it to Egypt
    to the burial place of my fathers and all my kinsmen.'*
    Julius said to him: 'I am prepared to do this very thing,
    *but I beg thee that thou wilt remember me
    in the places to which thou wilt go.'*
    And the saint Apa Epime opened his mouth, he blessed him
    saying: '*May God the Father of my Lord Jesus Christ bless thee, my
    brother Julius.
    Neither famine nor plague will exist in thy house
    nor will thy seed ever see punishment.'*

BA.HY.I.EPIM.B. 137.7

12. *When the saint Apa Epima had said these things,
    he turned his face back,* he saw the servants of Julius ( ),
    *he said to them: 'When they have cut off my head, secure my body
    well.
    Seek a ship and put me on it,*
    otherwise these impious ones will not transport me with them.
    *Take me to the South to the landing stage of Pmouche.
    Deposit me in that place.*
    Seek an ox and mount me on it.
    The Lord will send his angel as guide to the ox

until it brings me to the burial place of my fathers.
For the Lord has said to me: " Thy body will remain a long time there."
And guard yourselves lest men ask you "Where are you going" or
   "What is that?"
Do not say "It is a martyr" otherwise they will take my body from
   your hands
and they will not allow you to take it to the place which the Lord has
   prepared for me.'

MIN.EPIM.S. 33.4

13. *When the saint Apa Epime had finished praying,* (   )
   he said to them: ' *When my head is removed*
   protect my body well and *seek a boat and put me on it*
   and take me to the burial place of my fathers.'
   While he was saying these things
   behold Our Lord the Christ stood above him in great glory
   and the whole place was lighted seven times (more brightly)
   so that the multitude said: '*It is a fire which has come forth from*
      heaven in order to burn us.'
   The Saviour said to the saint Apa Epime: '*Peace to thee, O my*
      chosen one, Epime,
   be strong and have courage.
   Do not fear for I am with thee.'

BA.HY.I.EPIM.B. 152.24

4   THE EXECUTION

THEME

The culmination of the life of the martyr in his execution at the appointed
   time and place.

EPISODES

The appearance of the Saviour to encourage the martyr at the time of
   death.
The request by the martyr to the executioners that the sentence of death
   be pronounced.
The request by the martyr to the executioners that they fulfil that which
   they have been commanded.
The fastening of the gag to the mouth; the stretching out of the neck; the
   removal of the head.
The coming forth of blood and milk.

663

QUOTATIONS

1. *While the saint Apater was standing praying,*
   our Saviour, the Lord Jesus appeared to him.
   He said to him: '*Greeting Apater, my chosen holy virgin.*
   Have courage in all thy troubles.
   Yet another six days remain until thou fulfil thy martyrdom.'
   Apater said to him: '*My Lord and my God, there is a request which*
       I beg of thee.'
   The Saviour said to him: '*O my chosen one, Apater,*
   I swear by myself that what thou shalt request of me, I will give thee.'
   Apater said to him: '*I beg thee not to cause my sentence*
   to be given on the day of rest of a martyr.'
   The Saviour said to him: '*It shall be thus.*'

   HY.AP.IR.B. 107.16

2. *When the hegemon heard these things, he was greatly troubled.*
   He said to the saint Apater; 'Woe is me, my Lord.
   Let my soul live in thy presence,
   for I do not live any longer, but I shall die.'
   The saint said to him: 'Arianus, *do not fear to set aside the oath.*
   But pronounce sentence upon us.
   For behold, I see two angels standing by thee,
   one is that of light, one is that of darkness. (   )
   After I die, the King will send for thee in great anger
   because of the manner in which thou shalt return to the Lord.
   Thou also wilt be a martyr,
   for already thy crown is prepared for thee up in heaven.
   Behold the saint Philemon in prison.
   It is he who will teach thee the conflict.'

   HY.AP.IR.B. 108.21

3. And when they (Apa Sarapion and executioners) arrived before
       the town Pshati, the wind left them.
   They went aground on the left bank of the river
   and when midnight came they woke
   and found themselves aground on the right bank.
   And the angel of the Lord woke Orion the Cursor.
   He said to him: '*Rise, take Apa Sarapion to kill him.*
   This order is not from men but it is from the Lord Jesus Christ
   so that he does not pass this place (on his way) to the South.'

   HY.SAR.B. 328.17

4. *The saint, Apa Macarius, answered, he spoke to him in the power of*
    God saying: ( )
   ' *Behold for twenty-one days nothing of this world has entered my*
      mouth.
   And thou has said further: " *Who were these who spoke with thee?* "
   This was the great Archon, Michael the Commander-in-Chief of the
      power(s) of the heavens
   whom the Lord, Jesus Christ sent to me,
   he told me of the completion of my martyrdom in this place.
   Now therefore do thou hasten and pronounce on me my sentence,
   for behold, the Lord with His angels awaits me.'

HY.MAC.AN.B. 68.1

5. *He pronounced the sentence on him*
   that his head should be removed,
   and that he should be taken to an island in the sea and be left in it.

SOB.HEL.S. 64a.4

6. *The blessed man, when they brought him to the place in which he would*
      die,
   said to those who held him: 'I beg you, my brothers, to have patience
      with me for a little,
   that I may make a prayer to the Lord that He receive my spirit.'
   They then allowed him and *he cried out with a great voice*
   saying: '( ) *Let the torturers of Amente flee from me,*
   with the changing faces which I do not know,
   these which trouble the soul.
   Let the River of Fire which surges, cease in my presence until I cross it.
   Let all the evil powers flee. ( )
   Give a favour, O Lord to my body,
   so that all men who are sick of any illness,
   whether fever or chill or bodily wound or any evil sickness,
   if they will come upon my body and pray in thy name,
   thou wilt heal them. ( )'
   As he said these things,
   two soldiers took his two arms, they stretched him out.
   An executioner came, *he drew his sword,*
   he removed the (head) of the saint Apa Anub.
   There came from it blood and milk.
   He gave up the spirit, ( )
   on the Lord's day at the ninth hour of the day.
   Then Julius, the man of Kbehes waited until the middle of the night.
   He came to the body of the saint which was cast out,

665

he raised it, he placed it on a fine cloth,
he placed incense on it, with oil and wine.
He mounted it upon a boat with three servants.
He proceeded to the South with it for three days and two nights,
until they reached a village, Chetnoufi.
They came North, by the river.

BA.HY.I.AN.B. 239.22

7. After these things, the saint Apa Epima turned to the executioners
   he said to them: 'Come, my brothers and fulfil that which you have
      been commanded.'
   At that moment the gag was fastened to his mouth,
   his head was removed.
   There came forth from it blood and milk.
   And the place where his head was removed moved three times.
   The Lord Jesus took the soul of Apa Epima.
   He embraced him,
   He mounted him with Himself upon the chariot.
   He took him up to heaven.
   He made him sit upon his throne of glory.
   He placed on his head the imperishable crown of eternity.
   This is the manner in which the saint Apa Epima completed his
      martyrdom (   ) in the peace of God, Amen. (   )
   Then the servants of Julius took fine cloths with spices, which their
      lord had given them.
   They wrapped in them the righteous man
   They mounted him on a small boat, they proceeded South with him,
      until they reached the shore of Pmoushe.

MIN.EPIM.S. 34.4

8. After these things, the saint Apa Epime turned to the executioners.
   He said to them: '*Come, fulfil the command which has been given to*
      you.'
   And immediately they put a gag in his mouth.
   They dragged him.
   They removed his head.
   There came forth from his body blood and milk.
   And the Lord received his blessed soul,
   He embraced him,
   He placed him on the stole of the Archangel Michael.
   And He took him up to heaven with Him,
   He put a crown on him

666

in unspeakable glory in His Kingdom.
Then the servants of Julius brought forth fine cloths which their
  lord had given them, with choice spices.
*They wrapped in them the body of the holy man, they mounted it in a
  small boat,*
They proceeded with it to the shore of Shmoun.

BA.HY.I.EPIM.B. 153.28

9. And the holy man roused the soldiers,
  *saying to them: 'Come, my brothers, fulfil that which has been com-
    manded to you.'*
  And thus he stretched out his neck
  and the soldiers removed his holy head
  and immediately there came forth from it blood and milk.
  *And the Lord caused Michael to receive his blood and his milk in his
    stole of light*
  and the Lord received his soul in His own hand
  and He embraced him
  and He wrapped him in heavenly purples
  and He went up to the height with him.
  *And the whole Firmament was filled with holy angels and the chorus of
    the Holy Ones*
  and they sang hymns before him
  until He gave him as a gift to His good Father with the Holy Spirit.
  And He put on him his stole of light
  and a diadem of choice gold and it was studded with precious stones,
  and seven crowns upon it
  and they were plaited with blossoms of the Tree of Life.
  And He wrote his name with the First-Born for ever.
  *And He caused all the ranks of heaven and the companies of the Holy
    Ones to seat him upon the throne*
  and to make festival with him in the Heavenly Jerusalem.

BA.HY.II.GEO.DI.B. 257.18

10. *As the saint was saying these things*
  in the ardour of his heart, behold the Lord Jesus Christ appeared to him
  saying: 'Come now up to heaven and rest thyself
  *in the dwelling place which I have prepared for thee in the Kingdom
    of my Father in the heavens.*
  *O my chosen one, George, everything which thou hast asked I will
    grant them all to thee,*
  with many others which are greater than these.'

667

The saint George said to the executioners: '*Come now,*
complete the commandment which you have been given.'
And he stretched out his neck,
they removed his holy head.
There came forth water and milk.
The Lord Jesus received his blessed soul,
He kissed him, He took him up to the heavens with Him.
He gave him as a gift to His good Father with the Holy Spirit.
In that moment the earth shook to its foundation.
There were thunder and lightning which were terrifying
so that not one man passed forth from that place from great fear.

BA.HY.II.GEO.B. 310.1

11. *When he had finished the Amen,*
a voice came to him from heaven
saying to him: '*Come now O holy martyr of Christ thou saint Apatil.*
    Rest thyself with all the Holy Ones,
these with whom thou wilt receive the good things of Eternity,
to be a rest to you without end, in heaven and for ever.'
And when the saint Apatil heard these things
his spirit rejoiced within him, and *he urged the soldiers, saying to*
    them:
'*Complete that which you have been commanded.*'
And then when he had bent his knees he stretched out his neck in
    silence.
One of the soldiers pronounced on him the sentence of death
and when he gave him a blow with the sword which was in his hand,
he separated his holy head
and thus he left behind him this life.
He departed to Him whom he loved, the Christ.
He was with Him for ever.

BA.HY.I.AP.B. 107.26

12. And when the glorious martyr, Mar Azazail, had finished his prayer.
    and request to God,
   he traced three Crosses upon his face
   and in every direction he traced the Cross.
   He raised his voice, saying:
   'Lord, receive my soul in peace,
   that I will see thy face with joy.'
   And the martyr, Azazail said to the custodians:
   'Fulfil the command of your impious king.'

668

Then the custodians cut off the head of the glorious martyr,
    clothed by God, Mar Azazail.

MAC.AZ.SY. 35(85/86)

13. *When he had said the Amen*
    the Saviour appeared to him.
    He said to him: '*Take courage,*
    Apa Apoli, I am with thee until thou dost complete thy martyrdom
    so that thou come to me and I give thee the reward for thy sufferings.
    Do not hold thyself back
    so that I may receive thee up into the heavens in unspeakable glory.'
    Immediately the saint Apoli said to the soldiers:
    '*Hasten yourselves, come and complete your task.'*
    And he stretched out his neck.
    They removed his holy head with the blade of the sword
    and his head fell upon the earth.
    And Michael with Gabriel received his soul.
    And the Saviour embraced it,
    He took it up to the heavens in glory.

BA.HY.I.APOL.B. 247.5

14. *He turned his face to the East, he prayed:* ( )
    '*Do not put me to shame as I come before thee.'*
    The sweet voice of the Lord came to him immediately:
    '*Amen I say to thee, O my chosen one Helias,*
    that the heart of my Father is satisfied with thy contest.
    Behold those of heaven crowned before thee.
    Be strong thou who hast been strong. Be powerful thou who hast been
      powerful.'
    The holy Helias, when he heard these things,
    he crossed himself in the name of the Father and the Son and the
      Holy Spirit.
    And he stretched out his neck.
    They removed his head ( ).
    The angels and all the Holy Ones came forth before him.
    They embraced him
    and they sang the ode and alleluia until they took him to the city of
      Christ.
    When his head was removed,
    his body was taken and left on an island in the middle of the sea,
    until the day that God manifested it to two righteous monks
    in the land of Egypt in a vision,
    and they should go after his body and bring it to Egypt

669

and place it in the place which the Lord had prepared for him.
This is the manner in which he completed his martyrdom.
He went up to heaven in glory.
He received the imperishable crown in peace. Amen.

SOB.HEL.S. 64a.14

15. One of the soldiers seized his hair,
    he brought him forward, *he smote him with the sword,*
    he removed his holy head (   ).
    Raphael received his soul.
    He embraced it.
    He wrapped it in cloths of linen.
    He took it up to heaven in glory.

HY.EUS.B. 38.14

16. And Orion the Cursor rejoiced greatly. He rose, *he opened the door*
    of the hold.
    he brought the blessed Apa Sarapamon up,
    he brought him to the North of the town of Pshati.
    His head was removed in the presence of the town
    and each one cast a garment upon his body.
    And Orion the Cursor removed his head.
    There came forth water and milk.
    He completed his martyrdom (   ) in the peace of God.
    May his holy blessing be with us all forever, Amen.
    Orion the Cursor looked up with his eyes to the sky,
    he saw a great company of angels,
    singing with the soul of the saint, Apa Sarapamon,
    wrapped in a linen cloth
    and he watched them until they reached up to the heavens.

HY.SAR.B. 329.18

17. When Orion, the Cursor, heard this voice
    he had the blessed Apa Sarapion brought up from the hold of the ship.
    His holy head was removed.
    He, Orion the Cursor, divested a linen garment of his
    from those he wore.
    He caused the body of the blessed Apa Sarapion to be wrapped with
    honour
    Orion, the Cursor, prayed over it
    saying: 'Remember me, O my holy Apa Sarapion
    in the place to which thou wilt go.'

BA.HY.I.SA.PA.B. 87.17

18. When the Saviour had said these things to the General,
He caused Michael to take him so that he raised him.
And they took the soul of the Anatolian up to heaven (   ).
They wrapped him in a silken shroud of kings.
This is the manner in which the martyrdom of the saint, Theodore, the
Anatolian, was completed, (   ) in the Peace of God, Amen.

BA.HY.II.T.A.T.S.B. 114.24

19. *The soldiers immediately placed the gag in his mouth,*
they brought him to the place in which he should complete (his
course). (   )
*The blessed man turned to the executioners.
He said to them: 'Come, complete your service.'
Immediately the executioners came.
The blessed Apa Lacaron stretched out his neck.
They removed his holy head.
He completed his good course (   ).
There came a great light in that place.
The whole place spread perfume
because of the number of angels who had come for the soul of the
blessed Apa Lacaron.
The Saviour took his soul into the heavens with Himself
and His angels who followed Him.
And the whole chorus of Holy Ones came forth before him,
they embraced him until he was taken to the City
of our Lord and our God and our Saviour, Jesus Christ,

BA.HY.I.LAC.B. 20.17; *22.16

20. *When he was brought to the place where his head would be removed,*
he prayed and he signed himself with the Cross.
After this he stretched forth his neck,
his head was removed
and all those gathered with him bore witness, saying:
'*At that time we smelt a sweet smell,*
more precious than any upon the earth.'

BA.HY.I.TH.S.B. 193.1

5 INSTRUCTIONS ON BURIAL; ON BUILDING A SHRINE
THEMES

The appearance of the holy man to give instructions concerning the
burial of his body; the building of his shrine.
The giving of instructions concerning the burial of the Virgin.

EPISODES

The anger of the holy man at the removal of his body from its appointed place.

The carrying of the coffin containing the body of the holy man through the air to the place of burial.

The giving of instructions by the holy man to find his body and to perform the burial.

The giving by the holy man of instructions to build his oratory, shrine, martyrion.

The designation by the holy man of the site of the building.

The carrying out of the instructions by the hearers.

QUOTATIONS

1. (The brothers) after removing the body of the martyr at night,
   rose and ran with it upon (the banks of) the river
   seeking a boat, in order to sail
   before the men of that place knew and took him from them.
   As they were standing on the bank looking for a boat
   desiring to leave quickly,
   the holy man stood above them.
   He said to them: 'What are you doing? Have I done any harm to you?
   Have I not gone with you all this time by day and night,
   giving light to you like the Children of Israel,
   at the time when God over-shadowed them with a column of cloud by day
   and with a column of fire all night ( )?
   Why now do you wish to break the covenant which the Lord established?
   For it is He who wished that I should stay in this place in which I was laid,
   so that His Holy Name should be glorified by it.
   Therefore place my body in this stone coffin,
   board this ship which comes and sail.
   For He who once took Habbakuk from the lake of Babylon
   and Ezekiel from Babylon to Jerusalem,
   it is He who will cause me to dwell in the place from which you have removed me.
   The Lord Christ will give you the reward for your trouble
   and He will guide you and save you from all the afflictions of evil. ( )
   And I will be with you in all places where you go.'
   When he had said these things to them,

suddenly the holy body and the stone coffin were taken in the air.
They were placed in the dyke to the South of Paim at night.

BA.HY.II.IAC.P.B. 56.19

2. *There was a God-loving woman in that village,*
   who had practised the life of virginity since her youth,
   who was chaste, loving pilgrims and holy men.
   Her name was Theodora.
   The holy martyr of Christ, the saint Iakobus appeared to her
   in the form of the holy prophet, Daniel,
   with multitudes with him, wearing the garments of the Persians.
   When she saw them she was in a great fear.
   The saint Iakobus spoke to her, saying:
   '*Do not fear, I am Iakobus, from among the Persians,*
   I was not long since made a martyr for the name of Christ,
   for the Lord sent (me) to you.
   He gave me to you that I should be a strength and protector of all
       your village.
   Rise, go to the priest and to all the clergy
   and proceed to the South upon the road of the dyke.
   You will find a great stone coffin in which my body is placed.
   Take it and deal with it according to the will of God.'
   The chaste virgin rose, she came, she told the priest of the village
       all these things.
   He, with the clergy and all those of the village came
   with candles and censers full of incense and many sweet smells,
   he brought the saint Iakobus up in the coffin.
   They sang psalms over him until they brought him into that village
   and they laid him in the church with great zeal.
   They began to build a martyrion for him upon the dyke to the South
       of the village.
   They completed it in a few days ( ), a glorious church.

BA.HY.II.IAC.P.B. 57.27

3. (The Clergy and the rulers) *walked with him* (Eulogius)
   until they reached the place where they removed his (Macarius) holy
       head,
   to the north of Chetnoufi, the place where also he was buried.
   And he caused his body to be brought up.
   And he wept over him for a long time, he embraced him, he kissed his
       mouth.
   Then he put upon him much perfume and he buried him in a royal
       coffin

673

and he had arranged to bring him with him to Antioch.
That night the blessed Apa Macarius appeared to him,
wearing king's garments in great glory.
He said to him: 'Do not remove me from this village,
for indeed this is the place which the Lord ordained for me, until the
end of this aeon,
but do thou arrange for an oratory to be built me in that place where
my head was removed.
And thou also, my beloved brother, the Lord has already prepared for
thee thy crown like the martyrs,
because of the good thing which thou hast done to the Church.
Now do not give up, but add to these things which thou hast done
in Christ.
And to this village also in which my body dwells,
may the peace of Christ give rest for ever.'
Then Eulogius, when he rose in the morning, he did according to
what the saint Apa Macarius had commanded him.
And he brought forth a bag of gold.
He gave the gold to the clergy, that they should build the shrine in all
honour.

HY.MAC.AN.B. 75.20

4. *The brethren brought the body of Iakobus.*
 They laid it beside them in the place in which they were,
 celebrating great services around it morning, noon and evening.
 It happened at midday one day,
 while the holy man Abba Petrus was performing his liturgy,
 with the brothers who were with him,
 suddenly the martyr of Christ, the saint Iakobus appeared to them,
 with a multitude of martyrs wearing the garments of the Persians
 in the likeness of the picture of Daniel, the Prophet, with the Three
 Holy Children,
 and they were standing in their midst,
 singing psalms with them. ( )
 When the saint Petrus and the brethren with him saw them,
 they prostrated themselves,
 they worshipped the holy man.
 And the martyr of Christ, the saint Iakobus, said:
 '*This is my dwelling place, I will dwell in it* because I have
 desired it.
 This is the place which the Lord has ordained for me
 since I lay in the land of Persia.

Rise, come forth to the South of the village a short way,
and pray in that place.
For it is necessary that a martyrion be built for me in that place
and that my body be placed in it,
so that it should be a place of healing
for all those who shall come to the Lord within it
and pray in my name.'
The holy man went forth with the brethren.
They prayed, our father Abba Petrus made the sign of the Cross on the
    earth of that place,
he placed the body of the holy martyr Iakobus in that place
in a small dwelling,
for they had not yet built the shrine in that place.

BA.HY.II.IAC.P.B. 55.11

5. He (Andreas) slept. *Behold, the saint George appeared to him in a*
vision, saying: 'Andreas, Andreas, dost thou know me?'
He said: 'What is it my lord?'
He said to him: 'Dost thou not know me, who I am?'
He said to him: 'No,' although he knew him in the vision but he
    was troubled.
He rose, *he cast himself at his feet, he worshipped him,* saying:
'Thou art alive, indeed my lord, George.'
The saint George said to him: 'Thanks be to God,
my body is with you, *but I live in God through the Holy Spirit.*
Now therefore I have seen thee afraid and troubled, *because of the*
    shrine,
which thou hast undertaken to build in my name, so that thou wilt
    place my body in it.
I have come to thee to tell thee of a small sum from our fathers for
    thee to spend on the shrine.
Take courage, do not be faint hearted.
I will put in the heart of the men of this city that they help thee.
Rise, walk after me and I will make a line in the earth in the chamber
    of my house,
which thou didst disturb as thou didst place my body in it at first,
before thou didst take it to the church.'
Andreas appeared to rise and walk behind him.
The saint George appeared to take him into the chamber of his house.
He showed him the path, in which he had made the trace of his thumb.
He said to him: 'When thou risest tomorrow morning,
come into this place, dig in it one cubit.

675

Thou shalt find the blessing which the Lord has ordained for thee.'
When he had recovered from the vision, he roused his wife.
He told her all things which he had first seen in the vision.
They marvelled greatly.

BA.HY.II.MIR.GEO.B. 318.15

6. When the holy man, the Bishop and Confessor Abba Petrus, knew
   these things,
   he wished to leave Alexandria and go to the region of Maiouma of
   Gaza.
   As he was considering these things, behold, Saint Iakobus appeared
   to him, he said to him:
   'Do not go to Palestine, *but rise, go to the city of Pemje in Egypt*
   and stay in that place.
   For I have wished to dwell in that place
   according as the Lord wished to build for me a martyrion in that place.
   For I am he who will be for thee a guide on all roads on which thou
   goest,
   until thou dost place my bones in the place which I shall tell thee,
   in a small village, five stadia to the East of the city of Pemje,
   the name of which is Paim, according to the speech of the Egyptians.'

BA.HY.II.IAC.P.B. 53.28

7. *Then when our good Saviour had said these things over the body of*
   His mother, He wept.
   And we also wept with Him.
   He rose, He took hold of the heavenly garments,
   He shrouded her holy body, He with Peter and John,
   and the garments were fastened to her body.
   Then our Saviour spoke with the apostles saying:
   'Do you rise and bear the body of my beloved mother. ( )
   Let the rest of the apostles sing before her.
   Go you all forth with her, from the small to the great, to the East
   side of Jerusalem,
   in the Field of Jehoshaphat.
   You shall find a new tomb in which no man has yet been laid.
   Place her holy body in that place,
   keep watching it for three and a half days.
   Do not fear, I am with you.'
   Then when the Saviour had finished speaking with the holy apostles,
   He prayed,

David, the holy psalmist, said the Alleluia. (   )
Afterwards, Our Lord Jesus gave us Peace
and we all worshipped Him.
Then again David chanted saying:
'*Alleluia. (   )*'
Immediately our Saviour mounted upon His chariot of Cherubim,
while all the ranks of the heavens went behind Him, singing to Him,
so that the air was darkened through the quantity of perfume.
Thus He received the soul of His mother into His bosom,
wrapped in linen cloths, (   )
He went up to the heavens while we all looked after Him.
Immediately they raised the body of the Virgin,
and my father Peter bore her head while my father John bore her
feet.
And the rest of the apostles *with censers of incense in their hands,*
walked before us, while they sang,
and while all the virgins walked behind her. (   )
Then the body of the Virgin, the apostles carried it,
they put it into the tomb according to the word of Our Saviour,
and they remained watching it for three and a half days.

LA.DOR.MAR.B. 57.9

6 THE CULT OF THE SHRINE

(i) WRITING AND PREACHING

Writing a Martyrdom, manifesting the sufferings of the martyr, to be
his memorial.
Making a book and giving it to the shrine.
Providing a book on the day of commemoration of the martyr.
Writing an Apocalypse telling of the things seen in the heavens.
Hearing the Apocalypse in every place where it is preached.
Making provision for the writing of the Apocalypse.
Giving the book to the Church; keeping it as a phylactery.
Reciting the Apocalypse, or Martyrdom.

QUOTATIONS

1. (The Virgin said:) 'I swear, by the right Hand of my Son,
   O Paul, thou chosen one of God,
   that he who will write the words of this Apocalypse of what thou hast
   seen in the heavens
   will not taste any torture in the punishments which thou hast seen in
   Amente,
   except for the struggle alone of his going forth from the body.

677

And he who will recite it with faith
will have the handwriting of his sins erased,
and he who shall hear it and keep the commandments of my Son,
my Son will bless them in this world
and He will show mercy to them on the day of their visitation. ( )
I bear witness to thee that to every man who will do the will of my Son,
I am the first who will come forth to meet them
I will not allow them to be strangers
until they meet my beloved Son in peace.'

BU.AP.PAUL.S. 552.7

2. '*And it is necessary that thou shouldst see thy throne and thy house*
   before thou goest down to the world.
   And in every place in which thou shalt preach this Apocalypse in all
   the world,
   there will be many who will hear and repent
   and will not come to the punishments and the torments which thou hast
   seen.'

BU.AP.PAUL.S. 569.1

3. The angel of the Lord raised me,
   he brought me (down) upon the Mount of Olives.
   Then ( ) *I found the apostles gathered together with one another.*
   And I embraced them.
   I declared to them everything which had happened to me
   together with those things which I saw,
   with the honours which will be for the Righteous,
   and the fall and the overthrow which will happen to the wicked.
   Then the apostles rejoiced and were glad.
   They blessed God.
   They commanded us ( ) *that we should write this holy Apocalypse*
   for the profit and benefit of those that will hear them.
   And while the apostles were speaking with us,
   the Saviour, Christ, appeared to us
   upon the Chariot of the Cherubim.
   He said to us: '*Greeting my holy disciples,*
   whom I have chosen out of the world.'

BU.AP.PAUL.S. 572.29

4. The Saviour answered, he said:
   '*O beloved of the Father,*
   Amen, Amen I say to you

that the words of this Apocalypse will be preached in the whole world
for the profit of those that will hear it.
Amen, Amen, I say to thee, O Paul,
that to him who will make provision for this Apocalypse and write it
and leave it to be a witness to the generations to come,
I will never show (him) Amente and its bitter weeping
to the second generation of his seed.
And whoever will recite it with faith, I will bless him with his house.
On him who will scorn the words of this Apocalypse I will be avenged.
And let it not be recited except on holy days,
because I have revealed to you O my holy members,
all the mysteries of my Godhead.
Behold I have already told you all things.
Go now, depart and preach the Gospel of my Kingdom
because your course and your holy struggle approach.
Thou also Paul my chosen one,
thou wilt complete thy course
together with my beloved Peter ( )
and thou wilt be in my Kingdom for ever.
My power be with you.'

BU.AP.PAUL.S. 573.22

5. 'Now therefore, ( ), *if a man provides for the writing of the glorious*
   Covenant
   and gives it to the Church
   in the name of the Archangel Michael,
   or if he causes it to be written and keeps it in his own hands,
   neither sickness nor pestilence nor misfortune can enter his
   house in which it is, for ever.
   And upon his cattle and his fields and his orchards,
   no evil shall befall through any wild beast or mouse or blight upon
     his field,
   nor will any need arise in his house, nor among his sons, or his sons'
     sons, to the fourth generation.
   For the name of Michael will be upon them like a strong weapon. ( )
   Therefore let every one who will have written for himself a Covenant
     guard it as a phylactery
   so as not to lay it in a place wherein there is any unclean thing,
   for great is the power of these wonderful names.'
   When the angel of the Lord had said these things,
   he brought me down upon the earth.
   I ( ) stood upon the Mount of Olives

679

and he went up to heaven.
I marvelled greatly at those things which had been revealed to me.

B.M.TIM.S. 519.16

6. 'I say to thee (   ) *that if a man provides for this book*
of the pronouncement
and has it written and gives it to the Church
in the name of the Archangel Michael,
or if he gives an offering to the House of God,
or if he lights one lamp in the Church
in the name of the Archangel Michael,
or if he offers up incense
for his name,
in short, if he even gives one loaf of bread in *remembrance of*
   him, (   )
when he comes forth from the body (   )
he will not see torment in the punishments in which he is,
because of the merciful actions which he did
in the name of the Archangel Michael.
But he exists among the punishments like one who is in a house
   which is warm,
until God visits him and has mercy on him
and he is brought out of the punishments
and taken to the places of rest,
through the supplications of Michael.'

BU.M.TIM.S. 518.31

7. *When this man heard his* (George's) *Martyrdom being read,*
God opened his heart
and he gave heed to the place where God appeared to him (George)
saying: '*I swear by myself that all men who will extol thy afflictions,*
no evil will touch them because I know that they are flesh and blood.
All men who will undergo any compulsion, no evil will touch them. (   )
In any trouble, *if (a man) remember my name*
and the name of my Father in the Heavens and the Holy Spirit
and he remembers my youth George,
I will save him from all troubles.
Everyone who will write thy Martyrdom
and thy book manifesting thy day and all thy afflictions, which thou
   didst receive for my name,
I will write their names in the Book of Life.
He who will make an offering or give charity in thy name,

680

*or he who will make a book with his labours and give it to thy shrine
  in faith,*
he will be reckoned among my saints,
*and I will not let him lack any good things in this world in his whole
  life.*
I am the Lord God who (has spoken.)
I will glorify him who will build a shrine in thy name.
I will receive him into my Kingdom
and I will not forsake him for ever.
I will cause great miracles to happen in that place,
in the place where thy body will be laid.
I will cause people of the earth, the Jews and the Samaritans and the
  Persians and the sons of Esau, even the Barbarians, *to bring thee
  gifts.*
I will cause them all to come to thy shrine, bringing thee gifts.'

BA.HY.II.MIR.GEO.B. 315.10

8. '*Those who will write the book of your martyrdom*
   and the afflictions which you will receive for my name,
   I will write their names in the Book of Life,
   and no trouble will befall them in this world,
   no leper will exist in their houses for ever,
   nor blind man, even if they are great sinners.
   If they provide, on the day of your commemoration in this world,
   either a prayer book, or an offering, or a (gift of) first fruits or incense,
     or cummin, or oil,
   and give them to your holy shrine,
   I will erase their sins
   and I will give them to you as a favour.
   Even if someone (only) gives water to those that thirst on the day of
     thy commemoration,
   I will forgive him his sins and give him to you as a favour.'

HY.AP.IR.B. 92.16

9. '*He who will write the book of thy martyrdom,*
   manifesting thy conflicts and the afflictions which thou hast received
     for my name,
   I will tear up the handwritten list of his sins and I will write his name
     in the Book of Life.'

HY.EUS.B. 35.7

10. *And the Lord said to him:* '*They who shall write the book of thy*
      martydom in faith

681

and shall keep my commands,
I shall write their name in the Kingdom of the Heavens.
He who shall give commemoration offerings on thy day,
and who gives charity to those who are in need,
I shall remember when I shall come in my Kingdom.
And above all these thy name will be blessed
and those of thy country shall give it in joy to their sons.
And thy memory will remain to all the generations to come.
Be strong.
In a little while thou shalt be with all the Holy Ones in the Land of the
  Living.'
When He had said these things,
The Saviour hid Himself from him.

HY.ARI.B. 220.7

11. *Concerning those who buy reading-books*
  and give them to the House of God, whether small or large,
  it is a remembrance for ever without ceasing in the House of God.
  I say to you O Christ-loving people that any man who shall buy a
    reading-book
  and give it to the House of God,
  from the time in which it will be read in the Church, if that man is alive,
  immediately his name will be written in the Book of Life
  and he will be given his offering seven-fold as a blessing.
  If the man who has brought the book has gone forth from the body,
  if he has committed a small sin and he is taken to the punishments,
  from the time when the book is read in the Church,
  he will be brought up from Amente from the punishments among which
    he was
  and will straightway be given mercy.
  I beg you, O my beloved sons, all the Christ-loving people, at once
    men and women, old men and children,
  let us all provide this offering,
  so that we find mercy in the hour of necessity which will come upon us.
  Let each one provide this great good according to his power,
  because this is the unceasing remembrance for ever.

AM.CYR.AL.B. 186.10

(ii) SERVICES TO THE MARTYR

Building a shrine in the name of the martyr.
Giving the name of the martyr by men to their sons.
Invoking the name of the martyr by men for help in trials.

Bringing by men of commemoration-offerings to the shrine.
Making offerings at the shrine in the name of the martyr on the day of
his commemoration.
Lighting lamps, offering incense in the name of the martyr.
Giving first-fruits to the shrine in the name of the martyr.
Giving alms in the name of the martyr on his day of commemoration;
to the poor and weak, the widow and the orphan.
Feeding the hungry; clothing the naked; receiving strangers in the name
of the martyr.

BENEFITS ON EARTH IN RETURN FOR SERVICES TO THE MARTYR

Granting all requests made in the name of the martyr.
Granting salvation from trouble in this world.
Granting salvation from the snares of the devil.
Granting healing to anyone sick with any illness; possessed by devils;
blind, lame or deaf.
Giving a blessing on the village or house; that no misfortune would
befall the cattle, fields or orchards.
Granting relief from evil; that no wild beast, mouse or blight would
harm the fields.
Granting that there would be no lack of necessities in this world; no
lack of any good thing.

THE COMMEMORATION OF THE MARTYR ON EARTH

Causing the memory of the martyr to remain to all generations.
Causing the name of the martyr to be famous in the whole world.
Causing an archangel to serve at the shrine of the martyr.
Causing people to come to the shrine bringing gifts.
Causing kings to come to the shrine: causing the name of the martyr to
be celebrated in their houses.
Causing angels to preside over the commemoration day; to receive the
commemoration gifts.

REWARDS IN HEAVEN IN RETURN FOR SERVICES TO THE MARTYR

Wiping out, forgiving sins.
Erasing, tearing up the hand-written list of sins.
Granting that the torments of Amente would not be seen at the coming
forth of the soul from the body.
Transporting the soul over the River of Fire.
Taking the soul to the Third Heaven.

Bringing to the first hour of the Thousand Years.
Bringing to recline at the Feast of the Thousand Years.
Making inheritor with those in the Kingdom.
Making citizen with Christ in the Heavenly Kingdom.
Granting the blessing of the Eternal Offering in Heaven.
Receiving among the saints; reckoning among the saints.
Giving the good things of heaven.
Feeding with the fruit of the Tree of Life.
Spreading with the Stole of Glory; covering by angels with their wings
of light.
Clothing in the garments of heaven.
Placing with the Holy Ones in the Land of the Living.
Granting as favour, as son to the martyr in heaven.
Placing beside Christ for ever.

QUOTATIONS

1. The blessed man, when he heard his sentence, he gave thanks to
   God.
   Immediately the soldiers put the gag on his mouth,
   they brought him to the place where he would complete his course.
   He said to the executioners: 'Bear with me a short time *that I make
   a prayer to God.*' (   )
   The blessed Apa Lacaron stretched out his hands,
   *he prayed thus saying: 'My Lord Jesus Christ, do thou stand with me
   and give power to me until I complete my course.'*
   The Saviour Jesus appeared to him immediately,
   but no one knew Him except the saint alone.
   The holy man said to the Saviour: 'My Lord, and my God,
   behold thou hast heard me when I prayed to thee.
   *Now therefore, my Lord, I beg thee to fulfil for me that which I will
   request of thee. (   )'*
   *The Saviour then said to him: 'That which thou dost wish, I will fulfil
   for thee.'*
   The blessed Apa Lacaron answered, he said to Him: '*My Lord, I
   beg of thee*
   that thou wilt not allow my body to be destroyed in the earth,
   but thou wilt watch over it that it be safe
   and that a martyrion be built above it;
   and they who will build my martyrion,
   *that thou wilt give them the reward for their trouble in the Heavenly
   Jerusalem*
   and that thou wilt number them with thy Holy Ones.

If some one makes a vow to my shrine and keeps it,
do thou bless him with his whole house. (   )
If someone who is sick with any illness,
or one with whom there is a demon
enters into my shrine and worships over my body,
do thou grant him healing.
He who will write my Martyrdom to be a memorial for him,
do thou O my Lord erase the handwriting of the list of his sins.
And do thou save them from the evil snares of the devil.
And do thou place thy blessing and thy mercy,
and thy peace to remain in all their dwellings,
and do thou keep watch over them and write their names in the Book
    of Life. (   )
Do thou have mercy and bless everyone who will receive afflictions
and come to my shrine and pray over my body. (   )
And also, my Saviour, to me do thou give rest and repose. (   )'
When the blessed Apa Lacaron had finished saying these words,
the Saviour said to him: '*Be strong, thy afflictions have already*
    ceased,
I swear by myself to thee that all those things which thou hast said,
    I will fulfil,
those things which thou has not recalled I will do.
I will place my angels to keep watch on thy body by day and night
    receiving the commemoration (gift)
of those who will come to thy shrine bringing it to me,
I will bless each one according to his worth.'
When He had said these things, the Saviour embraced him,
He departed up to the heavens in glory.

BA.HY.I.LAC.B. 20.16

2. *And the Lord announced to them saying:*
   '*Every one who is in the lands, I will cause them to celebrate you on*
      the day of your remembrance.
   I will cause the kings with those who are in the high places to come
      and bring gifts to your sanctuary.
   Everyone who will invoke your names for a help to them,
   I will save them from all their afflictions.
   Everyone who will write your Martyrdoms to manifest the afflictions
      which you have received in my name,
   I will write also his name in the Book of Life.
   I will give him to you as a favour in my Kingdom.'
   When the Lord had finished saying these things,

He took the soul of the saint Theodore,
He removed it with Him up to the heavens,
while the angels sang after him.

BA.HY.I.TH.O.B. 61.5

3. 'When they take thee to thy village,
   I will send a delusion upon the men whom Arianus will send with
      thee
   so that they take thee to thy village in peace.
   There will be a shrine for thee in Panephre
   for thy prayers which were made there.
   There will be another one for thee in thine own house,
   for my peace and my blessing.
   And my blessing and my peace will be established in thy shrine for ever,
   for thou hast become a loved one to me with my Father and the Holy
      Spirit.
   All men who will serve in thy shrine
   I will cause Michael, the Archangel, to serve them at all times.
   Thy name and thy martyrdom will be celebrated in the house(s) of the
      kings of the earth
   because of thy valour which thou hast manifested in the presence of
      Arianus the hegemon.
   Everyone who will come into thy shrine in single-mindedness,
   that which will be asked in my name and the name of my Father, will
      happen to them.
   And all my angels will await the day on which thou wilt complete thy
      course,
   so that they will rejoice with thee in the Kingdom of the Heavens. (   )
   And thy sons who have become martyrs for my name because of thee,
   they will become fellow citizens with thee in the Heavenly Jerusalem.'
   And Apa Sarapion said to the Saviour: 'My Lord, I wish to ask thee
      a request.'
   The Saviour said to Apa Sarapion: '*O my beloved,*
   what thou wishest, ask it, it will happen to thee,
   for I know thy request which thou wilt ask of me.'
   The blessed Apa Sarapion said to him: '*My Lord I wish that thy*
      grace be in my shrine
   and the place in which my body will be placed, according to what thou
      hast said.
   O my Lord, *when someone comes to my shrine, sick of any illness,*
   with his offering in his hand and his lamp and his incense
   and he places them upon my grave and bathes,

686

do thou heal him from all illnesses,
whether fever, or chill,
or (if he be) convulsed or (with) broken head, or one troubled,
or one possessed by demons
or blind or lame or deaf
or one who is sick with any sickness.
Let thy mercy come upon them all and do thou cure them, my Lord
    Jesus.'
The Saviour said to the blessed man:
'*Everything which thou hast asked of me I will fulfil.*
I will place Michael, the Archangel, to serve in thy shrine in which thy
    body will be placed.
I will cause many cures to happen within the place where thy body will
    be manifested.
I will place my blessing in it for ever.'

BA.HY.I.SA.PA.B. 84.19

4. *When the saints saw the Saviour, their faces gave light like the sun*
    and they were filled with great joy.
    They said to the Saviour: 'Our Lord we wish that thou wouldst have
        mercy on us,
    so that every one who will ask thee a request in our name,
    that thou wilt grant it to them.'
    The Saviour said to them: '*My holy martyrs,*
    to every one who will satisfy a widow or a helpless one on the day of
        your commemoration,
    I will give the good things of heaven.
    All men who will give your names to their sons,
    I will bless and I will strengthen their hearts.
    All men who will undergo any trials
    and who say: "God of these saints Pirou and Athom, help us",
    I will save them from all their sufferings.
    After your martyrdom, many cures will happen in the shrine which
        will be built for you,
    I will place the Archangel Gabriel to serve in your shrine.'

HY.PI.AT.B. 169.13

5. *While Apa Epima was saying these words,*
    behold, the Lord Jesus came forth from heaven
    mounted upon a chariot of light.
    The whole Firmament was filled with angels.
    They came before the soul of Apa Epima.

The Lord cried out in a loud voice:
'Come up to me, my beloved Epima that I give thee thy reward
in return for thy sufferings which thou hast received for my name.'
When the saint saw the Lord, his heart rejoiced,
he said to Jesus: 'Hear me, my Lord,
that I ask thee my request before they remove my head.'
The Lord said to him: 'Speak my beloved one. Say what thou wishest
    to say.'
The blessed man said to Him: 'I wish that you shouldst grant my
    request.
If someone among my people commits a sin and he comes down upon
    my body
and he repents, do thou forgive him.
And he who will write my Martyrdom and manifest my memory,
do thou erase the handwriting of his (their) sins
and write his (their) name in the Book of Life.
And all men who shall give my name to their sons to give glory to my
    name,
do thou place thy blessing and thy grace, and thy peace to remain in
    their dwelling.'
The Saviour said to him: '*Everything which thou shalt ask I shall*
    grant thee.'

MIN.EPIM.S. 33.16

6. *The saint, when he saw our Lord, the Christ,*
   his heart rejoiced within him,
   he cast himself down, he worshipped Him.
   He said to Him: 'My Lord O my God, I wish that thou shouldst grant
       me a request.'
   The Saviour said to him: '*Everything which thou shalt ask, I will*
       give thee.'
   The saint said to Him: '*I wish that any man who will be sick in my*
       city from any sickness
   and will come to my shrine and worship over my body and pray to thee
       in my name
   that thou wilt grant them the cure.'
   The Saviour said to him: 'O my chosen one, Epime, I say to thee
   that not only in thy town, but *everyone in all places who will be sick*
       of any sickness
   and shall come and worship over thy holy body and pray to me in thy
       name,
   I will grant them salvation

and also I will cause thy name to be famous in the whole world.
I will cause multitudes of people to come forth from all places
and worship over thy holy relic.'

BA.HY.I.EPIM.B. 153.9

7. And when the custodians arrived at the place in which they sought
to kill him, he asked them to allow him a short time so that he
should pray, and kill him afterwards, and they gave him his wish.

And the glorious Mar Azazail knelt and made a genuflexion
towards the East, and prayed and said: 'Lord Jesus Christ, strong
God, who supports all and directs all things according to thy will,
good and long-suffering one, from thee I ask this request that in
every land in which is a portion of my bones, there will not enter
into it war, nor pillage, nor famine, nor pestilence, and that all
blows of anger should pass from it; that to the people or multitude
who honour my bones should come neither cold, nor heat, nor fires
nor locusts, ( ) nor evils, nor accidents nor any evil. Yes, Lord, he
who pronounces thy holy name and the name of thy servant,
Azazail, may his ways be made smooth, and cause him to reach the
Kingdom of Heaven. ( )

*   And they who read my history or listen and hear it or write my
eulogies, write, O Lord, their names and those of their deceased
ones in thy Book of Life. And cause them to hear thy (daughter of
a) voice rejoicing and saying to them: 'Your sins are forgiven you,
come and inherit the Kingdom of Heaven.' And let the believers in
every land be kept and turned from the evil one and his powers for
ever, Amen.'

MAC.AZ.SY. 28(61/62); *34(84)

8. '*I swear by myself with my holy angels*
that whoever will attend on thy body to bury it,
or take care that thy body is swathed,
I will swathe his body also in my Kingdom for ever.
He who will commemorate thee and write thy Martyrdom,
or give a reward for doing it,
I will write his name upon the Book of Life.
If he has committed sins also, I will forgive him.
He who will give bread to those who hunger, the poor and the weak,
because of thee, on the day of thy commemoration,
I God the Almighty, I will make him recline at the Feast of the
Thousand Years.
He who will clothe one who is naked,
or receive a stranger to himself in thy name,

I God the Almighty, I will wipe out all his sins,
whether murder, or fornication, or perjury, or theft, or any sins,
in short I will forgive him for thy sake.'
He commanded Michael the Archangel,
He stood him up without injury.
And the fire went, it became like cool water.
The Saviour placed His hand upon him,
He healed him,
He gave courage to him.
Apa Anub said to the Saviour: 'My Lord and my God,
I wish that thou wouldst command *that my body be taken to my*
   village
in the land of my fathers.'
The Saviour said to him: 'Everything which thou wilt request, I will
   fulfil.'
When the Saviour had finished saying these things to him,
He signed him with the Cross,
He filled him with power,
He went up to the heavens in glory.

BA.HY.I.AN.B. 216.16

9. '*Many cures will happen through thee.*
   The Lord will bless the place in which thy body will be placed, for
      ever and ever.
   All men who are ill with any illnesses,
   when they pray over thy body,
   we will grant them healing.
   He who shall swear falsely in thy sanctuary or will do a vain thing
      within it,
   we will take vengeance upon him and he will be in poverty for ever.'
   When Michael and Suriel and Raphael had said these things to him,
   they went up to the heavens in glory.
   The saint Apa Anub rose, he went to the prison.

BA.HY.I.AN.B. 222.1

10. '*Behold one whom I have prepared for thee*
   that he should prepare for burial thy body and send thee to thy village.
   Every man who shall write thy Martyrdom and thy conflicts,
   I will command Enoch, the Scribe of Righteousness,
   that he should erase the handwriting of all his sins,
   that I may write his name in the Book of Life
   and bless his possessions upon the earth.

THE ESTABLISHMENT OF COMMEMORATIVE RITUAL

He who shall promise a gift to thy shrine,
I shall bless him upon the earth
and repay them to him seven-fold in my Kingdom.
Any man to whom thy name is given in faith,
I will bless him and all his house
and I will save them from all evil.
All women and cattle,
when they suffer in childbirth,
and remember thy name I will hear them and give them living fruit.
The village in which thy body will be placed,
if they serve thee in my name single-mindedly, *I will bless that*
  village.
When they are ill they will be healed.
My peace will be in it for ever.
I will appoint Suriel to serve thy shrine
till the consummation of this aeon.'
When the Saviour had said these things to Apa Anub
He departed up to heaven in glory.
During all these things which the Saviour said to Apa Anub,
He caused the eyes of Julius to be opened.
He saw the Saviour saying all these words to the holy Apa Anub.

BA.HY.I.AN.B. 236.4

11. *As the blessed man was saying these things,*
    our Lord Jesus Christ came towards him mounted upon a chariot of
      light,
    while thousands of angels and tens of thousands of archangels preceded
      Him.
    The Saviour said to him: '*Greeting my chosen Theodore,*
    thou beloved of my good Father, take courage and do not fear,
    because indeed I am with thee in all thy afflictions
    and all the sufferings, which thou wilt receive for my name.
    Behold, I say to thee, O my chosen Theodore.
    that in return for these small sufferings which thou hast received for
      my name,
    I will cause thy name to be famous in the whole world,
    because of the number of wonders and cures
    which I will do through thee in all places.
    All men who are in any trials who will pray to me in thy name,
    I will hear them immediately,
    I will fulfil their requests.
    He who will do a kindness in thy name in any manner,

691

or will feed one who hungers,
or will clothe one who is naked,
or receive a stranger in thy name,
I will feed him with the fruit of the Tree of Life
and he will not lack the necessities of this world.
He who will build a shrine in thy name,
I will give him thanks in heaven.
He who will write the book of thy martyrdom
and the sufferings which thou wilt receive for my name
and the wonders which I will do through thee,
I will write his name in the Book of Life.
He who will give an offering or a first-fruits into the Church in the
    day of thy commemoration,
I will bless him in the eternal offering in the heavens.
He who will swear a false oath in thy shrine,
I will scorn him immediately.'
When the Saviour had said these things to the blessed Theodore,
He passed His hand over his whole body,
He healed him,
He embraced him,
He gave his Peace,
He went up to the heavens in glory,
while the angels sang to Him.

BA.HY.I.TH.S.B. 168.3

12. The saint Helias answered, he said to the Saviour:
    'My Lord, I do not wish to continue in the midst of godless heathen,
    lest my bones be scattered *and my memory disappear upon the*
        earth.'
    The Saviour said to him: '*Amen, I say to thee, O my chosen one,*
        Helias ( )
    in this way will my name be glorified through thee,
    because of the miracles which will happen in thy body. ( )
    And the sanctuary, in which will be placed thy body, will be for me an
        eternal temple.
    And to everyone who shall come into thy sanctuary, and will ask any
        requests in faith in my name,
    I will grant them to him.
    And men who are sick with any illness and *shall come into thy sanc-*
        tuary and make supplications in thy name,
    I will give the grace to them of healing.
    I will cause thy name to be renowned in all places,

*and I will cause great miracles and wonders to happen in thy burial
   place.'*
*When the Lord Jesus had said these things, (He departed) up to heaven
   in glory.*

SOB.HEL.S. 56b.12

13. '*I will cause many miracles and signs to happen through you
   in every place to which you will go.*
After your death also, *many signs of healing will happen through
   your bodies*
in the place where your shrine will be built.'

HY.PI.AT.B. 145.11

14. *In that hour, behold, the Son of God came forth from heaven with
   Michael.*
They went into the prison.
They found all the brothers with their hands outstretched, praying.
He greeted them all
and the whole place in which they were placed shone,
giving seven times more light than the sun.
The Saviour said to Apa Sarapamon 'Let thy heart take courage
for I am with thee in all things, my beloved Sarapamon.
I will cause Michael to serve thee.
Every place over which thy name is spoken,
I will cause Michael to serve it in all matters and all sicknesses.
Every one in whom dwells any illness,
who goes into thy shrine whole-heartedly and *prays to thee for their
   illnesses,*
I will hear them, whether they are fevered or chilled, ( )
let them bring a pot of water and a censer of incense and a full
   offering.
And let him give the pot of water to the priest
and let him make the offering over it for seven days with gratitude.
I will give healing to that man in thy shrine.
And he who will bury thy body,
or will take care of thy holy Martyrdom
and will write it truly with his labours,
*I will spread over him my stole of glory in the day of the Thousand
   Years.*
And glory and fame and blessing will remain in thy shrine for ever.
*I will cause thy name to be celebrated with all the generations of the
   earth.*

I will cause thee to receive a little more suffering for my name.
And the other brothers who are with thee, I will grant them to thee
  for ever.'
Afterwards the Saviour embraced the blessed Apa Sarapamon and the
  brothers who were with him.
He went up to the heavens in glory and splendour.

HY.SAR.B. 313.7

15. '*Blessed art thou, O my beloved George, thou strong one,*
    my good Father has written thy name on the chariot of the Holy Trinity,
    so that *those who will say: "God of George, help us and hear us"*
    thus thou wilt hear them.
    Blessed art thou, O my beloved George,
    for thou has manifested my name with that of my Father and the Holy
      Spirit,
    in the presence of the kings of the whole world.
    And I also, I will manifest thee in heaven, shining with light.
    I say to thee, my beloved, (   )
    by my right hand, O my beloved one,
    I will establish a covenant (   ).
    All the Holy Ones will recognise thee because of the glory which I will
      give thee, O my beloved one
    and they will all know that thou art George, the beloved of God
    and they will all worship thee according to the command of my Good
      Father.
    Behold now, O my beloved one, I have united thy name to mine
    so that it should be a port of salvation in the whole world,
    so that any men or women who fall into difficulties, (   )
    or any need, or very many afflictions,
    in a word, in any troubles which the sons of men may undergo
    and they cry out to me in thy name to the third time:
    "God of George, help us,"
    I will hear them immediately
    and I will fulfil everything which they will ask in their hearts.
    And all men who shall build a martyrion in thy name
    or (if one writes) a prayer-book of thy afflictions and thy conflict
    and gives it to the Church in thy name
    I will write his name in the Book of Life
    and I will cause him to be in the same place with thee in my Kingdom
      for ever.
    He who will give an offering or first-fruits to the Church in thy name,
    or will feed the hungry in thy name,

or (relieve) a widow on the day of thy glorious commemoration
I will give him help in this world
and I will cause him to rejoice with thee in the good things of my King-
  dom.
He who shall clothe a naked one in thy name,
I will clothe him in the garments of heaven.
He who will light a lamp in the Church in thy name, or incense,
I will cause my angels to give light to him as he comes to me in
  joy.
He who will give thy name to his son in faith,
will be satisfied.
He who will receive a stranger in thy name,
I will forgive him his sins
and I will receive him to me in my Kingdom, for ever.
I vow, by myself O George my beloved one, ( )
there is none who resembles thee among all those who have existed,
nor will there be one who resembles thee.
Hasten O my beloved one, to complete thy course,
that I may take thee up with me upon the chariot of Cherubim
and give thee as a gift to my Good Father and the Holy Spirit.
All those of heaven will rejoice with thee, for indeed they await thee.
Concerning thy body, I will cause commotions to happen now,
so that none of the crowd touch it at all until thy servants come to
  take it.
Behold thy mother and thy two sisters and thy bride, who was
  espoused to thee,
I have already taken to my Kingdom before thee,
so that they will not see thy death in this world,
but they see thee with thy father and thy grandfather
with the great glory which I will give thee in heaven in my
  Kingdom. ( )
I will cause thy kinsman to build for thee a shrine in thy city
and to place thy body within it in glory. ( )
And he (and thy king) will build for thee a tall shrine which is glorious
  in beauty
and he will give glory to thy Churches
and they will serve me in freedom in all the world for ever.
And I will cause to be built for thee many shrines in all the world.
I will cause all the tribes of the whole world to give glory to thee.
And I will cause thy name to fill the whole world.
And I will cause multitudes to bring gifts to thy shrine.
I will cause that festival be made for thee in the whole world,

especially on the day of thy commemoration, namely the day of thy consummation,

And on that day I have (? sealed) the wheat of the earth within it

and I have crowned the fruits of the earth on the day of thy coronation.

And also on the day of thy consecration is the beginning of the fruits of the earth. (   )

Thy name is excellent in heaven and also glorious upon the earth,

O my beloved George, my valiant soldier, for ever and ever, Amen.'

When the Lord had said these things to him,

he filled him with power and joy.

The blessed man rejoiced greatly and he was glad,

saying: 'I thank thee my Lord Jesus, because thou hast glorified me greatly above my worth.'

And He signed him with the Cross,

He hid Himself from him.

BA.HY.II.GEO.DI.B. 253.10

16. The Lord spoke to my father out of the Holy Place saying:

'*Every man who will give the name of my beloved Isaac to his son,*

my blessing will be in his house for ever.

It is well that thou hast come, O Abraham thou faithful one,

it is well that thy blessed and good root has come.

Now therefore, all requests which thou dost desire,

seek after them in the name of thy beloved son Isaac,

and they will be fulfilled for thee today to be a covenant for ever.'

My father Abraham said: 'Thine is the power, O Lord, the Almighty.'

The Lord spoke to my father out of the Holy Place, saying:

'*Every man who will give the name of my beloved Isaac to his son,*

or write his Testament and place it in his hand for a blessing,

my blessing will not fail in that dwelling for ever and ever.

Or if he feed a poor man who hungers

on the day of the commemoration of my beloved Isaac,

he will give him to you (as a favour) in my Kingdom.'

My father Abraham said: 'O Lord, God the Almighty,

if it is not possible for him to write his Testament,

let thy mercy reach him, for thou art merciful and compassionate.'

The Lord said to Abraham '*Let him give bread to those who hunger and the poor*

and I will give him to you in my Kingdom

and he will come with you to the first hour of the Thousand Years.'

696

Our father Abraham said: 'If he be a poor man and cannot find
    bread.'
The Lord said: 'Let him pass the night of my beloved Isaac without sleep
and I will give him to you as an inheritor in my Kingdom.'
My father Abraham said: 'If he be weak and this be impossible for
    him,
let thy mercy reach him in love.'
The Lord said to him; '*Let him offer up a little incense in my name*
and the day of the commemoration of my beloved Isaac
and I will give him to you as a son in my Kingdom.
And again, if he has not found incense
let him return to his Testament and meditate on it
on the day of my beloved Isaac thy son.
but again if he does not know how to meditate,
let him go and listen to them who read.
Again if he has not done one of these things,
let him go into his house and shut his door upon him *and make*
    supplication a hundred times,
and I will give him to you as a son in my Kingdom.
But what is better than all these
is *if he offer up a sacrifice in the name of my beloved Isaac.*
And again, *every one who will do all these things which I have said*
are inheritors with those who are in my Kingdom.
Everyone who will make provision for his life
with those who write his Testament,
or who does any compassionate act, even to a cup of water,
or he who writes his Testament
or who meditates upon it in faith with his whole heart
and believes all these things which I have said,
my power and the power of the Holy Spirit will be with them
and will guide them in all the world.
And there will be no distinction in my city
and I will give them as sons to you in my Kingdom
and they will come to the first hour of the Thousand Years.
I give Peace to you all, O my holy athletes.'
When He had finished saying these things,
all those of the heavens sang a hymn,

GUI.IS.B. 239.7

17. '*They who will provide for an offering*
    and give it to thy shrine on the day of thy commemoration, ( )
    I will bless also in the heavenly offering which is in the heavens.

697

And also he who will give bread into the hand of a poor man in thy
name,
I will not allow him to lack any good thing of this world all the days
of his life.
They who will give a cup of wine into the hand of a stranger or a widow
or an orphan
on the day of thy commemoration,
I will grant them as a favour to thee,
that thou shouldst take them to the Feast of the Thousand Years.
They who will write the book of thy going forth from the body
with all the words which have come forth from my mouth today,
by thy salvation, my beloved father Joseph,
I will grant them as a favour to thee in this world,
and also, when they will come forth from the body,
I will tear up the hand-written list of their sins,
so that they should not receive any torment,
except for the necessity of death,
with the River of Fire which lies before my father,
this which purifies all souls.
And if he is a poor man and has not (wherewith) to do those things
which I have said,
if he should beget a son, and name him Joseph,
giving glory to thy name,
neither famine nor pestilence will be in that house
because thy name is within it.'

LA.MOR.JOS.B. 31.4

18. *Our Saviour walked before us, He showed us the whole heaven,*
He showed us the good things and the joys
which are prepared within it,
which He had graciously given as favours to His beloved John,
so that He should bestow them upon everyone who should commemorate
John upon the earth,
because he was His kinsman and His forerunner.
I swear to you, I James, the brother of the Lord who record these
things,
that I shall not hide anything from you
of the good things which I saw and the joys
which are prepared in the Third Heaven,
these which God graciously gave to the saint John
so that he should give them to all those who will commemorate him
upon the earth.

Then Paul and Luke and Mark also were with us.
Then the good Saviour called the seven Archangels,
from Michael the great Archangel and Commander-in-Chief of the force of heaven to Sedekiel.
And He called to us the Apostles in order by our names
from Peter, our father, the chief Apostle, to Mark the Evangelist.
And He said to us: 'You, my Archangels and holy ministers and my Apostles, you were witnesses of my birth and my passion and
  my Crucifixion.
In the same way I give to you a testimony again.
*Behold I give the Third Heaven as a favour to John the Baptist, my
  companion and my kinsman.*
Therefore preach through the whole world that *all men who shall
  commemorate my beloved John upon the earth,*
*either with an offering, or alms-giving, or charity given to the poor or
  to his shrine in his name,*
*or who shall write the book of his holy memorial and give it to the
  Church,*
or who shall cover the table of his shrine with valuable cloths,
*thou (O John) shalt take them into the Third Heaven which I have
  bestowed upon thee,*
and thou shalt robe them in heavenly garments.'

BU.CH.JOH.S. 138.30

19. 'Amen I say to thee, *all men who shall commemorate thee upon the
    earth,* my kinsman John,
    I will not show Amente to them for ever, nor its punishments,
    as far as the River of Fire,
    over which all men shall cross whether righteous or sinner.
    *Behold this further favour I will give to thee, the ferry of this River of
    Fire which is the boat of gold.*
    *Those who will commemorate thee upon the earth, thou shalt ferry
    them in it on that River of Fire.* ( )
    Because of this, *all men who will perform thy commemoration upon
    the earth,* O John my companion and my kinsman,
    *whether with an offering, or first-fruits or any gift which they will give
    to thy shrine*
    in memory of thy holy name,
    I command thee to transport them on the River of Fire,
    in the boat of gold which I have bestowed upon thee.
    And thou shalt take them into the Third Heaven

699

that they may enjoy themselves among the good things which are prepared
and which endure for ever.'

BU.CH.JOH.S. 140.18

20. '*Every man who will light the lamp of the shrine of the saint John, or before his image,*
will be ferried across the River of Fire in the golden boat
which I have bestowed upon my beloved one, John.
These lamps shall burn before them, *giving light to them*
until they have passed over the roads of darkness
and are taken into the Third Heaven,
which I have given as a favour to my beloved John,
and they inherit the good things within it for ever.'

BU.CH.JOH.S. 143.15

21. 'I say to thee, O my beloved John, thou who wast worthy to baptise me with thy holy hands,
that if any one gives an offering of first-fruits to thy shrine in thy name,
or if he will give food to a hungry one in thy name,
or will give drink to a thirsty one, or will clothe a naked one in thy name
I will not show them Amente,
but thou shalt take them into eternal life.
And I will cause my angels to cover them with their wings of light,
and I will bestow on them the good things
which are in my Kingdom.
My Father shall bless thy right hand which thou didst place upon my head.
My tongue shall bless thy mouth, and thy tongue
with which thou didst say: "Behold the Lamb of God, who shall take away the sin of the world."
For I in truth am He.'

BU.CH.JOH.S. 140.3

22. It happened that when our Good Saviour had said these things to us *we rejoiced exceedingly*
at the great honours which God had bestowed upon John the Baptist.
He said to us also:' Come and I will show you the Paradise of the Third Heaven. ( )
These are the good things which I have prepared
for all those who will commemorate my beloved one and my kinsman, John, upon the earth. ( )

These are the things which God has prepared for those that love Him,
and those that love John His companion and kinsman.'

BU.CH.JOH.S. 141.26

23. *As the saint Abba Isaac was saying these things,*
behold the Lord Jesus came forth from heaven,
mounted on a chariot of light,
while thousands of angels sang hymns to Him.
He halted the chariot above the place where the saint was.
The Lord cried out with a loud voice:
'Come up to me, my beloved Isaac,
I will give thee thy reward
in exchange for the afflictions which thou hast suffered for my
name.
Any petitions which thou desirest to make
I will grant them to thee
for my Father is a giver who rejoices.'
When the saint Abba Isaac heard these things which the Saviour said
to him,
his heart was strengthened.
He spoke with the Saviour, saying: '*Hear me, my Lord,*
and satisfy my heart in what I ask of thee.
Thou knowest my Lord that my village is a small village.
Lest an enemy rise against it, *do thou send Michael the Archangel*
and help them and give power to them, and do thou destroy their
enemies.
When a man who has sinned comes and prays to thee over my body,
do thou forgive him his sins before the sun sets on that day.'
The Lord said to him: 'It shall be thus, my beloved one.'
The saint said to Him: 'I pray to thee concerning him who will swathe
my body in a shroud.
Do thou clothe his body in the time of his need, lest he be naked.
He who shall write my Martyrdom and manifest me,
do thou write his name in the Book of Life.
He who will give my name to a son of his with heart's desire,
do thou satisfy his heart.
He who will give an offering to my shrine,
do thou give to him from the eternal offering.'
When Abba Isaac had said these things,
the Saviour answered him with a voice of compassion,
saying: 'Amen, I say to thee that *everything which thou dost request,*
I will give to thee.

701

The other requests which thou hast not remembered, I will grant to
 thee.
Behold, Michael the Archangel, I have appointed him to the shrine
in which thy body will be placed, so that he should serve thee
in all requests for healing which men will seek through thee.'

BA.HY.II.IS.TI.B. 86.5

24. 'I will put thy memory in the hearts of God-loving men
 so that they build for thee a church in thy name and place thy body
  within it.
 And every one who is sick with those who are confined in prisons,
 when they say: "God of Apa Macarius of Antioch, do thou help us,"
 I will hear them and I will protect them with my wings of light.
 He who will build for thee a Church,
 I will build for him a church not made with hands in heaven.
 On the day of the placing of thy body within it,
 he who will provide an offering and first-fruits
 and alms to widows and the poor and the orphans on the day of thy
  remembrance,
 I will have him served with the good things of the Feast of the Thousand
  Years.
 He who will write the book of thy martyrdom
 and manifest the afflictions which thou hast received,
 I will write his name in the Book of Life.
 Blessed is the village which will receive thee;
 and the steward who will care well for thy shrine and not neglect thy
  church.
 I will grant him to thee as a favour.
 But if he be neglectful of thy shrine, *I will give him to the eternal*
  fire.
 I will confer a blessing of healing on thy shrine
 and I will heal men within it every Sabbath.
 Be strong and take power.
 My peace be with thee for ever, Amen.'

HY.MAC.AN.B. 66.11

7 FAVOURS GRANTED AT THE SHRINE

The granting of healing in answer to prayer.
The effecting of conversion, chastisement, forgiveness of sins.
The granting of the gift of writing.
The giving of instructions or relief; the granting of the favour requested.

QUOTATIONS

1. And when she (woman with swelling of breasts) was taken to the
     martyrion,
   she cried out with a loud voice, saying:
   '*My lord general, Saint Victor, I beg thee have mercy on me*
   and remove the affliction which is upon me, for *thou art a saint of*
     God.'
   At midnight, behold, the saint Apa Victor had mercy on her,
   he brought upon her a little sleep.
   She became unconscious.
   Then he came to her in a vision, bearing the honours of a king,
   while his face gave light like the sun,
   and a great perfume came forth from his mouth,
   a rod of light in his right hand.
   He said to her: '*O woman, dost thou wish for salvation?*
   When thou risest in the morning tomorrow take a little oil in a lamp.'

TIL.I.VIC.S. 46.19

2. *He* (a man blind in both eyes) *related to them everything which had*
     happened to him saying:
   '*It happened to me after I had entered this holy shrine*
   I cast myself down before the holy Sanctuary.
   I prayed the holy Archangel Gabriel.
   In that moment I felt a man's hand come down upon my face.
   It made the sign of the Cross on my eyes
   and immediately I saw and I heard a voice saying to me:
   '*Behold, I have granted thee the light of thine eyes, as thou didst*
     beseech me.'
   And I said: '*Who art thou my lord?*'
   He then said to me: '*I am Gabriel, the Archangel.*'
   And this is what I heard, but I did not see him who spoke with me.'

WOR.GAB.S. 188.13

3. *And thus he revealed himself to him who was paralysed, in a vision,*
   in the form of a man of light,
   whose face gave forth rays of light.
   He said to the man who was paralysed:
   'If thou dost greatly wish for healing (   )
   when thou knowest that they are all asleep,
   rise and drag thy hands and feet and go to the couch of the rich
     man (   ).
   And thou shalt obtain healing and walk upon thy feet then

703

and thou shalt be cured and go to thy house like one who was never ill.' ( )
And on the following night the Archangel Gabriel came to him
wearing a great kingly regalia which gave light more than the sun.
He spoke to him who was paralysed,
while an odour of great sweetness came forth from his mouth and he said to him: ( )
'Know this, that if thou dost not obey me,
thou shalt not cease from thy disease until thou diest.
But *if thou wilt do what I have commanded thee,*
thou shalt quickly be made whole.'
And when the Archangel said these things to him he departed from him.
At that moment he awoke in distress and fear.

WOR.GAB.S. 194.5

4. *And when he had fallen asleep,*
the holy Archangel Gabriel came to the youth in a vision,
wearing a glory of unspeakable greatness,
while a robe which gave forth rays of light, enveloped him.
He said to him: 'Behold I have taken away the pain from thee
and no suffering shall take hold of thee from this hour.'
The youth said to him: 'My lord who art thou.
surrounded thus with such great glory?'
He said to him: 'I am Gabriel the Archangel.'
And at that moment he disappeared from his presence.

WOR.GAB.S. 212.4

5. *At midnight, behold, the Archangel Gabriel appeared to the man in a vision*
in the form of a general of the king, wearing a robe of light.
He said to him: 'Dost thou know me, O man?'
The man answered: 'No, my lord.'
The Archangel said to him: 'If not, (know that) I am Gabriel, the Archangel,
into whose shrine thou comest daily, beseeching me to save thee from thy troubles.
It is I who have delivered thee many times from the snares of the Devil.
But since thou wast negligent yesterday and *thou didst not come to the shrine and pray,*
because of this, the Devil has brought upon thee this great affliction.
( )'

And when he had said these things,
he made the sign of the Cross on the whole body
of the man who had been burned with the fire.
And he said to him: 'Behold I have healed thee.
Do not again be negligent towards the Church lest worse than this
happen to thee.'
And when he had said these things he ceased to see him.

WOR.GAB.S. 232.17

6. *It happened one day, as they were performing the service in the mar-
tyrion of the saint Theodore,*
the Jew rose, *he went into the shrine,*
he mixed with the multitudes. No one knew him.
He stretched forth his hands to the priest. He took the body of Christ.
He did not eat it straightway but he took it on one side alone,
he looked at it, he found that it had become living.
He was afraid, he was in great doubt, he did not know what to do.
Suddenly the saint Theodore appeared to him, he said to him: ( )
'Dost thou know who I am?'
The Jew answered: 'No my lord.'
*The saint said to him: 'I am Theodore, the father of this
martyrion. ( )'*
The Jew answered, he said to the saint Theodore:
'I beg thee, my lord father,
show me the rules which I must perform that I be saved, with
everyone who is in my house.'
The saint Theodore said to him: 'This mystery which is in thy
hand,
do not eat it immediately, before thou art worthy to eat it,
but when thou wilt be worthy thou shalt eat from it without hin-
drance. ( )'
*And the saint Theodore signed him with the Cross, he departed from
him.*
Apollophanes waited until the service was finished.
He made his way to the priest. He said to him: 'My father, receive
this mystery.' ( )
The priest then received the Holy Mystery which was manifestly
flesh.

BA.HY.I.TH.S.B. 194.10

7. As the man who was petitioning God and Saint Theodore (to forgive his murder)
was at vigil at night in the shrine,

705

*sleep overcame him. He saw in a vision our good Saviour with Mary
  His mother,*
who had come into the martyrion of Saint Theodore
to visit those who were sick in the shrine and to heal them.
They went into the holy Sanctuary.
He saw Saint Theodore praying to the Saviour and the Holy Theotokos,
  Mary, saying:
'My Lords, have mercy on this man, that he may have rest
from his distress and his affliction and the suffering he endures.'
*And thus the good Saviour received the petition of the saint
  Theodore. ( )*
After this the Lord commanded the soul of the man who was killed
  in anger.
It came with three crowns in its hand.
It handed them to Saint Theodore, he placed them on the head of
  the man who was killed,
one for his ascetic practices and the afflictions he had received,
one for his endurance and his property which he had left behind him,
the other one for his blood which was shed thus.
The souls of the two men embraced one another.
The man was made free from his sins and *he obtained rest through
  the prayers of the saint, Theodore,*
the strong martyr of the Lord, Jesus Christ.

BA.HY.1.TH.S.B. 190.5

8. Puis de nouveau il (Romanus) dit: 'Saint père Euthyme, aie pitié
de moi et demande à Dieu qu'il me délivre de cette maladie très
amère.' Comme il avait fait cette prière et d'autres pareilles, il entre
en extase et voit un moine au poil tout blanc qui lui dit: 'Que
veux-tu que je te fasse?' Pris de frayeur et de joie, il dit: 'Qui es-tu,
maître?' Le moine lui dit: 'Je suis Euthyme, que tu viens d'appeler
avec foi. N'aie pas peur mais montre-moi ce dont tu souffres.' Il
lui montra son ventre. Alors, ayant joint les doigts tout droits,
l'être qui lui était apparu lui ouvre le ventre comme avec un glaive,
en tire une lamelle d'étain portant de certains caractères, et la pose
devant lui sur une tablette. Puis, lui ayant massé le ventre de la main,
il efface l'ouverture, le guérit et lui dit: '( ) Ne néglige plus tes
prières.' Sur ces mots, il disparut.

FE.III/I.EUT.G. 135(LVII)

9. Un jour ayant passé, la seconde nuit à la sixième heure, alors qu'il
était couché seul dans sa maison, réveillé et vaquant à de vaines

706

pensées, il voit soudain la porte de la maison s'ouvrir d'elle-même et entrer un moine âgé, resplendissant de lumière et illuminant la maison, accompagné de cinq moines plus jeunes, et tenant en main un bâton. Ce vieillard lui dit d'une voix sévère, avec un regard terrible: 'Dis-moi, homme perdu sans espoir, qu'es-tu allé faire au monastère d'Euthyme?' Comme il restait bouche close ne trouvant rien pour excuse, le saint dit aux plus jeunes; 'Soulevez-le.' Aussitôt, l'ayant saisi, ils le tinrent, à quatre, les membres étendus. Le vieillard donne alors au cinquième le bâton qu'il avait en mains et commande: 'Bats-le et dis: '( ) Ne méprise pas la longanimité de Dieu.' Quand il eut été longtemps battu et torturé, le saint dit à celui qui battait; 'C'est assez.' Puis, l'ayant saisi par les cheveux, il lui dit: ( ) 'Voici, cette nuit-même, nous te redemanderons ta vie.'

FE.III/1.EUT.G. 136(LVIII)

10. Un jour que j'étais assis sur mon siège accoutumé et tenais en mains les feuilles, vers la deuxième heure du jour, je fus pris de sommeil et je vois m'apparaître les saints pères Euthyme et Sabas dans le costume d'une sainte majesté qui leur était habituel. Et j'entendis saint Sabas dire au vénérable Euthyme: 'Voici donc Cyrille, il tient en mains ses notes sur toi, il montre le zèle le plus chaud, et cependant après tant de peines et de fatigues, il ne peut trouver de commencement à son ouvrage.' Le vénérable Euthyme lui repondit: 'Comment en effet pourra-t-il commencer ce livre sur moi, alors qu'il n'a pas encore reçu la grâce du style convenable pour ouvrir la bouche et parler?' Saint Sabas ayant dit: 'Donne-lui cette grâce, père', le vénérable Euthyme acquiesce, tire de son sein un alabastre d'argent et une sonde, plonge la sonde dans l'alabastre et m'en humecte trois fois la bouche. Le liquide injecté par la sonde avait l'aspect de l'huile, sa saveur etait plus douce que miel et vraiment une manifestation de la parole divine ( ), au point que, une fois réveillé par l'effet de cette douceur indicible, j'avais encore sur les lèvres et la bouche ce parfum et cette suavité spirituelle. Aussitôt je commencai d'écrire le prélude du présent ouvrage.

FE.III/1.EUT.G. 139(LX)

11. *It happened to me that when he came upon me this time,*
I became unconscious, I saw the saint George.
He came in to the Sanctuary, he took my hand, he encouraged me.
I saw this time that demon with my eyes, in the form of a man in my
 presence,
while the saint George gave him a great chastisement. ( )

707

and the demon gave a great cry from his nose, he departed and
  left, (   )
and the saint George went to heaven as I looked after him.

BA.HY.II.MIR.GEO.B. 325.10

II SALVATION FROM DEATH

1 IDENTITY ANNOUNCEMENT

THEME

The announcement by the Saviour of His name.

EPISODES

The appearance of the Saviour to rouse the holy man from sleep.
The appearance of the Saviour in answer to prayer.
The appearance of the Saviour in the middle of the night.
The appearance of the Saviour to the holy man in prison.
The appearance of the Saviour to the holy man during his martyrdom.
The appearance of the Saviour to the holy man confined in the hold of
  a ship.

QUOTATIONS

1. *In the middle of the night,*
   behold, the Good Saviour appeared to them,
   mounted on a chariot of light,
   with Michael on His right side and Gabriel on His left.
   And the whole place gave light
   seven times more than the sun.
   And the Saviour caused the holy Archangel Michael to touch them
     and rouse them.
   When they awakened from sleep they saw the light which surrounded
     them.
   They were afraid and they were disturbed.
   When the good Saviour touched them,
   He removed the fear from them
   and He said to them: ' Do not fear, (   )
   I am Jesus, the Son of the Living God.' (   )
   When the Good Saviour had said these things to them,
   He embraced them,
   He gave them Peace,
   He departed up to the heavens as they looked after Him.

HY.EUS.B. 9.9

2. *In the middle of the night,*
   while the holy men were in the prison,
   behold, our Lord Jesus Christ came down from heaven,
   with Michael on His right side and Gabriel on His left side.
   The whole prison was greatly lighted.
   The good Saviour answered, He said to them:
   'Greeting my chosen ones in the hour of greeting, (   )
   I am Jesus, who has sent His angel.
   He has saved you, He has taken you down from the hermetarion.'
   As our Lord Jesus Christ was saying these things
   the saints took courage,
   the chains which bound them were loosed, the stones fell down from
   them,
   they cast themselves down forthwith at the feet of our Lord Jesus, they
   worshipped Him.
   He embraced them, (   )
   He gave them Peace,
   He departed up to the heavens,
   while the holy men looked after Him.

   HY.PI.AT.B. 144.13

3. *When the holy Helias heard these things,*
   he raised his eyes,
   he saw Jesus mounted upon the chariots of Cherubim
   with Michael, the Archangel on His right and the holy Soterichos on
   His left
   with a robe of glory upon Him,
   such as no king of this earth would be able to wear.
   When the holy Helias saw these things he prostrated himself in the
   presence of the Lord. (   )
   And at that moment Jesus raised him, saying to him:
   'Arise my chosen one, Helias, I am Jesus who doth help thee. (   )'
   When the Saviour had said these things, *He gave him Peace,*
   He went up to the heavens in glory,
   while the holy Helias looked after Him.
   Then a great fragrance spread in the room in which the holy Helias
   was lying.

   SOB.HEL.S. 9b.22

4. *That night the Lord appeared to him,*
   He said to him: 'Be strong of heart, O Lacaron,
   for I am the Lord, Jesus Christ.

Be strong and have courage. ( )'
Thus the Saviour embraced him,
He gave him Peace,
He departed up to heaven in glory, with His holy angels.
The blessed Apa Lacaron kept vigil for the whole night until the light
　　dawned,
being strengthened in heart with the joy which the Lord had granted
　　him.

BA.HY.I.LAC.B. 4.3

5. *The blessed Apa Epima was sleeping one day in his house*
　　when behold, a youth of light stood above him.
　　He was troubled.
　　He said to him: 'Epima, Epima, open thy eyes and know who I am.
　　I am Jesus Christ, ( )
　　The Peace my Father gave to me as I came to the world, I also give
　　　　to thee.'

MIN.EPIM.S. 5.11

6. *It happened when the blessed Apa Epime was sleeping in his house*
　　he saw a youth of light standing above him.
　　He stirred his right side.
　　He roused him. The saint Apa Epime, *when he awoke,*
　　he saw a man of light standing above him.
　　He was troubled.
　　And he said to him: 'Epime, open thy eyes that thou mayest know
　　　who I am.
　　I am Jesus Christ, ( )
　　The Peace of my Father which He gave to me as I came forth from
　　　　Him,
　　I also give it to thee.'

BA.HY.I.EPIM.B. 126.4

7. It happened on one of the days in which he was in battle,
　　as he was sleeping in the night while his soldiers surrounded him,
　　behold our Lord Jesus Christ stood above him.
　　He stirred his side.
　　He said to him: 'Arise,
　　why art thou asleep, while the battle spreads abroad?'
　　When he rose up from sleep and he saw the Lord,
　　he was very afraid and he was troubled.
　　The good Saviour said to him: 'Dost thou know who I am?'
　　The blessed man said to Him: 'No, my Lord,

710

I beg thee to tell me who thou art, who art in this great glory.' ( )
The Lord said to him: 'I am Jesus, thy true King, ( )
then take courage, do not fear. ( )'
When the Saviour had said these things to him,
He gave him His Peace,
He went up to the heavens in glory with His holy angels.

BA.HY.I.TH.S.B. 158.20

8. *It happened one night, as the holy Basilides was standing vigil*
   and making his prayers, according to his custom,
   behold, the good Saviour appeared in the form of a beautiful youth.
   He said to him: *'Greeting my chosen one, Basilides,*
   greeting, O strong athlete in the contests. ( )'
   Basilides said to Him: 'Show me who thou art my Lord,
   who art in such great glory.'
   The Saviour said to him: 'I am Jesus Christ, whom thou dost serve and
   to whom thou art servant. ( )'
   When the Saviour had said these things to him,
   He filled him with power,
   He gave him Peace,
   He departed up to heaven in glory.

HY.EUS.B. 1.16

9. When the saint Apa Epima had said these things,
   his prayer was effective at the throne of God.
   His prayer entered into the ears of the Lord Sabaoth.
   The Lord Jesus came mounted upon a cloud of light,
   with Michael at His right side and Gabriel on His left,
   while a multitude of angels sang hymns to Him.
   He stood in the air above the boat.
   He said to the saint Apa Epima: *'Greeting at the time of greeting.*
   Courage at the time of courage.
   I am Jesus ( ).
   My Peace be with thee in all places, Amen.'
   When the Saviour had said these things
   He went up to the heavens in great glory
   while the angels sang hymns to Him.
   And the blessed man's heart rejoiced because he had seen the Lord.

MIN.EPIM.S. 12.22

10. *Behold, our Lord, Jesus Christ came to him,*
    mounted on a cloud of light,
    with Michael on His right side and Gabriel on His left side.

The Saviour answered, He said to Apa Epime: '*Greeting, my chosen
  one Epime,*
Be strong and have courage. ( )
I am Jesus thy King.' ( )
When the Saviour had said these things
He went up to the heavens in glory.
The blessed Apa Epime, when he had seen the Lord, his heart rejoiced.

BA.HY.I.EPIM.B. 133.25

11. *When he went forth in the hour of morning according to his
      custom,* ( )
Michael, the Archangel, appeared to him,
he said to him: '*Greeting, Paphnute, thou soldier of Christ.*'
Apa Paphnute also greeted him: 'Hail.' ( )
The Archangel said to him: '( ) *Take courage. Do not fear,*
for I am Michael, the Archangel, he who was with thy fathers.
I will be with thee also. ( )'
And he embraced him.
He went up to heaven
while his eyes followed him.

BA.HY.I.PAP.B. 110.17

12. *And behold, our Lord, Jesus Christ came down from heaven,*
mounted on a cloud of light.
He stood above the ship,
He said to the saint: 'Greeting, thou who art mine, Apa Didymus.
Be strong, O noble one, I am Jesus thy King. ( )'
And He gave him Peace. He went up to heaven in great glory.

HY.DID.B. 296.16

13. The Saviour said to him: '*Take courage, O thou who art mine,*
Apa Anub, my fighter in the battles.
Be strong, I am with thee,
I am Jesus thy King.'

BA.HY.I.AN.B. 235.23

14. *As the eunuch was sleeping in the same shrine with us, he prayed to
      the saint Theodore. ( )*
Afterwards he slept, he was unconscious for a day.
The saint Theodore came to him.
He said to him: 'O man dost thou know who I am?'

He said to him: 'No my lord.'
He said to him: 'I am Theodore, the father of this shrine.'

AM.CYR.AL.B. 175.7

15. *As he (a man accused of theft) said this (prayer),*
   the saint Theodore appeared to him on the road,
   in the form of a great general of the king.
   He said to him: 'Dost thou know me, O man, who I am?'
   The man said to him: 'No my lord.'
   The holy man said to him: 'I am Theodore, he in whose name thou
      prayest daily to God.'
   The man said to him: 'My lord, thou holy martyr, help me now in
      this hour of necessity.'
   The holy Theodore said to him: 'Do not fear, I am with thee.'

BA.HY.I.TH.S.B. 184.5

2   GREETING

THEMES

The greeting of the holy man as the chosen one.
The giving of courage and strength of heart to the holy man.
The giving of Peace to the holy man.
The blessing of the holy man.

EPISODES

The fear of the holy man at the appearance of the Saviour.
The prostration of the holy man upon the ground.
The embracing of the holy man by the Saviour.

QUOTATIONS

1. *At the moment, behold the Archangel Michael came down from heaven,*
   he embraced them all one by one.
   He turned to the saint Apa Sarapion.
   He said to him: *'Greeting, O best man of Christ the King. ( )'*
   And thus the Archangel Michael stretched forth his right hand
   over the body of the blessed Apa Sarapion, saying:
   'No torments will be able to prevail over thy body.' ( )
   After this Michael turned to the crowd of holy men, he said to them:
   'Take courage, let your hearts be strong ( )'.
   After this Michael embraced them.
   He gave them Peace.
   He went up to the heavens in glory.

713

The blessed Apa Sarapion *continued to give encouragement*
to the brother martyrs from the holy Scriptures
until the dawn rose.

BA.HY.I.SA.PA.B. 74.11

2. *That night Raphael, the angel, appeared to him,*
   he said to him: 'Greeting Paese, thou man worthy of love.'
   When he saw the Archangel, he prostrated himself, he worshipped him.
   He raised him
   and his face gave light like the sun.
   The holy ones saw the light,
   they were afraid, they worshipped the Archangel,
   he said to them: '*Peace be with you.*'
   Raphael blessed them. ( )
   The blessed Apa Paese said: 'Give power to me, O my lord father
   and I will give my body to the tortures of the Court of Justice.'
   The angel embraced him, he went up to the heavens.

TIL.I.PA.TH.S. 75.10

3. *As the saints were standing,*
   behold Gabriel the Archangel appeared to them.
   the whole place was lighted.
   The angel said to them: '*Greeting, O chosen ones of Christ,*
   be strong and take courage. ( )'
   When the angel had said these things,
   He gave Peace to them,
   he departed up to the heavens.

HY.PI.AT.B. 152.4

4. When they had said these things,
   behold, our Lord, Jesus Christ came forth from heaven,
   sitting upon a chariot of light,
   with Michael on His right side and Gabriel on His left side,
   while thousands of angels sang hymns to Him.
   He said to the holy men: '*Greeting in the time of greeting, my chosen*
   holy martyrs. ( )'
   When the saints saw the Saviour, their faces gave light like the sun
   and they were filled with great joy.

HY.PI.AT.B. 169.7

5. *While he remained in prison,*
   on that night the holy man was keeping watch
   and making great petitions up to God for the whole world,
   the Lord Jesus Christ appeared to him in unspeakable glory.

714

And He said to him: '*Greeting my chosen one, Macrobius.* ( )'
When the Saviour had said these things, *He gave him his Peace*
and thus *He departed from him in great glory.*
The saint Abba Macrobius *was in great joy in the prison when he had
    seen the Lord.*

HY.MACR.B. 233.3

6. *And he did not cease from beseeching, as he prayed until the middle
       of the night.*
   In the middle of the night,
   behold, the Archangel Michael came to him in the hold of the ship. ( )
   He said to him: 'Greeting, thou beloved one of God, Apa Anub. ( )
   Take courage, do not be faint-hearted. ( )'
   Immediately he gave him Peace,
   he departed up to the heavens in glory.

BA.HY.I.AN.B. 225.14

7. *At the eleventh hour of the night,*
   as the holy man Didymus was sleeping in his room,
   behold a man of light stood over him.
   He said to him in a sweet voice:
   '*Greeting, O noble Apa Didymus, the warrior of Christ,*
   Peace be to thee. ( )'
   When he had said these things to him,
   the man of light went up to the heavens in great glory.

HY.DID.B. 288.7

8. *In the middle of the night*
   an angel of the Lord appeared to him.
   The whole house became greatly lighted.
   The angel said to him: 'Greeting, Abba Isaac,
   the Lord be with thee.'
   The blessed man said to him: 'Thy blessing be with me.'
   He brought him outside his house. ( )
   When he had said these things, the angel departed up to the heavens.

BA.HY.II.IS.TI.B. 74.21

9. As the blessed Polycarp entered into the stadion,
   a voice came to him from heaven, saying:
   '*Polycarp, be of good courage and be strong.'*
   No one saw Him who spoke,
   but many of those present heard the voice.

BA.HY.II.POL.SM.B. 66.10

10. *Behold a voice came to them, saying:*
    '*Be strong, holy martyrs and go in peace.*
    Do not fear. My power and grace will be with you.'
    Thereupon they leaped with joy,
    they walked to the Kings *and the whole town was astonished at the*
        size of the crowds.

    BA.HY.I.TH.O.B. 58.1

11. In that hour the torches fell from the hands of the executioners.
    Behold a voice came to him from heaven saying to him:
    '*Be strong, thou who hast been strong,*
    take courage thou who hast taken courage,
    for my power will be with thee and no evil will be able to approach thee,
        O beloved of my Father.'
    In that moment the saint, Theodore jumped up,
    he ran, *he stood up before the hegemon.*
    He cried out saying: '*Shame on thee, O impious hegemon, thou and*
        thy scandalous kings.'

    BA.HY.I.TH.S.B. 174.13

12. *And in that hour Michael and Gabriel and all the host of angels came*
        forth from heaven,
    singing hymns to the Saviour who appeared over the branches of the
        Persea tree.
    He said to Apa Timotheus: '*Endure and do not fear, I am Jesus*'

    TIL.I.TIM.S. 115.6

13. *And in that moment Michael came down from heaven with Gabriel.*
    They went to him, they embraced him,
    They said to him: '*Be strong, thou saint Helias, no one will be able*
        to do thee harm. ( )'
    And the angels of the Lord embraced him.
    They went up to heaven in glory and in the peace of God. Amen.

    SOB.HEL.S. 28a.1

14. *When he had said the Amen,*
    behold, the Archangel Raphael stood at his right hand
    and he bore him upon his wings of light.
    He placed him down before the Tetrapylon of the town.
    He embraced him.
    He gave courage to him.
    He departed up to the heavens in glory.

    HY.EUS.B. 36.7

15. *The Lord appeared that night to him.*
He said to him: 'Be strong George, for I am with thee. (   )'
And the Lord embraced him,
He went up to heaven with His angels.

BU.GEO.C.S. 183.14

16. *That night the Lord appeared to the saint, George,*
He said to him: '*Be strong and have courage, my beloved George* (   ).'
and when He had embraced him,
He went up to heaven in great glory with the holy angels.

BA.HY.II.GEO.B. 275.19

17. *The Lord appeared to him that night* saying:
'*Be strong my chosen one, George and take courage. (   )*'
When the Lord had addressed him,
He went up to the Heavens with the holy angels,
while the strong martyr of Christ watched Him.
And he remained in vigil until the light broke
rejoicing in the gladness which the Lord gave him.

BA.HY.II.GEO.B. 284.5

18. *In that hour, behold, the Son of God came forth from heaven with*
Michael.
They went into the prison.
They found all the brothers with their hands outstretched, praying.
He greeted them all
and the whole place in which they were placed shone,
giving seven times more light than the sun.
*The Saviour said to Apa Sarapion: '*Let thy heart take courage. (   )*'*
Afterwards the Saviour embraced the blessed Apa Sarapion and the
brothers who were with him.
He went up to the heavens in glory and splendour.

HY.SAR.B. 313.7

3   RELEASING

THEMES

The removal by the Saviour of the cause of the torment.
The effect of the Saviour's intervention.
The invocation of the holy man as Saviour on earth after his death.

EPISODES

The removing of the fire from the holy man; extinguishing of the fire;
causing of the flame to become cool.

717

The bringing forth of the holy man from the place of torment.
The releasing of the bonds of the holy man.
The destruction of the dragon.

QUOTATIONS

1. *When he had said these things,*
   behold, the holy Archangel Raphael stood above him.
   He removed the flame of the fire from him.
   It became like cool dew.
   And he brought him some fruits of Paradise.
   He ate them.
   He grasped his hand.
   He brought him forth from the fire.
   He stood him up uninjured.
   He gave him courage.
   He gave him Peace.
   He departed up to the heavens while the saint Eusebius looked after
   *   him.*
   Then he rose straight away. He went upon the tribunal.
   He rejoiced with gladness like one who had risen from a feast.

   HY.EUS.B. 37.12

2. '*Now my Lord, send me thy holy angel to help me so that I am not*
   *   burnt in the fire.*'
   In that moment Michael the Archangel came down from heaven.
   He went into the furnace of the bath.
   He spread his robe of light over him
   and he did not allow the fire to touch him.
   And he caused the flame of the fire to become like a breath of cool
   *   dew at the hour of morning.*
   And the Archangel raised him,
   he gave courage to him,
   he loosed the irons which bound him
   and he consoled his heart with the mysteries and the good things of
   *   heaven.*

   HY.MAC.AN.B. 50.2

3. *The saint Apa Epima prayed to God in the midst of the fire*
   *   saying:* ( )
   '*Now therefore my Lord do thou hear me and save me in the midst of*
   this fire.
   For thine is the power and the glory for ever and ever. Amen.'

And at that moment Michael, the Archangel came forth from heaven.
He went into the stoke-hole of the bath to the saint Apa Epima.
He spread out his wings of light over him.
He caused the flame of the fire to become like a breath of dew in the
  hour of morning.
And Michael said to him: '*Be strong, O Saint Apa Epima.*
I am Michael whom the Lord has sent to thee so that I should help
  thee.'
At that moment the bonds were loosed from the saint.
He stood upon his feet.
He looked. He saw the angel of God.
His heart was strengthened within him.

MIN.EPIM.S. 23.2

4. *And at that moment, behold, Michael the Archangel came down from*
  heaven,
  he went into the stoke-hole of the bath to the Saint Apa Epime.
  He spread his wings of light over him
  and he caused the flame of the fire to become like a breath of dew
  which blows at the hour of morning.
  And Michael said to him: '*Be strong and have courage, O athlete*
  of Christ, the King.
  I am Michael whom the Lord has sent to thee to help thee.'
  In that moment the bonds were all loosed and he rose, he stood up
  upon his feet.
  It happened after three days while
  the saint Apa Epime lay in the stoke-hole of the bath
  while the Lord watched over him, (   )
  Armenius went to the bath (   ).
  While Armenius was speaking,
  behold the Archangel Michael carried the saint Apa Epime,
  he stood him up in his presence in the midst of the bath place.

BA.HY.I.EPIM.B. 143.22

5. *In the middle of the night,*
  behold Michael the Archangel broke the wall of the oven.
  He brought the blessed Apa Paese forth from it.
  He said to him: 'My beloved Paese, do not fear the torments because
  I am with thee.' (   )
  The angel of the Lord walked with him.

TIL.I.PA.TH.S. 78.25

6. *When the saint Apa Anub had completed the Amen,*
   behold, the Lord Jesus Christ came to him,
   mounted upon a chariot of light,
   with Michael on His right and Gabriel on His left side.
   He said to him: '*Be strong, O my beloved Apa Anub.*
   Do not fear, I am thy Lord, I am with thee.
   Do not be afraid.
   Behold, I have appointed for thee Michael, the Archangel,
   to stand and give power to thee. ( )'
   He commanded Michael the Archangel,
   He stood him up without injury.
   And the fire went, it became to him like cool water.
   The Saviour placed His hand upon him,
   He healed him,
   He gave courage to him. ( )
   When the Saviour had finished saying these things to him,
   He signed him with the Cross,
   He filled him with power,
   He went up to the heavens in glory.

   BA.HY.I.AN.B. 215.28

7. *The saint Apa Anub stretched forth his hands in the midst of the fire*
   saying: 'Hear me, my Lord Jesus Christ.
   I am thy servant and the son of thy maid-servant.
   Hear my voice now in the midst of this fire. ( )
   Send to me thy angel to give power to me
   for thine is the glory for ever, Amen.'
   At that moment, behold, the Saviour came forth from heaven,
   with Michael on His right side and Gabriel on His left,
   while the Cherubim and the Seraphim drew His chariot.
   At that moment the flame of the fire ceased and was extinguished
   and became like a breath of cool dew.
   He commanded Michael to bring up the justified one, Apa Anub,
     uninjured.
   The Saviour said to him: '*Take courage, O thou who art mine, Apa*
     Anub,
   My fighter in the battles.
   Be strong, I am with thee. ( )'
   When the Saviour had said these things to Apa Anub
   He departed up to heaven in glory.

   BA.HY.I.AN.B. 235.4

8. While he was burning, God ( ) *looked upon the strife of the saint Apatil*
and caused a cloud to surround him,
and by the pouring down of a flood of rain He at once extinguished the fire.
And behold a voice of the Lord came to Saint Apatil saying:
'Be strong, and have courage,
because *indeed I remain with thee to save thee and I will not forsake thee.'*
When the holy man Apatil heard this voice, *immediately a power of the Lord was added to him*
and the pains which were in his body ceased.
And thus he stood up in the presence of the hegemon
with no injury upon him.

BA.HY.I.AP.B. 94.11

9. As he was saying these things,
behold Gabriel the Archangel came forth from heaven,
he caused the fire to be quenched beneath them,
he gave the hand to the holy men,
he brought them up.
He said to them: '( ) *Be long-suffering, O beloved ones of the Lord* ( ).'
When he had said these things he disappeared from them.

TIL.I.TIM.S. 112.18

10. *The Lord remembered his servant, Abba Macrobius while he was still in the midst of the fire,*
and He sent His angel in the way He did so in the time of the three Holy Children, who were in Babylon.
And He extinguished the flame in the midst of the oven.
He caused the middle of the oven to be like a breath of cool dew
and it did not injure the saint in any way.
But he walked in the midst of the fire.

HY.MACR.B. 240.18

11. *In that moment, behold Michael the Archangel came down from heaven.*
He went to the middle of the burning fire of the oven
and he stretched out his wings of light over the saint Apa Sarapion.
And the fire became like cool water and a breath of dew which spreads forth.

721

And after three days, the hegemon commanded that the oven be
    opened. ( )
They did according to what he had told them.
When they opened the door of the oven they saw the saint Apa Sarapion
    standing safe in the midst of the fiery oven,
while his hands were outstretched as he prayed.
And they brought him up,
they stood him up in the presence of the hegemon uninjured.
The hegemon saw his face giving light like the sun,
while his body was red like a rose.

BA.HY.I.SA.PA.B. 71.15

12. Then he came down to the cauldron.
    He prayed to God saying:
    'Lord God, Almighty, the Father of my Lord Jesus Christ come to me.
        Do not remain apart from me.'
    In that moment, behold Michael the Archangel came forth from heaven.
    He quenched the cauldron.
    He caused it to be like cool water.

BA.HY.II.IS.T.B. 84.21

13. *As he said these things,*
    behold an angel of the Lord appeared to him in the midst of the
        cauldron,
    he extinguished the flame of the fire,
    he stopped the boiling of the sulphur and tar and it became like a
        breath of cool dew of heaven in the morning hour.
    And no injury was upon the saint at all.
    But he was singing and blessing God in the midst of the cauldron.

HY.ARI.B. 218.9

14. *While the blessed man was praying, God sent the Archangel to him.*
    He quenched the power of the fire.
    He brought him up.
    There was no injury upon him at all.

BA.HY.I.ANAT.P.B. 28.1

15. And it happened after three days,
    the King Maximus commanded and sent the prefect of his kingdom
        with his nobles.
    And they went towards the pit
    in which had been cast the holy man, Mar Azazail.
    They found the seals intact, and they removed them.

And they opened the pit
and they found the holy man healed,
and he was as if nothing had befallen him,
nor was there any scar on his body.

MAC.AZ.SY. 18(35)

16. *In that moment Michael, the Archangel stood above him,*
    he did not allow the fire or the boiling lead to touch him at all,
    but it became like cool water for him.

SOB.HEL.S. 52b.7

17. While the blessed Apa Paese was saying these things,
    Raphael the Archangel came forth from heaven.
    He stood on the right hand of the blessed Apa Paese.
    He caused the flame of the oven to be like a breath of dew which
        blows at the hour of morning.
    The holy man sat in the midst of the oven like one who has come in
        the heat and sat in a cool place.
    And the fetters which bound him were loosed.
    And the tar came off his body like cool water
    and his body was pure
    like one who had washed in a cool bath for a feast.

TIL.I.PA.TH.S. 78.12

18. *After the ninth hour,*
    while the fire surrounded him,
    behold Michael, the Archangel came down from heaven,
    he went to the midst of the fire,
    he caused the fire to depart from him.
    But the multitudes saw the blessed Apa Sarapion in the midst of the
        fire,
    with no injury upon his body.
    But his face gave light like the sun,
    his whole body was red like a rose in the days of Parmouthi.
    He rejoiced like one who had drunk wine.

BA.HY.I.SA.PA.B. 80.24

19. On the third day the hegemon said to those of the company:
    'Rise, let us see whether these impious ones are alive. ( )'
    Suddenly before the word came forth from his mouth, behold Michael
        the Archangel came forth from heaven.
    He released the bonds which bound the saints.

723

He placed them down, he stood them up in the presence of the hege-
*   mon,*
there being no injury upon them.

HY.PI.AT.B. 148.3

20. *As he was yet praying,*
    the great holy Archangel Michael appeared.
    He released him from the fetters and the pains which were in his body,
    he healed them in that moment.
    And immediately he stood up in the presence of the hegemon,
    without any injury being upon him.

HY.MACR.B. 236.6

21. *While he yet prayed thus,*
    behold the Archangel Michael came down from the heavens.
    He released the bonds which bound him
    and he healed his body (to be) as it was at first.
    And he said to him: '*Have courage O servant of Christ.*'

BA.HY.I.ANAT.P.B. 24.14

22. The saint, *when his flesh and his blood came down together,*
    was in very great distress, and as his heart was failing within him,
       he cried out ( );
    and immediately an angel of the Lord came to him,
    he healed him and all his bonds were loosed
    and in that moment he stood up in the presence of the hegemon.
    There was no injury upon him.

BA.HY.I.AP.B. 99.2

23. *A great fear fell upon all who were in his neighbourhood.*
    And behold the angels came, they released the holy man. They let him
       down from the cross.
    They carried away the cross.
    They left the saint Helias standing.

SOB.HEL.S. 62a.14

24. While the saint was saying these things,
    behold Michael came forth from heaven.
    He mounted on the boat with the saint Apa Epima.
    He released the bonds of the righteous man.
    He brought good things from heaven.
    He ate and drank and his heart rejoiced.

724

*When the animals saw the angel of the Lord, they cast themselves
    down at his feet ( ).*
Michael the Archangel of God cast off and landed the boat ( ) in
    the presence of Armenius. ( )
*He (Epima) said to him: 'God has sent his angel, he has saved me,
he has brought me to this place so that I may put thee to shame with
    thy abominable gods.'*

MIN.EPIM.S. 27.15

25. In that moment (Armenius) caused to be brought to him a lion,
    and a bear, and a panther, and a leopard.
    He mounted them upon a boat with the Saint Apa Epime,
    whose hands and feet were bound,
    and they pushed him out to sea for three days of travel.
    The saint Apa Epime was praying to God in the Song of Daniel.
    At the end of three days, the Archangel Michael brought the boat
        to the bank with the saint Apa Epime,
    while the animals licked his hands and his feet. ( )
    Apa Epime answered: 'Shame on thee, O Armenius,
    *for behold, My Lord, Jesus, the Christ sent his angel. He saved me
        from the sea and from the animals
    so that I should put thee to shame with thy abominable gods.'*

BA.HY.I.EPIM.B. 146.26.

26. The King commanded that they should bring him a small boat. He
    caused them to remove all its equipment,
    he caused the holy man Helias to be placed on board with the
        animals also.
    He caused him to be taken to the middle of the sea, bound down in
        the boat.
    The rope of the boat was cut. It was left tossing in the middle of the
        sea,
    while the holy man Helias was on board with the animals also.
    He turned his face to the East. ( )
    *As the saint Helias was praying, he saw the animals turning their
        faces to the East.*
    They cried out to God in their language.

SOB.HEL.S. 26a.19

27. *Immediately the serpents saw the justified one, Apa Anub, they
        came, they worshipped him.*
    Each one of the serpents was thirty cubits long

and like rods of wood, terrifying to see.
When the Count saw them, he rejoiced ( ).
And Michael the Archangel was standing with the youth Anub,
causing the beasts to be tame before him.
And the cell, which was dark, became light like the sun.
And he gave power to him.
He departed up to the heavens in glory.

BA.HY.I.AN.B. 232.24

28. *And at that moment, behold, the angel of the Lord took the form of*
    a dove of light.
    He struck with his wings of light in his face.
    His eyes were opened. He saw.
    He stood upon the tribunal
    as if he had not been tortured at all.

TIL.I.HER.S. 36.22

29. *Immediately, while the word was lying in his mouth,*
    he looked, he saw the archangel Michael, who came down from heaven.
    He signed to him, saying:
    'Theodore, Theodore, *do not fear, but cast thy spear after him* (the
        dragon).
    I will help thee until thou killest him with thy hand.'
    The saint then made the sign of the Cross on his spear.
    He cast it after him.
    Immediately Michael seized it, he fixed it in his head, he killed him.
    Straightway Michael said to him: 'Take thy spear. Do not fear. I
        am with thee.'

BA.HY.II.T.A.T.S.B. 151.28

30. As she was praying *she looked,*
    she saw the image of the saint, Theodore which was painted on the
        wall of the bath
    with the dragon depicted beneath his feet, his spear fixed in its head.
    She cried out saying: '*My lord saint Theodore, thou holy martyr of*
        Christ, help me in my time of need. (   )'
    Immediately God heard her prayer, He had mercy on her,
    He commanded the dragon depicted at the feet in the picture of
        the saint Theodore,
    it became a great black living snake, it came down,
    it seized in its mouth the throat of the bath attendant.

He did not pluck his mouth from him until he gave up his spirit.
And when she was saved through the wonder which happened to her,
the woman went forth whole,
telling through the whole city what had happened to her.

BA.HY.I.TH.S.B. 186.23

31. *As he said this, behold, the saint Theodore stood above him,*
mounted on his horse, his spear in his hand.
He pierced the head of the dragon with his spear.
He killed him. He left him lying dead. ( )
After this the saint Theodore blessed the man,
he went up to heaven from him.

BA.HY.I.TH.S.B. 197.16

32. (The God-loving woman) cried out saying: '*God of the saint*
Theodore, help me in this hour of need.' ( )
Behold the saint Theodore stood above her, in great glory.
The Devil, when he saw him, was afraid. ( )
He became invisible.
But the saint Theodore blessed the woman, he gave her courage,
he became invisible to her.

BA.HY.I.TH.S.B. 188.2

4   RESTORING

THEMES

The healing of the holy man.
The taking away of the afflictions of the holy man.
The uniting of the limbs of the holy man.
The restoring of the body of the holy man to be as it was before.
The putting to shame of the hegemon.

EPISODES

The signing of the holy man with the sign of the Cross.
The touching of the body of the holy man; the passing of the hand over
the body.
The bringing forth of the nails from the body of the holy man.
The finding of the body of the holy man to be whole and healthy.
The seeing of the holy man with his body red like a rose; his face giving
light like the sun.
The rejoicing of the holy man like one who had risen from a feast; who
had drunk wine.
The giving forth of a sweet smell by the body of the holy man.

QUOTATIONS

1. The Lord said to the blessed George: '*Greeting thou who art mine,
   George,*
   greeting, my beloved and that of my angels,
   greeting, thou fighter of the Kingdom of the Heavens. (   )'
   **When the Lord had said these things to him, He filled him with
   power and joy.*
   The blessed man rejoiced greatly and he was glad,
   saying: 'I thank thee my Lord Jesus, because thou has glorified me
   greatly above my worth.'
   And He signed him with the Cross,
   He hid Himself from him.

   BA.HY.II.GEO.DI.B. 252.18; *257.13

2. *When the Saviour had said these things to the saint Apa Epima,*
   *He signed his whole body with the Cross, lest torments prevail
   against him, (   )*
   He went up to heaven
   while the saint looked after Him.

   MIN.EPIM.S. 6.14

3. *When the Saviour said these things,*
   *He signed Apa Timotheus and his daughter with the Cross, with His
   fingers.*
   He withdrew to heaven.
   *And at that moment, Apa Timotheus was released from the Persea
   tree.*

   TIL.I.TIM.S. 115.24

4. *When the Saviour had said these things to him,*
   He signed him with the Cross,
   lest any torture should touch his body.
   He went up to heaven
   while he looked after Him.

   BA.HY.I.EPIM.B. 126.20

5. *As the saint Apa Epime lay in the prison,*
   *he stretched forth his hands, he prayed in his heart and he was giving
   glory to God.*
   Behold the Archangel Michael came down from heaven,
   he sealed his mouth and his tongue with the Cross
   and he spoke blessing God.

   BA.HY.I.EPIM.B. 129.14

6. *In the middle of the night*
   the holy Archangel Michael stood up above him.
   He said to him: *'Peace be with thee.*
   It is the Lord who has sent me to thee that I should heal thee.'
   The Archangel then stretched forth his hand over the body of the
      saint.
   He signed him with the Cross.
   He healed him and he gave power to him saying:
   'Do not fear. I am with thee until thou dost complete thy course.'

   BA.HY.I.EPIM.B. 130.18

7. *And at that moment the holy Archangel Gabriel came forth from*
      heaven
   wearing a robe of light.
   He took the youth from the mouth of the lion,
   he made the sign of the Cross on his side.
   He healed him of the wounds which the lion had given him with his
      teeth.

   WOR.GAB.S. 219.9

8. *It happened that when the blessed Helias finished praying, behold*
      Michael the Archangel came to him.
   He beat all the demons, he cast them forth on the mountain.
   And the Devil became a flame of fire and departed. ( )
   It happened when the saint Helias saw the angel standing up by him,
      he rejoiced greatly.
   He made the sign of the Cross in the name of the Father and the Son
      and the Holy Spirit.

   SOB.HEL.S. 44a.2

9. Then the noble Athom *raised his eyes to heaven,*
   he cried out saying:
   'My Lord, Jesus Christ, help me quickly
   and send thy angel so that he save me from this necessity, so that I
      put to shame this impious one.'
   Immediately, before the word had ceased in his mouth,
   behold Gabriel the angel came forth from heaven.
   He broke the hermetarion, he released the Saints,
   he signed their bodies with the cross,
   he healed them,
   he embraced them.
   He stood them up, in the presence of the hegemon,

THE CULT OF THE SEER IN THE ANCIENT MIDDLE EAST

there being no injury upon them.
The crowds, when they saw what had happened, they were amazed.

HY.PI.AT.B. 142.9

10. *My father spent forty days and forty nights*
without eating or drinking,
sitting upon a brick, within the dwelling-place
looking at a mirror in a window,
without closing his eyes for this forty days,
until they burst and poured out blood upon the ground.
The holy Archangel, who was Michael, came from the sky at the time
of daybreak
on the Sunday of the completion of the Forty Days.
He signed him with the Cross,
he ended all his sufferings. His eyes were restored.
Michael went up to the heavens in glory.

AM.PAUL.T.S. 767.5

11. *He raised his eyes up to heaven*
and he saw the Son of God with His angels surrounding Him,
each with a crown in his hand.
And He said to the saint Apa Macarius:
'*Be strong O thou who hast been strong, and take power O thou who*
has taken power. (   )'
When he had heard these words from the good Saviour, the Saint
Apa Macarius received the cup from the magician.
He signed it with the Cross in the name of the Father and of the Son
and of the Holy Spirit,
and he drank from it and it was sweet like honey and honeycomb.

HY.MAC.AN.B. 60.10

12. *The saint, Apa Ari looked upon his body.*
He raised his eyes up to heaven.
He said: 'My Lord, Jesus Christ. There is no God except thee. Come
thou and save me.'
As he said this, while he was upon the hermetarion and was being
beaten, the Saviour appeared to him.
He said to him: 'Be strong, O my chosen one, Apa Ari, in the good
fight. (   )'
When Jesus had said these things He touched his body,
He healed him of the tortures of the hegemon.
He departed up to the heavens in glory.

730

When the hegemon saw this miracle and this wonder, he was amazed with all the ranks.

HY.ARI.B. 205.3

13. As the Saint Apa Epima was saying these things
   as he hung upon the hermetarion, *his prayer travelled to the throne*
      of God.
   And his prayers went into the ears of the Lord Sabaoth.
   The Saviour Jesus called Michael, he said to him:
   'My faithful steward, *come, go and touch the body of Epima, my*
      servant
   and heal his body from all the torments of this shameless hegemon.'
   The Archangel Michael came forth from heaven.
   He stood on the right side of the righteous man.
   He said to him: '*Be strong, O noble Apa Epima.*
   God has heard thee.
   He has taken away all thy afflictions from thee, for I have been sent
      to thee to give power to thee.'
   As he said these things, he touched his body.
   The blessed Apa Epima ( ) cried out saying: '*Shame on thee, O*
      impious hegemon.'

MIN.EPIM.S. 9.21

14. *As the blessed Apa Didymus said these things*
   and his prayer reached the ears of the Lord Sabaoth,
   at that moment the holy Archangel Michael came down from heaven
   and he stood at his right hand.
   He said to him: '*Be strong, O noble Apa Didymus.*
   God has heard thy prayer.
   He has removed all thy afflictions from thee.
   I am Michael, who has been sent to thee to give power to thee,
   so that thou shouldst put to shame this impious hegemon with his
      soulless gods.'
   When he had said these things he touched his body.
   He healed him.

HY.DID.B. 291.7

15. The saint Theodore cried out saying:
   '*My Lord Jesus Christ, my God, help me in this hour of necessity.'*
   In that hour behold the Archangel Michael came from heaven,
   he touched the body of the saint Theodore.
   He healed him of the injuries which the executioners had given
      him.

BA.HY.I.TH.S.B. 173.4

V

16. *When he had said the Amen,*
   suddenly an angel of the Lord touched him,
   he healed him.
   His limbs became as before,
   no injury was upon him.
   The hegemon was amazed.

   BA.HY.I.AP.B. 98.9

17. *And behold the Lord came into the prison,*
   with myriads of His holy angels ( )
   and the Lord called to him thus, saying: ' My beloved George,
   rise up from thy sleep and thou art saved,
   there is no injury upon thee.'
   He jumped up immediately without harm in his body at all,
   but he was like one who had risen from a king's feast.
   And he cast himself down, he worshipped the Lord.
   Thus He took hold of him,
   He raised him and He embraced him,
   and He passed His hand upon his whole body,
   He filled him with power
   and He said to him: '*Take courage and be strong, my beloved one.* (   )'
   When He ceased saying these things
   the Saviour gave him Peace
   and He filled him with joy entirely.
   He departed up to the heavens with His angels,
   while the blessed man was looking after Him.
   And the justified one rejoiced greatly, praising God until the morning
       broke,
   because of the things which the Lord had told him.

   BA.HY.II.GEO.DI.B. 206.15

18. *The Lord Jesus saw his distress because indeed he had no power to*
       speak at all.
   Our Lord Jesus Christ came down from the high place of heaven
   and He spoke with him saying: 'I have strengthened thee, thou my
       beloved George,
   rise from all thy suffering, take power because I am with thee.'
   And the justified one rose.
   The Lord passed His hand over his whole body.
   He healed him
   and He gave him Peace.
   He departed up to the heavens in glory and splendour.

THE ESTABLISHMENT OF COMMEMORATIVE RITUAL

*The blessed man remained in the prison singing psalms until the light
   dawned.*
The soldiers and the tribunes who guarded him,
when they saw what had happened to the saint,
that he was healed, they marvelled.

BA.HY.II.GEO.DI.B. 208.24

19. *In the middle of the night the Lord with His holy angels came into
      the prison.*
   He passed His hand over his whole body.
   He healed him. He stood him up.
   He said to him: '*Take courage, O my beloved holy, strong one.*
   I am with thee with my good Father and the Holy Spirit. (   )'
   When the Lord had said these things to him,
   He embraced him and He filled him completely with power.
   He departed up to heaven in glory and splendour.

BA.HY.II.GEO.DI.B. 235.13

20. *As he was saying this behold Michael the Archangel came forth from
      heaven.*
   He broke the 'Asterion' in two.
   He united the limbs of the saint to one another
   *and he replaced for him the pupils of his eyes also (and made them)
      to be as before.*
   He stood him up uninjured.
   He said to him: 'Be strong, O Apa Anub.
   I am with thee, giving thee power
   until thou shalt receive the imperishable crown.
   This crowd will believe through thee.'
   When he had said these things to him,
   he departed up to the heavens.
   The blessed Apa Anub rose in the power of Christ, uninjured,
   while the whole crowd watched him.

BA.HY.I.AN.B. 219.8

21. *Thus also was the saint Iakobus, the servant of God,*
   while his head alone was standing with his chest and his belly
   and all his limbs were scattered on the ground in his presence
   and half of his body was dead beneath him. (   )
   *And in that hour he saw the Lord Jesus Christ standing above him,
   *saying to him: 'Blessing on thee because thou hast received affliction
      for a short time in this place.* (   )'

733

When our Saviour had said these things *He went up to the heavens in glory.*

BA.HY.II.IAC.P.B. 47.23; *49.13

22. He suffered greatly for his body began to be divided apart.
Then the holy martyr raised his eyes up to heaven, he prayed. (   )
When he had said these things, the Lord Jesus appeared to him at that moment.
He said to him: 'Be strong, O holy martyr, beloved of my good Father' (   )
He took the limbs of the holy man, He united them together
and He raised him again, so that no evil was upon him at all. (   )
Then He raised him, He stood him before the hegemon and the whole multitude.

BA.HY.I.LAC.B. 13.22

23. The hegemon, when he heard these things, caused the saint to be raised upon the hermetarion
and tortured until his flesh and his blood fell scattered upon the ground.
The saint raised his eyes to heaven. He prayed in his heart. (   )
In that hour behold Suriel, the angel, came down from heaven. (   )
He healed the wounds which he had received.
He gave Peace to him,
He departed up to heaven.
The executioners ceased from torturing him, they said to the hegemon:
'We are weary of torturing him, he does not feel at all.'

HY.EUS.B. 33.8

24. After these things he caused the skin of his head to be flayed as far as his nerves
and vinegar and ashes to be poured on his head.
And through the power of Christ he did not feel
but he prayed to God, saying: 'My Lord Jesus Christ, who made man according to thy likeness and thy image and made him of the bones and the nerves and the skin,
do thou hear me and send to me thy Archangel, that he unite my skin again in its place,
so that the impious one shall know that there is not another God except thee.'
Then immediately, as he prayed, the Archangel Michael stood over him

and he took the skin of his head, he joined it in its place again
and it was as it had been at first.
Thereupon the saint Anatolius said: '*Know, O impious one and doer*
    of evil, that thou art put to shame.'

BA.HY.I.ANAT.P.B. 26.9

25. He was bound hand and foot and cast into it,
    so that all his inner organs poured forth.
    The impious one smiled saying: 'Where is his God now?' ( )
    Immediately Michael came forth from heaven
    and when he touched the wheel, it disintegrated,
    he restored his limbs in place again.
    He stood him up healed, with no injury upon him at all.

BA.HY.I.ANAT.P.B. 26.27

26. *When the saint Apa Anub completed the Amen,*
    behold, the holy Archangel Michael came out of heaven
    with a crown of light in his hands.
    He said to the justified one, Apa Anub: '*Take courage and be strong,*
       O beloved of God, ( )
    I am Michael the Archangel, he who stands at the right hand of Al-
       mighty God.
    It is I who give power to all the martyrs until they receive their
       crown.
    It is I who give power to all the righteous and the anchorites until they
       complete their lives of virtue.
    Behold, thou seest thy crown of light in my hands
    until I place it upon thy holy head.'
    Then he passed his hand over his whole body, he healed him.
    He caused him to be as if he had not been tortured at all
    and he replaced his guts within his belly once more.
    He departed up to the heavens in peace.

BA.HY.I.AN.B. 208.26

27. *He caused six executioners to torture him until his blood fell upon*
    the earth.
    When the King saw, he smiled, he said to his nobles: '( ) Thus you
       may know that there is no God except Apollo and Artemis.'
    While the word was in his mouth,
    behold the Lord Jesus came forth from heaven,
    He with Michael, mounted upon a chariot of light.
    Michael took hold of the bowels of Apa Nahrow.

He placed them in his belly again.
He took him down, there being not one injury upon his body.
And his blood upon the ground hardened like that of Zacharias the
priest.
The whole city quaked from this side to that three times to its founda-
tions.

TIL.I.NAH.S. 5.25

28. The hegemon commanded that he be hung on the hermatarion *and*
    tortured until his bowels came forth from his belly.
    The blessed man raised his eyes to heaven saying:
    'Hear me, my Lord Jesus Christ and send me thy great Archangel
    Michael the holy one
    to help me in this hour of need.'
    In that hour, behold Michael the Archangel came forth from heaven.
    He enclosed the bowels within the belly of the righteous man again,
    and he brought him down from the hermetarion with no blemish on his
    body,
    nor was there any injury upon him at all.

BA.HY.I.LAC.B. 8.26

29. He, the noble one, *raised his eyes up to heaven*
    and he prayed, saying
    'My Lord Jesus Christ (   ) do not allow me to die now until I put to
    shame Arianus and his idols made by hand.'
    In that moment an angel of God stood at his right hand
    and he stretched forth his hand,
    he took his bowels, he returned them into his belly again.
    And he signed him with the Cross,
    he took him down from the hermetarion
    with no injury upon his body,
    but he was whole as if he had not been tortured at all.

BA.HY.I.PAP.B. 114.8

30. *He opened the belly of the righteous man with his hand, his guts fell*
    down upon the earth.
    At that moment, behold, a cloud of light made a shade over him.
    The angel of the Lord took his guts, he placed them inside his belly
    and he made his whole body smooth.
    He made it as if it had not been touched at all.

SOB.HEL.S. 53a.2

THE ESTABLISHMENT OF COMMEMORATIVE RITUAL

31. *As he was praying on these things,*
   behold, a great light shone in the place in which he was enclosed.
   And he saw a chorus of saints
   with the Lord Jesus Christ in their midst
   and the Lord said to him: '*Be strong and take power, O valiant*
      athlete. (   )'
   And the chorus of saints made their way,
   they drew out all the spikes from his body
   and he was healed.
   Immediately his whole body was whole,
   he sang psalms (   ).
   Then the Lord departed up from him and he sang psalms.

BA.HY.II.IAC.P.B. 33.21

32. *While the word was still in his mouth, Suriel the Archangel, came.*
   He stood in the midst of the prison.
   He said: 'Be strong O Anub,
   thou holy martyr of our Lord Jesus Christ, have courage,
   I am Suriel.
   It is the Lord who has sent me to thee
   that I should give power to thee in the afflictions
   which have been inflicted on thee
   and those which will come upon thee.'
   And he passed his hand over his whole body.
   He brought forth the nails which were in his body.
   He healed him.
   He gave power to him.
   He departed up to the heavens,
   as he (Anub) looked after him.

BA.HY.I.AN.B. 230.1

33. *The saint suffered greatly in this torment*
   and he said: '*My Lord Christ, the Son of the Living God,*
   remember me and do not forsake me.'
   And at that moment our Lord Jesus Christ appeared to him
   and He said to him: 'Greeting to thee, O my chosen one, Apa Macar-
      ius,
   my Peace be with thee, (   )
   for I am Jesus Christ, the Son of the Living God,
   who have come to bring good news to thee. (   )'
   And He passed His hand over his whole body,

He healed him,
he departed up to heaven in glory.

HY.MAC.AN.B. 41.4

34. *As the blessed man was saying these things,*
    our Lord Jesus Christ came towards him mounted upon a chariot of
       light,
    while thousands of angels and tens of thousands of archangels preceded
       Him.
    The Saviour said to him: '*Greeting my chosen Theodore,*
    thou beloved of my good Father, take courage and do not fear, (   )'
    When the Saviour had said these things to the blessed Theodore,
    He passed His hand over his whole body,
    He healed him, He gave him Peace,
    He went up to the heavens in glory,
    while the angels sang to Him.

BA.HY.I.TH.S.B. 168.3

35. *As he completed the prayer,*
    the flame of the fire burned greatly.
    The saint Theodore raised his eyes up to the heaven
    *and he said: '*My Lord Jesus Christ receive my soul to thyself in this*
       hour.'
    At that moment the fire became like cool water under the body of
       the saint Theodore.
    but his body was quite whole, as if he had not been cast into the fire
       at all.
    The holy martyr of Christ, the saint Theodore lay in the midst of the
       fire,
    not like flesh being burnt but like pure bread being baked,
    through the power of Christ which was with him.
    In that hour he gave his Spirit into the hands of Christ in peace
    and the whole road was filled with fragrance
    and a multitude of holy men were standing watching the soul of the
       saint Theodore
    as it was brought up to heaven
    to the place of rest of the Righteous with all the Holy Ones.

BA.HY.I.TH.S.B. 179.21

36. These things the angel said to him and approached his body and
    healed it. And the colour of his face was beautiful like the sun. And
    his breath was sweet like pure spices. And the angel ascended from
    his presence to heaven towards Him who sent him.

THE ESTABLISHMENT OF COMMEMORATIVE RITUAL

And after ten days the King commanded the custodians and said to them: 'Go, open the prison and see whether Azazail, the deceiver, is dead.' And the custodians went and opened the prison and they found Azazail, who was like a delighted bridegroom, when he has come forth from the bridechamber, while he rejoiced and was glad. And he exhaled from himself a goodly smell of spices which exceeded all sweet odours. And they saw him glorified and they were amazed at him.

MAC.AZ.SY. 26(54/55)

37. And the arrows which pierced the bodies of the holy ones came forth and fell to the ground.
And their bodies became whole and healthy like fruit trees (standing) in the field and flourishing.

TIL.I.TIM.S. 119.1

38. Then the brother monk asked the holy man: '*Whence is this man with long hair,*
surrounded by such glory?
Truly I have never seen one like him, full of glory and gentleness.
And now, when I seized his hands, and worshipped them,
a great power came in my body. I ceased to be weak
and I rejoiced like one who had risen from a feast.'

AM.PIS.KE.B. 355.10

39. *The saint Apa Epime was filled with joy and he spent the whole night praying and blessing God until the light appeared.*
When morning came the hegemon sat upon the tribunal. ( )
When he was brought, the hegemon saw that *he was rejoicing like one who had come from a feast.*

BA.HY.I.EPIM.B. 130.25

40. The blessed and noble *saint Theodore became like one who had risen from a feast*
as if he had not received any hurt at all,
through him who gave courage to him, Christ.

BA.HY.I.TH.S.B. 173.9

41. *The hegemon saw his face giving light like the sun,*
while his body was red like a rose.

BA.HY.I.SA.PA.B. 72.1

42. When morning came, the hegemon sent for Pteleme,
he was stood up in his presence.
His body was fresh and his face red like a rose
through the grace of God which surrounded him.

TIL.II.PTOL.S. 35.9

43. *But his face gave light like the sun,*
his whole body was red like a rose in the days of Parmouthi.
He rejoiced like one who had drunk wine.

BA.HY.I.SA.PA.B. 81.1

44. The brother said to Apa Pisentius:
'*Whence comes this brother who is hairy and with such grace sur-*
rounding him?
I have truly never seen such a one so gentle and filled with light.
And I say to thee, my brother, that at the moment that I grasped his
hands and kissed them,
a great power came into my body, I ceased to be powerless, I became
strong indeed.
I felt happy like one who has been in a wine shop.'

BU.AP.PIS.S. 81.4

45. *But he was flushed like those who rejoice in wine.*

BA.HY.I.ANAT.P.B. 27.6

46. *But his face was flushed like one who was drunk from wine.*

SOB.HEL.S. 44b.15

47. *Afterwards thou wilt return to the tribunal to contend for my name*
and put to shame this impious hegemon.

BA.HY.I.LAC.B. 14.11

48. *The saint Apa Heraclite prayed to God, saying:*
'*Hear me my Lord Jesus Christ and send thy angel to me that he may*
save me.
Do not leave me to die in the dark,
lest the impious one should say: "I have prevailed over him," ( )'

TIL.I.HER.S. 36.16

49. *Before he had finished praying,*
behold Michael, the great Archangel came down from heaven.
He delivered the saint,
the saint raised himself,

740

he stood up in the presence of the hegemon.
He cried out to him: 'Shame on thee, O impure dog.'

HY.ARI.B. 207.16

50. *Michael the Archangel broke a flat stone in the bath.*
    He raised the saint Apa Panesew upon his wings of light,
    he put him upon the pavement of the **bath**
    in the presence of the hegemon.
    The blessed man said to the hegemon:
    '*Art thou not ashamed to say these senseless words, O impious*
      Godless one?'

TIL.I.PAN.S. 96.21

5 RAISING FROM THE DEAD

THEMES

The fashioning of the body of the holy man with the hand that created
   Adam.
The reviving of the holy man from the dead with the breath of life.
The recalling of the holy man from the dead with the voice.

EPISODES

The gathering of the bones of the dead; the uniting of the limbs of the
   dead.
The taking of the dead man into the hand of the Saviour.
The breathing of the breath of life into the dead man.
The calling of the name of the dead man; the commanding of the dead
   man to rise, to stand on his feet.

QUOTATIONS

1. *A great disturbance happened, with fearful terror.*
   The sky was covered with cloud
   and there was a great fear so that the mountains suddenly moved, the
      earth shook,
   the sea was disturbed with waves and its waves were fifteen cubits high,
   Michael blew on the trumpet.
   Behold the Lord Jesus came upon his chariot of cherubim.
   He stood above the edge of the pit.
   He said to Michael, the Archangel: 'Go down to the pit. Gather
      the bones of my youth, George, ( )
   so that he should believe with his whole heart
   and know that *I am God, He who alone has power to save.*'

Michael went down to the pit, he assembled the holy body of the saint George.

The Lord took his hand saying:

'*George my beloved, behold the hand which created Adam the first man,*

it is this now which fashions thee again.'

The Lord blew into his face.

He filled him with life again.

The Lord embraced him,

He went up to heaven with His holy angels.

BA.HY.II.GEO.B. 281.9

2. *And in that moment the air became entirely dark.*

The sky was covered by cloud.

Thunder and lightning happened.

The whole earth trembled to its foundations.

The holy Archangel blew upon the trumpet,

the Lord came upon a chariot of Cherubim,

with ten thousands of angels

and he halted above the pit.

The Lord said to Michael: 'Say to this pit,

give me the blood and the bones and the flesh and the dust of the justified one, George (   )

so that he should know in his whole heart

that *I am the God of Abraham and the God of Isaac and the God* of Jacob.'

And Michael placed them in his presence.

The Lord received the bones in his hand

as he said: '*George my youth, the hand that fashioned Adam,*

it even now fashions thee, O my beloved George.'

And he blew in his face.

He gave him the breath of life

and the saint George rose from those who are dead.

The Lord embraced him

and He gave him Peace.

He departed up to the heavens,

as he looked after him.

BA.HY.II.GEO.DI.B. 215.1

3. *It happened in that moment, the air filled with clouds*

and there was a great disturbance,

so that the earth shook and the mountains were removed

and the sea rose fifteen cubits.

For the Lord came down from heaven, sitting upon the chariot of Cherubim.

He stood at the mouth of the pit.

He commanded Michael that he should bring the limbs of George together. ( )

'So that he will believe that *God has power to raise the dead after they are dead.*'

Then the Lord took George in His hand, He said to him:

'*George, the hand which fashioned Adam, the first man,*

whom I made from the earth in the East,

this it is which now will fashion thee.'

The Lord blew into his face a breath of life.

And when the Lord had embraced him,

He went up to heaven with His angels.

BU.GEO.C.S. 180.18

4. *Immediately behold, Michael, the Archangel came down from heaven,*
together with Suriel and Raphael.
They brought the limbs of his body.
They united them to one another.
And they blew into the face of the justified one.
He rose uninjured. ( )
When Michael and Suriel and Raphael had said these things to him,
they went up to the heavens in glory.
The saint Apa Anub rose, he went to the prison.

BA.HY.I.AN.B. 221.16

5. *The saint was not able to endure under all these torments.*
In that hour he gave up the Spirit.
The wicked and impious one Eutychian caused his body to be removed to a dunghill outside the town of Pshati.
They threw it there.
At that moment behold the Lord Jesus Christ, the Son of the living God
came forth from heaven with His holy angels.
He stood up above him. He called him three times.
saying: 'Macarius, Macarius, Macarius, my unwearied athlete,
my wise administrator, my devoted herald, my strong martyr.
I swear by myself that I will give glory to thee upon earth and in heaven. ( )'

743

And the good Saviour blew into his face.
He said to him: 'Receive a holy spirit.'
Immediately he rose, he stood up.
There was no injury to him at all.
And the Saviour embraced him,
He went to heaven in glory with His holy angels.

HY.MAC.AN.B. 54.1

6. *In this way the justified one gave up the spirit*
and his bones and his flesh were burned, they became ash together.
He caused his ashes to be taken upon a high mountain called Asurion
and scattered upon the mountain with the wind. ( )
Suddenly, behold, there came thunder and lightning with a great
disturbance
so that the earth was moved to its foundations.
Behold, Our Lord Jesus Christ came upon a cloud of light,
with His holy angels singing before Him.
The Lord commanded the four winds of the earth
to gather in for Him the dust of the body of the saint, George.
And the Lord called, in His Voice-of-God,
saying: 'George my youth, rise my beloved, from sleep,
because it is I who command thee.'
In that moment the blessed man arose like a bridegroom coming from
his bride-chamber.
The Lord embraced him.
He gave him Peace,
He departed up to the heavens in glory.

BA.HY.II.GEO.DI.B. 232.8

7. When the ministers of the Devil were at a short distance of thirty
stadia from the mountain,
there came thunder and lightning in the sky,
so that the whole mountain there was shaken.
Behold, the Lord came mounted on a cloud
and He said to the saint, George: 'My excellent, chosen one, rise
from sleep.'
And immediately the martyr of Christ arose.

BA.HY.II.GEO.B. 296.15

8. *As he was saying these things,*
behold the good Saviour appeared to him in the form of a youth,
with Michael and Gabriel and the rest of the seven archangels.

*He commanded the angel Suriel to bring to him the limbs of Eusebius,
the holy and glorious martyr.*
*Then Suriel the Archangel, gathered the limbs of the body of the
blessed man.*
He brought them to the presence of the good Saviour.
Then He called out over them in His sweet voice saying:
*'My beloved Eusebius, thou general of my good Father and the Holy
Spirit, rise up from this sleep, it is I who command thee.'*
Immediately the saint, Eusebius, rose from the dead.
And he flourished in his body so that no injury was upon him at all.
And he cast himself down, he worshipped the Saviour.
The Lord said to him: 'Be strong, O my chosen and glorious one. (   )'
When the Saviour had said these things to him,
He gave him Peace,
He departed up to the heavens in glory.
The saint then rose, he walked upright, he came to the place of
Maurianus, the hegemon.

HY.EUS.B. 34.9

9. After the soldiers had cast the body of the saint Apater upon the
mountain and departed.
Our Lord Jesus came forth from heaven in that moment.
He raised him, he embraced him.
He gave His Peace to him.
He departed up to heaven.
The saint Apater rose.

HY.AP.IR.B. 103.3

10. And the king commanded that he, (Macarius) be taken upon a very
high mountain
to be cast forth as food for the birds of the sky and the wild beasts,
so that they should eat his flesh.
And in that moment the Son of God came down from heaven
and He called with the voice with which He called Lazarus, saying:
'Macarius, my beloved, arise, I am thy Lord.'
Immediately he rose, he stood up upon his feet.
No harm had happened to him at all.
And He embraced him.
He went up to heaven with His holy angels.

HY.MAC.AN.B. 43.9

11. *A great disturbance happened in the air.*
The earth was moved to its foundations.

745

*Behold the Lord Jesus Christ came down from heaven with His holy
    angels.*
He stood over the place in which the cauldron was buried
and He said to Salathiel, the angel:
'Bring this cauldron up.'
When he had brought up the cauldron he placed it upon the ground.
The Lord of the Powers made answer over it saying:
'*George my chosen one, rise up. It is I who raised Lazarus from the
    dead.*
*In the same way now I command thee to rise and come up out of the
    cauldron.*
Stand upon thy feet.
I am the Lord thy God.'
*In that moment the truly strong man rose with great and mighty
    power*
like one who had received no injury at all.
All those who saw were amazed.
The Lord said to him: '*Be strong and take power, George my beloved,*
because there is great joy for thee in the heavens and on earth
*and before my good Father and before my angels, because of thy
    strife.*
Take courage because I am with thee.'
And He went up to heaven with His holy angels.

BA.HY.II.GEO.B. 287.10

12. *A great disturbance happened*
    so that the sky became dark and the stars did not give light.
    For the Lord came down with His angels upon the cauldron
    saying: 'I am the God who raised Lazarus from the dead.
    To thee also, O George, I say come forth from the cauldron
    and stand upon thy feet,
    there being no injury upon thee.'
    And in that moment the holy martyr George rose from the dead,
    as if there was no injury at all upon him.
    The Lord said to him: 'George, a great joy exists in heaven
    among the angels over thy strife.
    I will come to thee upon clouds to give power to thee
    like Abraham and Isaac and Jacob, my heirs.
    Take power and be strong.
    For I am with thee.'
    The Lord then went up to heaven with His angels.

BU.GEO.C.S. 185.17

13. (The Saviour) brought the body of the blessed Apa Sarapion up out
      of the cauldron.
    His limbs were united with one another.
    The Saviour stood above the limbs of the blessed Apa Sarapion.
    The Saviour cried out saying:
    'Sarapion, Sarapion, this is the hand which fashioned Adam, the first
      man.
    Now it will be that which fashions thee.'
    And at that moment, Apa Sarapion rose, he stood up,
    he worshipped the Saviour.
    The Saviour said to him: 'Rise, go to the town and confound the
      hegemon.
    Thou wilt receive great afflictions for my name
    but a great multitude will have faith in thee in my name.'
    The Saviour blessed him,
    He signed him with the Cross,
    He went from him up to the heavens with Michael and Gabriel,
    while the glory of God surrounded him.

HY.SAR.B. 304.1

III   HEAVENLY SIGNS

1   HEAVENLY LIGHT

EPISODES

The opening of the roof to give light before a revelation from heaven.
The appearance of light in the presence of a heavenly visitor: Christ,
    archangel or angel.
The lighting of the whole place.
The occurrence of light in the presence of holy men.
The occurrence of light at the birth or death of holy men.
The giving of light by the faces of heavenly visitors: Christ, archangels,
    angels, prophets, saints.
The giving of light by the faces of holy men: bishops, monks, martyrs.
The appearance of a heavenly visitor as a man of light, a youth of light.
The giving of crowns of light.
The wearing of robes of light, white robes, royal robes.
The appearance of a cross of light.
The appearance of heavenly visitors mounted on chariots of light.
The spreading of wings of light.
The appearance of heavenly visitors mounted on clouds of light.

QUOTATIONS

1. *At night, as the blessed John* (father of Theodore Stratelates) *was confined and lying in irons,*
   weeping in distress,
   behold, a light shone upon him,

   BA.HY.II.T.A.T.S.B. 106.24

2. *He looked up, he saw the roof as if it opened*
   and he saw as it were a beam of light coming down to him.

   GAR.ANT.S. 15.22

3. '*I prayed to God to reveal to me their work* (Macarius and two strangers).
   And the roof opened and there was a light like that at midday.
   But they did not see the light.'

   CHA.AP.PA.S. 72.8(239)

4. *He* (Macarius) *said:* '*I prayed to God that he would reveal to me their manner of work.*
   The roof opened.
   There was a light like that of day.
   But they did not see the light.'

   AM.MA.DO.B. 298.11

5. '*I prayed to God to reveal to me their manner of work* (Macarius and two strangers).
   The roof opened and there was a light like that of day.
   But they did not see the light.'

   AM.AP.MAC.B. 210.8

6. When he had said these things,
   that cave was filled with light
   which was brighter than the dazzling rays of the sun,
   and I was aflame with the brilliance
   and the fragrant odour of the incense.

   LOOK.MAR.SY. 18.6

7. *And when he* (Theodore) *was sitting meditating,*
   the cell in which he was became light. ( )
   Behold two angels taking the forms of men giving light, appeared to him.

   LE.PAC.B. 37.7

THE ESTABLISHMENT OF COMMEMORATIVE RITUAL

8. *And while the two were standing praying,*
   behold then the whole place became light
   and the old man was not able to bear the light.
   He fell upon the ground.

POR.IS.B. 335.17

9. *When I* (Apa Onnophrius) *came out of my monastery,*
   I looked, I saw a light in my presence.

BU.ON.S. 212.21

10. On the following night, when he rose to perform the service, accord-
    ing *to his custom,*
    behold, the whole place was made light as the hour of noon, in the
    days of summer.
    And Abba Macarius knew by the agreement that it was the Cherubim
    who had come to him.

AM.MAC.SC.B. 74.15

11. And in the middle of the night,
    suddenly a great light shone in the church
    and there was shed a sweet and fragrant smell,
    and the empty lamps themselves which were hanging there were
    lighted,
    and also a light appeared above the city. ( )
    The lamps remained lighted seven days and seven nights,
    without oil and without water.
    And the light and the sweet smell remained for a long time in the
    church.

NAU.JE.PE.SY. LXI.6

12. The King said to him: '*When thou didst enter in to me,*
    who were these who walked with thee?
    I saw two men walking with thee, while a great light surrounded thee
    and them,
    such as I have never seen.
    If they had not disappeared I should have died immediately with
    fear.'

POR.IS.B. 383.18

13. *And thus she* (Helen) *gave birth to her son*
    and there was a great light in the house in which he was born.

HY.JE.SI.B. 176.12

14. While they were considering with one another, *behold a great and indescribable light came forth in the sky.*
    It spread forth upon the date palms on which the holy ones were hung.

    TIL.I.TIM.S. 118.28

15. *We* (Christian priests) *watched until the sixth hour of the evening and every one went home.*
    As the King of Israel lives,
    we saw the light coming down upon him until it clothed the whole of that body (of the dead saint).

    BA.HY.II.JOH.PH.B. 178.10

16. When He had said these things, immediately He departed to heaven.
    And the heavens were opened, and the air shone,
    so that it is not possible to describe with human words, the splendour of that light.
    And when he had marvelled at these things which were said to him,
    straightway they beat (the board to summon) the brethren
    to the service of the night.

    BU.II.PAL.SY. 318.13

17. *Then after a time, Jesus the Son of the living God came down to Amente*
    and a cross of light preceded Him.
    The whole of Amente became lighted.

    BA.HY.II.GEO.DI.B. 227.12

18. *In the night of the holy Lord's Day,*
    behold our Saviour, Jesus came to him
    and the whole room became light.
    Apater leapt up when he saw the light.

    HY.AP.IR.B. 88.1

19. *In the middle of the night*
    an angel of the Lord appeared to him.
    The whole house became greatly lighted.

    BA.HY.II.IS.TI.B. 74.21

20. *In that hour, behold, the Son of God came forth from heaven with Michael.* ( )
    And the whole place in which they were placed shone,
    giving seven times more light than the sun.

    HY.SAR.B. 313.7

21. *As the holy Apanub was still praying, behold Michael, the Archangel,*
    came forth from the sky,
    The whole place gave light like the sun.
    Immediately the young boy fell upon his face before him and he was
    like one dead.

BA.HY.I.AN.B. 205.28

22. *As the holy men were standing,*
    behold Gabriel the Archangel appeared to them.
    The whole place was lighted.

HY.PI.AT.B. 152.4

23. *In the middle of the night,*
    behold, the Archangel Michael came to him in the hold of the ship.
    He caused the whole ship to give light in the night, as if it were the day.

BA.HY.I.AN.B. 225.16

24. *While he was saying these things*
    behold Our Lord the Christ stood above him in great glory
    and the whole place was lighted seven times (more brightly)
    so that the multitude said:
    '*It is a fire which has come forth from heaven in order to burn us.*'

BA.HY.I.EPIM.B. 153.3

25. In that evening, when they brought them to the prison,
    they saw a great light shining in the whole prison,
    like the sun in the days of Summer.
    And the rulers called the soldier who guarded the prison, they said
       to him:
    'Why dost thou light a fire in the prison?' (   )
    The soldier said to them: '(   ) Behold it is two days
    since they brought this Christian, Paphnute, in here
    and no darkness has been in it
    and its light has shone like the day and like the sun.'

BA.HY.I.PAP.B. 115.24

26. *Behold, our Lord Jesus Christ came down from heaven,*
    with Michael on His right side and Gabriel on His left side.
    The whole prison was greatly lighted.

HY.PI.AT.B. 144.13

27. Then in the middle of the night,
    the angel of the Lord, who held a lamp,
    lit up with its light all those in the prison,
    so that all those watchmen were astonished with its brightness.

BU.II.HIER.SY. 378.23

28. *In the third night then*
    when the holy man was with wounds,
    the Lord Jesus came to him in the prison with His holy angels.
    And the prison was filled with light.

BA.HY.II.GEO.DI.B. 217.18

29. *As he was praying on these things,*
    behold, a great light shone in the place in which he was enclosed,
    and he saw a chorus of saints
    with the Lord Jesus Christ in their midst.

BA.HY.II.IAC.P.B. 33.21

30. *Behold, our Lord, Jesus Christ came forth from heaven,*
    sitting upon a chariot of light,
    with Michael on His right side and Gabriel on His left side,
    while myriads of angels sang hymns to Him. (   )
    When the saints saw the Saviour, their faces gave light like the sun
    and they were filled with great joy.

HY.PI.AT.B. 169.7

31. *When he saw the Archangel, he prostrated himself, he worshipped*
    him.
    He raised him
    and his face gave light like the sun.
    The holy men saw the light,
    they were afraid, they worshipped the Archangel.

TIL.I.PA.TH.S. 75.12

32. He found the holy men, the blessed Elijah the Tishbite,
    with the blessed Pisentius who was lying sick.
    When the brother entered, he received the blessing of both.
    When he stood to pray, he was not able to raise up his eyes
    to look in the face of the blessed Elijah,
    because of the many rays of light which came from his face
    like lightning.

AM.PIS.KE.B. 354.6

33. He found the two holy men seated.
    Apa Pisentius was lying and the holy man Elijah was sitting beside
       him, paying him a visit.
    When the brother went in, he received a blessing from both.
    He stood, he was unable to look into the face of the prophet Elijah,
    because of the rays of light which flashed from his face like lightning.

                                                            BU.AP.PIS.S. 80.16

34. *I saw the angel who was with me change his form.*
    He burned with heat like a flame (   ).
    And seven eagles of light were standing on the right side of the
       altar, (   )
    and they sang hymns in a choir of blessing to the Father. (   )
    I saw a multitude of men, (   )
    and their faces gave light
    seven times more than the sun.
    and the hair of their heads was like white wool.

                                                          BU.AP.PAUL.S. 567.28

35. *One among the holy men spent forty days, without eating or drinking,*
    namely the man of God, Moses, the first prophet,
    and no one was able to look into his face because it gave light,
    like the sun at its rising.

                                                           TIL.II.PTOL.S. 35.18

36. And he also saw the light which went forth
    from the splendour of the face of the Lord,
    from the interior of the Holy Sanctuary.

                                                           NAU.JE.PE.SY.LVII.1

37. And they used to say
    that the face of the old man Sylvanus shone so brightly
    even as did the face of Moses,
    with the glorious splendour which he had received from God,
    that no man was able to look upon it with his eyes open.

                                                      BU.II.PAL.SY. 955(BEDJAN)

38. *Thus He received the soul of His mother into His bosom,*
    wrapped in linen cloths,
    sending forth flashes of light.

                                                          LA.DOR.MAR.B. 58.8

39. And one day, as was that poor man's custom,
    he (Priscus) went secretly outside the city
    to some enclosed garden-land, hidden by trees and reeds,
    to pray, in such a way that this nobleman observed him.
    And he went out after him secretly
    and as he was standing facing him,
    he saw him standing in prayer, with his hands stretched out to
        heaven.
    And suddenly a wonderful vision was laid upon his face
    and it flashed like lightning.
    And the rays of fire were going forth from his face
    and a wonderful bow of fire was stretched out above him,
    while he stood within it and a great light surrounded him.

                                                    BR.PRI.SY. 181.9

40. When they arrived at his cell,
    from it there reached them a sweet smell (   ).
    And the holy man John came forth immediately in their presence
    while his face was shining in the likeness of a seraphim.

                                                  NAU.JE.PE.SY. XXII.6

41. Once one of the brethren went to the cell of Abba Arsenius in Scete
    and he looked through the window and he saw the old man standing
        up
    and all of him was like fire.

                                                  BU.II.PAL.SY. 608.22

42. And when we came to the cell of the Saint Macarius, he looked up
    and we saw within his dwelling place, it was like a fire burning.
    And when we knocked at the door, the saint came forth.
    When we saw the radiance of his face we fell upon the ground.

                                                  AM.VER.MAC.B. 186.12

43. *He saw him whom he had previously seen black and in darkness,*
    with his whole body giving light as he came forth from the church.
    His face was shining, giving light.

                                                  CHA.AP.PA.S. 48.7(191)

44. And he saw the faces of sinners like charcoal,
    and he saw some of them whose faces were burning
    and their eyes red, full of blood.
    Others among them had their faces lighted and their garments were
        white,

THE ESTABLISHMENT OF COMMEMORATIVE RITUAL

Others while they were partaking in the body of the Lord *were on
  fire and burning.*
*Some became like the light which entered their mouths
and caused their whole body to be lighted, ( )
and their faces gave light and were dignified
and their garments were white.*
And when they also received the Holy Mysteries of Christ,
they became illuminated with light.

CHA.AP.PA.S. 58.10(211)

45. (The blessed Paul) saw that everyone who was entering
  was glorious in the appearance of (his) soul,
  and lighted in (his) face
  and that the angel of each one was rejoicing in him. ( )
  And then he saw that man whom he saw entering, ( )
  when he came forth from the church
  (he saw) his face lighted and his body white.

BU.II.PAL.SY. 298.17

46. '*At the time when I mount the throne, I see the sinners thus,
  with angels fleeing from them because of their evil smell.
  I see also the righteous clothed in light in the service
  while their faces are bright like light
  and like the sun giving rays of light.*'

AM.MAC.TK.B. 107.5

47. *His face gave light like the sun.*

BA.HY.I.SA.PA.B. 81.1

48. '*I* (John) *burned greatly with the heat and the thirst for water.*
  When my father had spent a long time at a great distance from me,
  *he returned to me, his eyes full of light like stars of the sky.
  And he was completely refreshed
  like one who has been stopping in a drinking place.*'

BU.AP.PIS.S. 98.12

49. The King with the twelve bishops, *when they saw the face of the
    Bishop which was giving light,
  knew that he had seen a vision.*

BA.HY.II.GEO.DI.B. 267.12

50. *When the saint saw this great vision, fear would seize him, with joy.
  Immediately his face would give forth rays of light,*

755

so that everyone marvelled saying:
'*God has made us worthy of a saint of such holiness.*'

POR.IS.B. 356.17

51. When Abba Sisoes was about to die
and the fathers were sitting in his presence,
they saw that his face was shining like the sun ( ).
And again his face shone twice as much ( ).
And again, suddenly, his face shone like the sun,
and all those seated were afraid ( ).
And immediately he delivered up his spirit
and there was lightning
and the whole place was filled with sweet perfume.

BU.II.PAL.SY. 643.13

52. *Behold an old man, whose face gave light like the sun*, approached me.

BU.AP.PAUL.S. 561.2

53. *At midnight he saw in a vision a man of light as if he were standing in
his presence, ( )
and his face gave light greatly.*

HY.JE.SI.B. 175.9

54. *And thus he revealed himself to him who was paralysed, in a vision,
in the form of a man of light,
whose face gave forth rays of light.*

WOR.GAB.S. 194.5

55. The man of light said to him:
'Save thy soul from her destruction in so far as she has set thee free,
withdraw thyself to thy land, for the sake of the disposition of thy
body.'

BA.HY.II.T.A.T.S.B. 112.5

56. *When they* (Pachomius and Theodore) *began to pray* (for a dying
catechumen)
*a great fear came upon them,
they saw a man of light standing in their presence
and he stretched forth his hands to them* saying:
'*Give me your perfumed prayers, that I take them to the Lord.*'
Immediately they fell upon the earth, they cried out to the Lord.

LE.PAC.S. 240a.2

57. *When they* (Pachomius and Theodore) *began to pray,*
    a great fear came upon them,
    they saw a man of light standing in their presence.
    He stretched his hand to them saying:
    '*Give me your perfumed prayers, that I take them to the Lord.*'
    Immediately they fell upon the earth,
    they cried out to God ( ) with great supplications and tears.

    LE.PAC.B. 86.15

58. '*Before I spoke to thee, an ecstasy came upon me.*
    A man of light came and stood before me.'

    BU.AP.PIS.S. 123.29

59. *As the holy man Didymus was sleeping in his room,*
    behold a man of light stood over him.

    HY.DID.B. 288.7

60. *It happened when the blessed Apa Epime was sleeping in his house,*
    he saw a youth of light standing above him.

    BA.HY.I.EPIM.B. 126.4

61. *The blessed Apa Epima was sleeping one day in his house*
    when behold, a youth of light stood above him.

    MIN.EPIM.S. 5.11

62. *When he had finished his service according to his custom,*
    he fell asleep for a short while
    and thus Christ appeared to him in a vision
    in the form of a beautiful youth giving light greatly.

    BA.HY.I.AP.B. 92.8

63. '*I suffered greatly because of the pain that was upon me, I looked,*
    I saw a very glorious man standing before me.'

    BU.ON.S. 208.26

64. *He saw a vision from the Lord thus:*
    he saw a man full of great glory standing in his presence.
    There was a sweet smell coming from his mouth.
    His face gave forth rays of light, like the sun.

    LEI.SIN.B. 61.12

65. *And again when he* (Theodore) *came to the place of the door of the*
    sanctuary,

49   757

he looked within, he saw in a vision
the place where the feet (stood) in the form in which it was manifested ( ).
He was not able to look in his face because of the great light which flashed in his presence.

LE.PAC.S. 281b.20

66. *And when he came to the place of the door of the church,*
he looked in, he saw a vision
and in the place of its feet, in the form in which it appeared to him,
it was like a sapphire stone which gave light.
And he was unable to look into his face,
because of the great light which flashed lightning
in his presence without ceasing.

LE.PAC.B. 163.9

67. *And we spent the whole night praying to God until the morning.*
When the morning came,
I saw his face which had changed and turned to become like another
man.
He became altogether like a fire and his form terrified me greatly.

BU.ON.S. 215.34

68. *Behold there appeared to him two saints*
shining greatly in glory and splendour,
while their faces were full of joy.

AM.MAC.SC.B. 107.10

69. *Before I spoke with thee an ecstasy fell upon me.*
I saw a multitude of orthodox bishops giving light like the sun,
standing in this courtyard, singing to God.

AM.PIS.KE.B. 415.13

70. *He* (Shenute) *saw in a vision a very beautiful woman,*
whose whole body gave forth rays of light like the sun.

LEI.SIN.B. 64.8

71. *Behold a multitude of angels came down from the sky*
with crowns of light in their hands.
They greeted the souls of the holy martyrs,
They placed the crowns of light upon them.

HY.MACR.B. 244.15

72. (Abba Amoi) *looked towards Abba John. Behold, he saw seven holy*
     angels,
   wearing bright robes in great glory and carrying seven crowns,
   giving forth flashes of lightning above our holy father Abba John
   and placing them upon his head, one after the other,
   filling him with great joy.

                                                   AM.JOH.K.B. 336.7

73. He saw seven angels, shining with light,
   carrying seven crowns of light,
   and they were flying above the head of the holy man, John.

                                                   NAU.JE.PE.SY. XVIII.17

74. *And the wife of the King saw great gatherings of angels*
   occupying the room with the holy man, the Archbishop.
   And she saw a great light like burning lamps.
   They were wearing white clothes
   And the holy Patriarch Isaac was in their midst.

                                                   POR.IS.B. 367.3

75. *He saw the form of our father Pachomius,*
   wearing a white garment like snow
   and two angels of the Lord gave much light. ( )
   'The garment which I saw on him in the vision
   was like royal purple and shone as lightning.'

                                                   LE.PAC.B. 157.28

76. And they saw the holy man and the angel with him.
   And they thought that this man was an angel
   because he was wearing a garment, white like the snow,
   while the holy man was wearing a garment of skin.
   Then the angel ascended to heaven.
   Then these men, from fear, fell upon the ground.

                                                   NAU.AAR.SY. 725.9

77. When the days were accomplished in which he (Isaac) should be
     baptised,
   according to the traditions of the Christians,
   his parents took him to the bishop of those times, who was a
     spirit-bearing man.

He, as he was baptising the holy child in the font
in the name of the Father and the Son and the Holy Spirit, the
  Consubstantial Trinity,
and his eyes were opened, he saw a cross of light over the head of the
  boy.

POR.IS.B. 305.7

78. When the old man Abba Zacharias saw the holy boy coming toward
  him,
  the Lord opened his eyes.
  He saw the sign of a cross above his head.

POR.IS.B. 313.3

79. When the priest came up from the fields, he put the ass into the stall
  he went up to the loft to give a bundle of grass to the ass.
  He saw the bundle of grass, which was placed over the boy,
  to have the form of a cross of light lying over him,
  giving forth rays of lightning.
  When the priest saw the wonderful vision he was amazed.

POR.IS.B. 315.6

80. Après cela, voici que soudain il apparut à tout le peuple, visibles à
  l'œil nu, trois croix dans le ciel au-dessus du cadavre, cependant
  que des colombes blanches volaient autour de lui.

FE.II.DAN.G. 164(XLVII)

81. As the saint Aba Isaac was saying these things,
  behold the Lord Jesus came forth from heaven,
  mounted on a chariot of light,
  while thousands of angels sang hymns to Him.
  He halted the chariot above the place where the saint was.

BA.HY.II.IS.TI.B. 86.5

82. *Behold the Lord Jesus came forth from heaven,*
  He with Michael, mounted upon a chariot of light. ( )
  The whole city quaked from this side to that three times to its founda-
  tions.

TIL.I.NAH.S. 6.1

83. *In the middle of the night,*
  behold, the Good Saviour appeared to them,

mounted on a chariot of light,
with Michael on His right side and Gabriel on His left.

HY.EUS.B. 9.9

84. *When the Saint Apa Anub had completed the Amen,*
behold, the Lord Jesus Christ came to him,
mounted upon a chariot of light,
with Michael on His right and Gabriel on His left side.

BA.HY.I.AN.B. 215.28

85. *As the blessed man was saying these things,*
our Lord Jesus Christ came towards him mounted upon a chariot of
light,
while thousands of angels and tens of thousands of archangels preceded
Him.

BA.HY.I.TH.S.B. 168.3

86. *While Apa Epima was saying these words,*
behold, the Lord Jesus came forth from heaven
mounted upon a chariot of light.

MIN.EPIM.S. 33.16

87. *While our Saviour was speaking with us,*
we heard hymns in the height.
Immediately we looked, we saw a great chariot of light.

LA.DOR.MAR.B. 61.7

88. *In that moment Michael the Archangel came down from heaven. ( )*
He spread his robe of light over him
and he did not allow the fire to touch him.

HY.MAC.AN.B. 50.5

89. *He saw Jesus mounted upon the chariots of Cherubim ( )*
with a robe of glory upon Him, such that no king of this earth would
be able to wear. ( )
Then a great fragrance spread in the room in which the holy Helias was
lying.

SOB.HEL.S. 9b.27

90. *And on the following night the Archangel Gabriel came to him*
wearing a great kingly regalia which gave light more than the sun.
He spoke to him who was paralysed,
while an odour of great sweetness came forth from his mouth.

WOR.GAB.S. 197.12

91. *And when he had fallen asleep, the holy Archangel Gabriel came to the*
      youth in a vision,
   wearing a glory of unspeakable greatness,
   while a robe which gave forth rays of light enveloped him.

WOR.GAB.S. 212.4

92. *And at that moment behold the holy Archangel Gabriel came forth*
      from heaven
   wearing a robe of light.

WOR.GAB.S. 219.9

93. *At midnight, behold the Archangel Gabriel appeared to the man in a*
      vision
   in the form of a general of the king wearing a robe of light.

WOR.GAB.S. 232.17

94. And in that night *I saw the holy Archangel Gabriel. ( )*
   He healed me, he departed up to heaven in a robe of light.

WOR.GAB.S. 239.5

95. *And that night he found himself as if in a vision and a man stood above*
      him,
   in a garment giving forth flashes of lightning
   and it was variegated of many colours.

AM.MAC.SC.B. 57.2

96. *Behold, the Archangel Raphael stood at his right hand*
   and he bore him upon his wings of light.
   He placed him down before the Tetrapylon of the town.

HY.EUS.B. 36.7

97. It was also said of him (Isaac) that *many times,*
   as he slept, he would see a cherubim of light,
   coming and clothing him with his wings.

POR.IS.B. 323.5

98. *I will cause my angels to cover them with their wings of light.*

BU.CH.JOH.S. 140.10

99. *And at that moment, behold, the angel of the Lord took the form of a*
      dove of light.
   He struck with his wings of light in his face.
   His eyes were opened. He saw.

TIL.I.HER.S. 36.22

100. Then he commanded that they should build a cross and that they
     should hang the holy man upon it. ( )
   *And at that moment a dove of light settled upon the right arm of the
     cross,*
   and another upon the left arm.
   They spread over him their wings,
   they sheltered him because he was naked.

   SOB.HEL.S. 61a.15

101. *At that moment, Michael, the Archangel came forth from heaven.*
   He went into the stoke-hole of the bath to the saint Apa Epima.
   He spread out his wings of light over him.

   MIN.EPIM.S. 23.15

102. *At that moment, behold, Michael the Archangel came down from
     heaven.*
   He went into the stoke-hole of the bath to the saint Apa Epime.
   He spread his wings of light over him.

   BA.HY.I.EPIM.B. 143.22

103. *In that moment, behold Michael the Archangel came down from
     heaven.*
   He went to the middle of the burning fire of the oven
   and he stretched out his wings of light over the saint Apa Sarapion.

   BA.HY.I.SA.PA.B. 71.15

104. *Michael the Archangel broke a flat stone in the bath.*
   He raised the saint Apa Panesew upon his wings of light.

   TIL.I.PAN.S. 96.21

105. *He gave it (the soul) into the hands of Michael, the holy Archangel,*
   he mounted it upon his wings of light.

   LA.DOR.MAR.B. 55.32

106. *When they say: 'God of Apa Macarius of Antioch,*
   do thou help us,'
   I will hear them and I will protect them with my wings of light.

   HY.MAC.AN.B. 66.13

107. After this we came to the middle of the sea.
   We were sitting speaking with one another of the greatness of God
   *and thus we heard the voice of the holy man Apa Shenute above us in
     the air* saying:
   '*Peace be with thee, O good shepherd* of the Church of the Great
     King Christ.'

*And we, recognising his sweet voice, we rose, we looked up to heaven
    above us.*
We saw a boat of cloud on which he rode in great glory,
with a pillow beneath his elbow as he lay upon it.
But we bowed our heads to him, we cried out saying: 'Bless us,
    our holy father, the Archimandrite and holy prophet of truth.'
And *we did not cease from looking after him as he proceeded South
in the air until our eyes failed to see him.*

AM.CYR.AL.B. 185.12

108. Then (the duke who was given the belt of Shenute to wear in battle)
        looked up in the air.
     He saw our father Shenute in the midst of a cloud of light,
     with a sword of fire in his hands,
     slaying the barbarians.
     And the duke went into the cloud beside our father Apa Shenute
     and in this way he overcame the barbarians with a great defeat.

LEI.SIN.B. 52.1

109. *Then at that moment Our Saviour commanded. He brought down a
        cloud of light.*
     *He mounted upon (it) and He commanded us the Apostles that we
        should mount the cloud with Him.*

BU.CH.JOH.S. 138.8

110. When the good Saviour had said these things,
     *He mounted upon the cloud, He commanded that we should mount
        with Him,*
     He brought us down, He set us upon the Mount of Olives.
     He stood, He prayed with us,
     He said to us: 'Peace be with you.'
     And when He had said these things to us
     *He went up to the Heavens in great glory while the angels sang hymns
        to Him.*

BU.CH.JOH.S. 143.26

111. *He opened the belly of the righteous man with his hand, his guts fell
        down upon the earth.*
     At that moment, behold a cloud of light made a shade over him.

SOB.HEL.S. 53a.2

112. *Behold, Michael came down from heaven with a cloud of light.* ( )
     He released the saint Helias.
     He mounted him upon the cloud of light, he took him up to heaven.

                                              . SOB.HEL.S. 54b.9

113. *And behold, our Lord, Jesus Christ came down from heaven,*
     mounted on a cloud of light.
     He stood above the ship.

                                              HY.DID.B. 296.16

114. *The Lord Jesus came mounted upon a cloud of light,*
     with Michael at His right side and Gabriel on His left,
     while a multitude of angels sang hymns to Him.

                                              MIN.EPIM.S. 12.24

115. *Behold, our Lord, Jesus Christ came to him,*
     mounted on a cloud of light,
     with Michael on His right side and Gabriel on His left side.

                                              BA.HY.I.EPIM.B. 133.25

2 HEAVENLY FIRE

EPISODES

The appearance of fire or lightning coming forth from the mouth.
The appearance of fire upon the finger-tips during prayer.
The appearance of a column of fire.
The ability to see fire upon the altar at the celebration of the Eucharist.
The appearance of garments, horses or horsemen of fire.
The appearance of angels with swords or spears of fire.

QUOTATIONS

1. (Macarius and two strangers) *The younger recited nine psalms of*
     six verses, each with alleluia,
   and at every verse a flame of fire came forth from his mouth
   and went up to heaven.

                                              AM.AP.MAC.B. 211.3

2. (Macarius and two strangers) *The younger recited five psalms,*
   six verses at a time, with one alleluia.
   At every verse a torch of fire came forth from his mouth
   and went up to heaven.
   The elder then did the same.
   When he began to open his mouth to recite a psalm,

                                              765

there came forth from his mouth as it were a great streak of fire,
which mounted up to heaven.

CHA.AP.PA.S. 72.20(239)

3. (Macarius and two strangers) *The younger said six psalms,*
   six verses at a time, each with an alleluia.
   And at every verse a flame came forth from his mouth
   and went up to heaven.
   In the same way also when the elder *opened his mouth to recite a*
        psalm,
   there came forth from his mouth, as it were, a rope of fire
   and it went up to heaven.

AM.MA.DO.B. 299.7

4. And afterwards, when he wished to speak to the brethren on the
        word of God, ( )
   a great flash of light came in the words,
   so that all the brethren were like men drunk with wine, ( )
   and he saw the words coming forth from his mouth
   like birds of gold, silver and precious stones,
   which flew over the brethren in secret
   and went into the ears of many of those who listened well.

LE.PAC.S. 156b.24

5. It happened again *when he was speaking,*
   telling them the words which he had heard from the Lord with their
        explanation,
   a great flash of lightning happened in the words
   which flashed forth light,
   so that all the brethren were exceedingly afraid because of the words
        of our father Pachomius,
   which were like a flash of lightning coming forth from his mouth.

LE.PAC.B. 96.2

6. *And he rose in the morning, he found Ephraim teaching*
   and as he heard him it was like a spring
   bubbling forth from his mouth.
   And the old man when he saw the vision
   knew that what came forth from his lips belonged to the Holy Spirit.

CHA.AP.PA.S. 42.21(178)

7. And fire came down from heaven,
   and it continued above his grave for many days

in the sight of every man,
and all those who saw it marvelled.

BU.II.PAL.SY. 656.11

8. When I Theophilus, the sinner, was a young boy of about fifteen
   years, I was commanded by my father to take five horses and some
   slaves and go out to the village before daylight. And when I myself
   had risen in the night to go down to our stable, in which were many
   horses, to take some to go out, as I had been commanded and when
   I arrived at the door, I looked and saw wonderful rays of light coming forth from the chinks of the door and from the windows. And
   when I saw it from a distance and was afraid and thought that our
   stable was on fire, I cried out, I ran. Then I looked through the
   chinks of the door and I saw a poor man standing on the horses'
   dung, on which he had slept, with his hands stretched out to heaven,
   and from his mouth and from each of his fingers rays of light were
   proceeding and the whole building was lighted.

BR.ANTI.SY. 172.12

9. It happened one evening.
   We saw a fire burning in his house.
   We spoke with one another
   saying: 'Then is our brother Pisentius lighting a fire?'
   We noticed this matter because it was not his custom, we rose,
   we looked in one of the windows of his house.
   We saw him praying,
   his hands stretched forth in the form of the cross,
   while his fingers burned like lamps of fire.

AM.PIS.KE.B. 360.10

10. And when the rulers heard these things, they went to the cell in
    which was Paphnute. ( )
    And when the door was opened, they saw that his out-stretched hands
    were like lamps of burning fire.
    And they embraced him. They spent the whole night in vigil with him.

BA.HY.I.PAP.B. 116.9

11. There was a sycamore tree above the cistern of water.
    Then the boy went down to the water
    and he prayed to God, with his hands stretched up to heaven.
    The shepherd who followed him hid himself behind the sycamore
    tree, so that he could see what the young boy was doing.

767

And the shepherd bore witness saying:
'*I saw the ten fingers of the young boy like ten lamps of fire.*'

LEI.SIN.B. 9.14

12. Then the old man rose, and spread out his hands to heaven and his fingers shone like ten candles; and he said: 'If you will, you could become a living flame.'

CHA.SA.L. 142(XII)

13. *It was said of our holy father Abba Pisentius that, when he stretched forth his hands in prayer,*
his ten fingers were burning like lamps of fire.

AM.PIS.KE.B. 351.8

14. And there was a ( ) upon the doorpost of the cell of Abba Macarius
and we saw a column of fire standing upon it,
which was shining and giving much light, rising up to the sky,
and as we walked, the column was diminished before us little by little.

AM.VER.MAC.B. 186.7

15. One day there overcame him amazement and alarm
and he saw a column of fire standing before the holy altar,
whose head reached up to heaven.

BRO.EP.SY. 32.4

16. And one night there appeared to him a glorious pillar of bright light
from the meeting-place of the brothers
and it reached to heaven.
And he also saw, as it were, a small spark round about the pillar,
and sometimes it shone and sometimes it was extinguished.

BU.PAL.SY.I. 630; BEDJAN.VII. 121

17. When he rose, the brothers saw him
in the likeness of a luminous column of fire.

NAU.JE.PE.SY. XXXI.2

18. It was said of him (Abba Pisentius) that when he was a young boy watching the sheep of his father,
God opened his eyes. He saw a column of fire which went before him. ( )
Abba Pisentius said to the boy who walked with him:
'*Didst thou see this column of fire which goes before us?*'

He said: 'No.'
Abba Pisentius cried out up to God saying: '*O God, open the eyes
of my brother also,
so that my friend also sees this column of fire even as I see it.*'
*God heard his prayer therefore, he opened the eyes of his friend.
He saw it and he marvelled greatly.*

AM.PIS.KE.B. 334.6

19. It was said of the holy man Apa Pisentius
that it happened, when he was young
as he was watching the sheep of his father,
*God opened his eyes.
He saw a column of fire before him.*
There were other small boys watching sheep with him.
He said to the small boys who were watching with him:
'*Have you seen the column of fire which is before us?*'
They said to him: 'No, we have not seen (it).'
He cried out up to heaven saying:
'*O God, open the eyes of these small boys
that they may see the column of fire as I myself saw it.*'
*And God heard his voice,
their eyes were opened, they saw it.*
For you see, O my beloved, that when God chose Moses from his
youth,
He spoke to him from a column of fire out of the Bush.

BU.AP.PIS.S. 85.29

20. *Then he prayed up to God saying: 'O Lord reveal to me this
matter ( ).'
And the Lord opened his eyes,
he saw a column of fire set up upon the earth, reaching up to heaven.*

AM.PIS.KE.B. 363.6

21. And when he besought God, he said:
'If it be thy will, my Lord, that I should remain, persuade me.'
And there appeared to him a pillar of fire from earth to heaven.

BU.II.PAL.SY. 678.10

22. 'Have I not gone with you all this time, by day and night,
*giving light to you like the Children of Israel
at the time when God overshadowed them with a column of cloud by
day
and with a column of fire all night?*'

BA.HY.II.IAC.P.B. 56.28

23. But one day, while he was offering the Oblation,
an Arab man, who had recently been baptised was present there.
And he saw that fire came down from heaven
and tongues of flame were hovering over the Oblation.

BR.JAM.SY. 265.2

24. *A great thunder came and lightning made flame in the heights*
so that the edges of the altar were filled with fire
and a great disturbance took place. ( )
And in that hour Michael and Gabriel and all the troups of angels came
forth from heaven.

TIL.I.TIM.S. 115.2

25. (The King) was passing with his multitude.
He came outside the door of the church. He looked within,
he saw the Archbishop standing before the altar,
while a fire surrounded him
and a light power was behind him, fortifying him.

POR.IS.B. 364.1

26. O who is able to tell the number of the visions and the mysteries
and the revelations which he saw at times.
For many times he would see the glory of the Lord upon the altar
like a fire.

DAV.JOH.KH.B. 343.16

27. As he mounted upon the altar, he began to make the Holy Offering,
a glory of the Lord appeared upon the altar like a fire.

DAV.JOH.KH.B. 354.11

28. Le vénérable et illuminé Euthyme, étant revenu après deux ans du
Rouba à la laure, offrait à Dieu un saint dimanche le sacrifice non
sanglant: Domitien était debout à la droite de l'autel, tenant le
flabellum liturgique. Comme donc s'accomplissait l'anaphore,
Térébon le Sarrasin, qui se tenait près de l'autel et qui s'appuyait
des mains au chancel du presbyterion, voit soudain qu'un feu
tombé du ciel s'était déployé au-dessus de l'autel, comme s'il
s'agissait d'un voile, et qu'il cachait le vénérable Euthyme et le
bienheureux Domitien: ce feu resta là depuis le commencement de
la doxologie du Trisagion jusqu'à ce qu'elle eût été achevée. ( )

Saisi donc de terreur, Térébon fuit en arrière, et, depuis ce jour,
il ne continua plus de s'appuyer sur le chancel du presbyterion.

FE.III/1.EUT.G. 99(XXVIII)

29. *As he* (Pachomius) *was still praying, an angel of the Lord appeared to him,*
    being very terrifying, with a sword of fire held drawn in his hand.

LE.PAC.B. 150.13

30. Then he saw again the angel of the Lord,
    standing in the midst of the monks,
    holding a sharp spear of fire.

NAU.JE.PE.SY. LVI.13

31. And the blessed man prayed all night
    and at midnight Khosrau saw horses of fire and horsemen, clothed
        in flame,
    saying to him: 'Rise, depart from our city
    and if also thou hast not done so when the sun rises,
    we will slay thee and all thine army.'

BR.JAM.SY. 263.8

3 HEAVENLY BEAUTY

EPISODES

The seeing of heavenly visitors wearing royal or military costume.
The seeing of the beauty of the inhabitants of heaven.
The seeing of beauty in the appearance of the ascetics.

QUOTATIONS

1. *Then he* (the saint Apa Victor) *came to her in a vision,*
   bearing the honours of a king,
   while his face gave light like the sun,
   and a great perfume came forth from his mouth,
   a rod of light in his right hand.

TIL.I.VIC.S. 46.26

2. *'My father was wearing a king's robe,*
   so that my eyes were blinded by reason of the light of his face
   and the radiance of his clothes which he was wearing.'

HY.AP.IR.B. 80.14

3. *And I saw one coming forth from within the Veil*
   who resembled a king.
   And he was wearing a golden diadem with seven crowns upon it.
   And he was riding a white horse

771

and he gave light many times more than the sun. ( )
*The soldier of God, the saint, George, came to me,
while his face gave light.*

BA.HY.II.GEO.DI.B. 264.2; *267.4

4. *The appearance of the costume of that angel as he stood was like a soldier,*
equipped with a sticharion.
At that moment he was not wearing his chlamis,
and his sticharion, which he was wearing, was of the type of a 'paragaudis,'
his 'medals' were very beautiful and all shining with light,
his belt was a palm's breadth in width and was very red
and gave flashes of lightning.

LE.PAC.S. 155b.9

5. *The appearance of the costume of that angel resembled the form of a soldier of the king,*
with a sword of fire in his hand and he gave much light.
And he wore a sticharion, for at that moment he did not wear his chlamis but on him was the sticharion.
There were great 'medals' on the sticharion, all giving light and very beautiful.
The width of his belt was a palm's breadth, it was very red, giving flashes of lightning.

LE.PAC.B. 94.26

6. *And she told him of the form in which he appeared to her* saying:
'*He appeared to me now, wearing a costume of a general, bearing much glory.*
There is no one like him among all the dignitaries on earth,
while the hair of his head is red and curled and his beard is pointed down,
being exceedingly beautiful in appearance.'

BA.HY.I.TH.S.B. 195.26

7. And after this they brought the man to the presence of the ruler and the ruler questioned him ( ).
(As the man was thinking to speak) the *saint Theodore the strong martyr came in at the door* of the praetorium,
in the likeness of a great general of the king,
with a volume of a book in his hand, bearing very great glory.
When the ruler saw him, he jumped up.

BA.HY.I.TH.S.B. 184.15

THE ESTABLISHMENT OF COMMEMORATIVE RITUAL

8. It happened in the night of the Sabbath the King was sleeping in his palace,
   behold, the saint John appeared to him as a noble general.

   BA.HY.II.JOH.PH.B. 179.16

9. *I saw another coming from afar*
   who was very beautiful,
   and his face gave light and he was smiling,
   while the angels sang hymns to him. ( )
   He said to me: ' ( ) *I am Job.*'

   BU.AP.PAUL.S. 555.23

10. *I looked, I saw another one who was taller than them all,*
    who was very beautiful. ( )
    (The angel) *said to me: 'This is Adam, the father of you all.'*

    BU.AP.PAUL.S. 567.18

11. *I saw another one whose angel was singing to him.*
    I said to the angel: 'Who is this who is beautiful in his appearance?' ( )
    He said to me: '*This is Moses the Law-Giver.*'

    BU.AP.PAUL.S. 553.27

12. *Another one came to me who was very beautiful in his appearance.* ( )
    The angel said to me: 'This is Lot.'

    BU.AP.PAUL.S. 555.5

13. Behold *three other* (men) *came from afar*
    and they were very beautiful in their appearance,
    and their angels were singing hymns to them. ( )
    (The angel) *said to me: 'These are the fathers of the people, Abraham,*
    and Isaac and Jacob.'

    BU.AP.PAUL.S. 552.23

14. And thus through divine Grace his body shone.
    And he possessed a healthy body,
    while by the Grace of Christ he was strengthened,
    so that those who beheld him, who did not know him,
    would not be persuaded of his austerity.

    BU.II.PAL.SY. 107.22

15. His slender frame was so well-knit by Grace
    that all who did not know his manner of life
    expected that he lived in luxury.

    LO.PAL.G. 47(1)

16. *When they saw his body, they marvelled at its appearance*,
    because he had not exercised and (yet) he was not weak
    as having come forth from fasts and battles with demons;
    he was the same in his appearance as they had known him before he
      retired.

GAR.ANT.S. 20.3

17. *He was beautiful in his appearance*.

BA.HY.I.LAC.B. 4.2

18. Voici ce qu'on dit de lui. Il avait l'air d'un ange, sa manière d'être
    était sans feinte et son caractère extrêmement doux. Pour ce qui est
    de l'aspect corporel, son visage était rond, brillant, blanc, avec des
    yeux perçants. Il avait la taille d'un nain et tout le poil blanc, avec
    une longue barbe qui allait jusqu'au ventre. Tous ses membres
    s'étaient conservés dans leur intégrité; ni ses yeux ni ses dents
    n'étaient gâtés d'aucune façon, mais il était tout ferme de corps et
    plein d'alacrité quand il mourut.

FE.III/1.EUT.G. 113(XL)

19. And like Jacob (Abba Arsenius) looked like an angel, having white
    hair, a man lovely to look upon, yet somehow dried up. He had a
    long beard which reached down to his waist; his eyes were dim with
    constant weeping; and although he was tall, his body was bent, for
    he died at the age of ninety-five.

CHA.SA.L. 158(XV)

4 MIRACULOUS EVENTS

EPISODES

The motion of holy men, walking on water, going through fire, travelling
  in the air, passing through closed doors.
The appearance of a hand giving directions.
The presence of perfume surrounding holy men, at the death of holy
  men.
The occurrence of earthquakes, thunder, lightning and darkness at the
  time of miraculous events.
The appearance of a vision between the horns of an animal.

QUOTATIONS

1. When he was at a little distance from the town,
     the holy man, Abba John, began to pray before God.
   And immediately, God sent him a cloud.

774

It carried him in its bosom and placed him
before the holy bodies of those Three Blessed Children in Babylon.
When the blessed man saw the power of the Holy Spirit
and how he had reached his goal immediately and without work,
he first began to pray before God and he offered Him worship and
  praise for what He had done.

NAU.JE.PE.SY. LVIII.10

2. The angel said to him: 'Follow me.'
And he descended to the great River Euphrates
and they both walked upon the waters.

NAU.AAR.SY. 721.12

3. And they said that many wonders were performed by him
and they testified about him that, on many occasions, he walked
  upon the water.
And further, he was found in an upper room with the brothers,
  having risen,
although the doors were shut
and he came to them in the air, by the speed of the angels. ( )
And at all times he was able to go wherever he wished, without
  trouble.

BU.II.HIER.SY. 413.4

4. Souvent aussi, dit-on, après être monté sur les eaux du fleuve, il
avait traversé le Nil n'ayant de l'eau que jusqu'aux genoux. Une
autre fois, passant par l'air il était arrivé près des frères sur la
terrasse bien que les portes fussent fermées. Souvent il arrivait sur
le champ au lieu où il voulait aller.

FE.IV/1.HIS.G. 73(X)

5. Abba Ammonas went once to Abba Anthony
and he mistook the road
and he sat down for a little and slept.
And he rose from his sleep and he prayed to God and said:
'I beg thee, Lord God, do not harm thy creature.'
And he raised his eyes and he saw the likeness of a man's hand,
hanging above him in the sky and showing him the road,
until he arrived and stood above the cave of Abba Anthony.

NAU.AMM.SY. 413.14

6. 'And I saw, as it were, a hand of fire, stretched out
and it drew a cross upon that wall.'

LOOK.MAR.SY. 15.2

7. And when his soul passed by all the hosts of demons,
   immediately I saw, as it were, a likeness of a hand of fire
   which was stretched out to him and I did not see him again.

   LOOK.MAR.SY. 21.5

8. While the blessed Apater prayed, (   )
   behold the place in which he stood all became light.
   He saw a hand beckoning him in the light.
   He walked after it.

   HY.AP.IR.B. 91.9

9. At that time, *when he was in the hole on the North side of the moun-*
   tain of Tsenti on the road,
   at that time there was great abundance upon the earth
   because of the sweet smell which was in the holy monasteries,
   especially because of our holy father, Abba Pisentius.
   It was he who gave light in our district of Heki
   and indeed he was a great one in our whole country.

   AM.PIS.KE.B. 344.1

10. When they (Abba Amoi and two elders) reached the dwelling place
    of Abba John,
    they smelt a very choice perfume from it. (   )
    After a long time, when he came forth,
    they saw his face giving light like that of an angel of God.

    AM.JOH.K.B. 341.2

11. I Pambo, the least of men,
    I smelt the sweet smell of that brother a mile before I reached him.

    BU.CYR.S. 130.12

12. *He gave up his spirit* (   ) at the tenth hour of the day.
    And there was a great fear at that hour and that place shook three
    times, (   )
    while perfume spread forth.

    LE.PAC.S. 95.2

13. *He gave up his spirit in great quietude and without trouble* (   ) *in*
    peace.
    Then a great fear came at that hour, with a sweet smell.

    AM.TH.B. 285.4

14. *There was a great light in that place.*
    The whole place spread perfume
    because of the number of angels who had come for the soul of the
      blessed Apa Lacaron.

BA.HY.I.LAC.B. 22.22

15. *At the time when they came for me in order to separate my soul from*
      my body,
    a great and mighty angel came (   )
    and also multitudes of angels (   )
    with sweet perfumes.

BU.BART.R.S. 35.6

16. *In that hour he gave his spirit into the hands of the Lord in peace*
    and the whole road was filled with fragrance.

BA.HY.I.TH.S.B. 180.5

17. *His head was removed*
    and all those gathered with him bore witness, saying:
    '*At that time we smelt a sweet smell,*
    more precious than any upon the earth.'

BA.HY.I.TH.S.B. 193.3

18. From his holy body there spread a sweet and fragrant perfume.

NAU.JE.PE.SY. LXXII.4

19. *When that God-loving servant went to the cave,*
    he found our thrice-blessed father, Abba John, (   )
    and there spread a marvellous perfume from his holy relic.

AM.JOH.K.B. 403.11

20. *Immediately our Saviour mounted upon His chariot of Cherubim,*
    while all the ranks of the Heavens went behind Him, singing to Him,
    so that the air was darkened through the quantity of perfume.

LA.DOR.MAR.B. 58.5

21. *Immediately when the soul entered heaven (   ),*
    its angel said: ' (   ) *No rest is given to the soul with whom I dwelt.*'
    The angels answered: 'Take it away, take it away from our midst,
    for *from the hour we saw it there was a great stench in our midst.*'

BU.AP.PAUL.S. 557.25

777

22. *A great disturbance happened when it was heard that they had taken Polycarp.*

BA.HY.II.POL.SM.B. 66.15

23. *In that moment the earth shook to its foundation.*
    There were thunder and lightning which were terrifying
    so that not one man passed forth from that place from great fear.

BA.HY.II.GEO.B. 310.16

24. *There came thunder and lightning in the sky,*
    so that the whole mountain there was shaken,
    Behold, the Lord came mounted on a cloud.

BA.HY.II.GEO.B. 296.17

25. *Suddenly, behold, there came thunder and lightning with a great disturbance,*
    so that the earth moved to its foundations.
    Behold, our Lord Jesus Christ came upon a cloud of light,
    with His holy angels singing before Him.

BA.HY.II.GEO.DI.B. 232.13

26. *A great disturbance happened in the air.*
    The earth was moved to its foundations.
    Behold the Lord Jesus Christ came down from heaven with His holy angels.
    He stood over the place in which the cauldron was buried.

BA.HY.II.GEO.B. 287.10

27. *A great disturbance happened*
    so that the sky became dark and the stars did not give light.
    For the Lord came down with His angels upon the cauldron.

BU.GEO.C.S. 185.17

28. *A great disturbance happened, with fearful terror.*
    The sky was covered with cloud
    and there was a great fear so that the mountains suddenly moved,
    the earth shook, the sea was disturbed with waves
    and its waves were fifteen cubits high.
    Michael blew on the trumpet.
    Behold the Lord Jesus came upon His chariot of Cherubim.

BA.HY.II.GEO.B. 281.9

29. *It happened in that moment, the air filled with clouds*
    and there was a great disturbance,

778

so that the earth shook and the mountains were moved
and the sea rose fifteen cubits.
The Lord came down from heaven,
sitting upon the chariot of Cherubim.

BU.GEO.C.S. 180.18

30. *In that moment the air became entirely dark.*
The sky was covered by cloud.
Thunder and lightning happened.
The whole earth trembled to its foundations.
The holy Archangel blew upon the trumpet,
the Lord came upon a chariot of Cherubim,
with tens of thousands of angels.

BA.HY.II.GEO.DI.B. 215.1

31. *When he completed the Amen,*
there was a great disturbance with fiery lightning
and those bones become lighted
and suddenly five men and nine women and ten children came forth
    from them.

BA.HY.II.GEO.B. 290.6

32. *The blessed one bent his knees, he made petitions to God.*
At that moment a great earthquake happened with thunder and light-
    ning.
A spirit of the Lord came on the earth in the bones and the dust
and five men and nine women and a small boy came forth.

BA.HY.II.GEO.DI.B. 226.12

33. *It happened that in the middle of the night*
an angel of light appeared to him in the prison.
And there was a great earthquake, so that the town moved to its
    foundations. ( )
And the whole place was filled with perfume which was very choice.

BA.HY.II.GEO.DI.B. 206.12

34. *And behold a voice reached him saying:* ' ( )
Amen, I say to thee, my chosen one Helias, that there is nothing
    higher than the symbol which thou has borne.'
And when Jesus finished speaking with him, there was thunder and
    lightning.

SOB.HEL.S. 61b.13

35. When a long time had passed, *as Plaketas was standing looking at the animal,*

wondering at the beauty of its greatness, at a loss how he should seize it,

the Lord showed him a sign, such that he could see it.

He revealed it to him in this form: as a sign of the Cross in the middle of its horns,

giving light more than the sun;

also in the middle of its horns was the likeness of the body which God bore in the womb of the Virgin. (   )

And he summoned Plaketas with a human voice through the animal, saying:

'O Plaketas, why dost thou pursue me?

Because of thee, therefore, I have appeared to thee by means of this animal.

For I am Jesus, He whom thou dost serve without knowing Him.

Thy good deeds, which thou doest, have come to my presence.

Because of this, indeed, I have manifested myself to thee. (   )

Because of this, I have come down upon the earth in the likeness in which thou seest me,

wishing to save the race of men.'

When Plaketas heard these things he was afraid, he fell down upon the earth.

When a long time passed he rose up alone,

wishing to know exactly concerning the marvel which had appeared and he said:

'*What is this vision which I have seen,*

and of what kind is this voice which I have heard?

Appear to me, O thou who speakest with me, that I may believe in thee.'

The Lord said to him: 'Attend, O Plaketas, *I am Jesus, the Christ, the Son of the Living God,*

He who made heaven and earth when they did not exist.

I made all matter which is beyond counting.

I am He who manifested the light.

I separated it from the darkness.

It is I who created the sun to give light by day and I established the moon and the stars to give light by night.

It is I who established the years and the divisions of time and the days.

It is I who fashioned man out of earth.

I manifested myself upon it in the flesh which I took for the salvation of men.

It is I who was crucified, I died, I was buried, I rose on the third day
   from the dead.'
When Plaketas heard these things he fell upon his face.
He cried out: 'I believe in the Lord, that it is thou who hast created
   all things (   ).
And thou art He who gives life to those who have died.'
Christ answered: 'If thou believest, go and make thy way to the high
   priests of the Christians
and seek from them the blessing through Baptism.'
Plaketas answered, he said to Him: 'Lord command me to speak
   these words to my wife and my sons,
that they also may believe in thee.'
The Lord said to him: 'Tell them and purify yourselves from defilement by taking the seal of Baptism
and do thou return to this place again
and I will appear to thee and I will tell thee the mysteries of salvation.'
Plaketas went down the mountain.
He went in to his house. When evening came *he began to speak to his
   wife and his sons*
of those things which he had seen in the visions
and the manner in which the Lord had appeared to him.
Immediately his wife cried out (   )
she said to her husband: 'Last night I also saw Him saying to me:
"Tomorrow thou and thy husband and thy sons will come to me."
And I knew that He was the God Jesus, the Christ, the God of the
   Galileans.
He wished to appear to thee in a miraculous way, through an animal,
so that thou shouldst be amazed by His power and believe in Him.'

BU.EUS.TH.S. 105.27

36. *When the saint* (Theodore) *heard these things* (a voice from heaven)
      he was amazed,
   especially when he heard the name of his father. (   )
   Immediately, behold, a hind appeared to him
   like the disc of the sun, as it rose on the horizon.
   *When the saint Theodore saw the young hind in this form, he was
      astonished.*
   Then he noticed the (vision) which was between the horns of the
      hind, which gave light.
   Immediately the lamb in the midst of the (vision) said to him:
   'Theodore, *I am the Lamb of God, He who takes away the sins of
      the whole world.*

781

I am Adonai, the Lord Sabaoth, the God of John thy father.'
When the holy man Theodore heard these things, he turned aside
    his horse, he turned back,
he came to a number of his soldiers, being troubled, he found them
    cast down like dead men from thirst, and also their animals.
The holy man Theodore came down from his horse, he offered a
    prayer saying: ' ( )
Do thou raise these who have fallen for my cause,
for thine is the glory for ever, Amen.'
Immediately, behold, a cloud of light poured dew upon them
so that their hearts were strengthened,
like some who have filled themselves with water which is cool and
    sweet.
Not one of them died, nor did their cattle.
But they prostrated themselves, they worshipped the saint Theodore.
They kissed his head, saying: 'Blessed is the hour when thou didst
    rule over us, O our lord Theodore.'
He said to them: ' ( )
Now come and see this animal which I have seen upon the summit of
    the mountain.
I never saw one such, the young hind which I saw is a great marvel.'
At once he walked with them, he brought them,
he showed them the hind which he saw.
They were amazed saying: '*We never saw one such in his beautiful*
    form.'
The saint Theodore did not know the interpretation of the lamb,
    which had spoken to him. ( )
They placed the hind in their midst, so that perhaps they might be
    able to lay hold of it.
The saint raised up his eyes to heaven, he prayed to the Lord concern-
    ing the young hind.
Suddenly he saw the Lord Christ in the likeness in which he saw Him
    upon the young hind,
when He took the form of the Lamb.
The holy man, Theodore, was amazed, through the marvel which he
    saw in the heaven
and that which he saw upon the hind, that they were one form.
Then he heard again a voice from heaven saying: '( ) *I am He who is*
    upon this hind, I am He who is in heaven.
I am the Lamb of God. I am He who takes away the sin of the world.
I am He who was baptised by John.
Behold, I have showed thee the glory of my form.

THE ESTABLISHMENT OF COMMEMORATIVE RITUAL

Give glory to the hind and know also my Incarnation in the womb of the Holy Virgin Maria and the manner of my crucifixion upon the Cross.

Thou shalt know that I am Jesus, the Christ,

the Son of the Living God, the God of John, thy father.

For it is necessary that thou shouldst see the face of John, thy father,

before thou completest thy martyrdom.

It is I who saved thee as thou wast pursuing the herd of camels,

namely the demons who were wishing to take thee to the barbarians, that they kill thee.

I am the hind whom thou hast seen upon the summit of the rock.

Now therefore be a strong man and become a martyr for my holy name.

Behold I have given thee and thy companion, the Anatolian, the favour of the blessing of my great Archangel Michael,

so that your souls should be at his right hand in heaven

and in all wars in which you will be involved, I will send my great Archangel Michael

so that he overcomes the enemies and destroys them before you,

until your names are famous upon the face of all the earth to all generations. ( )

Behold how great is the beauty of this hind.'

The holy man Theodore looked towards the hind,

he saw the (vision) of fire upon its horns in the form of a cross.

The saint Theodore answered, he said to him:

'O Lord, my God, thy likeness in heaven is that which I see;

it is thy likeness also upon the horns of this hind.

Now therefore, I beg thee let thy gift be with thy servant.'

The Lord said to him: ' ( ) *Now I have favoured thee*

with a famous name in heaven and upon the earth.

My power will be with thee.

Turn to thy band of soldiers.

Tell them to cease from pursuing the hind.'

BA.HY.II.T.A.T.S.B. 117.3

NOTES ON SECTIONS I–V

NOTES ON SECTIONS I–V

Archimandrite: the title of the superior of a monastery; see P. E. Kahle, *Bala'izah*, Vol. I, 1954, p. 33.

Assistant (helper); *boēthos:* a term applied to an official concerned with the collecting of taxes; see P. E. Kahle, *op. cit.*, p. 35.

Asterion: an instrument of torture, probably in the form of a wheel.

Beating the board: the method of summoning the monks to prayer; Coptic monasteries had no bells.

Blowing; *exsufflatio;* an act of exorcism.

Carob (*Ceratonia Siliqua*): the locust bean tree.

Chartulary: a term applied to an official or scribe, from *chartula:* a little paper, a bill.

Chlamis: an outer garment, worn by horsemen, adopted from Greece by the Romans, a military cloak.

Colobion, colobium (*tunica alba*): a sleeveless or short-sleeved tunic, worn by Roman emperors and adapted to ecclesiastical use.

Commemoration offering; *prosphora:* that which is brought or offered, gifts or sacrifices.

Cosmocrator: world ruler, a term used of deities and of the Roman emperor; the lord of this world; see *Eph.* 6.12.

Executioner; *quaestonarius:* a term derived from *quaestio*, a court of enquiry or trial for special criminal cases in Roman times.

Flabellum: a fan carried by Roman ladies; used in the Eastern liturgy.

Gag; *Chamos:* a cloth used by bakers to cover the nose and mouth; a fish hook.

Harp; *kidara:* a stringed instrument played in classical times at public games and processions.

Hegumenos: the title of the superior of a church or monastery; see P. E. Kahle, *op. cit.*, Vol. I, p. 3.

Hermetarion: possibly a type of gallows or a bed for torture; see W. E. Crum, *Coptic Dictionary*, 1939, p. 225a.

Lebiton: see *Colobion.*

Lention; linteum: a linen cloth.

Malabathrum: an oil; see A. Lucas, *Ancient Egyptian Materials and Industries*, 4th ed., 1962, Ch. XIII.

Monastery: for the designation of a monastery as a place *topos*, a rock *petra*, or a mountain, see P. E. Kahle, *op. cit.*, pp. 27–29.

Offering; *anaphora; oblatio:* the sacrificial portion of the Eucharistic liturgy of the Eastern Church.

Pallium: an outer garment, or cloak, worn in Roman times and adopted by the ascetics of the early Church.

Paragaudis: an ornament of dress.

Persea tree (*Mimusops Schimperi*): a sacred tree of ancient Egypt; deities were represented upon the branches of the *Persea* tree.

Sabbath: on the Sabbath and Lord's day, see Togo Mina, *Le Martyre d'Apa Epima*, 1937, pp. 89–111.

Scapulary; *epômis:* in classical times, the part of a woman's tunic which was fastened with a brooch on the shoulder.

Schema: a girdle of intertwined leather encircling the chest, passing over the shoulders and under the armpits; see F. R. Farag, *Sociological and moral studies in the field of Coptic monasticism*, 1964, p. 17, note 1.

Sindon: a loin-cloth.

Sitiohe: an Egyptian measure of land, equivalent to the Greek *aroura*, or about two-thirds of an acre; see W. E. Crum, *op. cit.*, p. 360A; A. Gardiner, *Egyptian Grammar*, 1050, para. 266.3.

Solidus: Roman coin, introduced by Constantine about 312 A.D.

Sticharion: a striped or variegated tunic.

Stola: a long robe worn by Roman matrons; later a generic term for ecclesiastical vestments.

Storax: a balsam; see A. Lucas, *op. cit.*, Ch. VI.

Synaxis: divine service; see W. E. Crum, *op. cit.*, p. 373b.

Table; *trapeza:* for meanings of this term, see J. Drescher, 'Graeco Coptica', Le Muséon, LXXXII, 1969, pp. 90–100.

Tetrapylon: a monument with four gates.

Tiara; *kidaris:* a Persian head-dress, probably the same as the royal *tiara* worn on solemn occasions.

Tribune; *bēma:* in Roman times a term for a platform on which magisterial personages sat when taking their chairs of office.

Veil; *katapetasma:* the designation of the Veil of the Temple and of the curtain before the door of the sanctuary in the Coptic Church.

Wheel; *trochos:* designation for a medal, circle or instrument of torture.

BIBLIOGRAPHY (GENERAL)

BIBLIOGRAPHY (GENERAL)

For ABBREVIATIONS, see p. 261.

ABRAHAMS, I. 'Name of God (Jewish)'. *ERE*, Vol. IX, 1917.

ALBRIGHT, W. F. *From the Stone Age to Christianity*. The Johns Hopkins Press, Baltimore 1940.

AMÉLINEAU, E. See ABBREVIATIONS (COPTIC TEXTS), pp. 262–263.

——*Lettres de Pierre Monge et d'Acace*. Mémoires de la Mission Archéologique Française du Caire. Tome IV. Monuments pour servir à l'Histoire de l'Égypte Chrétienne au IVᵉ et Vᵉ Siècles. Leroux, Paris 1888–86.

ARBESMANN, R. 'Fasting and Prophecy in Pagan and Christian Antiquity'. *Traditio*, VII, 1949–51, pp. 1–71.

ARMSTRONG, A. H. *Plotinus*. With an English Translation. I. *Porphyry on the Life of Plotinus*. Loeb Classical Library. W. Heinemann, London 1966.

BADAWAY, A. 'La persistence de l'idéologie et du formulaire paiens dans les épitaphes coptes'. *BSAC*, X, Cairo 1944, pp. 1–26.

BALESTRI, I. See ABBREVIATIONS (COPTIC TEXTS), p. 263.

BAYNES, C. A. *A Coptic Gnostic Treatise contained in the Codex Brucianus* [Bruce MS. 96. Bod. Lib. Oxford]. Cambridge University Press 1933.

BEDJAN, P. (Ed.) *Acta Martyrum et Sanctorum*, I–VII. Paris 1890–97.

BELL, H. I. *Egypt from Alexander the Great to the Arab Conquest, a study in the diffusion and decay of Hellenism*. Clarendon Press, Oxford 1948.

BOWRA, C. M. *The Greek Experience*. Weidenfeld and Nicolson, London, 1957.

BOX. G. H. *The Apocalypse of Abraham*. Edited with Translation and Notes from the Slavonic. Translations of Early Documents. Series I. Palestinian Jewish Texts (Pre-Rabbinic). SPCK, London 1918.

——*The Testament of Abraham*. Translated from the Greek Text with Introduction and Notes. With an Appendix containing a Translation from the Coptic version of the *Testaments of Isaac and Jacob* by S. Gaselee. Translations of Early Documents. Series II. Hellenistic-Jewish Texts. SPCK, London 1927.

BREASTED, J. H. *A New Chapter in the Life of Thutmose III*. Leipzig 1900.

——*Ancient Records of Egypt* 5 volumes, Chicago 1906–7.

BROCKELMANN, C. See ABBREVIATIONS (SYRIAC TEXTS), p. 266.

BROOKS, E. W. See ABBREVIATIONS (SYRIAC TEXTS), p. 266.

BUCHER, P. 'Les Textes des Tombes de Thutmosis III et d'Aménophis II'. Vol. I. in Mémoires de l'Institut Français d'Archéologie Orientale, Cairo 1932.

BUDGE, E. A. W. See ABBREVIATIONS (COPTIC TEXTS), pp. 263–264; (SYRIAC TEXTS), p. 266.

——*The Book of the Dead*. Kegan Paul, Trench, Trübner and Co., London 1898.

——*The Liturgy of Funerary Offerings.* The Egyptian texts with English Translations. Kegan Paul, Trench, Trübner and Co., London 1909.

——*The Book of Opening the Mouth.* The Egyptian Texts with English Translations. 2 Volumes. Kegan Paul, Trench, Trübner and Co., London 1909.

——*The Egyptian Heaven and Hell.* 2 Volumes. Vol. II. *The Short Form of the Book Am-Tuat and the Book of Gates.* Kegan Paul, Trench, Trübner and Co., London 1905.

——*The Mummy.* 2nd. ed. Cambridge 1925.

BURMESTER, O. H. E. 'The Baptismal Rite of the Coptic Church. A critical study.' *BSAC*, XI, 1945, pp. 27–46.

——*The Egyptian or Coptic Church. A detailed description of her Liturgical Services and the Rites and Ceremonies observed in the administration of her Sacraments.* Publications de la Société d'Archéologie Copte, Cairo 1967.

BUTTERWORTH, G. W. *Origen—On First Principles.* Koetschau's Text of the *de Principiis* translated into English, together with an Introduction and Notes. SPCK, London 1936.

CALVERLY, A. M., and BROOME, M. F. *The Temple of King Sethos I at Abydos.* Vols. I, II. London, Egypt Exploration Society and Chicago, University of Chicago Press 1933–35.

ČERNÝ, J. *Ancient Egyptian Religion.* Hutchinson's University Library, London 1952.

——'A note on the ancient Egyptian Family'. Studi in onori di Aristide Calderini e Roberto Paribeni. Vol. II. Studi di Papirologia e di Antichità Orientali. Milan 1957, pp. 51–55.

——'Egyptian Oracles' in *From a Saite Oracle Papyrus in the Brooklyn Museum* (ed. R. A. Parker). Brown University Press 1962.

CHADWICK, H. *Origen contra Celsum.* Translated with Introduction and Notes Cambridge University Press 1953.

CHADWICK, O. See ABBREVIATIONS (LATIN TEXTS), pp. 267–268.

CHAINE, M. See ABBREVIATIONS (COPTIC TEXTS), p. 264.

CHARLES, R. H. *The Ascension of Isaiah.* Translated from the Ethiopic Version, together with the new Greek fragment, the Latin versions and the Latin translation of the Slavonic. Edited with Introduction, Notes and Indices. A. and C. Black, London 1900.

——See ABBREVIATIONS (LATIN TEXTS); (ETHIOPIC, SLAVONIC, HEBREW TEXTS), p. 268.

COLSON, F. H. *Philo.* With an English translation. IV, IX. Loeb Classical Library. W. Heinemann, London, 1932, 1941.

CONYBEARE, F. C. *Philostratus—The Life of Apollonius of Tyana.* With an English translation. Loeb Classical Library. W. Heinemann, London 1912.

CRUM, W. E. *A Coptic Dictionary.* Clarendon Press, Oxford 1939. Reprinted 1962.

CUMONT, F. *Astrology and Religion among the Greeks and Romans.* Constable, London 1912. Dover Publications, New York 1960.

DANIÉLOU, J. *Les Figures du Christ dans l'Ancien Testament 'Sacramentum Futuri'* (*Rom. 6.15, d'après St. Hilaire*) Études de Théologie Historique Publiées sous la direction de Professeurs de Théologie à l'Institut Catholique de Paris, Beauchesne et ses fils, Paris 1950.

791

DANIÉLOU, J. *Message Évangélique et Culture Hellenistique*. Les Editions du Seuil, Paris 1961.

——*The Theology of Jewish Christianity*. Translated and Edited by J. A. Baker. The Development of Christian Doctrine before the Council of Nicaea, Vol. I. Darton, Longman and Todd, London 1964.

DAVIES, N de G. *The Tomb of Rekh-mi-Rē at Thebes*. New York Metropolitan Museum of Art, Vol. II, 1943.

DAVIS, M. H. See ABBREVIATIONS (COPTIC TEXTS), p. 264.

DE BUCK, A. *The Egyptian Coffin Texts*. University of Chicago Oriental Institute Publications. 3 Vols. Chicago 1935–47.

DE LAGARDE, P. See ABBREVIATIONS (COPTIC TEXTS), p. 264.

DELEHAYE, H. *Cinq Leçons sur la Méthode Hagiographique*. Société des Bollandistes. Subsidia Hagiographica 21. Brussels 1934.

——*Les Origines du Culte des Martyrs*. Société des Bollandistes. Subsidia Hagiographica 20. Brussels (1912). 2ᵉ edition 1933.

——*Les Passions des Martyrs et les Genres Littéraires*. Société des Bollandistes. Subsidia Hagiographica 13B. Brussels 1921. 2nd edition 1966.

——'Les saints d'Aboukir'. *Analecta Bollandiana*, XXX, pp. 448–450.

——*Sanctus. Essai sur le Culte des Saints dans l'Antiquité*. Société des Bollandistes. Subsidia Hagiographica 17. Brussels 1927.

DRESCHER, J. *Apa Mena. A selection of Coptic Texts relating to St. Menas*. Edited with Translation and Commentary. Publications de la Société d'Archéologie Copte. Textes et Documents, Cairo 1946.

——'Graeco–Coptica'. Le Muséon. LXXXII. Louvain 1969, pp. 85–100.

DU BOURGUET, P. 'Diatribe de Chenouté contre le Démon.' *BSAC*, XVI (1961–62), pp. 17–72.

ERMAN, A. *Die Religion der Ägypter*. Berlin and Leipzig 1934.

FARAG, F. R. *Sociological and Moral Studies in the Field of Coptic Monasticism*. Supplement I to the Annual of Leeds University Oriental Society. E. J. Brill, Leiden 1964.

FESTUGIÈRE, A. J. See ABBREVIATIONS (GREEK TEXTS), p. 267.

——*Antioche Païenne et Chrétienne*. Boccard, Paris 1959.

——*La Révélation d'Hermès Trismégiste*. 1. *L'Astrologie et les Sciences Occultes*. Librairie Lecoffre. J. Gabalda, Paris 1950.

FESTUGIÈRE, A. J., et NOCK, A. D. *Hermès Trismégiste. Corpus Hermeticum*. Texte et Traduction. Collection des Universités de France. Association Guillaume Budé, Paris, 1960.

FOUCART, J. 'Calendar (Egyptian)'. *ERE*, Vol. III, 1910.

——'Disease and Medicine (Egyptian)'. *ERE*, Vol. IV, 1911.

——'Festivals and Fasts (Egyptian)'. *ERE*, Vol. V, 1912.

FOWLER, H. N. *Plato*, With an English Translation. I. *Apology, Phaedo, Phaedrus*. Loeb Classical Library. W. Heinemann, London 1914.

FOX, P. *Tutankhamun's Treasure*. Oxford University Press 1951.

GARDINER, A. *Egyptian Grammar*. Oxford University Press, London 1950.

——*Egypt of the Pharaohs*. Clarendon Press, Oxford 1961.

GARITTE, G. See ABBREVIATIONS (COPTIC TEXTS), p. 264.

GASTER, M. 'Charms and Amulets (Jewish).' *ERE*, Vol. III, 1910.

GERHARDSSON, B. *Memory and Manuscript. Oral Tradition and Written Transmission in Rabbinic Judaism and Early Christianity* (Trans. E. J. Sharpe)

Acta Seminarii Neotcstamentici Upsaliensis XII. C. W. K. Gleerup(Lund). Ejnar Munksgaard (Copenhagen), Upsala 1961, Copenhagen, 1964.

GLASSON, T. F. *Greek Influence in Jewish Eschatology.* SPCK Biblical Monographs, No. 1, London 1961.

GRANT, F. C. *Hellenistic Religions. The Age of Syncretism.* Edited with an Introduction. Library of Liberal Arts. Bobbs Merrill and Co., New York 1953.

GRAVES, R. *Greek Myths.* 2 Vols. Penguin Books 1955.

GRENFELL, B. P., and HUNT, A. S. *Oxyrhynchus Papyri* XI. Egypt Exploration Society, London 1915.

GRIFFITH, F. Ll. *Stories of the High Priests of Memphis, The Sethon of Herodotus and the Demotic Tales of Khamuas.* The Clarendon Press, Oxford 1900.

GUIDI, M. I. See ABBREVIATIONS (COPTIC TEXTS) p. 264.

GUILLAMONT, A. See ABBREVIATIONS (SYRIAC TEXTS), p. 267.

——*Les 'Képhalaia Gnostica' d'Évagre le Pontique et l'histoire de l'Origénisme chez les Grecs et chez les Syriens.* Patristica Sorbonensia. 5. Aux Éditions du Seuil, Paris 1962.

HALPER, B. See ABBREVIATIONS (ETHIOPIC, SLAVONIC, HEBREW TEXTS), p. 268.

HARNACK, A. *The Mission and Expansion of Christianity in the First Three Centuries.* Translated and Edited by J. Moffatt. Theological Translation Library. Williams and Norgate, London 1908.

HARRISON, J. *Prologomena to the Study of Greek Religion.* Cambridge University Press 1903. Reprinted, Meridian Books, New York 1955.

HORNER, G. *The Statutes of the Apostles.* Oxford University Press 1904.

HURRY, J. B. *Imhotep, the Vizier and Physician of King Zoser and afterwards the Egyptian God of Medicine.* Oxford University Press 1928.

HYVERNAT, H. See ABBREVIATIONS (COPTIC TEXTS), pp. 263–265.

JANSSEN, J. M. A. *De traditioneele egyptische autobiografie vóór het Nieuwe Rijk.* Leiden 1946.

JONES, R. M. 'Flagellants.' *ERE,* Vol. VI, 1913.

JUNG, C. G. *The Integration of the Personality.* Translated by S. M. Dell. Kegan Paul, Trench, Trübner and Co., London 1940.

KAHLE, P. E. *Bala'izah. Coptic Texts from Deir El-Bala'izah in Upper Egypt.* 2 Vols. Published on behalf of the Griffith Institute, Oxford, by Oxford University Press, London 1954.

KAPELRUD, A. S. *The Ras Shamra Discoveries and the Old Testament.* Blackwell, Oxford 1965.

KING, C. W. *Plutarch's Morals.* Translated. Bohn's Classical Library, London 1882.

KUGENER, M. A. See ABBREVIATIONS (SYRIAC TEXTS), p. 267.

LACARRIÈRE, J. *The God Possessed.* G. Allen and Unwin, London 1963. (Translated from *Les Hommes Ivres de Dieu.* B. Arthaud, Paris 1961).

LAMB, W. R. M. *Plato.* With an English Translation. VIII. *Minos, Epinomis.* Loeb Classical Library. W. Heinemann, London 1927.

LANGTON, E. *Essentials of Demonology. A Study of Jewish and Christian Doctrine, its Origin and Development.* Epworth Press, London 1949.

——*Good and Evil Spirits. A Study of the Jewish and Christian Doctrine, its Origin and Development.* SPCK, London, 1942.

LEANEY, A. R. C. *The Rule of Qumran and its Meaning*. SCM Press, London 1966.

LEFÉBURE, E. *Les Hypogées royaux de Thèbes*, Paris, 1886–9, Annales du Musée Guimet, Vols. 9, 16.

LEFORT, L. TH. See ABBREVIATIONS (COPTIC TEXTS), p. 265.

——*Œuvres de S. Pachôme et de ses Disciples*. CSCO, Vol. 160, Louvain 1956.

LEIPOLDT, I. See ABBREVIATIONS (COPTIC TEXTS), p. 265.

LIETZMANN, H. *A History of the Early Church*. 4 Vols. Translated by B. Lee Woolf. Lutterworth Press, London 1961.

LINDBLOM, J. *Prophecy in Ancient Israel*. Blackwell, Oxford 1962.

LINDSAY, A. D. *The Republic of Plato*. Translated with an Introduction. Everyman's Library. J. M. Dent and Sons, London 1935.

LOOK, A. E. See ABBREVIATIONS (SYRIAC TEXTS), p. 267.

LOWTHER CLARKE. See ABBREVIATIONS (GREEK TEXTS), p. 267.

LUCAS, A. *Ancient Egyptian Materials and Industries*. 4th ed., revised by J. R. Harris. Edward Arnold, London 1962.

MACLER, F. See ABBREVIATIONS (SYRIAC TEXTS), p. 267.

MAYSTRE, C., and PIANKOFF, A, *Le Livre des Portes*. Vol. 1. in Mémoires de l'Institut Français d'Archéologie Orientale, Vols. 41–45. Cairo 1939–46.

MERCER, S. A. B. *The Religion of Ancient Egypt*. Luzac and Co., London 1949

MEYER, R. T. *St. Athanasius. The Life of Saint Anthony*. Ancient Christian Writers, Vol. 10. Longmans, Green and Co., London; The Newman Press, Maryland 1950.

MINGANA, A. *Early Christian Mystics*. Woodbrooke Studies. Christian Documents in Syriac, Arabic, and Garshūni. Edited and Translated with a Critical Apparatus. Vol. VII. Cambridge 1934.

MOSS, C. *Catalogue of Syriac Printed Books and Related Literature*. British Museum, London 1962.

MURRAY, M. A. *The Splendour that was Egypt*. Sidgwick and Jackson, London 1949.

MUSTAFA EL-AMIR. *A Family Archive from Thebes. Demotic Papyri in the Philadelphia and Cairo Museums from the Ptolemaic Period*. Cairo 1959.

NAU, F. See ABBREVIATIONS (SYRIAC TEXTS), p. 267.

NEUGEBAUER, O., and PARKER, R. A. *Brown Egyptological Studies*. VI. *Egyptian Astronomical Texts. III. Decans, Planets, Constellations and Zodiacs*. Brown University Press, Lund Humphries, London 1969.

NOCK, A. D. *Conversion*. Oxford University Press 1933. Reprinted 1963.

O'LEARY, De L. *The Difnar (Antiphonarium) of the Coptic Church* (Coptic text). 3 parts. Luzac and Co., London 1926–30.

——*The Saints of Egypt*. SPCK Press, London 1937

PAGET, R. F. *In the footsteps of Orpheus. The discovery of the ancient Greek underworld*. R. Hale, London 1967.

PETRIE, W. M. F. *Egyptian Tales translated from the Papyri*. Second series XVIIIth to XIXth dynasty. Methuen, London 1895.

PORCHER, E. See ABBREVIATIONS (COPTIC TEXTS), p. 265.

POSENER, G. *De la divinité du Pharaon*. Cahiers de la Société Asiatique. XV. Imprimerie Nationale, Paris 1960.

PUECH, H.-C. *Le Manichéisme. Son fondateur. Sa doctrine*. Musée Guimet.

Bibliothèque de Diffusion. Tome LVI. Civilisations du Sud. SAEP, Paris 1949.

RABIN, C. 'The Literary Structure of the War Scroll', in *Essays on the Dead Sea Scrolls*, ed. C. Rabin and Y. Yadin. Qumran Studies. Oxford University Press 1957.

RENDEL HARRIS, J. *The Odes and Psalms of Solomon*. Published from the Syriac Version. Cambridge University Press 1909.

ROBERTSON SMITH, W. *The Religion of the Semites*. Lectures on the Religion of the Semites. London 1889. Meridian Library. New York 1956.

ROBINSON, J. F. See ABBREVIATIONS (COPTIC TEXTS), p. 265.

RUSHTON FAIRCLOUGH, H. *Virgil*. With an English Translation. I. *Aeneid*. Loeb Classical Library. W. Heinemann, London 1916.

RUSSELL, D. S. *The Method and Message of Jewish Apocalyptic*. SCM Press, London 1964.

SCHMIDT, C. *Pistis Sophia*. Edita. Coptica Consilio et impensis Instituti Rask-Oerstediani II. Hauniae 1925.

SCHOLEM, G. G. *Major Trends in Jewish Mysticism*. Schocken, New York 1941.

SCOTT-MONCRIEFF, P. D. *Paganism and Christianity in Egypt*. University Press, Cambridge 1913.

SMITH, H. S. 'A Note on Amnesty.' *JEA*, **54**, 1968, pp. 209–214.

SOBHY, G. P. C. See ABBREVIATIONS (COPTIC TEXTS), p. 265.

SOTTAS, H. *La Préservation de la Propriété Funéraire dans l'ancienne Égypt avec le recueil des formules d'Imprécation*. Librairie Ancienne Honoré Champion, Paris 1913.

SRAWLEY, J. H. S. 'Eucharist (to the end of Middle Ages) 3. The Eucharist in the later Patristic period, 5th to 8th centuries.' *ERE*, Vol. V, 1912.

STEINDORFF, G. See ABBREVIATIONS (COPTIC TEXTS), p. 265.

TASKER, R. V. G. *Saint Augustine. The City of God*. John Healey's Translation Edited. Everyman's Library. J. M. Dent and Sons 1945.

TAYLOR, A. E. *Plato. Timaeus and Critias*. Translated into English with Introduction and Notes on the Text. Methuen and Co., London 1929.

TILL, W. See ABBREVIATIONS (COPTIC TEXTS), p. 266.

TISSERANT, E. See ABBREVIATIONS (ETHIOPIC, SLAVONIC, HEBREW TEXTS), p. 268.

TOGO MINA. See ABBREVIATIONS (COPTIC TEXTS), p. 266.

TOUSSOUN, O. '"Cellia" et ses couvents.' Mémoires de la Société Royale d'Archéologie d'Alexandrie. Tome VII.1. Alexandria 1935.

TURNBULL, G. H. *The Essence of Plotinus*. Based on the Translation by Stephen MacKenna. Oxford University Press, New York 1934.

VAN DER PLOEG, J. *Le Rouleau de la Guerre*. E. J. Brill, Leiden 1959.

VAN GOUDOEVER, J. *Biblical Calendars*. E. J. Brill, Leiden 1961.

VAN LANTSCHOOT, A. See ABBREVIATIONS (COPTIC TEXTS), p. 266.

——*Recueil de Colophons . . . Sahidiques*. Bibliothèque du Muséon. Tom. I, fasc. 1. Louvain 1929.

VERMES, G. *The Dead Sea Scrolls in English*. Pelican Books, 1962.

VÖÖBUS, A. *History of Asceticism in the Syrian Orient. Contribution to the History of Culture in the Near East. 1. The Origin of Asceticism. Early Monasticism in Persia*. CSCO, Vol. 184, Subsidia Tom. 14, Louvain 1958.

WENSINCK, A. J. *Legends of Eastern Saints chiefly from Syriac Sources.* Edited and partly translated. Vol. II. *The Legend of Hilaria.* E. J. Brill, Leiden 1913.

WHITE, H. G. EVELYN. *The Monasteries of the Wadi 'N Natrun.* Part II, *The history of the Monasteries of Nitria and Scetis.* The Metropolitan Museum of Art. Egyptian Expedition, New York 1932.

WIDENGREN, G. (Translation by C. Kessler). *Mani and Manichaeism.* Weidenfeld and Nicolson, London 1965.

WILDER, A. *Theurgia or the Egyptian Mysteries by Iamblichos.* Translated from the Greek. W. Rider and Son, London 1911.

WILLIAMS, C. A. *Oriental Affinities of the Legend of the Hairy Anchorite.* I, *Pre-Christian.* II, *Christian.* University of Illinois Studies in Language and Literature. Vol. X. No. 2. May 1925.

WILLIAMSON, G. A. *Eusebius. The History of the Church.* Translated with an Introduction. Penguin Books 1965.

WILSON, R. McL. See ABBREVIATIONS (GREEK TEXTS), p. 267; (ETHIOPIC, SLAVONIC, HEBREW TEXTS), p. 268.

WISSOWA, G. 'Divination (Roman)' *ERE,* Vol. IV, 1911.

WORRELL, W. H. See ABBREVIATIONS (COPTIC TEXTS), p. 266.

BIBLIOGRAPHY (MEDICAL)

BIBLIOGRAPHY (MEDICAL)

ANDERSON, E. W. 'Abnormal mental states in survivors, with special reference to collective hallucinations.' *Journal of the Royal Naval Medical Service*, **28**, 1942, pp. 361–377.

AZIMA, H., and CRAMER-AZIMA, F. J. 'Studies in perceptual isolation.' *Diseases of the Nervous System* (Monograph Supplement), **18**, 1957, pp. 1–6.

BEXTON, W. H., HERON, W., and SCOTT, T. H. 'Effects of decreased variation in the sensory environment.' *Canadian Journal of Psychology*, **8**, 1954, pp. 70–76.

BLUM, R. and Associates. *Utopiates, The Use and Users of LSD-25*. Atherton Press, New York 1964.

BRAUCHI, J. T. and WEST, L. J. 'Sleep deprivation.' *Journal of the American Medical Association*, **171**, 1959, pp. 11–14.

CAMERON, D. E. 'Studies in senile nocturnal delirium.' *Psychiatric Quarterly.* 1941. pp. 1–7.

CAMERON, D. E., LEVY, L., BAN, T., and RUBENSTEIN, L. 'Sensory Deprivation: Effects Upon the Functioning Human in Space Systems' in Flaherty, B. E. (ed) *Psychophysiological Aspects of Space Flight*. New York 1961, pp. 225–237.

CHRITCHLEY, M. 'The idea of a presence.' *Acta Psychiatrica et Neurologica Scandinavica*, **30**, 1955, pp. 155–168.

CROCKET, R., SANDISON, R. A. and WALK, A. (ed). *Hallucinogenic Drugs and their Therapeutic Use*. The Proceedings of the Quarterly Meeting of the Royal Medico-Psychological Association in London. February 1961. H. K. Lewis and Co. 1963.

DALTON, E. 'Mysticism and General Semantics' ETC.: *A Review of General Semantics*, XXII No. 4, 1965.

ELIADE, M. *Shamanism. Archaic Techniques of Ecstasy*. Translated by E. W. Trask. Routledge and Kegan Paul, London 1964.

ERIKSON, E. *Childhood and Society*. W. W. Norton, Chicago (1950) 1963.

FREEDMAN, S. J. and GREENBLATT, M. 'Studies in Human Isolation, II. Hallucinogens and other cognitive findings.' *United States Armed Forces Medical Journal*, II, 1960, pp. 1479–1497.

FREEDMAN S. J., GRUNEBAUM, H. U., STARE, F. A., and GREENBLATT, M. 'Imagery in sensory deprivation', in WEST L. J. (ed.) *Hallucinations*. 1962, pp. 108–117.

GOLDBERGER, L. and HOLT, R. R. Experimental interference with reality contact (perceptual isolation); method and group results. *Journal of Nervous and Mental Disease*, **127**, 1958, pp. 99–112.

GUSSOW, Z. 'A preliminary report of kayak-angst among the Eskimos of West Greenland; a study in sensory deprivation.' *The International Journal of Social Psychiatry*, **9**, 1963, pp. 18–26.

HARMAN, W. 'The Issue of the Consciousness Expanding Drugs.' From *Main Currents in Modern Thought*, 1963.

HUXLEY, A. *The Doors of Perception*. Chatto and Windus 1954.

HUXLEY, F. See CROCKET, R., SANDISON, R. A., and WALK, A. *Hallucinogenic Drugs and their Therapeutic Use*, 1963, pp. 174 ff.

KANDEL, E. J., MYERS, T. I., and MURPHY, D. B. 'Influence of Prior Verbalization and Instructions on Visual Sensations Reported under Conditions of Reduced Sensory Input.' Abstract, *American Psychology*, 13, 1958, pp. 334 ff.

LILLY, J. C. 'Mental Effects of Reduction of Ordinary Levels of Physical Stimuli on Intact Healthy Persons,' *Psychiatric Research Report of the American Psychiatric Association*, 5, 1956, pp. 1–9.

MASTERS, R. E. L., and HOUSTON, J. *The Varieties of Psychedelic Experience*, Holt, Rinehart and Winston 1966.

POLLARD, J. C., UHR, L., and WESLEY JACKSON, C. 'Studies in sensory deprivation.' *American Medical Association Archives of General Psychiatry*, 5, 1963, pp. 435–454.

SARGANT, W. 'Drugs and human behaviour.' *The Advancement of Science*, 22, 1966, pp. 681–687.

——'Witch doctoring, Zar and Voodoo; their relation to modern psychiatric treatment.' *Proceedings of the Royal Society of Medicine*, 60, 1967, pp. 1055–60.

——'The physiology of faith'. *British Journal of Psychiatry*, 115, 1969, pp. 505–518.

SAVAGE, C., JACKSON, D., and TERRILL, J. 'LSD, Transcendence and the New Beginning.' From the *Journal of Nervous and Mental Disease*, 135. 5. The Williams and Wilkins Co., Baltimore 1962.

SCHNECK, J. M. 'Hypnotic hallucinatory behaviour.' *Journal of Clinical and Experimental Hypnosis*, 1, 1953, 4–11.

SCOTT, T. H., BEXTON, W. H., HERON, W., and DOANE, B. K. 'Cognitive Effects of Perceptual Isolation.' *Canadian Journal of Psychology*, 13, 1959, pp. 200–209.

SMITH, H. 'Do Drugs have religious import?' *The Journal of Philosophy. LXI*, No. 18.

SMITH, S., and LEWTY, W. 'Perceptual Isolation Using a Silent Room.' *Lancet*, 2, 1959, pp. 342–345.

STAFFORD, P. G., and GOLIGHTLY, B. H. *LSD The Problem-solving Psychedelic*. Preface by H. Osmond, Introduction by D. Blewitt and Afterword by S. Krippner. Tandem Books, New York 1967.

TIIRA, E. *Raft of Despair*. Hutchinson, London 1954.

VERNON, J. *Inside the Black Room. Studies in Sensory Deprivation*. Souvenir Press, London 1963.

VERNON, J., McGILL, T. E., and SCHIFFMAN, H. 'Visual hallucinations during perceptual isolation.' *Canadian Journal of Psychology*, 12, 1958, pp. 31–34.

VOSBURG, R., FRASER, N., and GUEHL, J., 'Imagery sequence in sensory deprivation,' *American Medical Association Archives of General Psychiatry*, 2, 1960, pp. 356–357.

WALLACE, A. F. C. 'Cultural determinants of response to hallucinatory experience.' *American Medical Association Archives of General Psychiatry*, 1, 1959, pp. 58–69.

WEINSTEIN, E. A. 'Social aspects of hallucinations', in WEST. L. J. (ed). *Hallucinations*, 1962, pp. 233–238.

WEST, L. J. (ed) *Hallucinations*. Grune and Stratton, New York and London 1962.

——'United States Air Force prisoners of the Chinese Communists', *GAP Symposium No. 4*, July 1957, p. 270.

INDEX OF QUOTATIONS IN CHAPTERS I–V

For Editions cited see Bibliography

I. AUTHORS

'ABDISHO' HAZZAYA
    Treatises

	p. 159	50
	p. 172	222

AELIUS ARISTIDES
    Sacred Orations   II.31–32   198

APULEIUS
    Metamorphoses   XI.3, 4   226

ATHANASIUS
    Life of Anthony

	20	49
	89	111
	91	110, 112

AUGUSTINE

City of God	XXII.8	200
Confessions	IX.7.2	200
	VII.10.1–17.3	220

CASSIAN
    Conferences

	X.2	78
	X.11	61

CICERO
    de Divinatione

	2.58.119	45
	1.29.60ff.	46

CLEMENT OF ALEXANDRIA

Excerpta ex Theodoto	78.1–2	172
Stromateis	IV.IV.17	180
	V.XI.1	19
	VII.III.13	18
	VII.XI.68	18

CYPRIAN

Letters	LXIX.15	88
de Lapsis	8	181

DADISHO'
    On Solitude

	p. 80	33
	p. 81	30
	p. 82	30

DIODORUS SICULUS
    Bibliotheca Historica   1.27.3–6   204

EPIPHANIUS
    Panarion   26.13.2–3   214

EUSEBIUS
    History of the Church

	IV.15.40	208
	V.1.62, 63	218
	V.16.6–10	60
	VI.3.9	59
	IX.4.9	180

HARNACK A.
Mission and Expansion of
Christianity
Vol.I.Ch.III   64

HOMER
Odyssey   IV.561   138

IAMBLICHOS
The Egyptian Mysteries   I.III   221
                         II.V   76, 82, 221, 226
                         III.VII   44, 45, 223, 224, 229
                         III.VIII   222

IRENAEUS
adversus Haereses   V.33.2   187
                         V.33.3   140
Demonstrationes   83   216

ISOCRATES
Oration   V.117   4

JOSEPHUS
Antiquities of the Jews VIII.2.5   85

JUSTIN MARTYR
Dialogue with Trypho   II.LXXXV   88

ORIGEN
contra Celsum   VIII.58   156
de Principiis   I.I.9   51
                         II.XI.6   129
                         II.XI.7   130
Philocalia   II   19

PALLADIUS (Latin)
Sayings of the Fathers   VII.20   62
                         XI.10   111
                         XI.17   62
                         XV.9   114

PALLADIUS (Syriac)
Sayings of the Fathers   105   47
                         106   47
                         330   111
                         438   111
                         480   78
                         603   100
Questions and Answers   119   111
                         162   111
                         559   50
                         562   50
                         579   52
                         580   111
Appendix   23   85
                         35   61
                         68   81
                         104   88

PHILO

The Contemplative Life	II.11, 12	62
	II.III.20, 21	33
	III.26	54
	III.28, 29	58
	IV.34, 35	42
	VIII.64, 65	29
	XI.85, 87	62
Who is the Heir?	XVII.88	118
	LII.263	15
	LIII.263–266	16

PHILOSTRATUS

Life of Apollonius of Tyana	I.XVII	34
	II.XXXVII	46

PETER MONGUS AND ACACIUS

Letters	p. 223	97

PLATO

Apology	33C	7
	40E–41A	145
Critias	113C	138
	115A, B	138
Epinomis	977C, D	117
Minos	318E–319A	145
Phaedo	67C, D	214
	79C, D	8
	80E	23
	107D–108B	150
	110C–E	139
	111B, C	139
	111D–112A	168
	112E–113C	174
	113D–114B	175
Phaedrus	244A–D	7
	245C	8
	247C, D	119
	249B, C	10
	249E–250A	125
	250C	8
	250C, D	225
Republic	II.363	186
	VII.532	219
	IX.571	46
	X.615	170
	X.616	169
	X.621	197
Timaeus	71E–72B	7
	88C–89A	185
	89E–90D	120
	90D	5
	92C	5

PLOTINUS

Enneads	I.1.3	10

PLOTINUS—*cont.*
  Enneads—cont.

	IV.4.1	10
	IV.4.32	9
	VI.7.36	220

PLUTARCH
Alexander	I	23
On the apparent face in the Moon's orb	XXVIII–XXX	129
On the Cessation of Oracles	XXII	118, 125
	XXXVIII	13
	XXXIX	55
	L	45
On the E at Delphi	XVII–XVIII	105
	XX	205
On Isis and Osiris	XXVI	67
	XXVII	66
	XXXIII	75
	XXXV	65
	LXI	67
	LXXIII	67
	LXXIX	65
	LXXXI	231
On the Pythian Responses	XXIV	14

PORPHYRY
Epistle to Marcella	10	214
Life of Plotinus	23.15	11, 201
	23.25	145

TERTULLIAN
ad Martyras	2	35
Apologeticum	XXIII	68
de Anima	LII	44
	LIII	125

VIRGIL
Aeneid VI	282	170
	295	174
	548	168
	566	168
	616	169
	724	121

II. TITLES

Acts of Paul: Martyrdom	5	190
Acts of Thomas	168	191
Apa Mena	p. 141	189
Apocalypse of Abraham	XI	227
	XII	43
	XVIII	134
	XX	130
	XXI	130
	XXIII	141

Apocalypse of Elias	3.3	160
	4.13	171
	9.11	171
	13.1	176
Apocalypsis Mosis	37.3	175
Apocalypse of Paul	11, 12	151
	14	146, 153
	15, 16	154
	16	146
	46	131
Apocalypse of Peter	4, 5	167
	12	169
Ascension of Isaiah	V.8–14	208
	VI.15–17	231
	VII.22	186
	VII.25	161
	IX.16–19	215
	IX.22, 23	147
	IX.24, 25	186
11 *Baruch*	50.1–2	218
	51.8–10	161
Book of Jubilees	3.28	78
	4.17–20	194
	30.20–33	147
Book of Noah (Fragment of the)	106, 1–3	227
Christian Sibyllines	II.195–200	166
	II.285–295	169
Community Rule	XI	137
Damascus Rule	XIII	136
	IV	187
de dormitione Mariae	11	151
de morte Iosephi	13	152
	26	198
I *Enoch*	14.14–21	135
	17.1–6	164
	20.1–8	135
	21.1–10	164
	32.3E	139
	39.7b	222
	54.1–6	165
	67.5–7	165
	69.8–11	194
	71.1	17
	71.7–8	136
	75.1–2	136
II *Enoch*	17.1A	136
	22.1–3	227
	22A.8–10	161
	23.3–6	194
	29.4, 5	73
	55.1–2	113
	56.2	42
Epistle of the Apostles	51	215
IV *Ezra*	7.75–101	149

INDEX OF QUOTATIONS IN CHAPTERS I–V

V *Ezra*	42–47	127
VI *Ezra*	34–40	167
Hermes Trismegistus: Poimandres	I.24–26	122
	V.5	130
Historia Monachorum in Aegypto	VIII.55	104
Hymn to Rē		187
Messianic Rule	I	144
Muratori Canon		96
Mysteries of Saint John and the Holy Virgin	p. 69 (252)	99
Odes of Solomon	X.4–8	216
	XVIII.2–3	215
	XXI.1–3	215
	XXII.1–12	217
Of the Falling Asleep of Mary II	p. 96	155, 158
	p. 102	206
	p. 124	213
Of the Life of the Virgin III	p. 22	166
IV	p. 38	176
Pistis Sophia	256a–256b	213
	259b–261a	154
	262a–263a	153
	287a–289a	163
P. Oxyrhynchus	XI.1381	199
Psalms of Solomon	14.2	141
Pseudo-Clementines. Ad Virgines		98
Questions of Theodore	3	173
Qumran Hymns	III.5	202
	VI.10	140
	VIII.14	202
Song of the Three Children	26,27	207
Tale of Khamuas (*First*)	III.12–14	195
Tale of Khamuas (*Second*)	II.9–15	148
Testament of Abraham	IX	131
	XI	160
	XII	170
	XIV	173
	XVI	156
	XVII	157
	XX	213
Testament of Benjamin	4.1	186
Testament of Levi	3.4–8	135
	8.1–3	185
Testament of Reuben	1.1–6	112
	7.1–2	189
Vita Adae et Evae	XXV.1–3	134
	XXIX.2–4	140
War Rule	XI	165
	I	166

INDEX OF QUOTATIONS IN SECTIONS I–V

For Abbreviations see pp. 262 ff.

COPTIC TEXTS

AM.AP.ANT.B
322, 345, 457, 490, 494, 580.

AM.AP.MAC.B.
402, 470, 611, 748, 765.

AM.CO.ABR.S.
399.

AM.CYR.AL.B.
509, 585, 682, 713, 764.

AM.JOH.K.B.
284, 288, 298, 307, 317, 319, 328, 331,
414, 423, 468, 470, 471, 476, 500, 517,
759, 776, 777.

AM.JOH.LY.S.
475

AM.MAC.AL.B.
295, 300, 301, 303, 308, 320, 329, 331,
345, 357, 423.

AM.MAC.SC.B.
280, 293, 309, 353, 363, 403, 407, 409,
436, 472, 473, 480, 484, 486, 501, 515,
749, 758, 762.

AM.MAC.TK.B.
421, 451, 515, 531, 755.

AM.MAN.S.
481, 482.

AM.MAT.P.S.
390, 392, 504, 514.

AM.MA.DO.B.
295, 320, 328, 402, 470, 496, 510, 512,
536, 748, 766.

AM.MO.S.
378, 397, 465.

AM.PAUL.B.
404, 536.

AM. PAUL.T.S.
279,   283,   292,   293,   310,   326,
332, 333, 387, 434, 461, 466, 618, 730

AM.PIS.KE.B.
299, 306, 331, 348, 378, 441, 446, 452,
459, 487, 489, 502, 520, 608, 739, 752,
758, 767–769, 776

AM.TH.B.
514, 776

AM.VER.MAC.B.
365, 430, 455, 754, 768.

BA.HY.I.ANAT.P.B.
637, 722, 724, 735, 740.

BA.HY.I.AN.B.
360, 531, 620, 639, 642, 645, 660, 666,
690, 691, 712, 715, 720, 726, 733, 735,
737, 743, 751, 761.

BA.HY.I.AP.B.
632, 668, 721, 724, 732, 757.

BA.HY.I.APOL.B.
530, 669

BA.HY.I.EPIM.B.
532, 535, 628, 658, 661, 662, 663, 667,
689, 710, 712, 719, 725, 728, 729, 739,
751, 757, 763, 765.

BA.HY.I.LAC.B.
383, 436, 530, 544, 636, 645, 671, 685,
710, 734, 736, 740, 774, 777.

BA.HY.I.PAP.B.
531, 648, 712, 736, 751, 767.

BA.HY.I.SA.PA.B.
641, 647, 659, 670, 687, 714, 722, 723,
739, 740, 755, 763.

BA.HY.I.TH.O.B.
394, 395, 396, 530, 534, 623, 655, 686,
716.

BA.HY.I.TH.S.B.
391, 530, 631, 671, 692, 705, 706, 711,
713, 716, 727, 731, 738, 739, 761, 772,
777.

BA.HY.II.GEO.B.
335, 529, 616, 633, 635, 668, 717, 742,
746, 778, 779.

BA.HY.II.GEO.DI.B.
335, 529, 547, 617, 618, 632, 634, 644,
648, 667, 696, 728, 732, 733, 742, 744,
750, 752, 755, 772, 778, 779.

BA.HY.II.IAC.P.B.
651, 656, 673, 675, 676, 734, 737, 752,
769.

BA.HY.II.IS.TI.B.
647, 653, 702, 715, 722, 750, 760.

BA.HY.II.JOH.PH.B.
750, 773

BA.HY.II.MIR.GEO.B.
426, 676, 681, 708.

BA.HY.II.POL.SM.B.
320, 347, 365, 715, 778.

BA.HY.II.T.A.T.S.B.
388, 396, 404, 463, 530, 629, 671, 726, 748, 756, 783.

BU.ABB.S.
583.

BU.AP.PAUL.S.
557–563, 565, 566, 568, 570, 582, 585, 589–594, 599, 600, 601, 612, 613, 621, 678, 679, 753, 756, 773, 777.

BU.AP.PIS.S.
328, 331, 442, 460, 487, 502, 740, 753, 755, 757, 769.

BU.BART.R.S.
526, 557, 622, 777.

BU.CH.JOH.S.
566, 570, 620, 699, 700, 762, 764.

BU.CYR.S.
291, 292, 310, 326, 447, 497, 507, 509, 521, 618, 776.

BU.EUS.TH.S.
655, 781.

BU.GEO.C.S.
635, 717, 743, 746, 778, 779.

BU.M.TIM.S.
603, 612, 614, 615, 680.

BU.ON.S.
278, 279, 286, 294, 298, 309, 326, 334, 337, 459, 468, 506, 534, 547, 749, 757, 758.

CHA.AP.PA.S.
276, 279, 280, 291, 292, 294, 295, 298, 300, 302, 307, 308, 309, 310, 315, 317, 319, 325, 330, 332, 337, 338, 339, 340, 345, 346, 349, 350, 352, 360, 361, 366, 368, 372, 373, 376, 380, 384, 403, 416, 417, 418, 420, 430, 433, 435, 454, 456, 468, 470, 525, 539, 577, 579, 581, 610, 754, 755, 766.

CHA.MART.B.
274, 302, 307, 325, 390.

DAV.JOH.KH.B.
286, 298, 314, 319, 332, 339, 407, 440, 450, 451, 477, 478, 487, 497, 748, 770.

GAR.ANT.S.
291, 296, 297, 307, 308, 310, 325, 327, 329, 340, 345, 349, 367, 385, 387, 388, 392, 401, 405, 408, 409, 412, 413, 414, 415, 427, 429, 432, 433, 434, 457, 473, 493, 535, 579, 580, 748, 774.

GUI.DAN.B.
498, 508.

GUI.IS.B.
275, 367, 379, 499, 503, 510, 530, 559, 594, 603, 643, 652, 697.

HY.AP.IR.B.
302, 304, 324, 429, 448, 449, 468, 493, 533, 543, 654, 659, 664, 681, 745, 750, 771, 776.

HY.ARI.B.
451, 682, 722, 731, 741.

HY.DID.B.
397, 629, 662, 712, 715, 731, 757, 765.

HY.EUS.B.
535, 542, 651, 654, 670, 681, 708, 711, 716, 718, 734, 745, 761, 762.

HY.JE.SI.B.
317, 324, 377, 378, 462, 749, 756.

HY.MAC.AN.B.
332, 382, 472, 543, 610, 633, 658, 665, 674, 702, 718, 730, 738, 744, 745, 761, 763.

HY.MACR.B.
532, 637, 715, 721, 724, 758.

HY.PET.AL.B.
424, 464, 496.

HY.PI.AT.B.
532, 533, 638, 640, 646, 652, 687, 693, 709, 714, 724, 730, 751, 752.

HY.SAR.B.
535, 664, 670, 694, 717, 747, 750.

LA.DOR.MAR.B.
528, 588, 677, 753, 761, 763, 777.

LA.MOR.JOS.B.
524, 588, 698.

LE.PAC.S.
297, 303, 307, 312, 313, 314, 324, 328, 340, 341, 370, 371, 372, 380, 400, 412, 413, 414, 424, 453, 456, 457, 469, 479, 485, 491, 522, 523, 526, 434, 537, 544, 548, 553, 554, 597, 637, 756, 758, 766, 772, 776.

LE.PAC.B.
276, 296, 306, 314, 320, 328, 330, 341,
371, 380, 385, 386, 393, 400, 401, 424,
426, 432, 453, 470, 479, 485, 486, 488,
489, 491, 492, 524, 526, 538, 555, 577,
596, 598, 748, 757, 758, 759, 766, 771,
772.

LEI.SIN.B.
275, 301, 311, 318, 325, 332, 341, 347,
428, 439, 440, 443, 444, 445, 446, 448,
451, 466, 476, 482, 483, 493, 507, 521,
606, 757, 758, 764, 768.

MIN.EPIM.S.
338, 396, 529, 531, 628, 639, 652, 657,
662, 663, 666, 688, 710, 711, 719, 725,
728, 731, 757, 763, 765.

POR.IS.B.
300, 316, 317, 325, 333, 374, 375, 382,
447, 450, 452, 461, 466, 467, 471, 494,
748, 749, 756, 759–762, 770.

ROB.MAR.S.
533.

ROB.VIR.S.
334, 589.

SOB.HEL.S.
337, 391, 427, 533, 542, 627, 637, 640,
653, 665, 670, 693, 709, 716, 723–25,
729, 736, 740, 761, 763–65, 779.

ST.AP.EL.A.
574, 583, 604.

TIL.I.HER.S.
726, 740, 762.

TIL.I.JOH.LY.S.
291, 300, 360, 364, 401.

TIL.JOS.Z.S.
524, 586.

TIL.I.NAH.S.
736, 760.

TIL.I.PA.TH.S.
630, 714, 719, 723, 752.

TIL.I.PAN.S.
741, 763.

TIL.I.TIM.S.
630, 638, 658, 716, 721, 728, 739, 750,
770.

TIL.I.VIC.S.
703, 771.

TIL.I.WAN.S.
507, 534.

TIL.II.MAT.A.S.
506.

TIL.II.PTOL.S.
328, 649, 740, 753.

VAN.L.Q.TH.S.
451, 559.

WOR.GAB.S.
386, 460, 703, 704, 729, 756, 761, 762.

SYRIAC TEXTS

BR.AM.SY.
288, 313, 341.

BR.ANTI.SY.
767.

BR.JAM.SY.
421, 424, 770, 771.

BR.PAUL.SY.
406.

BR.PRI.SY.
754.

BR.THOM.SY.
299, 327, 362.

BR.ZAC.SY.
305.

BRO.EP.SY.
274, 287, 315, 326, 362, 366, 378, 383,
398, 467, 490, 768.

BU.II.HIER.SY.
273, 283, 288, 294, 298, 311, 315, 319,
325, 326, 334, 336, 337, 339, 341, 349,
355, 358, 362, 363, 377, 381, 389, 410,
421, 426, 461, 480, 484, 498, 752, 775.

BU.II.PAL.SY.
274, 277, 287, 290, 295, 297, 299–301,
303, 304, 310, 311, 315, 316, 318, 319,
321, 322, 323, 324, 329, 330, 336, 339,
341, 342, 344, 347, 349, 350, 351, 352,
353, 356, 359–63, 364, 365, 366, 368,
372–76, 377, 379, 382, 384, 386, 387,
392–94, 400, 409, 413, 416, 417, 419,
423, 427, 431–33, 435, 446, 455, 458,
468, 472, 488, 492, 494, 513, 526, 532,
536, 537, 578, 750, 753–56, 767, 768,
769, 773.

GU.EV.SY.
346.

KUG.SEV.SY.
311, 323.

LOOK.MAR.SY.
281, 282, 291, 297, 308, 335, 338, 350,
381, 409, 460, 467, 497, 500, 506, 522,
581, 748, 775, 776.

MAC.AZ.SY.
396, 636, 650, 669, 689, 723, 739.

NAU.AAR.SY.
407, 430, 475, 759, 775.

NAU.ABR.SY.
299, 306, 330, 483, 495, 514.

NAU.AMM.SY.
775.

NAU.JE.PE.SY.
284, 285, 299, 307, 318, 328, 331, 340,
341, 353, 354, 364, 369, 422, 444, 467,
468, 471, 476, 495, 500, 507, 519, 749,
753, 754, 759, 771, 775, 777.

NAU.JON.SY.
572, 573.

VAN.L.MAR.SY. (MUS.63)
551, 553.

GREEK TEXTS

FE.II.DAN.G.
276, 306, 398, 464, 474, 499, 510, 516,
760.

FE.II.HYP.G.
273, 277, 290, 311, 315, 334, 375, 384,
390, 511.

FE.III/I.EUT.G.
277, 388, 420, 464, 482, 492, 499, 578,
706, 707, 770, 774.

FE.IV/I.HIS.G.
295, 327, 330, 337, 347, 348, 358, 359,
363, 364, 365, 367, 369, 379, 382, 384,
389, 401, 403, 410, 420, 431, 434, 436,
448, 484, 498, 499, 535, 538, 574, 775.

LO.PAL.G.
275, 278, 288, 289, 290, 292, 296, 297,
298, 300–304, 306, 308, 311, 313, 315,
316, 317, 320, 321, 323, 324, 326, 327,
328–30, 332, 336, 339, 340, 341, 348,
356, 363, 364, 376, 377, 381, 382, 385,
402, 423, 427, 458, 482, 581, 773.

WIL.II.THOM.G.
275, 604.

LATIN TEXTS

CH.AD.EV.L.
318.

CHA.SA.L.
276, 287, 295, 304, 316, 324, 342, 345,
346, 348, 359, 362, 367, 384, 422, 509,
510, 768, 774.

OTHER TEXTS

CH.ASC.IS.E.
594.

CH.EN.I.E.
564, 568, 569.

CH.EN.II.SL.
540, 563, 569, 596.

MID.MOS.H.
527.

TIS.ASC.IS.E(G).
540, 541, 545.

WIL.II.PET.G.(E).
572, 604, 605.

GENERAL INDEX TO CHAPTERS I–V

The Index is basically an index of *subjects*, including the subjects covered by the extracts from published sources quoted in the Chapters. In addition, selected *personal names* have been included.

The letter *n* after a page-number indicates that the information will be found in a *note* on that page.

Aaron, Sons of, 144
Abaris, 43
Abbaton, Abbadon, angel of death, 155–8
    glorious appearance to the righteous, 171
    redemption from, 202
    seven heads, 157
Aboukir: shrine of John and Cyrus, 200
Abraham, Abram, 11, 173, 224
Abraham, Apocalypse of:
    Adam in Garden of Eden, 141
    appearance of archangel, 226–7
    expansion of Jewish race, 130
    fasting, 43
    seer raised above firmament, 130
    source of death imagery, 114
Abraham, Testament of:
    Adam enthroned in heaven, 159–60
    conversation with Death, 213
    intercession, 173
    pitiless angels, 170
    sight of whole creation, 131
    visits by Death, 156–7
    withstanding sight of Death, 158
Abstinence, 6, 59
Abu Simbel: inscriptions of Rameses II, 101
Abuse, terms of, 71–2
Abydos: boat journeys to, 188
Abyss:
    angel of, 171
    appearing at Last Judgment, 166
    fiery, 164
    sealed with seven seals, 171
Acacius, Archbishop of Constantinople, 97
Acheron, 121, 174–5
Acherusian Lake, 174–6
    washing in, 175
Acts of . . ., *see* under the names of the subjects, e.g., *Martyrs, Acts of*
Adam, 100, 141, 159–60, 173, 175
Adam and Eve, Life of:
    chariot of fire, 133
    fasting, 41–2
Admonitions:
    in funerary inscriptions, 107–8
    in narratives, 108
Adversaries, Book of, *see* Book
'Adversary': name of Satan, 73
Aelius Aristides, 198

Aeneas, Aenaeus, 145, 168, 170
Aeneid, see Virgil
Aeschylus, 150
'Age to come': replacing present age, 124
Ahriman, 98
Air: in elemental zone, 121
Alexandria:
    centre of culture, 15
    conflict of views among early Christians, 19
Alexandrian Church: Greek language used, 23
Alexandrian Fathers: cultural background, 25
Alexandrian Schools, 17–20
    human body despised, 100
    influenced by Plato, 8
Allegory:
    Bible as source, 58
    O.T. narratives interpreted as, 25
    use by Origen, 19
Ambrose of Milan, 192–3
Amente, 161–76
    accusers and advocates, 144
    all souls enclosed, 171
    boat journey through, 188
    changing faces of demons, 155
    demonic forms derived from rituals, 76
    demons encountered in, 68
    gate of, 148
    imagery derived from Zodiac, 154
    in Christian apocalyptic literature, 152
    journey through, 109
    names and formulae, 3
    Patriarchs in, 172–3
    prayers for journey, 151
    punishments averted, 196
    serpents in rituals, 75
    Setme in, 148
    soul punished by Spirit Counterpart, 154
    Virgin Mary delivered from torments, 206
Amulets:
    in pagan Egypt, 205
    use attributed to ascetics, 87
Ancestor worship, 243*n*29
    prohibition, 77

Anchorites, pre-Christian: hairy, 33
Andrew, the apostle, 84
Angelic robe, 31
Angels:
    accusing, 147, 160
    as advocates, 145; as intermediaries, 123; as mediators, 102, 104; as messengers of the deity, 92, 103; as protectors, 104
    ascetic life like life of angels, 47
    at death of ascetic, 115
    avenging, 166, 171
    beauty of, 226–7
    faces like leopards, 171
    fallen, 126
    foretellers of death, 112
    good and evil, 103, 123, 153, 154
    guides of souls, 126
    hierarchy of, 135
    imagination and, 234
    in visions, 81, 221, 226
    of light and darkness, 82, 158
    overcoming powers of the air, 153
    pitiless, 150, 170
    planetary, 165
    praying, 176
    punishment of, 164
    replacing stars, 92, 123
    resplendent with light, 221
    singing, 62, 116, 136, 146, 176
    unchangeability, 76
Animals:
    animal deities as demons, 67
    animal forms in Orphic under-world, 6
    attacks by, 80, 201–2
    clean and unclean, 69
    faces changing, 162
    gods in form of, 2
    horned, 232
    human attributes, 68
    in divination, 68, 69
    monsters slain byChristian saints, 77
    mummification, 210
    refusal to attack martyrs, 208
    sacred, 39, 67
    sacrifice of, 69
    typifying perfection, 162
    union of women with, 101
    world of, controlled by man, 6
    worship in late Egyptian religion, 64–5
    Zodiacal, 138
Anna, 101
Anointing:
    at death, 116
    in heaven, 42, 161
    thirty-six sites of, 177, 211
Anthesteria, festival of, 5
Anthony, Life of:
    death foretold, 112
    exhortation to live as though dying, 111
    funeral instructions, 110
    imagery of passage of soul, 154
    prototypes for *Lives* of saints, 23
Anthropomorphism, heresy of, 78

Anubis, jackal god, 67
Apis Bull:
    and Osiris, 67, 75
    burial, 65
    fertility cult, 39
Apocalypse of . . ., *see* under the names of the subjects, e.g., *Peter, Apocalypse of*
Apocalyptic literature, 16–17
    date of writing, 127
    first and third person used, 115
    form adopted, 17
    numbers used in, 28–9
    imagery, source of, 114, 127, 147
    see also under titles of individual works
Apollonius of Tyana, Life of, 23, 217, 228
Apollyon, 155
Apophthegmata Patrum:
    answers to disciples, 31
    brevity of speech, 34
    collection of narratives, 24
    exhortations, 37, 51–2, 87
    read by monks, 84
Apostles:
    exorcism by, 84–5
    seen at death of ascetic, 115
Apostles, Apocryphal Acts of, 84–6
    conflict between Christianity and pagan cults, 217
    exorcism, 87
    martyrdoms, 190–91
    read by lay communities, 84
Apostles, Epistle of: ascension, 215
Apuleius, 225–6, 227, 232
Aravoth, tenth heaven, 227
Archaism: reversion to, 234–7
Archangels:
    beauty of, 226
    Death in form of, 156–7
    hierarchy of, 135
    in visions, 81
    luminosity, 221
    punishment of wicked angels, 164–5
    singing hymns, 146
    unchangeability, 76
    watching over universe, 135
Archons:
    in visions, 81
    rulers over the living, 214, 216
    unchangeability, 76
Aretologies, 204
Arianus, 191
Aristotle, 9
Ark: measurements divinely dictated, 132
Artemis, worship of, 229
Ascension:
    in Hermetic literature, 122
    of Christ, 215–16
    of soul to heaven, 121, 132, 214, 216
    righteous ascending with Christ, 215
Ascetics and Asceticism:
    aphorisms, 24
    as 'dead men', 27
    as 'life of the angels', 26
    biography, 22–4; *see also* Martyrs; Saints

Ascetics—*cont.*
book-learning rejected, 63
burial by disciples, 31; in own garment, 113; in secret place, 110
celibacy, 32
cells, 34–5
deaths, accounts of, 113–14
delusions, 93
discipleship, 29–31
dwelling-place allocated, 105
environment, 27; detachment from, 36
fasting, *see* that heading
food *see* that heading
gifts bestowed by Deity, 57–63
hair, 33
illiteracy, 25
imagination and insight, 94
imagination control, 52–3
insanity, 93
intellectual development lacking, 63
last words, 113
life an act of self-destruction, 79
life conducive to beauty, 228
mental powers extolled, 51
miracles ascribed to, 53
modern medicine and, 48; modern man and, 236–7
nakedness, 33
pain disregarded in full consciousness, 37–8
periods of time in life of, 29
powers misunderstood, 53
recognition, 104
renunciation of ancient culture, 25–26
rest-prevention, 38
'saviours' of fellows, 63
self-enclosure, -isolation, -mortification, *see* those headings
silence, *see* that heading
singing, 61, 136
sleep-deprivation, *see* Sleep
solitude, *see* Self-isolation
standing posture, 35, 37, 38
sun, exposure to, 38
tears, 37
thought control, 49–50
training, 29, 81
visits to holy men, 141
way of life, 26–31
weakening body by labour, 36
Asclepius, Asklepios, 45, 198, 199, 217
Astrology:
Babylonian, 146–7
diffusion, 120
Hellenistic Middle East, 86
Jewish contact with, 123
Athanasius, 49, 81
Athletes: martyrs likened to, 181, 186, 188
Atlantis:
fruitfulness, 138
parallel, 141
Attainment: defined, 172
Augustine of Hippo, 182, 199–200, 210, 219, 220
Baal, Baalim, 69, 123, 133

Babylon:
astrology, 146–7
worship of heavenly bodies, 118
Banquet of the Thousand Years, 197
Banquets, heavenly, 186
perfumes used at, 230
Baptism:
after death, 173, 176
as exorcism, 176
before death, 116
dragon in iconography, 76
essential for salvation, 172
in River of Fire, 175
preparation for, 42
present-day Coptic rites, 211
unbaptised Patriarchs in *Amente*, 172
Bartholomew, Apocalypse of, 132
Baruch II:
fasting, 41
transformation of the dead, 161
Basil the Great, 182
Beauty:
heavenly, 225–8
of Atlantis, 138
of dress, 227, 228
of gods, archangels, angels, 226
of O.T. Patriarchs, 227
of sun, moon, stars, 227
of surroundings, 227
Beheading of martyrs, 190–1, 210
Benjamin, Testament of: crown as reward, 186
Bible:
Coptic translation, 25
exegesis, 19, 59, 103
imagery, 103, 122–3
inspiration to ascetics, 27
memorising and recitation, 25, 31, 58–9
symbolism, 28
Biblical references:
ii Chronicles, 221
Daniel, 16, 92, 207
Ecclesiastes, 17
Exodus, 224
Ezekiel, 14, 16, 134
Genesis, 101 *i*
Isaiah, 13, 16, 99, 114
Jeremiah, 16
Job, 73
i Kings, 222
ii Kings, 114
i Maccabees, 15
Proverbs, 17
Psalms, 14, 61, 74, 80, 87, 133, 202 215
Revelation, 137, 222
i Samuel, 14
Three Children, Song of The, 207
Wisdom, 17
Zechariah, 16, 92
Birth:
barrenness overcome by divine intervention, 100
death related to, 116
Egyptian queens impregnated by gods, 101

Birth—*cont.*
    great men fathered by gods or
    animals, 101
    light accompanying birth, 101
    rituals, 71
Bishops:
    canonisation, 192
    Order of, 107
Blood:
    drinking, 243n30
    'eating' prohibited, 69
Boat journeys, 176, 188
Boats:
    in apocalyptic literature, 175
    in Plato, 175
    in Virgil, 174
Body:
    centre of reference in ancient
    Egyptian religion, 161–2
    motion of, 184–5
    parts related to decans, 156
    preserved by Egyptians, 35
    restoring, 210–12
    rhythms, 177
Book, Books:
    burning of, 179
    of Adversaries, 147
    of Life, 147; erasing list of sins,
    187; writing martyr's name in, 188
    of the Living, 160, 176, 187
    power in, 195
    provision for writing of, 195
    writing of books beneficial in after-
    life, 255n48
    written by Thoth, 194
    written in heaven, 146, 194
Book of . . ., *see* under the third word for
    titles beginning *Book of* (e.g., *Gates,
    Book of*)
Bread:
    of life, 51
    universally eaten, 40
Burial:
    desert as burial place, 34
    inscriptions in burial chambers, 3
    instructions, 192–3
    of King, 188
    of Patriarchs, 189
    place located by animal, 243n27
    robe as shroud, 105
    site allocation, 105; by oracles, 189;
    by oxen, 189
    see also Mummification; Tombs
Busiris: boat journey to, 188
Buto, Lower Egypt, 244n49

Calendar:
    intercalary days, 136
    lunar and solar years, 136
    prophecy and, 28, 194
    writing and, 194
Callinicus: *Life of Hypatios*, 24
Camels: carrying coffin, 189
Canaanite tribes:
    gods condemned as demons, 70
    propitiation of demons, 69,
    sacrifices, 119
    throne in religion, 133

Cassia: in mummification preparation, 116
Cassian, John, 52, 61, 78
Castration, 98
Catechumen school, Alexandria, 17
Celibacy, 32
Cellia: community of monks, 30–31
Chalcedon, Council of, 25, 97, 246ns12, 13
'Changing faces', 155, 162
Chaos:
    angels imprisoned in, 164
    during last days of earth, 167
    punishment of the soul, 154
Chariot, Chariots:
    fiery, 133–4
    fiery wheels, 134
    in ascension of soul, 117, 121
    of cherubim, 131
    of light, 206, 223
Charon, 174
Chastity:
    identified with Christianity, 72, 84,
    98
    in Neoplatonism, 75
    obedience to divine law, 72
    pre-condition of intellectual life, 99
    resurrection as reward, 84
Cherubim:
    at death of ascetic, 115
    guarding throne, 136
    singing hymns, 146
    substitution for winged deities, 105
Choral singing, 61–2
Chosen race: recipients of divine guidance,
    102
Christ, *see* Jesus Christ
Chronology:
    Babylonian, 118
    see also Time
Chthonic deities, 5
Church the:
    authority based on revelation in
    Scriptures, 21
    control of soul and imagination,
    177, 232
    rituals protecting against disturbing
    experiences, 172
Churches:
    books for, 195
    call to build, 105
Cicero:
    dreams, 45–6
    statue of Herakles, 206
Clement of Alexandria, 17, 21, 29, 103
    baptism liberating from Fate, 172
    death-wish condemned, 180
    'gnostic' vision of God, 18
Cloud, Clouds:
    at Last Judgment, 166
    of fire, 224
    pillar of, 224
Cobra deity, 75, 244n49
Coenobitic movement:
    initiation of, 29
    training for solitude, 32
    way of life, 33
Coffins: inscriptions on, 3, 109; 'Coffin
    Texts', 248–53
Commemoration rituals, 110, 198

Communications from the divine to man, 102
Community Rule, see Qumran community
Constantine, 180
Continence, *see* Chastity
Coptic language:
    Lives of the Fathers, 24
    translation of Bible, 25
    words associated with images, 50
Covenant: legal element in Jewish religion, 11
Crocodile deity, 75–6, 244n50
Cross, sign of:
    before martyrdom, 191
    exorcism by, 201
    protection against pagan assaults, 211
Crowns, Crowning:
    'crowns of constancy', 128
    on Mount Zion, 126–7
    reward for righteousness, 185–6
Cyprian, of Carthage, 88, 181
Cyril of Jerusalem, 182
Cyril of Scythopolis, 24

Dadisho':
    dangers of solitary life, 30
    training for solitude, 32–3
Damascus Rule, see Qumran community
Daniel, O.T. Prophet, 41
Daniel the Stylite, Life of, 24
Darkness:
    at salvation of martyrs, 231
    fire imagery and, 224
    in life after death, 169–70
    outer, 162
    powers of, 165
David, O.T. King, 206, 213
Deacon, Order of, 107
Dead, the:
    as shades, 170
    cemeteries: cites of the dead, 132; necropolis, 105
    communication with, 3, 71; through dreams, 46, 192
    crossing Acheron, 174
    duties of the living towards, 107–8
    feared by the living, 159
    funerary inscriptions re-establishing the deceased, 3
    hostility of, 5
    invocation of, 196
    judges of the living, 108
    judgment of, *see* Judgment after death
    life after death a replica of earthly life, 137
    meeting with, 159
    offerings to, 197, 241n28
    oracular pronouncement from, 159
    participation in liturgy, 94; in world of the living, 27
    raising of, 217; at shrines, 218–19
    recognition after resurrection, 217–218
    rising at Last Judgment, *see* Resurrection
    rituals, 68

source of misfortune to living, 71
tomb as focus of cult, 35
Dead, Book of the, 109
    chapter concerning the head, 190
    'negative confession', 109; death-bed 'confessions', 26
    texts on mummy cloths, 116
    transformations of the dead, 160–161
Death:
    Angel of, 171
    angels appearing at, 158
    at appointed time, 212–13
    attainment of knowledge comparable to, 8
    faces of, 156–7
    fasting before, 42
    fear of, 114
    foretelling, 108, 112
    'labour' similar to that at birth, 116
    memory restored at point of death, 54–5
    of the wicked, 148–55
    preparation for, 113
    ritual experience of, 213
    salvation from 201–19
    separation of body, soul and mind, 128–9
    sleep as model of, 43
    terrifying form of, 155
    victory over, 158
    visits by, 156–7, 213
    wish for, 180–1
    withstanding sight of, 158
Decans, 155–6, 249n77
    as 'counsellors', 118, 156
    definition and relationships, 156, 252ns22, 23, 25
    invoked in healing, 156
Decius, Edict of, 179, 181, 207
Deir el Bahari: inscriptions of Amonhotep III and Hatshepsut, 101
Delphic Oracle, 7, 205, 223–4
Delusions:
    correction by older monks, 31
    danger of, in solitary life, 30
Demons, 64–80
    ambivalence, 66–7, 70
    appearance of smouldering fire, 221
    assault by, 79, 167
    attendant, 103
    changing faces and forms, 76, 155
    communal ritual and, 79
    conflict with, 163
    daevas and *deva*, 70
    danger to ascending soul, 121
    demonic retribution, 155
    demonic world obliterated by baptism, 177
    destructive powers, 177
    dominating souls, 154
    exorcism methods, 87; by self-inflicted pain, 85; by solitary effort, 76
    former gods as demons, 68
    forms, 74–6
    Hellenistic period, 64

Demons—*cont.*
    identified with vices, 52, 89
    image replaced by angels, 103
    in *Amente*, 68
    mode of activity, 78–9
    of unchastity, 84
    pagan temples infested by, 77
    physical ills inflicted by, 77
    possession by, 67–8
    propitiation, 68–9
    punishment of, 66
    purification by ritual, 69
    sexual temptations as, 74
    torment of and by, 72
    training for fight against, 35
    visible after exorcism, 86
    visions producing feelings of tumult, 81
Dendrites, 37
Descensus: Adam and Patriarchs raised to heaven, 173
Destiny:
    independence of, 153, 217
    rule of, 214
    rulers of, 152
Dēt, Tê, 148, 162, 163, 251*n*13
Devil, the, 77, 81
    see also Satan
Devils:
    casting out, *see* Exorcism
    imagination and, 234
    vices associated with, 242*n*4
Diocletian, 76–7, 179, 207
Diodorus, 116, 204
Dionysiac cults: preserving archaism, 20
Dionysius of Alexandria, 181
Disciples and Discipleship, 29–31
    authority of master, 81
    called to succeed master, 105
    journey to death-bed of master, 108
    recognition of perfection in master, 54
    witness at death-bed, 115
Diseases: recognition, 99
Dismemberment of martyrs, 188, 202; of Osiris by Seth, 211
Divination:
    and possession, 7
    animals used in, 68, 69
    in Hellenistic Middle East, 86
    inspection of sacrificial victims, 243*n*27
Doctrine: interpretation of, 96–8
Dodona: priestesses at, 7
Dragon, Dragons:
    demonic form, 75
    'dragon upon the water', 177; 'within the water', 76
    Hades as belly of dragon, 244*n*47
    killing by Herakles, 137; by martyrs, 189, 209
    of outer darkness, 162
    seven-headed, 157, 216
Dreams:
    affected by wine, 45–6
    communications from deity, 102
    dangers for the ascetic, 46–7
    dependence on bodily state, 45

    dreamer as actor or spectator, 55–6
    foods causing confused dreams, 241*n*40
    in healing ritual, 6
    inspiration for apocalyptic writers, 17
    recalled by memory, 54
    revelations in, 41, 44, 92, 192; prophetic, 12; modern, 236
Dress: beauty of, 227, 228
Drowning: cult of drowned persons, 110
Drug-taking: in twentieth century, 234
Drunkenness: accompanying ritual, 5–6; *see also* Intoxication

Earth:
    fruitfulness, 138
    in elemental sphere, 121
    last days, 167
Earthquakes: at salvation of martyrs, 231
Easter:
    forty-day fast adopted, 42
    preparation for baptism, 42
Eastern Saints, History of the, by John of Ephesus, 24
Ecliptic: division into 360 degrees, 118
Ecstasy:
    induced by music, 6; by choral singing, 61–2
    prophetic revelations, 12
    recalled by memory, 54
    supplanting reason, 15–16
Eden, Garden of:
    Adam in, 141
    image of paradise, 139
Egypt:
    agricultural wealth, 39
    conversion to Christianity, 24
    Coptic as liturgical language, 25
    foreign rulers as divine kings, 65
    Greek language official, 25
    Greek settlers Egyptianised, 65
    land ownership, 187
    marriage, 74
    persecutions in, 179
Egyptian religion, 2–4
    archaic practices re-introduced, 86, 210
    Ethiopian dynasty, 64
    heavenly banquets, 43
    life after death a replica of earthly life, 137
    local deities, 65
    see also Funerary cults
Elect, the: blessedness only for, 124
Elemental sphere:
    Deity and imagery of, 130
    passage through, 121
    viewed by seer, 141
    see also Spheres
Elias, Apocalypse of:
    Angel of the Abyss, 171
    avenging angels, 171
    boat journey across River of Fire, 176
    Egyptian imagery, 147
    gates and regions of heaven, 160
    Michael as intercesser, 173

Elijah, Elias, 13, 28, 30–31, 33, 41, 105, 114, 131, 141
Elisha, 114–15
Elisabeth, 101
Elysian Plain, 129, 138
Empedocles:
  ambivalance of demons, 70
  punishment of demons, 66
Enclosure, *see* Self-enclosure
Encomium:
  on St. Menas, 188–9
  used by early Fathers, 181
Enoch, O.T. Patriarch, 131
I Enoch:
  elect strong as fiery lights, 222
  fallen angels and disobedient stars, 126
  four places of Sheol, 141
  function of angels and archangels, 135–6
  Garden of Righteousness, 139
  heavenly house, 134–5
  knowledge of writing, 193–4
  leaders of the heads of thousands, 136
  righteous as companions of heavenly host, 159
  river of fire, 164
  spirit ascending to the heavens, 17
  source of imagery, 16–17; of death imagery, 114
II Enoch:
  appearance of Lord's face, 227
  beauty of angels and archangels, 226
  darkness in place of torment, 169
  date of writing, 127
  death foretold, 112–13
  fasting, 42
  Satanail thrown from height, 72
  transformation of seer, 161
  visits to regions of four elements, 141
  writing 366 books, 194
Ephraim Syrus, 61, 243*n*17
Epidaurus: sanctuary, 198, 199
Epimenides, 43
Erinyes, 53, 171
Esdras, *see* Ezra
Essenes:
  Bible study, 58
  obedience to divine authority, 81
Ethiopia: 'cradle of Egyptian civilisation', 64
'Ethiopian, The', *see* Nubian
Eucharist:
  divine appearance at, 95
  exclusion from 82
  in heaven, 187
  miraculous events connected with Elements, 246*n*14
  revealing man's true worth, 83
  transformation of Elements, 95
Eunuchs: highest place in heaven, 98
Eusebius:
  destroying of bodies to prevent resurrection, 218
  persecutions recorded, 179–80, 207, 210
Evagrius Ponticus, 30, 52, 56, 87

Excommunication, 82
Execution of martyrs, 179–80, 190–91
Exorcism, 83–6
  at grave of two martyrs, 199–200
  by apostles, 84–5; by casting down from height, 85; by invocation of martyrs, 209; by martyr's relics, 182; by music, 85; by self-inflicted pain, 88, 245*n*6; by sign of cross, 201; by speech, 85, 86
  healing by, 100
  in baptism, 176
  pagan ritual used by Christians, 87
  prayer before death, 191
  protection from River of Fire, 176
  Psalms recited, 87
Explorers: hallucinations: 235
Ezra Aocalypse:
  revelation to Moses on fiftieth day, 28
  IV *Ezra*—fasting, 41; journey of soul, 149
  V *Ezra*—crowning the elect 126–7,
  VI *Ezra*—clouds at Last Judgment, 166–7

Face, Faces:
  changing, 155–6
  four living creatures under fiery throne, 134
  giving light, 222
  of animals, 162; of avenging angels, 171; of death, 156–7; of Rulers of the Treasuries, 162–3; of the Lord, 227
Faith: substitute for knowledge, 18
Fasting, 241*ns*37–39
  and revelations, 96
  before death, 42
  days of, 40–42; periods, 132
  Egyptian ascetics, 39–40
  endurance feats, 40
  extension of time, 41
  in Apocalyptic literature, 41–3
  in Lent, 42
  preparation for prophecy, 12, 41
Fertility:
  cults, 39, 71
  promoted by martyr's relics, 182
Festivals:
  at four solstices, 137
  Egyptian, 245*ns*1, 2
Fields of Reeds and of Peace, 137
Fiery furnace:
  flame made harmless, 207
  imagery, 202
Fire:
  as punishment, 123, 201–2
  associated with prophecy, 133
  cataracts of, during last days, 167
  chariots of, 133–4
  columns of, 164, 224
  darkness and fire, 224
  demons as, 86
  divine communication and, 224
  divine fire, 222
  fiery transformation, 222
  heavenly, 223–5
  heavenly house of, 134–5

Fire—*cont.*
    in elemental zone, 121
    inspiration from breathing fumes, 223–4
    instrument of divine justice, 164
    lake of, 175
    pillar of cloud, 224
    pits of, 170
    River of, 170; at Last Judgment, 166; crossing, 176, 209; immersion in, 175; in prayers of The Virgin and Joseph, 151; luminaries of heaven as, 164; meanings, 174–5
        Throne of, 133, 134
        wheels of, 169
        wings of, 58
Food, Feeding:
    ascetics fed by disciples, 34–5
    deprivation, 39–43
    dreams caused by, 241*n*40
    funerary offerings, 39
    heavenly, 42–3
    representation of heavenly banquets, 43
    sign of Cross before eating, 88
    wild vegetation, 33
    see also Bread, Meat; Wine
Fornication:
    associated with paganism, 74
    condemnation, 71
    meaning changed, 72
    term of abuse, 71–2
Fruitfulness:
    of Atlantis, 138
    of earth, 138
    of paradise, 140
Funerary cults, 114–17
    banquets, 39
    boat journeys, 188
    description of ritual, 109
    endowments made before death, 105, 110
    imagery Christianised, 105
    imprecations against tomb desecration, 195
    inscriptions, 3, 107–8, 183, 195
    journeys to the south, 105
    offerings to the dead, 131–2, 241*n*28; of food, 39, 109
    purpose, 109, 177
    replaced by life of monastery, 106
    see also Mummification
Funerary paintings, 159

Gabriel, Archangel, 92, 135, 165
Gaianite heresy, 255*n*47
Galerius, Edict of, 180
Garden of Eden, *see* Eden
Garden of Hesperides, *see* Hesperides
Garments:
    changing in heaven, 161
    of truth, 185
    see also Robes
Gates:
    in *Aeneid*, 168
    in funerary texts, 160
    of heaven, 159–60; of righteousness, 176

passwords, 160
    seven gates of heaven in Mithraism, 159
Gates, Book of, 162
Gehenna: and Phlegethon, 168–9
George, martyr, 84, 86, 247
Gifts bestowed by Deity, 57–63
Gnosticism, 11, 17–18, 19
Gold, city of, 137
Golden gates, 159
Good and evil:
    angels and demons, 81–2
    in men, 82–3
Greek religion, 4–11
    sex in, 70
Greetings, 205–7
Gregory of Nazianzus, 182
Gregory of Nyssa, 182
Gregory Thaumaturgus, 210
Gregory the Great, 210
Guidance: in other world, 150
Guilt and propitiation, 73–4, 77

Habakkuk, 193
Hades:
    belly of dragon, 244*n*47
    descent of Christ, 215
    destroyed at Last Judgment, 166
    drunken banquet, 186
    journey of soul through, 17
    'Meadow of', 128
Hair: growth of, 33
Hallucinations and hallucinatory states:
    after states of possession, 86
    ascetic practices and modern knowledge, 26
    conscious thought and action precluded, 79
    dissolution of body as basis for, 163
    disturbing effects, 235, 259*n*5
    due to sensory deprivation, 235
    effects of environment, 235
    effects on primitive people, 260*n*8
    eradication through ascetic practices, 38, 81
    experimentally produced, 235, 259*n*5
    Hellenistic mystery cults, 32
    induced by pain, 37, 208
    modern experiences, 235
    rejection, 31
Hallucinogenic drugs, 234*ff*
    used in modern society, 259*n*7
Hallucinogeneric techniques, 234–6
Hand, Hands:
    in Roman funerary cult, 230
    of God, 230
Healing:
    abdomen, copper plate removed from, 201
    ancient modes perpetuated by martyr cult, 201
    ascetics as healers, 63
    as result of dreams, 199
    by demons, 156; by exorcism, 100; by scourging, 245*n*65; by divine intervention, 100, 199
    cults, 6, 198–201

Healing—*cont.*
    Egyptian gods of, 200
    incantations against disease, 85
    liberation from Fate, 217
    miraculous cures at shrines, 182, 200–201
    restoration of martyrs' bodies, 210
    through Mystery of raising dead, 213
    see also Diseases; Medicine; Remedies
Heaven:
    as city or garden, 185
    banquets and feasts, 186
    broad and narrow gates, 159
    city of, 132*ff*
    heavenly garments, 161
    in Plato, 5
    inhabitants, 94
    journey of soul through, 17
    Kingdom of, in Gospels, 49
    reunion in, 159
    seventh heaven, 126, 147, 215
    tenth heaven, 227
    thrones of, 132
Hebrew religion, *see* Jewish religion
Hegumens, Order of, 107
Hell:
    Christ's descent into, 173, 215
    earth as devil-filled hell, 64
    in apocalyptic literature, 16
    purification on way to heaven, 52
    source of imagery of, 178
Herakles, 137, 206
Hermas, Shepherd of, 82
Hermes, Mercury, 121, 125, 126, 128, 204
Hermetic literature, 122
    understanding visible universe, 130
Hermits, *see* Ascetics and Asceticism
Herodotus:
    Egyptian and Greek gods analagous, 65
    mummification procedures, 116
    oracles, 34
    sacrificed animals eaten, 39
Heroes:
    in Greek mythology, 6, 184
    legends and Christian biography, 22
Hesperides, Garden of, 137
Hezekiah, 99
Hippolytus, 169
Historia Monachorum in Aegypto, 24
    mutual recognition of ascetics, 104
Homer:
    dead, the, as shades, 170
    Elysian Plain, 138
    function of myths and Scriptures, 53
    meeting with the dead, 159
    study of, 4, 15
    Tartarus mentioned by, 168
Horus, 2, 66, 133, 204, 206
Hymns: of Coptic Church, 61, 243*n*18; of Ephraim, 61, 243*n*17; of Qumran, 140, 202
Hypatios, The Life of, by Callinicus, 24

Iamblichos:
    changeability of demons, 76

degrees of beauty of gods and angels, 226
    divine fire visible, 223
    divine unity as light, 220–21
    fasting described, 41
    fiery fumes, in Delphic oracle, 223–4
    gods and demons distinguished, 76, 81–2
    knowledge received during sleep, 44–5
    worshippers of Artemis, 229
Idolatry:
    condemned, 49, 72
    idols without sense perception, 78
    images prohibited by Mosaic Law, 12
Ikons: records of divine manifestations, 90
Images:
    new images of Christianity, 92
    pagan images overcome, 91
    power to create, 104
    ritual experience, 91
    visions as images of the divine, 93
    see also Idolatry; Revelations; Visions
Imagination:
    ascetic vision and, 52
    external control of, 217; by Church, 232
    sterility of, in modern times, 234
    visions as conscious creation of, 56
Imhotep, 198–9
Immortality: funerary cult, 109–110
Incense, 230–31
    ingredients, 230
Incubation cults:
    experience of divine as unity, 205
    healing, 99, 100, 198
    heavenly visitation, 203
    light of the gods, 220–21
    re-entering heavenly world, 225
    Serapis, cult of, 86
    similar method of healing in Christian shrine, 84–5
    sleep, fasting as preparation, 41
Individuality:
    deprivation by drugs, 236
    gradual emergence of individuals, 234
Insanity: demonic possession, 93
Inscriptions:
    aretologies, 204
    funerary, 3, 107–8, 183, 195
Intellect: sphere of, 122; *see* Spheres
Intercession: by Patriarchs and angels, 173
Intoxication:
    prevalence in Egypt, 40
    to obliterate self-consciousness, 5–6
    see also Drunkenness
'Invention' of bodies of saints, 110
Irenaeus:
    ascension of Christ, 215
    banquet in heaven, 187
    fruitfulness in world to come, 140
Isaac, O.T. Patriarch, 172–3, 196
Isaac, Apocalypse of: heavenly rewards foretold, 186
Isaiah, 126, 208

Isaiah, Ascension of:
  angel from seventh heaven, 126
  descent of Christ to Hades, 215
  earthly deeds known in seventh heaven, 147
  garments and thrones seen in visions, 186
  gates of heaven, 160
  sweet smell of the Spirit, 231
Isis, 2, 66, 133, 198, 200, 204, 210, 211, 225–6, 232
Islands:
  dwelling places of holy men, 141
  Isles of the Blest, 137
  resting places of martyrs' bodies, 191
  see also Atlantis
Isocrates: titles of gods, 4
Isolation, Self, *see* Self-isolation
Israel, Children of, *see* Jewish nation

Jacob, O.T. Patriarch, 172–3
Jahweh:
  angels as messengers, 92
  communication with prophets, 12
  enthronement of, 133
James, the apostle, 207
Jaoel, Archangel, 226
Jeremiah, 172–3
Jerome: power of martyr's relics, 182
Jerusalem:
  Heavenly, light of, 222
  New, predicted, 132
Jesus Christ, 28, 42, 97, 115, 173, 206, 215
Jewish nation:
  artificial creation, 71
  as tree with roots and branches, 140
  blood-ties, 72
  deity as expression of nationhood, 12–13
  expansion foretold, 130
  racial development in obedience to Law, 101
  single ancestor, 71
  struggle for supremacy, 92
Jewish religion, 11–13
  anger and vengeance of God, 70, 79
  God as judge and executioner, 72
  holy city, 132
  prohibitions, 69, 70
  transcendent God, 70
Job, 172–3, 193
John, the apostle, 84
John, Patriarch of Alexandria, 246n10
John Chrysostom, 182
John of Ephesus, 24
John the Baptist, 33, 101, 176, 193, 196
Joseph, the Carpenter, 151, 158, 196, 197–8
Josephus:
  Essenes and numbers, 29
  exorcism, 85
  failure of prophecy, 14
Jubilees, Book of:
  isolation of man from animal world, 78
  revelation to Moses on fiftieth day, 28

righteousness recorded, 147
  writing down signs of heaven, 194
Judaism, *see* Jewish religion
Judges:
  appointment of, 144
  just men as, 148
Judgment:
  cell as hall of judgment, 51–2
  in Egyptian religion, 3; in Judaism, 144; in Qumran community, 144
  of the ascetic before death, 115; of the living by the dead, 148
Judgment after death, 144–9
  at gate of heaven, 160
  in Christian apocalyptic literature, 145–7; in Egyptian religion, 36, 144, 148; in Plato, 144–5, 175
  rewards and punishments, 51, 148–151
  second judgments, 146
Judgment, Last, 111, 218
  disturbance of the elements, 231
  imagery, 166; imagery of individual experience transferred to universe, 167
  interval before, 197
  last days of earth, 167
  rising of the dead, 166
Julius of Kbehes, 189–90, 191

Khamuas, 148–9, 173, 194–5
King: embodiment of divinity, 2
Kingdom of Heaven, *see* Heaven
Kiss of Peace, 206
Kissing: social and ritual use, 206
Knowledge, gift of, 62–3

Land of the Inheritance, 187
Languages:
  gift of tongues, 55, 59–62
  misunderstandings caused by differences, 50, 63
Last Judgment, *see* Judgment, Last
Lausiac History, by Palladius, 24
Law in Judaism, 11–12, 51, 101
  Torah compiled, 14; study of, 14; calendar and prophecy in, 28
Leo the Great, Leon, 42
  Tome of, 97
Levi, Testament of: robes of office in vision, 185
Light:
  accompanying birth, 101
  chariot of, 206
  column of, 169
  environment illuminated, 222
  excluded from ascetics' cells, 35
  luminous qualities of angels, 222
  man of, 203, 223
  mystical vision of, 220–22
  of gods, angels, demons, 221
  of intellect, 219
  powers of light and darkness, 165
  wings of, 223
  youth of, 203, 223
Lightning: at salvation of martyrs, 231
Linen: mummy cloths, 116
Liturgy, Liturgies, 90

Liturgy—*cont.*
  participation of the dead, 94
  rituals of, 233
Liver, 247*n*20
  for divination, 201
  healing of, 201
Lyon: martyrdoms at, 207, 218
Macarius of Alexandria, 56
Macarius of Antioch, 184
Macarius of Egypt, 24, 111, 141–2
Madness: as gift of gods, 7
Manasseh, 208
Manichaeism, 40
  castration, 98
  influence on Syrian monks, 98
  physical existence denigrated, 98
Marriage:
  brother–sister, 243*n*34
  exogamy forbidden in Judaism, 71, 101
  with mother or sister, 71, 243*n*34;
  with nearest relative, 74
Martyrions, *see* Shrines
Martyrs, Acts of, 84
Martyrs and Martyrdom:
  animals subdued, 208
  as intercessors, 181–2; as threat to
  society, 180
  at death of ascetic, 115
  beheading, 190–1, 210
  benefactors to the living, 182
  boat journeys, 188
  conflict with pagan authorities, 201
  cult, 179–201; revealed by vision,
  196; rites, 185
  death and entry into heaven, 94,
  113
  depicted as types, not individuals,
  182
  discovery of bodies, 192
  dismemberment, 188, 210, 211
  eagerness for death, 180–81
  graves opening at Resurrection,
  218
  invocation of, 196
  Lives, 22; written on pagan models,
  48; based on panegyrics, 181
  martyrdom foretold, 184
  persecutions, 207
  persecutors put to shame, 211
  re-burial, 182
  recantation, 181
  reception in heaven, 188
  relics, 182; invested with divine
  power, 210
  restoration of bodies, 210–12
  resurrection of, 190, 191; foretold,
  184; as reward, 84
  rewards in heaven, 184–8
  saved by divine intervention, 211–
  212
  torments, imagery of, 201, 207–8,
  210, 218
  year, the martyrs, 179
Mary, Virgin, 101, 151, 158, 162–3, 166,
  176, 193, 206, 213, 244*n*46
Mary, falling asleep of: angels of light and
  darkness, 158

Maximinian, 179
Meat eating:
  abstention from, 241*n*32
  cooked meat unacceptable to ascetics, 40
  fasting and, 40
  sacramental communion, 241*n*33
  sacrificed animals eaten, 39, 69
Medicine:
  Egyptian writings on, 99
  Greek, 100
  see also Healing; Remedies
Meditation, 49
  Book of, 136
  last days spent in, 113
  means of joining community of
  heaven, 94
  thoughts spoken by Biblical personages, 96
Memorising, *see* Bible: memorising
Memory:
  gift of, 58–9
  means of attaining communion
  with the divine, 10
  of visions before birth, 125
  visions recalled, 54
Menander, 102
Menas, 188–9, 200
Mesopotamia, monastic life, 24
Messiah:
  foretold by Isaiah, 13
  in Apocalyptic literature, 16
  see also Jesus Christ
Methusaleh, 227
Michael, Archangel, 92, 131, 133, 135,
  145, 165, 166, 173, 195
Micah, O.T. Prophet, 193
Midrash, 135
Midst, the, 152, 154, 251*n*17
Miracles, 228*ff*
  ascribed to ascetics, 53, 63; at
  shrines, 182, 209
  healing arts replaced by, 100
  stories of holy men, 57
Miraculous cures, *see* Healing; Shrines
Miriam, O.T. Prophetess, 62
Monasteries:
  community dominating individual,
  94
  defence against attacks, 29
  earliest communities, 24
  founding, 105
  grave of holy man as site, 106
  head chosen under divine guidance,
  108
  narratives of founders collected,
  24
  rules of communities, 30; inscribed on tablet, 106
  training ground for hermits, 29–30
Monasticism:
  decay foretold, 58
  repressive forms, 52
  spread of, 30
Monks:
  reluctance to become priests, 107
  robes, 30–31; as shrouds, 105
  solitary, *see* Ascetics and Asceticism

821

Monophysite controversy, 246n8
Monotheism:
    and polytheism, 20
    as religion of the Jews, 11–12
Montanists, 242ns15, 16, 243n19
    revival of prophecy, 60, 62
    speaking with tongues, 55
Moon:
    as lowest planetary sphere, 128
    Babylonian deity, 118–19
    Jewish people and cult of, 123
    lunar year, 136
    purification of souls on, 128–9
Moses, 12, 17, 28, 41, 62, 106, 141, 172–3, 206, 222, 224
Moses, Apocalypse of: washing Adam in Acherusian Lake, 175
Mourning, Days of, 131
Mummification:
    aromatic substances, 116
    completion in forty days, 132, 250n91
    continued after prohibition, 210
    dehydration, period of, 116
    of animals, 39, 210
    'opening of the mouth', 109
    provision during life, 193
    removal of organs, 109, 116, 211
    source of imagery, 99, 116–17
    wrapping, 116, 192
Music:
    decline in everyday use, 13–14
    ecstasy induced by, 6
    exorcism by, 85
    liberating soul at death, 116
    lyre played before sleep, 231
Mystery cults:
    at Delphi, 205
    Hellenistic, 32
    Orphic, 20
    Pythagorean, 20
Mysticism:
    Alexandrian, 51
    Jewish, 134
    self-consciousness obliterated, 56
Mythology:
    Christian writers and, 26
    Homeric myths and the Scriptures, 53

Nabonassar, 118
Nakedness:
    endured by Origen, 59
    of ascetics, 33
Names:
    commemoration by, 3
    identity announcement, 204
    naming of children after martyrs, 196
    of God, 203–4; of martyrs, 196; of Saviour, 204
    personal names given to places, 97
    place-names, 246n15
    power residing in name, 203
    pronouncement of, 3, 203
    qualities handed down with name, 17
Nazirites:
    fasting, 40

    hair growth as sign of dedication, 33
Nebuchadnezzar, 33
Necessity:
    life pre-determined, 119
    life ruled by, 125
    wheel of, 169
Necromancers: death penalty for consulting, 72
Neoplatonism:
    attacked by Athanasius, 23
    continence, 75
    divine experienced only in the mind, 51
    fasting, 41
    god-like independence of earthly needs, 43
    influence of Plato on early Fathers, 9
    mystical experiences through intellectual effort, 56
    Old Testament interpreted as allegory, 103
    'separation of soul from body', 19–20
    soul imprisoned in body, 38
Neo-Pythagoreans:
    dreams dependent on bodily state, 45–6
    silence practised, 34
Nero, 190
New Year:
    Canaanite, 133
    Jewish, 133
Nicomedia: persecutions in, 179
Nile:
    as deity, 2
    flood, 53, 75–6; prayer for, 242n8
    sacred places, 90.
Nitria, mountain of, 239n6
    community of monks, 30–31
Noah, O.T. Patriarch, 227
Nubia, see Ethiopia
Nubian, the, 75, 76
Nudity, see Nakedness
Numbers:
    astrological numbers adopted by Jews, 123
    divine purpose revealed by, 28–9
    divine significance, 118
    essential to understanding, 117
    number of days spent fasting, 41
    universal significance, 132–3, 136, 137

Oceanus, 174
    'river of water surrounding the world', 141
Odyssey, see Homer
Oil:
    in animal sacrifice, 39
    in burnt sacrifice, 241n32
    see also Anointing
Ointment, see Anounting
Olives, Mount of: revelations received on, 132
Olympian deities, 4–5
Onnophrius, 99

Oracles:
    animals and birds, 90
    decline of, 13–21
    dreams, 6–7, 44
    fiery fumes, inspiration from, 223–4
    in Egypt, 34, 90, 245n1
    in martyr narratives, 189
    preparatory fasting, 41
    renewal of gift attributed to ascetics, 89
    similar role of holy men, 34
    solution of problems, 96
    transmission, 56–7
Organs, internal:
    in funerary inscriptions, 3
    psychic powers in, 17
    removal during mummification, 109, 116
Orgies, 186
Origen, 59, 69, 98, 132, 207
Origen, writings of:
    ascent of soul, 129
    decans invoked, 156
    individual struggle for perfection, 21
    solitary life superiority, 29
    soul and organs of sense, 51
Orion, the cursor, 191
Orpheus, 6
Orphic cults:
    man as divine, 5–6
    obliteration of self-consciousness, 6, 20
    sex as worship of life, 71
    underworld, relation to Christian hell, 53
Osiris, 2, 39, 65–7, 75, 109, 133, 148, 162, 188, 190, 204, 211, 250n92

Pachomius, 24, 29, 40, 47, 58, 61, 107, 169
Pahlavi texts, 98
Pain:
    conscious disregard of, 37–8, 163
    in exorcism, 85, 118
    in martyrdom, 208
    insensitivity to, 229
    removal of, 209
    self-inflicted, 35, 37
Palestine: persecutions in, 179
Palladius:
    influenced by Evagrius, 52
    Lausiac History, 24
Paphnute, 99
Papias, 140
Paradise, 137–42
    access to, 142
    created by ascetics, 233
    earthly, 129, 141
    expulsion from, 78
    four rivers of, 141
    fruitfulness, 140
    Garden of Eden as image of, 139
    in apocalyptic literature, 16
    light of, 141
    New Paradise, 159
    Paradise of Jubilation, 146; of the Fathers, 53
    place of instruction, 129

Trees of Life as saints, 140–41
Patriarchs, Old Testament:
    as intercessors, 173
    beauty of, 227, 228
    conception by divine intervention, 100
    death and succession, 113
    divine communications, 104
    in *Amente*, 172–3
    in heaven, 94, 173
Paul, Acts of: martyrdom, 190, 191
Paul, Apocalypse of:
    abyss opened by angel, 171
    angelic helpers, 153
    angels of righteousness, 150–51
    appearance of Paul in heaven, 131
    beauty of Patriarchs, 228
    demonic powers dominating soul, 154
    gates of heaven, 160
    judgment of the wicked, 146
    pain and injustice ending at death, 159
    pits as places of punishment, 170
    similarity to *Pistis Sophia*, 152
    souls brought before God for judgment, 145
Paul, the apostle, 84, 131, 190, 191
Pausanius: sanctuaries described, 198
Penitents, 82
Pentecost, 28
Perfection:
    attainment of, 53–4; by man's own efforts, 26
    possibility guaranteed by New Testament, 49
    self-perfection attained in isolation, 32
    tears as sign of, 37
    typified by animals, 162
    'way of perfection', 75
Perfume:
    environment of holy men, 231
    significance and usage, 230–31
    spreading at time of death, 116
    sweet smell in trance experience, 231
Pergamum, 198
Periods of time, *see* Time
Persecution of Christians, 179–80, 207; *see also* Martyrs and Martyrdom
Peter, Apocalypse of:
    chaos during last days, 167
    wheels of fire, 169
Peter, the apostle, 84
Peter Mongus, Archbishop of Alexandria, 97
Philip, Gospel of, 214
Philo of Alexandria:
    angels and demons, relationship between, 102
    Bible as allegory, 58
    coenobitic communities described, 33
    divine possession and human reason, 15–16
    dreams and memory, 54
    fasting by Therapeutae, 42

Philo of Alexandria—*cont.*
  ingredients of incense, 231
  numbers, sacred, 28–9
  singing, 61–2
  soul as counterpart of heaven, 118
  source of Neoplatonism, 9
  Therapeutae described, 28–9
Philostratus:
  dreams affected by wine, 45–6
  Life of Apollonius of Tyana, 23
  oracular manner of speech, 34
  unconfused dreams induced by fasting, 41
Phrygia: persecutions in, 179
Phylacteries, 195, 255n49
Physiology, human: basis of experience of the divine, 236–7
Pisentius, 99
Pistis Sophia:
  Destiny, liberation from, 153–154
  places of punishment, 162–3
  raising of the dead, 213
  seven-headed dragon, 157
  significance of, 155
  soul in life after death, 152–3
  Zodiac of hostile powers, 162; soul released from, 152
Pits:
  as places of punishment, 170
  immersion in, 201–2
  of fire, 170
Planets:
  as 'interpreters', 118
  Jewish people and cult of, 123
  planetary angels, 165
  planetary spheres, 128–9
  qualities of good and evil, 120
  relation to decans, 156, 252n22
  seer as interpreter of divine will, 122
  seven heads of Death and, 157
  seven planetary spheres and divisions of soul, 120
  synodal revolutions of, 118, 121
Plato:
  Absolute Good perceived, 219
  Atlantis, 138
  attendant demons, 103
  beauty in heaven and on earth, 225
  body a barrier to attaining truth, 8
  choice of way of life based on heavenly experience, 125–6
  divine harmony, 5
  divine madness, 7, 15
  drunken banquets in Hades, 186
  good demons, 67
  immortality of soul, 8
  influence survives, 5
  interval before reincarnation, 149, 197; journey of a thousand years, 197
  just men as judges, 145, 148
  knowledge and spiritual development, 18–19
  life work inspired by dreams and oracles, 7
  memory and communion with the divine, 10, 125

  motions of the universe, 5, 184–5
  number essential to understanding, 117
  philosophy as a form of death, 23
  prophets as spokesmen, not diviners, 7
  punishments in Tartarus, 170
  rivers of the earth, 168, 174
  separation of soul from body, 214
  tablets recording men's actions, 147
  universe a counterpart of soul, 5, 119, 184–5
  wandering of unguided souls, 149–150
  wheel of Necessity, 169
Plotinus:
  All-soul, 9
  divine light, 219–20
  identity of seer and seen, 11
  judges in heaven, 145
  Life by Porphyry, 201
  no memory in intellectual world, 10
Plutarch:
  decline of oracles, 13–14, 223–4
  dreams influenced by condition of body, 45
  Egyptian and Greek gods, 65–7, 75
  greetings of the god, 205
  historical biographies, 23
  ingredients of incense, 230
  memory and vision, 54–5, 125
  separation of body, soul and mind, 129
  triangle as pattern of all things, 117–18
Poetry:
  decline in everyday use, 13–14
  heroic, 6
  myths containing eternal truths, 4
Polycarp, martyr, 22, 207, 208
Porphyry:
  ascension of the soul, 214
  divinely inspired writing, 201
  identity of seer and seen attained by Plotinus, 11
Posidonius of Apamea, 120
Possession, 67–8
  and true divination, 7
  danger of possession by 'images', 93
  exorcism, *see* that heading
  insensitivity to pain, 229
  physical ills caused by, 73
  risk of injury and death, 79–80
  supplanting reason, 15–16
  see also Demons
Prayer:
  at martyrdom, 191
  at sunrise and sunset, 47
  bands, 255n49
  by the dying, 151
  for the dead, 108
  for the soul after death, 131
  Jewish prayers for guidance, 96
  repeated, against hallucinations, 38
  with outstretched hands, 224

Priests:
    as rulers over groups of ten, 136
    division between priests and lay-
    men, 106
    Order of Priest, 107; appointment
    to priesthood, 107
Processions:
    at festivals, 116
    ritual, in Ancient Egypt, 90–91
    to tombs, 116
Promised Land, 132, 139
Prophecy, 12, 57–8
    accepted as revelation, 59–60
    calendar and, 28
    failure of faculty, 14, 21
    memory and, 55
    Montanism, 60
    preparation for, 12
    renewal of gift, 15, 89
    Tree of Knowledge as source of
    power, 139
Prophetess: in Delphic oracle, 223–4;
    leader of choir of women, 62
Prophets:
    as interpreters of visions, 7
    at death of ascetic, 115
    death and succession, 113
    guilds, 12
    hand of God on, 230
    in apocalyptic literature, 16; in
    Hebrew religion, 12
    mouthpieces of deity, 56
    powers inherited, 114–15
    synonymous with seers, 12
Psalm-singing, 61
Pseudo-Clementine Letters, 98
Psychotherapy: drugs and techniques des-
    troying sense of individuality, 236
Punishments:
    at Last Judgment, 111, 168–77
    of angels, 164–5; of the wicked, 146
    places of, 162
    remission of, 171–3
    respite on Sabbath, 173
    wrong-doers sentenced by the
    wronged, 175
    see also Torments
'Pure Ones', 107
Purification:
    after death, 174–7
    in heaven, 176
    places of, 121
    see also Elemental sphere; Planets
Pyriphlegethon, 174
Pythagoras, 9, 34, 43, 45, 145
Pythagorean cult: universe mathematical,
    6, 117; experienced as divine, 20

Qumran community:
    agents for overthrow of disobedient
    angels, 165
    angels of light and darkness, doc-
    trine of, 82
    Community Rule, 82, 137
    Damascus Rule, 136
    discipline, 82
    Hymns, 140
    judgment by chiefs, 144

    list of the Elect, 187
    Messianic Rule, 144
    related to heavenly hosts, 137
    solar year governing way of life, 136
    torments, imagery of, 202
    War Rule, 165

Rachel, 100
Raising from the dead, *see* Dead, the
Raphael, Archangel, 135, 165
Rē, 71, 159, 185, 187, 189
Rebecca, 100
Receivers, avenging, 153–4
Remedies:
    instructions given by divine visitor,
    100
    knowledge deliberately forgotten,
    100
    Temple inscription by Solomon, 99
Reptiles: deities, 75–6
Restoring body, *see* Body, restoring
Resurrection, 212–19
    Egyptian gods, 212
    graves opening, 218
    in apocalyptic literature, 16
    of martyrs, 184, 190–91
    passive participation in, 231–2
    physical resurrection, 217–18
Retribution: in life after death, 148
Reuben, Testament of: deathbed instruc-
    tions, 112; regarding burial, 189
Revelations:
    authenticity, 96, 97
    see also Visions
Ritual:
    ascetics independent of, 33, 36
    battles, 116
    collective experiences and the in-
    dividual, 79, 93–4; and trance states,
    229
    commemorative, 179*ff*, 198
    description of funerary ritual, 109
    dramas, 90
    for the dead, 68
    in Egyptian religion, 2–3, 109
    lay participants, 106–7
    names in, 203
    of riddance, 5
    pagan ritual and divine protection,
    104
    protection against negative ex-
    periences, 172, 177, 233
    social and religious vitality pre-
    served, 27
River, Rivers:
    encircling world, 141
    of elemental sphere; of earth, 141
    of fire, *see* Fire
    of Paradise, 141
    of pitch, 166
    of the underworld, 174
Robes:
    of monks, as shrouds, 105
    of the priesthood, 185
    robing in heaven, 161
    symbolism, 30–31
Roman Emperors: Anti-Christ, 77; deifica-
    tion of, 120; image of the sun, 120–1

Rule of the Community, see Qumran Community

Sabbath: breaking of fast on, 41; respite of punishments on, 173
Sacrifices:
    animals, 39, 241*n*32; clean and unclean, 69; blood procuring fertility, 69
    divination by inspection of victims, 243*n*27
    human, 243*n*28; first-born, 74; infanticide prohibited, 101
Saints:
    Lives, 22; written on pagan models, 48
    see also Ascetics and Asceticism; Martyrs and Martyrdom; *and* under names of saints
Sallust: historical biographies, 23
Salpicius Severus: historical biographies, 23
Salvation:
    achieved by self-recognition, 203
    disturbances accompanying, 231
    from without, 216
    invoking Saviour's name, 204
Sarah, 100
Satan, 73, 74, 77, 88, 165
Satanail, 72–3
Saul, O.T. King, 85
Saviour, Saviours:
    apostles as, 217
    ascetics as, 63
    environment illuminated on appearance of, 222
    in pagan Egypt, 205–6
    Jesus Christ, 115, 173, 215
    Shed, lord of heaven, 205
Scetis, Scete, Shiet:
    narratives of the Fathers, 24
    'Paradise of the Fathers', 53
    site of, 239*n*6
Scriptures, *see* Bible
Seer, Seers:
    as interpreter of planetary power, 122
    dream visions, 20
    identification with the seen, 11
    names adopted by apocalyptic writers, 17
    raised above firmament, 130
    saints, martyrs, ascetics and seers, 233
    see also Ascetics and Asceticism; Martyrs and Martyrdom; Prophets
Seership:
    claims of apocalyptic writers, 16
    cults, 1–2; under Hebrews, 12
Self-consciousness:
    dependent on intellectual development, 1
    growth of, and demonic experience, 73
    loss intolerable to normal person, 236
    lost in union with the divine, 11
    meditation on Scriptures necessary for, 49

    obliteration of, 20, 56, 230; by drunkenness, 5; by ecstasy, 6
Self-destruction: ascetic life an act of, 79
Self-enclosure, 34–5
Self-immolation, 180, 253*n*6
Self-isolation, 31–5
    ascetics and group traditions, 27
Self-knowledge: source of healing power, 63
Self-mortification, 36–9
    exorcism by, 88
Sense-perception:
    in animals, 68
    polytheism based on, 20
Senses:
    barrier to attaining truth, 8
    Greek and Egyptian attitudes, 25–6
    organs of sense ascribed to soul, 51
Sensory deprivation, 48, 235, 259*ns*4, 5
Septimus Severus, 179
Serapis, cult of, 86–7, 198, 210
Serpents:
    destruction by martyrs, 189
    ritual use, 75
    three-headed, 157
Seth, 211
Sex:
    attitudes in different religions, 70–71
    condemned by Church Fathers, 72
    demons of unchastity, 84
    'Ethiopian' as image of licence, 75
    promiscuity, 71; offensive to Egyptians, 74
    temptations identified with demons, 74
Shed, lord of heaven, 205
Shenute, 24, 61, 242*n*16
Sheol:
    Abbaton and, 155
    place of darkness, 169
    places of, 141
Shepherd of Hermas, 82
Shiet, *see* Scetis
Shipwrecks, hallucinations following, 235
Shrines:
    benefiting locality, 182, 189
    cult of, 182, 193–201; based on funerary cult, 106
    exorcism at, 209
    favours granted at, 198–201
    locations indicated by divine agency, 103
    miracles and cures at, 198–201
    perpetuating names of martyrs, 196
    pilgrimages to, 197
    raising of the dead at, 218–19
    seer commanded to build, 126
    service to martyrs, 195–8
Sibyllines, Christian:
    after-life, 168–9
    Last Judgment, 166
Silence:
    ascetic discipline, 34
Singing:
    by ascetics, 61, 136; by Therapeutae, 61–2
    of angels, 62, 116, 136, 146, 176

Sleep:
death as, 112
deprivation, 43–7
healing during, 6, 198–9
heavenly visitation during, 203, 225–6
sleeping in tombs, 46; on floor, 59
see also Incubation cults
Solomon, *Odes of*:
salvation given from above, 214–15; through Christ's descent into hell, 216–17
seven-headed dragon, 157
Solomon, *Psalms of*, 140–41
'Son of God': name of Satan, 73
Soul:
ascension of, 214; through spheres, 128–9; completed, 132
assaults after death, 188
effluence of light, 152
fate revealed in books, 194
'fetching' of, 115–16
gender and person in narratives, 115
imprisonment in body, 8, 38
judgment of, 145–6
means of travel on journey to heaven, 121
punishment, 154
rational and irrational components, 46
return from heavenly to earthly world, 126
scattered members brought together, 214
'school for souls', 132
separation from body, 116, 124–7
spirit released from, 152
vision obscured by body, 124
wandering, 149–50
wrapping for journey to heaven, 116, 192
'Speaking with tongues', 55, 59–62
Speech:
divine power exercised by, 3
exorcism by, 85–6
Spheres:
elemental, 120; relation to rivers, seasons, cardinal points, places of Sheol, 141; purification of soul in, 121, 123, 128
highest sphere, 128, 130
of intellect, 122
Ouranos or eighth sphere, 120
seven planetary spheres, 120, 128–9; purification of soul in, 123
universe of three spheres, 119; imagery of, 127; corresponding to mind, soul and will, 127
see also Elemental sphere; Planets
Spirit, Spirits:
and soul, 116
'Counterpart', 152–4
'hand' synonymous, 230
Spleen: function of, 247n21
Stadium: imagery, 31, 188
Stars:
angels identified with, 92

as judges, 118
cults adopted by Semites, 119; dominance over man, 163; imagery in Old Testament, 122–3; abandoned by Jews, 92; destruction by Jews not effective, 123; obliterated, by Christian ritual, 178; imagery avoided in Christian writings, 185
destruction of, 164–6
disobedient, 126, 164–5
heavenly hosts, 123
heavenly house in terms of, 134
heliacal rising of, 118
highest sphere, 128
in Judaism, 122–3, 130; in life after death, 109; in Neoplatonism, 129
judgment obtained from, 144
leaders of the heads of the thousands, 136
melted by fire during last days, 167
parts of human body related to stellar deities, 99
rulers of Necessity, 125
Sons of Heaven, 137, 202
stellar deities of great size, 126
synchronising human activity with, 118
Statues: deified kings carried in procession, 90
Stellar cults, *see* Stars: cults
Stephen, the first martyr, 193, 200, 219
Sterility:
cause for reproach, 102
cured by divine intervention, 100
saints invoked, 101
Stoics:
doctrine in Patristic writings, 19
purification of soul in elemental sphere, 121
self-immolation, cult of, 253n6
Stylites, 37
Styx, river, 174
Suetonius: historical biographies, 23
Sun:
abode of souls after death, 121
as figure of faculty of reason, 15–16
Babylonian deity, 118–19
chariot of, 121
communal psychic life related to, 90
cult of, 2; Emperor as image of, 120–21; Jewish people and, 123
exposure to, 38
heavenly house in terms of, 134–5
highest planetary sphere, 128
journey of, 163
movements of planets, 118, 121
prayer at sunrise and sunset, 47
solar year, 136
Syria:
ascetics on columns and in trees, 37
persecutions in, 179

Tabennesi: monastic foundation of Pachomius, 24
Tabernacle:
measurements divinely dictated, 132
will of Jahweh made known in, 133

Tabernacles, Feast of, 133
Tablets:
    heavenly, 146–7, 187
    votive, 199
Tartaruchus, 146
Tartarus:
    Acheron, ferry to, 174–5
    in region of fire and hail, 121
    known to Homer, 167–8
    punishment in, 170
    regions of, at Last Judgment, 166
    watched over by Uriel, 135
Tê, see Dêt
Temple:
    measurements divinely dictated, 132
    remedies inscribed on wall, 99
Tertullian:
    gods as demons, 68
    Montanism, 60
    persecutions recorded, 179
    prison likened to a hermits' cell, 35
    sleep as model of death, 43–4
    soul during lingering death, 124–5
Thebais: martyrs, 179
Theodore, Questions of:
    date of, 95
    Patriarchs in Amente, 172–3
Theodore the General, martyr, 77, 97
Theodoret of Cyrus, 182
Theophilus of Alexandria, 78
Therapeutae:
    Bible study, 58
    choral singing, 61–2
    fasting, 42
    number symbolism, 28–9
Thomas, Acts of, 84
    burial honours, 192
    execution, 191
Thoth, 113, 194
Thought-control, 50
    training of ascetics, 81
Throne:
    as vehicle for deity, 133
    empty, 133
    enthronement and immortality, 133
    enthronement of Adam, 159–60; of
    Deity, 133; of Osiris, 133
    fiery, 133–5
    heavenly hosts around, 136
    reward for righteousness, 186
Thunder:
    at salvation of martyrs, 231
    seven thunders, 157
Time, periods of, 28–9
    annual cycle, 136
    divine significance, 118
    fasting periods, 28–9, 41–2
    mourning, days of and experiences
    of soul after death, 132
    Thousand Years, banquet of, 197–
    8; journey of, 197
Tombs:
    as hermits' cells, 34–5
    beneficial to neighbourhood, 110
    built during lifetime, 193
    desecration and punishments, 195
    focus of cult of the dead, 35

inscriptions at, 195
offerings at, 197
opening at resurrection, 218
paintings, 133, 188
priests as guardians, 197
processions to, 116
sacrifices at, 250n90
sleeping in, 46
Torah, 14, 28
Torments, 167–71
    at and before death, 150
    between first judgment and second,
    146
    everlasting, 111
    fiery, 123–4
    of martyrs, 181, 184, 201
    places of, 121, 132, 168–71
    redemption from, 202
    tormentors with changing faces,
    151, 155–6
Trance:
    collective ritual involving, 229
    induced by drugs, 234–5; by pain, 88
    inspiration for apocalyptic writers,
    17
    memory obliterated, 55
    pain made bearable, 208
    prophetic revelations under, 12
    sweet smell associated with, 231
Transformations of the dead, 160–61; of the
    seer, 161
Treasuries:
    of pitch, 166; of punishment, 162;
    of stars, 164; of sun, moon and stars,
    166; of thunder, 164
    Rulers of the, 162
Tree: of Knowledge, 139; of Life, 43
Twelve Patriarchs, Testament of the, 189

Ugarit, 133
Uriel, Archangel, 135, 164

Vices: seven principal, 242n4
Vienne: martyrdoms, 207, 218
Vigils, 47
Virgil:
    Aeneas in Tartarus, 170
    crossing the Acheron, 174
    meeting of seer with the dead, 159
    purification of the soul, 121
    underworld described, 168
Virgins: highest place in heaven, 98
Vision:
    faculty of, 1–13
    'gnostic', 18
    in Greek, Jewish and Egyptian
    religion, 19–20; in Orphic religion, 6
    thought and emotion, 52
Visions, 54–7
    conscious experience of the
    imagination, 143
    content Christianised, 95, 143
    dream visions stereotyped, 232
    essential characteristic of saints and
    martyrs, 94
    experiences of Hebrew prophets, 12
    inspiration to apocalyptic writers,
    17

Visions—*cont.*
    Jewish national destiny revealed by, 20
    mystical, 55–6
    of gods, angels and demons, 81–2; of light, 220
    prophets as interpreters, 7
    sharing, 56–7
    source of virtues and vices, 82
    waking experience, 56
Visitations, heavenly, 93–102
Voice: of invisible Deity, 102
Votive tablets, 199

Wakefulness:
    psychosis induced by, 258n3
    see also Sleep: deprivation
War Rule, see Qumran community
Warriors: martyrs likened to, 181
Watchers: archangels and fallen angels, 126, 249–50n88
Water:
    in elemental zone, 121
    transformed into fire, 167
West, the: entrance to *Amente*, 3; place of souls of departed heroes, 137
Wheel: fiery, 169; of Necessity, 169
Wicked, the: death of, 148–55
Wine:
    abstention from, 40, 59, 241n34
    dreams affected by, 45–6
    orgiastic drinking, 241n35
Wisdom: gift of, 62–3
Wizards: death penalty for consulting, 95
World, *see* Earth
Wrapping:
    in mummification, 116, 192
    of soul, 116, 192
Writing:
    and solar year, 194

    Egyptian, 194–5
    erased during judgment, 147, 187
    in apocalyptic literature 194–5
    knowledge of, and fall from divine status, 193–4
    of story of martyrdom, 195
    power in names in books, 195
    recitation of written formulae, 194
    rewards for, 195
    taught by angels (stars), 193
    under divine inspiration, 201
    see also Inscriptions

Xenocrates, 66–7

Zadok, Sons of, 187
Zechariah, O.T. Prophet, 193
Zion:
    nucleus of New Jerusalem, 13
    visions of Ezra, 126–7
Zodiac:
    Angel of the Abyss and, 171
    deities in each sign, 120
    demonic aspect, 158
    dissolution of, 164
    expression of laws of psychic life, 91, 127
    festivals at four solstices, 137
    imagery in apocalyptic literature, 124, 152; in journey of soul through *Amente*, 154; in Greek philsophy, 102
    numerology, 127, 184
    of deaths, 213; of hostile powers, 162
    restored, 202
    Treasuries: Rulers of twelve, 162–3; of stars, 164; of Tartarus, 166
    see also Decans
Zosimus, 141